CHARACTERISTICS OF
AND STRATEGIES FOR
TEACHING STUDENTS WITH
MILD DISABILITIES

SIXTH EDITION

CHARACTERISTICS OF AND STRATEGIES FOR TEACHING STUDENTS WITH MILD DISABILITIES

MARTIN HENLEY

Westfield State College

ROBERTA S. RAMSEY

Norwich University

ROBERT F. ALGOZZINE

The University of North Carolina at Charlotte

Upper Saddle River, New Jersey
Columbus, Ohio

Library of Congress Cataloging in Publication Data

Henley, Martin, 1943-
  Characteristics of and strategies for teaching students with mild disabilities / Martin Henley, Roberta S. Ramsey, Robert F. Algozzine. — 6th ed.
    p. cm.
  Includes bibliographical references and index.
  ISBN-13: 978-0-205-60838-6
  ISBN-10: 0-205-60838-8
  1. Learning disabled—United States. 2. Mainstreaming in education—United States. 3. Behavior modification—United States. I. Ramsey, Roberta S. II. Algozzine, Robert. III. Title.
  LC4705.H46 2009
  371.9—dc22

2008022251

Executive Editor and Publisher: *Virginia Lanigan*
Senior Editor: *Ann Davis*
Editorial Assistant: *Matthew Buchholz*
Production Editor: *Gregory Erb*
Cover Designer: *Linda Knowles*
Composition Buyer: *Linda Cox*
Manufacturing Buyer: *Megan Cochran*
Photo Researcher: *Katharine S. Cebik*
Editorial Production Service: *Marty Tenney, Modern Graphics, Inc.*

This book was set in Times by Modern Graphics, Inc. It was printed and bound by Hamilton Printing. The cover was printed by Phoenix Color Corporation/Hagerstown.

Pearson Education Ltd.
Pearson Education Singapore Pte. Ltd.
Pearson Education Canada, Ltd.
Pearson Education—Japan

Pearson Education Australia Pty. Limited
Pearson Education North Asia Ltd.
Pearson Educación de Mexico, S.A. de C.V.
Pearson Education Malaysia Pte. Ltd.

Photo credits appear on page 436, which constitutes an extension of the copyright page.

Merrill
is an imprint of

www.pearsonhighered.com

10 9 8 7 6 5 4 3 2 1

ISBN 13: 978-0-205-60838-6
ISBN 10: 0-205-60838-8

CONTENTS

CHAPTER FOUR

Students with Emotional Disturbance   116

PREFACE

This book is written for general and special education majors who want to learn how to effectively teach students with mild disabilities. Aside from speech and language problems, mild disabilities are the most common disabling conditions eligible for special education services. The mild disabilities include mild intellectual disabilities, emotional disturbance, and learning disabilities. Students with mild disabilities spend the major portion of their school day in general education classrooms. This means that the responsibility for educating these students is shared by general and special educators. The emphasis on inclusion makes it imperative that general and special educators share a common knowledge base about the nature and needs of these hard-to-teach students.

Our purpose is to provide, in a single volume, a comprehensive overview of educational practices that influence the identification, placement, and teaching of students with mild disabilities. No other text details both characteristics of and strategies for teaching students with mild disabilities. Our emphasis on characteristics separates this text from others in the same genre. Too often, key issues that influence the placement and teaching of students with mild disabilities are muddled by misinformation. One such issue is eligibility criteria. One of the most troublesome aspects of special education today is the misidentification of students as learning disabled. Many special education programs sag under the weight of misplaced students and unfulfilled expectations.In some cases, students with legitimate disabilities are overlooked. In other instances, problem learners are called learning disabled without sufficient supportive evidence. Both general and special educators need to develop a clear understanding of the types of learning problems that characterize students with mild disabilities.

The first part of this book addresses the characteristics of students with mild disabilities. Chapter 1 explains the basic principles of special education, including its history, legal mandates (including No Child Left Behind and IDEA 2004), and descriptions of various types of disabling conditions. Chapter 2 details those reasons and highlights similarities and differences found within the three mild disabilities. Chapters 3 through 5 present detailed information on each of the three mild disabilities, including practical teaching strategies for each. Although some states subscribe to a cross-categorical approach when serving students with mild disabilities, the reality is that learning problems are addressed by educators and parents in terms of one of the specific categories of mild intellectual disability, learning disability, or emotional disturbance. There are many reasons for this shifting back and forth between using and not using categorical terms to discuss students with mild disabilities.

The second part of this book describes effective teaching practices for students with mild disabilities. The research basis for instruction of students with mild disabilities indicates that effective teaching works for all youngsters regardless of the reason for their learning problems. Although categories of disabilities help determine eligibility for special education and provide direction for the prevention of mild disabilities, teaching concerns are best addressed cross-categorically. Such classroom practices as cooperative learning, peer tutoring, career education, and social skills instruction are equally effective for all learners, including those with mild disabilities.

Chapter 6 explains how to organize and implement inclusion programs. Chapter 7 looks at teaching from the needs of the learner, and Chapter 8 highlights instructional modifications. Classroom management practices are detailed in Chapter 9. The emphasis is on actions by the teacher that prevent discipline problems, and information on such classroom management practices as behavior modification and life space crisis intervention is presented. Chapter 10 extends the classroom management discussion to an analysis of social skills instruction. The final chapter, 11, describes the value of family-school cooperation. It describes programs for helping families and gives an overview of issues that surface when a family discovers that a child has a mild disability.

This book is organized with the needs of the reader in mind. Opening vignettes describe real-life scenarios. Figures and tables summarize information. Anecdotes help the reader get a feel for events that affect the lives of youngsters with mild disabilities. Activities support information within each chapter. We have attempted to achieve a writing style that is readable and intellectually stimulating. Many issues relating to the education of students with mild disabilities require thoughtful analysis. As in most educational concerns, the "right" answer is elusive. Our goal is to present an honest and straightforward picture of the issues that confront teachers and families as they strive to provide mildly disabled students with the education they need to live successful lives.

YOUR CLASS. YOUR CAREER. EVERYONE'S FUTURE.

MyEducationLab is a research-based learning tool that brings teaching to life. Through authentic in-class video footage, interactive simulations, rich case studies, examples of authentic teacher and student work, and more, MyEducationLab prepares you for your teaching career by showing what quality instruction looks like.

Multimedia assets on the MyEducationLab site include:

Video: The authentic classroom videos in MyEducationLab show how real teachers handle actual classroom situations.

Case Studies: A diverse set of robust cases illustrate the realities of teaching and offer valuable perspectives on common issues and challenges in education.

Simulations: Created by the IRIS Center at Vanderbilt University, these interactive simulations give you hands-on practice at adapting instruction for a full spectrum of learners.

Readings: Specially selected, topically relevant articles from ASCD's renowned *Educational Leadership* journal expand and enrich your perspectives on key issues and topics.

Student & Teacher Artifacts: Authentic preK-12 student and teacher classroom artifacts are tied to course topics and offer you practice in working with the actual types of materials you will encounter daily as teachers.

Lesson & Portfolio Builders: With this effective and easy-to-use tool, you can create, update, and share standards-based lesson plans and portfolios.

ACKNOWLEDGMENTS

We owe sincere thanks to our families, who supported us during the writing of this sixth edition. As always, we are in debt to our college students who, in their quest for knowledge and practical solutions, have pushed us to expand our awareness. We owe special thanks to our editors, Virginia Lanigan and Ann Davis. Their encouragement and support were instrumental in allowing this project to reach a successful conclusion. We also thank Matt Buchholz, editorial assistant, and the reviewers who provided helpful comments on the book: Maribeth Kasik, Governors State University; Maurice Miller, Indiana State University; Harold M. Waters, Southern Wesleyan University. Our copyeditor, Deidre Schaefer, did a marvelous job identifying and fixing grammatical and contextual errors. Finally, we want to thank our college and university colleagues who provide us with both inspiration and challenge. We are keenly aware that in the final analysis the value of our work rests on their judgment. We hope we have met their expectations.

ABOUT THE AUTHORS

Martin Henley, Ph.D. is the chairman of the Education Department at Westfield State College in Westfield, Massachusetts. He is a graduate of Syracuse University. In 1970, while at Syracuse, he was awarded a fellowship in to complete an M.Ed. program in urban education. Another fellowship awarded in 1972 allowed him to complete a Ph.D. program in special education. Martin has held a variety of positions in the field of education, including principal of an inclusive school for children with autism. He was a Head Start director, an urban school teacher, and a special education teacher. In addition to this text on mild disabilities, Henley has authored many articles on at-risk youth. His other books include *Teaching Self-Control: A Curriculum for Responsible Behavior, Creating Successful Inclusion Programs,* and *Proactive Classroom Management.* His most recent article "Teaching Self-Control" was published in the sixth edition of *Conflict in the Classroom.* Henley enjoys traveling and cooking. He is also an avid golfer and runner.

Roberta S. Ramsey, Ph.D., LPC is a retired professor of education, educational leadership, and special education with the Georgia University System. She continues to be active in education as a consultant, workshop presenter, and author. Her most recent endeavor was to research and design an online Master of Education program for Norwich University in Northfield, Vermont. She is known in Georgia for a strong leadership legacy as a professor at four state universities. As Chairperson of Graduate Special Education at Albany State University, she developed and provided the leadership for state approval of the master of education programs in behavior disorders, learning disabilities, intellectual disabilities, and gifted endorsement. She collaborated with a sister institution to create the specialist in education program for special education teachers. Throughout north Florida, Georgia, and southeast Alabama, she visits with teachers and administrators who are the product of her programs. This work was preceded by years of experience in many modes of instruction across the educational spectrum, and leadership roles at school and district level. She has served as a teacher at all levels from the kindergarten classroom to the college classroom with master of education students. As a principal, assistant principal, district representative for Section 504, and district staff officer in behavior disorders and specific learning disabilities, she has applied the things about which she has written for many years. As a Licensed Professional Counselor in Georgia, she continues an active relationship with the education and psychology communities. Her study guide for teachers faced with the Teacher Competency Test in their state was the first of its kind in the field and is still in use by special education teachers. She has been a professional consultant to the U.S. Department of Labor Job Corps program. With this book, she hopes to share a rich experience with aspiring teachers in general and special education.

Robert F. Algozzine, Ph.D. is professor in the Department of Educational Leadership at the University of North Carolina and co-project director of the U.S. Department of Education-supported Behavior and Reading Improvement Center. With over 25 years of research experience and extensive firsthand knowledge of teaching students with serious emotional disturbance, Algozzine is a uniquely qualified staff developer, conference speaker, and teacher of behavior instruction and effective teaching courses. As an active partner and collaborator with professionals in Charlotte-Mecklenburg Schools in North Carolina and as an editor of several journals focused on special education, Algozzine keeps his finger on the pulse of current special education research and practice. He has written more than 250 manuscripts on varied educational topics and authored many popular books and textbooks on how to manage emotional and social behavior problems. Through his work with Drs. Henley and Ramsey, Dr. Algozzine hopes to continue to help improve the lives of students with special needs and the professionals who teach them.

CHAPTER ONE

FOUNDATIONS OF SPECIAL EDUCATION FOR STUDENTS WITH MILD DISABILITIES

ADVANCE QUESTIONS

Answer the following questions as you read this chapter:

1. What factors led to the development of special education?
2. What are the key principles that drive special education today?
3. Why do some students receive special education?
4. Who is eligible for special education?
5. What are mild disabilities?
6. What are the advantages and disadvantages of classifying students for special education?
7. How do school personnel decide what special education services are appropriate for students with mild disabilities?
8. What are some key differences between general and special education?

VIGNETTE: JAKE, MARY, FELIPE

Jake always seems to be one step behind the other students in his 7th-grade class. Despite the slowness that is a part of Jake's performance and social development, his teacher enjoys having him in class. Because Jake is talkative with a good sense of humor, many of his schoolmates enjoy helping him. Jake's teacher likes teaching him because he responds favorably to efforts to help him develop new skills. Jake's classroom performance is similar to many students with mild intellectual disability.

Jake's class contains a mixture of students who are easy to teach and students who are hard to teach. Mary is one of the difficult kids. When she was younger she was diagnosed as "hyperactive," and she was put on medication to control her behavior. She comes from a home where both parents work hard to maintain a comfortable lifestyle. There is a lot of pressure put on Mary to succeed. Both of her parents are upwardly mobile professionals. Mary does not trust adults and often takes her anger out on her classmates. When she is not physically disrupting the classroom, Mary is socially withdrawn, isolated, and unhappy. Mary's teacher believes that Mary is emotionally disturbed.

Felipe also is difficult to teach—not because of what he does, but because of what he does not do. Felipe does not read or write as well as his 7th-grade classmates. He has never done well in reading, but his scores on ability tests and tests of achievement in other areas (e.g., mathematics) have always been average when compared to his peers. Now that Felipe is in junior high school, his difficulties are particularly troublesome, because he is expected to read and complete homework assignments in English, history, science, psychology, and economics. Felipe appears to have a learning disability.

Each of these students—Jake, Mary, and Felipe—is difficult to teach. They are constantly at risk of failing, and they are potential school dropouts. Jake, Mary, and Felipe have mild disabilities that are interfering with their progress in school.

Now that you have read the vignette about Jake, Mary, and Felipe, see how many problem-solving questions you can answer. For those questions you cannot readily answer, try to find some additional information to use in answering them as you read the chapter. The experiences of Jake, Mary, and Felipe are typical of students with mild disabilities.

1. What should be done to help students like Jake, Mary, and Felipe?
2. Who should teach them?
3. Should public schools provide special education services for students with learning problems like Jake, Mary, and Felipe?
4. What expectations would you have for students like Jake, Mary, and Felipe if you were teaching in their junior high school?
5. What is a mild disability?
6. Should students with mild disabilities be included in classes with students without disabilities?

Every classroom contains students like Jake, Mary, and Felipe. Helping students with learning problems is part of the motivation that stimulates many to become teachers. As one experienced teacher put it, "some teachers like the underdog." The purpose of special education is to help students achieve success in school. Special educators and their general classroom peers want to see all students stay in school, graduate, and succeed in life, but because of differences between the two systems of education, they sometimes work at cross-purposes. When special and general educators communicate and share responsibility for educating students with special needs, everybody benefits.

THE ROOTS OF SPECIAL EDUCATION

Origins of the national education system in America date from the colonial days. Early schools educated a select, limited segment of the population—white, male children of upper-class families (Smith, Price, & Marsh, 1986). Before 1815, schools serving this small proportion of school-aged youth were primarily church sponsored.

Public support of schools by local taxation began during the first half of the nineteenth century. Children previously excluded from schooling—middle class, poor, female, or culturally different—were included. During the mid-nineteenth century, states began enacting compulsory education laws (e.g., Rhode Island in 1840, Massachusetts in 1852). A change in the values and economic thinking of U.S. society was reflected by this Common School Movement.

These early common schools educated students of all ages in the same classroom. In the one-room schoolhouse, students of different ages, different abilities, and different backgrounds learned side by side. Horace Mann, the architect of American public education, believed universal education was the great equalizer. Cremin (1961) characterized this early vision:

> Mann's school would be common, not as a school for the common people—for example, the nineteenth-century Prussian Volksschule—but rather as a school common to all people. It would be open to all, provided by the state and the local community as part of the birthright of every child. It would be for rich and poor alike, not only free but as good as any private institution. It would be nonsectarian, receiving children of all creeds, classes, and backgrounds. (p. 10)

Mann's humanitarian ideal began to take hold, and by 1860, a majority of the states had established public school systems. Throughout this period of rapid growth, Mann advised that instruction be adapted to meet the needs of children who differed in temperament, ability, and interests.

As the United States grew, the one-room schoolhouse was replaced by graded elementary, middle, and high schools. Explicit academic requirements were established for each grade level of the common public school. Students were taught a specific curriculum and that curriculum was organized into graded units. Educators believed that grouping students by age would make the task of teaching easier (Sarason & Doris, 1979; Ysseldyke & Algozzine, 1982; Ysseldyke, Algozzine, & Thurlow, 2000). Achievement was determined by how well children learned the predetermined, graded curriculum. This curriculum-centered characteristic of the new schools made it difficult for many children to keep pace (Smith, Price, & Marsh, 1986; Ysseldyke & Algozzine, 1984).

SPEEDBUMP—Did you know that summer vacations originated so students could work the family farm during peak growing times?

Immigration and compulsory school attendance broadened the school-aged population to a larger, more diverse membership. Cultural and ethnic differences in students created a mismatch between teacher expectations and student performance. Some children adapted to school and learned; others dropped out. Many children worked in factories; others took to the streets. Few of the absent students were missed. Little concern was shown for children with learning problems and what we now refer to as "at-risk youth."

The influence of social reformers, such as Jane Addams, encouraged the establishment of alternative instructional programs for "special cases." The superintendent of the Baltimore schools wrote, "Before the attendance laws were effectively enforced there were as many of these special cases in the community as there is now; few of them, however, remained long enough in school to attract serious attention or to hinder the instruction of the more tractable and capable" (Van Sickle, 1908–1909, 102).

Early public educational programs offered two choices. Students either received and profited from instruction in lock-step, curriculum-centered classes or they were placed in special classes. Many administrators believed that these first **special education** programs were proper preparation for institutionalization. In a speech to the National Education Association, E. R. Johnstone (1908) stated that the special education class

> must become a clearing-house. To it will be sent the slightly blind and partially deaf, but also incorrigibles, the mental deficients, and the cripples. . . .The only thing to do is to give them the best of care and training possible. Keep them in the special classes until they become too old for further care in school, and then they must be sent to the institutions for safety. (Johnstone, 1908, 114–118)

A few early special programs were set up for children with specific disabilities, such as deafness or blindness. However, many early public school special classes were repositories for diverse youngsters who did not fit into the general classroom. In 1909, Elizabeth Farrell described students in her first special education class in New York City:

> The first class was made up of the odds and ends of a large school. There were the over-age children, the so-called naughty children, and the dull, and stupid children. They were taken from any and every school grade. The ages ranged from eight to sixteen years. They were the children who could not get along in school. They were typical of a large number of children who even today are forced directly or indirectly out of school; they were the children who were interested in street life; many of them earned a good deal of money in one way or another. While some of them had been in trouble with the police, as a class they could not be characterized as criminal. They had varied interests but the school, as they found it, had little or nothing for them. (Farrell, 1909, 91–96)

From the first decades of the twentieth century until the mid-1970s, students who did not fit in general education classes were ignored, placed in isolated special classes, or transferred to state institutions.

SPEEDBUMP—There is a saying "the more things change, the more they remain the same." Unfortunately, there are still programs where students are separated from their peers because they don't fit in. Many of them are like the streetwise type of youngster taught by Elizabeth Farrell over a hundred years ago.

In Pennsylvania, legislation provided for the exclusion of specific children from school. Children evaluated as uneducable because of below-average IQ scores were assigned to the Department of Public Welfare for training in state-run institutions. Most notable about the process of classifying and rejecting students who didn't fit the standard public school curriculum was the lack of due process in educational decisions.

In 1970, the Task Force of Children Out of School studied the Boston Public School System. The Task Force report—*The Way We Go to School: The Exclusion of Children in Boston*—found over ten thousand students excluded from public school classrooms because they didn't match school standards for the normal student. Patricia Reilly, age 16, was told to leave school because she was pregnant. Kathy Fitzgerald, age 9, was excluded from public school because she had a seizure disorder (i.e., epilepsy). Richard, 11 years old, was placed in a special class for the retarded because he was emotionally disturbed and no other program was available. These children were denied the right to an appropriate education because they were different. In 1974, the U.S. Congress estimated that over a million school-aged youngsters were denied a proper education in this country's schools.

The experience of being treated differently because one does not fit into society's vision of what is normal and accepted is difficult. Many move to the "land of opportunity," to "the other side of the tracks," to "the better part of town," or to "a good school" to overcome discrimination and to build a "better life" for themselves and their children. They hope to reclaim the dignity they are entitled to as human beings and citizens of a country for which dreams and ideals of individualism, equal opportunity, nationalism, and success prevail and are the basis for fundamental human rights and continuing social responsibilities. Too often it simply doesn't work out that way. Too often, differences and diversity that should be celebrated are the source of disparaging remarks, continuing intolerance, and disenfranchising treatment.

SPEEDBUMP—Having a disability is just another way of being different.

How could a nation based on equal opportunity for all its citizens support discriminatory practices toward children? The answer is found in attitudes. Prejudice, like creeping shadows, can take many forms. The public school system mirrors society. Schools reflect the attitudes and prejudices of teachers, administrators, and parents. Students with disabilities have special needs, and in the past those special needs have been used as a rationale to exclude them from mainstream life in American schools.

Education once intended for a small, elite sector of the population now is mandated for all children. During the past century, the curriculum-centered format of public schools has remained static while the needs of students have changed significantly. School dropouts, discipline problems, low achievement, and increased referrals to special education are a concern to educators and the public at large.

SPEEDBUMP—Passing standardized testing as a graduation requirement has created difficulties for many students, including those with special needs.

Diversity of students, simply defined as coming from a different background than your peers, is at odds with a system of education that requires conformity and assimilation of an unyielding curriculum. Smith-Davis (1989a) identified some important events and acts of legislation that enhanced diversity. The *Brown v. Topeka Board of Education* decision in 1954 radically altered the national school population. This landmark case, acted upon by the U.S. Supreme Court, decreed that "segregated but equal" school facilities for black and white schoolchildren were discriminatory and unconstitutional. *Brown v. Topeka Board of Education* reversed a prior decision rendered in *Plessy v. Ferguson* in 1894 that legalized separate schools based on racial lines.

The Civil Rights Act of 1964 gave support to advocates who pushed for the inclusion of students with disabilities in public schools (Smith-Davis, 1989a, b; Smith, Price, & Marsh, 1986; Ysseldyke & Algozzine, 1990). **Mainstreaming**, a term used to promote the integration of school-aged youth with disabilities into classrooms with their peers without disabilities, followed on the heels of successful efforts to deinstitutionalize programs for adults and children with disabilities. Placement of youth and adults with moderate and severe disabilities within community settings dramatized their capability to live normal lives. These changes diversified the student population in the nation's schools and emphasized the need for schools to accommodate children with special learning needs (Ysseldyke, Algozzine, & Thurlow, 1983; 2000), yet changes in public school practices toward students with disabilities have been slow to come. For instance, the steady increase each year in youngsters identified with mild disabilities and placed in special programs is testimony to the intractability of a system of education that looks first to blame the student for failure.

SPEEDBUMP—If you like to look at a situation from different points of view, you will like special education. It is interdisciplinary—combining such areas as politics, law, medicine, and psychology.

DIVERSITY

In 1987, 47 percent of the workforce was comprised of white Americans; by the mid-twenty-first century 85 percent of new workers will be African Americans. In the year 2020, almost half of the school-aged population will be young African Americans (Pallas, Natriello, & McDill, 1989). This "browning of America" is a reality that signals profound change in U.S. culture. Multicultural education, with its attendant emphasis on gender, race, and bilingualism is aimed at preparing today's youth for a future characterized by diversity. Ford (1992) defines multicultural education as school "practices and policies that transform the school so that male and female students, social class, racial, and ethnic groups will experience an equal opportunity to learn" (p. 108).

Multicultural Family Adaptation. Family adaptation researchers are just beginning to recognize culture as an important variable for exploration (Bennett, DeLuca, & Allen, 1996; National Research Council, 2001; Seligman, 1999). For example, African American families whose religions strongly influence their family traditions may appraise disability positively. "The optimism and belief that all children are important typifies African American culture and is reflected in family functions and reinforced in church and religious beliefs" (Rogers-Dulan & Blacher, 1995, 234). Within the Native Hawaiian culture, the spiritual orientation toward life may influence families to think that having a child with behavior disorders is "normal" and that this child is a valued member of the community, regardless of disability. The Native American assimilation of individuals with disabilities into the mainstream culture is reflected in the absence of native language "labels" or "classifications" for disabilities such as autism. Rather, descriptive statements commonly are used such as those by some Navajos, including "she runs away," or "he gets excited," or "he's in his own world" (Connors & Donnellan, 1998, 171).

Social support is defined as the community supports and resources "that the family may use to cope with a stressor situation" (McCubbin, McCubbin, Thompson, & Thompson, 1998, 20). Social support may include people, such as family and friends, and organizations, such as schools, churches, parent and sibling support groups, and medical services. Social support mediates the effects of the stressor on the health of the family (see McCubbin et al., 1998). The strong familial support needed to raise a child with behavior disorders is found in many cultures.

Native Hawaiians share a common concern for the well-being of all individuals in the tribal structure, which encompasses the immediate and extended family (McCubbin et al., 1998). Similarly, the foundation of the family structure in Filipino American families is built on cooperation and family support and allegiance, in which individual desires are sacrificed for the benefit of the family (McCubbin et al., 1998). Many individuals within the African American culture perceive caregiving for a dependent member as a responsibility to be shared among siblings and extended family members (Pruchno, Patrick, & Burant, 1997).

Fear of stigma also has been reported in African American families (Pruchno et al., 1997), who tend to access services provided by professional organizations less frequently than the majority culture (see Pruchno et al., 1997) and only after relying on family, friends, religion, and church support. The concept of "familismo" in Hispanic families relates to strong family cohesion. This familial cohesion may circumvent the use of professional services if family values conflict with standards of the majority culture (Blacher, Lopez, Shapiro, & Fusco, 1997). When Hispanic mothers of children with disabilities believe in their spiritual role as "sacrificing mothers," and if they receive strong support from their extended family, they may take upon themselves the responsibility of raising their child with little organizational support (Bailey, Skinner, Rodriguez, Gut, & Correa, 1999).

A diversity issue that affects all populations is lack of equal rights for women. Even though men and women have equal ability, men continue to be paid higher salaries and have easier access to promotion. Stereotypes about women begin in infancy, with pink birth ribbons signifying daintiness and beauty. These initial views are strengthened throughout childhood through toys, sports, and leisure activities. Consider a 9-year-old boy who chooses ballet over baseball or a 10-year-old girl who wants to play football. These youngsters will face opposition and ridicule as they attempt to oppose gender barriers. Look around your education classes. If you are an elementary or early childhood major, you probably have five times more females than males in your class. Why do more women than men select education as a major? An analysis of explanations will highlight some of the gender barriers girls and women must overcome in order to achieve an equal position in U.S. society.

SPEEDBUMP—One of the major issues educators as well as citizens will be dealing with in the future will be whether English should be the "official" language of the United States. What do you think?

As the debates continue about how diversity issues should be dealt with, the major hurdle to the educational progress of many people of color continues to be poverty. Hu-De-Hart (1993) succinctly illustrates the chasm that separates rich and poor in the United States: "Today 1 percent of the population of the United States has 'gained control' of more of the nation's wealth than the bottom 90 percent. This situation parallels the stark and painful inequality in much of the Third World" (p. 51). Multicultural proponents point to inequities of school funding as evidence that today's poor schoolchildren (many of whom are minorities) are at a distinct disadvantage in their preparation for tomorrow's workplace. Property taxes fund schools. Children who live in destitute communities are unable to break the cycle of poverty because their education is as bleak as their neighborhoods.

African American children, particularly males, are overrepresented in special education programs for students with **mild intellectual disability** and **emotional disturbance**. Paradoxically, females and children with limited English proficiency (e.g., Hispanic) are underrepresented in special education programs. This trend of over- and underrepresentation means that many African American children may be inappropriately placed (see Lloyd Dunn's remarks in Chapter 3, Mild Intellectual Disability), while females and Hispanic students who require special education are overlooked. The uneven distribution of students in special education has created a confusing picture about the educational needs of females of all races: African Americans, Hispanics, and Native Americans.

In an optimistic future scenario, the United States will be built on a strong foundation of respect for individual differences. The positive outcomes of multicultural education could help alleviate sexism and racism. In such a society all individuals regardless of gender, ethnic origin, sexual preference, or disability will have an equal opportunity to succeed. As educators, the choices we make now will determine our ability to adapt to fundamental changes in U.S. society.

ENDING HANDICAPPISM

Advocates for individuals with disabilities have used the word **handicappism** to refer to the disabling perception that a person is incompetent because of a physical or psychological impairment. When asked about their most difficult adjustments, adults with disabilities invariably comment about dealing with stereotypes. For example, friends and neighbors may refer to Elise Jones, who has a visual impairment, as "poor, blind Elise!" Condescending remarks about individuals with disabilities may be masked as sympathy, but the message is a clear illustration of handicappism. In fact, Elise's visual impairment is only a part of her individuality, not the sum total of who Elise is as a person.

Sooner or later, most of us will experience a disability. Old age, injuries, or illness are inescapable aspects of the human condition. Although the idea that at some point in your life you will experience a disability might seem remote, the simple truth is that we are not talking about infrequent or isolated cases. The number of U.S. citizens with disabilities is equal to the combined population of New York City, Los Angeles, Chicago, and Miami.

Individuals with disabilities are people first and people with a disability second. The label assigned to their disability should not be used to replace all their other characteristics. Franklin D. Roosevelt guided the United States through the Second World War from the vantage point of a wheelchair. Einstein was considered too slow to attend school with his peers. Thomas Edison had a learning disability. These extraordinary people were not limited by their disabilities. Throughout this book, we highlight the individual first and the disability second by our phrasing "student with a disability." We do this because language shapes expectations and expectations shape actions. Our persistent theme is that students with mild disabilities are more like their peers than different from them.

> **SPEEDBUMP**—Your language, your expectations, and your actions when you teach students with mild disabilities will determine their success or failure. Remember, a disability is a problem that can be overcome; don't handicap your students by limiting your expectations for their personal and academic growth.

Litigation and Legislation

Prior to the early 1970s, handicappism, the notion that individuals with disabilities were severely limited in their ability to learn, was the predominant educational perspective. Most notable about this view was that the lack of **due process** afforded students when educators either excluded them from school or placed them in dead-end special classes. Due process is a constitutional right guaranteed by the Fourteenth Amendment. During the 1970s, concern about the legal rights of students with special needs spurred several significant class action suits that challenged school evaluation and placement practices. A class action suit is litigation on behalf of a class or group of individuals. For example, when a small group of students who were classified as mentally retarded won a class action suit, all other students with intellectual disability within the court's jurisdiction benefitted.

> **SPEEDBUMP—**A class action suit affects all individuals who are in the same "class" as the litigants. Can you think of any other class action suits that have influenced public policy?

In *Diana v. California State Board of Education* (1970), the issue of Mexican American student overrepresentation in special classes for students with mild intellectual disabilities was addressed. The plaintiffs were nine children who came from homes where Spanish was the primary language. The class action suit alleged that Mexican American students had been improperly categorized as mildly retarded on the basis of invalid IQ testing. In a consent agreement, the opposing parties agreed that schoolchildren should be tested in their native language. This case laid the groundwork for future lawsuits based on cultural bias in educational evaluations.

The following year, 1971, fourteen families sued the state of Pennsylvania on the basis that their children with intellectual disability were denied equal access to a public education. This case, *Pennsylvania Association for Retarded Children (PARC) v. Commonwealth of Pennsylvania*, was prompted by the state policy of denying a public education to youngsters with intellectual disability. During the legal proceedings, parents described their futile attempts to fight a system that arbitrarily and callously excluded their children from school.

Nancy Beth Bowman was expelled from kindergarten because she wasn't toilet trained. The 15-year-old daughter of Leonard Kalish was never allowed to enroll in school. It cost him $40,000 to have her educated in private schools. The parents of David Tupi said their son was expelled from school without notice. One morning the school bus simply stopped coming to pick him up. The three-judge panel, in a consent decree, ruled that the state could not predetermine educability. In their decision the judges stated that Pennsylvania must:

1. Admit all children with intellectual disability into public school.
2. Place students with intellectual disability in general classrooms when possible.

■ ■ ■ ■ ■ ▬▬▬▬▬▬▬▬▬▬▬▬▬▬▬▬▬▬▬▬

HIGHLIGHT 1.1

Francis enjoyed going out to eat with his friends. However, he often encountered difficulties because few restaurants were accessible to his wheelchair. Curbs, narrow doors, stairs, and small public restrooms were all obstacles for Francis. One evening Francis and his friends were ordering dinner. When the waitress came to Francis, she asked one of his friends, "What would he like to eat?" The waitress assumed that because Francis was in a wheelchair he was incapable of ordering his own dinner! Just as physical obstacles impaired Francis's ability to live a normal life, so did stereotypes by well-meaning but thoughtless people. A disability is born but society handicaps.

3. Make all school records accessible to parents.
4. Provide preschool programs for children with intellectual disability when such programs were available to nondisabled children.
5. Precede all placement decisions with a hearing to allow parental participation and consent.

The PARC decision emphasized the due process rights of parents to review and challenge placement decisions regarding their children.

In *Mills v. The Board of Education of the District of Columbia* (1972), litigants challenged the exclusion of children identified as mentally retarded, emotionally disturbed, learning disabled, visually impaired, hearing impaired, and physically disabled from Washington, D.C., schools. As in the *PARC* case, Mills demonstrated the unconstitutionality of school exclusion procedures. Both the *PARC* and *Mills* "right to education" cases highlighted the right of students with disabilities to due process in educational decisions.

By 1973, 31 similar court cases constituted a groundswell of political activism on behalf of students with disabilities (Taylor & Searle, 1987). It was clear to Congress that schools could no longer be allowed to violate the Fourteenth Amendment rights of students with disabilities. The Fourteenth Amendment states that "no state shall make or enforce any law which shall abridge the privileges or immunities of citizens of the United States; nor shall any state deprive any person of life, liberty, or property without due process of law."

FEDERAL LAWS

Section 504 of the Rehabilitation Act of 1973

Several federal laws have significantly influenced the education of children and adults with disabilities. The first of these is the Rehabilitation Act of 1973 that protects individuals from being discriminated against because of a disability. Within public schools Section 504 of this law is often used to provide support services for students who have a disability that is not included in the Individuals with Disabilities Education Act (IDEA), for instance students with ADHD.

Section 504 of the Rehabilitation Act of 1973 states:

> No otherwise qualified individual with a disability . . . shall, solely by reason of her or his disability, be excluded from participation in, be denied the benefits of, or be subjected to discrimination under any program or activity receiving Federal financial assistance. . . . [Language of Section 504 of the Rehabilitation Act: 29 U.S.C. 794(a) (1996)]

Section 504 is a brief but powerful provision of the Rehabilitation Act of 1973 that extends to individuals with disabilities the same kind of protection extended to individuals discriminated against on the basis of race and gender (Huefner, 2000). Originally targeted at employment discrimination, the scope of Section 504 is broad, addressing protection in many areas (e.g., public school education, higher education, social services, health care, transportation). Because most school districts in the country accept federal funds, public education was greatly influenced by Section 504.

The relationship between Section 504, the **Americans with Disabilities Act** (ADA), the **Individuals with Disabilities Education Act** (IDEA), and the **No Child Left Behind Act** is presented in Table 1.1. Basically, any person with a disability (i.e., physical or mental impairment that limits major life activities) is eligible for Section 504 assistance. This group is broader than the group eligible for federal assistance under IDEA and special education guidelines (i.e., all students with disabilities receiving assistance under IDEA are eligible for 504 support, but not all students receiving assistance under 504 are eligible for support under IDEA).

Individuals with Disabilities Education Act (IDEA)

The culmination of many years of struggle on behalf of children with disabilities occurred on November 29, 1975, when President Ford signed Public Law 94–142, the Education for All Handicapped Children Act (EHA). This landmark federal legislation mandated a **free and appropriate education** for students with disabilities aged 3 to 21. The EHA has been called the "first compulsory special education law," and much of what happens in special education today is a direct response to the provisions embodied in it (Ysseldyke, Algozzine, & Thurlow, 2000). Since first enacted, the EHA has been amended to further emphasize the rights of individuals with disabilities and their families. Today the EHA is known as the Individuals with Disabilities Education Act (IDEA). Despite the name change and other amendments, the basic rights and provisions it afforded students with disabilities and their families have remained largely the same: the right to free and appropriate education, the right to due process, and the right to education in the least restrictive environment.

SPEEDBUMP—If it wasn't for this law, you probably would not be taking this course. IDEA changed the educational landscape in this country.

BOX 1.1
AMERICANS WITH DISABILITIES ACT

The year 2000 represented a milestone for the nation's disability community; July 26 marked the 10th anniversary of the Americans with Disabilities Act (ADA). The ADA guarantees access, accommodation, and removal of barriers to help people with disabilities fully participate in society. For people with disabilities, the ADA is analogous to the Civil Rights Act of 1964. This law provided individuals with disabilities a declaration of liberty from the days when they had little hope of competing on a level playing field with their peers without disabilities. It provides the foundation of nondiscrimination against people with disabilities in the areas of employment, state and local governments, public accommodations, and telecommunications.

TABLE 1.1   Scope of Key Legislation Affecting Students with Disabilities

INDIVIDUALS WITH DISABILITIES EDUCATION IMPROVEMENT ACT (IDEA) (2004)

This education act reauthorizes federal financial assistance to state and local education agencies to guarantee special education and related services to eligible children with disabilities.

Who is protected?	Children ages 3–21 who are determined by a multidisciplinary team to be eligible within one or more of 13 specific categories of disability and who need special education and related services. Categories include autism, deafness, deaf-blindness, hearing impairments, intellectual disability, multiple disabilities, orthopedic impairments, other health impairments, serious emotional disturbance, specific learning disabilities, speech or language impairments, traumatic brain injury, and visual impairment.
Responsibility to provide a free appropriate public education (FAPE)?	A *FAPE* is defined to mean special education and related services. Special education means "specially designed instruction, at no cost to the parents, to meet the unique needs of the child with a disability. . . ." Related services are provided if required for the students to benefit from specially designed instruction. States are required to ensure the provision of full educational opportunity to all children with disabilities. IDEA requires the development of an individualized education program (IEP) document with specific content and a required number of specific participants at an IEP meeting.
What are the procedural safeguards?	IDEA requires written notice to parents regarding identification, evaluation, and/or placement. Further, written notice must be made prior to any change in placement. The act delineates the required components of the written notices.
What is the due process?	IDEA delineates specific requirements for local education agencies to provide impartial hearings for parents who disagree with the identification, evaluation, or placement of a child.

NO CHILD LEFT BEHIND ACT (2002)

Signed into law in 2002, this new law contains sweeping changes in the Elementary and Secondary Education Act. The act contains four basic education reform principles.

Responsibility to provide a system for educational accountability?	States create their own standards for what students should learn in each grade. Beginning in 2002, states began testing students in grades 3–5, 6–9, and 10–12. By 2005, tests were administered in grades 3–8 in math and reading. All students including those with mild disabilities are to be held to the same curriculum and assessment standards.

(continued)

TABLE 1.1   Continued

Who is protected?	Federal aid is contingent on an increase in proficiency in math, reading, and science among all students. States must maintain goals and assess results for various categories of students based on poverty, ethnicity, disability, and limited English proficiency.
What are the procedural safeguards?	Students attending Title I schools that fail to improve have the option to attend a better school in the same district.
What is the due process?	Schools have more flexibility in allocating resources and teacher professional development. Students who choose to attend persistently failing schools can use Title I funds to obtain supplemental educational services from public or private sectors.

AMERICANS WITH DISABILITIES ACT OF 1990 (ADA)

This act is a civil rights law to prohibit discrimination solely on the basis of disability in employment, public services, and accommodations.

Who is protected?	Any individual with a disability who (1) has a physical or mental impairment that substantially limits one or more life activities; (2) has a record of such an impairment; or (3) is regarded as having such an impairment. Further, the person must be qualified for the program, service, or job.
Responsibility to provide a free appropriate public education (FAPE)?	However, ADA protections apply to nonsectarian private schools, but not to organizations or entities controlled by religious organizations and ADA provides additional protection in combination with actions brought under Section 504 and IDEA. Reasonable accommodations are required for eligible students with a disability to perform essential functions of the job. This applies to any part of the special education program that may be community based and involve job training/placement.
What are the procedural safeguards?	The ADA does not specify procedural safeguards related to special education; it does detail the administrative requirements, complaint procedures, and the consequences for noncompliance, related to both services and employment.
What is the due process?	The ADA does not delineate specific due process procedures. People with disabilities have the same remedies that are available under Title VII of the Civil Rights Act of 1964, as amended by the Civil Rights Act of 1991. Thus, individuals who are discriminated against may file a complaint with the relevant federal agency or sue in federal court. Enforcement agencies encourage informal mediation and voluntary compliance.

SECTION 504 OF THE REHABILITATION ACT OF 1973

This is a civil rights law to prohibit discrimination solely on the basis of disability in programs and activities, public and private, that receive federal financial assistance.

TABLE 1.1 Continued

Who is protected?	Any person who (1) has a physical or mental impairment that substantially limits one or more major life activities, (2) has a record of such an impairment, or (3) is regarded as having such an impairment. Major life activities include walking, seeing, hearing, speaking, breathing, learning, working, caring for oneself, and performing manual tasks.
Responsibility to provide a free appropriate public education (FAPE)?	An "appropriate" education means an education comparable to that provided to students without disabilities. This may be defined as regular or special education services. Students can receive related services under Section 504 even if they are not provided any special education. Section 504 does require development of a plan, although this written document is not mandated. The IEP of IDEA may be used for the Section 504 written plan. Many experts recommend that a group of persons knowledgeable about the students convene and specify the agreed-upon services.
What are the procedural safeguards?	Section 504 requires notice to parents regarding identification, evaluation, and/or placement. Written notice is recommended. Notice must be made only before a "significant change" in placement. Following IDEA procedural safeguards is one way to meet Section 504 mandates.
What is the due process?	Section 504 requires local education agencies to provide impartial hearings for parents who disagree with the identification, evaluation, or placement of a student. It requires that parents have an opportunity to participate in the hearing process and to be represented by counsel. Beyond this, due process details are left to the discretion of the local education agency. It is recommended that districts develop policy guidance and procedures.

Source: Adapted from ERICDigest E537, Henderson, K. (1995).

Free and Appropriate Education. By law, school personnel must prepare an **individualized education program** (IEP) for every student receiving special education services. The IEP must include certain information about the child and the educational program designed to meet his or her unique needs. The IEP documents that a student is receiving an "appropriate education. In a nutshell, this information is (U.S. Department of Education, 2000a):

- **Current performance.** The IEP must state how the child currently is doing in school (known as present levels of educational performance). This information usually comes from the evaluation results such as classroom tests and assignments, individual tests given to decide eligibility for services or during reevaluation, and observations made by parents, teachers, and related service providers. The statement about "current performance" includes how the child's disability affects his or her involvement and progress in general education.

- **Annual goals.** These are goals that the child can reasonably accomplish in a year. Goals may be academic, address social or behavioral needs, relate to physical needs, or address other educational needs. The goals must be measurable; meaning that it must be possible to measure whether the student has achieved the goals.
- **Special education and related services.** The IEP must list the special education and related services to be provided to the child or on behalf of the child. This includes supplementary aids and services that the child needs. It also includes modifications (changes) to the program or supports for school personnel—such as training or professional development—that will be provided to assist the child.
- **Participation with students without disabilities.** The IEP must explain the extent (if any) to which the child will *not* participate with children without disabilities in the general class and other school activities.
- **Participation in state and districtwide tests.** Local educational agencies must measure student progress with state- or districtwide assessments used for students without disabilities.
- **Dates and places.** The IEP must state when services will begin, how often they will be provided, where they will be provided, and how long they will last.
- **Transition service needs.** Beginning when the child is age 16 (or younger, if appropriate), the IEP must state what transition services are needed to help the child prepare for leaving school.
- **Discipline.** When disciplining students with disabilities, a school must determine if the behavior was a result of the disability before taking action.

> **SPEEDBUMP—**The amount of paperwork and time it takes to develop an IEP is a serious concern for school principals and educators.

Due Process.   By law, students with disabilities and their families are guaranteed rights of due process (see Figure 1.1). This means that these students and their families have the same Fourteenth Amendment rights enjoyed by all citizens. School personnel cannot change the educational placement of students with disabilities without the informed consent (i.e., written permission) of the students' parents or guardians. Parents also are entitled to independent assessments and impartial hearings when decisions about their children are being made. If needed, states must provide mediation services to resolve disputes with families regarding special education services.

Least Restrictive Environment.   Students with disabilities must be educated in the **least restrictive environment**. This means that students with disabilities should be educated to the maximum extent feasible with students without disabilities. Students with disabilities receive special education in a variety of settings. Some are enrolled full time in general education classes and receive only indirect services from special education personnel. Some students with mild disabilities are pulled out of their general education classes daily to go to resource rooms for special education services. Still others are enrolled in self-

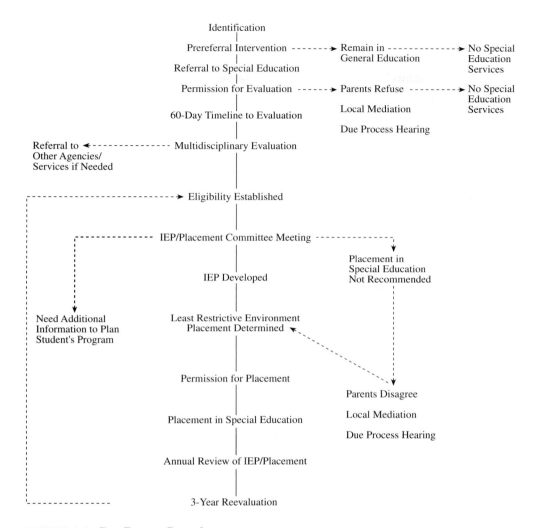

FIGURE 1.1   Due Process Procedures

Source: Georgia Department of Education, 1989.

contained special education classes but, to the maximum extent possible, attend general education classes for part of the school day for certain kinds of instruction. For example, a student might be enrolled in a special class but attend a general education class for instruction in math, music, art, or physical education. Figure 1.2 lists key provisions of IDEA. In addition to IDEA, other significant federal legislation promotes the rights and services for individuals with disabilities. The mandate for a free, appropriate public education for adults with disabilities also is paralleled in the Vocational Rehabilitation Act of 1973 (P.L. 93–112). Section 504 of this act made it illegal for institutions or organizations that receive federal funds to discriminate against citizens with disabilities.

FIGURE 1.2   Major Provisions of IDEA

Due Process Provisions
Right to examine all pupil records
Right to independent assessment of pupil
Right to written notice of any program change
Right to impartial hearing on any school decisions

Protection in Evaluation Provisions (PEP)
Right to individual assessment before placement
Right to assessment with appropriate instruments
Right to unbiased assessment and team decisions

Individualized Education Program (IEP) Provisions
Right to written statement of present functioning
Right to written statement of goals
Right to written statement of services expected
Right to written statement of expected time frame
Right to participate in program development

Least Restrictive Environment (LRE) Provisions
Right to education in general education classroom to the maximum feasible extent

IDEA.   In 1990, Congress amended the EHA in several significant ways. The Individuals with Disabilities Education Act (IDEA) (Public Law 101–476) replaced the original title of the law. The name change reflects the need to emphasize the person first and the disability second. Also, individuals who receive special education up to age 21 should not be referred to as "children" as in the original title: Education of Handicapped Children Act. Amendments in IDEA included an expansion of related services such as therapeutic recreation, social work services, and rehabilitation counseling. Transition services were mandated to be written into IEPs. Transition services begin at age 16. These services coordinate rehabilitative services— for example, supported employment and independent living—beyond the school years. The purchase or leasing of customized equipment to support educational services (e.g., computers, wheelchairs, adaptive equipment) also is authorized by this federal law. The Individuals with Disabilities Education Act adds students with autism and traumatic brain injury to the list of populations provided special education.

Americans with Disabilities Act

In 1990 Congress passed the Americans with Disabilities Act (ADA). This national law provides individuals of all ages with protection from discrimination due to a disability. The ADA is sweeping in authority. Sometimes referred to as "the civil rights act for the disabled," ADA applies to a variety of venues including public services, transportation, private sector employment, public accommodations, and communications. ADA requires that every sort of public accommodation from automatic bank machines to football bleachers be accessible to individuals with disabilities.

> **SPEEDBUMP—**The next time you go to a restaurant or sporting event see how many accommodations you can identify.

No Child Left Behind Act

On January 8, 2002, President George W. Bush signed into law the No Child Left Behind (NCLB) Act. This reauthorization of the Elementary and Secondary Education Act set challenging new academic standards for the education of this country's youth. The Act is based on four education reform principles:

1. Stronger school accountability is needed for student improved learning.
2. Local schools need increased flexibility in order to respond to specific student needs.
3. Expanded options should be made available to parents.
4. Teaching methods should have a strong positive research basis. (www.nclb.gov)

Throughout the 670-page document a central theme is repeated: Schools and teachers are accountable for the academic achievement of *all* students including those who receive special education services. Some highlights of NCLB in relationship to special education students are:

1. Students with disabilities must be included in each state's new accountability system.
2. State plans must be coordinated with the Individuals with Disabilities Education Act.
3. Academic standards apply to all students including those with disabilities.
4. Special education students must meet each state's proficient level of academic achievement by 2014.
5. States must report graduation rates for students with disabilities and at least one other academic indicator.

In December of 2004, President George W. Bush signed the reauthorized IDEA into law. The provisions of the act became effective on July 1, 2005, with the exception of some of the elements pertaining to the definition of a "highly qualified teacher" that took effect upon the signing of the act. The final regulations were published on August 14, 2006, and required the alignment of IDEA and the NCLB (U.S. Department of Education, 2007a). From early beginnings in isolation and discrimination, individuals with disabilities have taken their rightful place in the mainstream of the U.S. education system.

SPEEDBUMP—A child comes home from his first day of school. His mother asks, "Well, what did you learn today?" The kid replies, "Not enough. They want me to come back tomorrow."

At-Risk Students.   By now it should be clear that legal mandates to educate and provide services to individuals with disabilities have been the driving force to provide equal opportunities for all school-aged children. The IDEA is being reviewed continually in state and federal courts. For example, overrepresentation of African American students in special classes and the use of IQ tests to identify African Americans and Hispanics as mildly "retarded" have been scrutinized by federal courts. Such key provisions as "appropriate education" and "nondiscriminatory assessment" also have spurred important judicial decisions. Table 1.2 lists some court cases that have shaped refinements of special education services to students with mild disabilities.

Unreported in the special education data are **at-risk students** who may or may not have received some type of compensatory education. At risk is the phrase used for students who fall through the cracks between special education and general education. Unless a student is found eligible under IDEA for learning disabilities, emotional disorders, or intellectual disability (or other exceptionality listed in IDEA), the youngster is not required to have an individualized educational program. Additionally, the disability must interfere with school progress. The 2004 reauthorization of IDEA allows schools to use up to 15 percent of special education funds for underperforming students in general education classrooms.

> **SPEEDBUMP**—In IDEA, the term mental retardation is used; throughout this text we use the term "intellectual disability." The explanation is in Chapter 3. In the meantime can you figure out why the authors prefer intellectual disability rather than mental retardation?

Several categories of children with disabilities are at risk. Even though they have a condition or a documented disability, they may not be eligible for special education as defined in IDEA. For instance, a child with an emotional disorder may not meet the federal criteria for "intensity and degree," or, despite an emotional problem, a student might be making adequate grades.

Many students are protected under Section 504 of the Rehabilitation Act and the Americans with Disabilities Act (ADA). However, they are not covered by the stringent procedural safeguards available under IDEA. The safeguards include the right to remain in the current placement, nondiscriminatory evaluation, an individualized educational plan, an impartial determination as to the appropriate placement, and other due process protections (Rothstein, 1995).

Youth with social maladjustments (e.g., incarcerated youth) do not qualify for special education under IDEA unless a disability is documented. There is disagreement over whether to identify or even attempt to separate youth with social maladjustments from other youth who meet the federal definition of emotional disturbance.

ADHD.   Another category of children who require significant assistance in schools, but for whom there is no category in special education, are those with attention deficit/hyperactivity disorders (ADHD). In order to assess public opinion about whether ADHD should be a separate special education disability, the 1990 amendments to IDEA required that the U.S. Department of Education solicit comments about the issue. It was decided that this condition would not become a separate disability category under IDEA. Several reasons were given, including the fact that many youngsters with ADHD qualify for special education services as learning disabled. Some youngsters with ADHD receive special education services under the category "other health impairments."

Youth who are addicted to drugs and alcohol are protected under IDEA only if they qualify for special education and related services under one of the disability categories.

TABLE 1.2 Selected Judicial Decisions Since Passage of Public Law 94–142 Focus on Students with Mild Disabilities

1975	*Issac Lora et al. v. The Board of Education of New York et al.* Nondiscriminatory assessment procedures must be used when placing minority students with emotional problems in special education programs.
1976	*Frederich L. v. Thomas* (Philadelphia). Class action suit that reaffirmed the right of students with learning disabilities to have appropriate education programs.
1979	*Larry P. v. Riles* (California). Intelligence tests banned in California when assessing African American students as mildly retarded. Disproportionate numbers of African American students were placed in special classes for the mildly retarded.
1981	*Luke S. and Hans S. v. Nixe et al.* (Louisiana). Prereferral interventions, curriculum-based assessment, and direct classroom interventions were mandated for students with mild disabilities.
1982	*Board of Education of the Henrick Hudson School System v. Rowley.* This Supreme Court decision clarified "appropriate" education by determining that the intent of P.L. 94–142 is to open the doors of public schools to students with disabilities, not to provide opportunities for students to reach maximum potential. Due process procedures to determine an appropriate education were reaffirmed by the Court.
1984	*Smith v. Robinson.* This Supreme Court decision restricted the ability of students and their families to recover legal fees incurred in due process hearings. This decision was negated in 1986 when Congress passed the Handicapped Children's Protection Act, which restored the courts' authority to award legal fees to parents who succeed in lawsuits or administrative hearings.
1984	*Marshall et al. v. Georgia.* Judge Edenfiel ruled that the overrepresentation of African Americans in special classes was not discriminatory. In his view, lower socioeconomic conditions rather than discriminatory assessment and placement practices was the reason African American students were placed in programs for the mildly mentally retarded. This was the first court case that highlighted the need to include a measure of adaptive behavior within the classroom as part of the criteria for determining mild intellectual disability.
1985	*Burlington v. Department of Education, Massachusetts.* The Supreme Court found that parents had the right to public school reimbursement of private school tuition if the public school program rejected by parents was inappropriate.
1988	*Honig v. Doe.* The Supreme Court decreed that school systems may not unilaterally exclude children with disabilities from the classroom for dangerous or disruptive behavior. Any programmatic changes because of behavior disturbances must follow due process procedures outlined in P.L. 94–142. In drastic situations the school can suspend a student for up to 10 days.
1989	*Daniel R. R. v. State Board of Education.* District and appeals courts upheld the hearing officer's decision that general education curriculum was beyond abilities of a student with retardation and that he would receive little benefit from mainstreaming. The courts found that for some children placement in general education environment would not provide a free appropriate education.
1990	*Moore v. District of Columbia.* Reversing an earlier decision, the federal appeals court ruled that prevailing parents were entitled to recover attorney fees when a final resolution of their special education dispute came at the administrative hearing level.

(continued)

TABLE 1.2   Continued

1993	*Zobrest v. Catalina Foothills School District.* The court held that provision of a sign language interpreter in a parochial school was not an entitlement under IDEA; the decision was reversed in a finding that services of an interpreter were part of a general government program that distributed benefits to any child qualifying for services regardless of the school the student attended.
1997	*K.R. v. Anderson Community School Corp.* The Seventh Circuit court decided that a student with severe disabilities was not entitled to a publicly funded personal assistant while attending a parochial school. The ruling set forth that under the IDEA, students with disabilities who choose to attend religious school need not receive the full range of services they would receive if they attended public school, but they must receive some services.
1999	*Cedar Rapids Community School District v. Garret F.* During the school day, Garret required services of a specially trained nurse because of his health needs. The school district, believing that they were not obligated under IDEA to provide continuous nursing care, refused to provide the services. The Supreme Court held that the school district had to pay for the nursing services required by Garret when he was at school.
2003	*Lewisville Independent School District v. Charles W. and Gay W. ex rel. Charles W.* The Fifth U.S. Circuit Court of Appeals determined that an intellectually superior 7th grader with pervasive developmental disorder received FAPE, despite the parents' belief that the child could make better grades and should attend a private school for children with disabilities. The court determined that his IEP was individualized, addressed all his special needs, and resulted in both academic and nonacademic progress.
2004	*C.J. v. Indian River County School Board.* The court agreed with the hearing officer's determination that a student presenting with bipolar disorder and oppositional defiance disorder was not eligible for special education because there was no support for a finding of emotional disturbance. Although the student exhibited behavior and feelings that were inappropriate under normal circumstances, the behaviors were intermittent in the school setting. The student's behavioral problems, suspensions, and hospitalizations did not interfere with her learning and she performed well, above average in most of her classes. Unilateral placement in a residential facility was largely for noneducational reasons.

These students, like other categories described, are at risk, and although they do not qualify for special education under IDEA, they are entitled to protection under Section 504 of the Rehabilitation Act or the ADA.

What determines whether a person is entitled to protection under Section 504? The individual must meet the definition of a person with a disability, which is

> any person who (i) has a physical or mental impairment which substantially limits one or more of such person's major life activities, (ii) has a record of such an impairment, or (iii) is regarded as having such an impairment.

If the person meets the definition of a person with a disability under Section 504, "reasonable accommodations" must be made by recipients of federal financial assistance. Public school systems receive this assistance, so teachers must make accommodations that are educationally beneficial for these students. The usual remedy when a violation of Section 504 is proved is the termination of federal assistance, which means loss of federal funding to the school system.

WHO RECEIVES SPECIAL EDUCATION?

In the United States, school-aged children with disabilities are entitled to a free, appropriate public education. It is illegal to discriminate against individuals with disabilities. An individual cannot be denied an education or a job because of a disability. *Special education is mandated to provide services to students who have been identified as unable to progress effectively in the general classroom as a result of that disability.* It is important to note that the presence of a disability alone is not sufficient reason to initiate special education services. Special education is warranted only after all attempts to help a youngster within the confines of the general classroom have proved ineffective.

In the first textbook dealing with the "education of exceptional children," Horn (1924) observed that mental, temperamental, and physical differences were the bases for some students needing special education. Today, many states organize their special education departments along similar categorical lines. A category is a descriptor or label assigned to a group of students. Although the names of the categories vary slightly from state to state, special education is generally provided for children within each of the following categories:

1. Students with visual impairments or blindness
2. Students with hearing impairments or deafness
3. Students with deafness and blindness
4. Students with orthopedic impairments
5. Students with multiple disabilities
6. Students with language or speech impairments
7. Students with learning disabilities
8. Students with emotional disturbances
9. Students with mental retardation
10. Students with autism
11. Students with traumatic brain injury
12. Students with developmental delay
13. Students with health impairments

Physical/Sensory Disabilities

Special learning needs in areas of physical abilities (e.g., seeing, hearing, moving) are the basis for several categories of students with special needs. Most of us take normal vision and hearing for granted. The expression "20/20 vision" is used to describe normal visual functioning. Vision is measured by having people read letters or discriminate objects at a distance of 20 feet. The task is not difficult for most people. There are people, however, who must stand closer to see what others see easily from 20 feet away. These differences in visual functioning are the basis of deciding whether a student is blind or visually impaired. There are also people who even at a louder volume cannot hear what can easily be heard by the majority. Between normal hearing and deafness are various degrees of hearing loss, and it is these differences in degrees of hearing that are the basis for another category of exceptional students (i.e., deaf or hearing impaired).

How different does vision or hearing have to be before a person is considered blind or deaf? A person who, even with correction (e.g., glasses), must be 20 feet from a target that a person with normal vision can see at 200 feet or more is considered blind. People with corrected vision better than 20/200 but not better than 20/70 are considered *visually impaired*. Ability to hear is measured along two scales: intensity and frequency. Intensity or loudness is measured in decibels (dB), and frequency or pitch is measured in hertz (cycles per second). Moores (1982) defines deaf and hard of hearing in terms of the effects on hearing loss:

> A deaf person is one whose hearing is disabled to an extent (usually 70 dB or greater) that precludes the understanding of speech through the ear alone, without or with the use of a hearing aid. A hard of hearing person is one whose hearing is disabled to an extent (usually 35–69 dB) that makes difficult, but does not preclude, the understanding of speech through the ear alone, without or with a hearing aid. (p. 17)

For practical purposes, deafness means the absence of hearing in both ears; people with deafness have great difficulty hearing conversational speech without the assistance of a hearing aid. People with hearing impairments experience significant difficulty in hearing.

There are other disabling conditions that are of a physical nature. For example, *arthritis* is a measurable inflammation of a joint that limits movement. *Cerebral palsy* is impaired motor function due to brain damage; it produces difficulties in motor control that are observable in movement of large and small muscle groups. *Seizure disorder* (i.e., epilepsy) is also a brain disorder that results in convulsive episodes and periods of unconsciousness. Other health impairments include severe orthopedic problems that adversely affect educational performance and limit strength, vitality, or alertness. Special education may be provided to people with physical differences caused by congenital anomalies (e.g., spina bifida) as well as other general health and physical problems (e.g., heart disease, asthma, diabetes, traumatic brain injury, autism).

Intellectual Disabilities

Differences in intellectual performance or mental abilities are the bases for identifying a special need. To be considered intellectually disabled, an individual must demonstrate subaverage intellectual functioning and delayed social development. Intelligence tests frequently are used to determine if an individual's intellectual performance is below that of peers. Students with scores from 50 to 75 on an intelligence test fall within the mild range of intellectual disability. Students with more complex forms of intellectual disability are categorized as mildly, moderately, severely, or profoundly disabled. Besides the differences in severity linked to IQ scores, students with moderate to profound intellectual disability usually have communication and health problems. We refer to these students as having a developmental disability because they have serious physical and medical complications that are identified by a physician at birth or soon afterwards.

Students with intellectual disabilities demonstrate deficits in adaptive behavior (i.e., social development). Adaptive behavior generally refers to the way in which an individual functions in his or her community. As with intelligence tests, adaptive behavior evaluations are based on age-group comparisons. Formalized inventories of functional abilities (such as dressing oneself, using the telephone, or independently moving about the neighborhood) help educational evaluators determine adaptive behavior. Any determination of intellectual disability must include a measure of intelligence and a measure of adaptive behavior skills.

Just as there are students with low intelligence test scores, there also are students whose intellectual performance is above that of their classmates. Historically, **giftedness** was determined by high IQ test scores. This approach is no longer favored by many educators because intelligence tests sample too narrow a range of abilities. Creativity, musical talent, leadership skills, and problem-solving abilities are a sample of talents not measurable through intelligence testing. More recently, experts in the field of giftedness recommend a multidimensional approach to establishing criteria for identification of students with special gifts or talents. According to Renzulli, Reis, and Smith (1981), in order to be identified as gifted, students should demonstrate:

1. High ability including measured intelligence evaluation
2. Creativity in the development and implementation of innovative ideas
3. High task commitment—perseverance or diligence

Students with special talents are not viewed as needing special education services; consequently, they do not receive federally mandated special education.

■ ■ ■ ■ ■ ▬▬▬▬▬▬▬▬▬▬▬▬▬▬▬▬▬▬▬▬▬▬▬▬▬▬▬▬▬▬▬▬▬▬▬▬▬▬

HIGHLIGHT 1.2

Evan is a 14-year-old resident of a Catholic residential facility for youngsters who require child care in Syracuse, New York. Tall and athletic, Evan is a leader among the other boys. Mark Costello, a first-year child care worker, describes his response to Evan's invitation to come see the puzzle he has just completed.

As Evan led me over to a card table sitting in the middle of the living room, it was obvious how proud he was of his accomplishment. Eager to lavish him with praise, I looked down at the table to see the three hundred jigsaw pieces carefully connected after many evenings of effort. Pride quickly turned to confusion, however, when it became apparent that the picture was face down on the card table.

"What picture, Mr. Cos?" Evan asked.

"Do you see the picture on the top of the box the pieces came in, my friend?" I asked.

"Sure, what about it?"

"Well, that picture is now upside down on this card table and you, old buddy, have just completed one heck of a tough task."

While the other boys were trying to read Evan's reaction to this perplexing bit of news, I began to internalize my first real lesson about the significance of intellectual disability. Naïve but determined, he had stuck to a task few if any youths of normal intelligence could tolerate. Was this just a glimpse of his true potential? How hard it was that night to convince Evan of how proud we were of his somewhat tarnished accomplishment.

From *Confessions of a Special Eddie: Reflections in Appreciation of Human Difference*, p. 19, by T. Mark Costello, copyright 1994, New York: Wizard Press. Reprinted with permission.

> **SPEEDBUMP—**Do you think federal law should mandate special education programs for gifted children?

Gifted programs exist in some school systems because of state or local leadership and funding. Four groups of students are underrepresented in gifted education programs: culturally different, female, disabled, and underachieving (Patton, Kauffman, Blackbourn, & Brown, 1991).

How different do measures of intelligence have to be before an individual is considered intellectually disabled or gifted? Differences in scores on intelligence tests and measures of adaptive behavior are evaluated in the same way as differences in scores on hearing, vision, or physical performance tests. Standards for normal intelligence and adaptive behavior are set by testing large groups of individuals. Professionals then set criteria for intellectual disability or giftedness that are based on mean intelligence scores and adaptive behavior ratings. For example, the common standard for normal performance is a score of 90–110 on an intelligence test; scores below 75 or above 130 are generally considered indicative of intellectual disability and giftedness. It is important to remember that special education services for students identified as gifted are not mandated by federal legislation. Figure 1.3 traces the normal curve distribution of IQ scores.

Academic Disabilities

With the categories of intellectual disability and gifted, it is assumed that the individual's performance on achievement tests will be consistent with the performance on intelligence tests. This means that if a student obtains a high score on an intelligence test, high performance on an achievement test also is expected. If students perform poorly on intelligence tests, it is expected that their achievement test scores also will be low. There are students

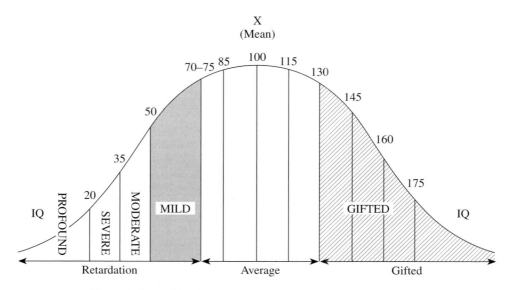

FIGURE 1.3   Normal Curve Distribution of IQ Scores

whose performance on achievement tests is not consistent with their performance on intelligence tests. When the difference between ability (e.g., intelligence test performance) and achievement (e.g., reading, math) is significant, the student may be identified as **learning disabled**. Students with learning disabilities comprise one-half of the entire special education population.

SPEEDBUMP—Why do you suppose so many students are identified as learning disabled as compared to the other disability categories?

How different do scores on ability tests and scores on achievement tests have to be before a student is classified as learning disabled? Although officials of the federal government have provided guidelines for use in identifying students with learning disabilities, no specific criteria have been provided for judging when discrepancies between ability and achievement are severe enough to call a student learning disabled.

Students are considered eligible for special education if they meet guidelines spelled out in state regulations. Due to a lack of consistent criteria between and within states, it is likely that many students in special education programs for students with learning disabilities are misidentified.

Communication Disabilities

Just as there are differences in the reading, writing, and mathematical skills of students, there are also differences in the ways students speak and express themselves. Some people speak clearly, enunciating each part of their speech. Others speak quickly, making it difficult for listeners to understand them. Some children use speech as a means of making their desires, feelings, and opinions known. Others are less adept at verbalizing personal needs. There are accepted ages at which children are expected to demonstrate the use of various forms of communication. For example, most children understand approximately one thousand words, combine their words into simple sentences, and understand concepts related to language (e.g., on, off, later) by the time they are 2 years old. By the age of 7, children are expected to use culturally acceptable grammar when speaking; language at this age is much like that used by family and friends. Differences in language and communication skills are measured by performance on tests and classroom observations of student interaction. Differences in language development and communication skills commonly are observed in children of all ages. When these differences adversely affect educational performance, the individual may be entitled to special services provided for students with language impairments.

How different does language have to be before a student is considered language impaired? Many students in this category receive special services for such problems as lisping, stuttering, and mispronunciation of individual words (e.g., they say "wabbit" instead of "rabbit," "pasketti" instead of "spaghetti," or "bud" for "bird"). Some of these students have voice tones that are too low, too high, too nasal, too harsh, or too hoarse. There are no absolute standards for determining when an individual's speech is "too" nasal or "too" harsh or when it will adversely affect educational performance. When speech mannerisms cause difficulties for the listener, a student may be referred for speech therapy. Some teachers are more adept than others at understanding differences in the language produced by their students. Similarly, the context in which speech occurs influences the judgments made about it. Recent government figures indicate that there are more students in this category than in any other besides learning disabilities. This is probably not surprising for a category based on differences in speech clarity or tone.

Emotionally Disturbed

Just as standards for normal intellectual performance have evolved within the educational system, standards for how students should act in school and society also have evolved. Standards for normal behavior are based more on what is judged acceptable in a specific setting than on judgments about how an individual performs on a test. Demonstrating intellectual performance that is sufficiently above or below normal is the basis for being identified as gifted or mentally retarded. Demonstrating unacceptable behavior in school is the basis for being identified with behavior disorders or emotional disturbance.

Just how different does behavior have to be before a student is considered **emotionally disturbed**? Based on what you have learned about the other conditions of special education, your answer may be "behavior that is significantly different from the behavior of their peers." You are right, but you will have trouble explaining behavioral differences. There are no numerical standards for normal behavior. There are no tests to measure the normality of behavior. Classroom observations by teachers carry the most weight in identifying students with emotional/behavior disorders. However, what is acceptable behavior for one classroom may not be acceptable in another, and what is acceptable behavior for one teacher is not necessarily acceptable for another.

Many students with emotional problems sit undetected in general education classrooms. Although 1 percent of students receive special education services because of emotional disturbance, mental health experts estimate that from 6 to 10 percent of the school-aged population have an emotional problem serious enough to warrant mental health care. Chief among these emotional problems are depression, posttraumatic stress disorder secondary to abuse and attention deficit disorder with hyperactivity (Forness, 2001).

HOW MANY STUDENTS RECEIVE SPECIAL EDUCATION?

Since 1976, the U.S. Department of Education has maintained a database on the number of children with disabilities served in special education programs. In 1990, several of the disability category labels within IDEA were revised: learning disabled was changed to specific learning disabilities, mentally retarded became mental retardation, and hard-of-hearing and deaf were combined to become hearing impairments; in other revisions to the regulations, multihandicapped was changed to multiple disabilities, and autism, traumatic brain injury, and developmental delay were added as separate categories.

More than six million students aged 3 to 21 receive special education services in public school or private settings (Twenty-seventh Annual Report to Congress). In thinking about the number of students involved, consider that it is about the same as the total full-time undergraduate enrollment in all U.S. colleges and universities. The number of students who receive special education is more than the combined population of North Dakota, South Dakota, Montana, Nevada, Idaho, and Wyoming.

There has been a steady increase in the number of students aged 6 to 21 receiving special education services. In 1992, 4,499,824 school-aged students were placed in special education programs; in 2003, the overall figure had increased to 6,046,031 students (see Table 1.3). Included in this figure are 269,596 children ages birth to 2 who received early intervention services and 680,142 children aged 3 through 5 who received preschool services; the total number of children benefitting from special education in 2000 was 6,995,789 (U.S. Department of Education, 2007b). The number of students classified with specific learning disabilities, speech or language impairments, intellectual disability, and emotional disturbance has decreased in recent years, while the number with multiple disabilities, other health impairments (including ADHD), and autism has increased. In 2003, for all racial/ethnic groups, the largest disability category was specific learning disabilities (U.S. Department of Education, 2007b). Specific learning disabilities, speech or language impairments, intellectual disability, and *other health impairments* were among the five largest disability categories for all racial/ethnic groups. Autism appeared in the top five disability categories only for the Asian/Pacific Islander racial/ethnic group. The percentage of the population receiving special education and related services varies by race/ethnicity. In 2003, the percentage receiving special education (i.e., risk index) was largest for American Indian/Alaska Native students (13.8 percent), followed by black (12.4 percent),

TABLE 1.3   Growth in Numbers of Students Ages 6 Through 21 Served Under IDEA

DISABILITY CATEGORY	1991–1992	2000–2001	2003–2004
Specific learning disability	2,247,004	2,887,217	2,866,908
Speech or language impairments	998,904	1,093,808	1,129,260
Mental retardation	553,262	612,978	582,663
Emotional disturbance	400,211	473,663	484,479
Multiple disabilities	98,408	122,559	132,645
Hearing impairments	60,727	70,767	72,048
Orthopedic impairments	51,389	73,057	68,234
Other health impairments	58,749	291,850	452,442
Visual impairments	24,083	25,975	25,879
Autism	5,415	78,749	141,002
Deaf-blindness	1,427	1,320	1,670
Traumatic brain injury	245	14,844	22,534
Developmental delay		28,935	66,267
All disabilities	4,499,824	5,775,722	6,046,031
Percent with specific learning disabilities, mental retardation, or emotional disturbance	71	69	65
Percent with specific learning disabilities, speech or language impairments, intellectual disability, or emotional disturbance	93	88	84

Note: Reporting in the autism and traumatic brain injury categories was optional in 1991–1992 and required beginning in 1992–1993; developmental delay category is available only for children under age 10. The table does not include students receiving special education early intervention or preschool services.

white (8.7 percent), Hispanic (8.2 percent), and Asian/Pacific Islander (4.5 percent) students. The average cost to educate a student with a disability is $12,639 per year (U.S. Department of Education, 2002). Reasons for the increase in students identified as having special needs include the following:

1. Poverty-related issues, such as inadequate health care
2. An increase in cultural and linguistic diversity in the schools
3. An increase in the numbers of students identified with specific learning disabilities
4. The addition of new categories of students eligible for special education
5. Variations in school referral and evaluation procedures

Special education's growth has continued to increase the demand for special education teachers (U.S. Department of Education, 1999; 2007b).

The growth of special education services has caused other problems. For example, school personnel have to decide how to pay for the increasing numbers of students. Because the cost of educating students with special needs may come at the expense of educating students in general education, school personnel face hard choices when allocating funds. The growth of special education is attributed directly to passage of the IDEA, which mandates a "free and appropriate public education" for all students with disabilities.

For years many school districts organized their special education programs along categorical lines (e.g., emotionally disturbed, learning disabled). Recently public schools have made a greater effort to include students with disabilities in general education classrooms. The "inclusion" movement is based on the premise that students with disabilities will make greater progress if they are allowed to learn alongside peers without disabilities. The 1997 reauthorization of IDEA stated that special education students should be educated in general education classrooms to the maximum appropriate extent. Inclusion efforts continue to show results. During the 1984–1985 school year, only 25 percent of students with disabilities aged 6–21 spent more than 80 percent of their day in general education classrooms. By 1998–1999, almost half of all students with disabilities spent more than 80 percent of their time in general education classrooms and this figure has remained constant for many years (U.S. Department of Education, 2001; 2007b). Unfortunately, the inclusion trend is not without problems. Forty-two percent of general education teachers feel inclusion is "not workable" due to deficiencies in teacher attitude, teacher preparation, and administrative support (Henley, 2004).

> **SPEEDBUMP**—Because of the constant rise in the special education population, the demand for teachers licensed in special education continues to grow as well.

STUDENTS WITH MILD DISABILITIES

Many people experience mild vision, hearing, or other physical problems but they are not typically among those receiving special education services. Students with mild disabilities who do receive special education are those typically included in the federal categories of specific learning disabilities, intellectual disability, and emotional disturbance. Students with language or communication impairments is another large category of mild disabilities; however, because their difficulties are primarily treated by speech clinicians rather than teachers in general or special education classrooms, information about them is not included in this book.

We do not use the term **mild disabilities** to imply that these students do not have serious learning problems or that their problems are less important than those of other students. We use this term for these students because many of their characteristics overlap, many of the interventions used with them are effective with all of them, and many of them can be educated effectively in general education classrooms with support rather than full-time assistance from special education teachers. The three mild disabilities are mild intellectual, learning disability, and emotional disturbance.

Students classified with learning disabilities, mild intellectual disability, or emotional disturbance account for about than two-thirds of all students with disabilities (U.S. Department of Education, 2007b), and they share many characteristics. For example, students with learning disabilities often have problems with reading comprehension, language development, interpersonal relations, and classroom behavioral control (Lerner, 2000). These same characteristics are common in teacher descriptions of students receiving special education in the categories of mild intellectual disability and emotional disturbance.

If you think that these characteristics also can be found in students who do not receive special education services, you are correct. It is a thin and sometimes arbitrary line that separates students with mild disabilities from other students. Many classroom problems are interactional: the result of a mismatch between teaching and learning style. The behavior, expectations, and attitude of the general classroom teacher is a key component in determining whether a student is referred and evaluated as having a mild disability. For example, some characteristics of learning disabilities, such as dyslexia (i.e., an impairment in reading ability), are neurologically based; other characteristics, such as distractibility, can be based on teacher perception of student performance. A student with dyslexia will be dyslexic in every classroom; on the other hand, a student identified as distractible and hyperactive in one teacher's classroom may have less difficulty attending in another classroom. How can this happen? Some teachers are more adept at engaging students in their schoolwork than others. In special education, never underestimate the power of good teaching to "cure" a mild disability.

Whether it helps students with mild disabilities to be categorized is controversial. Over the years, each of the three subgroups of mild disabilities has been separated by distinct identification criteria, different teaching methods, teacher certificates linked to a single disability, and different special education placements. Each category is represented by separate professional organizations and advocacy groups and their efforts influence the number and types of services provided to students with disabilities. The American Association for Individuals with Developmental Disabilities and the Council of Children with Behavior Disorders are two examples of disability-specific organizations. Researchers develop expertise within a single category of mild disabilities and report their findings in journals that specialize in intellectual disability, learning disabilities, or emotional disturbance.

Still, students who are placed in different categories of mild disabilities share many common traits. Lack of interest in school and low motivation are two traits displayed by many youngsters categorized as having a mild disability. It also is clear that instructional practices proved effective for students in one category of mild disabilities can be useful with students within another category. Such instructional strategies as peer tutoring, phonemic awareness, and cooperative learning can help students learn regardless of how their mild disability is categorized.

There are advantages and disadvantages to classifying students by specific categories of mild disabilities. Special educators sometimes use the term "labeling" to describe this categorization process. Is it a good idea to label students? We will present the facts about both sides of this issue. Ultimately you will need to make your own professional decision about labeling students with such terms as intellectual disability, learning disabilities, and emotional disturbance. Whether to place a student into a mild disability category is an issue you will be faced with throughout your career as a teacher.

LABELING

Students identified as having problems in school either will meet **eligibility criteria** for special education services or will be unofficially labeled with such negative adjectives as "lazy," "unmotivated," "slow learner," or "behavior problem." In the latter case, neither the teacher nor the student will get help. The student will remain in general education and most likely continue to fail in school. There is an increased probability that the student will eventually drop out of school (see Figure 1.4).

In most states, a student is identified as requiring special education when school evaluation data match the student with a specific disability category that is outlined by state education regulations. This classification process assumes that assigning a student a categorical name implies knowledge about the characteristics of the student's learning problem. This categorical approach to providing help has been roundly criticized by many educators who claim that labeling a student does more harm than good. What students are called determines what services they receive and where they will receive them. Because this classification process alters the school experience of many students, professionals have researched and described the advantages and disadvantages of the labeling associated with it.

Advantages of Labeling

The advantages of labeling were more obvious in the formative years of special education (mid-1940s to early 1970s) than they are now. For instance, without the category of learning disabilities, advocates for these children would have had no rallying point to promote educational programs. Imagine how ineffective scientists would be in raising money for cancer research if they had no name for it. The advantages of labeling can be summarized as follows:

1. Federal and local funding of special education programs are based on categories of disabilities.

FIGURE 1.4 Children with Disabilities Remain at Risk

Although it is true that special education has created a base of civil rights and legal protections, children with disabilities remain at risk of being left behind.

■ Young people with disabilities drop out of high school at twice the rate of their peers.

■ Enrollment rates of students with disabilities in higher education are still 50 percent lower than enrollment among the general population.

■ Most public school educators do not feel well prepared to work with children with disabilities. In 1998, only 21 percent of public school teachers said they felt very well prepared to address the needs of students with disabilities, and another 41 percent said they felt moderately well prepared.

■ Of the six million children in special education, half of those who are in special education are identified as having a "specific learning disability." In fact, this group has grown more than 300 percent since 1976.

■ Of those with "specific learning disabilities," 80 percent are there simply because they haven't learned how to read. Thus, many children identified for special education—up to 40 percent—are there because they weren't taught to read. The reading difficulties may not be their only area of difficulty, but it's the area that resulted in special education placement. Sadly, few children placed in special education close the achievement gap to a point where they can read and learn like their peers.

■ Children of minority status are overrepresented in some categories of special education. African American children are twice as likely as white children to be labeled mentally retarded and placed in special education. They also are more likely to be labeled and placed as emotionally disturbed.

Sources: U.S. Department of Education, 2004; U.S. Department of Education, 2002.

2. Labeling enables professionals to communicate with one another because each categorical label conveys a general idea about learning characteristics.
3. The human mind requires "mental hooks" to think about problems. If present categorical labels were abolished, a new set of descriptors would evolve to take their place. There is ample evidence of this in the evolution of the term "mildly retarded."
4. Labeling the disability spotlights the problem for the public. Labeling can spark social concern and aid advocacy efforts.
5. Labeling may make the majority without disabilities more tolerant of the minority with disabilities. In other words, the actions of a child identified as having intellectual disability might be tolerated, whereas the behavior of a peer without intellectual disability would be criticized.
6. Labeling has led to the development of specialized teaching methods, assessment approaches, and behavioral interventions that are useful for teachers of all students. (Hallahan & Kauffman, 1982)

DISADVANTAGES OF LABELING

Because of IDEA, students with disabilities have made significant gains in public schools. These advances have been accompanied by problems inherent in officially designating someone abnormal. Make no mistake about it; these labels stick. Once a child is categorized with intellectual disability, emotional disturbance, or learning disabilities, that information will be forwarded to every new teacher in the child's cumulative folder. Along with the label comes the stigma of being considered deficient. For this reason alone, assigning a student to a category for special education purposes is a fateful step that should not be taken unless all other options have proved unsuccessful. The disadvantages of labeling are summarized as follows:

1. Labels shape teacher expectations. Imagine what your reaction would be if the principal informed you that the new student in your class is mildly mentally retarded. Studies on teacher expectations have demonstrated that what teachers believe about student capability is directly related to student achievement.

2. All children have some troubling behaviors. Labels can exaggerate a student's actions in the eyes of a teacher. A teacher may overreact to behavior of a labeled child that would be tolerated in another.

3. Labels send a clear message: The learning problem is with the student. Labels tend to obscure the essence of teaching and learning as a two-way street. Some students placed in a mild disability category have nothing wrong with them. They are the unfortunate recipients of ineffective schooling.

4. Labels perpetuate the notion that students with mild disabilities are qualitatively different from other children. This is not true. Students with mild disabilities go through the same developmental stages as their peers, although sometimes at a slower rate.

5. Teachers may confuse the student with the label. Labels reflect categories of disabilities. Categories are abstract, not real, concepts that are general enough to incorporate many different individuals. More than two million students may be identified with specific learning disabilities, but as individuals, each is a unique human being. When a student is placed in a category, a teacher who knows some of the characteristics of a category may ascribe all known characteristics to each labeled child. This is stereotyping. **Stereotypes** harm students when teachers rationalize low achievement by citing characteristics of the label. An example is the teacher who explains away a teaching-learning problem by stating, "We can't really expect Mary to remember too much math because she is 'intellectually disabled.' "

6. Students cannot receive special education services until they are labeled. In many instances, the intervention comes too late. The need to label students before help arrives undermines a preventive approach to mild learning problems.

7. Diagnostic labels are unreliable. Educational evaluation is filled with quirks. States use different descriptive criteria for the same categories; many evaluation instruments have questionable validity and reliability; specific labels go through trends (for example, at one time learning disabilities was considered a white, middle class category and African American students were overrepresented with mild intellectual disability).

8. Labels often put the blame (and the guilt) for a student's learning problems squarely on the parents' shoulders. In many cases, this is unjustified because students may be mislabeled or teachers may not fully understand the many different causes of mild disabilities.

WHAT TO TEACH STUDENTS

The purpose of IDEA is to ensure that all students with special needs receive a free and appropriate education—however, Congress did not define what it meant by the term "appropriate." The legislators recognized that there is no one instructional approach that is best. Instead they viewed appropriate as a process rather than a product. Whether a program is appropriate is based on the ability of the school system and parents to work out a mutually acceptable individualized education program.

Individual Education Program

An individualized education program (IEP) must be written for each student receiving special education. Special education includes many services related to classroom instruction, such as transportation, occupational therapy, counseling, and adaptive equipment. Assessed instructional needs of each student determine the areas for which an IEP is developed.

Each school district may develop its own IEP format as long as the required information is included. The IEP must be developed within a meeting by participants stipulated by legislation. The IEP team is a group of individuals composed of:

1. The student's parents or guardians
2. At least one general education teacher (if the child is, or may be, participating in the general education environment)
3. At least one special education teacher, or, where appropriate, at least one special education provider of such child
4. A representative of the local educational agency who is qualified to provide, or supervise the provision of, specially designed instruction to meet the unique needs of individuals with disabilities; is knowledgeable about general curriculum; and is knowledgeable about the availability of resources of the local educational agency
5. An individual who can interpret the instructional implications of evaluation results
6. At the discretion of the parent or the agency, other individuals who have knowledge or special expertise regarding the student, including related services personnel as appropriate
7. Whenever appropriate, the student

SPEEDBUMP—If you ever get an opportunity to attend an IEP meeting, take advantage of it. You will learn a lot about what it is like from a parent's point of view to have a child in special education.

In the case of students with mild disabilities, the IEP is usually determined by the portion of the general education curriculum with which a student is having difficulty. A student with a specific learning disability might have an IEP that emphasizes reading and mathematics. A student with emotional disturbance would have an IEP that emphasizes self-control and adjustment to classroom routines. An adolescent with mild intellectual disability might have an IEP that describes vocational goals and objectives.

WHERE TO TEACH STUDENTS

When Congress passed IDEA, the media hailed it as a **mainstreaming** law. This caused considerable concern among teachers and administrators who feared this would lead to dumping students with disabilities into general classrooms. News people inadvertently misled the public. The term "mainstreaming" is not mentioned in the law. Congress believed that students with disabilities should be educated with students without disabilities whenever feasible. The law states that students should be educated in the least restrictive environment. The intent of the least restrictive environment mandate is to assure that students are not segregated because of their disabilities and to give them every opportunity to have a normal school experience. More restrictive settings, such as self-contained special classes and residential programs, should be utilized only when a student's needs are so complex that he or she would not receive an appropriate education in a less-restrictive environment. Evelyn Deno's *Cascade of Services* (Figure 1.5) provides a visual representation of the relationship between least and most restrictive settings. Level I is least restrictive. Each succeeding level establishes more distance between special and general education services.

It is the responsibility of each school system to provide a continuum of educational services ranging from least to most restrictive. We will briefly describe the types of special education services you can expect a school system to provide.

General Education Classroom Placement

Placement in the general education classroom with supportive services (e.g., materials, consultation, team teaching) is the least restrictive environment in the hierarchy of services. If a student spends less than 21 percent of the school day outside the general classroom receiving special instruction, the federal government defines the placement as a general classroom. Students with learning disabilities usually spend most of their day in the general classroom. Full-time placement in general education often is described as an **inclusion** program. Speech clinicians, social workers, special education teachers, and school psychologists may consult with the general classroom teacher on student needs and progress.

> **SPEEDBUMP—**If you visit an inclusion program, take note of how often special education students are actually included in normal classroom routines.

Resource Room Placement

Resource rooms are commonly referred to as **pull-out programs**. The resource room is a special education classroom located within the student's school. A youngster goes to the resource room on a scheduled basis to receive tutorial help from a special education teacher. Students may spend from 21 to 60 percent of their school day in a resource room. Typically, resource room teachers teach fundamental skills and/or tutor students in the academic subjects that were the source of the referral. It is the resource room teacher's job to take a lead role in the development and implementation of IEPs for students placed in this

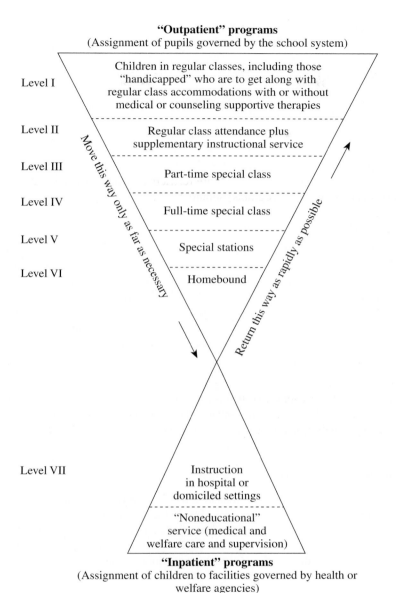

"Outpatient" programs
(Assignment of pupils governed by the school system)

Level I — Children in regular classes, including those "handicapped" who are to get along with regular class accommodations with or without medical or counseling supportive therapies

Level II — Regular class attendance plus supplementary instructional service

Level III — Part-time special class

Level IV — Full-time special class

Level V — Special stations

Level VI — Homebound

Move this way only as far as necessary

Return this way as rapidly as possible

Level VII — Instruction in hospital or domiciled settings

"Noneducational" service (medical and welfare care and supervision)

"Inpatient" programs
(Assignment of children to facilities governed by health or welfare agencies)

FIGURE 1.5 Cascade of Services

Source: "Special Education as Developmental Capitol" by E. Deno, *Exceptional Children 37,* 229–237. Copyright © 1970 by the Council for Exceptional Children. Reprinted with permission.

setting. The majority of students who receive resource room help remain in the general classroom for most of their school day (U.S. Department of Education, 2002; 2007b).

Special Class Placement

Special classes are **self-contained** programs located in a public school system. They are sometimes called **segregated programs** because only students with disabilities are enrolled. Students are usually grouped in special classes by categories of disability. The special class is the most criticized of special education placements when it is used for students with mild disabilities. Although students with specific learning disabilities are not usually placed in special classes, students with mild intellectual disability and especially emotional disturbance sometimes are placed in these programs.

Special Day School Placement

Alternative high school programs, special education early childhood programs, and private day programs are examples of special day school placements. Students are transported to these special education programs at the school system's expense. Public school systems sometimes contract with private vendors to provide special education services for students with low-incidence disabilities such as autism or multiple disabilities. In addition to the disadvantages inherent in segregation, students who attend special day school programs may spend lengthy amounts of time being transported from home to program and back home again.

> **SPEEDBUMP—**Why do you suppose students with emotional disturbance are placed in more separate special education classrooms than students with learning disabilities?

Homebound Programs

Students who are ill or require intensive medical services are educated by itinerant teachers at home. With the passage of P.L. 99–457 in 1986, incentives were created to develop individualized family service plans for infants and toddlers with disabilities at home. P.L. 99–457 (Handicapped Infant and Toddler Program, Part H) amended the Education for All Handicapped Children Act to extend special education services to preschoolers in the 1991 school year.

Other Domiciled Settings

Some hospitals have their own special education programs. Only a small percentage, less than 1 percent, of all special needs learners are restricted to hospital care (U.S. Department of Education, 1999; 2007b). More than 450,000 adolescents are incarcerated in correctional facilities across the country each year (Margolis, 1988). Many of these young people are from minorities and the uneducated. If a special need is identified, an incarcerated youth up to age 21 has the same right to special education services as students in the public school system. In their book *Special Education in the Criminal Justice System* (1987),

Nelson, Rutherford, and Wolford suggest that this population is underserved and that there may be a higher prevalence of mild disabilities among prisoners than the general population. Within the past few decades, some special educators have argued that an adjudication of delinquency (i.e., socially maladjusted) may be a disability in itself (Benson, Edwards, Rosell, & White, 1986; U.S. Department of Education, 1999). Correctional facilities include prisons, jails, and detention centers. DiGangi, Perryman, and Rutherford (1990) reported that 42 percent of offenders in a state juvenile facility required special education.

Residential Programs

When a student requires intensive, around-the-clock treatment, residential programs are an option. Residential placements are expensive, however, and it can cost a school system over $50,000 a year to send one student to a residential facility for a year. One program for students with severe disabilities in Providence, Rhode Island, costs in excess of $135,000 a year. Ironically, the funding mechanisms in some states actually create incentives for such restrictive placements by providing reimbursements that increase in proportion to time in a special education program.

Blackman (1989) reported that in Illinois, "it frequently costs a school district less money to send a child to a private day, often a residential school, than educating the child within the school district" (p. 461). Illinois set aside money to fully reimburse school districts for room-and-board costs incurred as a result of residential placements. Despite the additional expense, residential placements cannot match the quality of public school special education programs. Private school teachers often are uncertified or inexperienced. They work longer hours (usually through the summer) and for less pay than public school teachers. Union representation, a sine qua non of public school life, is virtually nonexistent in private, residential facilities. In 1997, less than 1 percent of students with special needs were placed in residential programs (U.S. Department of Education, 1999; 2002; 2007b).

■ ■ ■ ■ ■ ▬▬▬▬▬▬▬▬▬▬▬▬▬▬▬▬▬▬▬▬▬▬▬▬▬▬▬

HIGHLIGHT 1.3
AN EDUCATIONAL OASIS ON RIKERS ISLAND

In the halls of the Adolescent Reception Detention Center on Rikers Island, there are rapists and muggers, murderers and thieves awaiting judgment—but when Sharon Jones looks at the teenagers there, she sees mechanics and writers, printers and scientists. "Whatever they might be to other people, to me they're students," said Ms. Jones, principal of the Rikers Island Educational Facility, a surprising oasis of order, possibility, and education for young men who mostly never before appreciated the value of school and who mostly never before bothered to attend. Ms. Jones believes that if the offenders at Rikers Island are not educated, "you might as well

set a permanent place with them in a prison mess hall." The school has a newspaper and a literary magazine that is printed in the school's print shop. There are seven computer labs and an auto shop—and there is no violence.

"I was really into autos back at home, but I had the bad influence of my environment and I let it rule me," said Danny, awaiting trial at Rikers Island. "Then I see my teacher in here and I think, 'Oh man, I really made a mistake with my life.' But if there was no auto shop here, I don't think I would learn any lesson being incarcerated because I would have nothing to keep me interested" (Fein, 1995).

HOW TO TEACH STUDENTS WITH MILD DISABILITIES

The laws and court decisions that mandate an appropriate educational program for youth with disabilities are equally beneficial for general education students. Working together, general and special educators can improve the education of all students. Some special educators have proposed a merger of general and special education. They believe that the splintering of educational services in schools has diminished efforts to help difficult-to-teach students (Stainback, Stainback, & Forest, 1989). If the ideal is the establishment of an appropriate education for students with disabilities, can this be accomplished in the general education classroom with collaborative efforts of general and special educators? The movement to educate all students together has addressed this concern and is discussed in more detail in Chapter 6.

Both general and special educators are aware that the education system is in a state of transition as educators determine the best strategies for helping students with mild disabilities. Therefore, the future focus may shift from where (setting) and why (rights) students are placed in special education to a focus on *how* to educate successfully those students who are difficult to teach. Smith-Davis (1989a) defined the following factors as critical in making these decisions: (1) curriculum, (2) instruction, (3) methods, (4) materials, (5) options, (6) alternatives, and (7) instructional roles and relationships. In order to understand how these factors can make a difference in the realm of general education, it is necessary to understand the current status of the field.

Comparing General and Special Education

Many students end up in special education, not so much to meet unique individual needs but because special education is one of the few services available to help children unable to meet general education requirements (Sarason & Doris, 1979; Ysseldyke & Algozzine, 1982; Ysseldyke, Algozzine, & Thurlow, 2000). This practice neglects preventive efforts to solve classroom problems. Often, the only way a teacher can get help for a student (or for him- or herself) is to refer the youngster for special education evaluation.

There are differences between the two systems of general and special education. Basically, special education is adaptive to the individual needs of students. Concepts such as individualization, specialization, heterogeneity, and lifelong learning are among those that drive practices in special education. In contrast, general education is group oriented, global, norm referenced, and presents standardized curriculum.

Since 1975, special education has grown as a subsystem of general education. This growth has tended to accentuate differences between the two systems. Students have received special services, but not without cost. The stigma of being identified as deficient, along with a loss of general classroom instructional time, has pushed some students with mild disabilities further down the ladder of school success. If general and special educators can find ways to work together, the combination of knowledge and expertise will benefit all students. The following chapters will focus on the unique characteristics of students with mild disabilities. Using this knowledge as a base, in ensuing chapters we describe those strategies that can help general and special educators work more closely to assist students with mild disabilities in reaching their fullest potential.

SUMMARY

Special education serves students with disabilities. Students with mild disabilities constitute the majority of students in special education programs. These students have problems and characteristics that make success in school difficult without special assistance. Students with mild disabilities have problems that are basically educational in nature. Today, more than two-thirds of the students served in special education programs are classified with specific learning disabilities, mild intellectual disability, or emotional disturbance.

Early special education programs sometimes consisted of isolated special classes or custodial placements that left much to be desired in terms of good instruction and sound educational practices. With the advent of Individuals with Disabilities Education Act (IDEA) and its subsequent supplements and amendments, special educators focused on providing appropriate education for students with mild disabilities. As a result of this monumental legislation, students who receive special services are entitled to education that is as much like normal as possible. Cooperation between general and special educators is the best strategy for ensuring the success of educational interventions for students with mild disabilities.

ACTIVITIES

1. Based on what you have learned in this chapter, answer the following questions:
   a. Do you think special education is good for students even if they are separated from their peers and placed in separate programs?
   b. Did you in the past or do you now know any students like Jake, Mary, and Felipe. How were they similar to the students in the vignette? How were they different?
   c. Of the three mild disabilities, which do you think is most problematic in terms of providing appropriate educational services?
   d. If you were going to become a special education teacher, which kind of student would you prefer to work with Jake, Mary, or Felipe?
2. For many years the practice of labeling students by categories of disabilities has been a controversial practice among educators. What do you think of this practice? In small groups of three to four, reflect and share your views on your time in elementary or secondary school. Can you remember times when students were separated from their peers because they had a special education label? What are the similarities and differences of separating students by disability and other traits such as race or religion?
3. In small groups share an episode in your life when you felt "different" or out of place. Where were you? How did people treat you? How did you feel? How did this situation affect your behavior? Can you see any similarities between your experience and being identified as disabled?
4. Draw a flow chart that illustrates the key principles of IDEA.
5. Do you have any friends or family members who have received special education services? Was special education a good experience? Do you think these individuals benefitted from special education? Did they have any problems because they were in special education? What are the advantages to being in special education? What are the disadvantages?

CHAPTER TWO

OVERVIEW OF STUDENTS WITH MILD DISABILITIES

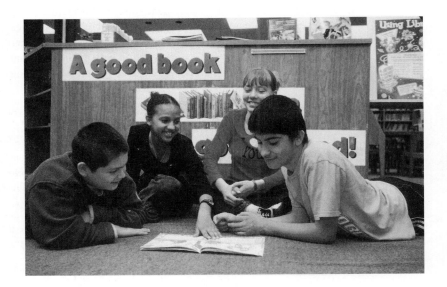

ADVANCE QUESTIONS

Answer the following questions as you read this chapter:

1. What is the difference between noncategorical and cross-categorical identification of students with mild disabilities?
2. What common characteristics do students with mild disabilities have?
3. What are the advantages of categorizing students by disability type? What are the disadvantages?
4. What are organic and what are environmental causes of mild learning and emotional disabilities?
5. Who is served under Part B of the Individuals with Disabilities Education Act? Who receives Public Law 99–457, Part H services?
6. What are the characteristics of Asperger's syndrome, ADHD, nonverbal learning disorder, and pervasive developmental disorder?

7. Who are the special populations at risk of educational and school failure? Describe these two main groups of students.
8. In which instructional settings are students with mild intellectual, learning, and emotional disabilities primarily taught?
9. Explain the due process procedure that must be followed when making decisions about who will receive services in special education.
10. List student behaviors required for success in the general education classroom.
11. What are some effective strategies for modifying classroom instruction?

Students with mild disabilities are those who are served in special education in the categories of learning disabilities, mild intellectual disabilities, or emotional/emotionally disturbances. These students are referred to as having a mild disability because many of their special learning needs and characteristics go undetected until they reach school age. The majority spend some time within general education classrooms. Others receive special services in a special education classroom one to several periods a day. Whether you are a general or special education teacher, you will have students with mild disabilities in your classroom.

VIGNETTE: TALE OF THREE STUDENTS

Karl's 3rd-grade teacher reported that his academic abilities were significantly delayed. In reading, Karl had difficulty blending letter sounds and recalling content from reading and listening. Mathematics also was a problem for Karl, although he experienced some success with basic facts. He had difficulty mastering reasoning and problem-solving skills. His teacher estimated that he was 2 to 3 years behind his classmates in academics. Karl's teacher also reported that he had poor social skills. Working cooperatively with classmates and controlling impulses were two areas in which Karl experienced difficulty. His teacher stated that Karl's "immaturity" and social withdrawal were a source of frustration to her. His IQ was 69. Karl has been identified as a student with mild intellectual disability.

Jackie was in constant trouble because she did not turn in assignments or complete work in class. Her 5th-grade teacher reported that her academic performance suffered due to her incomplete work. Jackie was a source of frustration to her teacher and family. Although Jackie's teacher tried to handle most discipline problems herself, she sent Jackie to the principal's office an average of three times per week. Jackie's teacher described her as "sullen and hostile." When she was in these moods, she talked out in class, refused to work, and became disruptive. Jackie had been involved in several fights in school and on the bus; one was enough to get her suspended from school. Jackie was identified as a student with an emotional disturbance.

José was 8 years old. His IQ was 110. His teacher reported that José had average intelligence and a good understanding of spoken language. He was extremely verbal and often engaged in long conversations on a variety of topics; however, José's performance in spelling and written language was comparable to students who were 3 years younger than he. He was unable to reproduce letters legibly. Although he readily recognized each letter of the alphabet, he had difficulty both remembering what the letters looked like and executing the motor patterns necessary to form each letter. When José was given a set of letters to copy, his written product often was illegible. José's fine motor coordination and memory difficulties extended into the area of arithmetic. He understood mathematical concepts but had difficulty reproducing numbers and remembering basic facts. His acad-emic performance in math was approximately 2 years below his peers. José has been iden-tified as a student with a learning disability.

Answer the following problem-solving questions about the three students in the vignettes, Karl, Jackie, and José.

1. Can you identify differences between the three students?
2. What are the social and adaptive differences shown by Karl, Jackie, and José?
3. How could these learning and behavior differences influence decisions regarding the least restrictive environment and an appropriate educational plan?
4. Are Karl, José, and Jackie more similar or different in terms of their educational needs?

CROSS-CATEGORICAL CHARACTERISTICS OF STUDENTS

Special education labors under the weight of two contradictory beliefs. The first is that each student is unique in his or her individual learning needs. That is why all students are required by law to have an individual education program. The second belief is that there are **homogeneous** groups of mild disabilities that can be described, classified, and reme-diated. The **categorical** system led to the formulation and separation of mild intellectual disability, emotionally disturbances, and learning disabilities. We can see the results of this bipolar perspective in the debate over whether students with mild special needs are best served in special education or general education programs.

It's reasonable to categorize students with **developmental disabilities** (e.g., autism) because at the more severe learning level, emotional characteristics and etiological roots are identifiable. However, at the mild level, there is overlap between learning and emo-tional characteristics of students. Historically, certain characteristics have been attributed to students with mild disabilities. Table 2.1 shows categorical descriptions of students with mild disabilities. These characteristics are not descriptive of individual students. They are general characteristics of mild intellectual disability, learning disability, or emotional/emotional disorder.

Table 2.2 identifies generally accepted instructional strategies for students with mild disabilities across the three categories of mild intellectual disability/emotional disturbance, and learning disabilities. The categorical approach to teaching students with mild disabil-ities begins to unravel when researchers investigate what happens in special education classrooms. Hallahan and Kauffman (1982) found that instruction matched to characteris-tics of specific mild disabilities is largely nonexistent. The authors observed:

> Anyone, who happens to look in on each of three special classes or resource rooms for mildly disturbed, mildly retarded, or learning disabled children is not likely to see very

TABLE 2.1 Generally Accepted Categorical Descriptions of Students with Mild Disabilities

	MILD MENTAL RETARDATION	EMOTIONALLY DISTURBED (ED) BEHAVIORAL DISORDERED (BD)	LEARNING DISABLED
Cognitive	Subaverage intellectually. Eligibility criteria: 2 SDs below the mean (50–75 IQ); often demonstrate short memory span, difficulty transferring learning, inability to project beyond the present situation, poor reasoning skills, poor abstract thinking, attention deficits.	Average to low-average intelligence scores; behavior interfaces with test scores.	Average or above average intellectually. Mental processing dysfunctions affect thinking and learning abilities.
Academic	Delayed academically. Demonstrates expectancy of failure, has slow learning rate, repeats unsuccessful strategies or behaviors, does not attempt new tasks.	Behavior interfaces with school achievement. Weak, average, or superior academic performance.	Have processing deficits. Lack generalization skills, demonstrate learned helplessness, work slowly on tasks, may or may not have developed coping skills.
Adaptive	Eligibility criteria specifies poor adaptive skills. Hyperactive, low tolerance/frustration, easily fatigued, moral judgment comparable to mental age. Delayed community-family adaptive skills.	Discipline problem. May have anxiety, fears, physical pain. May be unhappy or depressed.	Learn to compensate for deficiencies. Dependency needs. Outer directed.
Social	Socially and emotionally immature. Unfavorable self-concept. Lacking in self-esteem. Susceptible to peer influences.	Poor peer relations. Disruptive behavior/conduct problems. May be shy/withdrawn or aggressive. Disturbing behavior demonstrated in various settings. Often elicit emotional responses in others.	Lack social insightfulness. Poor self-esteem. Susceptible to peer influences. Often feel inferior but want acceptance.

(continued)

TABLE 2.1 Continued

	MILD MENTAL RETARDATION	EMOTIONALLY DISTURBED (ED) BEHAVIORAL DISORDERED (BD)	LEARNING DISABLED
Perceptual-Motor	Delayed developmental skills affect perception and motor abilities.	Intact perceptual and motor skills generally.	Impaired perceptual and motor abilities. Eye–hand coordination problems. Awkward. May lack orientation skills.
Language	Speech/language delayed or deficient. Poor social communication.	Spoken content problems (e.g., profane, argumentative, disrespectful language).	Receptive, integrative, and expressive language difficulties. Deficient processing abilities. Poor social communication.
General Characteristics	Manifest problems adapting to the environment. Lag behind in most academic areas. Perform best at physical/motoric skills.	Display behavior that is persistent and incompatible with cultural norms to a significant extent. May have concomitant academic deficits.	Manifest specific learning problems in one or two academic areas. May have concomitant negative behavioral manifestations.

Note: These characteristics have historically been attributed to each category. Individual students' profiles will vary considerably.

different teaching techniques being used. . . . The appropriate teaching strategies and the materials used are very nearly the same for each of the three areas. (p. 435)

Similarly, Ysseldyke and associates (1982) suggested that a student diagnosed as having a learning disability may *not* require instructional treatment different from that of youngsters with intellectual disabilities or emotional disorders. The authors also state that many students without disabilities can benefit from specialized instruction designed for students with mild disabilities.

> **SPEEDBUMP—**A noted special educator once said if you want to discriminate between a student with a learning disability and a student with a reading problem, you might as well flip a coin.

Generalities about Mild Learning Disabilities

Some generalities can be made about students with mild disabilities—who they are and who they are not.

TABLE 2.2   Summary of Instructional Strategies by Functional Domains

	MILD MENTAL RETARDATION	BEHAVIOR DISORDER	LEARNING DISABILITY
Cognitive	Identify stage of cognitive development. Match teaching style to student level of development and learning style.	Make lessons relevant by connecting to meaningful experience outside of school.	Teach metacognitive, "how-to-learn" skills. Teach study skills.
Academic	Provide early childhood education. Teach thinking/problem-solving skills. Teach functional/career skills.	Focus on enhancing motivation to learn. Provide emotional support. Build on student experiences.	Teach students self-monitoring strategies. Analyze products and performance for learning disability clues.
Language	Emphasize intuitive skills and high interest in reading. Use systematic analysis of skills and progress. Respect cultural differences.	Emphasize congruent communication: "sane" and "I" messages. Accept student feelings; promote expression of feelings.	Utilize alternatives to phonics such as whole language and right-hemispheric activities. Identify specific language processing deficits and teach coping skills.
Social	Emphasize activities to build confidence and self-esteem. Teach social skills.	Establish a proactive behavior management program. Teach social skills.	Teach social perception skills. Teach social behavioral skills.

■ **Students with mild intellectual disabilities, learning disabilities, and emotional disturbance are the largest subgroup of students receiving special education services.**

Since 1976, a prevalence figure of 11 to 12 percent for special education students has been reported by the U.S. Department of Education (2007). We estimate that of the number of students identified, those with mild disabilities are approximately 80 percent of the total special education population. The population of students with mild disabilities receiving special education constitutes approximately 9 percent of the total school population.

■ **Students with mild disabilities are identified during school years.**

Mild disabilities usually are unrecognizable before entering and after exiting school. The physical appearance of these students is like that of students without disabilities. There are no differences in facial features or body dimensions. Students with mild disabilities are, in almost all respects, physically normal children who have encountered learning problems. Consequently, they remain unidentified until entry into public school, and they mesh into the mainstream of society upon leaving school. Acquaintances and employers usually don't make a connection between social and work difficulties and the fact that, at one time, an individual received special education services.

■ **Evaluations of mild intellectual, emotional, and learning disabilities are inconsistent.**

Education is not precise in pinpointing students with mild disabilities. Consider a scenario in which a virus would be identified by different criteria in the various states. An infected child traveling cross-country would be diagnosed as sick in one state and healthy in the next. Despite the difference in diagnosis, the child would still be ill.

This is the problem with mild disabilities. Because there are no standard state criteria, some students are diagnosed accurately while others are misevaluated as false positives or false negatives. A *false positive* means that some students are incorrectly identified as having a mild disability, whereas, with a *false negative*, some students who have a mild disability are overlooked.

Unreliable evaluations are complicated by the diversity of behaviors that are subsumed under the category learning disabled. Everybody has trouble in school at one time or another. As James Ysseldyke, an authority on special education assessment practices, pointed out, at one time or another 80 percent of all American schoolchildren could be identified as having a learning disability.

Similar troublesome problems are observed across these categories when we must determine which mild disability category fits a student. An analogy could be that of a preschool child attempting to put geometric shapes into the right holes of a container. When the particular objects do not fit into any of the holes, he just pounds on them or pushes harder to make them go in. Perhaps a hypothetical student with mild disabilities is like a square shape (Figure 2.1). We try to shove her into the circle representative of mild intellectual disability, or, seeing at least two straight sides, we try to push her into the triangle representative of learning disabilities. If that does not work, then we try the behavior rectangle because, even though it does not have all sides equal, it does have four sides like a square. The child may not have the exact dimensions of the category, but she is similar enough to all three that we figure if we just try hard enough, she can make a fit with one of them.

Common characteristics of students with mild disabilities are listed in clusters in Figure 2.2.

■ **Students with mild disabilities are those who are most likely to be taught in a general education classroom inclusion program.**

Special education services for students with mild disabilities usually are provided in the general classroom and/or in a combination of general and special education services. For these students, the key issue is the effectiveness of the education they are receiving in both types of classrooms.

For every study that presents gains by students with mild disabilities in general education classrooms, there is a contradictory study that demonstrates gains through services from placement in resource rooms (Fuchs & Fuchs, 1986; Marston, 1988; Villa, Thousand, Stainback, & Stainback, 1999; Henley, 2004). Educators are attempting to refocus this murky picture by shifting the viewfinder from where students are educated to what teaching methods work best. In subsequent chapters, you will find that many strategies that work well with students in general education are just as useful for teaching students with

"Oh dear, some of these kids don't **fit** into the categories."
"No problem— —we'll just stuff 'em in."

FIGURE 2.1   School Category Machine

Illustration by Lois Creech.

mild disabilities, and vice versa. Good teaching is a constant that cuts across both special and general education.

■ **Similar instructional strategies work with both general and special education students.**

Effective instructional approaches that have found common ground among teachers of students with mild disabilities as well as general educators include cooperative learning, peer tutoring, social skill instruction, phonics, career education, and behavior modification. Students within all three mild disabilities categories participate in inclusion programs in which they are instructed together in large or small groups with their general education peers. Similar behavior management approaches are used with all students with mild disabilities including functional behavior assessment, positive reinforcement, and positive emotional supports.

SPEEDBUMP—If you had to select Karl, Jackie, or José for your inclusion classroom which student would you choose?

FIGURE 2.2   Common Characteristics of Students with Mild Disabilities

The following characteristics will vary from one student to another but are generally the same across the categories of mild intellectual disability, emotional disturbances, and learning disabilities. They are clustered under psychological, educational, and social characteristics.

Psychological Characteristics

- Mild disability undetected until beginning school years
- Cause of mild disability is difficult to detect
- Physical appearance the same as students in full-time regular education
- Poor self-concept

Educational Characteristics

- Lack of interest in school work
- Prefer concrete rather than abstract lessons
- Weak listening skills
- Low achievement
- Limited verbal and/or writing skills
- Right hemisphere preference in learning activities
- Respond better to active rather than passive learning tasks
- Have areas of talent or ability that are overlooked by teachers
- Prefer to receive special help in regular classroom
- Higher dropout rate than regular education students
- Achieve in accordance with teacher expectations
- Require modifications in classroom instruction
- Distractible

Social Characteristics

- Experience friction when interacting with others
- Function better outside of school than in school
- Need adult approval
- Have difficulties finding and maintaining employment after school
- Stereotyped by others
- Behavior problems exhibited

CROSS-CATEGORICAL DISABILITIES

The following four disabilities—ADHD, pervasive developmental disorder, Asperger's syndrome, and nonverbal learning disorder are examples of cross-categorical learning problems. None of these is mentioned specifically in IDEA. For students to receive special education services, a school system must find a match with the federal disability categories. For example, if Asperger's syndrome is evaluated as mild the student could receive services under the category learning disability. If the Asperger's is moderate to severe in it limitations the category autism might be used to provide services.

Despite the differences in nomenclature the behavioral and learning characteristics of these youngsters are similar. All, for instance, are likely to have difficulty with peer relationships. Impulsivity is another common problem, as are following directions and completing assignments. Research-based social skill programs, effective reading programs, and data-based behavior management plans work equally well for all of these students.

ATTENTION DEFICIT HYPERACTIVITY DISORDER

Attention deficit hyperactivity disorder (ADHD) is an example of a condition that cuts across categories. Many youngsters with ADHD do not receive special education services because ADHD is not listed as a disability in IDEA. Some receive special education services under the category of "other health impaired," while still other youngsters with ADHD are categorized as emotionally disturbed, emotionally disturbed, or learning disabled. More recently, many school systems have avoided the knotty problem about whether students with ADHD should receive special education by utilizing Section 504 plans (see Chapter 1). These plans provide educational services without all of the due process procedures required under IDEA.

Whether a youngster with ADHD is provided with special education, a 504 plan, or no extra help can depend on several factors, including how rigorous parents are about getting services, how disruptive the student's behavior is, and the severity of learning problems. If the problem is perceived as primarily academic, the student might be classified as learning disabled. If the problem is perceived as primarily emotional, the student might be classified as emotionally disturbed. If the condition does not interfere with academic progress, no special education services are provided. ADHD often coexists with other childhood problems such as dyslexia, depression, bipolar disorder, and anxiety disorder (Gilbert, 2000).

The prevalence of coexisting learning disabilities and ADHD is approximately 25 percent (Fowler, 2002). Learning disabilities may occur more often with ADHD-IA, primarily students with attention problems, than with students with ADHD-HI, primarily hyperactive (Figure 2.3). Lerner and associates (1995) estimated that 40 to 60 percent of ADHD students have coexisting oppositional defiant disorder (ODD), while approximately 20 to 30 percent of students develop the more serious conduct disorder (CD). The *Diagnostic and Statistical Manual of Mental Disorders (DSM-IV),* published by the American Psychiatric Association (1994), specifies the following guidelines for determining if ADHD is present:

- The onset of symptoms occurs no later than 7 years of age.
- Symptoms are present in two or more situations.
- Symptoms do not occur exclusively during the course of a pervasive developmental disorder, or schizophrenia or other psychotic disorders, and is not better accounted for by a diagnosis of a mood disorder, anxiety disorder, dissociative disorder, or personality disorder.
- Symptoms have been present for the past 6 months.

FIGURE 2.3   Diagnostic Criteria for Attention Deficit Hyperactivity Disorder (ADHD)

The diagnostic criteria for attention deficit hyperactivity disorder (ADHD) was revised in the fourth edition of *The Diagnostic and Statistical Manual of Mental Disorders* published by the American Psychiatric Association. Three types of ADHD are specified.

1. **ADHD-IA.** *Primarily inattentive.* This subtype refers to children who have primary problems with attention.
2. **ADHD-HI.** *Primarily hyperactive and impulsive.* This subtype refers to children who primarily display behaviors of hyperactivity and impulsivity.
3. **ADHD-C.** *Combined.* This subtype refers to individuals who have attention problems and exhibit symptoms related to hyperactivity and impulsivity.

In order to be diagnosed, each type requires that the person display at least *six of the following nine symptoms.*

ADHD-IA Subtype. Symptoms of inattention.

- Fails to give close attention to details, makes careless mistakes
- Has difficulty sustaining attention
- Does not seem to listen
- Does not follow through or finish tasks
- Has difficulty organizing tasks or activities
- Avoids or dislikes tasks requiring sustained effort
- Loses things needed for tasks
- Is easily distracted by extraneous stimuli
- Is often forgetful in daily activities

ADHD-HI Subtype. Symptoms of hyperactivity or impulsivity.

Hyperactivity

- Fidgets with hands or feet, squirms in seat
- Leaves seat in classroom or other situations
- Runs about or climbs excessively
- Has difficulty playing or engaging in leisure activities quietly
- Talks excessively
- Acts as if "driven by motor" and cannot sit still

Impulsivity

- Blurts out answers before questions are completed
- Has difficulty waiting in line or awaiting turn in games or activities
- Interrupts or intrudes on others

ADHD-C. Combined Subtype.

Sources: American Psychiatric Association, 1994; Lerner, 1997.

ADHD is a presumed neurobiological disorder involving a network of brain structures that control inhibition and focus attention (i.e., frontal lobe, caudate nucleus, and thalamus). While research in etiology continues, evidence to date suggests that ADHD has a genetic factor and is likely caused by a chemical imbalance in the brain. Individuals with ADHD have difficulties with the brain's executive functions, which include planning, staying focused on a task, overriding emotional impulses, and short-term memory gaps. Although some students are successful because they persevere with school tasks, students with ADHD have difficulty attending to tasks that they find frustrating or uninteresting. Impulsive and inattention characteristics of ADHD are presented in Chapter 4. Although hyperactivity often appears to diminish with age, problems with attention can continue through adulthood. The following three disabilities, like ADHD, often are included as mild disabilities, although the category assigned will vary with individual students.

SPEEDBUMP—Students with ADHD seem to populate every classroom. Why do you think so many children are identified with ADHD?

PERVASIVE DEVELOPMENTAL DISORDER

Pervasive Developmental Disorder (PDD) is a term used to describe a group of neurological and biological conditions. These conditions are characterized by delays in social, communication, and cognitive development. Pervasive developmental disorders include Asperger's syndrome (high-functioning autism), childhood disintegrative disorder (Heller's syndrome), hyperlexia, Rett's disorder, and pervasive developmental disorder, not otherwise specified. Autism is the main PDD recognized and studied. In fact, the terms autism and pervasive developmental disorder often are used interchangeably. *Autism* (usually a general term) and *autistic disorder* (a specific term) do not necessarily mean the same thing to all people. Autistic disorder is a severe and pervasive form of PDD. Moreover, there is no clear understanding about how these disorders are caused. Conner (2003) states that causation theories include biochemical, electrophysiological, and structural differences within the brain. Recent studies have implicated abnormal levels of neurotransmitters (serotonin or dopamine), phenylketonuria, epilepsy, ventricular enlargement, and brain stem abnormalities.

Two diagnostic categories are listed in the *Diagnostic and Statistical Manual of Mental Disorders*, Fourth Edition. These are:

1. **Autistic disorder**—considered the primary disorder in which most children are diagnosed. This diagnostic category has specific criteria and symptoms that are fairly similar from one child to the next.
2. **Pervasive developmental disorder, not otherwise specified (PDD-NOS)**—a category for children who meet the general description for pervasive developmental disorder, but not the criteria for autistic disorder. (Conner, 2003)

The majority of children with pervasive developmental disorder exhibit behaviors in the moderate range (somewhere between mild and severe). Those with the most severe

■ ■ ■ ■ ■

HIGHLIGHT 2.1

Jerome is 16 years old. He has barely scraped through school. His reading and calculating skills are on par with those of an average 10-year-old. Each year his teachers promote him, hoping that their successor will have more luck in teaching Jerome. Jerome's poor academic skills are counterbalanced by his leadership ability. The other students look up to him because he is tough but kind. In the inner-city school Jerome attends, this is a charismatic combination. When Jerome leaves school at the end of the day, he walks home through a maze of drug dealers, winos, and storefronts girded with iron gates. His mother would like to move Jerome and his two sisters to a nicer neighborhood, but her salary as a fast food restaurant worker barely provides the family with rent and food money. Jerome is street-wise, and lately he has begun to make extra money by selling crack. All his teachers agree that Jerome is a good kid, who, with a few opportunities, could be a success; but, in educational jargon, he is a functional illiterate. Jerome is at risk of graduating from high school unable to read a newspaper.

impairments are usually diagnosed with autistic disorder. Diagnosis of the most pervasive form, autistic disorder, may involve profound mental retardation, cerebral palsy, and a pattern of severe impairments across intellectual, adaptive, social, language, and motor functioning. The least pervasive forms of pervasive developmental disorder are characterized by less-severe impairments in one or a few areas, such as expressive or receptive language (Conner, 2003).

ASPERGER'S SYNDROME

One type of pervasive developmental disorder is **Asperger's syndrome.** Asperger's syndrome (AS) generally is recognized as a neurological and biological disorder, characterized by normal intelligence and language development, but accompanied by autistic-like behaviors and marked deficiencies in social and communication skills. The autistic-like behaviors include restricted and repetitive patterns of behavior, interests, and activities. These children have trouble making transitions or changes and thus prefer sameness. They seem to experience difficulties in determining appropriate body space and in reading nonverbal cues (body language). They often are overly sensitive to sounds, tastes, smells, and sights (see Figure 2.4).

By definition, persons with AS have normal intelligence and some exhibit exceptional skills and/or talents in specific areas. Because individuals with AS perceive the world differently, their behaviors often seem odd or unusual. They excel in literal language usage. Most are unable to apply this rich vocabulary in social or pragmatic settings. They seem to perceive the world differently due to their neurobiological differences. This leads to behaviors that often seem "odd" or "eccentric." Unfortunately, these behaviors sometimes are seen as intentional or bad.

Asperger's syndrome contrasts with autism or autistic disorder in that there are no clinically significant delays in language, cognition, self-help skills, or in adaptive skills, other than social interaction. Some professionals refer to Asperger's syndrome as high-

FIGURE 2.4   Diagnostic Criteria for Asperger's Disorder

1. Qualitative impairment in social interaction, as manifested by at least two of the following:

   ■ Marked impairments in the use of multiple nonverbal behaviors such as eye-to-eye gaze, facial expression, body postures, and gestures to regulate social interaction
   ■ Failure to develop peer relationships appropriate to developmental level
   ■ A lack of spontaneous seeking to share enjoyment, interests, or achievements with other people (e.g., by a lack of showing, bringing, or pointing out objects of interest to other people)
   ■ Lack of social or emotional reciprocity

2. Restricted repetitive and stereotyped patterns of behavior, interests, and activities, as manifested by at least one of the following:

   ■ Abnormal preoccupation with one or more stereotyped and restricted patterns of interest that is abnormal either in intensity or focus
   ■ Rigid performance of routines or rituals that do not appear to have a function
   ■ Stereotyped and repetitive motor mannerisms (e.g., hand or finger flapping or twisting, or complex whole-body movements)
   ■ Persistent preoccupation with parts of objects

3. The symptoms cause clinically important impairment in social, occupational, or personal functioning.
4. There is no clinically important general language delay (the child can speak words by age 2, phrases by age 3).
5. There is no clinically important delay in developing cognition, age-appropriate self-help skills, adaptive behavior (except social interaction), and normal curiosity about the environment.
6. The patient does not fulfill criteria for schizophrenia or for another specific pervasive developmental disorder.

Sources: American Psychiatric Association, 1994; Kirby, 2003.

functioning autism (HFA) and others describe it as a nonverbal learning disability (NLD). AS is named for a Viennese physician, Hans Asperger, who described a pattern of behaviors seen in some young boys in a paper published in the 1940s. We now know that this syndrome is more prevalent in males. AS was added to the DSM-IV in 1994. Because it was virtually unknown until this time, many persons originally diagnosed with ADD or ADHD have been rediagnosed with AS. Likewise, AS shares many of the characteristics of HFA, NLD, or PDD-NOS; therefore, many individuals diagnosed with one of these have been rediagnosed or found to have a dual diagnosis.

Lois Freisleben-Cook (2003) provides a more "down-to-earth" description of persons diagnosed with AS. They have a wonderful vocabulary and often talk like "little professors"; however, their literal vocabulary does not usually convert into socially appropriate speech in a pragmatic sense. Motor dysfunction often is reflected by clumsiness. In social interactions, persons with AS may demonstrate gaze avoidance and actually turn away at the same moment when greeting another. Most would like to socially interact with others, but must be taught appropriate ways of doing so. Because the characteristics often are very similar, the educational strategies given earlier in this chapter for ADHD and PDD can be effectively used with individuals with AS.

NONVERBAL LEARNING DISORDER

Nonverbal learning disorder (NLD) is a type of PDD known as a neurological and physiological impairment originating in the right hemisphere of the brain. Similarly to other types of PDD, individuals with NLD experience early vocabulary and speech development, remarkable rote memory skills, attention to detail, development of early reading and spelling skills. In addition, persons with NLD tend to have eloquent verbal expressive abilities and strong auditory retention (NLDline, 2003; Nonverbal Learning Disorders Association, 2003).

There are primarily four areas in which persons with NLD have dysfunctional abilities. These include motoric, visual-spatial-organizational, social, and sensory skills (NLDline, 2003, 1):

1. **Motoric.** Lack of coordination, severe balance problems, and difficulties with graphomotor skills.
2. **Visual-spatial-organizational.** Lack of image, poor visual recall, faulty spatial perceptions, difficulties with executive functioning,[1] and problems with spatial relations.
3. **Social.** Lack of ability to comprehend nonverbal communication, difficulties adjusting to transitions and novel situations, and deficits in social judgment and social interaction.
4. **Sensory.** Sensitivity in any of the sensory modes: visual, auditory, tactile, taste, or olfactory.

Misdiagnosis of NLD is prevalent. This is partly due to the fact that many individuals with PDD develop secondary neurobiological disorders—anxiety disorders, panic disorder, obsessive-compulsive disorder, posttraumatic stress disorder, phobias, and depression, as well as suicidal tendencies. Once again, early intervention is very important.

SPEEDBUMP—Do you know any children who have been identified with the one of these four disabilities? If so, how do the textbook descriptions match up with the reality? If you have a student with one of these disabilities in your class when you become a teacher, what kind of support services do you think you will need? Where could you go to get more information to help you teach such a student?

---

[1]Definition of executive functioning: Neuropsychological functions including, but perhaps not limited to, decision making, planning, initiative, assigning priority, sequencing, motor control, emotional regulation, inhibition, problem solving, planning, impulse control, establishing goals, monitoring results of action, self-correcting.

CAUSES OF MILD DISABILITIES

There are two major causes for mild intellectual, emotional, and learning disabilities: **organic** (biological) and **environmental** (Figure 2.5). In the chapters on mild intellectual disability, emotional disturbances, and learning disabilities, we discuss organic and environmental causes and what the literature states about them.

Under the category of organic are included pre-, peri-, and postnatal factors, genetic factors, and maturational lag. These are the contributors that originate within the body. We include under environmental reasons for mild disabilities factors such as poverty, nutrition, toxins, language differences, sensory deprivation, emotional problems, and inadequate education. Although some environmental factors (e.g., toxins) cause organic dysfunction, the point of origin is environmental.

The more severe the disability, the sooner the problem is identified. In fact, it is not unusual for a parent of a child with a developmental disability to learn of this at birth. The appearance of the infant may differ from that of normal babies, with enlarged head circumference, tell tale facial features, or inadequate response to visual or auditory stimuli. Several medical tests are now in use with expectant mothers to provide information about possible abnormalities in their unborn fetus. These include ultrasound scans (the recording of tissue densities by sound waves), amniocentesis (examination of amniotic fluid and culturing of fetal cells), chorionic villus biopsy (examination of fetal cells in placental tissue), fetoscopy (the surgical placement of an endoscope into the uterus), and blood analysis (analyses of embryonic cells that migrate from the fetus into the mother's bloodstream).

As mentioned earlier, however, mild learning and emotional disabilities usually are not discovered until children enter school. The schedule and routines of classroom life

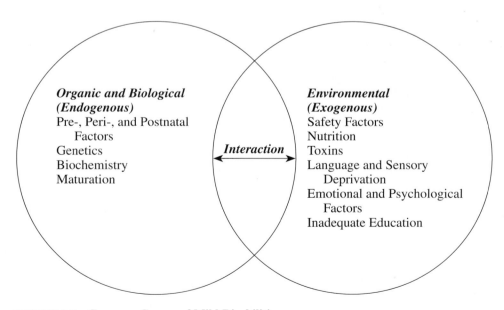

FIGURE 2.5   Common Causes of Mild Disabilities

serve as a backdrop to compare children's ability to cope with various academic and social demands. Such mild learning problems as distractibility or delayed social development
become apparent when students are unable to sit for lessons or follow classroom routines.

Fortunately, educational intervention is not contingent on identifying and curing the
cause of a problem. Educational intervention begins with the identification of a student's
strengths and weaknesses in thinking, behaving, concentrating, using language, and functioning in other areas. Once an educational assessment profile of an individual student is
compiled, teachers can select any one of numerous educational strategies to enhance learning. No one plan works for all students even though their functional problem may be the
same. For example, one student who is identified as hyperactive may respond to a program
that uses positive reinforcement to extend the student's ability to concentrate. Another student with hyperactivity may flourish in a classroom that provides methods such as learning centers and peer tutoring, while still another might respond best to medication.

An informed understanding of causal agents can prove beneficial in the identification of students who are at risk for developing learning or emotional difficulties. For instance, students who live near toxic waste discharge run a high risk of developing a
disability (Croser & Seiter, 2003). Better knowledge about etiology provides educational
programs with information to prevent learning problems. An example is the Head Start
preschool program aimed at ameliorating the effects of poverty, such as inadequate nutrition and lead poisoning.

Organic Causes

Pre-, Peri-, and Postnatal Factors.   Mild disabilities may be caused by prenatal, perinatal, and postnatal agents. Learning problems have been traced to the following prenatal
conditions:

- Maternal endocrine disorders (e.g., hypothyroidism, diabetes)
- Maternal–fetal blood type incompatibilities (i.e., Rh factor)
- Maternal age, reproductive readiness, and efficiency
- Maternal cigarette smoking
- Maternal drug and alcohol abuse
- Rubella
- Radiation exposure
- Anoxia
- Accidents (Pasamanick & Knoblock, 1973)

Infants born of mothers who have consumed alcohol during pregnancy may develop
fetal alcohol syndrome. This disability is characterized by intellectual delay and other serious learning problems. Prenatal and postnatal growth deficiencies are present in approximately 50 percent of babies born to mothers classified as severely and chronically
alcoholic, with an unknown number of babies affected by a lesser degree of alcohol abuse
during pregnancy and nursing (Smith, Price, & Marsh, 1986; Umbreit & Ostrow, 1980).
Abstinence from alcohol consumption during pregnancy is recommended by obstetricians.

Researchers have attributed various pre- and postnatal factors to mild disabilities. Maternal malnutrition can harm the development of the fetus's central nervous system and modify the growth and biochemical maturation of the brain (Hallahan & Cruickshank, 1973; Silver, 1989). Secondary cigarette smoke and substance abuse by nursing mothers have been reported as cumulative, postnatal toxins (Silver, 1989; Smith-Davis, 1989a, b).

Genetics. There is some evidence that dyslexia, a type of learning disability that impairs a student's ability to read, occurs in family lineages. Schizophrenia, a severe emotional disturbance, also appears to have, in some instances, a genetic component. Some forms of mental retardation leave unmistakable genetic tracers. Riley–Day syndrome is an inherited form of mental retardation that occurs principally among people with Jewish backgrounds. Marfan's syndrome is a rare, inherited disorder that causes visual impairments and mild intellectual disability.

As neuroscientists and geneticists become more adept at chromosome and gene identification, they will unravel the mystery of why some individuals develop learning disabilities and other mild learning disorders. In the meantime, the code word is caution when making assertions about an individual's innate, inherited characteristics. When any disorder appears with regularity in different generations of the same family, environmental influence cannot be dismissed as a causal factor. Home life, readiness for school, adequacy of teaching, motivation, and attitude toward learning are the deciding factors in a large number of cases of students with mild learning disorders.

Biochemistry. Despite its durability, the human body is a delicately balanced organism. The way our body functions depends on how well approximately 100,000 different chemicals work together. In order for the body and mind to function in unison, these chemicals must mesh in rhythmic patterns that assure optimum performance of all body organs. An imbalance in one area, such as glucose metabolism, will adversely affect mood, perception, and thinking. In the flurry of educational evaluations that precede a determination of special education services, physiological reasons for a learning problem often are overlooked. Vitamin deficiencies, allergic reactions, and abnormal mineral levels (e.g., iron deficiency) are just a sample of biochemical explanations for why students fail to develop normal learning and socialization skills.

It also is possible that many behaviors that are considered disturbing in school are stress related. Hans Seyle (1975) defined *stress* as the nonspecific response of the body to a demand. By this he means that regardless of the type of stressor experienced, the biochemical reactions of the body are the same. The student who views reading as a threatening activity or who perceives the teacher as hostile may instinctively resort to a flight-or-fight response. Withdrawal, apathy, resentment, moodiness, and anger are nonverbal responses to stress that are common both inside and outside the classroom. The ability of the teacher to identify physical signs of a youngster in distress (e.g., eyes with dilated pupils or increased muscle tone of the body) is important because many students do not have the verbal facility to describe feelings like panic, tension, and anxiety. Students with emotional disturbances, in particular, are apt to act these feelings out rather than communicate them verbally.

Educators, both general and special, have been reluctant to accept biochemical explanations for learning problems. There are two reasons for their indisposition. First, possible biochemical causes for learning problems are difficult to track down. Hair analysis, for example, can pinpoint mineral deficiencies, but the procedure requires expertise that is outside the range of most family physicians. Second, educators, in general, simply do not accept biochemical explanations for learning problems because the evidence largely is anecdotal. For example, although Feingold's (1975) and Crook's (1980) research on how specific foods can cause allergic reactions and learning problems caught on with parents, educators remained unimpressed. School menus, which weekly offer schoolchildren large doses of preservative-laden and chemically treated foods, graphically illustrate a lack of concern about biochemical contributors to learning problems.

Maturation.   Although it is common knowledge that children physically develop at different rates, parents and educators sometimes overlook the fact that children's nervous systems follow the same idiosyncratic pattern as height and weight. Differences in development are not uniformly equal. Small children in a classroom may have quick reflexes, while larger children may lag behind others in the ability to coordinate movement. This developmental lag is normal and, eventually, as the students' nervous systems mature, they will be on an equal physical footing with others in the class. Developmental delay is more serious with some children, presumably because there is an irregularity in the physical development of their nervous system.

Much is written about developmental lag and mild learning and emotionally disturbances in relationship to recent brain research. Within the brain, some reasoning abilities are localized in specific areas. For instance, in most individuals, the language center of the brain is in the left frontal and temporal lobe of the neocortex. A slight anomaly to a small area of the brain can be responsible for problems in such abstract skills as calculating and reading. Often these problems are detectable only in a formal learning environment, such as a classroom.

Hynd and Hynd (1984) contend that developmental anomalies exist in all brains. Not all brains develop in the same way (e.g., time stages, growth sections), and not all parts of the brain develop uniformly within a single individual. These researchers contend:

> While it is easy for psychologists and educators to conceive of separate distributions for IQ, reading achievement, math achievement, personality, and so on, it seems almost impossible for these same professionals to conceive of a separate distribution of neurological development. It is almost as if an assumption is made that everyone was born with a perfect unblemished cerebral cortex. (p. 491)

This statement has several implications. First, rather than assuming that students with mild disabilities have organic deficits, consider the possibility of developmental lag that, given time, can "catch up." Second, educational modifications can stimulate development in schoolchildren while maturation proceeds. Third, if all brains are "blemished" in some fashion, learning disabilities may be contextual. In school, the context is verbal skills. Thus students with language-based learning disabilities stand out, while students with deficits in musical or artistic abilities would be overlooked.

Environmental Causes

Environmental factors can enhance a child's learning potential or retard progress. The most rapid developmental growth in physiological, intellectual, emotional, motor, and linguistic functioning domains occurs during preschool years (Healthy Children Project, 2005).

Trauma.   Physical safety is necessary for the healthy growth and development of any child. A complicated delivery, early injury, illness, or falls and accidents can be traumatic and show their effects as the child develops learning readiness. Harmful events can occur even under well-supervised medical and familial conditions. Nevertheless, accidents frequently occur during times of inadequate supervision at home, on the playground, and even in school.

Nutrition.   Many different children are at risk of learning problems as a result of poor nutrition. Poor children, children of teenagers, migrant children, and children in rural areas are most likely to develop learning and behavior problems as the result of poor nutrition. Some of the symptoms of a lack of a proper diet are listlessness, irritability, fatigue, and inability to concentrate. Although poor nutrition slows metabolism and restricts the functioning of the central nervous system, the effects are reversible. The most prevalent nutritional disorder in the United States today is iron deficiency. Mothers of iron-deficient children tend to be younger, less educated, poor, and depressed. Iron-deficient children have short attention spans and behavior problems. Drinking cow's milk rather than mother's milk or formula can harm infants. Uneducated families who are unable to afford formula sometimes feed their infants cow's milk or sweetened beverages such as carbonated colas.

Allergies, which come about as abnormal responses to substances within the environment (e.g., food, chemicals, inhalants, dust, mold, selective foliage), have been associated with learning and behavior problems. Mayron (1979) estimated that 60 to 80 percent of this nation's population has suffered an allergic reaction to food at some time during their lives. Megavitamin therapy has many advocates. However, research validating this approach is mixed with some researchers showing positive results and others showing no improvement. Other dietary deficiencies correlated with learning and emotionally disturbances include deficiencies in protein, zinc, magnesium, and calcium.

The cumulative aspect of nutritional effects most aptly is illustrated and summarized by Crook (1980) (see also Figure 2.6):

> If you don't use the right kind of fuel in your automobile, it won't run properly. It may sputter, jump, jerk, and knock. Similarly, the poor performance of the inattentive, overactive child is often caused by improper "fuel": too much sugar and other junk food and insufficient amounts of essential nutrients, including complex carbohydrates, essential fatty acids, vitamins, and minerals.

SPEEDBUMP—Do you think that a steady diet of nonnutritious food can contribute to a mild disability? The next time you go to the grocery store make a list of ingredients found on labels of hot dogs, frozen pizza, and ice cream. Bring the lists to class and compare your findings. Look up some of the chemicals on the Web and discuss your results.

FIGURE 2.6   Cars and Kids Don't Run on Bad Fuel

Illustration by Lois Creech.

Toxins.   Environmental pollution is a contributory source for mild disabling conditions. Toxins found in the environment that have a strong likelihood for causing intellectual, learning, and emotional problems include hydrocarbons (from coal, petroleum, and natural gas) (Mayron, 1979), lead (from such sources as paint, plaster, automobile exhausts) (Smith & Patton, 1989), and mercury (from factory-contaminated waterways) (Peterson, 1987). Contamination from toxic waste sites and landfills contribute to learning problems as well. A follow-up study of 425 children treated for lead poisoning in the Chicago inner-city area reported 39 percent with neurological damage, 54 percent with recurrent seizures, 38 percent with mental retardation, and 13 percent with cerebral palsy (Wallace, 1972). Oil and chemical spills continue to be studied for negative effects on development and learning.

Although high doses of radiation are known to be deadly, effects from low-level radiation are not so easily determined. Pregnant mothers, however, are advised to avoid unnecessary dental, chest, and other body X-rays because of possible damage to the developing fetus—and, though not well understood, evidence has linked radiation from fluorescent lights and televisions to learning and behavior problems (Smith, Price, & Marsh, 1986). In addition, the pollution of air, soil, and water has resulted in the contamination of many foods. Animal products especially are apt to contain insecticides and other toxic substances. These toxic substances may place a further burden on a child's developing immune and nervous systems.

Language and Sensory Deprivation.   Intellectual learning and emotional development are delayed by the absence of sensory, linguistic, and cognitive stimulation. Children learn through interaction within their environment (Piaget, 1950). During infant and preschool years, overlooked health problems such as ear infections can hinder involvement in activities that are important to the development of academic readiness. Regular trips to the pediatrician or family physician are necessary to detect subtle hearing and visual difficulties. Unfortunately, many poor or uneducated parents are unable to provide preventive health attention for their children.

Children can develop verbal language problems when adequate models are unavailable to them during early years while speech is forming. Deficits occur in homes where there is language deprivation. For example, if a primary caregiver does not initiate speech or respond to a youngster's speech efforts, the child's language will suffer. English language learners encounter many educational difficulties because their primary language is not English. Detecting mild disabilities among English language learners is difficult because assessment of verbal abilities plays a key role in determining if a student has a mild disability.

Emotional and Psychological Factors.   Many children with mild learning, intellectual, and emotional disorders exhibit lack of self-esteem, insecurity, low frustration tolerance, and impulsive behavior. Home life that at an early age is unstable, abusive, or psychologically stressful contributes to poor emotional and social development of the young. Furthermore, some children are slow to respond to maternal bonding and nurturing. Sometimes these children will not allow themselves to be comforted during stressful times (Ainsworth, 1989).

Mary Ainsworth studied infant-mother bonding at the baby's 12 months of age. Ainsworth found that infants respond differently to their mothers. In an experiment called the "strange situation," Ainsworth analyzed infant reaction when their mother left them in an observation room. Securely attached infants cried when the mother left and greeted the returning mother with pleasure. Avoidant infants gave the impression of independence and did not seem to be affected by the mother leaving or returning. Insecurely attached infants clung to their mother and cried profusely when their mother left. However, upon the return of the mother, insecure infants resisted all attempts to be soothed and would angrily arch away from the mother's comforting embrace.

Without intervention, these attachment patterns persisted. Insecure and avoidant infants often become problem children. At age 2, they tend to lack self-reliance and show little enthusiasm for problem solving. From 3 to 5, they have poor peer relations and little resilience. At 6, insecure and avoidant children are apathetic and unmotivated. Ainsworth has found that teachers tend to treat securely attached children in age-appropriate ways. Teachers tend to excuse and infantilize insecurely attached children. With avoidant children, Ainsworth found, teachers are controlling.

Ainsworth's research is valuable because it highlights the interactional aspect of social-emotional growth. Significant adults in a child's life, whether they are parents or teachers, help mold a youngster's personality by the way they respond to his or her behavior. A teacher who ignores a child because "she just wants attention" or gets angry at a child who is "immature" unwittingly is contributing to the development of the offensive behaviors. Child abuse, inconsistent nurturing, neglect, and poverty all play a role in contributing to the development of avoidant and insecure children. The effect of an early unnurturing or depriving living environment may result in youth who lack motivation for learning and are unconcerned about others. Further unacceptance may be shown by teachers who have a differing value system coupled with intolerance for youth who are disturbing in the classroom.

> **SPEEDBUMP—**Does your state have mandated reporting procedures if a teacher suspects child abuse?

Inadequate Education.   Negative expectations for students with mild learning and behavior problems are handicapping factors in the classroom. Poor instructional programming, disorganized teaching practices, and low expectations for educational outcomes of children with mild disabling conditions contribute to learning difficulties. Hallahan and Kauffman (1994) include the following teacher behaviors as contributors to school failure: insensitivity to individuality, requirement of conformity to rules and routines, inappropriate and inconsistent disciplinary practices, reinforcement of inappropriate behaviors, and emphasis on student inadequacies.

Insufficient development of prerequisite readiness skills occur both in home and school environments. The absence of intellectually stimulating experiences and lack of exposure to materials that will be used in school contribute to academic delay (Smith & Patton, 1989). Lack of readiness for school coupled with desultory teaching in school almost guarantees school failure.

> **SPEEDBUMP—**A 4th grader was asked the following question—"What is the process used to make water safe to drink?" He answered, "Flirtation makes water safe to drink because it removes pollutants like grit, sand, dead sheep, and canoeists."

POPULATIONS AT RISK

Infants, Toddlers, and Preschoolers

When crafting IDEA, Congress recognized that early intervention is effective for young children with disabilities and through IDEA authorized several programs to establish a coordinated service-delivery system for children with disabilities from birth through age 5.

Under Public Law 99–457, at the state's discretion, infants and toddlers, ages birth to 2, are eligible for early intervention services if they currently are experiencing developmental delays or are at risk of having such developmental delays. Preschoolers, children aged 3 to 5, are entitled to special education if they have developmental delays in physical, cognitive, communication, social, emotional, or adaptive development. In 2001, 599,678 preschoolers received special education services (U.S. Dept. of Education, 2003).

IDEA defines children with disabilities as those

> with mental retardation, hearing impairments including deafness, speech or language impairments, visual impairments including blindness, serious emotional disturbance, orthopedic impairments, autism, traumatic brain injury, other health impairments, or specific learning disabilities . . . who, by reason thereof, need special education and related services.

Two significant developments outside of IDEA have begun to impact on the way in which preschool services are provided. One of these is the Americans with Disabilities Act (ADA) and the other is the concept of "developmentally appropriate practice." The ADA mandates that preschoolers with disabilities cannot be excluded from a public day care or kindergarten facility because of a disability, and that reasonable accommodations are to be given children with disabilities according to need. The ADA became effective in 1992. The ADA is discussed later in this section as we talk about school-aged children with disabilities.

At-Risk School-Aged Youth

School efforts to help at-risk students have focused almost exclusively on children and youth from low socioeconomic backgrounds. The term **compensatory education** is used to describe federal programs that are targeted for disadvantaged children who are at risk of academic failure.

About 25 percent of school-aged youth needs significant assistance to benefit from education, but only about half or 12 percent of these fit the IDEA definition (Rothstein,

1995). Two criteria must be met in order to qualify for special education. A youngster must

1. qualify for one of the disability categories listed in the law.
2. The presence of a disability alone does not necessarily mean that special education assistance is needed, if the student is making adequate educational progress.

The 12 percent reported by Rothstein as requiring significant assistance in order to benefit from education and who do not qualify for special education are considered "at risk." Some receive reading and math assistance from compensatory education programs, such as Title 1. Some are referred to as slow learners or underachievers. Others have chronic discipline problems or frequently are truants. All have a high probability of becoming school dropouts.

Students at risk is a generic term that describes a range of problems of school-aged youth. Low achievement, retention in grade, truancy, and behavior problems are indicators that a student may be at risk of school failure. Approximately 15 percent of all high school students leave school before their graduation date; thus, after infants, the most vulnerable at-risk population is adolescents. A student is at risk when failure is likely to occur—either in school or in life. Whether a youth is at risk is a function of the family and community as much as school actors. Problems linked to family and society include drug abuse, deficient school readiness skills, emotional problems, absenteeism, and family turmoil. Retention, low achievement, behavior problems, and absenteeism are school variables that are characteristics of students at risk.

School Dropouts

Students with emotionally disturbances have a higher rate of dropout than any other type of disability (Warner, 1991). Older secondary students are more likely to drop out than younger secondary students, although the latter group has a sizable proportion of students who also dropped out of school. Students with disabilities who drop out are less likely than those without disabilities to eventually earn a high school diploma.

Warner (1991) studied factors that influence retention. Schools and communities can apply some of these findings to assist at-risk students who might be potential dropouts.

- Students who received individual attention such as tutoring or counseling were more likely to remain in school.
- Smaller classes, tutoring, and other services increased the chances that students would succeed in general classes.
- Students in general classes were less likely to have high absenteeism or to be retained in grade if classes were small or if they had help from an instructional aide.
- Students who received job-specific vocational education performed better in school and at work than those who did not, had significantly lower absenteeism, and were significantly less likely to fail a course, miss school, or drop out.
- Students who socialized with other students outside of school and were involved in extracurricular activities were less likely to fail a course, miss school, or drop out.

When a student is identified as at risk of education failure, the educational response often has been to place the student in a special education program rather than a compensatory education program. For instance, since the passage of the Individuals with Disabilities Education Act, the number of all learning disabled students has increased beyond all reasonable expectations. However, as Slavin (1989b) points out, labeling students learning disabled is no guarantee that their problems will be remediated:

> This increase (in learning disabled students) represents the entry into the special education system of low achievers who would not have been served in special education in the past. In other words, special education has assumed a substantial burden in trying to meet the needs of students at risk of school failure. Yet research comparing students with mild handicaps in special education to similar students left in regular classrooms finds few if any benefits for this expensive service. (p. 15)

A better response to at-risk students is to identify effective teaching practices from all sectors (general, compensatory, and special education) and use these methods with all students receiving education in the mainstream (for example, cooperative learning based on planned student groupings, and peer tutoring work with students who are accelerated, average, at risk, and have mild disabilities). Unsuccessful teachers need to be retrained in effective teaching practices. Teachers must be willing to work with a broad spectrum of students, including those identified as at risk or with a mild disability. The gray area between students with mild disabilities and at-risk students may have been expanded by 1997 changes to IDEA, which permit states to use "developmental delay" as eligibility criteria through age 9, rather than a specific disability category. Experience with noncategorical criteria suggests that without the accountability of having to substantiate a specific mild disability, the numbers of students placed in special education will increase.

Perhaps the most difficult challenge is to convince teachers that their responsibilities to youth do not end at the schoolhouse door. Most of the problems of at-risk students begin in the home and community. Teachers who make home visits and who value parental participation in school activities are capable of understanding the needs of at-risk students more clearly than teachers who have little interest in their students' lives outside of school.

SPEEDBUMP—What is the dropout rate in your state? Do you have friends who have dropped out of school? If so, why did they drop out? How are they doing now?

PROBLEMS WITH LEARNING

Identification of Learning Problems

Identification of a student's learning problem occurs when comparisons are made within the general peer population about a student's academic or emotional characteristics. Teachers hold expectations for student behaviors, and those who exhibit behaviors that differ significantly are singled out. Salend and Lutz (1984) identified student behaviors required for success in the general classroom. These behaviors are grouped into the following major areas:

1. **Interact positively with other students.**
   Work well with others.
   Respect feelings of others.
   Play cooperatively.
   Share materials and property.
   Avoid fights.
   Refrain from stealing.
2. **Follow class rules.**
   Remain quiet while others are talking.
   Use appropriate language.
   Tell the truth.
   Keep hands and feet to self.
   Use time wisely.
3. **Display proper work habits.**
   Follow directions.
   Seek assistance when appropriate.
   Initiate assignments independently.
   Attend to task.
   Persist at difficult tasks.
   Attend regularly.
   Have materials ready.

Students with mild disabilities are identifiable by academic and social behaviors that deviate from those of their classmates; however, these students are not always so obvious. Imagine three groups of children working on an assigned worksheet. Students in one group appear to be concentrating on what they are doing and are busily writing answers on a worksheet. In the second group, students are working on task, concentrating, and recording answers about 50 percent of the time. Students in the third group are off task, staring into space, or jesting with each other while they ignore the worksheets on their desks.

Students at the far right end of the continuum are displaying disturbing academic and social behaviors at a high rate, duration, or intensity; these students easily are identified by their nonconforming behaviors. It would make things simpler if a certain portion of the continuum could be designated as representative of the characteristics and traits of students who are special education candidates. Unfortunately, identification of students with mild disabilities is not this simple. Imagine that some of the students at the left side of the continuum appear to be working appropriately, but closer inspection shows no rhyme or reason for the answers they are writing. Others appear to be working on task, but are drawing doodles on their worksheets.

These students often fall further and further behind. Their learning problems are not as noticeable, and they are tolerated by the teacher. Students like these often are told to pay attention, listen, and try harder. Because they have no obvious disability, they are mistaken for being lazy or apathetic. These children are at risk because if they are not identified as deviating from the norm in their learning, they are likely to fall increasingly further behind age-mates in school.

SPEEDBUMP—If things were not to improve for Karl, Jackie, or José, who do you think would be the most likely to drop out of school?

Prereferral Intervention

Federal legislation requires that sincere efforts be made to help the child learn in the general classroom. In some states, school-based teams of educators are formed to solve learning and behavior problems in the general classroom. These informal problem-solving teams have a variety of names that include concepts of support (school support teams, student support teams), assistance (teacher assistance teams, school assistance teams, or building assistance teams), and appraisal (school appraisal teams) (Pugach & Johnson, 1989b).

Regardless of what the teams are called, their purpose is similar. Teacher assistance teams are created to make professional suggestions about curricular alternatives and instructional modifications. These teams may be composed of a variety of participants, including general education teachers, building administrators, guidance counselors, special education teachers, and the student's parents. The team composition varies based on the type of referral, the needs of the student, the availability of educational personnel, and state requirements.

Modifications are tried in an attempt to accommodate the student in the general classroom. Modifications are based on the presumption that learning problems can occur because of a mismatch between teaching and learning style. Students have different learning styles (see response to intervention in Chapter 5). Whereas one student might benefit from phonics instruction, another student could be baffled by the system of blending sounds to make words. The second student might excel at a reading approach that emphasizes children's literature. Effective instruction recognizes differences in how students learn. The strategies shown in Table 2.3 for modifying general classroom instruction are effective with students at risk, students with mild disabilities, and students without learning problems.

Implementation and results of any intervention that is tailored to meet the unique needs of a student should be documented. Anecdotal records, test results, and samples of work help team members assess progress during regularly scheduled meetings. Thus, appropriate changes within the classroom environment and teaching approaches are attempted prior to or in lieu of special education referral. At this time, focus remains on what can be done in the regular classroom to assist the student. Special education labels are not considered; only modifications that might help the student to progress in the general classroom.

TABLE 2.3   **Strategies for Modifying General Classroom Instruction**

Strategy 1	Provide active learning experiences to teach concepts. Student motivation is increased when students can manipulate, weigh, measure, read, or write using materials and skills that relate to their daily lives.
Strategy 2	Provide ample opportunities for guided practice of new skills. Frequent feedback on performance is essential to overcome student feelings of inadequacy. Peer tutoring and cooperative projects provide nonthreatening practice opportunities. Individual student conferences, curriculum-based tests, and small group discussions are three useful methods for checking progress.
Strategy 3	Provide multisensory learning experiences. Students with learning problems sometimes have sensory processing difficulties; for instance, an auditory discrimination problem may cause misunderstanding about teacher expectations. Lessons and directions that include visual, auditory, tactile, and kinesthetic modes are preferable to a single sensory approach.
Strategy 4	Present information in a manner that is relevant to the student. Particular attention to this strategy is needed when there is a cultural or economic gap between the lives of teachers and students. Relate instruction to a youngster's daily experience and interests.
Strategy 5	Provide students with concrete illustrations of their progress. Students with learning problems need frequent reinforcement for their efforts. Charts, graphs, and checksheets provide tangible markers of student achievement.

Referral to Special Education

Referral is the process through which a teacher, a parent, or some other person formally requests an evaluation of a student to determine eligibility for special education services. Six factors that influence a decision to refer are:

1. Student characteristics, such as the abilities, behaviors
2. Individual differences among teachers in their skill in dealing with learning or behavior problems
3. Need for special education assistance with a student who is exhibiting emotional or learning problems
4. Availability of specific special education programs
5. Parents' demand for referral or opposition to referral
6. Institutional factors that may facilitate or constrain teachers in making referral decisions

Fewer students are referred when school districts have complex referral procedures, lengthy paperwork, special education classes filled to capacity, psychological assessments backlogged for months, and mandates to decrease special education placements can limit referrals.

Multidisciplinary Evaluation and Eligibility

If instructional modifications in the general education classroom have not proved successful, a student may be referred for a multidisciplinary evaluation. The evaluation is comprehensive and includes norm- and criterion-referenced tests (e.g., IQ and diagnostic tests), curriculum-based assessment, systematic teacher observations (e.g., behavior frequency checklist), samples of student work, and parent interviews. The results of the evaluation are twofold: to determine eligibility for special education services and to identify a student's strengths and weaknesses in order to plan an individual education program.

Eligibility is based on criteria defined in federal law or state regulations. Identification of a mild disability occurs in many states when a student's evaluation results correspond with established eligibility criteria for learning disabilities, mild intellectual disability, or emotional disturbances. As mentioned previously, there is variation in state eligibility criteria.

Evaluation by a multidisciplinary team is the means by which eligibility criteria is determined. A variety of professionals including a speech-language pathologist, school psychologist, special education teacher, and guidance counselor can be involved in the multidisciplinary evaluation. The wording in federal law is very explicit about the manner in which evaluations must be conducted and about the existence of due process procedures that protect against bias and discrimination. Provisions stated in the law include:

1. Testing of children in their native or primary language
2. Use of evaluation procedures selected and administered to prevent cultural or ethnic discrimination
3. Use of assessment tools validated for the purpose for which they are being used (e.g., achievement levels, IQ scores, adaptive skills)
4. Assessment by a multidisciplinary team utilizing several pieces of information to formulate a placement decision
5. Rule out lack of appropriate instruction in reading
6. Use processes that determine if student responds to scientific, research-based intervention

According to the law, parents *must:*

1. Be notified before initial evaluation or any change in placement by a written notice in their primary language describing the proposed school action, the reasons for it, and the available educational opportunities
2. Consent, in writing, before the child is initially evaluated
3. Consent, in writing, to classification and placement in least restrictive environment

Parents *may:*

1. Request an independent educational evaluation if they feel the school's evaluation is inappropriate
2. Request an evaluation at public expense if a due process hearing decision is that the public agency's evaluation was inappropriate
3. Participate on the committee that considers the evaluation, placement, and programming of the student

All students referred for evaluation for special education should have on file the results of a relatively current vision and hearing screening. This will determine the adequacy of sensory acuity and ensure that learning problems are not due to a vision and/or hearing problem.

Evaluation methods correspond with criteria for special education disabilities. For example, a multidisciplinary evaluation for a student being evaluated for mild intellectual disability would include the individual's intellectual functioning, adaptive behavior, and achievement levels. Other tests are based on developmental characteristics exhibited (e.g., social, language, and motor).

A student evaluated for learning disabilities is given reading, math, and/or spelling achievement tests, an intelligence test to confirm average or above-average cognitive capabilities, and tests of written and oral language ability. Classroom observations and samples of student work (such as impaired reading ability or impaired writing ability) also provide valuable indicators of possible learning disabilities.

Eligibility for services in emotionally disturbances requires documented evidence of social deficiencies or learning deficits that are not due to intellectual, sensory, or physical conditions. Therefore, any student undergoing multidisciplinary evaluation for this categorical service usually is given an intelligence test, diagnostic achievement tests, and social and/or adaptive inventories. Results of behavior frequency lists, direct observations, and anecdotal records collected over an extended period of time often accompany test results.

Additional information frequently used when making decisions about a child's eligibility for special education include:

- Developmental history
- Past academic performance
- Medical history or records
- Neurological reports
- Classroom observations
- Speech and language evaluations
- Personality assessment
- Discipline reports
- Home visits
- Parent interviews
- Samples of student work

If considered eligible for special education services, the child's disability should be documented in a written report stating specific reasons for the classification decision.

Periodic reevaluations of a student's progress are required by law and serve the purpose of determining the growth and changing needs of the student. During the reevaluation, continued eligibility for services in special education must be assessed, using a range of evaluation tools similar to those used during the initial evaluation. All relevant information about the student is considered when making a decision about continued eligibility. Although these procedures are traditional methods for providing special education, a more systematic strategy has been recently implemented. It is called response to intervention and its focus is as much prevention as remediation.

SPEEDBUMP—The special education referral and placement seems really complicated. How would you streamline the process? Refer to the flow chart on page 17.

SUMMARY

Students with mild disabilities are those who receive services in special education for learning disabilities, emotional disturbances, and mild intellectual disabilities. Regardless of the category in which they are receiving services, these students have similar learning needs. In fact, unless you are informed about each one's specific exceptionality classification, you may not know whether a particular student is identified as mild mentally retarded, learning disabled, or emotionally disturbed. Because of this, some states now deliver services under cross-categorical systems. Students with mild disabilities generally are more alike than different.

Generalities can be made about mild disabilities. Students with mild intellectual disability, learning disabilities, and emotionally disturbances are the largest subgroup of students receiving special education services. In fact, the total group of students with mild intellectual disability, emotional/emotionally disturbances, and learning disabilities comprise the majority of the total special education population. Second, students with mild disabilities are served primarily during their school-aged years. Mild disabilities often are unrecognized before and after school years. Third, the categories for mild intellectual disability, emotional disturbances, and learning disabilities are unreliable. As demonstrated with ADHD, many psychological, educational, and social characteristics overlap. Although many students with mild disabilities receive special education services, there are some who are incorrectly identified as having a mild disability and others who have a mild disability but are overlooked. Finally, students with mild disabilities are most likely to be placed in the general classroom. Effective collaboration between general and special education teachers is vital.

Causes for mild disabilities can primarily be subdivided into two major categories: organic (biological) and environmental. Particularly vulnerable populations of at-risk students are identified: infants, preschoolers, and adolescents. Existing and new compensatory education and special incentive programs can offset school failure. The inability of some students to keep up and make successful progress within the educational system results in an increased number of school dropouts at the secondary level.

A series of mandated steps must occur before a student can be delivered services in special education. The full sequence of procedural steps includes identification of learning problem, prereferral intervention, referral, evaluation, eligibility and classification, development of an individualized education program, placement, and reevaluation.

ACTIVITIES

1. Do a community survey of the city or town in which your college is located. What industries or businesses produce by-products such as toxins or pollutants that might be harmful to children? What agencies advocate for children's welfare in your community? Invite a representative of a local child advocacy group to speak to your class.
2. Invite a teacher from an early intervention program or Head Start program to visit your class. Prepare questions about the identification and services for at-risk infants, toddlers, and preschoolers.

3. Review the chapter opening vignette about Karl, Jackie, and José. In small groups, make a list of organic or environmental agents that might account for the learning problems of each student. Compare lists and discuss.

4. Inquire about services on your college/university campus for students with mild disabilities. Which students have services and how are the services provided? Are there students with disabilities who do not have services?

5. Invite a special education teacher to come to one of your classes. Ask them to comment on categorical versus cross-categorical approaches to teaching students with mild disabilities. In addition, ask these teachers to talk about inclusion versus resource room delivery of services to students. If the teachers are using the inclusion model, are they involved in consultative or coteaching approaches? Ask them to explain how they implement the various models.

6. ADHD is not considered a disability in the Individuals with Disabilities Education Act. Does this seem fair? Gather information from the Internet on ADHD. Present a position to support the following: "ADHD should be included as a special education category" or "ADHD should continue to be excluded as a special education category." Discuss the pros and cons of each statement.

CHAPTER THREE

STUDENTS WITH MILD INTELLECTUAL DISABILITIES

ADVANCE QUESTIONS

Answer the following questions as you read this chapter:

1. How has IQ testing influenced social and education practices in the United States?
2. What is a mild intellectual disability?
3. What are the causes of a mild intellectual disability?
4. Why is adaptive behavior important in defining a mild intellectual disability?
5. What does the "6-hour retarded child" mean?
6. Why is there an overrepresentation of African American males in special education programs for students with mild intellectual disabilities?
7. What are the cognitive, social, language, and academic characteristics of students with mild intellectual disabilities?
8. How can teachers improve the functional, social, and academic skills of students with mild intellectual disabilities?

VIGNETTE: LARRY

Larry was 9 years old. Each day he boarded a yellow school bus for a half-hour journey to George Washington Elementary School. When he arrived at school, he walked past a series of cheery, primary-grade classrooms and entered a small room at the end of the hall. In this, the special education classroom, Larry struggled with reading and arithmetic. He had difficulty sitting still and attending to lessons. Because of his distractibility, he was a discipline problem. Despite these negatives, Larry's schooling provided him with a safe and secure routine for 5 hours a day.

Larry, his mother, and his 2-year-old sister shared a single room in a rundown tenement, which also was inhabited by drug addicts and prostitutes. Hunger, anxiety, and depression were a way of life for Larry in this bleak world. Even a trip down the hall to the communal bathroom was a hazardous journey. Larry never knew his father. His mother tried to make do on her salary from a fast food restaurant, but it barely provided enough money to live on. She tried several times to find a full-time job, but she was handicapped by her lack of formal schooling.

Larry was one of many children who strained the resources of the city's social and educational services. His teacher described him as "depressed" and "apathetic." "Even when he smiles," she reported, "his eyes are sad." Larry was evaluated as a student with a mild intellectual disability soon after he began school at George Washington Elementary School 6 months ago. Larry's chaotic and insecure life made the prognosis bleak. His teacher felt that school could offer Larry an orderly environment, a nutritious lunch, and emotional stability. "I don't know if Larry will ever learn to read," she said, "he has been in three different schools in the past 2 years, and I doubt if he will be here much longer."

This teacher's remarks underscore how unfavorable social conditions can overwhelm the best educational intentions. Larry's mild disability is an example of the negative consequences of poverty on the health and well-being of young children. Intellectual development is stymied by a lack of such basic requirements of normal development as intellectual stimulation, medical services, good nutrition, and emotional security.

Now that you have read the vignette about Larry see how many problem-solving questions you can answer. If necessary, refer to other sources of information about the effects of poverty on the quality of life of children. See, for example, *Savage Inequalities* (1991) and *Amazing Grace* (1995) by Jonathan Kozol, *Children in Jeopardy: Can We Break the Cycle of Poverty?* (1996) by Irving B. Harris, and *Child Care and Child Development: Results from the NICHD Study of Early Child Care and Youth* (2005) by the NICHD Early Child Care Research Network.

1. What can teachers do outside of school to promote the social welfare of young people?
2. What kind of social programs can you identify in your community that offer assistance to homeless youth?
3. What can teachers do in school with students like Larry? Is Larry's situation an isolated case?
4. What services support the development of poor children in your community?

5. What can undergraduates in teacher preparation programs do to support children in their community?
6. Why is poverty still a major concern in the United States?
7. What are specific negative effects of poverty on child development?

BACKGROUND

Approximately 600,000 students with an intellectual disability participate in special education programs throughout the country (National Center for Education Statistics, 2007). The majority of these students, an estimated 80 percent, have a **mild intellectual disability**. Although mild intellectual disabilities are found among all ethnic groups, minorities, especially African American males, are overrepresented.

Because of their lack of success in school, students with mild intellectual disabilities lose confidence in their ability to learn. Motivation is a persistent problem for teachers. Although individual students differ significantly, generally students with mild intellectual disabilities exhibit problems in academics and social adjustment. Such specific problems as distractibility, weak verbal skills, and speech disorders are common to this population. In appearance, these students are normal. Most are not identified as having a disability until they enter school and begin to fall behind their age-mates in learning. After they leave school, these young people merge with the general population. In the mainstream of society, they often are not identified as disabled due to the absence of physical features associated with more severe forms of intellectual disabilities such as Down syndrome.

For over 50 years, the term **mental retardation** was used by professionals to describe an intellectual disability. A change in terminology was initiated by the American Association on Intellectual and Developmental Disabilities (AAIDD), formerly known as the American Association on Mental Retardation (AAMR). The AAIDD is the oldest and largest professional organization in the country comprised of professionals in the field of intellectual disabilities. This chapter was renamed to conform with the thinking of AAIDD. However, the term mental retardation has not been changed in the federal law IDEA. The department of education stated their reasoning in the *Federal Register* (2007):

> . . . we do not see a compelling reason to change the term (mental retardation). However, states are free to use a different term to refer to a child with mental retardation, as long as all children who would be eligible for special education and related services under the Federal definition of mental retardation receive FAPE (free and appropriate education). (p. 46550)

The following definition of mental retardation appears in the Individuals with Disabilities Education Act (IDEA):

> Significantly subaverage general intellectual functioning, existing concurrently with deficits in adaptive behavior and manifested during the developmental period, that adversely affects a child's educational performance.

> **SPEEDBUMP—**The use of two terms, one by the government and another by the leading professional organization, is certain to cause some confusion, such as when collecting data. Can you think of any other problems that could develop?

Although all states must identify a student with an intellectual disability before placement in special education, the previous definition is not mandated. Each state has the latitude to establish its own criteria. The issue of terminology has been a central clinical and political issue in the field of intellectual disability. "Moron," "imbecile," and "idiot" were considered humanitarian classifications by the scientific community during the early twentieth century. Until the 1970s, "mongolism" was the clinical term used by researchers and lay people alike to identify individuals with Down syndrome. This crossover between intellectual disability and ethnicity encoded in mongolism was no accident. The view that minorities were intellectually inferior extended beyond feeblemindedness to clinical forms of intellectual disability as well. As Gelb (1997) observed, "the typological logic of scientific racism was a major influence on the social sciences in the late nineteenth and early twentieth centuries" (p. 449).

According to Steven Taylor (2007), the term "intellectual disability" is less stigmatizing than terms that were used in the past such as mental retardation, feebleminded, mildly retarded, and educably retarded. Name change of a disability is not new, but rather an attempt to keep ahead of prejudices that can develop when a term has been used for an extensive period of time. For instance, in 1914, Henry Goddard, director of the Vineland Training School in New Jersey, promoted the use of the term moron to replace feebleminded because it was more scientific. Over the years, moron was replaced by educably retarded, which in turn was replaced by a mild mental retardation. Someday in the near future educators will probably feel the need to find a better term to replace intellectual disability.

> **SPEEDBUMP—**The next time you hear the use of moron as an insult, think about Henry Goddard.

Lloyd Dunn

In 1968, Lloyd Dunn, president of the Council for Exceptional Children, the nation's largest professional special education organization, gave a memorable speech at the council's annual conference. Dunn urged educators to reevaluate their view of students with mild intellectual disabilities. He criticized special education placements that placed such students in what he called "dead-end" special education programs. Dunn characterized students with mild intellectual disabilities as children of poverty who were denied equal access to educational opportunity in general education classrooms. (It should be noted that Dunn, like others during this era, referred to these students as educably retarded.) Dunn called for the elimination of self-contained special education classes for students identified with a mild intellectual disability. He said that disability labels too often were used by educators to explain away the school's inability to educate African Americans, Native Americans, Hispanics, and other nonstandard-English-speaking students. Dunn was particularly forthright in his condemnation of the use of intelligence testing to categorize these hard-to-teach students (1968):

> Again the purpose has been to find out what is wrong with the child in order to label him and thus make him eligible for special education services. In large measure this has resulted in digging the educational graves of many racial and/or economically disadvantaged children by using the WISC or Binet IQ score to justify the label "mentally retarded." This term then becomes a destructive, self-fulfilling prophecy. (p. 9)

Dunn's speech alerted educators to the need to reexamine practices for diagnosing and educating students with mild intellectual disabilities. The use of **intelligence tests** to identify students with intellectual delay and the educational treatments that follow are so closely knit that an understanding of one is virtually impossible without knowledge of the other (Zucker & Polloway, 1987).

Alfred Binet

In 1904, Paris school officials asked Alfred Binet and his colleague, Theodore Simon, to identify students in need of special education. The overall goal was to select students with learning problems and place them in special classes to help them with what Binet called "mental orthopedics." Binet was a fervent believer in the power of education, and he agreed to the project because he saw an opportunity to improve school services for slow learners. Previously, Binet had attempted to measure intelligence of schoolchildren by following the accepted "objective" method of calculating head size with a tape measure. He soon found that the pseudo-science of "craniometry" could not provide information to accurately select slow students. The differences he found in head sizes of students designated by teachers as the smartest or dullest were insignificant.

> **SPEEDBUMP**—Alfred Binet is one of the most revered psychologists of all time. Many of his ideas about intelligence were derived from journals he kept noting the qualitative difference in the intelligence of his two daughters. It is ironic that his greatest contribution is a quantitative intelligence test.

Binet changed tactics and decided to follow the practical strategy of presenting youngsters with problems in abstract reasoning. He tested students on a variety of tasks, including counting money, classification, and choosing "pretty" faces drawn on cards. Binet's procedure was empirical; that is, he did not start from a theory of intelligence, rather he experimented with an array of tasks until he was satisfied that he could derive a "mental level" that would indicate a child's potential for school achievement. Because of the high priority placed by schools on verbal skills, items on Binet's original test emphasized language-based cognitive skills. This accent on language skills as a primary indicator of intelligence still persists in **IQ tests** today.

A Brief History of Intelligence Testing

The turn of the century in the United States was a time of rapid cultural and social change. Vast numbers of immigrants provided industry with cheap labor. As slums, teeming with thousands of poor immigrants, sprang up in major cities, social reform became a national necessity. While educators tried to cope with students who were different, some U.S. psychologists focused their attention on the relationship between intelligence and social status. In Vineland, New Jersey, Henry Goddard founded the New Jersey Institute for Feeble-Minded Boys and Girls to investigate the influence of heredity on intelligence. After a visit to Paris in 1907, Goddard imported Binet's intelligence scale and used it to classify residents into categories of mental deficiency. To the already existing groups of "idiot" and "imbecile," he added a new term, moron, to describe the highest functioning level of intellectual disability. It was the moron or feebleminded group that became the centerpiece of Goddard's research.

In 1912, Goddard set out to detect feebleminded immigrants. He selected Ellis Island as his research site. Goddard intended to use the intelligence test to identify individuals who because of their limited intellectual capacity would likely contribute to the spread of pauperism and crime. Each day thousands of immigrants poured through the massive disembarkation building in New York harbor. Goddard sent two associates to test immigrants as they passed through customs. Candidates for testing were selected by visual inspection. Goddard believed that an individual's posture, facial characteristics, and dress provided clues about his or her mental ability.

Goddard's associates administered intelligence tests to 22 Hungarians, 35 Jews, 50 Italians, and 45 Russians. When the scores were tabulated Goddard found that 83 percent of Jews, 80 percent of Hungarians, 79 percent of Italians, and 87 percent of Russians were feebleminded! He dismissed language as an explanation because the Jews had been tested by a Yiddish-speaking psychologist, and their scores were as low as the other groups. Goddard did not consider testing conditions a contributing factor, rather he concluded that many immigrants were genetically inferior (Gould, 1981).

Goddard's views on the genetic character of feeblemindedness were reinforced by his infamous Kalikak Study (1912). Goddard claimed to have traced the offspring of a Revolutionary War soldier, Martin Kalikak, to an impoverished community located in the Pine Barrens of New Jersey. He claimed that these uneducated and dirt-poor residents of this isolated area were the descendants of a sexual liaison between Kalikak and a "tavern wench." Goddard compared the intellectual abilities and economic lives of the Pine Barren residents with the legitimate descendants from Kalikak's marriage. The legitimate Kalikak clan produced lawyers, business professionals, and doctors. The illegitimate Pine Barren descendants were characterized as sexually immoral, alcoholics, and mentally retarded. Goddard's research provided powerful arguments for the heritability of intellectual disability. In 1981, Goddard's study was discredited because he failed to consider environmental factors (Taylor & Searle, 1987). Stephen Jay Gould (1981) discovered that the photographs displayed in Goddard's research had been retouched to give the Pine Barren residents a sinister and dimwitted look.

SPEEDBUMP—Goddard is not the only psychologist who distorted data to provide evidence for inherited intelligence. Cyril Burt, who many considered the "father of educational psychology," contrived data on twins separated at birth. In many instances, the twins never existed.

Other psychologists, including Lewis Terman, continued Goddard's work with intelligence testing and came to the same conclusions about the **heritability** of feeblemindedness in Mexicans and African Americans. After the publication of his Stanford-Binet Intelligence Test, Terman, in a speech at Harvard University, made his ultimate claim for the role of intelligence testing and **social engineering** (Kamin, 1977):

> In the near future intelligence tests will bring tens of thousands of these high grade defectives under the surveillance and protection of society. This will ultimately result in curtailing the reproduction of feeblemindedness and in the elimination of an enormous amount of crime, pauperism, and industrial inefficiency. It is hardly necessary to emphasize that the high grade cases, of the type now so frequently overlooked, are precisely the ones whose guardianship it is most important for the State to assume. (p. 47)

Politicians gave Terman's notion of guardianship a macabre twist by initiating a number of state sterilization laws. In 1907, the Indiana legislature passed a law that allowed the state to sterilize prisoners and orphans. Beginning with the preamble, "Whereas heredity plays a most important part in the transmission of crime, idiocy, and imbecility . . . ," this, the first of many state sterilization laws, was passed amid high hopes of controlling the spread of intellectual disability.

It was the "high-grade defectives," or the feebleminded, identified through intelligence tests, that were the primary targets for sterilization. In a 1911 sterilization law, Iowa listed criminals, rapists, idiots, the feebleminded, imbeciles, lunatics, drunkards, drug fiends, epileptics, syphilitics, and moral and sexual perverts as primary targets for sterilization. Any adult who was institutionalized or any child who became a ward of the state was a potential candidate for sterilization. From 1907 to 1972, over 60,000 "social misfits" were sterilized in the name of social reform (Houts, 1977; Taylor & Searle, 1987; O'Brien, 1999).

SPEEDBUMP—Hitler instituted a similar plan in Nazi Germany to eliminate "mental defectives."

By the 1930s, Binet's procedure for measuring intelligence was fully Americanized and in the process distorted. Instead of a measure to identify students for special education, the intelligence test was used as an "objective" measure of innate intelligence. Binet's concept of environmental stimulation to increase intelligence was turned inside out as low IQ became synonymous with intractable dullness. Between 1928 and 1929, 65,000 intelligence tests were administered in Los Angeles elementary schools. Youngsters whose scores ranged from 75 to 50 were placed in special classes for the "educable feeble-minded" (Hendrick & MacMillan, 1987). Immigrant and minority children were placed in segregated special classes at a higher rate than their middle-class, white peers.

The tenacity with which educators clung to the IQ test as a valid measure of intelligence is remarkable. When pressed, most scholars admit that IQ tests don't measure intelligence. Today's psychologists are more likely to think about intelligence as a complex interplay of cognitive abilities including tenacity, social skills, and creativity. These and other cognitive attributes are manifested differently in each individual. Who would you rather tune up your car: a person with a Ph.D. in English or a certified mechanic? The Ph.D. would impress with a knowledge of Coleridge, Wordsworth, and Emily Dickinson, but be unable to distinguish a torque wrench from a monkey wrench. *New York Times* columnist David Brooks (2007) said:

> . . . judging intelligence is less like measuring horsepower in an engine and more like watching ballet. Speed and strength are part of intelligence and these things can be measured numerically, but the essence of the activity is found in the rhythm and grace and personality of an idiosyncratic blend of emotions, experiences, motivations and inheritances. (p. C5)

There is no correlation between an individual's IQ and success in life after school—yet, despite its shortcomings, the IQ test still serves the purpose for which it was originally intended by Alfred Binet. Because they emphasize verbal skills, intelligence tests are reasonably good predictors of school achievement. For this reason—until a more efficient method is developed to measure intelligence—IQ scores remain the most frequently used standard for identifying a mild intellectual disability.

> **SPEEDBUMP**—Educators are measuring intelligence the same way they did almost a hundred years ago.

DEFINITION AND IDENTIFICATION

Two primary characteristics are needed to identify an intellectual disability: **limited intellectual functioning** and **adaptive behavior impairments**. Limited intelligence usually is indicated by a score that is at least two standard deviations below the mean on a standardized intelligence test. Adaptive behavior refers to an individual's adjustment to everyday life including such practical skills as preparing meals, dressing, managing housekeeping activities, and using the telephone. Over the years, the definition of an intellectual disability has been modified several times. The **AAIDD** defines intellectual disability in the following way. The AAIDD definition is similar to the definition in IDEA with more emphasis on practical skills (2007):

> An intellectual disability is characterized by significant limitations both intellectual functioning and adaptive behavior as expressed in conceptual, social and practical adaptive skills. (www.aaidd.org)

The AAIDD recommends keeping the following assumptions in mind when making decisions regarding the presence of an intellectual disability.

- Valid assessment considers cultural and linguistic diversity, as well as differences in communications and behavioral factors.
- The existence of limitations in adaptive skills occurs within the context of community environments typical of the individual's age peers and is indexed to the person's individualized needs for supports.
- Specific adaptive limitations often coexist with strengths in other adaptive skills or other personal capabilities.
- With appropriate supports over a sustained period, the life functioning of the person with intellectual disability will generally improve.

To summarize, a mild intellectual disability is reflected in difficulties in learning and performing certain daily life skills. Scores of 70 to 50 on one or more individually administered intelligence tests are considered the mild range. Because the standard deviation for most IQ tests is approximately 5, the AAIDD believes that it is appropriate to use a cutoff point of 75 rather than 70. Test scores and other information are reviewed and evaluated by teams of school professionals. However, limited intelligence, as usually measured by an IQ test alone, is an insufficient basis for identifying intellectual disability—the individual also must demonstrate limited **adaptive skills** (see Table 3.1).

> **SPEEDBUMP**—The following section on the 6-hour retarded child shows what can happen when only intelligence test scores are used to identify a mild intellectual disability.

The 6-Hour Retarded Child

The need to ascertain a youngster's adaptive behavior outside of school before making an educational diagnosis of a mild intellectual disability was highlighted by the research of

TABLE 3.1   Adaptive Skills

SOCIAL	PRACTICAL
Interpersonal skills	Meal preparation
Responsibility	Housekeeping
Self-esteem	Transportation
Gullibility	Dressing
Follow rules	Taking medication
Avoid victimization	Money management
Obeys laws	Telephone use
Naïveté	Personal hygiene

Source: Adapted from American Association on Intellectual Disability, 2002.

Jane Mercer (1973). In an 8-year study in Riverside, California, Mercer found that the majority of youngsters identified with a mild intellectual disability were poor. When Mercer examined classification of students by race, she found a disproportionate number of Mexican Americans and African Americans placed in special classes for the mildly retarded.

SPEEDBUMP—Keep in mind this was before the change in terminology from mild mental retardation to mild intellectual disability favored by the authors.

Mercer coined the term **6-hour retarded child** to describe the students in her research. At home and in the community, the 6-hour retarded child was considered normal; in school, the same child was considered retarded. Why was there a discrepancy in views? Mercer concluded that the schools failed to take a youngster's adaptive functioning outside of school into account. In Mercer's judgment, the lack of attention to socialization skills outside of school resulted in the mislabeling of many minority students. Mercer's research highlighted the need to take adaptive behavior into account before making an evaluation of a mild intellectual disability.

Types of Intellectual Disabilities

It is important to discriminate between a mild intellectual disability and other levels of moderate and severe intellectual disability. One demarcation point is IQ score. As stated earlier, an IQ range from 50 to 75 indicates a mild intellectual disability. As IQ scores move below 50, the degree of intellectual disability is more severe. Students with IQs below 50 usually demonstrate observable physical and behavioral anomalies. For instance, there are over 350 inborn errors of metabolism that can lead to an intellectual disability (e.g., Down syndrome, Tay Sachs syndrome, and Prader-Willi syndrome). About 25 percent of moderate to severe intellectual disabilities are **organic** in nature. These inborn intellectual disabilities are permanent and in most cases the individual will require lifelong services. This does not mean that a student's intellectual ability has a permanent limit. With early detection and sophisticated educational intervention, students with such organic intellectual disabilities as Down syndrome continue to grow intellectually, although at a slower pace than their peers.

Within the a mild range of intellectual disability, the majority of students are not identified as having a disability until they enter school and begin experiencing academic and social difficulties. The vast majority of these students have no visible physical trait that would indicate an intellectual disability. In these cases there is no reason at birth to suspect the development of a mild intellectual disability. It is the **environment** these youngsters grow up in that impedes their intellectual development. Although such childhood traumas as high fever and brain injury can cause a mild intellectual disability, the majority of students with mild intellectual disabilities have had their normal intellectual development stymied by **poverty**. For the most part, students identified as having a mild intellectual disability experience delay in their development; they are not permanently disabled. With proper health and educational intervention, they can overcome their initial impairments and go on to lead productive lives.

Armor (2003) cites the following at-risk factors that contribute to a mild intellectual disability: low parental IQ, lack of cognitive stimulation, inadequate nurturing, poor nutrition (e.g., breast feeding), and dysfunctional family dynamics. Because poverty plays such a key role in mild intellectual disabilities, the etiology is primarily environmental (i.e., see Table 3.2 for comparison of environmental and organic intellectual disabilities). Although poor children are more at risk of an intellectual disability than their more affluent peers, it is important to remember that a family's income is not a predictor of quality parenting. It is indeed remarkable that so many poor families are able to persevere and raise children who go on to live successful lives.

Poverty is the leading cause of a mild intellectual disability. According to Armor (2003), the major at-risk factors for a mild intellectual disability include: low parental IQ, lack of cognitive stimulation, neglect, nutrition deficiencies, dysfunctional family structure, teenage pregnancy, and low birth weight. All of these factors are more prominent among poor families than among middle class or affluent families. Because poverty plays such a key role in mild intellectual disabilities, the etiology is primarily environmental (i.e., see Table 3.2 for comparison of environmental and organic intellectual disabilities).

SPEEDBUMP—If we could eradicate poverty, we would eliminate most cases of mild intellectual disabilities.

Prevalance

Approximately 10 percent of the total 6,634,000 students with disabilities ages 3–21 are identified with an intellectual disability (Digest of Education Statistics, 2007). This is about 1 percent of the entire public school population. There is variation among the states in the numbers and percentages of students identified. Recall that states are not required by law to

TABLE 3.2   **Comparison of Environmental and Organic Mild Intellectual Disability**

ENVIRONMENTAL INTELLECTUAL DISABILITY	ORGANIC INTELLECTUAL DISABILITY
Primary cause is environmental	Primary cause is biological
Normal physical appearance	Physical anomalies
Subtle health complications	Obvious health complications
Identified after beginning school	Identified at birth or soon afterwards
Developmentally delayed	Developmentally disabled
After school, able to merge into the general population	Disability is chronic and often requires lifelong support
Higher prevalence among poor with African Americans overrepresented	Cuts across all socioeconomic and ethnic groups
Subject to misidentification	Demonstrates clearcut medical diagnostic criteria
Not recognized as a disability in all countries	Universally recognized as a disability

apply the uniform criteria for mild intellectual disabilities outlined in IDEA. Oklahoma has more students ages 6–21 identified intellectually disabled than any other state—50,630. Conversely, the more populated state of New Jersey identified 6,238 students with intellectual disabilities. Generally southern states with smaller populations tend to identify more students with disabilities than higher populated states in the northeast (U.S. Department of Education, 2004). Reasons for this variation include assignment of students with a mild learning problems to categories other than intellectual disability (e.g., learning disabilities), higher poverty rates, differences in criteria, and variations in IQ score cutoff points.

Since 1999, IDEA allows each state to identify some disabled students from the age of 6 to 9 as **developmentally delayed**. In all likelihood, this classification will prompt a decrease in prevalance figures for students with mild intellectual disabilities as school systems switch to the more descriptive and less-stigmatizing term.

CAUSES OF MILD INTELLECTUAL DISABILITIES

Intellectual and adaptive behavior deficits are caused by a variety of different factors. Two conditions cause intellectual disability. These include organic problems prior to, during, and after birth, and environmental problems that result in delays in development. A summary of organic and environmental causes is presented in Table 3.3; more detailed information is presented in the following sections.

Organic Causes

Although we describe two groups of causes—organic and environmental, the boundary between them is not always clear. For example, because drugs have an effect on the unborn child similar to the effects of infections and genetic disorders, we have grouped them with organic causes. It also could be argued that drugs are part of serious environmental circumstances that are common for some families living in poverty and therefore should be included with other environmental causes. The edges are blurred but the problems are clear-cut.

Drugs.   From the moment of conception, a child is vulnerable to influences that can stunt normal development. A pregnant mother's health is a crucial determiner of a healthy child.

TABLE 3.3   **Summary of Causes of Intellectual Disabilities**

ORGANIC CAUSES	ENVIRONMENTAL CAUSES
Drugs	Toxins
Infection	Diet
Genetic	Inadequate health care
	Environmental deprivation

Whatever a pregnant woman puts into her body will eventually be absorbed into fetal tissue. Alcohol and cocaine especially are dangerous to the fetus. Even small amounts of these drugs pose a threat to the fetal nervous system, especially during the first trimester of pregnancy.

Drug abuse cuts across all socioeconomic levels and poses an immediate threat to the nervous system of an unborn child. Because drug abusers neglect their bodies in general, the fragile nervous system of the fetus may be jeopardized by malnutrition, iron deficiency, or anoxia. Newborn infants of drug abusers often are addicted to whatever drug the mother was using. The National Institute on Alcohol Abuse and Alcoholism estimated that annually 1,500 of three million newborns are born with fetal alcohol syndrome (FAS). Thousands of other children will have some of the characteristics of FAS, including prenatal and postnatal growth deficiencies, intellectual disability, and fine-motor impairments. Low birthweight (less than 5.5 pounds) can lead to a variety of health problems, including mild intellectual disability. Teenage pregnancies and inadequate prenatal care— for instance, smoking—can result in low birthweight.

Infections. Several forms of a mild intellectual disability are caused by **maternal infection**. Retardation can result from the mother's being infected with rubella (German measles). The effects can range from mild to severe intellectual disability. Toxoplasmosis is caused by a protozoan infection of a pregnant woman. The protozoa sometimes is found in cat litter. Toxoplasmosis can cause a mild to severe intellectual disability, along with a variety of health problems. Cytomegalic inclusion disease is caused by a viral infection. The child's intelligence can range from normal to severely retarded. Cytomegalic inclusion disease also can cause visual and hearing problems. Microcephaly often accompanies this disease. Kernicterus is a form of neonatal brain damage that is caused by the destruction of fetal red blood cells in utero. The principal cause of kernicterus is Rh incompatibility, but drugs, infections, and enzyme abnormalities also have been identified as etiological factors. Although a mild intellectual disability sometimes is present, such other symptoms as disturbed speech articulation and athetoid cerebral palsy can lead to a misdiagnosis of a mild intellectual disability in an individual with normal intelligence. Children who run high fevers for an extended period of time are also at risk of brain damage that can result in a mild intellectual disability.

Genetics. In the past, many pediatricians and educators assumed that children with inherited intellectual disability disorders were moderately to severely disabled. Although this may sometimes be true, it is a mistake to assume that **inherited intellectual disability** exists at any specific level—mild, moderate, severe, or profound. Inherited disorders are genetic in origin. Some are found in specific ethnic groups. For example, Riley-Day syndrome occurs principally within Semitic groups. Autonomic nervous system function is impaired, and children are usually small with poor coordination. Emotional problems are common, but intelligence can range from above-normal to moderate intellectual disability.

Approximately 5,000 infants are born with Down syndrome each year in the United States. Infants with Down syndrome are born to women over 35 years of age in approximately 80 percent of cases. Women over the age of 35 have babies with Down syndrome in about 1 out of every 400 births. In 95 percent of cases, Down syndrome is caused by a chromosome imbalance, resulting in three number 21 chromosomes instead of two. Intellectual disability can range from mild to severe. Down syndrome is one of the most common forms of clinical intellectual disability. Since the institution of preschool special education programs, children with Down syndrome, as well as other inherited disabilities, have demonstrated an increased ability to learn and participate in age-appropriate activities. Some Down syndrome children score in the normal range on IQ tests.

Fragile X syndrome occurs in 1 of 1,000 males; however, many cases may go undiagnosed. This sex-linked disorder occurs in males four times as often as females. Individuals with fragile X do not produce a protein, FMRP, which is crucial in nerve cell function and learning. The name "fragile X" is derived from a break in the long arm of the X chromosome. Characteristics of fragile X syndrome may include delayed language development, hyperactivity, mood disorders, a long narrow face, and prominent ears. Other forms of inherited intellectual disability include Prader-Willi syndrome, Marfan's syndrome, oral facial digital syndrome (OFD, Type I), and Klinefelter's syndrome. Each of these clinical forms of mild intellectual disability is complex in its educational, medical, and psychological symptoms. Seizures, behavior disorders, metabolic problems, organ dysfunctions, motor problems, speech disorders, and emotional disturbance can combine in any number of ways in specific individuals (Lemeshow, 1982).

One of the greatest difficulties for children with clinical intellectual disability is overcoming the social stigma of their physical appearance. Children with Down syndrome, for instance, might be placed in self-contained special classes based on the fact that they "look" retarded. Limited expectations for success, along with isolation from nondisabled peers, can become a self-fulfilling prophecy of failure for these youngsters. Adolescence, with its emphasis on being attractive and popular, can be a particularly painful period. The aphorism "nature disables but society handicaps" aptly describes the constant struggle of these children for acceptance by their peers without disabilities.

Environmental Causes

The majority of students with mild intellectual disabilities are poor and have no observable organic impairments. Poverty contributes to a mild intellectual disability by limiting access to experiences that lay the foundation for cognitive development and educational achievement. Consequently, a mild intellectual disability is as much a social as an educational problem. A combination of factors contributes to a mild intellectual disability among the poor. Because it is difficult to pinpoint a specific cause, these youngsters are referred to as having socioeconomic or nonspecific retardation. African Americans and Hispanics constitute the highest ethnic percentage of students with mild intellectual disabilities; 33 percent of African Americans and 30 percent of Hispanics live in poverty (Center on Budget & Policy Priorities, 2000). See Table 3.4 for government-established poverty guidelines.

Toxins.   Lead and other heavy metals, such as mercury, poison children through inhalation, ingestion, and skin contact. The toxin is absorbed by central nervous system tissue, where it can cause a variety of learning problems. Lead poisoning causes irritability, listlessness, clumsiness, and distractibility. Verbal and attending skills are most vulnerable to lead's toxic effects. A child can get **lead poisoning** by drinking from water pipes that are

TABLE 3.4   Poverty Guidelines, 1999

SIZE OF FAMILY UNIT	FORTY-EIGHT CONTIGUOUS STATES ($)	ALASKA ($)	HAWAII ($)
1	8,240	10,320	9,490
2	11,060	13,840	12,730
3	13,880	17,360	15,970
4	16,700	20,880	19,210
5	19,520	24,400	22,450
6	22,340	27,920	25,690
7	25,160	31,440	28,930
8	27,980	34,960	32,170
Each Add'l Person	2,820	3,520	3,240

Source: Children's Defense Fund, 2000.

soldered with lead. Lead also is found in plaster and paint. Children are exposed to lead from carbon monoxide exhaust in automobiles and factory emissions. The National Center for Disease Control estimates that 890,000 U.S. children ages 1–5 have elevated blood lead levels, and more than one-fifth of African American children living in housing built before 1946 have elevated blood levels (CDC, 2007). A blood test can detect elevated levels of lead.

Although all children are exposed to lead in some form, poor children are most susceptible to lead poisoning. Old, dilapidated buildings and houses often are covered with lead paint. The cars on major highways that circle over inner-city ghettos spew hydrocarbons into the air. Eventually the lead soaks into the soil, which remains contaminated for decades. Children playing in yards or playgrounds near highways and factories are at risk of lead poisoning. Table 3.5 lists vulnerabilities of school-aged children.

SPEEDBUMP—Lead poisoning and ADHD symptoms are similar.

Diet.   A proper diet is necessary for normal growth and development. Nutrition is most important during fetal, neonatal, and early life, when body cells are dividing, organs are forming, and developmental reflexes are beginning. Lack of proper **nutrition** in early development can contribute to growth retardation, intellectual delay, and behavior disorders. Winick (1976) found that malnutrition is a widespread problem in the United States, particularly among low-income African Americans, Native Americans, and Hispanics. Although research has not proved that malnourishment alone causes a mild intellectual disability, it is evident from studies of Third World children that there is a significant relationship between proper nutrition and normal development (Edgerton, 1979).

Health.   A number of overlapping health issues put children in poverty at risk. The lack of adequate **health services** for these children is well documented. Infant mortality rates

TABLE 3.5   Vulnerabilities of School-Aged Children

AGE	VULNERABILITIES	WHAT TO LOOK FOR
2–6 years	Brain, lungs, small intestines, immature detox capacity	Pesticides, floor-level air pollutants, lead, mercury, allergens
6–12 years	Brain, lungs	Air pollutants, arts & crafts, pesticides
Adolescent	Brain, lungs, rapid growth, sexual maturation	Occupational hazards, drug abuse, air pollutants, arts & crafts, trade school hazards, pesticides

Source: Adapted from American Association on Intellectual Disability, 2002.

and percentage of low-birthweight infants are higher among the poor, as are teenage birth rates. Low-birthweight infants are underdeveloped and vulnerable; children born to teenage mothers confront a host of environmental and developmental difficulties, including diminished learning opportunities, inadequate nurturing, and frequent illness. A child born to an unmarried, teenage, high school dropout is 10 times as likely to grow up in poverty as a child born to an intact family. Mothers who lack health insurance are less likely to seek out medical advice. Some youngsters only see a doctor when their illness is so severe that they require emergency room care. Among these youth, common childhood ailments such as asthma, ear infections, fevers, and infectious diseases fester without the benefit of medical intervention. The sum total of these environmental risk factors can contribute to cognitive delay, which upon entry to school can result in a diagnosis of a mild intellectual disability.

Deprivation.   The cultural gap between the lives of poverty-level children and the middle-class standards of school puts these youngsters at a disadvantage. This particularly is true in the case of minorities, especially non-English–speaking students. Most discouraging are the conditions that many American youth must adapt to within areas ravaged by poverty. Consider the following description reported by Jonathan Kozol in his guided tour of East St. Louis (1991):

> East St. Louis begins at the Monsanto fence. Rain starts falling as we cross the railroad tracks, and then another set of tracks, and pass a series of dirt streets with houses that are mostly burned out shells, the lots between them piled with garbage bags and thousands of abandoned auto tires. . . . The waste water emitted from the sewage plant, according to a recent Greenpeace study, "varies in color from yellow-orange to green." The toxic substances that it contains become embedded in the soil and the marshland in which children play. Dead Creek, for example, a creek bed that received charges from the chemical and metal plants in previous years, is now a place where kids from East St. Louis ride their bikes. The creek, which smokes by day and glows on moonless nights, has gained some notoriety in recent years for instances of spontaneous combustion. . . .

"Nobody in East St. Louis," Ahmed says, "has ever had the clout to raise a protest. Why Americans permit this is so hard for somebody like me, who grew up in the real Third World, to understand. . . ."

"I'm from India. In Calcutta this would be explicable, perhaps. I keep thinking to myself, 'My God! This is the United States!' " (p. 17)

When considering the negative effects of poverty, it is clear that a mild intellectual disability is as much a social as an educational problem.

Poor children may begin school with delayed language development, inadequate reading readiness, and short attention spans. Some are latchkey children; when they finish school for the day, they return to empty homes where they must care for themselves. The gut-wrenching reality of poverty is that formal education has little meaning to a youngster whose daily existence is a struggle for survival.

> **SPEEDBUMP**—Although some of these descriptions might seem far-fetched, they are unfortunately true.

In *The Longest Mile* (1969), Rene Gazaway documented the inexorable slide toward intellectual disability in isolated, rural Appalachian communities, or "hollows" where **environmental deprivation** was a way of life. In Duddie's Branch, Gazaway found rampant illiteracy, malnutrition, disease, and isolation. The culture was so impoverished that for some time Gazaway thought that many adults were mute. In the course of a day, a typical family exchanged no more than a half dozen words. Children under 6 showed little curiosity or imagination. They spent most of the day together without the benefit of adult guidance or playthings. Gazaway provided the following description of a youngster's life in Duddie's Branch:

> Hollow parents are completely indifferent to the expanding demands for more formal and informal educational experiences. Not one child from Duddie's Branch has ever seen a sandbox. None has played with finger paints, puzzles, or blocks. Their "toys" consist of broken bottles, sharp metal, discarded tin cans. Ask them about Goldilocks, and they will look at you in bewilderment—they never heard a fairy tale. I made a bean bag from an old rag and asked some of the older boys to catch it. They had difficulty. With an old string ball and a heavy stick, I tried to involve them in batting practice. I was unsuccessful. Not only do games fail to interest them, they are almost completely unable to participate in most activities. They could not be taught to whistle, or even sing a simple tune. (Edgerton, 1979, 55)

> **SPEEDBUMP**—The authors are aware that this is a dated study, but the description is compelling and unmatched. Remember the movie "Deliverance"?

Gazaway went on to describe the inability of these children to count, draw a geometric shape, discriminate right from left, or identify pictures of common animals. In this community, characterized by disease, hunger, lack of stimulation, neglect, and minimal verbal interaction, few children could be expected to score over 70 on an IQ test. Duddie's

Branchers were trapped in an unchanging cycle of intellectual disability. Adults with a mild intellectual disability parent children who will soon become retarded themselves, and the cycle continues.

Since *The Longest Mile* was published in 1969, both state and federal government combined have infused millions of dollars into highway construction to relieve the isolation of Appalachia, but a high rate of school dropouts continues to sustain functional illiteracy and undermine political initiatives. Hampered by an inability to do simple arithmetic calculations, read a recipe, or fill out a job application, functionally illiterate parents struggle to provide their children with the basic necessities. A national survey in the state of Kentucky reported that 30 percent of the adults in Appalachian counties were functionally illiterate (Kilborn, 2000).

For children of poverty, success or failure hinges on the teacher's ability to adapt to the students' needs. This begins with an understanding of a youngster's life outside of school. When a student can see a connection between life in and outside of school, then there is a reason to learn. There are too many distractions on the streets for disadvantaged youngsters to sit still for 18 years of unmeaningful schooling. The identification of a youngster ensures the delivery of special education services, yet provision of special education is no guarantee of success. Instead, it is the quality of these services that will make

■ ■ ■ ■ ■

HIGHLIGHT 3.1
A PROFILE OF POVERTY

In a large northeastern city, one elementary school encapsulated the miserable union of poverty and inadequate schooling. The neighborhood around the school resembled the aftermath of a battle scene. Shop windows were boarded, abandoned automobiles lined the streets, and the stamp of despair was etched in the faces of middle-aged men hunched in doorways. The school playground looked like a suburban landfill. Mattresses, old tires, and appliances were piled high amid broken bottles and overfilled garbage bags. Any child who played in this area risked serious injury. The outside of the school resembled a fortress with heavy metal doors and wire-mesh windows. It was a cheerless yellow building covered with graffiti.

Teachers, the majority of whom were white, punched time cards and talked of weekends away from the chaos of the inner city. In one classroom the teacher made several tentative attempts to get his 6th-grade charges to sit down and have a group lesson. After it was clear that no one was listening, he sat down with two students in the corner of the room and helped them with some math problems. The rest of the "class" wandered around or amused themselves with solitary activity. A teenage girl doodled on the blackboard. She carefully drew an arm with a clenched fist. A hypodermic needle jutted from the bulging biceps. Another girl stared into the tiny holes of an oval pencil sharpener attached to the wall. For 15 minutes, she slowly turned the handle as she peered inside, occasionally giggling to herself. When queried about the total disorder, the teacher's response was plain, "I'm just happy they come to school, at least they are safe for a while; anything after that is a bonus."

a difference. The task for both regular and special educators is to convince disadvantaged youngsters that there is a good reason to persevere in school.

DISPROPORTIONATE REPRESENTATION OF MINORITIES

African American males continue to be identified as mildly intellectually disabled at a higher rate than their overall attendance in the public schools. Among adolescents, African American students accounted for 21 percent of the total number of students in special education programs, and they represented 16 percent of students in general education (Wagner, Carneto, & Guzman, 2003). The intersection of poverty, racism, and questionable diagnostic procedures presents a complex problem for educators. Are minorities overrepresented in special education programs because of their higher poverty rate or are diagnostic procedures culturally biased? Educators have argued both sides of this thorny issue since Dunn drew national attention to the problem in his address to the Council for Exceptional Children in 1968.

Only the most ardent political advocate would argue that overrepresentation of minorities is purely discriminatory in origin. Many minorities live in poor urban and rural areas. The deleterious effects of poverty are bound to hinder normal development of many youngsters and result in special education placement. Between 1983 and 1996, numbers of students identified as mentally retarded declined from 13.3 percent to 11.3 percent among families living *above* the poverty line. During the same time span, students identified as mentally retarded and living *below* the poverty level increased from 17.4 percent to 18.4 percent (Fujiura & Yamaki, 2000). Other population-based studies have found "no increment risk associated with racial/ethnic group beyond the overlap with poverty and family" (Fujiura, Yamaki, & Czechowicz, 1998).

Friend and Cook (2000) summarized concerns about **overrepresentation** of African Americans, finding that although African American students represent 14.8 percent of all the students in school ages 6 to 21, they represent 19.8 of all students served as having disabilities defined by IDEA. The disproportionate representation of this group is particularly striking in (1) the intellectual disability category, in which African Americans represent 33.8 percent of all those identified; (2) the emotional disturbance category, in which African Americans represent 26.7 percent of those identified; and (3) the developmental delay category, in which African Americans represent 25.5 percent of those identified (Friend & Cook, 2000, 92).

The case for discrimination is supported by further evidence that despite the legal mandate for multidisciplinary assessments, limited-English–speaking youngsters continue to be tested in English. Despite widespread knowledge of the "6-hour retarded child" phenomena, some school districts still identify students as a mildly disabled without gathering additional information on adaptive behavior outside school. Finally, concerns about the cultural fairness of IQ testing continues to spark serious reservations. For example, a judicial decree in California prohibited IQ testing of African American students when making an educational assessment for a mild intellectual disability (*Larry P. v. Riles*, 1979). As long as IQ tests remain the primary assessment tool for determining a mild intellectual disability, arguments about both validity and cultural fairness will persist.

CHARACTERISTICS

The following sections describe learning characteristics of students with mild intellectual disabilities. The first section, *cognitive*, reviews the research on the development of thinking skills. The next section on *mental processing* describes how students with a mild intellectual disability interpret, store, and use sensory information. The section on *academics* explains how students succeed or fail in school. The *communication* section describes the relationship of language ability to school achievement. The *perception/motor* section explains how attention and memory influence learning. Finally, the section on *social-adaptive* skills discusses the special problems of living with the label intellectually disabled. Through a review of each of these sections, you will find that students with a mild intellectual disability are more similar to than different from students without disabilities. Variations between learners with a mild intellectual disability and other students are differences in degree of ability rather than differences in kinds of ability.

Cognitive

What is intelligence? This is a question that continues to confound scholars in science and education. While scientists study the brain, educators study the mind. Neuroscientists calculate that the brain is composed of a hundred billion neurons, with 500 trillion connections between these microscopic carriers of information. At the molecular level of brain function, thoughts are electrical impulses coursing through neural networks at the speed of light. Teachers in classrooms, psychologists in research laboratories, and employers in business provide ample descriptions of the thinking abilities of individuals with a mild intellectual disability. These descriptions of thinking skills vary depending on the point of view of the observer. For example, a teacher might describe problems with abstract material, while a psychologist will report a subaverage mental level. An employer, meanwhile, might complain about difficulty following directions.

Within the context of everyday life, a suitable definition of intelligence is the ability to adapt to the demands of specific settings and individuals. This social systems view of intelligence, with its emphasis on adaptation, is different from the psychometric (i.e., IQ) concept of intelligence that prevails in schools. In the former, intelligence is a function of survival and of getting along with others; in the latter, intelligence is a score on a test.

Psychometry is the measurement of intellectual ability by mental tests. Mental tests provide an intelligence quotient (IQ) and mental age (MA) but present limited information about how an individual thinks. Because the first mental test devised by Binet was meant to screen slow students, revisions of the original intelligence test continue to focus on school-related skills. For example, the Wechsler Intelligence Scales for Children-Revised (WISC-R) measures verbal and performance skills, including information questions, arithmetic, memory, and speed in putting together puzzles. To judge intellectual capacity based on performance on 14 subtests on the WISC-R (or its latest revisions) provides a limited view of the nature of intelligence.

Sternberg (1990) described student cognitive ability in terms of thinking styles. Many learning problems could be eliminated, according to Sternberg, if teachers examined more carefully the mismatch between their teaching style and their students' thinking style. He maintained that any subject can be taught in a way that is congruent with a student's thinking style. Students who prefer what Sternberg calls the "executive" thinking style like to be told what to do and are good at recalling facts. These students make a good match with teaching methods that emphasize memorization and objective examinations. On the other hand, students who are more "legislative" in their thinking respond best to learning tasks that require imagination, planning, and creative problem solving. Teachers might confuse thinking style with quality of intelligence. When a legislative-thinking student is taught by an executive-style teacher, the student is at a disadvantage. According to Sternberg, teachers need to pay closer attention to the differences in how their students think.

Piaget's Theory. The cognitive theory of Jean Piaget (1950) offers another method for understanding the development of thinking. Piaget's theory describes four phases of intellectual development. Each phase is distinctively different in terms of *how* the individual perceives and interprets information. The *sensory-motor* stage is the initial phase of mental development. It begins at birth and typically develops through infancy. (All age indicators are only approximations. There is a good deal of variability in when individual children move onto the next stage of development.) As its title suggests, learning is linked to sensory input and evolving motor abilities. During this stage, the infant organizes and constructs a sense about how the world operates through imitation and play.

> **SPEEDBUMP**—When Piaget was a young man he worked in Alftred Binet's lab as an assistant. Piaget's job was to ask children questions, mark their answers, and move on. He kept falling behind in his work because he was more interested in children's wrong answers than their right answers. In one of the most intriguing encounters in science, Binet called Piaget into his office and fired him!

The second stage of cognitive development, the *preoperational*, begins around age 2. At this point the child develops the ability to think symbolically through language, deferred imitation, games, and art. Ideas are tied to perceptions. For example, a pile of leaves that is scattered may appear to be "bigger" to a 4-year-old than if the leaves were pushed close together because it covers more space. The preoperational thinker's view of the world still is characterized by the egocentrism of infancy. For example, clouds are alive because they move, and the sun sets, as a 4-year-old put it, "because kids get tired."

During the primary school years (ages 7 to 11), most children are *concrete operational* thinkers. A child can mentally manipulate such symbols as numbers and words, but the child's thoughts still are tied to concrete here-and-now experiences. The opportunity to experiment with materials, to select topics of interest, and to investigate relationships, coupled with an increased need to share ideas verbally, characterizes thinking during this stage.

Formal operations is the final stage of cognitive development. Piaget described the onset of this stage around adolescence. At the formal stage, the young adult has developed the ability to reason logically, to analyze, and to search for solutions among an array of possibilities.

Cognitive research with individuals with intellectual disability demonstrated that their reasoning abilities are better characterized as developmentally delayed than deficient (Henley, 1985). Stafford and Klein (1977) noted in their comprehensive review of cognitive research:

> An important aspect of Piaget's orientation is that it enables one to shift from the deficit notion . . . to understanding where the retarded may be in terms of developmental structures. This positive view enables us to look at what retarded children are rather than what they are not; what they know rather than don't know. (p. 308)

The major impact of Piaget's view of intelligence is that children interact and view their world in a distinctively different manner depending on their stage of cognitive development (Figure 3.1). The application of cognitive developmental theory to the instruction of learners with a mild intellectual disability requires a close look at what goes on in classrooms. Piaget described learning as interactive. Children require opportunities to learn through trial and error. They use language to compare perceptions and make adjustments to their egocentric view of life. A teacher-directed, sit-still-and-listen classroom does not match the cognitive abilities of children at the sensory-motor, preoperational, or concrete stage of intellectual development.

Reid (1978) analyzed education methods from a Piagetian perspective and observed that many education techniques work in opposition to the natural abilities of students. Rigidly sequenced curricula, concern for the "right" answer, drill, and memorization are formal operational strategies that overshoot the cognitive strategies of students who are at the preoperational or concrete operational stage of thinking. The neglect of educators to consider underlying developmental processes in their teaching can create a conceptual gap between the curriculum and the mediating cognitive structures of the student. The overall effect can be a loss of motivation and continued dependency on adults to provide information and solutions to problems. Educators who view the cognitive development of learners with a mild intellectual disability from a Piagetian perspective modify classroom activities to match the learning capabilities of their students.

Mental Processing

Thinking is a complex process. Suppose a stranger asks you for directions. As you picture a route in your mind, the visual center of your occipital lobe is activated. Then you mentally translate your vision into a series of steps while your left hemisphere analyzes each part of the stranger's journey. Words take shape next, and instantaneous messages flash back and forth between the parietal lobe and frontal lobe. The mouth region of the motor cortex fires signals to your tongue, jaw, and larynx. Finally, as you speak, the auditory cortex of the temporal lobe tracks your words and sentences to ensure that you are accurately describing the correct route.

This brief illustration describes the multiple tasks the brain performs in **mentally processing** the steps of a simple communication. When a deficit exists in these processing skills, even everyday tasks can become overwhelming. Much of the pioneering research on processing skills was done using patients who had suffered brain injuries. Researchers

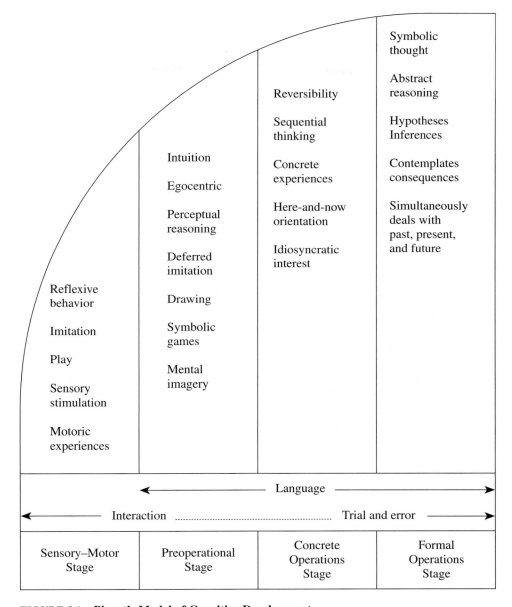

FIGURE 3.1   Piaget's Model of Cognitive Development

Sources: Adapted from Wyne & O'Connor, 1979.

would pinpoint the damaged area of the brain, determine what processing skill was impaired, and draw a conclusion that the damaged area was responsible for that specific processing disability. With individuals who had no obvious brain damage, judgments about deficits in processing skills were hypothetical. Ellis (1963), for example, theorized that individuals with intellectual disability were deficient in some processing skills and had normal abilities in others. The challenge for researchers was to determine which processing skills were intact and which were deficient.

The previous section on cognition described the developmental view of how students with mild intellectual disabilities think. Researchers who espouse the developmental view of a mild intellectual disability report a slower rate of cognitive development rather than specific deficits in mental processing. It is likely that the developmental and deficit theories are to some extent both correct. Present research methodologies are muddled by divergent statistical procedures and grouping of subjects by mental age rather than type of intellectual disability (i.e., putting students with socioeconomic and clinical intellectual disability in the same category because they have similar IQ scores).

When researchers discriminate intellectual disability by etiology, a clearer picture begins to emerge. For instance, research conducted on students with intellectual disability with an organic etiology, such as Williams syndrome, Prader–Willi syndrome, and fetal alcohol syndrome, produced evidence of diverse mental processing problems not found in students with a socioeconomic mild intellectual disability (Dykens & Kasari, 1997; Uecker & Nadel, 1998).

Advances in **biotechnology**, including PET scans, magnetic resonance scans, and CT scans, allow neuroscientists to observe the thinking brain in action. Although the research costs for such advanced equipment are still prohibitive, these technologies are certain to play a future role in clarifying the relationship between mental processing skills and intelligence. The mapping of the human genome will add to this body of knowledge by allowing future researchers to compare and contrast thinking abilities of students based on genetic markers rather than IQ scores.

Testing is a common method for identifying processing deficits of students with a mild intellectual disability. However, many tests that are used to measure mental processing skills have validity and reliability problems. Teacher observations are the most common source of information about mental processing problems. Deficient memory skills, short attention span, distractibility, and impaired abstract thinking commonly are attributed to students with a mild intellectual disability, yet teachers' observations of student actions are biased by their expectations for "normal" classroom behavior. In a classroom, where students spend inordinate amounts of time sitting, listening, and writing in workbooks, even small amounts of bored or distracted behavior can be misinterpreted as a mental processing problem.

SPEEDBUMP—A university professor asked his students the following exam question—"What is the difference between ignorance and apathy?" The professor had to give an A+ to the student who answered "I don't know, and I don't care."

—Richard Pratt, *Computer Weekly*, July 20, 1990

Accurate identification of the processing skills needed to succeed in school is far from complete. Until the 1970s, attempts to evaluate processing skills and deficits were hindered by overreliance on the need to infer abilities from samples of behavior. Sometimes the behaviors were answers to questions on a test; at other times the behaviors were actions in the classroom. The difficulty with these indirect assessments of processing skills is that there were other factors, such as teacher bias and inadequate theory, that distorted judgments about processing skills.

With positron emission tomography (PET scans), neuroscientists can directly observe the brain in action. Through the use of computer-enhanced imagery, physicians are able to observe the brain of a patient in the act of thinking. A radioactive tracer in the bloodstream lights the computer projection of the patient's brain in vivid colors that correspond to the part of the brain that is engaged. When the patient is talking, the left frontal lobe and motor cortex are highlighted in red. When the patient is listening, the left temporal lobe projection turns red and surrounding inactive brain tissue is colored a dim blue on the computer monitor. Although this procedure is too expensive to use in schools, the knowledge gained from PET scan research on mental processing and learning is certain to benefit researchers in their work with all students.

Academics

In some ways the classroom experience for students with mild intellectual disabilities has changed; in other ways it has remained the same. Twenty years ago, students were labeled educable mentally retarded and placed in self-contained special education classrooms or state-sponsored training schools. Although the label "educable mentally retarded" has been dropped, in some school systems, the placement of students in self-contained classrooms still persists, particularly within inner-city school districts (U.S. Department of Education, 2002).

In the past, students with a mild intellectual disability were often exposed to a watered-down curriculum. Special education teachers would present the regular school curriculum but at a slower pace, with emphasis on drill and repetition. Students subjected to this tedious instruction frequently failed to show any significant gains in academic skills. Failure brought on motivational problems and a high dropout rate. Researchers began to detect a characteristic phenomenon, which they referred to as "**learned helplessness**." Students lost faith in their ability to learn and gave up when a task seemed difficult. Today, new approaches to curriculum for students with mild intellectual disabilities have emerged with an emphasis on functional and thinking skills. (More information about these approaches is included in the section on teaching strategies.)

SPEEDBUMP—Learned helplessness is discussed a great deal in this text because it is so pervasive with students who struggle with school work.

An equally vital academic strategy is **early childhood education**. Two types of early childhood programs play a significant role in alleviating conditions that contribute to intellectual disability: programs that target children at risk because of poverty and programs for developmentally disabled and delayed children provided through IDEA. Early childhood programs that target poor children, such as **Head Start**, provide health, family training, and educational services to preschool children. Entrance criteria for Head Start is based on income guidelines; entrance criteria for special education early intervention programs is based on the identification of a disability.

Over the years, a strong research base has substantiated the positive effects of early childhood programs to stimulate cognitive development of high-risk disadvantaged youth and students with disabilities. For example, a longitudinal study of early childhood for poor children, the Carolina Abecedarian Project (Ramsey, 1998) reported numerous benefits when they compared project young adults (21 years) with individuals who had not participated in early childhood programs. Included among the positive findings were higher scores on tests of cognitive ability, enhanced language development, higher academic achievement in reading and math, and increased enrollment in postsecondary school education. Young people at risk of socioeconomic mild intellectual disability clearly benefit from early childhood preschool experiences as do children with clinical intellectual disability. Various studies have demonstrated an increase from 13 to 20 points in measured IQ of children enrolled in early childhood programs as compared to nonparticipating peers (Kotulak, 1996).

Communication

Robert Ornstein, the neuroscientist, once observed that students are not judged on how well they use their brains, but on how well they use their mouths. Rational thought involves more than verbal abilities. The **neocortex** of the human brain is divided into two halves, the left and right hemispheres. For most individuals, the left hemisphere is the language center. In the left frontal, parietal, and temporal lobes of the brain, mental activity is expressed through listening and speech. The right hemisphere is the creative, intuitive part of the brain. While the left hemisphere solves problems through analysis, the right hemisphere integrates information and searches for holistic solutions. Neither half is superior to the other; both work together to produce rational thought.

The majority of school activity, including reading, speaking, and writing, requires a preponderance of left-hemisphere language skills. Therefore, a preschool child who is not provided with such language activities as bedtime stories, listening to music, and guided conversations with adults is at a distinct disadvantage upon entering school. Because so many students with a mild intellectual disability are poor, minorities, and speak English as a second language, their opportunities to develop the language skills required for a successful school experience may be limited.

Secondary teachers expect students to follow oral directions, recall information from lectures, locate information in textbooks, and take notes. In elementary classrooms, students are expected to listen to the teacher, answer questions correctly, read silently, and write. The one-sided emphasis on verbal skills favors the middle-class child and handicaps the poor child. Disadvantaged learners may not begin school with the middle-class language background that is a prerequisite for successful classroom participation.

Language Deficient versus Language Different. Bernstein (1961) described poor children's language as a "restricted code," which was ill-suited for subtle shades of thought or meaning. Poor children, he said, were unprepared for rational thought when parents dealt with them in an authoritative, impulsive manner. Thus the disadvantaged child fails to learn such abstract concepts as causality and long-range planning. Bernstein's view of the deficient language development of children of poverty was used by some educators in this country to explain the inadequate school performance of poor African American children.

Bereiter and Englemann (1966) believed that a deprived environment retarded speech and that deficient speech led to deficient thought. School failure was the cumulative result. The "language deficient" perspective of African American children's speech focused attention on remedial efforts to teach them "white standard English." For instance, DISTAR, a sequentially structured preschool program, was used to teach language development to poor inner-city children. The TV show *Sesame Street*, which is designed especially with poor children in mind, adopted the deficient-language hypothesis by teaching new vocabulary, labeling objects, and presenting basic school readiness skills.

> **SPEEDBUMP—**How many parents believe that sitting their young child in front of a TV for hours at a time will make up for a lack of play and interaction?

Lobav, Cohen, and Lewis (1968) reported that poor and middle-class students are more alike than different in the way their language develops. Lobav carefully scrutinized how disadvantaged African American children learned to speak. He found that their language, which he described as black standard English, progressed through a logical sequence of syntax and structure. Lobav reported that the speech of his subjects followed a normal pattern of development. Their language was not deficient, only different from white middle-class language. The language different hypothesis advocated by Ginsburg (1972) highlighted the structural and functional conflicts between how poor children speak and the expectations placed on them by schools embedded in middle-class language. One example of structural conflict is the use of white standard English in reading texts. A student might encounter difficulty when the teacher expects the child to pronounce words as they appear in the text. Functional conflicts occur when, as Robinson noted, students persist in using speech in school that is accepted by peers because to do otherwise would be considered "unmanly."

The proposition that black standard English is a legitimate dialect was carried one step further in 1996 when the Oakland, California, school board unanimously declared Ebonics a language. The Ebonics controversy was fueled by attempts to solicit federal funds for Oakland schoolchildren based on the premise that they should receive assistance in the same way any non-English–speaking youngster would via bilingual classes. The Ebonics movement divided African American leaders. Some felt validation of black standard English would be the first step to improve scholastic achievement. Others, including the political activist Jesse Jackson, said that legitimizing Ebonics would limit the ability of

African American students to compete against people with fluent verbal skills. The debate faded after both federal and state officials opposed funding that would support Ebonics in California classrooms.

English Language Learners.   When English is a second language, it is difficult to determine whether a mild disability exists. Language assessment of **English language learners** is improving, particularly for Spanish-speaking youngsters. Still, it is difficult to identify a language deficit in a bilingual or non-English–speaking youngster. Assessment of language disorders analyzes a variety of skills, including auditory discrimination, articulation, verbal expression, and comprehension of complex relationships. According to Langdon (1983), "the purpose of testing a non-English- or limited-English-proficient student is to determine his or her proficiency in the native language and to compare it with the performance in the second language, when appropriate" (p. 39). The objective is to determine whether lack of proficiency in English is due to a general language disorder or is a reflection of normal difficulties in learning a new language.

As numbers of non-English–speaking students strain the resources of public schools, determining the source of academic problems will continue to challenge educators. For instance, in California, there are 90 distinct language groups and nearly 400,000 limited-English–proficient students in public schools (Cegelka, Lewis, & Rodriguez, 1987). When these students fail to progress satisfactorily, standard testing procedures used to identify a mild intellectual disability almost certainly will indicate a disability, unless special measures are used to take language differences into account. This is because most standardized tests of intelligence primarily assess language skills. Misdiagnosis can take two forms: false positive and false negative. In the former, students are incorrectly assessed as a mildly disabled, whereas in the latter situation, a mild disabilities are overlooked.

To accurately assess a language disorder among non-English–speaking students, both languages are assessed by a clinician who is fluent in each. Assessment instruments are translated into the student's native language, and, if a language disorder is found, remediation begins in the student's native language (Langdon, 1983). Figure 3.2 contains a list of tests that have been translated into Spanish.

The itinerant lifestyles of many of non-English–speaking students make it difficult to assess a mild intellectual disability and other disabling conditions. Baca and Harris (1988) estimated approximately 80,000 migrant children in need of special education. They concluded that only 8,000, or 10 percent, of these children receive special education services. Because of limited English proficiency, poverty, and inadequate health conditions, migrant children are especially vulnerable to a mild intellectual disability. In a study of migrant education, Barresi (1984), found that:

1. Only 10 percent of children with a mild disabilities were identified.
2. Identification occurs late in the school career.
3. Students were placed in the wrong special education programs.
4. Gaps in services existed because of different administrative procedures between school districts. (Baca & Harris, 1988)

The number of **culturally and linguistically diverse students** will continue to increase in the nation's schools. Urban schools, in particular, will be faced with increased numbers of

FIGURE 3.2   Tests Used by School Systems that Are Translated into Spanish

Bilingual Syntax Measure
Ber-Sil
Dos Amigos Verbal Language Scales
Del Rio
Leiter International Performance Scale
Language Assessment Scales
SOMPA
WISC-R
Boehm Test of Basic Concepts
Carrow Test of Auditory Comprehension of Language
Peabody Picture Vocabulary Test
Woodcock–Johnson Psychoeducational Battery
Bender–Gestalt
PEOPLE
Austin Spanish Articulation Test
Columbia Mental Maturity Test
Raven Progressive Matrices
Woodcock Language Proficiency Battery

underachieving students with cultural and language differences. Schools need to keep pace with the changing student population. If teaching techniques do not change to take into account such meaningful circumstances in children's lives as their language and culture, special education will become inundated with children identified as a mildly disabled. Many of these children will not have intellectual deficiencies. Rather, they will be the product of an educational system that was unable to adjust to the changing needs of its student population.

> **SPEEDBUMP—**The movement of youngsters from one community to another is one of the most serious problems faced by urban educators today.

Perception/Motor

Perception is a combination of attention, memory, and thinking. As an illustration, without looking, list the names of the authors of this textbook. Even though you look at the cover of this book on a regular basis (at least your professor hopes this is the case), you probably found naming each author a difficult task. Perception begins with selective attention. You can look at many features of your environment day after day (e.g., the color of the walls in your classrooms), but if you do not concentrate and willfully commit the sensory input to memory, your brain will not encode the information, and it will be forgotten.

Familiarity, interest, color, and movement are a few of the factors that influence perception. As infants mature, they learn to discriminate specific details from a background of competing stimuli. This figure-ground discrimination is an essential perceptual skill for successful school performance. Students with poor figure-ground discrimination skills may have trouble selecting individual letters from a line of words, become confused by oral directions, or become distracted by movement in a classroom.

Inadequate teaching often is overlooked as a contributor to presumed deficits in attention and memory. Students who are expected to maintain attention during dull and repetitious lessons are unlikely to remember what they read or heard only moments before. Ineffective teachers use general characteristics of students with mild intellectual disabilities as a rationale for individual learning problems. A vicious cycle of low expectations and unsuccessful learning evolves when teachers use a disability as an explanation for a student's learning difficulty. A teacher who remarks, "Well, Susan simply can't retain concepts because she's a intellectually disabled," is overlooking the significant role of effective teaching in helping students learn.

SPEEDBUMP—No one is so disabled that he or she cannot learn one more thing.

Teaching that includes active student involvement with learning tasks, guided practice sessions, and systematic error-correction procedures will produce successful results that can overcome deficits in organizing perceptual information (Algozzine & Maheady, 1986).

The ability to coordinate perception with movement is a fundamental skill required for learning. The fact that he named the first phase of intellectual development the sensory-motor stage is a clear indication of the importance Piaget attached to early perception-motor experiences. Lack of perception-motor stimulation at a young age may delay intellectual development. The delay can be so subtle that negative consequences may be overlooked until the school years, when a youngster is compared to peers in such tasks as reading, writing, and physical education.

Perception-motor problems can manifest themselves in a variety of ways, including poor coordination and inadequate fine-motor skills. Research on motor-skill performance of students with mild intellectual disabilities consistently reports difficulties with such activities as running, throwing, and jumping (Dobbins & Rarick, 1977; Holland, 1987). Poor performance in physical education classes can negatively affect student self-confidence and motivation to persevere. Conversely, physical education and recreational skills can promote student self-confidence by enhancing awareness of body coordination and performance. Such programs as Outward Bound and rope climbing increase perception and attention skills of students while providing them with challenging and successful experiences.

Social-Adaptive Skills

Categorical labels, such as intellectual disability, reinforce the tendency to classify students in terms of the single dimension ascribed by the label. The social needs of students with a mild intellectual disability may be overlooked because their "problem" is viewed in terms of subaverage intellectual functioning, yet there is nothing retarded about the emotions of these students. Students identified with a mild intellectual disability have normal feelings. They want to be liked, accepted, and valued as human beings. Their self-esteem is strongly influenced by their status and day-to-day activities in school (Dupont, 1978).

Many students spend a significant portion of their day out of the mainstream of normal school activities. A study of students with a mild intellectual disability in northern Illinois found that more than 90 percent of the students were in regular classrooms less than half the day (Polloway et al., 1983). The stigma of spending most of the day in a special education classroom, isolated from normal school activities, can have a corrosive effect on a youngster's self-esteem. Like all other students, youngsters with a mild intellectual disability want to be liked and accepted, yet studies of regular education students' perceptions report nonacceptance or rejection of students identified as a mildly retarded (Kuveke, 1983).

The majority of students with a mild disabilities are identified by an educational assessment after entering school. At the precise time in their young lives when they are most in need of success, these youngsters experience failure and the added indignity of being identified with such labels as learning disabled or a mildly retarded. The stress of dealing with school failure, peer rejection, and segregation as a learner with a mild intellectual disability can cause students to lose faith in themselves as competent individuals. Failure in school leaves a strong impression. When Reynolds and Miller (1985) compared students identified as a mildly disabled with nondisabled students, they found the special needs students showed significant signs of depression and learned helplessness. The findings suggest that students with a mild intellectual disability are vulnerable to feelings of inadequacy because of their failure in school and their prolonged exposure to peer disapproval (Epstein, Cullinan, & Polloway, 1986).

Wehmeyer, Kelchner, and Richards (1996) noted that lack of optimism undermines autonomous actions. Subsequently, such students are unable to manage their lives and are limited in pursuing quality-of-life experiences. They lack what researchers call "self-determination." Everyday experiences such as paying a bill, returning an item to customer service, or asking a friend to socialize can seem overwhelming.

These students exit or graduate high school handicapped in their ability to find work, live independently, and enjoy everyday experiences that many of us take for granted, such as riding a bus to the mall. In order to encourage self-determination, Wehmeyer and Schwartz (1997) recommend that teachers "provide activities that challenge the student and promote optimism by supporting student initiation of activities and allowing choice" (p. 254).

SPEEDBUMP—"Between the optimist and the pessimist the difference is droll: The optimist sees the doughnut, but the pessimist sees the hole." McLandburgh Wilson as cited in Augarde (1991) p. 229

Placement decisions often are based on educator perception of student social functioning. Hughes and associates (2002) postulated that the reason that less than 10 percent of students with intellectual disability are educated primarily in general education classrooms is the "narrow repertoire of social interaction behavior" (p. 533). Researchers' observations within informal school settings, such as lunchroom and hallways, indicate that without interventions, students with intellectual disability infrequently interact with their nondisabled peers. Differences in how students socialize verbally were observed in both groups of students. For example, general education students stayed focused on a topic longer than disabled students; also, students with intellectual disability engaged in more inappropriate motor activity during conversations. This research builds on many studies that have emphasized the need for specific social skill training coupled with planned interventions such as school "buddy" programs, peer tutoring, and incorporation of social skill curriculums within the academic program.

TEACHING APPROACHES

Students with mild intellectual disabilities often need assistance to connect academic learning to real-life experiences (i.e., functional skills) and adjust how they approach learning activities (i.e., school adaptive behavior). They need assistance learning the content and skills that many of their peers learn without special educational activities (Ysseldyke & Algozzine, 1995). Of course, many of their characteristics overlap with those of students with learning disabilities or emotional disturbance. Therefore, many of the approaches used to improve basic academic skills (e.g., reading, writing, and arithmetic), communication (e.g., language and speech), and behavior (e.g., attention to tasks, disruptiveness) of these other students also are useful when working with students with mild intellectual disabilities. Effective teachers of students with intellectual disability set high expectations and focus instruction on functional activities designed to promote success with real-life problems. A summary of general interventions used by teachers with students with intellectual disability is presented in Figure 3.3. Some general principles of effective teaching, general procedures for improving thinking skills, teaching reading, school adaptive behavior, leisure, and work skills are discussed in the following sections.

FIGURE 3.3   General Interventions for Teaching Students with Mild Intellectual Disabilities

1. Expect to see progress; a mild intellectual disability is not a permanent, unalterable condition.
2. Many students come to school without readiness skills; don't assume they know what you are talking about.
3. Identify a student's level of cognitive functioning (i.e., preoperational, concrete, operational), and match teaching approaches to learner's characteristics.
4. Always connect abstract ideas to life experiences.
5. Avoid dull, repetitive work. Provide novelty in lessons.
6. Provide maximum opportunities for learning in the least restrictive environment.
7. Remember that the label "mentally retarded" is demeaning and promotes stereotyping.
8. Keep in mind there is more to intelligence than the narrow range of skills assessed by IQ tests.
9. Insist on a measure of adaptive behavior before a student is evaluated as mentally retarded.
10. Provide students with functional, career-oriented learning experiences.

Instructions

Given the array of students with different language skills and backgrounds who populate classrooms, and the amount of listening that students are expected to do, teachers face a formidable challenge when instructing their students. Teachers, however, sometimes are unclear in their lessons. An analysis of teacher talk by Nelson (1988) found that false starts, repetitions, lack of clarity, and abstract language were common aspects of teacher talk. Students with a mild intellectual disability may have attention and memory deficits that further impair their ability to understand teachers' explanations.

Robinson (1989) recommended the use of **advance organizers** to help alert students to important material. She proposed the following guidelines for the use of advance organizers:

1. Alert students to the transition to a new activity.
2. Identify topics or activities students will do.
3. Provide an outline or other organizational framework.
4. Clarify teacher expectations for student participation.
5. Provide background information regarding how this lesson relates to previous activities.
6. State the concepts to be learned.
7. Give examples of concepts.
8. Highlight the relevance of topic.
9. Introduce new vocabulary.
10. Specify the desired general outcomes of the activity.

These 10 steps provide the student with a direct and simple framework for listening and understanding teacher expectations for successful classroom participation. They are highly effective with many students.

Student memory can be enhanced through the use of verbal rehearsal and self-questioning. Rehearsal requires the student to repeat directions silently several times. This strategy can help a student follow teacher directions. Self-questioning is a strategy useful for all students. After a passage is read or a lesson is taught, the student reviews key elements by asking:

What is the story (lecture) about?
Who is in the story (lecture)?
Where did the events take place?
When did they take place—in what order?
Why is this information important or useful? (Robinson, 1989, 150)

Teaching requires clarity. Many students, including those with language differences or deficits, need help in listening and remembering. The simple technique of asking students what they learned in class today can help a teacher determine what students do or do not understand.

Thinking Skills

Documented evidence continues to point to effective decision-making and problem-solving skills as an academic weakness in students with mild intellectual disabilities. Concerns about these critical cognitive abilities have provided an impetus for development of cognitive curriculums.

Guided teaching of thinking skills is a general procedure used in educating students with a mild intellectual disability. Goldstein (1974) advocated the direct teaching of problem-solving skills. A major hurdle for many individuals with a mild intellectual disability is adapting to the social demands of life after school. Goldstein's social learning curriculum utilized a "logical inductive strategy" to teach students a hierarchical procedure for problem solving. Within this system, students learned to label, detail, infer, predict, verify, and generalize.

Goldstein's approach is significantly different from the traditional teacher-directed lessons so often encountered in academic programs for students with a mild intellectual disability. In a teacher-directed lesson, the teacher

1. tells the student what is to be learned
2. tells the student what to do
3. calls on students to respond
4. evaluates student answers
5. corrects wrong answers

In a teacher-directed lesson, each step is controlled and monitored by the teacher. Goldstein believes that teacher-directed lessons undermine student confidence in their own thinking abilities. Students with a mild intellectual disability sometimes are characterized as field dependent in their thinking. This means they do not trust their own perceptions or judgments.

These students are easily influenced by peers and authority figures. By emphasizing individual problem-solving, critical-thinking programs such as Goldstein's logical-inductive strategy can help develop self-reliance and improve reasoning abilities. Reuven Feurenstein's instrumental enrichment program (1980) teaches thinking skills by providing learners with strategies for using such cognitive skills as analysis, categorization, and inference. Students develop tools and habits of thinking that allow them to process information, see connections, visualize spatial and temporal relationships, and increase their reasoning ability (Feurenstein, 1980). Through a process of mediated learning, teachers use paper-and-pencil exercises that focus on specific cognitive functions. Students receive feedback through self-correction, peer interaction, and teacher's assessment. Feurenstein's systematic method requires training in mediation practices and an introduction to cognitive and affective factors that affect student performance. Advocates of Feurenstein's methods claim that they effectively ameliorate cognitive problems experienced by students with varying disabilities including autism, intellectual disability, and attention deficit disorder.

Reading

The teaching of reading by phonics is an example of a left-hemispheric approach to language development used in schools. Phonics teaches the sounds of letters, how those sounds blend to make syllables, and the combination of syllables to make words. In the reverse procedure—decoding—students are expected to decipher new words by sounding out each letter to complete a whole word. This auditory, analytical, sequential approach to reading is fine if it takes advantage of preexisting language abilities, but what about the child who does not master the phonics approach? For students who lack good auditory and analytic abilities, phonics and eventually reading can be difficult to master.

Marie Carbo found that economically disadvantaged readers tend to be tactile-kinesthetic learners. Their approach to reading is best described as "global." These students have excellent visual and integrative skills that enable them to acquire sight vocabularies. They demonstrate an intuitive awareness of word patterns. Carbo (1987b) observed that "global learners learn to read most rapidly through such activities as writing stories, reading books of their own choosing, engaging in choral reading, writing and performing in plays, and listening to tape recordings of interesting and well written books" (p. 432). The global reading style described by Carbo is an example of right-hemisphere abilities and is an apt description of the approach to learning observed by teachers of disadvantaged, underachieving students (Dennison, 1969; Kohl, 1967).

Mandelbaum (1989) reviewed best practices in teaching reading and found that a combination of functional reading lists with interesting reading material best met the needs of students with a mild intellectual disabilities. Several principles of effective teaching summarized by Mandelbaum are:

1. **Demonstrate rather than tell.** The teacher and student discuss, read, and answer questions together about a story on the student's reading level.
2. **Provide for successful practice.** Make sure students use reading materials that will sustain at least an 80 percent success rate.
3. **Use direct instruction.** Teacher-led group instruction should demonstrate the skill to be learned, provide practice with feedback, and allow for independent student practice.
4. **Plan for high levels of task involvement.** Reading in unison, choral reading, and high-interest readings improve fluency and comprehension.
5. **Ignore errors that do not matter. All errors are not equal.** Every word does not have to be read correctly. Focus only on errors that change the meaning of a sentence. Provide sufficient time for a student to analyze a word and decode.
6. **Give independent assignments that relate to the lesson.** Most workbooks and dittos focus on isolated skills unrelated to stories. Avoid the drudgery of worksheets unless relevant and necessary.
7. **Integrate subject matter.** Use themes or webbings to cluster concepts.
8. **Measure behavior change.** Plot and graph reading improvement in terms of median of number of words read correctly each minute.
9. **Provide opportunities to learn achievement formats.** Formats vary widely, and students need practice with the procedures that will be used to evaluate their skills.

In a report of the National Reading Panel (1999), hundreds of research studies on reading were assessed using scientific evidence-based criteria. The results indicated that phonemic awareness, systematic phonics instruction, guided oral reading, and silent oral reading produced significant gains in reading comprehension among at-risk learners. Disadvantaged and special education students, in particular, benefitted from the recommended approaches. Although the panel was primarily concerned about instruction for students identified as learning disabled, it is evident that their findings are equally valuable for all students who have delayed reading abilities.

Functional Skills

Students with mild intellectual disabilities respond to the same instructional methods as other students. They may require more time to achieve satisfactory levels of performance and typically require special instruction and extra practice to generalize what they have learned to settings other than the classroom. Sometimes they simply need to be taught how to approach academic tasks. For these students, basic academic skill instruction must go beyond basal readers and traditional worksheets. Effective teachers of these students design instructional and practice activities so that they relate to functional use in everyday life, including home and community living. Ysseldyke and Algozzine (1995) provide a detailed set of tactics for improving these functional skills; some of them are summarized with others from Smith, Finn, and Dowdy (1993) in Table 3.6.

Recall that according to a widely accepted view of intelligence, children interact differently depending on their stage of development (see Figure 3.1). This means that using concrete objects and manipulatives helps many children learn concepts more easily. It also means that while some students pass through the concrete stages of learning more rapidly than others, the need for these stages is extended for students with intellectual disability and other developmental disabilities. Some ideas from Smith, Finn, and Dowdy (1993) for ways to extend instruction in important areas of mathematics are illustrated in Table 3.7.

TABLE 3.6   Summary of Functional Skill Interventions

FUNCTIONAL SKILL AREA	INTERVENTION DESCRIPTION
Reading	Have students use community signs, local store directories, local restaurant menus, newspapers, local street signs, Yellow Pages, and other everyday materials for reading practice.
Mathematics	Have students use newspaper advertisements, mail-order catalogs, menus, and other everyday materials for basic skill and problem-solving practice. Use real objects and manipulatives often when teaching math concepts.
Writing	Have students keep diaries of school events, local news stories, classroom visitors, and other everyday activities for writing practice.
Listening	Use real objects or pictures to teach sounds or names. Give students directions to follow in sentences that require movement around the room or manipulation of real objects. Read directions to students and have them make the object described in the directions.

TABLE 3.7   Instructional Activities for Extending Learning in Mathematics

GOAL: CLASSIFYING OBJECTS BASED ON CHARACTERISTICS OR UNIQUE FEATURES

■ Have students place blocks into groups based on size, color, texture, shape, name, or other attributes.
■ Have students place small toys into groups based on size, color, texture, function, or other attributes.
■ Have students sort coins, paper money, school supplies, books, or other common objects.

GOAL: LEARNING ONE-TO-ONE CORRESPONDENCE

■ Have students match sets of different objects using numbers to create sets (3 coins = 3 bottle caps).
■ Have students match sets of objects with numbers used to represent them (3 coins = 3).
■ Have students find as many target sets as possible in a large group of objects (all groups of 3 similar objects in a set of 100 or more).

GOAL: ORDERING OBJECTS ON THE BASIS OF SOME CHARACTERISTIC

■ Have students arrange a box of pencils from shortest to longest.
■ Have students arrange coins from smallest to largest in size.
■ Have students arrange sports team members from shortest to tallest.

GOAL: LEARNING THAT ORDER DOESN'T CHANGE RELATIONSHIPS BETWEEN OBJECTS

■ Have students combine sets of items to represent relationships.

4 dimes + 3 dimes = 7 dimes	4 clips + 3 clips = 7 clips
3 dimes + 4 dimes = 7 dimes	3 clips + 4 clips = 7 clips
7 dimes − 4 dimes = 3 dimes	7 clips − 4 clips = 3 clips
7 dimes − 3 dimes = 4 dimes	7 clips − 3 clips = 4 clips

Adaptive Behavior

Adaptive behavior refers to the ability to be independent and socially responsible (Reschly, 1989). This means that students with intellectual disability require a curriculum that teaches social skills, self-direction, and health and safety information. Effective teachers of these students design instructional and practice activities that they need to succeed in school and other adaptive life experiences. Most incorporate the following teaching procedures (Meese, 1994):

1. They carefully select skills that maximize the likelihood of a student's success.
2. They provide clear statements of the skills to be learned and reasons for learning them.
3. They demonstrate the new skills using a variety of methods (e.g., videotapes, films, live demonstrations), models (e.g., high-status peers, siblings), and situations.
4. They provide plenty of examples and nonexamples of expected behaviors.

5. They provide opportunities for practice under their supervision so students can receive supportive and corrective feedback and avoid practicing errors.
6. They provide recognition and rewards for successful demonstration of newly learned skills.

Some specific activities for improving adaptive behavior skills are summarized in Table 3.8.

Daily Living and Work Skills

Self-care, including activities of daily living and being successful at a job, are important adaptive behavior skills that are the focus of instruction for students with a mild intellectual disability. Self-care skills include managing personal finances; caring for personal needs; buying clothing, food, and other personal items; and getting around in the community. Job-related skills include following directions, being punctual, beginning assignments promptly, staying on task, and completing assignments; these sometimes are addressed with functional academic interventions.

Here are some ways to improve self-care skills:

1. Teach students to differentiate coins and other money.
2. Teach students to make and receive change.
3. Have students practice physical fitness activities.
4. Have students practice personal grooming skills.
5. Teach consumer economics.
6. Teach traffic and safety rules.
7. Teach students to use public transportation.

TABLE 3.8   Summary of Adaptive Behavior Interventions

ADAPTIVE BEHAVIOR AREA	INTERVENTION DESCRIPTION
Social Skills	Have students take part in role-playing activities related to using appropriate social skills. Have them practice greeting friends, exchanging information, engaging in small talk, and other social and communication skills. Reward them for doing so.
Self-Direction	Teach students how to ask for help in school and community settings. Provide practice using these skills in small groups and real-life situations.
	Have students keep track of occasions in which they made a decision on their own, and discuss the outcomes of what they did. Share alternatives between and among classmates.
Health and Safety	Have students role-play emergency situations and generate, discuss, and practice alternative solutions.

Here are some ways to improve work skills:

1. Teach students that attendance and punctuality are important.
2. Reward students for being on time and for high attendance.
3. Have students record their own attendance.
4. Reward students for completing tasks on time.
5. Have students keep records of completed assignments.
6. Have students complete job applications.
7. Provide rewards after completion of smaller tasks.
8. Set liberal standards for task completion.

Students with mild intellectual disabilities experience difficulties in many areas of school and life functioning. There is no magic in instructional activities that work with these students. In many ways, what effective teachers do with them is just like what they do with everybody else—and, whenever necessary, they modify what they do to accommodate the special learning needs of their students. Given quality instruction, students with a mild intellectual disability can learn to overcome many of their problems and can be successful and productive in school and life. Priorities are high expectations and functional learning experiences.

SUMMARY

A mild intellectual disability is both a social and an educational problem. The majority of children identified as a mild intellectually disabled are poor, with African Americans over-represented. Although many students with mild intellectual disabilities have no identifiable organic or neurological problems, the health-threatening conditions of poverty clearly put these children at greatest risk. The deleterious effects of such factors as low birthweight, deficient diet, and improper prenatal care can be offset by health and educational intervention for children and their families. There are two categories of mild intellectual disability: environmental and organic.

Characteristics of children identified with a mild intellectual disability can vary from one state to another. Although the American Association of Intellectual Disability published guidelines for identifying a mild intellectual disability, individual states establish their own criteria. Consequently, the prevalence of students identified as a mildly retarded varies from state to state. This means that some students who need special education services may go without, and other students without disabilities receive services.

Students with mild intellectual disabilities are characterized by slower cognitive development; academic deficiencies, especially in reading; and deficits in adaptive behavior. Because success in school depends so much on verbal skills, some students—children in poverty and children from non-English–speaking families in particular—encounter difficulties. An individual student may demonstrate specific learning problems in mental processing, social adaption, and perception. However, students with a mild intellectual disability show a great deal of variability in learning characteristics, and generalizations about their abilities or disabilities can lead to stereotypes and negative teacher expectations.

Students with a mild intellectual disability score in a range of 50 to 75 on IQ tests, and they have deficits in social skills outside the school setting. Quality of educational programming depends on the teacher's ability to motivate students who have a history of school failure. Academic programs that emphasize functional skills provide adolescents with a reason to stay in school. Younger children learn best when teachers match instruction to their cognitive abilities. Programs that attempt to remediate specific deficiencies, such as poor memory, through drill and repetition fail to consider the point of view of the learner. Students with a mild intellectual disability need practice in developing their own thinking abilities. School programs that help students with a mild intellectual disability gain confidence in themselves as learners are most successful in helping them to adapt to life after school.

The cycle of destitution that has characterized mild intellectual disabilities throughout the past century will be broken when disadvantaged learners graduate from school with employable skills. Education is the best offensive strategy in the war on poverty. When regular and special educators work together to keep learners in the mainstream of school life, teacher and student expectations for success are enhanced. As Lloyd Dunn (1968) eloquently pointed out, the interests of poor children are not served by labeling them retarded and relegating them to isolated special education classrooms. Ultimately it is the quality of educational programming, not the label pinned on the student that determines success or failure.

ACTIVITIES

1. Imagine you are colleagues of Alfred Binet. In small groups of three to four, list 10 specific mental skills that you believe make up intelligent thinking. Then for each skill listed, describe how you would go about measuring a person's ability. For example, suppose you list short-term memory. A method for measuring might be asking an individual to repeat a sequence of numbers. Compare each groups' skill list. Discuss the pros and cons of different measurement techniques.

2. Many young people who are identified as having a mild intellectual disability are poor. What are some ways that poverty causes mild intellectual disabilities? Brainstorm ways that we as a society could improve the lives of poor children to decrease mild intellectual disabilities among this population. Do a Web search and identify an organization or an individual that has taken a leadership role in combatting poverty. What do you think teachers who teach in impoverished areas can do to improve the lives of their students?

3. Think about a time you encountered an individual with an intellectual disability. How old were you? Where did this happen? How did you recognize the presence of an intellectual disability? How did you feel about this individual? As a group, discuss how attitudes of the nondisabled toward individuals with intellectual disabilities are shaped and how these attitudes influence the lives of disabled individuals.

4. Are there local or state branches of professional organizations that represent individuals with intellectual disabilities in your area? If so, ask a member to visit your class and talk about the purpose of the organization, membership composition, and services offered to members.

5. Suppose you are a teacher (pick your own grade level) and you are told that a new student with a mild intellectual disability has been assigned to your class. What difficulties can you

anticipate this student might have academically and socially? How could you prepare yourself to help this student deal with the curriculum and his or her new classmates? Select one curriculum area at your grade level (for example, fractions in 5th-grade math). Describe a teaching method that you think might help this student and explain why you selected this approach.

6. Read Highlight 3.1 again. Which of the teaching approaches described in this chapter do you think would be most appropriate for the students? As an educator, where would you begin to make positive changes?

7. Watch the video *Charlie* starring Cliff Robinson. Discuss the effect of a mild intellectual disability on Charlie's life. Do you think it was ethical to try to enhance Charlie's intelligence? What was the most difficult part of Charlie's old life? What was the most difficult part of Charlie's new life? How did you feel about the conclusion?

CHAPTER FOUR

STUDENTS WITH
EMOTIONAL DISTURBANCE

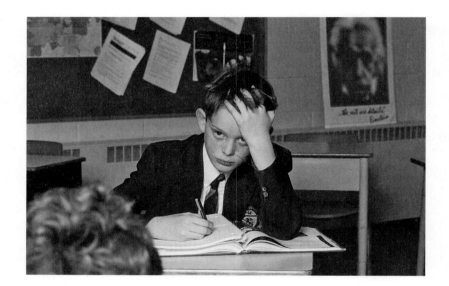

ADVANCE QUESTIONS

Answer the following questions as you read this chapter:

1. What types of students are included in the category of emotional disturbance?
2. What are some of the main components of definitions of emotional disturbance?
3. How many students are included in the emotional disturbance category?
4. What causes emotional disturbance?
5. What are some characteristics of students with emotional disturbance?
6. What strategies are used by teachers of students with emotional disturbance?
7. What can teachers do to improve the problems of students with emotional disturbance?
8. What aspects of cultural diversity are important to consider when meeting the needs of students with emotional disturbance?

VIGNETTE: PROBLEM BEHAVIORS

Fred Peterson has been a teacher for over 20 years: each of his classes has had at least one problem student. This year it was Selena. Selena could always find a way to avoid schoolwork. For example, one day Fred told the class to begin work on the math sheet he had provided each of them. "Excuse me, Mr. Peterson," said Selena. "Can I go to the bathroom?" Fred had a policy of letting students move freely throughout the school, so he let her go. About 15 minutes later, she returned and asked if she could wash the blackboards. Fred mentioned it was probably a better idea to start on her worksheet. At this suggestion, Selena grew angry. She walked up to Fred, balled the worksheet in her fist, and threw it at Fred. "Do your own damned worksheet," she shouted, and she ran out the classroom door.

Alan is a senior in high school with decent grades. He is on the basketball team, and he has a lot of friends. Lately he and a few buddies have started smoking marijuana on the way to school in the morning. Alan maintains that after 12 years of boring classes, it's fun to go to "high" school. Ms. Hildago, his homeroom teacher, can tell when Alan has been smoking because his eyes are red and glassy. She has tried talking to Alan privately but to no avail. Alan either denies he smokes or walks away. Alan's behavior in his classes is erratic. He jokes around, makes snide comments, or just spaces out. Ms. Hildago is hesitant to discuss Alan's situation with the principal because she's afraid Alan will be expelled.

Alice has been teaching kindergarten for 10 years, but she has never had a class like this one. Several youngsters have attention problems caused by alcohol use by mothers during pregnancy. Raymond, although talkative and outgoing, is unable to handle scissors or even extra fat crayons. Louis gets a sticker just for sitting still for 10 minutes. He is constantly careening around the room, bumping into other children, and starting fights. Fay tries hard to do well, but she can't follow directions. She is frequently confused about what she's supposed to be doing. Alice is unable to give Fay all the individual attention she requires.

Now that you have read the vignette about some teachers of students with problem behaviors, see how may problem-solving questions you can answer. For those you cannot readily answer, try to find some additional information to use in answering them as you read the chapter. The experiences of Fred Peterson, Ms. Hildago, and Alice are typical of teachers of students with **emotional disturbance.**

1. What should be done to help students like Selena, Alan, Raymond, Louis, or Fay?
2. Who should teach them?
3. Do all schools provide special education services for students with emotional disturbance?
4. What expectations would you have for students like Selena, Alan, Raymond, Louis, or Fay if you were teaching them?
5. Should students with emotional disturbance be included in classes with students without disabilities?

Experiences like these illustrate the kinds of "problems" that cause students to be identified with emotional disturbance. Disturbing behaviors, noncompliance, or an inability to adjust to classroom routines are common reasons for students to be referred for special education. Each year, Phi Delta Kappa, a national education organization, commissions a Gallup Poll of the public's attitudes toward education. In all of the surveys, discipline (i.e., controlling disruptive behavior) is a major concern.

At one time or another, every teacher has a student who has conflicts with rules for proper behavior in school. The decision to evaluate a student for special education services on the basis of classroom behavior is a matter of frequency and intensity of the disturbing actions. The more "acting out" the behavior, the more likely a student will be referred for special education. The following behaviors are those most likely to attract unfavorable attention in the classroom:

1. Exhibits physical and verbal aggression toward classmates (fighting, instigating arguments)
2. Exhibits verbal aggression toward teacher and the other authority figures (profanity, negative names)
3. Refuses to cooperate in classroom group activities
4. Intentionally damages classroom materials
5. Uses classroom materials to create disruptive sounds and noises

A student who is shy or withdrawn may have serious problems but if she continues to follow classroom directions and completes her schoolwork, they may be overlooked. Depression and suicide are too common among today's schoolchildren to be ignored. Latchkey children (children who return home from school to empty houses), students with learning problems, and students experiencing chronic family problems are particularly vulnerable. Guetzloe (1988) summarized the causes of suicide among children:

> Any problem that contributes to feelings of depression, worthlessness, helplessness, or hopelessness has the potential to trigger suicidal behavior in a vulnerable individual. Among the many factors that have been cited as contributing to youth suicide are isolation, alienation, loss, physical or psychological abuse, disturbance in peer relationships, substance abuse, rejection, incarceration, disorganization, availability of weapons, fear of punishment, fear of failure, knowledge of suicide, and humiliation. (p. 26)

U.S. Surgeon General David Satcher stated that one in 10 children suffers from mental illness (Satcher, 2000). Among special educators there is concern that not enough is being done to help **students with emotional problems**. This concern is equally shared by general classroom teachers who spend a large portion of their day trying to manage youngsters' behavior. Table 4.1 lists at-risk factors associated with emotional problems.

SPEEDBUMP—Does it surprise you that so many young people experience emotional problems? There is good news too. Thanks to caring adults, many at-risk youth are capable of overcoming difficult experiences and go on to live productive lives. See www.resiliency.psu.edu for more information.

TABLE 4.1   In School At-Risk Indicators of Emotional Problems

INTERNALIZED EMOTIONAL PROBLEMS (DEPRESSION, SUICIDAL)	EXTERNALIZED EMOTIONAL PROBLEMS (AGGRESSIVE, CONFRONTATIONAL, SOCIALLY MALADJUSTED)
Anxiety	Chronic discipline
Lacks friends	Lack of empathy or compassion
Incomplete work	Gang attachments
Mood swings	Angry outbursts
"Learned helplessness"	Poor academic performance
Interest in cults	Conflicts with authority figures
Inordinate attraction to fantasy	Bullying
Indolent	Frequent absences
Bully victim	Physical aggression
Frequent absences	Damaging property
Inappropriate affect (e.g., crying)	Obscene language
Obsessive/compulsive behaviors	Ignore teacher warnings
Shyness	

OUTSIDE OF SCHOOL AT-RISK INDICATORS OF EMOTIONAL PROBLEMS

Premature birth
Maternal depression
Poverty
Neglect, physical, sexual, or emotional abuse
Foster home placement
Chronic discipline problem
Frequent temper tantrums
Loss of appetite/overeating
Long periods of isolation watching TV or on computer
Sleep disturbances/nightmares

Source: Compiled from Gresham, MacMillan, & Bocian, 1996, 277–292.

FOUNDATIONS OF EMOTIONAL DISTURBANCE

Hyman and D'Alessandro (1984) highlighted the complex interaction of environmental and individual factors that contribute to behavior disorders and classifications of emotional disturbance. They found that causes often rest outside the student's ability to control. Their assessment still has value today.

Included among **environmental causes** are inadequate parenting, overcrowding, racism, lack of employment, overexposure to violence through television and other mass media, peer pressures, and specific social, political, and bureaucratic factors that ignore the needs of the young. Schools contribute to behavior problems through **ineffective teaching**, poor school organization, inadequate administrative leadership, inappropriate curricula, overuse of suspensions, and other punishments. Within the individual student, Hyman and D'Alessandro cited inborn traits, such as **neurological impairments**, that may disrupt interactions with others, ultimately causing behavior disorders. Poor self-esteem and frustration with learning are also student responses that accelerate behavior disorders. When attempting to understand students' problems, we also must take into account the troubled systems (family, school, community) that interact with and shape children's development (Apter, 1982; Erickson, 1998; Kauffman, 1997; 1999). Placing students in a special education program will produce mixed results if, at the end of the school day, youngsters return home to an abusive father, a tormented mother, or a neighborhood permeated with drugs and violence.

There is a fine line between normal and abnormal, right and wrong, mental illness and mental health. Often the force that pushes an individual into one or the other of these categories does not originate in their own behavior. Others with whom they interact are instrumental in shaping, defining, managing, and manipulating feelings and behavior. This is the crux of the human dilemma. We need to interact with others to grow and learn, yet the nature of those interactions, which are often shaped by forces outside our control, help determine the kind of person we will become.

Behavior disorder, emotionally disturbed, antisocial, opposition defiant disorder, and **conduct disorder** are some terms professionals use to explain special needs of students who cannot cope with the social demands of school or society. The current federal category for providing services to these children is emotional disturbance. Over the years, special education has accumulated a large body of research on the causes and treatment of students with emotional disturbance. Before we discuss these different conceptual models, we examine the historical roots of this disability and its treatment.

Historical Perspective

Human history is replete with strange stories of how people have dealt with emotional disturbance. There was a time when the treatment of insanity was worse than the condition. Early medicants believed that by boring holes in the head (a method called *trephining*), the devil or other evil spirits would be released and leave the body. Hippocrates first classified mental problems using mania, hebephrenia, and melancholia as terms to describe separate conditions. He also is credited with offering the first theory for the cause of mental problems, blaming an imbalance of body fluids for strange behavior (Rhodes & Tracy, 1972a, b).

Through the ages, theories of causation of emotional disturbance ranged from witchcraft to science. One of the first environmental causes was identified in the Middle Ages, when it was discovered that hatters were driven "mad" from the mercury they used to condition felt. When mercury use was discontinued, so was the observance of "mad hatters." As Restak (1984) noted, "Over the centuries, schizophrenics have been burned at the stake, chained in dark dungeons, starved to death, and drowned" (p. 273). Discoveries that vitamin B6 deficiencies and syphilis caused emotional disturbance helped move treatment out of the shadows and into the medical laboratory. About 1890, Kraeplin identified an advanced form of emotional disturbance that he called "dementia praecox." This term was used to refer to adult mental illness, and the classification system surrounding it became the forerunner of the scientific classification system that is in place today (Algozzine, Serna, & Patton, 2001). After Kraeplin introduced dementia, a psychologist, DeSantis, recommended that a new term be designated for the childhood version of this condition. He suggested "dementia praecocissima," and the study of childhood emotional disturbance was given a life of its own.

SPEEDBUMP—Remember the "Mad Hatter" from *Alice's Adventures in Wonderland*? Well now you know where Lewis Carroll got the idea for the tea party character.

Shortly thereafter, another psychologist, Heller, observed a severely debilitating, degenerative condition in infants characterized by a loss of motor and language abilities. This condition was labeled as Heller's syndrome. In 1943, Leo Kanner observed odd, stereotyped behaviors in young children. The children, although uncommunicative and aloof, appeared to have average or above average intelligence. This condition became known as early infantile **autism**. A once-rare condition, autism is now a shorthand term for a variety of milder related conditions called "autism spectrum disorders" (see Chapter 2). By 1952, the American Psychiatric Association produced a document listing the major types of mental disorders. Childhood disorders did not appear in the first *Diagnostic and Statistical Manual* (*DSM-I*), but the second edition (*DSM-II*) contained a category titled Behavior Disorders of Childhood and Adolescents. Most students with emotional disturbance do not exhibit the kinds of severe debilitating conditions that were first identified by early psychologists and physicians. Such disabilities as childhood schizophrenia and autism exist; however, they are severe disabilities and are not included in our discussion of mild disabilities.

DEFINITION AND IDENTIFICATION

Professionals use a variety of terms to describe students with emotional disturbance. Classroom teachers use terms based on observations combined with judgments about classroom behavior. Frequently used are such terms as *immature*, *hyperactive*, *needs attention*, *inappropriate*, or *withdrawn*. Psychologists are more clinical in their approach. Using the *Diagnostic and Statistical Manual of Mental Disorders*, Fourth Edition *(DSM-IV-TR)* (American Psychiatric Association, 2002) as a reference, psychologists match student behavior to specific criteria for such conditions as adjustment disorders (e.g., difficulties dealing with a stressful event), impulse control disorders (e.g., unable to control feelings of rage), and mood disorders (e.g., severe swings in mood or behavior). Figure 4.1 lists some of the specific disorders that may be used to justify a special education placement. Keep in mind that not only does a disorder have to be identified but that there must be evidence that the disorder is interfering with academic progress. For example, a student who is being treated with medication for depression might be able to maintain satisfactory grades and thus not qualify for special education services.

The term **emotional disturbance** means a condition exhibiting one or more of the following characteristics over a long period of time and to a marked degree that adversely affects a child's educational performance. The Individuals with Disabilities Education Act provides this set of guidelines for determining if a student is eligible for special education services for emotional disturbance.

- An inability to learn that cannot be explained by intellectual, sensory, or health factors

FIGURE 4.1   Synopsis of Selected Behavioral and Emotional Disorders in Children

Opposition Defiant Disorder—A pattern of negativistic, hostile, and defiant behavior lasting at least 6 months. Included among eight listed behaviors are often losing temper, often angry and resentful, deliberately annoys people. (Four or more of the eight behaviors must be present.)

Conduct Disorder—A repetitive and persistent pattern of behavior in which the basic rights of others or major age-appropriate social norms or rules are violated. Specific behavioral criteria is listed under the following: aggression to people and animals, destruction of property, deceitfulness or theft, serious violation of rules.

Attention Deficit Hyperactivity Disorder (ADHD)—There are three types of ADHD: inattention, hyperactivity-impulsivity, and combined. Each type has a list of symptoms that persist for 6 months or more. Inattention is characterized by six or more of nine traits including difficulties with sustained attention, listening, following directions, memory, and finishing tasks. Hyperactivity-impulsivity is characterized by six or more of nine traits including fidgeting, excessive talking, constant moving, impatience, and interrupting others.

Asperger's Syndrome—A developmental disorder characterized by unusual preoccupation with a topic that excludes other interests. Behavioral traits include repetitive routines, oddities in speech, inappropriate social behavior, and uncoordinated motor movements.

Bipolar Disorder—Bipolar disorder is characterized by mood swings from elation to sadness. Changes in energy and behavior mirror mood swings. Some signs of the manic stage include extreme irritability, increased energy, euphoric mood, spending sprees, and increased sexual drive. During the depressed phase, individuals express feelings of guilt, worthlessness, and helplessness. Normal sleep routines are impaired and appetite is adversely affected. Mood swings are interspersed with normal moods. Diagnosis is based on how often (three or more times a day) mood swings occur each day and within a week. Children and adolescents experience very fast mood swings.

Early-Onset Depression—Almost one-third of 6- to 12-year-olds with depression develop bipolar disorder within a few years. Some of the signs of early-onset depression are chronic sadness, withdrawal from friends, poor school performance, frequent physical complaints, lack of energy, changes in eating and sleeping habits, and increased agitation.

Sources: Compiled from National Alliance of Mental Health, 2004; National Institute of Mental Health, 2004; National Institute of Neurological Disorders and Stroke, 2004.

- An inability to build or maintain satisfactory interpersonal relationships with peers and teachers
- Inappropriate types of behavior or feelings under normal circumstances
- A general pervasive mood of unhappiness or depression
- A tendency to develop physical symptoms or fears associated with personal or school problems

The term includes schizophrenia but does not apply to children who are socially maladjusted, unless it is determined that they have an emotional disturbance. States are not mandated to use the federal criteria to identify students, however many do so. Many special educators are critical of the federal definition, but to date no suitable replacement has been crafted.

Issues and Concerns

Unfortunately, the criteria fall short of being a conceptually clear representation from which to develop meaningful identification procedures and treatment practices. For example, how do educators identify "an inability to learn which cannot be explained by health factors," or what constitutes a "general pervasive mood of unhappiness"? And what about students who perform in school but still have emotional problems? Morse (1985) put it this way:

> Note that a definition including educational performance leaves out those who have no school problems or problems that do not affect achievement, and this can be a significant number. The idea that all disturbed children must have an educational problem in behavior or achievement is a significant error. The other error lies in implying that when children have problems in school, these problems are primarily school related. The fact is that problems are often generated outside the school environment and brought to school. (p. 43)

Perhaps most contentious to some special educators is the omission of "socially maladjusted students" from the ranks of students who qualify for special education services. In addressing this problem, the Executive Committee of the Council for Children (1987) with Behavioral Disorders had this to say:

> This exclusion of the **socially maladjusted** from special education seems to be based on several assumptions. These include: (a) There is a significant population of youngsters whose antisocial behavior is more related to a general social phenomenon than a specific handicapping condition; (b) it is possible to consistently differentiate such students from those who are truly handicapped by virtue of their behavior; and (c) it is important that special education not automatically incorporate a group specified as "in trouble" by other systems, such as the juvenile justice system.

The position of the council is that an adjudication of delinquency does not mean a disability is present. Some students with delinquent behavior do have mild disabilities, and they have an equal right to federal services mandated by Congress for all school-aged youngsters (U.S. Department of Education, 1997; 1998; 2003). Indeed, comprehensive surveys of incarcerated youngsters indicate that mild disabilities are more prevalent among youthful offenders (Nelson, Rutherford, & Wolford, 1987; Rutter, Giller, & Hagell, 1998).

SPEEDBUMP—Do you think that gang members who break the law should be placed in special education because they are socially maladjusted?

The lack of clear direction in determining who receives special education services for social or emotional behavior problems is highlighted by a survey that found states use a total of 17 different terms to describe this population (Knitzer, Steinberg, & Fleisch, 1990). Most state definitions used to refer students with social or emotional difficulties tend to have several general similarities. They suggest that the disturbances or disorders that exist within the student's behavior patterns cause academic and social problems that in turn affect the youngster and peers. Although these state definitions help professionals to know who should be identified as requiring special education, the actual process of identification is not facilitated by any one definition in particular. Most definitions do not have clearly stated operational criteria that can be dovetailed into a special educational assessment.

Levels of Emotional Disturbance

A systematic application of operational criteria results in the identification of two types of children with emotional disturbance. Type I is characterized by the types of behavior problems found typically in public schools. This student may be a problem in school but not at home. The behavior may be a response to an inappropriate or unmotivating school environment, and it may be responsive to positive environmental strategies. Type II may be characterized by the more comprehensive form of disturbance typically not found in general classrooms. This student's behavior will be problematic at home and school, and it may exhibit itself with regularity in both favorable and unfavorable environments. The behavior will not be immediately responsive to environmental management strategies. The behavior may be traced to organic inadequacies, as in the case of youth with childhood schizophrenia. A possible diagnostic comparison between Type I and Type II students with emotional disturbance based on the suggested operational criteria is presented in Table 4.2.

Hallahan and Kauffman (1977) suggested that the categories referred to as learning disabilities, emotional disturbance, and mild intellectual disabilities were similar. The characteristic behaviors of each disability also are similar (Neisworth & Greer, 1975). Whereas the Type I child may be similar in many respects to students with learning disabilities and mild mental retardation, it would seem that the Type II child would be unique.

PREVALENCE OF EMOTIONAL/BEHAVIORAL DISORDERS

Of the 6,046,031 students with disabilities (ages 6 through 21) receiving special education services in 2003–2004, 484,479 were included in the category of emotional disturbance,

TABLE 4.2   Comparison of Type I Behavioral and Type II Emotional Disturbance

TYPE I (BEHAVIOR DISORDERS)	TYPE II (CLINICAL EMOTIONAL DISTURBANCE)
General class has not been beneficial, but placement there is a preferred goal.	General school placements have not been successful; outside placements common.
School counseling services often prove beneficial.	External counseling services are typical.
Common behavioral problems evident in assessment records.	Clinical diagnoses and problems recorded.
Problems often reported in only one classroom or only at school.	Problems evident at home, school, and in other environments.
Evidence that interventions are effective with selected problem behaviors.	Evidence that problems are very resistant to common interventions.

reflecting about a 2 percent increase per year over the preceding 10-year period (U.S. Department of Education, 2007b). This represents about 8 percent of the special education students and about 1 percent of the general school-aged population. The overall prevalence of this group of students has been relatively constant over the last 10 years (Ysseldyke, Algozzine, & Thurlow, 2000). There is considerable variation from state to state in the percentage of the school-aged population identified with emotional disturbance (EdD). Prevalence figures can range from about 2 percent in some states to less than 0.5 percent in others. Forness (2001) reported that the majority of students with emotional problems sit undetected in general education classrooms.

The prevalence of students with emotional disturbance tends to fluctuate considerably across states and local school districts depending on several factors. The nature of the definition and criteria used to identify students has a major impact on the rate of identification and numbers of identified students; for example, when the Bower definition was originally used, the rate of occurrence of behavior disorders was estimated to be 10 percent (Reinert, 1976).

Rubin and Balow (1971) found that 41 percent of the students they studied were identified chiefly by their inability to meet the demands of school behavior expectations. Their findings are analogous to Jane Mercer's description of the "6-hour mildly retarded student." (See Chapter 3.) The results of the Rubin and Balow study indicated that some students may be regarded as disturbed or behavior disordered by their teachers in school. Outside of school, their behavior is adaptive to the demands of their environment.

> **SPEEDBUMP**—Does this description remind you of a classmate? Just as some students don't fit into school academically others don't fit in socially. Does that mean there is something "wrong" with them?

The 6-hour student with emotional disturbance, identified by Rubin and Balow, is an illustration of the widening cultural gap between poor children and the demands of school. As an illustration, consider a 10-year-old who lives in a ghetto neighborhood. What are the environmental conditions that this youth must deal with on a daily basis? The widespread reports of violence, drug use, and gang membership in poverty-stricken neighborhoods suggest that survival dictates an aggressive attitude. A 10-year-old who cannot take care of himself could quickly become prey to any passerby who fancied his sneakers, jacket, or money. In order to survive, our 10-year-old must learn to stand up for himself; he must project an image of toughness and nonchalance in the face of danger.

Now let's project this same streetwise youth into a 5th-grade classroom. His teacher has just demanded to know why he did not complete his homework. The youth is trapped between the demands of the adult authority and the expectations of his classmates, who eagerly await his response. Our 10-year-old is no fool, he knows that his mettle is inadvertently being challenged by the teacher, so he replies, "Do your own homework." The teacher's authority has been challenged, and the teacher responds by sending the young rebel to the principal, who suspends him for the rest of the day. A cycle of hostility now is perpetuated that could lead to a special education referral because of inappropriate behavior.

Kelly, Bullock, and Dykes (1974) reported teacher-perceived prevalence rates of 12.6 for mild behavior problems, 5.6 for moderate problems, and 2.2 for students with severe emotional disturbance. This general ratio has been reported elsewhere (Glidewell & Swallow, 1968). Paul and Epanchan (1991) cite additional research that indicates a prevalence rate of 11 percent of the total school population. This amounts to an estimate of six to eight million students with emotional disabilities.

Males consistently outnumber females. One interpretation of these data is that females are better adjusted than boys. It is far more likely, however, that cultural experience plays a significant role. Males tend to develop aggressive ways of expressing their problems, whereas females learn to express problems such as anger and hostility in a more covert fashion. Promiscuity, drug abuse, and depression are not the type of behaviors that teachers see, but that does not mean that they do not exist.

Several factors indicate that the number of students receiving special education for emotional disturbance will continue to increase as it has in recent years.

Item: One out of every five children grows up in poverty. Poverty contributes to broken homes, proliferation of drugs, violence, and homelessness. Millions of American children will be required to adapt to desperate environmental demands. The same behaviors that are adaptive on the streets will be disruptive in school.

SPEEDBUMP—The United States has the highest poverty rate in the industrialized world.

Item: The United States is becoming a multilingual nation. While schools attempt to deal with the steady increase in non-English–speaking students, the cultural gap between home and community continues to widen. Students are alienated from the affairs of schooling, and this alienation is acted out in classrooms.

Item: Inner-city schools continue to present the greatest challenge to educational reform. The social and emotional turmoils that infect these schools require the best teachers available. However, few young people who enter the teaching profession want to risk their psychological or physical safety teaching in ghetto schools. Without a massive infusion of educational and social support, inner-city schools become hotbeds of chaos.

Item: Violence and neglect permeate the lives of many American children (see Figure 4.2).

The personal fallout from children's violent lives presents an overwhelming challenge to U.S. policy makers. However, there is no national agenda with the specific aim of creating safe havens for children. According to the *National Needs Analysis in Behavior Disorders,* "The most glaring concern that exists in the area of behavior disorders is the staggering number of children with behavior problems who remain unserved" (Apter, 1982, 7). This concern continues today.

To summarize, almost 500,000 students are identified as requiring special education due to emotional disturbance. Many of these students are diagnosed with conduct disorder.

FIGURE 4.2   Mental Health At-Risk Factors

- Mental health problems affect one in every five young people.
- One in every 10 young people age 9 or older, or about 4 million, has a serious emotional disturbance that severely disrupts daily life.
- Among children, boys and girls are at equal risk for developing depression.
- Children who develop depression often have a family history of the illness, many times a parent who had depression at an early age.
- Once a young person experiences a major depression, he or she has a greater risk of developing another depression or mental health problem within the next 5 years.
- Untreated mental health problems can lead to suicide, which is the sixth leading cause of death for 5- to 14-year olds.
- An estimated two-thirds of all young people with mental health problems are not getting the help they need.
- Mental health problems can—and should—be treated.

For more information, contact:
SAMHSA's National Mental Health Information Center
800-789-2647

Source: Available at http://mentalhealth.samhsa.gov/publications/allpubs/fastfact5/default.asp. Retrieved March 12, 2008.

Anxiety disorder and depression disorder follow in prevalence (Greenbaum, Dedrick, Friedman, et al., 1998), yet many children go unserved because their behavior is not disruptive in the classroom or their behavior does not fit categorical criteria for special education. America's children and youth are in a state of emergency. As children become more vulnerable, the need for effective educational and community programs continues to grow.

ATTENTION DEFICIT HYPERACTIVITY DISORDER

Since **hyperactivity** was first described in 1902 by Dr. George Still as "an abnormal defect of moral control," it has been one of the most discussed behavior disorders encountered by teachers and parents. The *Diagnostic and Statistical Manual of Mental Disorders* (*DSM IV*) describes hyperactivity as a symptom of attention-deficit hyperactive disorder (ADHD). According to the *DSM IV*, the onset of hyperactivity occurs before age 7, persists for at least 6 months, and must include a subset of some of the following symptoms: fails to give close attention to details, often does not seem to listen to what is said, often fidgets with hands or feet or squirms in seat, and often talks excessively.

William Cruickshank (1986) described two types of hyperactivity: sensory hyperactivity and motor hyperactivity. Distractibility is one of the primary characteristics of sensory hyperactivity. A student with sensory hyperactivity has an exceedingly short attention span, sometimes less than a minute. The student's attention is literally tugged back and forth by the visual and auditory stimuli of classroom activity. Unable to discriminate figure-ground relationships, either visually or auditorily (i.e., separating the object from its background), this student encounters severe problems with the simplest task. The printed page of a book, with its angled letters, spaces between letters, and pictures, is a visual minefield for a student with impaired figure-ground ability. The student is unable to stay focused on the sequential arrangement of letters and words.

According to Cruickshank, students with motor hyperactivity "seem to fall apart at the seams." They are constantly twisting, squirming, bending, and manipulating anything they can get their hands on. Hallways, playgrounds, or other open spaces, with the abundance of stimuli, cause the hyperactive student to overreact by running, yelling, and generally making a nuisance. Requesting such a student to sit still for 10 minutes is asking the near impossible. Needless to say, a student with sensory and/or motor hyperactivity is a severe test of a teacher's patience and creativity. Cruickshank (and many other researchers) believed that hyperactivity is a neurological disorder that is outside a youngster's ability to control. With estimates of hyperactivity ranging from 3 to 10 percent of school-aged students, it is plain to see how the problem of hyperactive students would attract teachers, pediatricians, and parents to treatment with drugs. Recent research using computational neuroanatomical techniques have confirmed Cruickshank's beliefs about a biological cause of ADHD. Shaw and colleagues at the National Institute of Mental Health did MRI scans on 223 children with ADHD and 223 control children. The researchers found "marked delay" in cortical development. In summarizing their findings the researchers said, "The delay was most prominent in prefrontal regions important for control of cognitive processes including attention and motor planning" (Shaw, Eckstrand, Sharp, et al., 2007).

SPEEDBUMP—Cruickshank established a special program for hyperactive children at Syracuse University. He designed a low-distraction classroom with covered windows, a carpet, and soundproofed walls. Children were seated at desks with side panels so they could see only their work. By today's standards the schoolwork was tedious and boring. However, for many years afterwards, the Cruickshank low-distraction classroom was a special education mainstay.

The *DSM-IV* criteria describe three types of ADHD:

1. ADHD primarily of the hyperactive-inattentive type
2. ADHD primarily of the hyperactive-impulsive type
3. ADHD of the combined type

Teachers, parents, and health professionals often work with children and young adults exhibiting behaviors related to activity, inattention, and impulsivity. The developmental variation commonly observed in these individuals is presented in Figure 4.3 and a variety of intervention methods are part of the special education they receive when properly diagnosed and treated.

Many hyperactive students are treated with Ritalin, a stimulant. Ritalin is classified as a Schedule II drug, meaning that it is regarded as an easily abused drug. Its manufacture is regulated by the Drug Enforcement Administration. Kohn (1988) reported that three-quarters of a million children are receiving the drug because of ADHD. Ritalin helps some students to concentrate by activating areas of the brain that help focus attention, plan,

FIGURE 4.3   Development Variation in Hyperactive Behaviors

Inattention

Developmental Variation

Young children have short attention spans that increase with age.

Inattention should be appropriate for the child's level of development and does not indicate a problem if it does not impair functioning.

Common Development Presentations

In early childhood, the child has difficulty attending, except briefly, to a storybook or quiet task such as coloring.

In middle childhood, the child may not continue with a task that he or she does not want to do such as read an assigned book, do some homework, or complete a household chore.

The adolescent is easily distracted from tasks that are undesirable to perform or complete.

Other Information

Infants and preschoolers usually have very short attention spans and normally do not persist with activities for long periods of time.

Diagnosing inattention is difficult in very young children.

Attention span varies greatly with interests and skills.

Inattention may be more an indication of interest or skill than a marker for a behavior problem.

Impulsivity

Developmental Variation

Young children are normally very active and impulsive; some need constant supervision to avoid injury.

Constant activity may be stressful to adults who lack energy or patience to tolerate their behavior.

During school years, activity may be high during play situations and impulsive behavior may occur with peer pressure.

High levels of hyperactive/impulsive behavior do not indicate a problem if they do not impair functioning.

Common Developmental Presentations

In early childhood, the child runs in circles, doesn't stop to rest, may bang into objects or people, and asks questions constantly.

In middle childhood, the child plays active games for long periods of time and may do things impulsively, especially when excited.

The adolescent engages in active social activity for long periods of time and may be involved in risky behavior with peers.

Other Information

Activity and impulsivity normally increase with hunger and fatigue.

Activity and impulsivity normally increase in new or anxiety-provoking situations.

Activity and impulsivity should be judged in the context of the expectations of others; when expectations are unreasonable and caregiver stress levels are high, perceived levels may be exaggerated.

Activity levels for some children are high from birth and continue high throughout development.

Sources: Adapted from American Academy of Pediatrics, 1996; 2000, 1158–1170.

and organize thoughts. Barkley (1977) found that approximately 75 percent of children with ADHD who take Ritalin or other psychostimulants showed short-time improvement, but found evidence still lacking to support long-term positive results. A recent synthesis of research literature by Swanson and associates (1993) sorted out expectations for effects of stimulant medication on children diagnosed with ADHD (Figure 4.4).

Some possible negative effects of stimulant medication are:

1. Some students don't improve and others worsen.
2. Although concentration may improve, the linkage with improved academic achievement has not been firmly established.
3. Placebos often (up to 40 percent of the time) work as well as Ritalin.
4. Physical side effects such as stunted growth, elevated blood pressure, facial tics, insomnia, and weight loss have been reported.

Underlying the pros and cons of drug treatment for hyperactivity is the more basic question: Is there a safer, more effective method for helping students control their hyperactivity? In some instances, the problem may be the classroom. When students labeled as hyperactive are placed in school programs that promote movement and concrete activities, problems of hyperactivity may diminish. These classrooms utilize learning centers and small-group activities. Students with hyperactivity are able to learn because the routines of the environment allow them to move around and manipulate materials.

Other more controversial approaches to decreasing hyperactivity in students with ADHD include elimination diets to remove allergens and decrease of sugar consumption. Evidence to support diet therapy is largely anecdotal. Widespread testimony by parents and professionals about the effect of food on behavior is difficult to ignore, yet the established medical community is not satisfied with the lack of hard evidence connecting diet

FIGURE 4.4   Effects of Psychostimulant Treatment for Children with ADHD

Temporary Management of Symptoms

Decrease in overactivity.
Improved attention.
Decrease in impulsivity.

Associated Improvements

Improvement in deportment.
Improvement in social interactions.
Improvement in academic productivity.

Other Observations

Response to medication cannot be predicted from neurological signs, biochemical markers, or physiological measures.
Side effects are infrequent.
Higher-order thinking processes and skills show scant improvement.
There is no long-term improvement in adjustment.

and hyperactivity. Despite medical disclaimers, parental reports like the following continue to fuel the debate.

> A mother described the effect of nitrates, a common food preservative: "I can always tell when my daughter (seven-year-old) has eaten a hot dog or baloney sandwich. She is off the walls, and it takes at least an hour for her to calm down." A college professor reported the effects of sugar on his six-year-old daughter, "Forget giving her dessert before bedtime. Just peanut butter on apple slices will keep her bouncing out of her bed and awake till 10:00 P.M." (Henley, 1986)

Table 4.3 lists some commercial foods that contain minimal amounts of sugar and preservatives. Many are part of dietary treatments prescribed for some children with emotional disturbance.

Factors that influence classification with emotional disturbance also can play a role in hyperactive behavior. Life in a **dysfunctional family**, where a youngster is continually exposed to chaotic living situations and warped interpersonal ties, will raise a student's stress level. The normal reaction to stress is flight or fight. For a student who is experiencing chronic stress, flight in the form of hyperactive behavior may be a futile attempt to adapt to an unpredictable lifestyle.

Over the years, educational strategies have run the gamut from controlling techniques such as elimination of extraneous stimuli coupled with behavior modification to focusing on the "whole child" by monitoring diet, identifying stress factors, and allowing guided movement in the classroom (Armstrong, 1998). The rise of Ritalin usage and other stimulants to control ADHD has spawned a cottage industry of books, pamphlets, and research monographs that extol the benefits and disadvantages of medication. In 1993, the United States consumed three times the amount of Ritalin used throughout the rest of the world (Valentine, 1994). Frankenberger (1998) synthesized the often-contradictory findings regarding **stimulant medication** use. The following are some of the claims about stimulant medication and the research findings:

- *Claim—Stimulant medication has a positive effect on cognitive functioning.* A review of 84 studies found stimulant medication sometimes improved short-term cognitive functioning in laboratory tests, but the results were inconclusive in terms of classroom behavior. Other researchers found no improvement in cognitive functioning.
- *Claim—Stimulant medication has a positive effect on achievement.* Results are mixed. Short-term gains have been documented. Best results are when medications have been used in conjunction with remedial teaching. Many studies found no improvement in achievement.
- *Claim—Stimulant medication has a positive effect on reading achievement.* As compared to overall achievement, the results with reading seemed somewhat more promising. Two studies documented improvement, two studies showed no improvement, and one study documented temporary improvement.
- *Claim—Stimulant medication has a positive effect on behavior.* Behavior appears to be most positively influenced by stimulant medication. In one reported study, 75 percent of hyperactive students improved. Many anecdotal reports by teachers and

TABLE 4.3   Partial List of Foods Found in Supermarkets that Are Free of Artificial Coloring, Flavoring, and Preservatives

Cereals
Cheerios
Quaker Oats, Puffed Rice, and Puffed Wheat
Post Grape Nuts
General Mills' Kix
Kellogg's Raisin Bran

Crackers
Hi-Ho
Krispy Saltines
Premium Saltines
Cheese-Its
Nabisco Graham Crackers (not Honey Graham)
Pepperidge Farm Cookies

Ice Cream
Ben & Jerry's
All Natural Hendries
All Natural Breyers
All Natural Dolly Madison
All Natural Stop & Shop

Canned Juices
100% juices such as pineapple, grapefruit, cranberry, apple, tomato. Check label to be sure that no sugar, coloring, etc., added.

Salad Dressing
Walden's

Popsicles, etc.
Hood's Orange (all natural)
Welch's Grape
York Peppermint Patty Sticks

Frozen Waffles
Golden Harvest (at Stop & Shop and Shop Rite)

Sausage
Jones or fresh ground

Soda
Seven-Up
Soda water
Country Club Ginger Ale

Jelly
Smuckers
Polaner

Candy Bars
Reese's Peanut Butter Cups
Mound's
Almond Joy
York Peppermint Patties
Planter's Peanut Bars
Bit-O-Honey

Frozen Juices
Juicy Juice
Minute Maid orange juice and lemonade
Stop & Shop Lemonade
Welch's Grape Juice
Many brands of orange juice; look at label

Gum
Wrigley's

Cocoa
Swiss Miss Cocoa Mix
Hershey's Pure Cocoa

Peanut Butter
Smucker's
Teddies

Mayonnaise
Cain's

Spaghetti Sauce
Prince

Sharp Cheese
"Helluva" Good Cheese

Margarine
Shedd's Willow Run
Natural food store margarine (colored with carotene, which is natural)

Hot Dogs (without nitrates)
Wild Wind

Maple Syrup—100% Pure
Vermont Maple Orchards

parents support the positive effect of stimulants on hyperactive behavior. However, such negative side effects as weight loss, interrupted sleep, and loss of appetite also are commonly reported.

Educational Approaches for ADHD

Whether stimulant medication is administered or not, the classroom teacher still needs to improve the achievement of students and help them learn to cope with some of the deleterious outcomes associated with hyperactivity, distractibility, and impulsivity. What follows is a brief synopsis of educational strategies used by general and special education teachers to help students with ADHD.

- **Cognitive Behavior Modification (CBM).** The objective of CBM is to teach students problem-solving strategies and self-control techniques. Students are instructed in a step-by-step procedure to monitor and direct their behavior. For example, students are taught to deal with conflict by (1) calming down before reacting impulsively; (2) identifying feelings and expressing feelings in an appropriate manner; (3) setting positive goals for themselves; (4) thinking of alternative solutions to problems; (5) trying a plan and evaluating results (Greenberg, 1998). The overall goal is for students to spontaneously think through situations in which they feel the impulse to act quickly.
- **Social Skills Training.** Students with ADHD develop impulsive habits that interfere with their ability to manage interactions with peers and adults. The purpose of social skills training is to rectify social skills deficits through direct and indirect instruction. This proactive approach seeks to change students' disruptive behavior by focusing on teaching new skills rather than the reactive approach of trying to eliminate bothersome behaviors. For example, a student who acts out impulsively might benefit from learning to verbalize his or her feelings (i.e., proactive), rather than being sent to timeout each time the offending behavior occurs (i.e., reactive). Social skills curriculums (see Chapter 10) employ a variety of instructional techniques including modeling, step-by-step scripts, classroom meetings, reinforcement, and emphasizing social skills embedded in the regular curriculum; for example, using science to teach how to anticipate consequences or using children's literature to teach conflict resolution.
- **Contingency Management.** Based on principles of behaviorism, students are rewarded when they demonstrate socially appropriate behavior. Contingencies also can include negative consequences for inappropriate behavior. Positive consequences can include praise or tangible rewards. Reprimands or ignoring the behavior are examples of frequently used negative consequences. Teachers must be vigilant to ensure that negative consequences are logical and match the inappropriate behavior. For example, a logical consequence for throwing food in the cafeteria is eating lunch alone in the classroom for 3 days rather than doing additional homework. Other applications of behavior theory to ADHD include token economy, response cost, and contingency contracting.

- **Structured Activity and Movement.** Planned classroom activities that allow students to move about, converse with others, and interact with concrete materials help students with ADHD sustain attention and reduces the stress of trying to constantly restrain motor activity. Some frequently used techniques are learning centers, planned student interactions, art, music, kinesthetic activity, games, and authentic learning experiences such as teaching ratios by making orange juice from concentrate (Reif, 1998).
- **Self-Management Strategies.** Students with ADHD lack organizational skills for sustaining attention and completing projects. Direct instruction in time management helps students learn to divide a task into subunits. By monitoring due dates incrementally, teachers help students set realistic time lines and avoid procrastination. Helping students learn how to organize materials is another key self-management strategy. Filing papers, scheduling, keeping notes in binders, and periodical inventory of materials are frequent self-management organizational objectives. Teaching study skills such as active reading (i.e., writing down questions and comments rather than simply highlighting), webbing of chapters, reviewing key topics and subtopics, and developing test taking skills are helpful strategies.
- **Classroom Accommodations.** The physical layout of a classroom is the single most important element in focusing attention. Textbooks with shiny paper particularly are problematic under fluorescent lights. Also, the hum and the flickering of fluorescent lights is a distraction and they should be replaced with incandescent lights. Soft, classical music in the background can be soothing. "Natural" sound recordings can have a similar effect. Student seating should be adjusted to cut down distractions from high-traffic areas. Sitting at tables may present a problem for some students. Carrels with side panels help eliminate visual distractions. Some teachers report that overhead projectors help cut down on visual distractions by reducing the "clutter" that sometimes fills up chalkboards (Flick, 1998). Directions should be given slowly with frequent requests for the student to provide restatements. When worksheets are used, students benefit from fewer problems to complete, lined paper helps with handwriting, and computer software offers myriad possibilities from word processing to games that reinforce academic skills.

CAUSES OF EMOTIONAL DISTURBANCE

The search for understanding the causes and treatment of emotional disturbance has followed many roads (Erickson, 1998). Each distinctive field of knowledge—biophysical, psychodynamic, psychoeducational, and behavioral—has contributed, in a synergistic fashion, to an overall understanding of emotional disturbance (see Table 4.4). During the early years of special education, theorists tended to pitch their tents in a single conceptual camp. They fortified their encampments with rigorous defenses, and with equal vigor, hurled conceptual assaults at each other. Thus graduate students would burn the midnight oil as they debated the relative merits of Bruno Bettelheim's psychodynamic view versus B. F. Skinner's behavior modification techniques for treating troubled children.

The first model addressed, the **biophysical**, makes a clear case for understanding that emotional disturbance can occur when something goes wrong with the delicate mechanism of a child's body.

TABLE 4.4 Summary of Causes of Behavior Disorders

	BIOPHYSICAL	PSYCHODYNAMIC	BEHAVIORAL	PSYCHOEDUCATIONAL
Emphasis	Biological and physical systems	Stages of psychological development	Behavior antecedents and consequences	School adaptation and behavior change
Etiology	Genetics, nutrition, biochemistry, neurology	Conflict in development, traumatic experiences	Learning systems, conditioning, reinforcement, punishment	Conflict in development compounded by expectations
Diagnosis	Identify area(s) of biological or physical dysfunction	Identify critical phases in development or insight into origins of conflict	Identify controlling conditions within learning trials	Identify controlling influences in development
Assessment	Medical and physical exams	Psychological exams	Observations	Observations
Instruction/ Treatment	Medical and physical treatments	Psychological counseling	Behavior therapy	Reeducation
Goals	Correcting system dysfunctions	Reduction of conflict	Arranging conditions of learning	Individual and system change
Some Major Figures	Rimland Feingold	Freud Erikson Redl Bettelheim	Pavlov Skinner	Hobbs Long Morse Wood

Biophysical Causes

Throughout history, physical and biological factors have been identified with some of the conditions that are part of the broad classification known as emotional disturbance (Erickson, 1998). Researchers have linked genetics and emotional disturbance; Schwartz (1979) pointed out that evidence exists to support the role of heredity in shaping behavior and personality. This conclusion is based on findings that sex-linked differences are evident in many types of emotional disturbance. For example, hyperactivity, antisocial behaviors, and conduct disorders more commonly are identified in boys than in girls.

Thomas and Chess (1977) followed several groups from childhood to adulthood and found that their behavior patterns were relatively constant. About 40 percent were made up of the "easy child" whose characteristics included adaptability, high tolerance for frustration, and positive responses to change. The "difficult" child (about 10 percent) was characterized by irregular biological functions, negative behaviors, poor adaptability, and negativism. The "slow-to-warm" child was characterized by limited responsiveness, flat emotional responses, and unsatisfactory interpersonal relations. These findings were presented as support for the position that behavioral characteristics are predicated on biophysical differences among people.

The popularity of **psychoactive drugs** to treat behavior disorders is testimony to the widespread acceptance of the biophysical approach. Physicians prescribe drugs, and they rely on parents and others to monitor the effects those drugs have on problem behaviors. School personnel are in a crucial position to monitor a successful drug therapy program. Teachers maintain consistent contact in situations that allow for comparisons of student behavior, so observations by teachers are exceptionally valuable. The drug-monitoring process requires systematic observations and recordings of a student's behavior at various points during the school day.

Interest in using drugs is based on general knowledge about the ways chemicals influence behavior. For example, the amino acid tryptophan is converted into the neurotransmitter serotonin by chemical reactions that are regulated by enzymes (e.g., tryptophan hydroxylase); serotonin is believed to influence aggression, depression, and normal sleep patterns (Restak, 1984).

Stimulants, such as methylphenidate hydrochloride (Ritalin), dextroamphetamine sulfate (Dexadrine), and magnesium pemoline (Cylert), as well as antihistamines, such as diphenhydramine hydrochloride (Benadryl), are used to treat problem behaviors related to overactivity. Antidepressants and antianxiety drugs, such as imipramine hydrochloride (Tofranil), oxazepam (Serax), and chlorpromazine hydrochloride (Librium), are used to control problem behaviors related to mood disorders.

Experiments with lithium, a drug originally used to treat gout, indicated a calming effect with aggressive animals. In the laboratory, Siamese fighting fish, rats, and mice showed decreased hostile behavior when treated with lithium. Outside the laboratory, experiments with lithium demonstrated interesting and controversial results with aggressive prisoners. In an experiment in the maximum security prisons at Vacaville and Sacramento, California, 27 inmates were administered lithium. Although diverse in family backgrounds and personalities, the inmates were similar in their recurrent violent behavior and quick tempers. Restak (1984) described changes in both prisoner behavior and attitude after 9 months:

> The results showed a decline in disciplinary action for violent behavior. Among fifteen of twenty-two subjects, the number of disciplinary acts for violent behavior were reduced. Even more interesting than the decrease in violence, however, were the reports offered by several prisoners in Dr. Tupin's study. One man stated, "Now I can think about whether to hit him or not." Another said, "I have lost my anger." Each of the Lithium dosed prisoners demonstrated an increased capacity to reflect on the consequences of his actions, a quality Dr. Tupin refers to as a "more reflective mood." (p. 142)

Stimulants, minor tranquilizers, and anticonvulsants commonly used for children with emotional disturbance are in Appendix B. Each class of psychoactive medication includes generic and brand-name drugs, common dosages, expected effects, and side effects. Whenever students are given drugs to treat behavior problems, the underlying premise is that chemical body processes are being altered. Imbalances in the biochemical system are believed to be the source of the problem. Drugs are prescribed by physicians to bring abnormal body chemicals into proper levels of balance and thereby change behavior. The more disturbing the behavior, the greater the likelihood that drug treatment will be accepted as a needed procedure. In the case of students with mild disabilities, the use of drugs can and has created controversy.

Psychodynamic Causes

Some educators believe that problems related to personality development are the cause of social and emotional behavior problems of children and youth (Rhodes & Tracy, 1972a, b). Generally, these professionals have received training from psychiatrists and psychologists who believe that the inner conflict principles first developed by Sigmund Freud can be used to explain and treat emotional disturbance. The **psychodynamic** view describes the evolving personality in terms of the relationship between three strong intrapsychic forces: id, ego, and superego. The *id* is the pleasure seeking, impulsive force that is dominant in childhood. The *superego* is the conscience; it represents moral and ethical beliefs. The *ego* mediates between the id and the superego and shapes judgments about reality. The ego guides actions by taking into account the natural consequences of behavior. The id, ego, and superego act as a system of checks and balances on individual behavior.

Consider the following illustration of the id, ego, and superego relationship. A teenager walks through a shopping mall and sees a Swiss Army knife sitting on a counter. His impulse (id) is to pick the knife up and put it in his pocket. His conscience (superego) tells him it is wrong to steal, but his id is winning the battle. "I'll go to church and it will be okay," he thinks. Meanwhile his reality-testing instincts (ego) tell him to look around. He sees several mirrors arrayed along the store walls. Now the struggle is on between id and ego. The teenager walks away without the knife because he decides the knife was not worth the risk.

Freud described **neurosis** (emotional disturbance) as a conflict between the ego and the id. The person is at war with her- or himself. The goal of psychodynamic treatment is to bring the id, ego, and superego into harmony. As Freud explained, "A man should not try to eliminate his complexes but get into accord with them; they are legitimately what direct his conduct in the world" (Seldes, 1985, 151). Over the years Freud's theory has been expanded and modified by some of the greatest thinkers in the field of psychology. A list of contributors to psychodynamic theory reads like a *Who's Who* of twentieth-century thought—Carl Jung, Alfred Adler, Erik Erikson, Anna Freud, Erich Fromm, and Bruno Bettelheim are just a sample of the writers and therapists who were heavily influenced by psychodynamic theory.

Fritz Redl and David Wineman were two of the first practitioners to successfully apply psychodynamic principles to the treatment of aggressive youth. In *Children Who Hate* (1951), Redl and Wineman described how the self-control (ego development) of adolescents collapses under the impact of specific environmental or psychological triggers. Redl and Wineman catalogued 22 separate self-control challenges that all children need to cope with in order to continue their emotional development. Using colorful language such as "gadgetorial seduction" and "warfare with time," Redl and Wineman presented a roadmap for identifying self-control weaknesses in specific youngsters. Their descriptions of ego functions provide classroom teachers with a clinical model for anticipating when and where a student will lose self-control (Henley, 1987).

The psychodynamic point of view underscores the need to understand *why* students are disruptive. It emphasizes the connections between how a student feels and how a student acts. The classic psychodynamic treatments are play therapy for children and individual psychotherapy for youth. For educators who saw the value of psychodynamic principles, it was necessary to develop treatment procedures that would be useful in the classroom, where teachers must manage groups of children. Psychoeducational treatments were born out of the need to merge behavior management with psychodynamic theory.

Psychoeducational Causes

Proponents of the **psychoeducational** perspective believe that problem behaviors result from underlying psychological disturbances, and that adaptive behaviors must be learned for successful accommodation in schools. Knoblock presented a succinct description: "A psychoeducational framework assumes that behavior is caused, that there are reasons why children act as they do. Early psychoeducators like Berkowitz and Rothman believed that children's feelings were the source of observed behaviors. Now it is recognized that behaviors should be analyzed in the context of specific environments as well . . ." (Knoblock, 1983, 107). There is a balance between concern for causes of behavior and acquisition of adaptive skills in the psychoeducational treatment model.

This integrated philosophy is illustrated in the principles of Project Re-Ed (Hobbs, 1966):

1. Students should be kept busy in school; successful completion of purposeful activities is central to reeducation.
2. Students should spend as much time as possible in positive, therapeutic environments; neighborhood schools with supportive personnel are preferred in efforts to reeducate students with behavior problems.
3. Supportive teacher-student interactions are a key to establishing academic success; teachers learn this by working with students in positive relationships.

Psychoeducators believe the student-teacher relationship is the fundamental building block for change. Out of this relationship comes mutual trust and a willingness on the part of both teacher and student to accept the needs of each other. Behavioral and emotional difficulties are viewed developmentally. Using cognitive and emotional developmental milestones as a guide, the psychoeducator attempts to identify developmental strengths and weaknesses. Classroom accommodations are made that capitalize on student abilities in order to move a youngster along the normal developmental continuum. Self-concept development, the teaching of social skills, and normalization of a youngster's school experience are all components in the psychoeducational treatment model.

Some social development programs, including *Life Space Crisis Intervention* (Long, Wood, & Fecser, 2001), and *Teaching Self-Control: A Curriculum for Responsible Behavior* (Henley, 2004) have translated psychoeducational principles into functional systems for assessment, goal setting, and teaching. These models assume that students have the internal resources to change, and that appropriate environmental supports can nourish and maintain student emotional growth. These treatments assume that change begins within the individual and that the ultimate goal is to teach students to accept responsibility for their own behavior. A counterpoint to the psychoeducational treatment approach is the behaviorist model, which focuses almost exclusively on the manipulation of environmental conditions to shape student behavior.

Behavioral Causes

During the 1960s, educators and psychologists recognized the importance of **behavioral** principles of learning. The key points of behavioral theory and practice can be summarized as follows:

1. Behaviorists view inappropriate and appropriate behavior as learned. Behavior is a response to a person's interaction with the environment.
2. Learning occurs when environmental conditions reinforce a specific behavior. Learning takes several forms, including imitation, modeling, and operant conditioning (i.e., consequences that shape behavior).
3. Inappropriate behavior is learned through environmental conditioning and new, appropriate behaviors can be learned with proper arrangement of the conditions of learning.
4. Effective implementation of behavior treatments in classrooms requires observable descriptions of behavior to be changed, targeting of new behaviors, systematic application of reinforcers, and collection of pre- and postdata to determine treatment effectiveness.

Behaviorists do not attempt to understand behavior problems using underlying personality constructs (e.g., id, ego, superego) nor do they ascribe hypothetical causes (e.g., inner conflict) to behavior. In explaining behavior, behaviorists prefer to deal with observable actions (e.g., what happens before and after the behavior) rather than theoretical (e.g., arrested development) explanations. The emphasis on observable, known causes for behavior rather than possible, unknown causes has been a catalyst to replace the term **emotionally disturbed** with the classification **behavior disorders** in many states. Whereas the former term implies a person knows the reason for a behavior (i.e., disturbed emotional development), the latter makes no claim about causality but simply points to a problem associated with an individual's behavior. To clarify reasons for the behavior, the behaviorist would conduct a **functional behavioral assessment** to identify variables that cause it. To design an effective intervention, the behaviorist systematically would control all or some of these variables and observe changes in the behavior. This process of applying principles of behavior theory is known generally as behavior modification or applied behavior analysis.

Operant conditioning is a form of behavior modification used to change student behavior in the classroom. Operant conditioning is based on the premise that actions are shaped or changed by their consequences. The operant is the behavior (e.g., listening, hitting, laughing), while the consequences (e.g., praising, punishing, or ignoring) either reinforce or eliminate the operant.

SPEEDBUMP—During World War II, B. F. Skinner, the originator of operant conditioning, invented a pigeon-guided bomb. He found that marijuana seeds were the best reinforcers to train his pigeons. The guidance system worked, but the Army thought the idea silly. A few months after rejecting Skinner's idea, a lone bomber dropped an atomic bomb on Hiroshima.

Individuals can modify their own behavior. Cooper, Heron, and Heward (1987) provide the following example of behavior, which is modified by the consequences it produces.

> When an infant moves her arms through space, setting in motion the mobile dangling in her crib, she is literally operating on her environment. The mobile's movement and sound are stimuli produced by the child's behavior, consequences of her batting at the toy with her hands. If continued observation of the baby reveals an increased rate of arm swinging when the mobile hangs in her crib, her behavior would be described as an operant. (p. 21)

Behavior can be modified spontaneously, for example, when a student invents a shortcut to solve math problems. Behavior also can be shaped systematically, for instance, when a teacher awards tokens for finishing classroom tasks. Behavior can be modified ineffectively, as when a teacher's verbal reprimands reinforce an acting-out behavior. The principles of operant conditioning are always the same; the key is knowledgeable application. Many teachers, both special and regular education, use operant conditioning practices in their classrooms on a regular basis.

Schroeder and Riddle (1991) list the basic components of operant conditioning. The following is an adaptation of their definitions.

1. **Positive reinforcement:** presenting a consequence that increases the probability of a behavior in the future. Example—a student who shares toys in a play area of a classroom because of favorable reaction from other children.
2. **Punishment:** presenting or withdrawing a consequence that decreases the probability of a behavior in the future. Examples—a reprimand (i.e., presenting a stimulus) or keeping a youngster in class during recess (i.e., withdrawing a stimulus) in order to stop disruptive classroom behavior.
3. **Negative reinforcement:** increasing the probability of a behavior by removing an unpleasant consequence. Example—students who complete homework for 5 consecutive days are excused from taking a weekly math quiz. Negative reinforcement is often confused with punishment. Example—a student is sent into the hall for disrupting the class. The teacher is negatively reinforcing the misbehavior when the child continues to act up in the future in order to avoid an unpleasant classroom activity.
4. **Extinction:** decreasing the probability of a response by withholding a previously reinforcing stimulus. Example—classmates don't laugh when a student makes a sarcastic comment in class.
5. **Differential reinforcement of other behavior (DRO):** decreasing the probability of a response by reinforcing the omission of it; sometimes referred to as *omission training*. Example—a student who is disruptive is given a token for every 5 minutes the behavior is not emitted.
6. **Satiation:** decreasing the probability of a response by reinforcing it excessively. The reinforcer no longer maintains the behavior. Example—a teacher uses a novel reading series to encourage student effort. In a short while, student effort diminishes as the novelty wears off.

Often these treatments are used in combination to shape behavior in the classroom; for example, a teacher might use both positive and negative reinforcement to encourage a youngster to comply with classroom rules. Positive reinforcement could take the form of verbal praise immediately following the desired behavior, and negative reinforcement would consist of a decrease in corrective comments from the teacher. A comprehensive elaboration of each component of operant conditioning is outside the scope of this book. For more details, read Macy's *Behavior Management from Theoretical Implications to Practical Applications*, Second Edition (2004).

DISTURBED OR DISTURBING?

When a student is disruptive in a classroom, does that mean that the student has a disability or are there alternative explanations? Consider the following behaviors: talking out of turn, swearing at the teacher, throwing objects, running out of the room, or refusing to do an assignment. Those behaviors are commonplace in chaotic classrooms, but they occur infrequently in classrooms where teachers demonstrate effective group management skills.

Frederic Jones (1987) studied teacher-student interactions in hundreds of elementary and secondary classrooms. Many of his observations were done in inner-city schools and alternative programs for students with behavior disorders. One might expect Jones to report many examples of behavior disorders such as hostility, impulsiveness, or aggression. He didn't. Jones and his colleagues characterized the majority of student activity as "massive time wasting." Students walked around the room, "goofed off," and talked whenever they felt like it. In poorly managed classrooms, these behaviors occurred every 20 seconds. In well-managed classrooms, the same behaviors were noted once every 2 minutes. Jones found that teachers in poorly managed classrooms lost 50 percent of their instructional time dealing with disturbing behaviors (Charles, 1989). Jones concluded that many disruptive behaviors were symptomatic of mismanaged classrooms.

The classic study by Wickman (1929) is the first major investigation that attempted to identify specific behaviors that educators perceived bothersome or disturbing in their work with children. Behaviors identified were characterized as those that offended moral standards (e.g., stealing, cheating, lying) and challenging teachers' authority (e.g., defiance, impertinence). Ramsey (1981) analyzed 33 replications that followed this seminal study and concluded that classroom orderliness and recognition of authority are of primary importance to teachers so that they can do their job, which is to teach students.

The notion that teachers can cause behavior problems is underscored by Jacob Kounin's research. Kounin (1977) found classroom disruptions were correlated to teacher expertise. Kounin reported that the following teacher behaviors contributed to discipline problems: making verbal comments about minor disturbances such as dropping a pencil, getting sidetracked by a single student's behavior, forcing students to do boring and repetitious activities, and becoming angry or punitive when students misbehaved. Conversely, Kounin observed that teachers positively influenced appropriate classroom behavior by smooth transitions between lessons, keeping track of all student behavior in the classroom at the same time, and providing novelty in lessons. Teachers who were liked by their students had the least behavior problems.

The **interactional perspective** of disturbing/disturbed behaviors underscores the need to evaluate both the individual and the setting. Behavior is a function of the individual interacting within the environment. Although disturbing behavior may begin with the individual student, the way in which the teacher responds is crucial in preventing further problems. Organization of classroom space, routines, and lessons influence student behavior. Imagine a 7-year-old youngster with ADHD attempting to conform to a classroom in which students are expected to sit quietly at their desks and complete assignments consisting of workbooks and written exercises. In this classroom, the student is at a disadvantage by her learning problem. She is unable to sit still and concentrate. Why force a student to do something that is outside her limits? Suppose we move the same student into a classroom where she can walk around and work at learning centers that feature manipulative materials. In the latter classroom, our 7-year-old no longer is restrained and she is engaged in concrete tasks that match her developmental abilities. This interactional perspective is summarized by the principle that behavior is a function of the individual interacting within the environment.

When a student's behavior is properly evaluated, the context within which the behavior occurs is examined. Special education historically has provided individual services for students rather than classroom support to the regular classroom teacher. The entire special education service delivery system is geared to find something wrong with the student, yet for years special educators have recognized that disturbance is often in the eye of the beholder. In 1967, William Rhodes remarked that behavior is often more "disturbing" than "disturbed." He contended that disturbance is a function of where and with whom a student interacts (Rhodes, 1967).

School records and case histories brim with examples of the influence of adult expectations and perceptions on the lives of students classified as behaviorally disordered or emotionally disturbed. For example, Apter (1982) provide the following description of a "disturbed" student.

> We worked with an adolescent boy with an IQ of approximately 80. He has the misfortune to be born into a family of extremely high achievers who expected him to go to Princeton University. He was attempting an academic program in high school and failing miserably. From his father's point of view, he was just lazy. His mother babied him. His older brother teased him. His teachers criticized and demeaned him. He stayed up long hours to study but couldn't keep up. His health began to suffer. Finally, he became deeply depressed and attempted suicide. Fortunately, following this episode, a careful examination of this boy's ecosystem (home, family interactions, community, school, teacher behavior) resulted in greater understanding on the part of all parties concerned. (p. 72)

In analyzing this story, it is difficult to identify the source of the problem. Did the family's expectations and behaviors produce the student's problems? Did his behavior and expectations influence others' perceptions of him? Would he be a problem in another family? Would he be a problem with other teachers? The complex nature of human interactions clearly leaves the source of the disturbance unresolved in this case study, and this is true for most students with behavior disorders as well. Table 4.5 illustrates how four different theories influence analysis and treatment of disturbing behavior.

TABLE 4.5   There's Always a Reason for Behavior: Four Theoretical Explanations

Behavior: Sixth grader Manuel frequently disrupts class through attention-seeking behaviors such as making sarcastic remarks and inappropriate jokes.

THEORETICAL PERSPECTIVE	HYPOTHETICAL EXPLANATION
Psychoeducational Theory	Manuel is frustrated by his attempts to develop friendships. His attention-seeking behavior is an awkward attempt to gain other students' acceptance. This social-emotional conflict typically surfaces in insecure students during adolescence.
Behaviorist Theory	Each time Manuel makes a wisecrack, the other students laugh and snicker. Their response serves as positive reinforcement for his disruptive behavior.
Biophysical Theory	Manuel lives in a rundown area of town. The state freeway bridge runs almost directly over his subsidized public housing unit. Over the years, lead has gradually accumulated in Manuel's nervous system. Manuel's impulsivity is caused by lead poisoning.
Psychodynamic Theory	Manuel's self-control problems are triggered by situations that remind him of past failures. Most of his inappropriate remarks occur in situations where he is expected to read. He is insecure about his weak reading skills. This insecurity increases his anxiety which he acts out through impulsive behavior.

Source: Henley, M. (2005). *Classroom Management: A Proactive Approach.* Upper Saddle River, NJ: Prentice Hall. Reprinted with permission.

THE ECOLOGICAL MODEL

When trying to understand students with social and emotional behavior problems, one can get caught up in the chicken or the egg paradox. Does the behavior problem lead to negative responses from others, which ultimately result in an emotional disturbance? Or are the behavior problems caused by an emotional disturbance? Or is the student simply a disruptive individual without an emotional problem? These questions may seem to be rhetorical verbal games best suited for clever banter, but, in fact, how teachers and administrators view students and determine the answers to these questions can mean the difference between a student getting special education services, no help at all, or becoming a school dropout.

What is conspicuously absent from the general special education connection is a focus on prevention, which is discussed in greater detail in Chapter 9 and Chapter 10. Additional help for the classroom teacher would improve classroom management practices. Community centers could provide mental health and networking services for troubled families. Greater attention to the needs of children in general would produce a concentrated effort to mobilize national attention and resources to battle such childhood perils as loneliness, fear, abuse, addiction, and school failure.

The view that treatment of behavior disorders must take into account all features of a student's life (including school, family, and community) is called the **ecological model**.

Educators who embrace the ecological perspective believe that in order to understand troubled children, teachers need to consider all facets of their lives (Apter, 1982):

> From this outlook emotional disturbance is not seen simply as the necessary result of intrapsychic conflict (psychodynamic model) nor as the inevitable product of inappropriate social learning (behavior modification model). Instead, according to the ecological model, disturbance resides in the interaction between a child and critical aspects of that child's surrounding environment, that is, the child's system. More specifically, ecological theorists believe that what we know as emotional disturbance or behavior disorders actually result from discrepancies between a given child's skills and abilities and the demands or expectations of that child's environment. (p. 2)

The ecological model emphasizes the need for comprehensive preventive systems within and outside of school to make adjustments in the parts of a student's life that can cause behavior disorders. As Apter (1982) acknowledged, change strategies should be aimed at increasing competence instead of reducing deficits. Well-baby clinics, parent effectiveness training, community development programs, sex and drug education programs, and teenage counseling programs are examples of change strategies that focus on prevention while increasing the competence of young people (Heller & Monahan, 1977).

Clearly the ecological model cannot work without community and political support. The long-range view of looking at troubled social systems requires a broad-based constituency. It requires a commitment to social change and social policies that often are not shared by politicians or the populace in general. The road to social change is riddled with pitfalls.

A case study in the pitfalls of prevention is illustrated by the work of Spencer Holland, a psychologist at Morgan State University in Baltimore. Holland recommended educational intervention specifically aimed at African American male students. African American males have the highest dropout rates, get the lowest grades, and exhibit more discipline problems than any subgroup of students. Holland argued that lack of adequate male role models was a primary cause of troubles encountered by African American males (Chmelynski, 1990):

> The most common reasons cited for the academic and social failings of young black males are that such boys come from poor, single-parent, female-headed households; that they have no positive male role models; and that they view the (school) as feminine and not relevant to their daily lives. (p. 16)

One extension of Holland's reasoning is that referral for special services for behavior problems may be related to females teaching males. Teacher ratings of behavior are the most influential component in school evaluations of behavior disorders. Teachers rate boys as "acting out" more often than girls, and boys are more likely to be evaluated as having a behavior disorder (Walker, Ramsey, & Gresham, 2004). When one matches the overrepresentation of boys in the category of behavior disorders with the overrepresentation of females among teachers, a likely hypothesis is that referrals for social and emotional problems are gender related.

Some schools, influenced by Dr. Holland's work, took a hard look at gender issues in classrooms. Several school systems responded to this problem by providing African

American male students with positive male role models. African American businessmen, professionals, and tradesmen volunteered as role models for students in Baltimore, Detroit, Miami, Milwaukee, San Diego, and Washington, D.C., schools. The role models tutored students, took them on field trips, and provided them with the male mentoring that was conspicuously absent in the youngsters' lives.

These volunteer programs proved so popular that school officials in Dade County, Florida, and Detroit considered starting African American male academies. The possibility of schools just for African American male students quickly produced widespread critical reactions. Specters of sexism and segregation raised by the National Organization of Women (NOW) and the National Association for the Advancement of Colored People (NAACP) caused many advocates to reconsider education programs that single out only African American boys. Proponents of the programs contended that the situation for young African American males was so dire that radical measures were in order. Holland argued that whereas African American girls have role models in their mothers and teachers, boys searching for role models in their inner-city neighborhoods find that the only successful males are drug dealers or criminals (Chmelynski, 1990). As this case study of prevention illustrates, it is easier to refer a disruptive student for special education services than it is to try to change school practices or redirect social policies.

> **SPEEDBUMP—**There is a tremendous need for teachers who are trained and motivated to work with students who have emotional problems.

The advantage of the ecological model is that it focuses attention on the interactional aspects of behavior disorders. David Witcher was a teacher at Batchler Middle School in Bloomington, Indiana; his comments in the August 1988 issue of the Council for Children with Behavior Disorders newsletter are revealing:

> For the past eight years, I have been a public school teacher in special education programs for so-called emotionally handicapped children and adolescents. Even after working on over a hundred cases, I still cannot tell why one student qualifies for my special services while another does not.

As long as ineffective teaching practices continue and urgent social issues are ignored, many students whose behavior problems could be prevented will be classified with emotional disturbance and placed in special education programs.

CHARACTERISTICS

Students with emotional disturbance exhibit a wide variety of characteristics that makes teaching them difficult (Erickson, 1998; Kauffman, 1997; 1999). A description of functional characteristics is somewhat hampered by the differences in professional perceptions of these youngsters. We all interpret what we see, hear, and understand in terms of the assumptions we hold about the world around us. Keep this in mind when you hear professors and teachers discussing students with emotional disturbance. A professional who is solidly in the behaviorist camp does not recognize feelings as important aspects of a student's behavior. If a behaviorist were to describe the functional priorities of a youngster, feelings would be at the bottom of the list. At the same time, a professional who is devoted to the psychodynamic treatment approach would describe a youngster's functional abilities in terms of interpsychic conflicts between id, ego, and superego. The observable actions that are the foundation of the behaviorist treatment model are minimal in the psychodynamic view. A key point to remember is the power of the observer (i.e., teacher, professor, psychologist) of student's behavior to determine if a behavior is disturbing or disturbed.

Students with emotional disturbance are identified by their severe deficits in perception, communication, and behavior. Such behaviors as delusions and lack of effect are marked examples of the extreme behavioral disturbances in seriously emotionally disturbed students. Students with mild behavior disorders are quite different. Before they entered school, the majority of these youngsters seemed capable of adapting to the social demands of formal education. (We hope at this point this theme sounds familiar.) Basically students with emotional disturbance exhibit behaviors that interfere with productive interpersonal relationships, they are unable to adapt to classroom routines, and they cause classroom disruptions. These students have behavior excesses or deficiencies that make regular school progress difficult to achieve without special education.

Consider this example: Mrs. Stone, a junior high school teacher, has just passed out a sheet of math problems to be completed by each of her students. Frank's response is clearly excessive. He looks at the paper, throws down his pencil, and angrily states, "What do you think I am, a genius or something?" After this preamble, he proceeds into a harangue supported by four-letter words and no-holds-barred attacks on Mrs. Stone's professional and personal integrity. He ends up with an ultimatum suggesting that "nothing or nobody" can make him do the worksheet.

In this episode, we see grist for everybody's theoretical mill. Frank's behavior is clearly inappropriate, and a behaviorist would work to eliminate outbursts and reinforce appropriate school behaviors. The psychodynamic-oriented professional examines the relationship between Frank and Mrs. Stone. Counseling might be directed at helping Frank cope with females in authority positions. From a psychoeducational point of view, Mrs. Stone is setting Frank up for failure by using worksheets when Frank is developmentally unable to handle such abstract work. Classroom modifications that include work-related functional skills and supported employment would be directed at changing Frank's attitude toward school. The biophysical model suggests that we examine Frank's medical history. Perhaps he has allergies that set off impulsive and aggressive behavior.

In the following sections, we describe functional characteristics on which most professionals agree. The brevity of this section is testimony to the need of professionals to consolidate theoretical models in order to present a less fractured and more comprehensive description of students with emotional disturbance.

COGNITIVE

Students classified with emotional disturbance usually score in the low-average range (75–100) on standardized tests of intelligence. Some professionals argue that emotional problems can cause individual students to perform poorly on intelligence tests. Anyone who is accustomed to taking standardized tests readily reports feelings of anxiety prior to and during testing. For children with minimal ability to cope with stress, an IQ test can be overwhelming. These students will give up, guess wildly at answers, or refuse to continue.

Students with behavior disorders proceed through the same stages of cognitive development as other children: sensory-motor, preoperational, concrete, and formal. Selman (1980) applied Piaget's developmental scheme to social perception, and he suggested that children go through four stages before they are fully capable of socialized thought. Paul and Epanchin (1991) summarized Selman's model:

> First, the child is in a fully egocentric state and is unable to differentiate the points of view of others. Second, the child can consider other people's ideas in a rudimentary way and realizes their thoughts can be different from his own. However, he has difficulty understanding exactly what the differences are. Third, although the child cannot consider others and his own perspectives simultaneously, he can sequentially consider first his own perspective and then another's perspective. Finally, the child is able to think about both perspectives at the same time in an integrated manner, as well as having a "third person" perspective in which he can figuratively step back from the interaction and examine both sides' point of view. (p. 195)

As children develop cognitively, they are more capable of understanding a situation from another's point of view. They recognize how their behavior affects others. They are able to identify their own feelings, and they empathize with the feelings of others (Erickson, 1998).

Students with emotional disturbance are delayed in their social-cognitive development. They literally forget their own contributions to conflict. Their memories seem to evaporate when they are asked to recall how their actions contributed to a classroom disruption (Henley & Long, 1999). They seem to be able to recall only the behavior of others while they remain steadfast in their own innocence. These students cannot apply past experiences to present situations. As often as a student will experience peer retribution for teasing or belittling others, the student does not change tactics that goad others into retaliation. They do not understand how their behavior affects others in a negative way. Students with these types of delay are unable to learn from the experience of others, and they possess minimal strategies for solving social problems. If another youngster is disapproving, the student with emotional and social problems will maintain a fixed and predictable response such as a temper tantrum, sulking, scapegoating, or fighting.

These students need practice in developing social problem-solving skills. Included among these needed skills are anticipating consequences, learning from past experiences, and understanding how their behavior affects others (Henley, 2004).

Academic

Many students with emotional disturbance do not like school. Some professionals believe these students fail because they have not developed academic survival skills (e.g., finishing tasks, following directions, adjusting to classroom routines). Other professionals maintain that emotional problems (e.g., anxiety, low self-esteem, depression) prevent students from doing well. Although researchers tend to focus on independent variables—for example, task engagement—when in reality a given student could be limited by all these characteristics.

For the classroom teacher, the main difficulty is motivation. These students have limited faith in their ability to learn. Their whole school experience has been testimony to their inadequacies. Because their behavior has been a consistent liability, they have internalized feelings of worthlessness. This makes learning a formidable task. Suppose you were on a ski slope taking your first lesson, but you were absolutely convinced you were going to fall. How far do you think you'd make it down the slope without falling? When it comes to learning, students with emotional disturbance see themselves as always falling down.

> **SPEEDBUMP**—Mandated testing required by the No Child Left Behind Act makes it even more difficult for students to achieve. About 50 percent of these students with emotional problems drop out of school.

More than anything else these students need success in school. Learning requires risk taking and a willingness to change; students with social and emotional behavior problems have spent much of their lives resisting change. Sameness, even if unpleasant, provides security. For a student with emotional disturbance, learning to read can be a fearful experience. Reading may mean loss of control because it is change, and if one thing about a person's life changes, what is next? Fritz Redl and David Wineman (1951) called this resistance to change *newness panic*. The student is overwhelmed by apprehension when confronted with new or different experiences. This makes teaching students with emotional disturbance difficult.

A secure classroom environment is the first priority. Unless psychological and physical safety is maintained, the student will be overcome by real or imagined threats and the ensuing anxiety will disrupt learning. Next, the students need to derive some personal meaning from school activities. As discussed in the previous section, students with emotional disturbance are egocentric. Schoolwork that relates to their day-to-day lives enables students to personalize their learning. Teachers can make learning relevant by emphasizing students' interests, using humor, and developing functional lessons to teach skills. Activities such as rope climbing and challenge courses help to develop risk-taking behavior and enhance self-confidence. Finally, students need reminders of their progress. Positive feedback about emerging skills helps to consolidate gains and encourages perseverance.

Think of student development as a series of upward spiraling circles. Be prepared for regression following progress. This natural cycle of growth and backsliding is normal (Long, 1986). When teaching students who have social and emotional problems, it is easy to overlook how far they have come. Others who have a long-range view, such as administrators or counselors, can help keep intermittent reversals in perspective.

Many special education teachers are cloistered with eight to ten students in a single classroom. These teachers are expected to bring their students up to grade level, while also teaching them how to behave properly. This is a difficult task. Students are put in special education programs because they need to learn new behaviors. In a special class, there are no models for appropriate behavior. Regrettably, the reality of the situation is that the teacher is "keeping the lid on" a group of youngsters that other teachers won't tolerate in their classrooms. The burnout rate among teachers of students with emotional disturbance is extremely high.

Despite the negative programmatic aspects of self-contained classrooms, these socially isolating environments serve the administrative purpose of making the problem go away. Unless the emphasis in regular classrooms changes to preventive discipline and the teaching of prosocial behaviors becomes a legitimate part of the curriculum, the label emotional disturbance will continue to be a one-way ticket into segregated, self-contained special education programs.

Communication

For students with emotional disturbance, words are both sword and shield. Their verbal outbursts of hostility outrage others, while their facile excuses keep them, in their own minds, free of responsibility. The inability to communicate feelings in a socially appropriate manner results in resentment and misunderstandings between these students and others. Resentment, fear, apprehension, and other tumultuous feelings are acted out rather than discussed. At the same time, students with emotional disturbance can use language in finely executed performances of manipulation. Students who are hostile know just what to say to get others to respond in kind. For example, students who whine and complain cause others to withdraw from them.

Like a crafty salesperson, troubled youngsters solicit feedback that reaffirms their position. The more angry or caustic the teacher or student response, the more secure a youngster is in the knowledge that others are indeed out to get him or her. The student with emotional disturbance needs negative feedback to keep his or her world steady and predictable. Why change one's behavior if it is clear that others are unable to change theirs? As long as teachers threaten, criticize, and shout, a student with a behavior disorder remains in control. The student pulls the strings, and the adults and peers in the classroom put on the show.

Ginott believed teachers can short-circuit this closed system of emotional turmoil through "congruent communication." Charles (1989) defined **congruent communication** as "a harmonious and authentic way of talking in which teacher messages to students match the students' feelings about situations and themselves." Students need teachers to model communication methods that highlight verbal expression of feelings in appropriate ways. For example, Ginott advocated "sane messages." When addressing student disruption, sane messages describe the situation rather than criticizing the student. Sane messages give students the opportunity to assess a situation and to understand why a behavior is disruptive. Sane messages describe the area of concern rather than blaming, preaching, or criticizing students. As an illustration, two students are arguing about who is first in line; an "insane message" is, "You two are always causing trouble; both of you sit down and wait for everybody else to leave." In this situation, the students may feel attacked, and they have no opportunity to learn from the situation. A contrasting sane message would be, "When you act like that it takes longer for all of us to get to lunch; you have to take turns." The explanation provides insight into *why* the teacher is disturbed and describes a more acceptable behavior.

According to Ginott, through modeling, the teacher helps students to express their feelings and communicate their needs. "I messages," for example, help students understand that teachers do indeed have feelings. Statements like "I am disappointed" or "I am angry" are better than "You are a nuisance" or "You ruin everything for everybody else." Teachers accept and acknowledge feelings when they avoid negative communication modes such as sarcasm and verbal insults. One of Ginott's more novel observations is the perils of praise. Praise creates a dependence on others for approval. Judgmental praise such as "You are a good girl" or "I really like the way you are acting" reinforces the need to look to others for self-worth. What of the student on the other side of the room who was equally "good"? Ginott underscores the need for teachers to understand that for every student who stands in the spotlight, 20 or so are going to feel left out. Charles (1989) has summarized Ginott's main points:

1. Good classroom discipline begins with the teacher's self-discipline.
2. Use sane messages when correcting misbehavior.
3. Teachers at their worst attack and label student characters.
4. Teachers should model the type of communication they expect from students.
5. Anger and other feelings should be expressed in sane ways.
6. Avoid sarcasm and be judicious with praise.
7. The best teachers build self-esteem and help students to trust and express their own feelings.

Social-Adaptive

A student is referred for special education services for emotional disturbance when a teacher notes frequent and chronic behavior that is markedly different from peers. Difference in behavior is based on teacher expectations and judgments. Authoritarian teachers prize student behavior that is compliant and conforming. Teachers who depend on workbooks, worksheets, and other repetitive instructional materials view students who don't "stay on task" as disturbing. Teachers who encourage students to ask questions, express their opinions, and participate in group discussions would more likely view a passive and quiet student as disturbing.

Behavior should not be separated from the context in which it is viewed or judged. Apter (1982) emphasized the interactional aspect of behavior disorders when he commented that ". . . what we know as emotional disturbance or behavior disorders actually result from discrepancies between a given child's skills and abilities and the demands or expectations of that child's environment" (p. 2). A student who is loud and aggressive may be disturbing in school, but on city streets he could be a leader. Students who are unable or unwilling to adapt to the expectations of classroom life are most likely to be referred to special education.

Achenbach and Edelbrook (1981) distinguished between internalizing and externalizing behavior problems. Internalized problems are those manifested when a student turns inward because of emotional or social conflict. Anxiety, fears, social withdrawal, and immaturity are examples of internalized problems. Aggression, noncompliance, and open hostility are examples of externalized behavior problems; they are more obvious (and get more attention) because they are disruptive.

Externalized behaviors, because they are the most difficult to deal with, are more frequently used as indicators of behavior disorders. Although all children may fight, bully, or argue, students classified with behavior disorders engage in these behaviors repeatedly. Teachers refer students because they find disciplinary measures are ineffective in controlling or minimizing externalized behaviors. Though less frequently noted, such internalized behaviors as poor self-esteem, moodiness, depression, and social withdrawal also are difficult to change. Internalized students often are overlooked in teacher's judgments about who has an emotional problem.

As children pass through developmental stages of social maturity, they acquire self-control skills that help them to restrain their impulses, assess social reality, manage group pressure, deal with stress, and solve problems in relationships. Impulse maintenance includes the ability to deal with frustration, to self-regulate behavior, and to understand that temptations are accompanied by consequences. When assessing social reality, youngsters need to be realistic about rules and routines, evaluate the effect of their behavior on others, take responsibility for their possessions, and remain reasonable about such gratifications as praise and attention. Peer-management skills include staying calm when others have lost control, managing competitive challenges, and participating in and furthering group activities. Stress management requires coping with anxiety, adjusting to new situations, separating past trauma from present events, and accepting responsibility for actions. Finally, social problem-solving skills include learning from experience, noting one's effect on others, and drawing inferences from others' experiences (Erickson, 1998; Henley, 2004). (These skills are discussed in greater detail in Chapter 10.)

The less capable a student is in each self-control skill, the more likely the youngster will encounter social problems in school. Teachers who understand that the misbehavior they encounter in the classroom is based on frustration or stress are likely to demonstrate what Fritz Redl and David Wineman (1951) referred to as symptom tolerance. Simply stated: when teachers don't personalize disruptive behavior but try to understand not only the behavior but the child as well, dealing with the behavior is easier. When teachers believe a child is intentionally being disruptive or mean or selfish, it is difficult to squelch the adult impulse to "put the kid in her place"; "show him who is boss"; or "not let the kid run all over me." No child chooses to be unhappy in school; every child wants to be liked and admired. By working to understand the students you deal with, you will find the best way to deal with their behavior. Some general suggestions for teaching students with behavior disorders are presented in Figure 4.5.

SPEEDBUMP—Have you seen the movie *Dangerous Minds*? It is based on a true story. The teacher, Ms. Johnson, learns not to take misbehavior personally. It is one of her most important insights.

POSITIVE BEHAVIOR SUPPORT

Positive behavior support (PBS) is a schoolwide system that defines, teaches, and encourages appropriate behavior in children (OSEP Center on Positive Behavioral Interventions and Supports, 2005). In schools that have been successful building PBS systems, the

FIGURE 4.5   Suggestions for Teaching Students with Behavior Disorders

1. Recognize the differences between disturbing and disturbed behavior.
2. Look for classroom routines, lessons, and discipline practices that may contribute to behavior problems.
3. Consider diet, allergies, and other physical causes for disturbing behavior.
4. With hyperactive students, change classroom routines before going along with drug treatment.
5. Trust is the basis for social–emotional growth. Work to develop a trusting relationship with a disturbing student.
6. Use behavior modification in a systematic fashion. Don't use behavior modification as a way of rationalizing punishment.
7. Make a home and neighborhood visit of each student in your class and determine adaptive skills required for environments outside of school.
8. Present lessons in a format that connects to the personal experience of your students.
9. Assess the impact of such real-life issues as teenage pregnancy, drugs, and depression on your students.
10. Model the language and behavior that you want to foster in your students.

following procedures have been established (Colvin, Kame'enui, & Sugai, 1993; Lewis & Sugai, 1999; Sugai & Horner, 1999; Todd, Horner, Sugai, & Sprague, 1999).

1. Identify a small number of clearly defined behavioral expectations and present them as positive, simple rules. For example, follow all adult directions promptly or be respectful to yourself and others.
2. Teach the behavioral expectation to all students in the school using the same instructional formats applied to other curriculum content: Present the general rule, discuss the rationale for the rule, describe and rehearse positive examples (right way), describe and model negative examples (wrong way), and provide opportunities for students to practice the right way until they demonstrate fluent performance.
3. Acknowledge appropriate behavior on a regular basis using formal systems (e.g., tickets, rewards) or social events (e.g., Friday Fun Time). When teachers are successful in creating a positive behavior learning environment, their interactions with students are positive four times as often as they are negative.
4. Establish clear procedures for providing information to students that their behavior was unacceptable. Students, teachers, and administrators all should be able to predict what will occur when behavioral errors are identified.

PBS interventions are proactive and designed to prevent problem behavior by altering a situation before problems escalate while concurrently teaching appropriate alternatives (Safran & Oswald, 2003). When *universal schoolwide interventions* are designed for all students, positive effects also can be achieved for individuals with severe difficulties. PBS also can be applied as *secondary-level interventions* with small groups of students and in specific settings such as hallways, playgrounds, and cafeterias or as *tertiary-level interventions* with individual students experiencing chronic difficulties. Although research offers several guiding principles, individual schools must collaboratively shape PBS to fit their own unique needs; the key factors to be included are using collaborative team problem solving and research-based interventions, using multiple data sources for planning and evaluating, and using positive strategies to reduce punitive disciplinary practices.

Students with emotional disturbance receive special education because they have mood and social problems that require attention from teachers, parents, and other professionals if they are to be successful in school (Ysseldyke & Algozzine, 1995; Erickson, 1998). **Emotional problems** stem from unproductive personal ways of managing stress or activities (e.g., inappropriate types of behaviors or feelings, tendency to develop physical symptoms or fears). For example, one child's response to having to wait for the school bus might be to become impatient while another's might be to become very anxious. Low self-esteem and limited self-control are common emotional problems of students with behavior disorders. **Social problems** are unproductive ways individuals respond in situations involving interactions with other people (e.g., inability to maintain satisfactory interpersonal relationships). Disruptiveness is a common social problem of students receiving special education for behavior disorders.

Treatment Approaches

When you look in classrooms, you probably will see evidence of many approaches used in combination. For example, one student may be taking medication to control hyperactivity and other students may be participating in a behavior modification system designed to reinforce work completion. The teacher is likely to have the room organized in a manner that encourages student participation through learning centers or discussion groups. You may see many self-concept materials on display. One or two of the students may be in counseling either in school or after school at private agencies.

If you were to look at the teacher's lesson plans or the students' IEPs, you should see goals and objectives that center on improving interpersonal skills and reducing behavior problems. You also would see academic textbooks and other instructional materials that are the same as those used in general education classrooms. Finally, if you observed the teacher working with the students, you would see the same type of positive teaching behaviors you would expect to see in any classroom—special or regular. The differences that have come to be identified with some students are a function of assumptions people have about the nature of emotional disturbance. This perspective is evident in the diversity of definitions that are used to describe troubled students in today's schools.

Distribution of Emotional Disturbance. The prevalence of emotional disturbance is reflected in the numbers of children who are served under the Individuals with Disabilities Education Act of 1997 and rates of identification and placement differed among cultural groups (U.S. Department of Education, 2002; 2007b). For example, for the 2000–2001 school year, white students made up 62.3 percent of the students served; 19.8 percent were African American; 14.5 percent were Hispanic; 1.9 percent were Asian/Pacific Islander; and 1.5 percent were American Indian/Alaska Native (U.S. Department of Education, 2002). In the 2003–2004 school year, emotional disturbance was also among the five largest disabilities for all racial/ethnic groups except Asian/Pacific Islander and African

American students were 2.3 times more likely to receive special education and related services for emotional disturbance than all other racial/ethnic groups combined. (U.S. Department of Education, 2007b).

SUMMARY

Emotional disturbance in students are one of the three prevalent mild disabilities identified in schools. Students are referred for special education programs when their behavior is perceived to be disturbed or disturbing. Teachers like Fred Peterson, Ms. Hildago, and Alice often report that these students are among the most difficult to teach. There are no absolute standards to judge the presence of normal or abnormal behavior. Frequently, judgments represent opinions about the appropriateness of behavior in a specific classroom. Normality and abnormality are relative concepts that are derived from the interaction of the actor, the observer, and the environment. Reactions to behavior vary according to the skills, expectations, and tolerance of the teacher. A single indication of the relativity inherent in the category of emotional disturbance is the variance in state prevalence figures and differences in state criteria for identifying students.

Over the years, the study of emotional disturbance has been based in four theoretical viewpoints. The biophysical perspective emphasizes the relationship between body chemistry and behavior. The psychodynamic is concerned with feelings, family history, and relationship building. The psychoeducational framework is developmental in nature. It integrates clinical insights in behavior with practical methods for managing behavior. The behaviorist position views observable behavior as the critical element. Treatment strategies are focused on modifying environmental factors that reinforce appropriate behavior.

A synthesis of these models highlights the interactional nature of emotional disturbance. The ecological model promotes the notion that children are influenced by many different environments and that any attempt to help children with social or emotional problems must focus on all key elements in a youngster's life.

ACTIVITIES

1. Invite teachers such as Fred Peterson, Ms. Hildago, and Alice who work with students with behavior disorders to your class. Ask them to describe the behaviors of the students with whom they work. How do these behaviors differ from those of general education students? Ask them to talk about special interventions that might be done in general and special education classrooms. What recommendations would each of them make about teaching both social and academic skills?

2. As a class, brainstorm a list of disruptive classroom behaviors. Identify each behavior as disturbed or disturbing. Are some behaviors rated as both disturbed and disturbing? Does the degree of intensity and duration influence perceptions of whether a particular behavior is rated as disturbed or disturbing? Now look at the behaviors from a different point of view. Rate each on a 1–5 scale of disturbance based on the perception of a traditional educator who controls his or her classroom so that students sit in rows and must remain quiet and comply with all teacher directives. Then do the same exercise based on how you think a

proactive teacher—one who uses cooperative learning, activity centers, and differentiated instruction—would rate each behavior. Do you have different ratings based on different perceptions? Discuss your findings.

3. Beat the authors! Go online and locate publishers and organizations that provide information on emotional disturbance. Review four or five sites. See if you can locate information not provided in this chapter. Email the principal author at mhenley@wsc.ma.edu and describe what you discovered. Explain briefly why it should be included in the next edition of this text. You will get a rapid reply and be notified if you will be credited in the next edition of this text.

4. In teams of three or four, review the five chapters that comprise this section of the text. For each chapter, write 10 fill-in-the-blank questions. Be certain the answer is the only one that clearly fits the question. Arrange the questions in order of difficulty and put in the categories of learning disabilities, emotional disturbance, foundations of special education, mild intellectual disabilities, and overview of mild disabilities. Play classroom *Jeopardy*.

5. View a video of the film *White Oleander*. Discuss the difficulties faced by foster children. What type of emotional problems are likely to develop from exposure to dysfunctional relationships? Is Astrid a survivor, disturbed or disturbing? What social and school policies could best serve children like Astrid? Do you think the film is an accurate portrayal of foster care?

CHAPTER FIVE

STUDENTS WITH SPECIFIC
LEARNING DISABILITIES

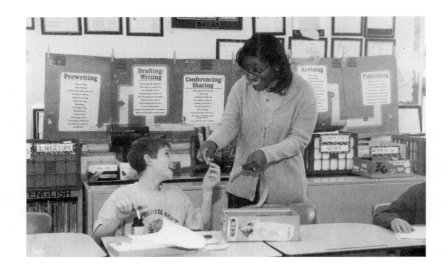

ADVANCE QUESTIONS

Answer the following questions as you read this chapter:

1. What are the most common terms used to describe learning disabilities today?
2. Why do you think students with learning disabilities were "misclassified"?
3. How has brain research contributed to our knowledge of learning disabilities?
4. What are believed to be causes of learning disabilities?
5. How is learning disabilities defined? How did IDEA 2004 change the way in which students with learning disabilities are determined eligible?
6. What are the pros and cons of using the discrepancy approach and the response-to-intervention (RTI) approach when identifying students eligible for specific learning disabilities?
7. What is the prevalence of learning disabilities? Can you explain the relationship between identification criteria and the numbers of students who receive special education?
8. What are the primary characteristics of students with learning disabilities?

9. What are the general interventions and instructional procedures used by teachers of students with learning disabilities?

10. What are some specific activities that teachers use to improve academic and interpersonal skills of students with learning disabilities?

11. Identify major characteristics of young adults who have learning disabilities. Compare the characteristics of young adults with learning disabilities to those of children with learning disabilities.

12. What are some suggestions that might be helpful to college students with learning disabilities?

VIGNETTE: DAVID

David, an active and friendly child, progressed through preschool with some minor behavior problems. His year in kindergarten was without incident, and his parents recalled that he was excited and happy to be going to school. He was particularly fond of the learning games and activities that the teacher had the children play.

It was surprising then, when during 1st grade, David displayed ambivalence about school. Some days he seemed excited about going. On other days, he cried to stay home. David's parents talked with his teacher about his scratchy-looking printing and his problems with reading and spelling vocabulary words. The teacher always assured them that David was ahead of the class in math, and in fact, the teacher was impressed with the way in which David could add and subtract numbers in his head.

By 2nd grade, it was apparent that David was unable to associate sounds with letters of the alphabet. The letters he wrote down for his spelling words showed little relationship to the sounds that the words made when spoken. Interestingly, David still was well ahead of his classmates in math. He did make careless mistakes aligning numbers when writing them down during seatwork. His teacher said that he needed to space his numbers more carefully so that he wouldn't make addition or subtraction errors—and if he would just try as hard in reading and spelling as he did in math, he would do fine.

When David entered 3rd grade, he was unable to read or spell on grade level with his classmates and was making poor grades in these subjects.

Finally, in 4th grade, David's teacher referred him to the prereferral assistance team for prereferral interventions. The team studied David's learning capabilities and performance, and made suggestions about ways in which David could best learn. Instead of using phonics and trying to teach him sound–symbol relationships, the team recommended a sight approach. In addition, David's teacher used line cues to help him in his number spacing in math so that his numbers didn't get out of line and appear so confusing to him. The teacher talked with David's parents about his pattern of school problems and asked them to confirm that David's hearing was all right. These techniques seemed to help, but David needed more intense instruction using similar types of learning strategies. (Refer to Figure 5.4 and Table 5.4 for ideas about special instructional strategies.) Thus, David's teacher referred him for a special education evaluation.

Now that you have read the vignette about David, see how many problem-solving questions you can answer. For those that you cannot readily answer, think about them as you read the chapter. David's story typifies that of other youngsters with learning disabilities.

1. Why do you think that David's attitude toward school became more negative each year?
2. Why was David having difficulties with spelling and reading? Why was math a better subject area for him?
3. How was David's handwriting affecting his school work?
4. How did the prereferral assistance team assist David's teacher in working with him? How did their suggestions help?

FOUNDATIONS OF LEARNING DISABILITIES

Of the current disability categories named in the Individuals with Disabilities Education Act, specific learning disability is the fastest growing and most controversial condition. Since 1975, millions of students have been identified as "learning disabled" and treated in public schools and clinical programs by educators, psychologists, and physicians.

Because each profession tends to view phenomena from a distinctive perspective, it is difficult to get professional agreement about what a learning disability is and how it should be treated. To a pediatrician, a learning disability is a mild neurological disorder. To a teacher, a learning disability is a reading, writing, or math deficiency. To an ophthalmologist, a learning disability is a visual tracking problem. To a speech-and-language pathologist, a learning disability is a deficit in vocabulary and syntactic development. Each of these professionals will evaluate, describe, and treat learning disabilities in terms of his or her own professional point of view. Much of the confusion can be cleared up by recognizing that there are many types of learning disabilities. Throughout the past 40 years, many different terms have been used to indicate a learning disability (Table 5.1).

One type of specific learning disability is **dyslexia**, an impairment in reading ability. Students with dyslexia have difficulty decoding letters. For example, a student might not be able to tell the difference between letters that have a similar shape such as b, p, and d, or the student might confuse the sounds of long and short vowels such as o and e. Many educators believe dyslexia is caused by crossed signals in the area of the brain that interprets and gives meaning to words. A mild neurological impairment is the most widely accepted explanation for the cause of a learning disability. It is important, however, not to jump to conclusions too quickly about the diagnosis of dyslexia. It is common for children to mispronounce letters and numbers as their nervous systems are maturing.

> **SPEEDBUMP**—Do you know anyone with a learning disability? If so, does this person have problems with reading? Under what circumstances have you heard people using the term *dyslexia*?

Terms used to identify specific learning disabilities typically begin with the prefix *dys*, which means an impairment in a particular ability, as in *dysfunctional* (Table 5.2). Mild neurological dysfunction cannot be proved by a standardized test. A neurological examination (including a detailed medical history, an examination of cranial nerves, an

TABLE 5.1   Terms Used to Describe Learning Disabilities Over the Past 40 Years

Attention Deficit Disorder	Perceptual Handicap
Minimal Brain Dysfunction	Behavior Disordered
Hyperactivity	Hyperkinesis
Educationally Handicapped	Impulsive
Strauss Syndrome	Strephosymbolia
Dyslexia	Word Blindness
Psycholinguistic Disorder	Multisensory Disorder
Neurologically Handicapped	Slow Learner
Reading Disability	Dyscalculia
Dysgraphia	Dysphasic
Organic Brain Dysfunction	Puzzle Children
Minimal Cerebral Palsy	Neurologically Immature
Developmentally Delayed	Mildly Handicapped
Hypoactivity	Language Disordered
Delayed Learner	Neurophrenia
Congenital Alexia	Diffuse Brain Damaged
Association Deficit Pathology	Organicity
Primary Reading Retardation	Maturation Lag

assessment of motor function, and an electroencephalogram [EEG]) *may* be able to confirm a neurological basis for a student's learning problems.

Other types of learning disabilities are more generalized in terms of behavior or cognitive difficulties. Students who are hyperactive or distractible sometimes are called *learning disabled*. Students who are disorganized and have difficulty following directions may be identified with learning disabilities. Poor coordination, problems with short-term memory, perceptual problems, limited concentration, speech deficits, inadequate verbal skills, and problems with becoming easily frustrated are just a sample of characteristics that have been attributed to learning disabilities.

Distinguishing the student with learning disabilities from the underachiever is a major challenge facing educators today. In recent years, almost 5 percent of the school population of students aged 6 to 17 received special education services because of a presumed learning disability. Although the U.S. Department of Education has consistently stated that a range of 2 to 3 percent is a more reasonable **prevalence** figure for learning disabilities, the actual number of students identified across the nation and served in the specific learning disabilities category continues to increase. Many students may be misclassified with specific learning disabilities, while others remain unidentified.

Early Research on Learning Disabilities

Barsch was one of the first professionals to point out the need to look more closely at learning disabilities as a possible explanation for the failure of some children to make adequate progress in school (1968):

TABLE 5.2   Specific Learning Disabilities

Each of these specific learning disabilities is generally believed to be caused by an impairment in nervous system functioning.

Dyslexia	A language-based reading disability. The individual has trouble understanding words, sentences, and/or paragraphs.
Dysgraphia	Difficulty forming letters correctly or within a defined space. Mirror writing is a severe form of this impairment.
Dysacusis	Impairment in understanding and deriving meaning from speech.
Dyskinesia	Clumsiness or poor coordination.
Dyscalculia	A mathematical disability in which a person has difficulty solving arithmetic problems and grasping math concepts.
Dyslogia	A linguistic disturbance characterized by faulty formation or expression of verbal ideas.
Dysphasia	An impairment in the ability to produce or comprehend language. It can affect either written or spoken language function.
Dysnomia	Difficulty in searching for and thinking of a word to express a thought or idea.
Dysrhythmia	Poor rhythm or the loss of ability to move with rhythm.
Auditory and Visual Processing Disorders	Sensory disabilities in which an individual has difficulty understanding language in these modalities despite normal hearing and vision.
Nonverbal Learning Disability	Well-developed verbal and auditory abilities accompanied by difficulties in coordination, visual–spatial organization, and social relationships.
Hyperlexia	Precocious reading ability with concurrent difficulties in communication and social skills.

> The failing learner is no longer a statistic of minor significance. Academic failure, learning inefficiency, anxiety barriers, dismissals, expulsions, dropouts, reading retardation, and a host of other problems are rampant on the educational scene. The percentages of failing students is increasing annually. . . . The problem is immediate upon the educational terrain: the confrontation is compelling and vibrant and the pressure for action is inescapable. (pp. 7, 10)

Barsch's remarks, which appeared in the first issue of the *Journal of Learning Disabilities*, signaled a shift toward considering the possibility that some problem learners had a learning disability. Barsch's comments linked 30 years of research with brain-injured individuals to remedial services for students in public schools.

Misclassified Mentally Retarded Students.   In the 1950s, Samuel Kirk discovered that a number of persons had been **misclassified** as mentally retarded at the Wayne County Training School in Northville, Michigan. Kirk could not justify classifying these pupils as having mental retardation for several reasons. First, the intelligence quotient (IQ) scores of these students were too high; second, after intensive remediation in reading, they made extraordinary progress. Similar gains were rarely made by their counterparts with mental retardation.

> All of the children I taught . . . were classified as mentally retarded. In all of these cases my purpose was to show through the results of remediation that these children should have been classified as learning disabled instead of mentally retarded, since they were normal in some respects but had specific disabilities. (Kirk, 1976, 260)

Many of these individuals eventually left the institution and became self-supporting (Kirk, 1976). These misclassified individuals inspired Kirk to do further research to determine the nature of their disabilities. Kirk's findings paralleled earlier research on patients with brain injuries. In the early 1930s, Kurt Goldstein had observed perseveration, figure-ground confusion, and forced responses to stimuli in adults who had suffered brain injury (Goldstein, 1942).

SPEEDBUMP—Isn't it strange that people could actually be misclassified as mentally retarded? How could such a thing happen? What is the term that the authors use in place of mentally retarded?

Heinz Werner (1944) and Alfred Strauss and Laura Lehtinen (1947) followed similar research avenues. They identified and described exogenously brain-damaged (i.e., point of origin of disability outside the body) children with mental retardation. The disabilities of these children could not be traced to genetic causes. Their behavior was characterized as perceptually disordered, impulsive, distractible, and repetitive. This condition became known as *Strauss syndrome*. Later, during the 1960s, William Cruickshank (1967) was instrumental in changing the focus of research from exogenous retardation to minimally brain-damaged (MBD) children with normal intelligence. Cruickshank's identification of Strauss syndrome characteristics in children with average intelligence was a pivotal turning point in the study of learning disabilities (Figure 5.1).

Supporters of Learning Disabilities.   The movement to gain recognition for children with Strauss syndrome took a giant step forward in 1963 when Kirk proposed the term **learning disability** in a speech at a special education parents' conference. Previously, professionals had used many different terms to identify the same children. By using the term *learning disabilities* as an umbrella concept to cover children who had been variously called minimally brain damaged, perceptually handicapped, minimally brain dysfunctional, or language delayed, advocates were able to join forces and push for federal legislation to provide remedial school services for those students.

Critics of Learning Disabilities.   The category of learning disabilities evolved as a means of addressing a condition that did not fit into preexisting classifications of exceptionality (e.g., mental retardation, emotional disturbance). Some educators think that the label is a convenience because students with learning disabilities usually have average or above intelligence, and primarily come from middle-class backgrounds. The critics

FIGURE 5.1   Strauss Syndrome, Characteristics of Brain-Damaged Children

These are general behaviors that Strauss and Werner believed characterized brain-injured children. These characteristics influenced the later work of William Cruickshank with nonretarded children and led to treatment in classrooms that were devoid of distractions. Study carrels, which still are found in many resource rooms, are artifacts of instructional programs that were designed to focus the attention of students who exhibited Strauss syndrome characteristics.

1. Forced responsiveness to stimuli—Any noise or movement distracted the child: a pencil dropping on the floor, the sound of cars driving outside a window, a student passing by. This is different than distractibility caused by boredom.
2. Pathological fixation—The child perseverated. Once engaged in a motor task, the child repeated movements over and over. An example is a student who rubs a hole in a work sheet with an eraser. Perseveration can affect thinking, talking, or movement.
3. Disinhibition—Excessive motor activity. Now commonly referred to as hyperactivity. Strauss found that children with brain damage were attracted to specific features of objects. The "bounciness" of a ball or the "jabbiness" of a pencil would seduce the child into bouncing or jabbing.
4. Dissociation—The child was unable to integrate or see the "whole picture." For example, a student would have difficulty seeing how the parts of a puzzle fit together. The child was disorganized. This integration problem inspired Werner's famous Marble Board experiments where students were asked to repeat patterns of red and black marbles on 11-inch squares with 10 lines and 10 holes to each line. Children who were unable to copy the patterns were identified as dissociated in their conceptual reasoning.

Sources: Derived from Farnham-Diggory, 1978; Bruner, Cole, and Lloyd, 1978.

believe that the identification of a learning disability is a way for students to get special education services without anyone being held accountable for the problem. The student is blameless because the problem is assumed to be neurological in nature. Parents are blameless because the learning problem is not caused by inadequate parenting. Finally, teachers are blameless because the students' presumed neurological impairment, rather than inadequate instruction, is the reason for school failure.

Coles (1989) suggested that the term *learning disabilities* is popular because it explains and justifies poor school performance by focusing on presumed characteristics and attributes found within the child. Bartoli (1989) proposed that instead of leaning on neurological dysfunction solely, we also should consider the child's learning curriculum, classroom dynamics, our means of testing student progress, the overall school climate, teacher-parent relationships, family socioeconomics, and the values of the community. In other words, we need to look at the child's entire learning situation and environment.

Brain Research

The human brain weighs less than 5 pounds, and it can store more information than all the libraries of the world. In appearance, it resembles a soft, wrinkled walnut. It communicates with itself through 10 billion neurons and a hundred billion neuron connections (Restak, 1984). Neuroscientists approach the study of the brain with the same awe most of us reserve for space travel and exploration of the universe. We have much to learn about brain function, thinking, and learning disabilities. Modern technology, through the use of computerized axial tomography (CAT) scans and positron emission photography (PET) scans, can provide a detailed picture of brain function in living patients. Unfortunately, these medical techniques are far too complex and expensive to be helpful to school evaluation teams.

It is possible to detect brain anomalies in persons with severe learning disabilities. In 1861, Paul Broca, a French neuro-anatomist, exhibited the brain of a deceased patient who had a severe communication impairment. His intelligence was average and he showed no indication of emotional disturbance. Broca called his patient "Tan-Tan" because those were the only words the man could utter. Tan-Tan understood speech and communicated through gestures. Only Tan-Tan's speaking ability was impaired. The brain Broca exhibited had observable damage in a circumscribed 2-inch area of the left hemisphere, including the lower portion of the frontal lobe, the lower portion of the parietal lobe, and the upper part of the temporal lobe. Broca convinced his colleagues that Tan-Tan's speech impairment (known today as *aphasia*) was the result of an insult to the brain. Broca was one of the first contributors to the theory that language ability is localized in the left hemisphere of the brain (Restak, 1984).

SPEEDBUMP—What an odd story. Why don't you get on the Internet and see if you can find out anything more about Tan-Tan or Paul Broca. Carl Sagan wrote an interesting story about what Paul Broca did with his own brain in the book called—of course—*Broca's Brain*.

The Russian psychologist Aleksandr Luria believed, as Broca did, that certain mental abilities were localized in specific areas of the brain. For instance, visual images are centered in the occipital lobe in the brain. Any damage to the occipital lobe will result in a visual impairment. Luria's work on memory, particularly with his most famous patient "S," documented the relationship between visual imagery and memory.

Luria's work with patients who suffered from ***dyscalculia*** (impaired ability to do arithmetic) demonstrated how defects in spatial logic, mathematical planning, and calculating could be traced to defects in specific areas of the brain. For example, Luria presented the case of an artillery commander who lost the ability to add, subtract, divide, and multiply after a bullet wound. Surrounding brain tissue was unblemished and other mathematical skills, such as counting and logic, were unaffected. In another illustration, Luria described a female patient who was unable to plan how to solve sequential problems. She became confused when given a three-part problem like: a boy is 8 years old; his father is 30 years older; and the mother is 10 years younger than the father—how old are they? Luria reported that this patient's thinking ability improved after surgical removal of a brain tumor (Farnham-Diggory, 1978; Restak, 1984).

Specific areas of the brain control discrete cognitive functions (Figure 5.2). Robert Sperry's (1968) work with split-brain patients detailed the different ways that the right and left hemispheres of the brain process information. Sperry studied individuals whose corpus

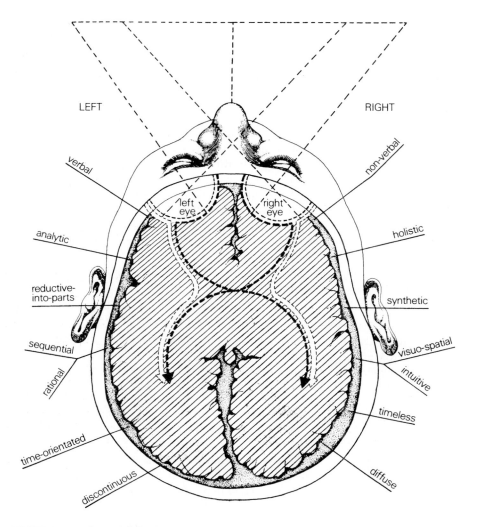

FIGURE 5.2   Areas of the Brain

Source: Hamptden-Turner, Charles. *Maps of the Mind.* London: Mitchell Beazley, 1981. Reprinted with permission.

callosums were severed by surgery in order to diminish uncontrollable seizures. The *corpus callosum* is the bundle of nerves that connects the left and right hemispheres of the brain. It is the line of communication that allows the hemispheres to communicate with each other. Sperry found that the left hemisphere specializes in dealing with things in sequence; the right hemisphere deals with things all at once. The left hemisphere often is characterized as the logical, verbal, and analytical half of the human brain. The right hemisphere is characterized as the intuitive, holistic, and visual half of the brain.

Robert Ornstein, who studied under Sperry, found that his subjects were right- or left-hemispheric oriented; that is, they had a preferred mode of thought. Using EEG measurements of electrical activity in individuals from different occupations, Ornstein discovered that artists relied more on their right hemisphere even when the task required left-hemisphere capabilities. The opposite was true of lawyers; that is, even when the task required right-hemispheric thought, the lawyers tended to process the information through their left hemisphere. Ornstein concluded that the hemispheres are specialized for information processing and that individuals gradually develop a hemispheric preference.

Ornstein also found that the hemispheres of most right-handed people are specialized for specific types of thought along the lines outlined by Sperry—but left-handed individuals, according to Ornstein, sometimes do not follow the standard left-right hemisphere localization of function. According to Ornstein (1978):

> Left-handers often show a reverse specialization, in which some information is processed in the opposite hemisphere from the one used by right-handers. Some left-handers appear to have brains organized like those of right-handers, while others show no specialization at all. Ambidextrous people seem to have the least specialization of all the groups we have tested. (p. 81)

Students with learning disabilities sometimes have a developmental history of mixed dominance (e.g., favoring neither the right nor the left hand). Perhaps the "reverse specialization" that Ornstein discovered in left-handers may provide a clue as to why left-handed children are identified with learning disabilities at a greater rate than right-handed youngsters. In applying his findings to schools, Ornstein (1978) observed:

> Even a casual look at the results of hemisphere research shows that the ways of thinking that seem to be primarily the province of the left hemisphere are used extensively in the basic subjects of the school curriculum. The realization that schools spend most of their time training students in what seem to be left hemisphere skills, and that most educators and taxpayers regard what seem to be right hemisphere skills as frills, has caused many people to wonder whether our educational system is unbalanced. (p. 82)

Ornstein's research indicated that there may be a mismatch between how students process information and how information is presented by teachers. If some students have a preferred mode of right-hemispheric thinking, they will be at a distinct disadvantage in classrooms where the teacher relies heavily on sequenced learning, verbal skills, and analysis of problems (i.e., left-hemispheric material). This supposition is supported by the work of Sally Smith (1980) at the Lab School, a special school for students with learning disabilities in Washington, D.C. Smith has found that her students respond to activities in which the arts (right-hemispheric thinking) are used to teach academic skills. Smith's observation (1980) that ". . . the child with the hidden handicap of learning disability also has a hidden talent in an artistic area because he has learned unique ways of looking at things," sounds very much like Ornstein's description of individuals who prefer right-hemispheric modes of thought.

> **SPEEDBUMP**—This idea that some students are right-hemispheric oriented and some left is controversial. What do you think about yourself? Would you put yourself into either of these two categories?

More recent evidence from the National Institute of Mental Health (NIMH) (1996) shows that most learning disabilities do not stem from a single, specific area or hemisphere of the brain. Rather, difficulties occur when attempting to bring together information from various regions of the brain. These difficulties stem from subtle disturbances in brain structures and functions. For example, a recent study sponsored by NIMH (2003) found an absence of functional linkages between the occipital lobe, which recognizes letters, and the angular gyrus in the left hemisphere, which processes language. Interaction between these regions enables an individual to read.

The NIMH stated that some disturbances in brain structures begin before birth. During pregnancy, the fetal brain develops from a few all-purpose cells into a complex organ made of billions of specialized, interconnected nerve cells called *neurons*. During this evolution, things can go wrong that may alter how the neurons form or interconnect (NIMH, 1996).

Brain development continues throughout pregnancy and therefore is vulnerable to disruptions. If the disruption occurs early, it may be fatal to the fetus, or the infant may be born with disabilities. Disruptions can occur from such occurrences as maternal diseases, trauma, and heredity. If the disruption occurs later, when the brain cells are becoming specialized, errors may occur in the cell make-up, location, or connections. Some of these "errors" are thought by scientists to contribute to learning disabilities. In 1999, scientists identified the first gene linked to dyslexia. Although not considered the only gene that contributes to dyslexia, the discovery confirms a genetic basis for some cases. They mapped the gene DyX3 to chromosome 2 by studying a large Norwegian family in which 11 of 36 members had dyslexia (*New York Times*, Sept. 7, 1999).

SPEEDBUMP—The fetus is vulnerable to toxins during pregnancy, which is why it is so important for pregnant women to avoid alcohol and other drugs. What would you do if you saw a pregnant woman drinking a beer?

Causes of Learning Disabilities

IDEA does not recognize environmental, cultural, or economic factors as primary reasons for a learning disability; however, these factors do impact youth and can cause subsequent disorders. For example, a child born into an impoverished environment may have parents who are economically deprived and educationally deficient. Lack of knowledge about nutrition or exposure to toxic substances (e.g., lead in paint) can cause neurological damage. Insufficient prenatal or inadequate perinatal care, as well as untreated postnatal diseases or trauma (e.g., infections), are contributors to learning disorders. Thus, detrimental environmental factors and biological conditions are interrelated (Smith et al., 1986).

Many of the organic origins of intellectual disabilities can overlap as possible contributors of specific learning disabilities and behavior disorders as well (Ramsey, Dixon, & Smith, 1986). For example, postnatal disorders of encephalitis and meningitis can cause attention disorders, behavior disorders, and mental retardation. Hyperactivity, visual impairments, and deafness can be caused by measles or whooping cough. Anoxia, or oxygen deprivation, can cause brain damage, with resulting learning or behavior disorders. Furthermore, genetic factors may precipitate learning disabilities.

Silver (1989) reported findings from a study of children with learning disabilities who were attending the TRI-Services' Center School in Chevy Chase, Maryland; the Chelsea School in Silver Spring, Maryland; and Pine Ridge School in Williston, Vermont. He calculated that the frequency of learning disabilities was 4.5 times higher among adopted children; according to his study, 17.3 percent of adopted children versus 3.9 percent of biological children. He reported that many adopted children are born out of wedlock to indigent young women. Such mothers are likely to receive less-adequate nutritional and medical care during pregnancy and insufficient emotional support. Pregnancies of young, indigent mothers usually are stressful, and Silver concluded that the mother's tension and anxiety could adversely affect the fetus. Children born to such mothers are slow to mature and sometimes develop learning disabilities.

The fact that learning disabilities tend to turn up in families, some even generations apart, indicates a genetic link. Many times educators have identified learning problems in children only to find that one of their parents had the same problem in school. For example, a young boy is identified as having a problem linking phonetic sounds to letters they represent. It turns out that the boy's father had the same problem when he was trying to learn to read during early grades—or a girl has difficulty expressing herself, and it so happens that her mother always has had this problem. A parent with an expressive language disorder might talk less or use distorted language. In this situation, the child acquired the same problem due to environmental reasons because her mother was a poor language model from which to learn. Of course, it could have also been genetic. In this case, it is difficult to say which was the primary cause—environment or genetics.

A youngster who has difficulty in learning does not necessarily have a specific learning disability, and if a learning disability does exist, other causes are possible. The National Center for Learning Disabilities (NCLD) *IDEA 2004 Parent Guide* suggests looking into other sources as well. This guide includes (NCLD, 2007):

- The school's approach to teaching basic academic skills like reading may not be achieving adequate results for all students.
- Your child's previous learning may not have prepared him or her sufficiently for the lessons the teacher is presenting.
- Cultural and/or language differences can present a barrier to communication with the teacher and prevent access to learning materials.
- Another condition, such as attention difficulties, poor hearing, or vision, may be affecting learning.

DEFINITION AND IDENTIFICATION

In 1975, Congress delayed the passage of the original federal special education law several months while it wrangled with experts and parents over a suitable definition for a learning disability. The expression that a camel is a horse created by a committee aptly applies to the federal definition of a learning disability. It appeases everyone but pleases no one. It is vague in some parts and too specific and exclusive in others. According to the 2004 federal guidelines implemented under (IDEA), *specific learning disability* means

> a disorder in one or more of the basic psychological processes involved in understanding or in using language, spoken or written, which may manifest itself in an imperfect ability to listen, think, speak, read, write, spell, or do mathematical calculations.

The term includes such conditions as perceptual handicaps, brain injury, minimal brain dysfunction, dyslexia, and developmental aphasia. The term does not include children who have learning problems that are primarily the result of visual, hearing, or motor handicaps, of mental retardation, of emotional disturbance, or of environmental, cultural, or economic disadvantage (see P.L. 108–446, 2004 reauthorization of IDEA).

> **SPEEDBUMP**—Virtually no professional is happy with this definition. What are some problems that you can spot?

Major Concepts and Key Phrases

The federal definition for learning disabilities has been criticized because it is broad based and includes undefined terminology. It is helpful to understand the thoughts and concerns that existed when the major concepts and key phrases were first proposed and put into practice in 1975.

Basic Psychological Processes.   This phrase has yet to be specifically defined but refers to the processing functions that any learner must have intact in order to receive, integrate (i.e., organize, associate, store, retrieve), or express information. It infers that learning problems of students in this category are of a neurological nature and that development is uneven due to subtle disorders of mental processing.

Language Based.   The federal definition states that the disorder is language based and occurs in learning situations that involve oral language, listening comprehension, written

■ ■ ■ ■ ■

HIGHLIGHT 5.1
WHAT IS A LEARNING DISABILITY?

In order to help you understand the difficulty in defining a learning disability, here is a brief quiz. First question—what is a table? Nice going—you figured that out without much trouble. When you can see, feel, and eat off something, it's not hard to define. Let's try another. What is the wind? That's a little harder. You can't see the wind, and you don't use it very often (except for some kite flying or sailing if you're fortunate) but you can feel the wind, and it's a common part of life. But did you give a specific definition or did you just describe what it means to you? The more abstract a concept, the further removed from direct experiences (our senses), the harder it is to come up with one definition. Let's extend this thinking to one more question. What is eternity? Now there's an abstract concept. We'll have to accept a lot of different views on this one. We have the same problem with the term "learning disabilities." It is a very abstract idea, and it is interpreted in many different ways.

composition, writing, spelling, reading (e.g., vocabulary, word-attack skills, decoding, comprehension), or arithmetic (e.g., calculation, reasoning, general problem solving). Due to each student's specific processing deficit, uneven abilities are manifested in these language-based areas highlighted in academic tasks.

Inclusion Clause.   The federal definition specifically includes examples of presumed central nervous system deficits like perceptual handicaps, brain injury, minimal brain dysfunction, dyslexia, and developmental aphasia. These deficits are representative of more severe disabilities, and are not typically identified during educational assessment of students with mild learning disabilities.

Exclusion Clause.   The federal definition excludes intellectual disability, emotional disturbance, visual impairments, organic hearing dysfunctions, and motor disabilities as primary causes of learning disabilities, even though these conditions *can coexist* with learning disabilities. According to the definition, a learning disability cannot be attributed to conditions such as environmental, cultural, or economic disadvantage. This part of the exclusion clause is particularly perplexing because it is difficult to determine whether a student's underachievement is due to a subtle central nervous system disorder, delayed developmental growth, inadequate teaching, or a lack of environmental opportunities.

Intellectual Ability.   It is common to hear teachers define a student with learning disabilities as a youngster with *average or above* intelligence who is underachieving. This is misleading, and the results show up in educational programming. As an illustration, a child with Down syndrome has a clear neurological impairment, but rarely does one hear learning disabilities discussed as a contributor to academic problems. Any learning problems a student with Down syndrome has with reading or math are attributed to his or her intellectual disability. The possibility that the student might have dyslexia or some other specific learning disability can be overlooked. For many years, William Cruickshank, a pioneer in the field of learning disabilities, argued against assuming that only children with average or above-average intelligence have learning disabilities.

Achievement.   A learning disabled child is presumably not up to "grade level" in one or more academic subjects. Grade-level work is what 50 percent of the children in a particular grade are doing (p. 5). If grade-level measures are accurate, half the class will always have a discrepancy between their ability and achievement. This leaves us to ponder what a *severe* discrepancy is. According to Smith (1991), 57 percent of the states provide guidelines on how to quantify severe discrepancy. Two or more years below grade level is common. In almost half of the states, the meaning of severe discrepancy is left in the hands of local school systems. Lerner (2000) pointed out that a 1-year delay in reading at age 6 could be more severe than a 3-year delay at age 16.

SPEEDBUMP—This is a lot to remember. To help, focus on this: Average IQ and below-average grade level is the first signal that a learning disability could exist.

The Discrepancy Controversy

Public Law 108-446, the 2004 reauthorization of IDEA, addressed concerns regarding the identification of students when the discrepancy formula was used to determine a learning disability. Before IDEA 2004, a student was identified as having a specific learning disability if a severe discrepancy between achievement and intellectual ability was found. The new bill states (Council for Exceptional Children, 2004):

> A local educational agency shall not be required to take into consideration whether a child has a severe discrepancy between achievement and intellectual ability in oral expression, listening comprehension, written expression, basic reading skill, reading comprehension, mathematical calculation, or mathematical procedures. (p. 14)

Instead of utilizing IQ and achievement tests to determine if a learning disability exists, the language in IDEA 2004 suggests that school systems use scientific, researched teaching methods as an intervention. If there is no progress, then a determination of a learning disability is acceptable (NCLD, 2007).

Problems with the Discrepancy Requirement.   The **discrepancy requirement** had been part of the federal special education regulations since its inception. Simply stated, since 1975, it had been assumed that a severe discrepancy between intelligence and achievement indicated a learning disability. Because both intelligence and achievement can be measured by testing, the discrepancy formula was mandated.

Utilization of the discrepancy formula has not solved all the problems in identifying students with learning disabilities. For instance, students must fail for a long period of time before they can be found eligible for special education services. "Equally important is the growing evidence that the discrepancy requirement is particularly problematic for students living in poverty, students of culturally different backgrounds and those whose native language was not English" (NCLD, 2007, 2). Too many referrals to special education programs and an overidentification of students with learning disabilities are also major problems that evolved from the discrepancy approach. Many general education students are under grade level. If teachers take "below-grade level" to mean that students need special education, referrals are quick to follow. This often leads to students being mistakenly placed in special education. Hopefully, making the discrepancy requirement *optional* will lead to improvements in identification practices and will yield better results for students.

Response to Intervention

The 2004 reauthorization of IDEA authorizes utilization of the **response to intervention** as an alternative to the discrepancy formula. The response-to-intervention (RTI) process is a multitiered approach to providing services and interventions to struggling students. The RTI process has the potential to limit the amount of academic failure that any student will experience and to increase the accuracy of special education evaluations. The NCLD provides the following three-tier framework for an RTI process in the IDEA *2004 Parent Guide:*

Tier 1: Screening and Group Interventions. At-risk students are identified using universal screenings and/or results on state- or districtwide tests. These students receive supplemental instruction, or interventions, generally delivered in small groups during the regular school day in the general education classroom. Student progress is closely monitored using a validated screening system such as curriculum-based measurement. At the end of no more than 8 weeks, students showing significant progress resume the regular classroom program. (This step may be divided into two separate tiers in a four-tier model.)

Tier 2: Targeted Interventions. Students who do not make adequate progress in the regular education classroom in Tier 1 are given more intensive services and interventions. These services are provided in addition to instruction in the general curriculum. Interventions are presented in small-group settings. Early grades interventions, kindergarten to 3rd grade, are primarily in reading and math. This intervention time period is longer but should not exceed one grading period. Students who show inadequate progress at this level are considered for more intensive interventions at Tier 2. Ideally, parents are involved in the earliest stages of RTI. The process is explained to them in face-to-face meetings, written intervention plans are provided, and parent consent is obtained.

Tier 3: Intensive Interventions and Comprehensive Evaluation. At this level, students receive individualized, intensive interventions that target individual skill deficits. Students who do not make adequate progress with these targeted interventions then are considered for eligibility as required by IDEA. Data collected at all tier levels are included when making the eligibility decision. (This step can be divided into two separate tiers.)

IDEA allows parents to request a formal evaluation to determine eligibility for special education services at any point in a RTI process. In other words, an RTI process cannot be used to deny or to delay a formal evaluation for special education.

Pros and Cons.   Scanlon and colleagues (2003) summarized the pros and cons of the RTI approach. Some of the potential positive aspects of RTI are:

- Students will get systematic instructional help sooner rather than waiting until after the student has a lengthy history of failure
- There will be an emphasis on data-based student performance and monitoring of student progress; theory and practice will be more closely aligned as school systems utilize research-based interventions; and the discrepancy formula is particularly ineffective in identifying learning disabilities in adolescents and girls.

Drawbacks to the RTI approach include:

- No research-based instructional approaches are sufficiently validated
- Learning disabilities will be correlated with low academic achievement
- The push for reading proficiency will cause educators to overlook learning disabilities in other areas such as math and oral expression; and implementation and monitoring will be particularly difficult to accomplish in secondary schools.

Gresham, VanDer Heydon, and Witt summarized (2005) concerns about RTI as a means of clarifying the muddled picture of learning disabilities:

Apart from the need for controlled outcome research in other academic areas, there is still the question of whether RTI is a legitimate basis for ruling in or ruling out the presence of a learning disability. Does the fact that a child responded adequately to an intervention rule out that he or she did not have a disability? Does this mean the child's learning difficulties were caused exclusively by poor instruction? Does the fact that the child did not respond adequately to an intervention mean that he or she has a "true" learning disability? (p. 27)

Until a solid, cost-efficient scientific technique such as brain imagery technology is designed to identify a learning disability, professionals will continue to examine and refine available educational methods. RTI is a step forward because it provides early intervention for reading and other academic problems.

Prevalence of Learning Disabilities

Prevalence rates in the 13 special education categories relate to the numbers or percentages of students possessing a defined disability within the total population. In almost every public school classroom, there are at least two students identified as learning disabled. According to the National Institutes of Health, learning disabilities affect one in seven people (Coordinated Campaign for Learning Disabilities, 2000). More than 6 million school-age children in the United States receive special education services (U.S. Department of Education, 2003). Of these, almost half (48.3 percent), a total of 2.8 million students with disabilities reported in the 6 to 21 age group are served as specific learning disabled (NCLD, 2007).

SPEEDBUMP—Approximately half of all special education students have a learning disability! Does this make sense to you? Why do you think so many students are identified with a learning disability?

The number of students classified as learning disabled varies from state to state (Algozzine & Korinek, 1985). Hallahan and colleagues (2007) compared interstate variability of prevalence rates for special education categories from 1984 to 1985 through 2001 to 2002. They were surprised to find that specific learning disabilities prevalence rates were consistent from state to state; yet it is still clear to practitioners that students found eligible for services because of a learning disability in one school district or state might not meet the requirements in another.

A continued trend of increases in the category of learning disabilities is attributed to:

1. The broad and vague wording of the federal definition for specific learning disabilities.

2. Social acceptance and preference for the learning disabilities classification (rather than intellectual disability or emotional disturbance).
3. Differing criteria used by states for qualification for services. (Sigmon, 1989)

Added to this list of possible reasons for the increase in numbers are reasons offered by Lyon in 1996:

4. Financial incentives to identify students for special education.
5. Inadequate preparation of teachers by colleges of education, leading to overreferral of students with any type of special need.

CHARACTERISTICS

Each student with learning disabilities has unique characteristics, as do students without learning disabilities. Student characteristics are categorized within functional domains. These domains include cognitive abilities, processing skills, academic achievement, communication development, perceptual-motor skills, and social-adaptive skills. All domains interact; no functioning areas operate independently.

Each student needs to be viewed holistically. If one part of an auto malfunctions, the rest of the vehicle will not function properly. Compensations can be made, but the malfunctioning part affects the overall service the car gives; for example, have you ever tried to go somewhere only to find that your car would not start because the battery was dead? You quickly learned that the best-performing engine will not function at all because the starter would not turn over. You may have used a jumper cable to start your car—which means you were able to temporarily bypass the main problem. However, sooner or later, the battery had to be replaced. People with learning disabilities are a heterogeneous group of individuals who have deficits in one or more of the functional domains. The problem can be bypassed or overlooked for a period of time—but sooner or later, the specific disorder has to be addressed.

Students with learning disabilities do not have an easily identifiable problem. We cannot assume that the problem simply resides within the student. We have to look at all of the interactive components within the child's learning environment; for example, what task is the child being required to perform? If it is above his or her functioning level or if instruction is inappropriate, the student may fail. Curricular and task components should be analyzed as assiduously as learner behavior. Learner characteristics by functional domains are presented in Table 5.3, along with general instructional interventions for students with learning disabilities. We will have more to say about teaching in sections that follow.

Cognitive

There is overlap between cognitive functioning, intellect, and processing of information. **Cognitive** refers to a wide spectrum of thinking skills (e.g., memory, analysis, deduction). Jacobs (1984) defines cognition as the active process of mental awareness and thinking. Some of these skills are sampled by an intelligence test.

TABLE 5.3   Teaching Students with Learning Disabilities

	COGNITIVE	ACADEMIC	ADAPTIVE	SOCIAL	PERCEPTUAL/ PERCEPTUAL MOTOR	LANGUAGE
Learner Characteristics	Normal or above-average intelligence.	Uneven pattern of academic performance.	Some degree of field dependency.	Susceptible to distraction. Social imperception.	Difficulties with learning modalities and eye-hand coordination. Inadequate gross or fine motor skills.	Difficulty in reading or language skills.
Instructional Intervention	Adapt instruction to individual cognitive abilities.	Identify entry-level skills for each academic area.	Emphasize independent strategies for learning.	Teach self-management skills. Make social skills training situational.	Adjust instruction to individual learning styles and physical capabilities.	Provide opportunities for language stimulation activities.

Children without disabilities approach learning by asking themselves questions, organizing information, and using environmental cues. This process of thought is called **metacognition** (Ryan, Short, & Weed, 1986). Students with a learning disability typically do not acquire the skills of learning how to think through problems naturally. These students can be taught how to organize their thoughts through metacognitive training.

Students with deficient metacognitive strategies may appear to be passive learners or apathetic. Teachers may describe students with learning disabilities as 'dependent', 'impulsive', or 'disorganized'. A negative cycle occurs when a student's academic progress is limited by his or her inadequate metacognitive strategies. The youngster becomes soured toward learning, and teachers come to think of the child as unmotivated. This cycle of failure can be changed by teaching metacognitive strategies (Levine, 1990).

Metacognitive training teaches students *how* to learn. Deshler and associates (1983) suggested teaching students study skills like scanning, outlining, note taking, time management, and questioning. Tarver (1986) said metacognitive training includes instruction in various (1) self-monitoring strategies (e.g., self-questioning, self-interrogatives, self-checking); (2) self-instructional strategies; and (3) executive strategies (e.g., selecting the strategy most appropriate to the task or problem at hand).

SPEEDBUMP—Staying organized is often a problem for students with learning disabilities. What are some ways you keep your time and work organized? Share ideas with your classmates and make a list of organizational tips.

Lloyd (1980) emphasized the positive benefits of using self-instructional training. This involves training in use of self-verbalization to apply academic strategies. The student is taught to ask him- or herself: "Am I paying attention?" "What is the problem asking me to do?" "What is my plan for solving this problem?"

Mental Processing

Processing skills relate directly to cognitive skills. A problem may occur in one or more of the perceptual neuro-pathways activated during learning. In school, these perceptual neuro-pathways are primarily visual and auditory. Educators use terms such as visual discrimination, auditory memory, visual closure, auditory sequencing, and auditory blending to describe the interplay between how a student perceives something and the mental processing that must occur in order to understand it.

SPEEDBUMP—Just think of all the subtle operations your brain engages in while you read this sentence.

Receptive processing utilizes subskills that are essential to learning. These include attending to task and being able to discriminate what is heard or seen (Ramsey, 1995a). As students read or listen, they must select which facts and concepts are important and which are less critical or relevant. Students with learning disabilities are likely to miss cues (Levine, 1990). Distractibility sometimes is confused with attending. The problem is not lack of attention; rather, the problem is too much attention on a single stimulus. Instead of reading a book, a student is attracted to coughing, a pencil dropping, or a door opening.

In order to read, a child must be able to perceive individual phoneme sounds and to correspond these sounds with letter symbols. Students also must learn to associate groups of letters with English language sounds, and store words with definitions, along with other memory recognition and recall tasks. Over the school years, memory becomes increasingly automated. Learning higher skills depends on effortless recall of previously learned skills (Levine, 1990). Thus, the importance of practice as students learn and attempt to further learning is evident.

Discrimination refers to the ability to differentiate one stimulus from another (e.g., an object, an item, a sound). When asked to identify the letters "m" and "n," the child must visually perceive that there are two humps in "m" and only one in "n." Children learn to discriminate by color, shape, pattern, size, position, and brightness. Eventually students must be able to visually discriminate letters and words to learn to read. This requires intricate visual-processing skills such as figure-ground discrimination. Figure 5.3 lists typical problems students with visual-learning disabilities encounter when reading and spelling. Notice in Figure 5.4, an example of figure-ground discrimination, you can see the vase or the faces, but not both simultaneously.

Academics

The decline of the academic status of students with learning disabilities has been the focal point of much research (Deshler, 1978; Koppitz, 1972–1973). The impact that delayed

FIGURE 5.3   Typical Reading and Spelling Patterns of Students with Visual-Processing Difficulties

- Confuse letters that differ in directionality (b-d, p-q)
- Confuse words that can be reversed (was-saw)
- Limited sight vocabulary; unrecognizable from word configuration
- Lose place reading, especially when moving gaze from the end of the line on the right side to the beginning of the next line on the left side
- Omit letters and words because they were not visually noted
- Insert and substitute letters erroneously as well as omit them
- Have difficulty learning irregular words that cannot be sounded out phonetically
- May find it easier to read words when learning to spell them first
- Sometimes experience difficulty recalling the shape of letters when writing them
- Spell phonetically but inaccurately (cof-cough; bisnis-business)
- Can spell difficult phonetic words but not simple irregular phonetically spelled words

FIGURE 5.4
Figure-ground discrimination.

developmental cognitive functioning has on academic progress was addressed in a study by Speece, McKinney, and Appelbaum (1986). They concluded that students with learning disabilities, even though they showed average intelligence on tests, did not catch up with their peers after 3 to 4 years of remedial services.

The disparity between academic performance and intellectual ability characterizes students with learning disabilities. The federal definition specifies academic areas in which learning disorders are manifested during school experiences. Reading, mathematics, spelling, and writing are listed.

Learning disabilities may occur in the following academic areas:

1. Reading: The majority of students with learning disabilities exhibit 2 or more years delay in their reading ability.
2. Spoken language: Delays, disorders, or discrepancies in listening and speaking.
3. Written language: Difficulties with reading, writing, and spelling.
4. Arithmetic: Difficulty in performing arithmetic functions or in comprehending basic concepts.
5. Reasoning: Difficulty in organizing and integrating thoughts.
6. Organization skills: Difficulty in organizing all facets of learning. (NICHCY, 2000, 18)

Instructional procedures need to match the learning style of students in order for them to achieve success in learning to read (Ratekin, 1979). Because reading skills are necessary in every subject area (e.g., science, history, geography), Wong (1985) suggests that learning strategies be combined with teaching school subjects. Palinesar (1982) recommended that reading comprehension can be improved by teaching students self-monitoring strategies, such as reciprocal questioning and summarization skills (i.e., metacognition). However, to use self-questioning skills, a student must have an adequate knowledge base in the particular subject matter. The acquisition of knowledge may be hampered due to inattention, decoding problems, vocabulary deficiencies, poor reading comprehension skills, and inadequate instruction in content areas (Wong, 1985).

What is the best method for teaching reading? This is a question that confronts every educator who works in a primary or elementary classroom. Students who struggle with reading need to be exposed to the best research-tested reading approaches available. Working with a collaboration of reading organizations, and funded by the federal government, the Center for the Improvement of Early Reading Achievement (CIERA) identified five reading approaches that met scientific-based criteria for effective reading approaches (2003). The five are:

Phonemic awareness instruction
Phonics instruction
Fluency instruction
Vocabulary instruction
Text comprehension instruction

Each of these approaches have advantages and disadvantages. For example, phonemic awareness instruction teaches students to become aware of how sounds work in words. *Phonemes* are the smallest parts of the sound in a spoken word that distinguishes the word's meaning. Changing the "b" in "but" to an "h" in "hut" changes the meaning of the word. Some common phonemic awareness terms are: phoneme manipulation, blending, and segmenting. Phonemic awareness is effective with young children and it can help children regardless of their economic status. Many special educators use the phonemic awareness approach with students identified with dyslexia. Phonemic awareness instruction is better suited to small groups than individual or large-group situations. Older students might find the sounding and blending exercises tedious or too immature for them.

Edge and Burton (1986) cite studies in which many students with learning disabilities are able to perform such computational skills as adding, subtracting, multiplying, and dividing, but they lack the ability to use these computational skills in problem-solving situations. These authors further point out that students need to know how to apply computational skills to financial situations that occur in everyday life.

Spelling disorders have been studied by a number of researchers. A major type of difficulty is the incorrect utilization of standard rules in a phonics approach to spelling. Boder and Jarrico (1982) refer to these errors as phonetically inaccurate (PI). PI spelling errors contain inaccurate phoneme-grapheme (i.e., sound-symbol) correspondences. Letters of the alphabet (i.e., symbols) that correspond with phonemic sounds are not used in the spelling of words. Cicci (1983) concluded that these errors must reflect an underlying language disorder. Horn, O'Donnell, and Leicht (1988) determined that an excessive number of PI disorders is characteristic of persons with learning disabilities; however, other factors, such as inattention and carelessness, also might contribute to this problem (see Figure 5.5).

Communication

Language disorders usually interfere with academic achievement, not only in subject areas like reading, spelling, language arts, and mathematics, but also in listening, thinking, and

FIGURE 5.5   Typical Reading and Spelling Patterns of Students with Phonetic-Processing Difficulties

- Lack ability to analyze the sequence of sounds and syllables in words; often the sounds become reversed in words
- May misunderstand phrases in songs and rhymes like "Hosé can you see?" for the first line of the U.S. national anthem
- Poor ability to remember individual sounds or sequences of sounds
- Difficulty blending individual sounds into words
- Difficulty substituting sounds in one word for sounds in another word, whether in initial, final, or medial position (e.g., man-fan; cat-cut; tan-tag)
- Experience problems remembering sounds of individual letters and sounds represented by regular and irregular letter combinations
- Unable to quickly retrieve letter sounds while analyzing words so that the beginning sound of a word is forgotten by the time the individual recalls the last letter of the word (naming problem)
- Limited sight vocabulary because the student has difficulty memorizing words without being able to use phonetic cues
- Guesses at unfamiliar words rather than using word-analysis skills
- Spelling attempted more by sight than by ear
- Correct spellings occur primarily with words that the individual can visualize
- Bizarre spellings occur, because phonetic patterns cannot be applied
- Extraneous letters and omitted syllables occur when spelling

expression. Recall that language is identified as the broad-based disorder in learning disabilities in the federal definition.

Language is a complex phenomenon. It refers to the ways in which a person receives, comprehends, and transfers thoughts to another person and to oneself. Five components are traditionally identified in the study of language: phonology, morphology, syntax, semantics, and pragmatics. Youth with learning disabilities may have difficulties with basic speech sounds (phonemes), units of meaning (morphemes), sentence structure (syntax), relationships between words, grammatical forms, and underlying meaning (semantics), and everyday context usage (pragmatics).

> **SPEEDBUMP—**Most professionals think learning disabilities are primarily language based because so many students have reading problems. Do you agree with this analysis?

Perceptual-Motor

Some students with learning disabilities have coordination problems. They may appear awkward or clumsy when attempting ordinary childhood activities like riding a bicycle, skipping, and jumping rope. Children with learning disabilities usually develop these skills, but later than their age-mates. Problems with fine motor skills may become apparent when these children are cutting with scissors and manipulating small objects. Motor problems are most evident in school during physical education and during handwriting and art activities (Lewis & Doorlag, 1987).

Perception is the ability to process (or use) information received through the sense organs of the body. Deficits within the perceptual realm can cause cognitive and motor difficulties. For example, a child may incorrectly copy simple geometric designs. If she cannot see her errors, a problem might exist in her perceptual (input) mechanism, whereas a child who can acknowledge her errors but cannot correct them may have a deficiency in her motor (output) mechanism. Likewise, a child who is unable to write on a paper at his desk what he sees on the chalkboard or in a textbook may be experiencing cross-modal difficulties. The difficulty rests in the ability to transfer from one modality to another (e.g., visual to motor, auditory to expressive).

According to Jacobs (1984), perception, memory, and attention are integrative processes and are used collectively to obtain information from the environment and make it meaningful. Perception is the differentiation of distinctive features with filtering of irrelevant information. Attention is affected by a person's capacity to organize and make sense of information (Reid & Hresko, 1981b). Memory is dependent on attention and how well information has been received and associated with experience. Perception, attention, and memory are necessary prerequisites for learning. Jacobs suggests that each individual uses unconscious metacognitive strategies to organize and remember new information.

Dysgraphia is a term that describes the impaired handwriting skills some children demonstrate when attempting to form letters of the alphabet. The child can see accurately what to write but cannot manage correct writing movements (Bush & Waugh, 1982). An example is mirror writing. Each letter is symmetrical but backwards. This condition is not to be confused with children who have poor handwriting skills of a temporary nature due to late maturation or those who write poorly due to carelessness or lack of practice.

SPEEDBUMP—Leonardo da Vinci often used mirror writing when keeping notes. Some believe he wanted to hide his ideas from prying eyes. Others think writing from right to left was less messy because when writing from left to right his sleeve would drag across the manuscript and smear the ink.

During the formative years of learning disabilities research (1950s–1960s), perceptual-motor differences in underachieving children with average intelligence were considered indicators of a minimal brain dysfunction. When hard-to-teach children were unable to match peers in such tasks as copying geometric shapes, researchers believed that a learning disability represented by perceptual-motor processing difficulties was present. Treatment programs were developed based on the premise that the presumed perceptual-motor dysfunction would be remediated by having students practice such worksheet tasks as connecting dots, tracing lines, and finding hidden objects in pictures. Perceptual-motor training declined in the early 1970s when basic assumptions of this approach were unsupported by research. Perceptual-motor training failed to improve academic skills, and tests used to identify perceptual-motor dysfunction were found to be unreliable.

Social/Adaptive

Social skills underlie one's ability to adapt to the environment. Students with learning disabilities demonstrate adaptive behavior problems through such difficulties in school performance as lack of self-control, poor self-esteem, and inadequate interpersonal relationships. Adaptive behavior skills shape friendships, communication, and vocational choices (Weller, Strawser, Buchanan, 1985). Social competence comprises an umbrella of social skills that one needs in order to be accepted in social situations (Hops, 1983; McFall, 1982). A socially adept person selects appropriate skills in particular circumstances and uses social skills in ways that lead to positive outcomes (Deshler & Schumaker, 1983; Larson & Gerber, 1987). Taking appropriate actions and making appropriate responses in social situations requires the use of adequate social perception, social knowledge, and social performance. Some individuals with learning disabilities lack the ability to perceive social situations correctly, show deficiencies in social "know-how" skills, and fail to act appropriately. These students require instruction in the use of social skills (Wojnilower & Gross, 1988).

Several factors have been suggested as contributors to social problems of children with learning disabilities. Carlson (1987) reported studies that showed those with learning disabilities have processing deficits in social comprehension and misinterpret social situations. Specific cognitive functions may be affected in some persons with learning disabilities that cause an impaired ability to understand or empathize with another person's feelings, make inferences about social cues, or predict and evaluate consequences for social behavior (Schumaker & Hazel, 1984). Both are problem areas related to perceptual and cognitive deficiencies. Such students adopt an egocentric perspective and exhibit an inability to shift the focus away from themselves (Derr, 1986). An overwhelming number of studies indicate problems including social competence, and personal failure in social interaction (Bryan, Donahue, & Pearl, 1981) and peer relationships (Bruininks, 1978; Bryan, 1974).

Researchers report that delinquent behaviors and antisocial acts characterize a significant number of adolescents with learning disabilities (Bryan, Werner, & Pearl, 1982; Larson & Gerber, 1987; McConaughy, 1986). Even as children, these youngsters evidently lack the skills and inner control to handle age-appropriate tasks and to manage their own behavior (McWhirter, McWhirter, & McWhirter, 1985). Because of this, they receive negative feedback from family and neighbors. Thus, by adolescence, it is not surprising when students with learning disabilities exhibit behaviors that are out of step with prevailing values (see Table 5.4).

Zigmond, Levin, and Laurie (1985) reported tardiness, absenteeism, and off-task behavior by high school students with learning disabilities. Ysseldyke and his colleagues (1982) observed no differences in the classroom behaviors of elementary nonlearning-disabled children and those with learning disabilities. Contrary to this finding, other researchers found that children with learning disabilities, when compared to nonlearning-disabled elementary students, spend more time off-task (McKinney, McClure, & Feagans, 1982) and engage in more nontask-related behaviors (Sherry, 1982).

APPROACHES FOR TEACHING STUDENTS WITH LEARNING DISABILITIES

Students with school achievement problems have been around for a long time and a variety of teaching strategies have been proposed. Contemporary intervention practices stem from three major theoretical models: the psychological process model, the behavioral model, and the cognitive/learning strategies model (Poplin, 1989). In general, treatment models evolve in response to how the problem of learning disabilities is conceptualized. Authorities within each model highlight different student characteristics. Early conceptualizations and corresponding treatment practices were based on the assumption that underlying causes of learning failure were neurological.

Psychological Process Model

In the 1960s, educators focused their efforts directed toward remediating deficits in perceptual skills. Such perceptual skills as auditory discrimination and visual sequencing were emphasized in remediation programs (Coles, 1989; Poplin, 1989). Treatment was provided in highly structured pull-out programs or special classes. Teachers focused on changing behaviors that interfered with learning such as distractibility, impulsivity, inadequate figure-ground discrimination, deficiencies in recall of words, disorders of symbolic processes (e.g., using letters or numerals), and an inability to categorize or generalize. Psychological process tests and remediation materials proliferated. In 1971, Newell C.

TABLE 5.4   What to Look For: Some First Signs of Trouble Keeping Up with the Flow of Expectations

	LANGUAGE	MEMORY	ATTENTION	FINE MOTOR SKILLS	OTHER FUNCTIONS
Preschool	Pronunciation problems Slow vocabulary growth Lack of interest in story telling	Trouble learning numbers, alphabet, days of week, etc. Poor memory for routines	Trouble sitting still Extreme restlessness Impersistence at tasks	Trouble learning self-help skills (e.g., tying shoelaces) Clumsiness Reluctance to draw or trace	Trouble learning left from right (possible visual confusion)
Lower Grades	Delayed decoding abilities for reading	Slow recall of facts Organizational problems Slow acquisition of new skills Poor spelling	Impulsivity, lack of planning Careless errors Insatiability Distractibility	Unstable pencil grip Trouble with letter formation	Trouble interacting (weak social skills) Trouble learning about time (temporal disorganization) Poor grasp of math facts
Middle Grades	Poor reading comprehension Lack of verbal participation in class Trouble with word problems	Poor, illegible writing Slow or poor recall of math facts Failure of automatic recall	Inconsistency Poor self-monitoring Great knowledge of trivia Distaste for fine detail	Fist-like or tight pencil grip Illegible, slow, or inconsistent writing Reluctance to write	Poor learning strategies Disorganization in time or space Peer rejection
Upper Grades	Weak grasp of explanations Foreign language problems Poor written expression Trouble summarizing	Trouble studying for tests Weak cumulative memory Slow work pace	Memory problems due to weak attention Mental fatigue	(Lessening relevance of fine motor skills)	Poor grasp of abstract concepts Failure to elaborate Trouble taking tests, multiple choice (e.g., SATs)

Source: Levine, 1990.

Kephart described the student with perceptual disabilities in the preface of his book, *Slow Learner in the Classroom:*

> He does not see what we think we show him; he sees something different. He does not hear what we think we are saying to him. He does not make the connections as we do between bits of information which we think we are presenting in such a beautifully organized fashion. His central nervous system is treating these items in a different way. (p. 23)

Teaching methods that evolved from this orientation emphasized three primary approaches to correcting processing problems (Lerner, 1985): (1) strengthening the areas of processing deficits (e.g., students with visual-processing problems were provided exercises designed to improve visual-processing skills); (2) using processing strengths to overcome problems (e.g., students with auditory-processing problems were taught using primarily visual approaches); or (3) strengthening weak areas and using strong areas simultaneously.

Behavioral Model

In the 1970s, educators became disillusioned after seeing only slight progress being made by students who were assessed and taught by psychological process model methods. Test results were unsuccessful in differentiating students with learning disabilities from their low-achieving peers, and psycholinguistic and perceptual process training models were unable to provide evidence of improved ability to perform academic tasks. The behavioral model emerged from a need for social skills training coupled with a general lack of academic achievement in regular classrooms.

Proponents of the behavioral model proposed direct instruction of academic and social skills. Prerequisite processing abilities were minimized in delivery of special education services. The remediation of inadequate sensory processes was replaced by a functional approach to teaching. Programmed texts, short-term objectives, task analysis, and criterion-referenced tests were developed as educational materials during this decade (Poplin, 1989). The purpose of these materials was to provide the regular classroom teacher with a practical, sequenced approach to academics.

> **SPEEDBUMP—**Section II of this text will provide you with many specific ideas for teaching and managing behavior, a good reason to keep this text for your professional library

Improving Behavior.   Norris G. Haring, while director of the Children's Rehabilitation Unit at the University of Kansas Medical Center, argued for the use of **behavior modification** because it deals with observable behaviors and immediate consequences. According to Haring, achievement-oriented behaviors increased when events (e.g., reinforcers) were arranged to follow targeted behaviors (Haring & Phillips, 1962). Careful arrangement of reinforcers, Haring maintained, was a more practical way to teach students with learning disabilities.

Ogden Lindsley taught the use of **precision teaching** in instructional settings while at the University of Kansas. According to Lindsley (1964), precision teaching is a type of instruction that directly measures student performance on a daily basis. Students are administered probes (i.e., skill samples) each day that correspond to their instructional objectives. These frequent measurements provide a systematic method for planning instruction. In addition, Lindsley encouraged the use of contingency management, which is similar to behavior modification. **Contingency management** is an "if–then" type of arrangement that incorporates carefully selected reinforcers to follow specified target behaviors.

Behavior modification, precision teaching, and contingency management were transferred from the laboratory setting into the classroom in an effort to identify observable and measurable student behaviors. The goal was to teach by contingency (i.e., an "if–then" type of reinforcement) rather than concentrating on undetectable neurological causes. By looking at task requirements, adding contingencies, and observing the learners' responses, behaviorists believed that students could be more effectively taught. Observable behaviors related to learning (such as staying on-task, being in seat, or raising one's hand to talk) were targeted for reinforcement.

During the 1980s, academic achievement advocates remained the primary force in teaching students with learning disabilities. The notion that instruction should focus on acquisition of academic skills and the application of these skills into everyday functioning skills was widely accepted among special educators. Yet, this academic remediation approach had its limitations. It was characterized by critics as too teacher directed and student passive. Critics maintained that behavioral treatments bred student dependency. Poplin (1989), for instance, felt that students should develop autonomous ways of learning in order to adequately prepare for self-sufficiency after school.

Cognitive/Learning Strategies Model

Cognitive strategists emphasize a self-monitoring approach to learning. Self-questioning, self-checking, self-correcting, self-evaluating, and self-reinforcing are components of *cognitive strategies*. Students are taught such learning skills as outlining, organizing time, memorizing, studying, and generalizing conceptual information from one setting to another. Teaching students "how" to learn is paramount (Reid & Hresko, 1981). Presently, two cognitive/learning strategy models predominate: *cognitive behavior modification* and the *cognitive strategy model*.

Cognitive Behavior Modification.   Donald Meichenbaum at the University of Waterloo in Ontario, Canada, is a primary contributor to the cognitive behavior modification (CBM) approach. Meichenbaum (1977) emphasized teaching students a variety of self-instructional strategies (e.g., self-questioning, self-checking), a variety of self-guidance strategies (e.g., "What do I have to do? I have to find the main idea in this paragraph."), and a variety of executive strategies (e.g., reflection about one's own array of strategies and selecting the strategy most appropriate to the task at hand). The goal is to train students to use verbal statements and images that prompt, direct, and maintain their behaviors (Lovitt, 1989).

In Meichenbaum's "What's my problem? What's my plan?" problem-solving program, students are taught to verbalize statements of self-correction, self-evaluation, and self-reinforcement (Meichenbaum & Goodman, 1971). Hallahan and Kauffman (1982) outlined Meichenbaum's self-instructional procedure:

1. **Cognitive modeling.** The adult model performs a task while verbally self-instructing.
2. **Overt, self-guidance.** The student performs the same task by imitating instructions spoken by the model.
3. **Faded overt self-guidance.** The student softly repeats the instructions spoken by the model.
4. **Covert self-instruction.** The student performs the task while silently self-instructing.

Tarver (1986) theorizes that gradual fading of speech from overt (outward) to covert (inward) will change the student's spoken language into the inner language that typically regulates thought. According to cognitive behavior modification advocates, modeling and imitations of inner language improve thinking skills.

Cognitive Strategies.   Passive learning seems to be a characteristic of many students with learning disabilities (Torgesen, 1977). Thus, it was important to know how students approach learning. Cognitive strategists recommend that students be taught "strategy behaviors" necessary to perform academic tasks (Poplin, 1989; Wong, 1979).

Knowing how one knows, **metacognition**, is stressed in the cognitive strategy model. The following guidelines detail Meichenbaum's (1985) techniques for teaching *metacognitive strategies:*

1. Teachers need to adopt metacognitive outlooks. They should have the attitude that self-instructional thinking skills exist and can be taught.
2. It is important that teachers be aware of their own metacognitive skills and make students aware of these. Teachers let students down when they fail to assist them in developing the metacognitive skills that they themselves find effective.
3. Teachers need to conduct a task analysis of the skills to be taught. This requires reducing the desired metacognitive skills into a series of simpler subskills.
4. Teachers must be aware that generalization of the learned metacognitive skills will not simply occur; learning opportunities that cut across various settings (e.g., home, community, work) must be included.

A major criticism of teaching students with learning disabilities is that many do not learn generalization and maintenance skills (Lovitt, 1989; Poplin, 1989). What is taught in one training site or classroom has not been proven to carry over sufficiently to other settings or circumstances. When skills do not carry over, maintenance, or sustained use of them, diminishes. Some suggestions for assuring generalization include tasks that place responsibility for learning on the student. These include (1) student self-instruction, (2) student self-rehearsal, (3) practice in multiple settings, (4) dividing skills into manageable portions, (5) student self-monitoring, (6) teacher feedback about performance, (7) skills taught to mastery level, and (8) teacher reinforcement of skills acquired.

Contemporary thinking about best practices for teaching students with learning disabilities combines academics with cognitive learning strategies. In other words, it is important that teachers focus on academic skills while simultaneously teaching students how to learn, how to manage their own behaviors in school, how to generalize information from one setting to another, and how to acquire study skills techniques such as scanning, outlining, taking notes, and time management. Some suggestions for teaching students with learning disabilities are presented in Figure 5.6.

YOUNG ADULTS

It was once thought that the problems encountered by children with learning disabilities ended upon reaching adulthood. It has become evident that a learning disability persists as individual lives evolve.

FIGURE 5.6   Suggestions for Teaching Students with Learning Disabilities

1. Teach the student to organize materials and assignments. Use lists to establish work priorities. Teach study skills.

2. Help the student to think through steps in completing a task. Use questions such as the following as a guide: "How much time do I have to complete a task? What materials will I need? Who can I ask for help?"

3. Overlook minor errors in written work such as spelling and handwriting. Emphasize quality of ideas and perseverance.

4. Provide right-hemispheric activities such as art, drama, and images to represent ideas. Don't overemphasize such left-hemispheric functions as verbal reasoning, logic, and sequential arrangement of ideas.

5. Provide emotional support to help ease the frustration of a learning disability.

6. Provide options during tests such as untimed or oral exams. List answers to multiple-choice questions vertically rather than horizontally.

7. Give clear and concrete directions. Have the student repeat instructions back to you.

8. Link new ideas to the student's experience.

9. Use multisensory materials. Repeat concepts, but use novel presentations rather than drill.

10. Collaborate with parents.

It was not until the 1970s that the need for providing college programs for students with learning disabilities was recognized. Gertrude Webb at Curry College in Milton, Massachusetts, was one of the first to develop college services for those with learning disabilities. Her pioneer efforts and the development of the Program of Assistance in Learning at Curry College inspired other colleges and universities to develop similar programs (Mangrum & Strichart, 1984).

For students who graduate high school and want to go on to college Section 504 of the Rehabilitation Act of 1973 (P.L. 93–112) (refer to Chapter 1) has promoted college learning disabilities programs. The requirement states that colleges receiving federal assistance may not discriminate against any qualified individual.

> No otherwise qualified handicapped individual in the United States, shall solely by reason of handicap, be excluded from participation in, be denied the benefits of, or be subjected to discrimination under any program or activity receiving federal financial assistance.

The Americans with Disabilities Act (P.L. 101–336) extended these provisions to private colleges and universities.

Characteristics

The characteristics and special needs of learning disabled young adults in college differ little from the characteristics and needs they had when much younger. The domains discussed in this section include cognitive, language, perceptual-motor, academic, work/study habits, and social/affective.

Cognitive.   The college student with learning disabilities may have difficulties with sequencing, understanding abstract concepts, reasoning, short- and long-term memory, organization, and generalizing (Mangrum & Strichart, 1984). Difficulties often are experienced in processing information. These can occur in the receptive, associative, or expressive learning modalities (Ramsey, 1995a).

Language.   The weaknesses children with learning disabilities experience in receiving, processing, and acquiring language skills continue to be a problem (Smith, 1983). The young adult may have trouble grasping what is spoken, expressing appropriate vocabulary, understanding words in context, clear and precise written expression, sentence structure, punctuation, and written composition (Mangrum & Strichart, 1984).

Perceptual-Motor.   Educators working with students with learning disabilities at colleges report that perceptual-motor problems continue. These students may have trouble locating information and performing tasks that require motor coordination. One particular problem they may encounter is the form in which tests may be given. For example, tests that require students to fill in circles or to grid in answers may penalize students who actually know the information that is being tested but cannot perform the fine motor tasks required to show evidence of their knowledge (Hobbs, 1982).

Academic.   Because of deficits in basic skill areas, the student with learning disabilities may have difficulties reading required material, spelling, handwriting, and math (Mangrum & Strichart, 1984).

Work/Study Habits.   Smith (1979) reports that the college student with learning disabilities may continue to have problems organizing and budgeting time, completing work and getting work started, and establishing long- and short-term goals. This student also may suffer from test anxiety (Mangrum & Strichart, 1984). Note taking may present a serious problem as well (Roberts, 1983).

Social/Affective.   The social difficulties experienced by youngsters with learning disabilities continue to follow them into adulthood. They have difficulties establishing good relationships with others, reading body language, expressing their own feelings, and relating to authority figures (Mangrum & Strichart, 1984). Social implications of behavior problems extend beyond academic programs. A national survey revealed that 44 percent of incarcerated adolescents had a history of learning disabilities (McConaughy, 1986).

Likewise, young people with learning disabilities frequently suffer from poor self-concepts and tend to feel insecure and frustrated with life. They may have difficulties meeting responsibilities, curbing impulsive behavior, and maintaining motivation (Mangrum & Strichart, 1984).

SPEEDBUMP—What services does your college or university provide for college students with learning disabilities? If you have 25 or more students in this course, probably at least two students have a learning disability. Obviously there is nothing wrong with their intelligence but they do have to work hard to keep up—why?

Alternative Strategies

Some of the higher education services offered students with learning disabilities include:

1. Assessing students to determine deficit areas, in order to provide appropriate services.
2. Using tape recorders for lectures.
3. Providing students with an outline as an aid for organizing content.
4. Photocopying class notes.
5. Allowing testing modifications (e.g., administered orally, additional time, less items, isolated seating).
6. Purchasing textbooks in advance so they can begin reading earlier.
7. Using taped textbooks.
8. Securing tutors to help students understand and master the content of subject areas.
9. Having another student take notes.
10. Offering special courses to students according to their needs. These might include writing courses, study skills, or instruction in college survival. See Figure 5.7 for teaching suggestions.

SUMMARY

The search for appropriate terminology that would identify learning disabilities continues to challenge educators. The first terms used to describe this population emphasized medical- and neurological-processing deficits. The most popular and widely accepted name was *minimal brain dysfunction*, or *MBD*.

In 1962, Kirk suggested the name *learning disabilities*. This new classification was intended to distinguish persons with learning disorders and average intelligence from other exceptionality categories, especially mental retardation. Many students were identified as mentally retarded during the 1940s and 1950s, because the category *specific learning disabilities* didn't exist. The classification was adopted following Kirk's use of the term to link together students with average intelligence and presumed mild neurological disorders.

The federal definition is widely used in providing appropriate public education to students who are eligible for services because of a learning disability. With the reauthorization of IDEA 2004, schools now have the option of employing the discrepancy

FIGURE 5.7 **Suggestions for Faculty Who Teach College Students with Learning Disabilities**

1. Provide students with a detailed course syllabus the first week of class.
2. Clearly spell out expectations before the course begins (e.g., grading, material to be covered, due dates).
3. Start each lecture with an outline of material to be covered in that period. At the conclusion of class, briefly summarize key points.
4. Speak directly to students, and use gestures and natural expressions to convey further meaning.
5. Present new or technical vocabulary on the chalkboard or use a student handout. Terms should be used in context to convey greater meaning.
6. Add stories and examples to illustrate or provide examples to information being taught.
7. Role-play, act out, draw, or utilize some other media or activity to build meaning to conceptual material.
8. Give assignments BOTH orally and in written form to avoid confusion.
9. Announce reading assignments well in advance for students who are using taped materials.
10. Help students find community resources, like the Talking Book Center (affiliated with the National Organization for the Blind) where they can get tape-recorded reading materials (e.g., textbooks, newspapers, magazines).
11. Facilitate use of tape recorders for note taking by allowing students to tape lectures.
12. Make use of self-correcting materials, which provide immediate feedback.
13. Provide study questions for exams that demonstrate the format, as well as the content, of the test. Explain what constitutes a good answer and why.
14. If necessary, allow students with learning disabilities to demonstrate mastery of course material using alternative methods (e.g., extended time limits for testing, oral exams, taped exams, individually proctored exams in a separate room).
15. Let students use a simple calculator, scratch paper, a thesaurus, and/or a speller's dictionary during exams and formal writing exercises.
16. Provide adequate opportunities for questions and answers, including review sessions.
17. Modify the amount of practice work required when needed.
18. Be sure students are being taught skills relating to how they can more efficiently and effectively:
    a. study
    b. manage time
    c. take notes
    d. proofread their work
    e. take a multiple-choice, true-false, or essay test
    f. cope with stress
    g. engage in decision making and problem solving
19. Encourage (or require) students to use campus support services (e.g., preregistration, assistance in ordering taped textbooks, alternative testing arrangements, specialized study aids, peer support groups, diagnostic consultation, study skills training, and academic tutorial assistance.
20. Capitalize on each student's strengths.
21. Provide opportunities for success in a supportive atmosphere to help build self-esteem.
22. Allow flexibility in classroom procedures.

between intelligence and academic achievement approach or choosing scientific, re-searched methods inherent in the response-to-intervention (RTI) track. Pros and cons are being expressed for both of these choices for determining individual eligibility for specific learning disabilities.

Characteristics of students with learning disabilities are classified by developmental domains of functioning. These functioning domains include cognitive skills, academic achievement, language and communication development, perceptual and perceptual-motor skills, and social/adaptive skills. Students with learning disabilities demonstrate learning difficulties in at least one of these functioning domains.

From the 1940s into the twenty-first century, treatment models continued to evolve in response to theories about the causes of learning disabilities. Programs were developed during the 1960s that attempted to ameliorate perceptual deficits. This approach is called the psychological-process approach. Interaction between the learner and the environment was the major emphasis during the 1970s. This is the behavioral approach. Arranging the environment, reinforcing appropriate behavior, and using systematic instructional ap-proaches in the teaching of academic skills are components of this model. Contemporary thinking states that it is important to teach academics, but it is also necessary to teach stu-dents how to learn, how to manage their own behaviors in school, and how to generalize information from one setting to another. Cognitive/learning strategies models emphasize the need to produce self-sufficient, independent learners for a lifetime.

Learning disabilities do not end when students exit schools. Characteristics of young adults with learning disabilities continue to define their needs for assistance with educa-tion (vocational or college), study skills, social skills, personal development, and career pursuits.

ACTIVITIES

1. Reread the vignette about David. Answer the questions asked about him as a class activity.
2. Divide the class in half. Give half of the class a reading passage that appears to them like it might to a student with a learning disability. The other half of the class needs to be given the reading passage in a normal format. Discuss with the class later how it felt for both groups of students—those with an assumed learning disability and those assumed normal in reading skills.
3. Do a Web search of the following terms: dyslexia, dysgraphia, dyscalculia, and dysphasic. Answer the following questions: How are these conditions similar? How are they different? How would each condition affect a student's ability in reading, writing, mathematics, and verbal skills?
4. Interview a student on campus who has a learning disability. Ask the following: What was the student's public school experience? Was he or she satisfied with their special education services? Did the individual feel stigmatized? What teaching accommodations helped? How does the individual deal with his or her learning disability today?
5. Invite a college student or an adult (professional) with a diagnosed learning disability to come speak with your students. Ask the person to talk about ways in which they have learned to make accommodations and/or modifications in order to be successful.

6. Look for journals that discuss techniques for working with students with learning disabilities, such as the *Journal of Learning Disabilities, Learning Disabilities Quarterly, Learning Disability Focus,* and *Remedial and Special Education.* Read several articles from different journals if possible, and discuss techniques about working with students with learning disabilities in general and special education classrooms. Talk about approaches suggested for academic and social skills training. Discuss suggestions about collaboration with other educators, support personnel, and parents.

7. There are two major professional organizations as well as a major parent-professional organization in the field of learning disabilities: The Division for Learning Disabilities of the Council for Exceptional Children (1920 Association Drive, Reston, Virginia 22091); the Council for Learning Disabilities (P.O. Box 40303, Overland Park, Kansas 66204); and the Learning Disabilities Association (4156 Library Road, Pittsburgh, Pennsylvania 15234). Write to these organizations for their directories and literature. Determine the purposes, membership, and services offered by these organizations.

8. Find out if there are active state and local branches of these national organizations in your area. If there is a local organization, arrange to visit one of those meetings. Try to determine concerns that the group is currently addressing in your community. Ask a representative from the group to visit your class and speak about the organization's purpose, membership composition, and service.

9. Join the Student Council for Exceptional Children. Find out when and where the annual state CEC conference is going to be held, and suggest that the local chapter send representatives. Volunteer to attend as a representative, and while at the conference, attend the meeting for the Division for Learning Disabilities.

CHAPTER SIX

THE INCLUSIVE CLASSROOM

ADVANCE QUESTIONS

Answer the following questions as you read this chapter:

1. What comparisons can you make between least restrictive environment and inclusion?
2. What are four steps for setting up an inclusion program?
3. How do collaborative consultation and cooperative teaching support inclusion?
4. Describe co-teaching.
5. Discuss role responsibilities in the collaborative consultation and cooperative teaching models.
6. How would you organize a peer tutoring program?
7. What is cooperative learning and how would you use cooperative learning in the classroom?
8. What are some common issues that general and special educators deal with?

VIGNETTE: MONROE ELEMENTARY SCHOOL

Monroe Elementary School is located in a large northeastern city. Despite a 92 percent poverty rate and a 22 percent special needs population, Monroe was recognized as one of five most improved schools in the state. Throughout this 384-student K–5 school, students with special needs are taught alongside nondisabled students in general classrooms. The spirit of Monroe Elementary School is emblazoned on the banner that hangs over the front entrance: "Some goals are so worthy it's glorious to fail."

A co-teaching approach is used in each classroom. Rather than pulling students out for resource room delivery services, the special education services come to the students. In Kensington's classrooms, teachers work side-by-side. Teachers utilize their individual strengths and to experiment with new ideas. All students, regular and special education alike, benefit from the delivery of instruction by these co-teachers. Frequent use of cooperative learning and peer tutoring provides each student with the opportunity to help another.

Each day begins with a morning meeting. This gives youngsters an opportunity to share their experiences and goals for the day. In order to encourage self-direction, students are allowed to make some choices within activities. The classrooms are organized in such a manner as to promote student and adult movement. Chairs and tables are arranged in small groups. Much of the learning takes place at learning centers designated as "science," "math," and "language arts." Support professionals include the adjustment counselor, the speech-and-language teacher, the Title I teacher, and the physical therapist. They work with small groups and none makes a distinction between special education and general education students.

Teachers enjoy working together, and their efforts have been validated by positive test scores. Recently 26 percent of the city's public school 4th-grade students were proficient in language arts, and 12 percent were proficient in mathematics. In comparison, 48 percent of Monroe's 4th graders were proficient in language arts and 37 percent were proficient in mathematics. The sense of community and the belief that together they are doing good work are the hallmarks of the Monroe success story.

Successful programs like the one developed at Monroe Elementary School demonstrate that inclusion programs can be successful. However, it took several years of development and most importantly administrative support to raise Monroe to such a level of distinction. For every Monroe, there is an inclusion model that has failed due to lack of preparation. Teachers need to learn how to work together; they need in-service training to prepare them for cooperative learning and peer tutoring activities—and they need an administration that provides leadership.

1. Is there a Monroe success story near your college or university? If so, make time to visit and talk directly with teachers about how their programs developed
2. Would you like to work in an inclusion program? What are the benefits? Are there disadvantages? Can you anticipate some of the issues you would have to deal with?

3. Simply calling a program "inclusion" does not make it so. Learn to discriminate the features that separate successful and nonsuccessful programs

4. Monroe is a total school inclusion program. What other ways do you think there might be to organize an inclusion program?

LEAST RESTRICTIVE ENVIRONMENT

Inclusion means keeping students in general education classrooms rather than having them receive services in separate special education classrooms. It comes from the "least restrictive environment" provision of the law. When students are educated in the **least restrictive environment**, they are taught in classrooms that most closely approximate a normal learning situation. For many students with mild disabilities, the least restrictive environment is a general education classroom with special education support services. For students who require more intensive **remedial help**, the least restrictive environment might be part-time resource room instruction with the majority of their school day spent in the general classroom. When students with special needs are placed in full-time special classes or alternative special education programs, they are in the *most* restrictive environment. Their opportunities to associate with full-time general education students are limited.

When a student with a mild disabling condition is placed in a special education program, there is a presumption that it is a temporary situation. Placement in a special education program is no badge of distinction for child or parent. Indeed, if parents suspected that, once identified as having a special need, their youngster would be permanently tracked in special education, it is unlikely that they would be so eager to have their child receive special education services.

When students with disabilities are kept out of the mainstream of normal school life, it underscores the differences between them and students without disabilities. Indeed separate special education programs are sometimes classified by such categories of disabilities as emotionally disturbed, developmentally disabled, or emotionally disturbed. When a student is grouped with eight to 10 other "emotionally disturbed" students and isolated in a special classroom that is located in a secluded area of the school, it is unlikely that the student will either feel or act "normal." Table 6.1 details placements for students with disabilities.

The intent of the least restrictive environment provision of the law is to ensure that a student's special education program is as normal as possible. Recent revisions to IDEA have underscored the need to keep students in general education classrooms. However, under law each school system still is required to provide a continuum of special education placements. Figure 6.1 lists special education programs for learners with special needs ranging from least to most restrictive environments. Once the bold line is crossed, a student is out of the mainstream of the normal public school experience, and the prospects for return to general education are bleak.

SPEEDBUMP—This might be a good time to return to Chapter 1 and review the descriptions of each type of special education placement.

BOX 6.1
SPECIAL CHILD—ME (ODE TO MY TEACHER)

Written by Marsha Sykes, General Classroom Teacher

Pine Castle Elementary School, Orange County School System, Orlando, Florida

I'm a special child . . . you know—that quiet one in your room.
Or maybe I'm the loud one—or the sad one filled with gloom.

It really doesn't matter—but I'm in your room this year.
It's sometimes hard to spot me—but WHY?—is not too clear.

I cry out in frustration—or my silence is TOO serene.
I get attention when I'm noisy—you KNOW I'm on the scene!

You might find me in a corner—where I'll really try to hide.
My dad's an alcoholic—he beat Mom last night . . . I CRIED!

Maybe I'm from that broken home—my Mom works hard, you see.
My homework, friends, behavior—a lot's left up to me!

I've been tested—I'm a GENIUS!—but you've always known that's true.
The school psychologist just told Mom—my IQ's one-forty-two!

I'm laughed at 'cause I make mistakes—my classmates call me dumb.
I TRY and TRY—but I guess they're right—my IQ's eighty-one!

And then there's me—I'm SLD!—to you I'm not amusing!
The line goes right—but I go left!—this world is so confusing!

I might not see—I might not hear—my English might be broken.
My speech teacher's proud of me—I correctly pronounced "quotient!"

I'm "AVERAGE," have two parents—though rare—I fit the "norm!"
Ironically . . . I'm the one STANDARD curriculum's designed for!

YES, I'm in your class of twenty-six! But I'm SPECIAL, can't you see?
It takes HARD WORK and SPECIAL SKILLS to teach a child like me.

Your job's so tough—so much to do—you must spread yourself so THIN!
Counseling, parenting, advising, teaching—how will it ALL fit in?

Whole language, exciting math and science, sex ed . . . YOUR JOB'S IMMENSE!
I don't know how you'll do it all—BUT TRY—MY HOPE'S INTENSE!

And so, if in your daily plans—SKILLS AND CONCERN for ME, you provide,
I'll grow . . . I'll learn . . . I'LL LOVE YOU SO— AND YOU'LL SEE ME BEAM WITH PRIDE!

Source: Ramsey, R. S. (1995b).

Wang and Baker's (1986) meta-analysis of 11 empirical studies on students placed in general education classrooms showed more positive results when compared to placements in special education classrooms. There are several reasons why students with disabilities perform better in general education classrooms.

TABLE 6.1   Percentage of Students Ages 6–21 with Disabilities Served in Different Educational Environments

		1999–2000 SCHOOL YEAR			
		SERVED OUTSIDE THE REGULAR CLASSROOM			
DISABILITIES	ALL STUDENTS WITH DISABILITIES	< 21 % OF THE DAY	21–60% OF THE DAY	> 60% OF THE DAY	PUBLIC SEPARATE FACILITY
Specific learning disabilities	50.4	48.3	67.4	39.2	9.9
Speech or language impairments	19.2	35.5	4.6	5.0	2.5
Mental retardation	10.8	3.2	11.3	26.9	23.3
Emotional disturbance	8.2	4.5	6.8	13.3	32.9
Multiple disabilities	2.1	0.5	1.4	4.5	16.8
Hearing impairments	1.3	1.1	0.9	1.5	3.6
Orthopedic impairments	1.3	1.2	1.0	1.7	2.3
Other health impairments	4.5	4.2	5.2	3.8	2.1
Visual impairments	0.5	0.5	0.3	0.4	1.1
Autism	1.2	0.5	0.6	2.9	4.9
Deaf-blindness	0.02	0.01	0.01	0.05	0.2
Traumatic brain injury	0.2	0.2	0.2	0.4	0.3
Developmental delay	New category; data not yet compiled				

Source: U.S. Department of Education.

1. The research on the ineffectiveness of tracking students by ability groups demonstrates that students perform better academically in heterogeneous groups than in homogeneous groups (Lewis, 1990; Massachusetts Department of Education, 1991).

2. Modeling enhances learning. Students naturally imitate their peers. Good peer models provide teachers with success examples that can help encourage students with learning problems to strive harder.

3. Teacher expectations for success go up in relationship to perception of a student's capability. Mainstreamed students may benefit from increased teacher expectations because the student is perceived to be ready to succeed in the regular classroom.

4. Teachers who were used as mainstreaming research subjects may try harder to succeed with their students. The "Hawthorne Effect" (i.e., trying harder to excel because of the perceived special status of being a research subject) is well documented in research annals.

5. How students feel about their abilities has a lot to do with success. Students in special education programs may feel stigmatized. This can affect motivation and perseverance, two crucial elements in school success.

6. Teachers who agree to accept mainstreamed students may be more skilled than their colleagues.

Least Restrictive

↑	I
	N
	T
	E
	G
	R
	A
	T
	E
	D
		1. Full-time general class/
		   room placement with
		   support services.*
		2. Resource room (pull-out)
		   program for part of the
		   day, and general education
		   placement without special
		   education services the rest
		   of the day (Mainstreaming)

↓	S
	E
	G
	R
	E
	G
	A
	T
	E
	D
		3. Full-time placement in
		   self-contained special
		   classroom in regular
		   school.
		4. Special day or alternative
		   school program outside
		   of regular school.
		5. Homebound/Hospital.
		6. Residential facility.
		7. Correctional facility.

Most Restrictive

FIGURE 6.1   Continuum of Special Education Placements

*Inclusion

INCLUSION

Inclusion is a movement designed to bring special education services into the general classroom. This is a significant change from the traditional practice of having students receive special services in resource rooms or self-contained special education classrooms and then return to general education classrooms without special education support. See Figure 6.2.

According to Will (1986), four negative consequences are unintentional by-products of separate special education services.

1. Fragmented instruction. Students who do not meet eligibility criteria for specific remedial programs fall through the cracks and receive no special help. Financial incentives determine program choices. School systems put the child where the money is with too little regard for educational need. Many who receive special services are put in pull-out programs, others in self-contained classrooms. Meanwhile, there is a lack of coordination between general and special educators. Consequently remedial and special education students fall further behind in their studies. Each minute they spend in a special program, students miss a minute of regular classroom instruction. Likewise, students who could use

FIGURE 6.2   Key Definitions

Least restrictive environment: Students with disabilities must be placed in appropriate education programs to meet their individual needs. Every effort should be made to place students with special needs in general education programs. Parents and the school system together select from a continuum of special education placements to determine what is the least restrictive setting for a student.

Mainstreaming: Students with disabilities placed in general education classrooms either full- or part-time without special education support.

Inclusion: Students with disabilities placed in general education classrooms full-time with special education support services provided.

extra help are overlooked because their learning problems are not severe enough to qualify for remedial or special education. The present system of general education emphasizes remediation rather than prevention of learning problems.

2. Dual systems. Special and general education have separate administrative structures, distinct budgets, and separate training for teachers. The duality of these systems creates a gap between the general and special educator. Building principals do not feel ownership of special programs because of separate financial, administrative, and decision-making procedures. Special education teachers feel estranged from general teachers because they tutor students in resource rooms or teach small groups of students in self-contained classrooms. The physical isolation of special education classrooms minimizes contact, communication, and mutual problem solving. With these constraints it is difficult to foster a sense of shared responsibility for the instructional needs of special learners. Learning becomes jeopardized when special and regular instruction do not complement each other.

3. Stigmatization of students. Schools are social environments. Isolation of students from their peers decreases self-esteem and increases negative attitudes about school. All children want to be accepted and feel they belong. Low expectations for success, failure to persist on tasks, learned helplessness, and continued school failure are some of the negative consequences of separating students into categories of "special needs."

4. Placement decision as battleground. The Individuals with Disabilities Education Act is based on the premise that parents have much to contribute in making school-based decisions. Requirements for special programs can place teachers and parents in opposing positions. Parents get stereotyped as "pushy" if they fight to get a youngster into special education and "uncaring" if they don't attend school meetings. The cumulative effects of these misunderstandings are a series of adversarial, hit-and-run encounters between parents and educators.

> **SPEEDBUMP**—If special education students could choose their own placement, do you think they would request a special education or general education class?

Stainback and Stainback (1984) recommended a unitary system of education to replace the splintered approach of providing help through regular, special, and other remedial programs such as migrant, bilingual, and Title 1 programs.

Several sources spurred the movement toward inclusion. Many parents and professionals argued that inclusion in school is best preparation for inclusion in the community. This point of view was bolstered by research studies such as the one conducted by Baker, Wang, and Walberg (1994) that reported students with disabilities performed better academically in general education than in special education classrooms. Furthermore, the least restrictive environment provision of federal law clearly intended that students with disabilities be educated alongside nondisabled students to the maximum feasible extent.

The reauthorization of IDEA in 1997 required that the general education classroom be the first option in determining where special education services should be delivered and school systems had to justify why a student was not placed in the general education classroom.

> **SPEEDBUMP**—This change in the law was the catalyst for a quiet revolution with long-range effects on all students, their teachers, and school systems. Can you guess what one of those effects might be? Hint: Think NCLB and mandated testing.

Some of the documented benefits of including students with disabilities in the general classroom are:

- Students with physical disabilities achieved IEP goals more effectively within inclusive rather than separate special classrooms (Miller, 1996).
- Students who receive special education services in the general classroom do better academically and socially than comparable students in noninclusive settings (Baker, Wang, & Walberg, 1994).
- The academic progress of students without disabilities is not hampered (Staub and Peck, 1994).
- Documented benefits for students without disabilities include tolerance for individual differences, growth in social skills, improved self-concept, and enhanced interpersonal skills (Staub and Peck, 1994).

When inclusion is properly organized, personnel, money, and material resources are reallocated for use in the general education classroom. General education teachers assume greater responsibility for the education of special populations. One of the major rationales for inclusion is that it provides a better academic environment for students with mild disabilities than either pull-out (resource room) programs or separate special education classes.

Organizing Inclusion Programs

Careful planning precedes the implementation of successful inclusion programs. Inclusion will not work if teachers are coerced to comply or if special and general educators are not given ample time to plan together. Students cannot be included with the expectation that simply seating students with mild disabilities next to other youngsters in a general class-room is a formula for success. There are five basic strategies that help ensure an inclusion program will work for both teachers and students. By following the guidelines of communicating with parents, understanding student needs, and evaluating progress, teachers will increase the probability of a successful inclusion program.

Communicate with Parents.   Parents play a vital role in student achievement. Parents of students with mild disabilities attend individual education program conferences, participate in decisions regarding type of special services, and approve placement changes. Lack of communication between teachers and parents can foster misunderstandings and adversarial positions. Parents are concerned about their youngster's progress in school. They want to be kept informed and need to know that the teacher respects their views.

Often the only time parents hear from the teacher is when something is wrong. A weekly note indicating classroom successes, a home visit, or a monthly phone call to review student progress can bridge the communication gap between home and school. Parents can provide information on a student's interests, likes, dislikes, and time spent outside of school. When parents feel that the teacher values their input, crossover learning between school and the family is more likely to occur. A productive teacher-parent partnership can be a powerful alliance for change and growth in a youngster's life.

SPEEDBUMP—Parents play a key role in special education. You will learn more about this in Chapter 11.

Understand Student Needs.   Full-time entry into a general classroom can be an anxiety-provoking experience for a student. Special education programs provide a safe haven from the demands of normal school routines, and special education students may experience "newness panic." Some students withdraw, while others act out in uncharacteristic ways. It is not unusual for a recently included student to regress to disruptive behaviors that the special education teacher thought were eliminated. The first few weeks is not the time to evaluate the viability of the inclusion decision. The included student needs reassurance that a few bumps in the road will be tolerated.

When a student is identified as having a mild disability, it sometimes is difficult to remember that the student has the same developmental needs of other children. Students with mild disabilities are more alike than different from nondisabled students. A student with dyslexia has difficulty reading, but this academic activity is a small slice of a youngster's daily experience. Students with dyslexia play Little League, get into trouble, and sing in church choirs, just like other children. All adolescents share a common need for group approval and independence from authority. These developmental needs are just as immediate in a youngster with an emotional or behavior disorder as with other adolescents. Interpreting a youngster's behavior from a developmental perspective rather than an assigned school label provides a clearer picture of a youngster's actions.

Evaluate Progress.   Enormous amounts of time and money are spent by school systems to assess the educational status of children referred for special education. Norm-referenced tests measure how they compare in academics to their peers. Criterion-referenced tests pinpoint specific strengths and weaknesses in academics. Psychological tests attempt to determine whether a student has mild mental retardation, a learning disability, or an emotional disturbance. Observations detail learning styles and student ability to adapt to classroom routines. These are the most common evaluation procedures used to identify and place youngsters in special programs.

The need to evaluate progress for any student participating in an inclusion program does not diminish. However, evaluation methods shift to curriculum-based assessment. Samples of student work, observations of student interaction, and charting of student progress provide detailed evaluative information. Students' individual education programs are reviewed to match learning objectives with classroom work. Evaluation also includes assessment of teaching behavior. Does the teacher provide enough time for the student to answer questions? Are classroom materials adapted to meet student needs? Is the student seated in an area of the room that makes it easier to concentrate and follow teacher directions? Is the teacher providing enough hands-on activities to help students master specific skills? These are a sample of questions that could guide observations of teaching methods in an inclusion program.

COLLABORATION

Medical patients generally appreciate knowing that their physician has collaborated with other medical professionals about their condition. Perhaps the physician requested a second opinion. Independent views from another professional with a similar background provides reassurance that someone else has given opinions from his or her knowledge and experience. The same is true of building construction. It is reassuring to have another carpenter, plumber, or roofer offer his or her opinion about repairs that may be necessary. Having several car mechanics discuss an automobile's malfunction also is helpful.

Why should it be any different in education? **Collaboration** should be explained to parents as a school team or committee voluntarily meeting together to review all facets of the child's condition, history, and instructional methods previously used in order to develop the most appropriate plan for the youngster. In order to design this plan and work toward a mutual goal, all participants need to be heard on an equal basis and have their area of experience and expertise heard by all members. This includes the essential data that parents can give the team about their child and his or her background, plus current likes, abilities, skills, and so on. Supporting collaboration in one's school helps to foster an important outlook upon meeting the needs of individual students (Fishbaugh, 1997; Friend & Bursuck, 1999; Friend & Cook, 2000).

> **SPEEDBUMP—**When you visit a school, ask about inclusion. Investigate to determine if collaboration is really working. If you are a general education major, take as many special education electives as you can in order to strengthen your marketability.

The term collaboration and its derivatives (i.e., collaborate, collaborative) are used fairly commonly and interchangeably in education, but the terms can differ in the way they are applied in other areas. Simply stated, *collaborate* means "to work together." The word *collaboration* has taken on the meaning of referring to "the event or act of working together." In education, the term has been primarily applied to "persons who work together in order to make inclusion work" (Friend & Bursuck, 1999; Friend & Cook, 2000). With collaboration, there is an interdependence among participants. The act of collaborating provides support and an opportunity to brainstorm ideas with other members who come from a different orientation or training.

Specifically, a team or committee meet to discuss or to *collaborate* about ways of serving students and their families so that student needs will be met. Educators, parents, and other professionals meet to plan programs and interventions, to monitor student progress, or just to problem-solve issues that come up and affect the youngster with special needs. This meeting is referred to as *collaboration*. In some states like Alabama, classes in which students with disabilities are included are referred to as *collaborative classes*, and the special education teachers who consult or co-teach with the regular classroom teacher are called *collaborative teachers*.

Because of the various ways in which it is applied, the term collaboration sometimes is used carelessly. For example, two or more educators discussing a child's progress is not always a form of collaboration. According to Friend and Cook (2000), most people agree that collaboration is "working together in a supportive and mutually beneficial relationship." These authors also offer some guidelines for determining what is true collaboration. They have delineated six defining characteristics, which together add to this definition and expand it. Collectively, all must exist for true collaboration to exist.

Characteristics of Collaboration

Collaboration is voluntary. This first characteristic refers to a person's attitude. The meeting or planning session may be held due to a mandate or requirement of the law, but the voluntary part refers to persons being present and involved because they want to be there, or because they sense the need for them to work with others in order to make it possible for the child's special needs to be met (Friend & Cook, 2000; Mostert, 1998).

Collaboration requires parity among professionals. Parity means equality. In this situation, parity means that each person's contribution during the collaborative event is accepted on an equal basis. That doesn't mean that all suggestions should be accepted—just listened to. Each person has equal power in making decisions (Friend & Bursuck, 1999).

Collaboration is based on mutual to goals. All teams or committees generally have specific purposes or reasons for meeting. During collaboration, these are translated into goals. For example, a multidisciplinary special education team meets to determine for what services, if any, a student is eligible—or having established eligibility, the multidisciplinary team meets to develop an IEP for the student or decide which educational setting the student should be placed in order to have his or her needs best met.

Collaboration depends on shared responsibility. Sharing responsibility for making decisions when working together toward a mutual goal does not mean that everyone shares equally in accomplishing the tasks outlined. Responsibility is assumed by persons most related to the tasks outlined (Friend & Cook, 2000; Mostert, 1998).

A school guidance counselor may assume responsibility for meeting with a youngster with ADHD, both individually and with a regularly scheduled ADHD group. Because the counselor is knowledgeable about this condition, he or she might plan to make suggestions to the special education and general classroom teachers about activities they could effectively incorporate into various parts of the curriculum during the school day. These activities would be those directed toward meeting the child's goals and would be helpful to other students as well.

Collaboration includes shared resources. All members of a collaborative team have different types of experience and expertise that they would be able to share with the group. For example, knowledge about a particular technique might be something that one person would be able to share; whereas, the time and accessibility to the student in order to carry out the technique would be in someone else's realm of knowledge.

Collaboration means sharing accountability for outcomes. All participants or team members are accountable for the outcome (Friend & Bursuck, 1999; Friend & Cook, 2000; Mostert, 1998). The outcome may be positive or it may turn out negative; regardless, all members are responsible and accountable.

INCLUSION MODELS

Every profession has models for putting theories to work. Economists have supply-and-demand models for explaining changes in financial trends. Psychologists use developmental models to explain human behavior. Like a blueprint, a model provides a set of instructions for the application of an idea. Education has many models. There are instructional models, assessment models, and discipline models.

In education, a model is judged in terms of its usefulness. An elaborate model of instruction may be well researched, but if it requires too much teacher time or is too expensive to implement, teachers will look someplace else for ideas. Teachers like practical ideas that increase student competence. A good idea for one teacher may seem esoteric or nonfunctional to another. Teachers adopt models that match their professional philosophy and personal values.

A set of guidelines for inclusion qualifies as a model when it has proved effective in a variety of educational programs. This is no easy task because circumstances vary so much from region to region, system to system, and from school to school. There are two inclusion models used to deliver services to students in the general classroom. The first, the consulting teacher, provides services primarily to teachers, and only indirectly through the classroom teachers to students. The second, the **co-teacher**, supports a method by which the general classroom teacher and special education teacher plan, teach, and evaluate together. The following two topics, consultation and instructional practices, describe inclusion models that have proven useful in many classrooms. Each approach can stand on its own or be combined with other models and strategies. Ultimately, the choice of an inclusion model depends on how well it matches the needs of students, teachers, and parents.

SPEEDBUMP—If you are getting tired of studying while others are out having fun, think about this quote by Sigmund Freud: "As regards intellectual work, it remains a fact, that great decisions in the realms of thought and momentous discoveries and solutions of problems are only possible to an individual, working in solitude."

Consulting Teacher

The **consulting teacher** model is an alternative to the pull-out approach to special education services (Phillips & McCullough, 1990). Instead of working directly with special needs students (e.g., in a resource room), the consulting teacher plans with the general classroom teacher to facilitate inclusion. Some of the responsibilities of the consulting teacher include observing in the general classroom, sharing materials with the general classroom teacher, demonstrating instructional techniques, coordinating programs, and presenting in-service workshops for general educators.

The consulting teacher provides intervention at the site of the learning problem. Both the student with the learning problem and the instructor with the teaching problem can be helped within the general classroom. Consultation can remedy such disadvantages of pull-out programs as fragmentation of instruction and stigmatization of students. It provides a viable means for educators to jointly own the problem of a difficult learner. Through a process of shared problem solving, collaborative consultation crosses over boundaries that have traditionally separated general and special educators.

Consulting requires careful scheduling and administrative support. Consulting is ineffective if the classroom teacher and consulting teacher do not have adequate time to plan. The building principal controls each classroom teacher's schedule. Administrative support in terms of release time and a nonjudgmental view toward teachers who are working with a consultant are two prerequisites for successful implementation of this model.

Consulting also requires diplomatic communication skills on the part of the consultant and a readiness to cooperate on the part of the consultee. Any "helper" has a power advantage over the person who is being helped. The need for consultation, if not handled properly, can imply weaknesses in the ability of the recipient. Imagine the following scenario. A 24-year-old special education teacher has just completed graduate training as a teacher consultant, and her first assignment is a teacher who is a 20-year veteran of the public schools. The teacher was selected by her principal because she has a higher-than-average referral rate for special education services, and the principal wants to establish an inclusion model. It is clear, without drawing out this illustration any further, that a successful outcome is problematic. How will the general classroom teacher feel about this "rookie" observing in her classroom and offering suggestions for changes in instruction? How will the consultant deal with the general classroom teacher's attitude toward outside help? Can consulting work when the general classroom teacher has not directly requested outside assistance?

Consulting works when there is genuine collaboration among all parties (e.g., general classroom teacher, consultant, special services teachers). There are superb and mediocre teachers in both special and general education. For the consulting teacher model to be useful, there needs to be a commitment to sharing of expertise and resources on both sides of the fence (Mastropieri & Scruggs, 2000; Pugach & Johnson, 1989a; Thomas, Correa, & Morsink, 2001). Trust must precede collaborative problem solving. Consultant teachers should be selected from the ranks of the most experienced and respected teachers in a school system. Pinning the title "consultant" on a teacher who lacks the expertise or interpersonal skills to work with classroom teachers will disrupt rather than facilitate mainstreaming efforts. Ultimately, the success of the consulting teacher model depends on a mutual sharing of ideas, methods, and responsibilities between regular and special educators.

Co-Teacher Model

Co-teaching means that the general education teacher and the special education teacher work together in the regular classroom. Both work directly with students and share teaching responsibilities. They co-teach. There are several advantages for this type of service delivery to students with special needs who otherwise might be pulled out of the regular classroom to receive special education.

- The general classroom and special education teachers plan lessons together.
- The general classroom and special education teachers instruct students in the same room.
- Special education teachers work with all students, not just the ones with identified special education needs.
- Regular classroom teachers are given instructionally relevant information about students that helps them to adapt and modify classroom instruction and activities.
- Students with special needs are able to participate in regular class activities because appropriate modifications and accommodations have been identified and put into place.
- Regular classroom and special education teachers have mutually agreed-upon roles and responsibilities concerning instruction and classroom maintenance.

Friend and Cook (2000) outlined six basic approaches for co-teaching. A brief description of each is given. Some are more appropriate in some situations than others; each should be reviewed by the co-teachers to see which would be most effective when teaching certain subject content, when leading learning activities, when remediating skills, when working with drill and practice, when working with particular student behaviors, and so on. Each classroom has its own combination of students and student strengths and needs (Vaughn, Bos, & Schumm, 1997; Vaughn, Schumm, & Argulles, 1997).

One Teach, One Observe.   One teacher primarily manages the classroom while the other observes. The teacher who is observing can do data collection, record student learning characteristics, and so on.

One Teach, One Drift.   One teacher instructs the class while the other intermingles among students, offering specialized assistance. Both teachers need to take active and passive roles at some time.

The co-teaching roles of the second teacher in *one teach, one observe* and *one teach, one drift* are both considered supportive roles in these first two co-teaching approaches. In Figure 6.3, these are referred to as *one teach, one support*.

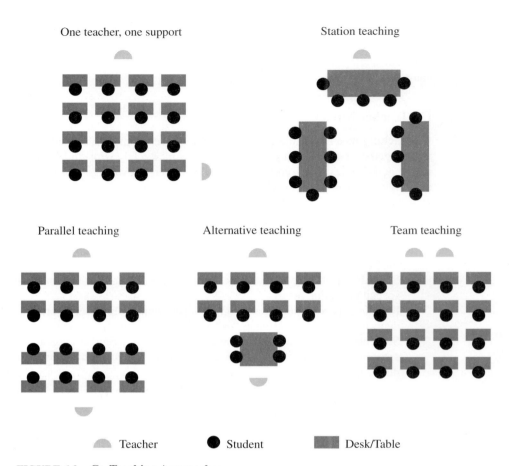

One teacher, one support

Station teaching

Parallel teaching

Alternative teaching

Team teaching

Teacher   Student   Desk/Table

FIGURE 6.3   Co-Teaching Approaches

Source: Friend, M., and Bursuck, W. D. *Including Students with Special Needs: A Practical Guide for Class-room Teachers.* Boston: Allyn and Bacon, 1999, p. 83. Reprinted with permission.

Station Teaching.   Both teachers deliver instruction in teaching stations. Students can work independently at the third teaching station or with a volunteer, student, or paraprofessional.

Parallel Teaching.   The class is divided in half, with each teacher taking a similar number of students to teach. Each teacher is teaching the same information, but in a different manner. For example, the special education teacher might bring in outlines, highlighted materials, and manipulatives with which to instruct students.

Alternative Teaching.   One teacher manages the major group of students, while the other has a small group pulled aside. The group membership changes according to the purpose of the group, which might be to preview or review material being learned, to provide social skills training, or for enrichment.

Team Teaching.   Two teachers are actively involved in managing instruction with the whole class. Both teachers assume responsibility for teaching subject content areas. Variations to this approach have been around for a long time.

For example, in tag-team teaching, one teacher instructs the class in English and then the other teacher instructs math. The first teacher then might teach social studies while the other teacher prepares to teach science. The teacher might each be grading papers or preparing lessons for his or her subject area while the second teacher is teaching. The students can remain in the same classroom or change classrooms in order for part of the students to receive instruction in one subject area while the other part of the class receives instruction in another subject area.

The Co-Teaching Plan

When two or more teachers work together, there are some topics that need to be addressed and discussed. To work out this "game plan," the teachers need to collaborate about the following topics or concerns (Burrello et al., 1996; Dover, 1994):

- Subject area or class (What is being co-taught?)
- Co-planning (Where, when, and how often will the team collaboratively plan? How will feedback about student progress be discussed?)
- Textbooks and instructional materials (What textbooks and materials will be used? What types of instructional support will be given and to whom?)
- Co-teaching approaches (When will the various types of co-teaching approaches be put into action? What type is needed for various kinds of teaching content and classroom learners? How will classroom space be utilized?)
- Instructional accommodations, modifications, and adaptations (What types might be needed for individual learners for the content being taught?)
- Responsibilities of each team member (What needs to be done? Who will do it?)
- Parity (How will personal space be decided? Will the teachers be looked upon as equals by the students?)
- Methods and materials (What materials will be used with the students? Will there be books and materials on diverse functioning levels? Will content be presented according to student functioning levels? What types of materials will be assigned for drill and practice and for homework?)
- Student responsibilities and expectations (What actions and reactions are expected from students? What are the overall setting demands? Will any of these be modified for individuals?)
- Classroom rules and discipline plan (What are the rules? What procedures will be used for enforcing these rules? Is there a difference in teacher tolerance levels?)
- Testing of students (How and when will content be tested or activities assessed?)

- Evaluation of students (Who will grade which papers or assignments? How will student grades be decided?)
- Role and responsibilities of the paraprofessional (Will the role and responsibilities of the paraprofessional change as a result of having a co-teacher in the classroom?)
- Substitute plans for each in-class team member (What will happen when a team member is absent?)

Tips to Remember About Co-Teaching

Each co-teacher has his or her own unique areas of experience and expertise. We should not expect regular classroom teachers to know the specialty areas in special education, nor should the special education teacher be expected to be a content expert. Good co-teaching teams do not just happen; it takes good collaborative planning, implementation, and follow-up evaluation (Ramsey, 1998).

- Allow for and respect differences in technique. One teacher may not approach a task exactly like another teacher would. Differences can be looked at in a positive manner.
- Keep a balance of special needs students in proportion to general education students. Special needs and other at-risk students should comprise about 20 to 25 percent of the class.
- Follow the schedule. Other co-teaching arrangements may be planned so everyone's schedule must be held to as much as possible in order not to disrupt plans for another class with another teacher.
- Expect a few problems along the way. Some changes will need to be made as the co-teaching experiences occur.

> **SPEEDBUMP—**Co-teaching can be satisfying or frustrating. Much depends on how well the two professionals communicate.

COLLABORATIVE INSTRUCTION

Teachers never cease to puzzle about how to teach students with varying abilities. Students are so different in personality, motivation, work habits, and interests that even the best teachers are challenged to keep all their students involved in learning. The selection of peer tutoring and cooperative learning is based on the flexibility each provides for teaching students who are different. These are a sample of worthwhile **collaborative teaching** approaches for maintaining students with mild disabilities in the general classroom.

Peer Tutoring

One of the best ways to learn something is to teach it to someone else. **Peer tutoring** can be equally effective for students with and without mild disabilities. For example, Maheady,

Sacca, and Harper (1988) established a classwide peer tutoring program for 50 10th-grade social studies students. The students ranged in age from 15 to 17 years. Weekly study guides developed by regular and special education teachers were used as the basis for half-hour tutoring periods, three times a week. Progress was measured by weekly quizzes. The researchers reported that the implementation of classwide peer tutoring (CWPT) resulted in an increase in test scores for both special and regular education students.

Peer tutoring places the responsibility for learning on the student. This is a potent change for students with mild disabilities who often become passive learners. With a tutor, students accustomed to sitting alone at their desks waiting for the teacher are directly involved in their learning. Peer tutoring provides individualized instruction. The nonthreatening aspect of peer tutoring encourages students to admit a lack of understanding without concern about adult evaluation. Working with another student provides a youngster with opportunities to discuss, question, practice, and evaluate learning with immediate feedback. Jenkins and Jenkins (1981) described seven steps to implement a peer tutoring program.

1. Determine which children are to be tutored. Start small. Begin with four or five students who like to work with others. Slow development of a tutoring program gives the teacher opportunities to restructure tutoring sessions as needed. Tutoring is not for everyone. Students who are serious behavior problems may not respond well to working with fellow students.

2. Prepare the school for tutoring. The principal and teachers who are involved in the program must be convinced that a tutoring program will not disrupt regular school activities. A written proposal outlining scheduling and monitoring procedures will ensure that all participants are clear about each person's role. Accountability is a major issue in schools. The tutoring program developer should reassure the other teachers that time used for tutoring will not detract from the tutor's classroom performance.

3. Determine a time for tutoring. Daily sessions of one half-hour produce the best peer tutoring results. Peer tutoring within the classroom does not present the scheduling difficulties that occur when two separate classes are involved. Working out a program between classrooms requires careful negotiation of time and space, two valuable commodities in schools. Establish a set time each day for tutoring sessions. When a program is initiated, adjustments in plans almost always are required. This is a normal consequence of implementing a novel idea. Build in a first-week evaluation, with the expectation that adjustments in schedules will be needed.

4. Inform parents about the program. Parents are always curious about school programs that vary from traditional teacher instruction. In public schools, even minor changes can have a ripple effect. Some teachers, particularly those who are not involved in the program, may be suspicious of its value. It is best that parents receive written notice about peer tutoring rather than hearing about it from their children or other parents. Such a letter would contain a brief description of the program skills that students will learn, program supervision methods, and evaluation procedures. Invite parents to school to observe the tutoring program in action.

5. Design lessons and a measurement system. Decide what content tutors are to teach; then specifically detail tutoring methods. For example, a reading lesson might involve 5 minutes of listening to oral reading followed by the tutee writing a list of words she found difficult. Then the tutee could write a sentence containing each word. Tutors need clear guidelines for their work. Avoid unstructured tutoring sessions where the students are not sure of their responsibilities. Detailing student progress on daily charts is a recommended procedure for keeping track of program effectiveness.

6. Conduct tutor training. Although tutorial skills will vary with age and content, there are some general training needs applicable to all tutors. Each tutor should be clear about punctuality, confidentiality, and positive regard for the tutee. Schoolwork needs to be evaluated in a systematic manner. The tutor will need to understand how progress is measured. Daily charts, percentage of correct answers, or random samples of behavior are examples of data that tutors commonly are asked to maintain.

The tutor will require training. A natural tendency to prompt or do the work for a tutee can be addressed by the teacher modeling proper instructional behavior. The tutor is a helper. This requires the ability to interact in a positive manner. Some key interpersonal skills are active listening and praising good effort. Change behaviors that intimidate or cause the tutee to feel incompetent. Model error correction behaviors that encourage sustained effort.

7. Maintain tutor's involvement and interest. Frequent reminders of the tutor's positive contributions can be gleaned from tutee progress charts. Special recognition at assemblies or through the awarding of certificates will serve the dual purpose of rewarding tutors and encouraging other students to be involved with the program. Teaching is no less a difficult endeavor for a youngster than it is for an adult. Periodic group meetings with tutors can provide the program developer with opportunities for refining the program and boosting morale.

Peer tutoring is cost effective, and it provides a student with individual attention. If conducted in a thoughtful and systematic manner, peer tutoring can increase school achievement and motivation of both students.

> **SPEEDBUMP—**Think about all the time teachers spend trying to stop students from talking to each other. The drive to socialize is a natural urge in us all; it makes more sense to channel this urge than to thwart it.

Cooperative Learning

When students lack control over their learning, motivation to persevere is undermined (Gough, 1987). **Cooperative learning** is a method of structuring small groups of nondisabled and disabled students so that all the individuals achieve a learning goal through mutual planning and decision making.

Cooperative learning can be used with all age groups to teach any part of the curriculum. Putnam and her colleagues (1989) compared 50 studies of cooperative, competitive, and individualistic learning situations. Cooperative learning produced more instances of positive relationships between students with and without disabilities. Students work in groups and ask questions, share ideas, clarify thoughts, experiment, brainstorm, and find solutions with their classmates (Salend, 2001). Benefits from cooperative learning include: increased student motivation, higher test scores, and enhanced social skills (Johnson & Johnson, 1986; Putnam et al., 1989; Slavin, Madden, & Leavey, 1984; Smith, 1987).

There are four steps to establishing cooperative learning groups in the classroom:

1. The teacher selects members of each learning group. Cooperative learning groups are heterogeneous in composition with a balance between males and females, high and low achievers, and active and passive students. A typical group would include three to six students with no more than one student with a mild disability. The balance of the groups is crucial to ensure that each group has strengths to offset individual academic or social weaknesses.

2. The teacher directly teaches cooperative group skills. Most students are conditioned to earn grades based on individual work, often in competition with other students. Such familiar refrains in classrooms as, "Pay attention to your own work," or "No talking while we are working" are antithetical to cooperative learning. The teacher who uses cooperative learning wants students to talk and work with each other. Cooperative learning requires such interpersonal skills as the ability to trust and work with others, good listening skills, acceptance and support of others, and the ability to resolve conflicts constructively (Johnson & Johnson, 1990).

Some students may have difficulty making the transition from passive, teacher-directed learning to cooperative learning activities. Roy Smith (1987) found he needed to teach his junior high school students how to work cooperatively. He described six steps for teaching cooperative skills:

a. Identify the specific skills group members will need to demonstrate; for instance, listening or providing information.
b. Help students become aware of the need for cooperative skills.
c. Help students gain a clear understanding of each skill.
d. Provide students with situations in which to practice cooperative skills.
e. Give students descriptive feedback on their performance of each skill.
f. Persevere in practicing the skill. Role playing, group discussions, brainstorming sessions, and observer feedback of group activities are samples of classroom methods that help students acquire and reinforce cooperative group skills.

3. The teacher assigns cooperative group activities. There is a difference between small-group work and cooperative learning. In typical small-group activities, students are given an assignment with little attention paid to how they will work together. A common complaint about small-group activities is that a few students do all the work. In cooperative group activities, students work together toward a common goal, and the group tasks are equally divided among group members. One approach to subdividing group participation is the "jigsaw" strategy. The group is given an assignment, and each member has part of the materials needed to complete the task; for instance, the assignment could be a group report on drugs. Each student would have a different source of information, such as a medical reference book, newspaper clippings, magazine articles, and an encyclopedia.

Another approach for beginning cooperative groups is to assign each member a specific role to facilitate the group work. One student would be responsible for reviewing suggestions, another would question individual members to elicit their ideas, while a third group member could be responsible for keeping the group on track. When students are experienced in cooperative learning, it is possible to turn virtually any part of the school curriculum into a collaborative learning experience.

4. The teacher evaluates group efforts. In cooperative groups, students learn that they sink or swim together. There are two levels of group assessment:

   a. Did the group accomplish its goal?
   b. How well did the group work together?

Products such as a classroom presentation or tests where individual scores are averaged to give a group score are examples of ways teachers have evaluated group goals. Self reporting by groups or observer feedback on group dynamics can provide information on group interaction. Group evaluation should be criterion referenced. Before the group work begins, the teacher should clearly outline the criteria used for group evaluation. For example, a cooperative group activity on drug abuse could conclude by members summarizing each other's contributions.

Tateyama-Sniezek (1990) cautions against investing too much enthusiasm in cooperative learning as a tool to increase academic achievement of students with mild disabilities. She points out that more studies need to be undertaken that include students with mild disabilities in cooperative learning groups. Stephens and Slavin (1991) took issue with Tateyama-Sniezek's findings. They pointed out that when group rewards and individual accountability both are included in cooperative learning activities, the outcomes for students with and without disabilities are positive.

Both peer tutoring and cooperative learning groups capitalize on students as classroom resources. The active involvement of students in their own learning enhances mainstreaming efforts by fostering social relationships between students, increasing student motivation, and supporting the acquisition of skills. A poster in the classroom of a teacher who used cooperative learning activities summarizes the impact of collaborative learning strategies. It simply states, "None of us is smarter than all of us" (Smith, 1987, 664).

COMMON GROUND

Schools must change in order to meet the demands of the future. Demographic trends indicate increased poverty among students. A growing proportion of students are nonwhite and non-English speaking, and there is an increase of students from single-parent families. If the schools of the future are to meet the growing demands of hard-to-teach students, changes must occur in present school practices that serve to separate students (and teachers) into groups of "haves" and "have nots."

General and special educators can collaborate to teach all children. There are contact points where key issues faced by regular and special educators rub together. All educators, whether special or regular, must deal with problems of teacher expectations, standardized tests, classroom organization, discipline, and dual systems of administration. The ability of educators to meet these challenges and solve them together will set the course for an improved educational system for the students of the twenty-first century.

Teacher Expectations

Research on effective instruction indicates the powerful effect of **teacher expectations**, both positive and negative, on student performance. When students are labeled as deficient and put in "special" programs, the message is clear: there is something intrinsically wrong with this student. Labels like mentally retarded and learning disabled become explanations for why a student is difficult to teach. Students then are grouped with other "deficient" learners, and teacher expectations for the group decline. Conversely, when teachers believe that learning problems are temporary hurdles that can be overcome by adapting teaching methods, there is an expectation that success will come with hard work. When teachers have high expectations, the performance of students is enhanced.

However, what about teacher expectations of themselves? Two Rand Corporation studies found that positive teacher opinions of their own ability had a beneficial effect on students' learning (Armor et al., 1976; Berman et al., 1977). McDaniel and Dibella-McCarthy (1989) described the teaching style of these confident teachers:

> High efficacy teachers maintained high academic standards, had clear expectations for students, concentrated on academic instruction, maintained on-task behavior, and demonstrated "withitness." They combined a secure classroom environment with a strong academic orientation. . . . High-efficacy teachers allocated twice as much time to whole group instruction as did low-efficacy teachers. (p. 35)

Teachers who believe in their own ability have good group-management skills. They encourage student participation and have less discipline problems. Perhaps most important, high-efficacy teachers are problem solvers. They view a student's learning difficulties as a temporary problem, and they try different teaching approaches until they get results. Teacher preparation programs that concentrate on developing high-efficacy skills will provide young teachers with the tools needed to help all learners in the regular classroom.

Classroom Organization

Between kindergarten and 12th grade, a student will spend more than 11,000 hours in school. How much of this time is actually spent learning? According to researchers who have studied life in schools, only a fraction of a school day is allocated to instruction, and students spend even less time engaged in learning activities (West Ed, 2000). Out of a typical 390-minute school day, teachers spend less than half that time teaching. In their survey of 2nd-, 3rd-, and 4th-grade classrooms, Ysseldyke and Algozzine (1984) found that students have few opportunities to do independent work, and they spend a lot of time in such passive activities as listening and waiting.

Goodlad (1984) reported that students spend as little as 12 percent of their school day questioning, reading, writing, or engaged in some other activity that reflects active learning. He said that a good deal of what goes on in schools is like painting by numbers. The teacher gives directions, and students follow them in robotlike fashion. He described the emotional tone of these classrooms as flat. The climate of these rooms lacked joy and warmth. Goodlad noted that although teachers verbalize the need for students to become independent thinkers, many teachers exhibit a need to control student decision making.

More attention needs to be directed toward how classrooms are organized. When the teacher controls every action, from distribution of materials to collecting lunch money, precious instructional time is wasted. Students must be actively involved in their learning to succeed. Such active teaching strategies as cooperative learning projects, learning centers, and peer tutoring allow teachers to move about the room and guide student learning. By shifting the class-room instructional norm from "frontal teaching" to student-centered activities, teachers can increase instructional time and allow learning to proceed at the student's pace.

Standardized Tests

Chester Finn, past assistant U.S. Secretary of Education in charge of research, characterized standardized testing in the United States as the "Lake Wobegon" effect. He observed that in the mythical Minnesota town popularized by the humorist Garrison Keillor, all the children are "above average." Finn's comment was prompted by national achievement scores that each year showed a rise in average test scores for all schoolchildren. In their zeal to demonstrate how much their school systems have improved, this statistical paradox has been conveniently ignored by many educators (Fiske, 1988).

Neill and Medina (1989) summarized the case against standardized tests:

> At best, standardized testing is hopelessly inadequate for promoting school reform. At worst, such testing will preclude reform. In either case, the continued domination of testing will mean that millions of students—primarily those most in need of improved education—will be dumped into dead-end tracks and pushed out of school. (p. 695)

The 2004 reauthorization of IDEA mandated that students with disabilities be included in state- and districtwide assessments. These mandates reflect the push for equal access and high standards for all students. They also highlight the need for teachers to be knowledgeable about test accommodations, test preparation, test administration, outcomes, and legal and ethical concerns surrounding high-stakes exams (Washburn-Moses, 2003).

The Council for Exceptional Children (CEC), the primary professional organization for special education, has long supported including students in state- and districtwide assessments. The results of these assessments can help determine if the schools are providing quality instructional programs for the special education students, or if additional resources or professional development are needed to improve the programs.

To ensure that students with disabilities are assessed fairly and appropriately, CEC states that:

- Students with disabilities must be assessed with high expectations.
- Whatever accommodations are necessary to facilitate this must be provided.
- Alternative assessments must be provided for the small percentage of students with the most significant disabilities.
- Individualized decisions must be made within the framework of general assessment, assessment with accommodations, or alternate assessments. (*Today*, 2003, 1)

The No Child Left Behind (NCLB) Act has given schools additional accountability responsibilities with their students with disabilities. The NCLB mandates that a majority of students with disabilities (1) be included in state- and districtwide assessments, and (2) show annual improvement in the test scores of students with disabilities.

High-stakes tests are a concern to special educators. High-stakes testing refers to the requirement that students must pass an exam in order to move from one grade to the next or earn a high school diploma. As of 2008, 25 states require students to pass an exam to receive a high school diploma, and seven require that students pass a test to be promoted to a certain grade level (National Education Association, 2001). This means that students with disabilities *must* be provided with sufficient access to the general curriculum and be given tests that are valid and adequately measure student knowledge, rather than reflect their cultural diversity, linguistic diversity, or disability exceptionality. Middle and high school teachers need to ensure that students are taught course content as well as basic skills, such as reading, writing, and arithmetic.

Assessment reporting must make sure that individual accountability is differentiated from accountability focused on the school as a whole. School system accountability must never be the sole basis for making individual educational decisions. The IEP team should make the determination about participation in assessment testing based on individual needs. Teachers, related service personnel, paraprofessionals, administrators, parents, and students must cooperate in the planning, application, and evaluation of an appropriate assessment and accountability system, including its application to students with exceptional needs in order to guarantee its successful implementation (*Today*, 2003, 5).

Educators should keep in mind that alternatives to standardized tests are available. Curriculum-based assessment, classroom observations, and student portfolios provide more detail about student learning than standardized tests. Evaluation of student performance can improve when assessment paints a picture of student as learner rather than student as test taker.

SUMMARY

Inclusion and least restrictive environment are terms that address the importance of integrating students with disabilities with their nondisabled peers. Inclusion means educating students with disabilities in the general education classroom with special education support. There are two models of support in today's schools used to implement inclusion and these are called collaborative consultation and co-teaching.

The legal mandate for inclusion is based on the least restrictive environment provision, reaffirmed in the latest amendments to IDEA. All students want to be viewed as normal by peers and teachers. With special education delivered in the general classroom, all students do not have to be pulled out for special instruction in the resource room or placed in segregated "special" programs. Inclusion eliminates the artificial division that is created between students with disabilities and their peers when they are needlessly removed from their general classroom. However, a continuum of special education placements is necessary in order to teach those students for whom inclusion does not work.

Inclusion can be an effective educational intervention. A well-planned inclusion program helps develop both academic and social skills as well as or better than pull-out or self-contained special education programs. Planning an inclusion program includes communicating with parents, understanding student needs, preparing students for a change, and evaluating student progress.

Sound general educational practices such as cooperative learning and peer tutoring work equally well with students with mild disabilities. Consultation strategies offer teachers and students alternative strategies to achieve inclusion programs.

Both special and general educators have a stake in realigning their efforts to teach students with mild disabilities. The inclusion movement breathed new life into mainstreaming efforts by focusing attention on the benefits of merging special and general education efforts for students. It is clear by now that uninspired teaching does as much to create learning problems as do the characteristics of individual students. By focusing attention on ways of enhancing classroom learning environments, educators can best serve the needs of all students.

ACTIVITIES

1. Arrange to meet with several general classroom and special education teachers of students with mild disabilities. Ask them questions about how inclusion works for them. What special needs do students with mild disabilities have in their general and resource classrooms? Are their needs similar? Do the teachers collaborate with each other as they plan for the students' instruction? Do both participate in developing the students' individual education programs?

2. Visit the campus library. Locate major journals in special education. Look for articles on inclusion. In particular, look for inclusion models and ways in which inclusion concerns have been resolved. Identify articles that present effective ideas about adapting and modifying instruction in the regular classroom.

3. While visiting your campus library, look through journals that publish articles about special education teachers who function as consultants. What would the role of the special education teacher be like in this capacity compared to functioning in a direct service delivery role? How would a special education consultant deliver indirect services to general classroom teachers?

4. Examine the parallels between the civil rights movement and the disability rights movement. Identify leaders in both movements. What sort of heroic deeds inspired individuals to back these movements? How were the movements similar and different?

5. Read Burton Blatt's pictorial essay on institutionalization, *Christmas in Purgatory*. Discuss the impact of this exposé on the lives of individuals with disabilities and their families. Discuss how society's views of disabilities has changed since the publication of Blatt's advocacy work in the early 1970s. Contact the Center for Human Policy at Syracuse University to provide information on the disability advocacy movement (www.thechp.syr.edu).

CHAPTER SEVEN

LEARNING AND TEACHING

ADVANCE QUESTIONS

Answer the following questions as you read this chapter:

1. How will you implement a response-to-intervention (RTI) program?
2. How does student perception influence attitudes about school? How does a developmental perspective help teachers understand their students?
3. What is student-centered learning? What are some things to consider when implementing student-centered learning?
4. What is the connection between direct instruction and effective school research?
5. How does a teacher differentiate instruction to fit each learner's needs?
6. What is the purpose of precision teaching?
7. How can students learn for a lifetime by using learning strategies?
8. How can recent research on brain function improve teaching?

9. What types of assistive technology are accessible to classroom teachers?
10. What is a "functional curriculum"?
11. How does a teacher determine which instructional approach to use?
12. What does current research state about math and reading?

VIGNETTE: JERRY WILLIAMS AND ANN BROWN

At the beginning of the school year, a classwide screening test in reading was administered to the 1st-grade classrooms at Jefferson Elementary School. Both Jerry Williams's and Ann Brown's scores fell below the school's cut-off level used to identify students at risk for reading failure. RTI was initiated. Jerry, Ann, and several of their classmates were monitored for 5 weeks to determine if they could succeed with the school's reading curriculum, which consisted of a well-known basal reader series. Their teacher, Mr. Singh, used curriculum-based measurement to see how well they did. Both Jerry and Ann were found unresponsive to Tier 1 general education and in need of additional support.

Mr. Singh met with the Williamses, and the Browns, Jerry's and Ann's parents. He explained to the parents at both of these meetings why the school was concerned about their child's lack of reading progress. The parents were asked to give written consent so that their children could enter Tier 2 of the school's RTI program. Parents received a written intervention plan that provided details about the intervention program. The selected intervention was phonemic awareness instruction. Jerry and Ann received tutoring "four times each week for 45 minutes each session for 8 weeks."

Progress monitoring was done weekly. The parents received a report that included graphs of their child's progress every 2 weeks. The graphs enabled the parents to "see" the individual progress being made by their child. They were told that they could ask questions about the progress reports at any time. The parents also were told that they could request a formal evaluation if they thought their child might have a disability and need special education under the Individuals with Disabilities Education Act (IDEA).

Jerry made good progress. He was determined to do well and he returned to Tier 1 general education. The Williamses were told that the school would continue to monitor his progress on a weekly basis. They were assured that if Jerry did not continue to progress as expected he could reenter the Tier 2 phase again.

Ann's parents, the Browns, requested information and materials that they could use at home while their daughter received the preventative tutoring on Tier 2. Ann's mother worked with her every school night for half an hour on phonological sounds, letter-sound recognition, and sight word recognition. Mrs. Brown used flash cards, adapted learning cards, and word games. Still, Ann continued to have many of the same reading difficulties.

Mr. Singh met with Mr. and Mrs. Brown to explain their concerns about Ann's lack of response to Tier 2. The possibility of a learning disability was discussed. Mr. Singh explained that if Ann continued to fall behind her classmates, she might have to repeat 1st grade. The school principal asked for written consent to conduct a special education screening to gather more information about Ann. Testing measured Ann's language-processing skills. An above-average score on an IQ test and an age-appropriate measure of adaptive behavior ruled out a mild intellectual disability. Several classroom observations, along with progress monitoring records of Ann's performance in Tier 1 and Tier 2, were added to the information pool. A multidisciplinary school team including a school psychologist, reading specialist, special education teacher, and Ann's general education teacher, Mr. Singh decided that Ann met the federal criteria for a specific learning disability and she was eligible for special education. The team developed an IEP for Ann. Written consent was provided by the Browns for special education services to begin. At this point, Ann entered Tier 3 where a special education teacher began a more intensive intervention program with her.

The special education teacher, Mr. Jackson, worked with Ann in a pull-out program for an hour each day, both one-to-one and in small groups. He utilized an intensive phonics approach that focused on letter-sound associations, letter-sound correspondence, and graphophonemic relationships. Ann's progress was monitored twice weekly and the Browns were provided a written report each grading period. The graphs in the monitoring reports showed the parents the progress that Ann was making in reading. Mr. Jackson enhanced Ann's special education program by adding 20-minute computer software reading sessions, three times a week. Ann's mother and father continued to work with her at home to supplement and to reinforce the special education services she was receiving.

Ann's progress continues to be monitored and reported to her family. If Ann's reading level improves sufficiently, the school team will meet to determine whether Ann might discontinue special education services and receive all reading instruction in the general education 1st-grade classroom with continued monitoring.

1. Do you know how to implement an RTI program for your students? Tell what happens at the different tier levels.
2. Can you explain why Jerry was put back into the monitoring phase for general education? What instructional methods would you recommend for him?
3. How was Ann identified as having a specific learning disability? (Refer back to Chapter 5.)
4. Which instructional methods and techniques could Ann's special education teacher use? Which instructional methods and techniques could her general classroom teacher utilize?

TODAY'S SCHOOLS

Each morning, 55 million students troop off to school. They arrive on foot, in cars, and in an armada of yellow school buses. Bells ring; children file into classrooms; the teacher closes the classroom door, calls for attention, and another school day begins. What happens next? Other than sleeping and watching television, no activity demands as much of adolescents' time time as school. Even though teachers and students spend almost a thousand hours together each year, our knowledge about what transpires inside classroom walls is fragmentary.

Some teachers spend most of their day standing or sitting in the front of the classroom. Their primary teaching tools are lecture, texts, workbooks, and worksheets. Other teachers appreciate the need for students to be active learners. These progressive teachers mix student-centered learning with direct instruction. They are flexible and are more adept than "frontal teachers" at modifying their instruction to meet the needs of individual students. Teachers who vary their teaching methods are more successful than those who depend on one or two "tried-and-true" ways of teaching.

Proactive teachers generally are more receptive to innovations. They are ready to try new interventions and programs like the RTI program. Having special education teachers bring in special teaching methods and ideas is not threatening to these general education classroom teachers. They welcome the special innovations and skills that these teachers add to their classroom. Inclusion thrives under the auspices of proactive classroom teachers.

SPEEDBUMP—Did you have any teachers that fit the proactive mold? How were they different from other teachers?

Ask any teacher what schools are for, and you are likely to get a variety of answers ranging from the basic—"Schools are to teach skills for life"—to the enthusiastic—"Schools are to help kids learn about themselves and the world around them." However, what do the students who, from ages 5 to 18, spend 12,000 hours in classrooms think about school?

Student Perceptions of School

Noyes and McAndrew (1971) interviewed students throughout the country and asked them, "What are schools for?" A typical response was:

> We go to school because it is the law. They make you stay until you are sixteen, and by then you may as well go on since you probably only have another year or two anyway. The point of it, I guess, is to get a diploma so you can go to college. (Noyes & McAndrew, 1971, 321)

The overall **perception** of the students in this study was that the purpose of school was preparation for college. Students did not view school as a place that would meet their personal needs. They gave different versions of the same theme—figure out a way to get through school with the least resistance.

In elementary school, White found that student and teacher perceptions about the purpose of school differ. Whereas teachers value the content of the curriculum, students pay more attention to teacher judgments of their work. In the words of one student:

> . . . you have to have a half-inch margin on your papers . . . you put the headings on the right not on the left, and line it up . . . the cover should be felt if you want an A . . . you can't hand in papers that aren't neat, she'll really mark you down . . . you have to write out "remainder" or it's wrong. . . . (White, 1971, 341)

Students measured their progress by grades rather than what they learned. When he was a special education teacher, one teacher had a straightforward reminder regarding the importance of grades to students:

> The director of our program had accepted the teachers' recommendation that we substitute descriptive evaluations for grades. The students participated in assessing their learning. Students met with the teachers to determine if their work in each subject showed improvement. Peter and I had a conference at my desk about his progress. "Do you think your reading has improved?" I asked him. "What do you mean?" he replied. "You know, are you getting better at reading?" I asked. "How should I know," Peter said, "you're the teacher. It's your job to give me a grade so I'll know if I've learned anything."

Peter's comment illustrates the distance between teacher and student perspectives about school. Students are not connected to their learning in the ways adults imagine. They learn the rules of school and how to get by, but curriculum as adults understand it does not have the same meaning to students. Whereas teachers want students to learn, students want to get the teacher's approval, receive good grades, and enjoy the company of their friends. Sometimes they are excited about learning; sometimes they are bored. At all times, students realize that their fate is essentially in the hands of the teacher. Some students cope with the inequality of power and perform at a level that will satisfy both teacher and parents. Others fall by the wayside. These failures are eventually classified as students at risk, school dropouts, or students with mild disabilities.

> **SPEEDBUMP**—Do you agree or disagree with this analysis? Can you think of any ways that you perceived school differently than your teachers? How about now in your college classes?

What are the characteristics of classroom life that create such a discrepancy between how teachers and students view learning? It should come as no surprise that students view grades as the purpose of their school experience. From the time they receive their first report card until they take the Scholastic Aptitude Test (SAT) in high school, students continually are reminded of the importance of grades. Tests are as indigenous to life in schools as chalk, blackboards, and textbooks.

Some teachers' efforts are best characterized as test rather than curriculum driven. These teachers teach to improve test scores rather than to stimulate a love of learning. As long as school-based quizzes and national achievement tests continue as the key measure of success in school, students will concentrate on grades as their most important goal.

Child and Adolescent Development

"What did you do in school today?" When a father asked his 6-year-old daughter Margaret this question, she answered, "Well, we had lunch in the cafeteria, we lined up for the bus, and we had folder work on Thursday and we had fun together, me, Brian, all my friends." She added, "That's not all but I forget the rest."

Margaret's response illustrates another major difference between the way in which teachers and students view school. When she thinks about school, Margaret considers its most gratifying aspects—lunch, friends, and a side reference to her studies, "folder work." Children are not miniature adults. There are significant developmental differences between teachers and their students. One developmental distinction is in perceptions of goals.

While adults take the long view, students look at the future from short range. Teachers are concerned with distant goals; students are concerned with here and now. For a 5-year-old, 20 minutes is an endless wait. Summer for a 12-year-old seems to extend into the distance, an uninterrupted progression of sunny days and steamy nights. To the freshman and sophomore, high school appears as if it will never end. Time limits have slight meaning to teenagers who perceive themselves as immortal.

Within this context of time without end, parents and adults pound away at such themes in high school as "You need to learn math in order to get a good job," or they tell primary-grade children, "If you finish your work in 20 minutes, you will get free time at the end of the week." Each of these messages leaves a faint impression on students who are unable to fathom the mystery of work today for tomorrow's reward. Child and adolescent development lend weight to Einstein's view that time is relative. Discipline, grades, and learning are fundamental classroom issues that teachers approach as long-range preparation for work or college, while youngsters jolt forward one day at a time with eyes cast on more substantial concerns, such as watching the clock hands on the wall slowly creep toward dismissal.

SPEEDBUMP—Do you remember staring at a clock waiting for school to end for the day? Name three things you can do when you become a teacher to make school work interesting for your students.

Developmental differences between students and teachers are accepted and valued in many early childhood programs, but teachers and administrators sometimes lose track of child and adolescent development. This neglect by school personnel creates a gulf between teachers and students that can have dire consequences. To paraphrase Robert Sternberg (1990), ignore students' developmental differences at our peril—and theirs.

Part of growing up is learning to take on the perspective of those who are older. Primary-school–aged children learn to be less egocentric as they acquire the ability to perceive a situation from another's point of view. Students in elementary school are here-and-now oriented. It isn't until adolescence that students can begin to consider future goals.

Developmental needs dictate priorities to students, and these priorities can put a student in conflict with adults. For the teenager, relationships, intimacy, and getting a driver's license are major concerns. Adolescence is a time of "grandiose ascension." Teenagers fly high above the mundane matters of the everyday world as they experience new mental and physical abilities they never imagined they would possess (Bly, 1990). Many teenagers perceive parents as old fashioned and too strict. When bad things happen, teenagers are reluctant to face them head-on. Denial is a useful defense mechanism for skipping over the hardships of a family's divorce, a mother's addiction, or a father's neglect. This is why depression and drug abuse are such developmental hazards for adolescents. Adolescents are more likely to act out their emotional struggles than to reflect or talk to others.

In high school, acceptance by one's peer group can be more pressing than getting homework done. The teenager confronts the social dilemma of breaking free from the bonds of adult authority at precisely the same time that parents and teachers are demanding responsible behavior. This pulling in opposite directions usually leaves both adults and adolescents perplexed. Even though developmental changes are at times baffling, these changes help explain why the meaning of school is interpreted differently by teachers and students (Hersch, 1998).

STUDENT-CENTERED LEARNING

In his widely acclaimed book *A Place Called School*, John Goodlad (1984) laments the lack of vigor in U.S. classrooms. He describes some teachers as **frontal teachers**. By this he means they seem rooted to the front of the room, where, like ship captains, they oversee all classroom activity. In describing the culture of school, Goodlad characterizes the teacher as a virtually autonomous person who controls almost every aspect of classroom life. Students labor alone, solitary figures in groups, with little to say about how they spend their days. Many students, Goodlad said, engage in a narrow range of passive behaviors such as listening to the teacher, writing answers to questions, and taking tests or quizzes. Goodlad was not the first educator to describe public schools as havens of autocracy that demand conformity. Demands for changing schools to be more student centered seem to provide a counterpoint to reform recommendations that insist teachers get back to the basics. For every statement about empowering teachers, such as Hunter's direct instruction model, there is the inevitable reaction to empower students.

SPEEDBUMP—Why avoid becoming a "frontal teacher"?

Glasser (1985) argued that schools should become more responsive to student needs. According to Glasser, student apathy and unwillingness to participate in classroom activities is a direct response to student impotence. As an illustration, Glasser pointed out that no one has to coerce students to work hard at extracurricular activities. Yearbooks, science fairs, athletics, and debate clubs represent a few manifestations of activities that students engage in with enthusiasm. Glasser maintained that the opportunity to exercise control of extracurricular activities increases motivation and involvement. He articulated four student needs that schools should strive to fulfill in the classroom (1985):

1. Students need to belong. They need to feel a part of a larger community and to feel that they are valued by the group.
2. Students need power. They need to make decisions and have responsibilities.
3. Students need freedom. They need to feel self-reliant and in control of their own destiny.
4. Students need fun. They need to have joy and humor, and they want to work for personal satisfaction.

Notice that none of these needs relates to specific parts of the academic curriculum; rather Glasser is focusing on deeper, developmental needs. It's at the developmental level where student-directed and teacher-directed advocates split. Teachers who formalize student-directed learning in their classrooms assume a developmental view of education.

Preschool education is the only sector of public education that holds to a strong developmental outlook. Once students begin 1st grade and continue through middle and high school, developmental views on how young people learn and what their psychological needs are get mired in a curriculum logjam (Elkind, 1986). Teachers wilt under the pressure to get a student "ready" for the next grade. Achievement tests, basal readers, and an endless array of workbooks provide the grist that students must grind their way through in traditional, curriculum-centered classrooms. In high school, the winds of curriculum pick up pace as teachers bend to pressure to prepare students for graduation and college entrance requirements. The pressure to pass standardized achievement tests increased with the passage of the NCLB.

In a **student-centered** classroom, it is unlikely that students would select the same topics mandated by the school system for each grade. Here lies the dilemma for the student-centered teacher.

What the priority specific curriculum requirements that are best taught through teacher-directed lessons, or student-centered activities that may overlook content measured in standard tests of achievement?

A negotiated solution is workable. Teachers can merge both approaches. Direct instruction on the periodic table is more likely to grab a student's attention after a few experiments in a chemistry laboratory. Classroom discussions about the pros and cons of *Roe v. Wade* can provide the same insight into the judicial system of our country as that covered by a mundane chapter in a social studies text. Cooperative learning projects can cover the same content as a lecture on algebraic equations.

Student-centered classrooms look different than teacher-directed classrooms. Furniture is arranged to enhance student conversation in small groups; cooperative learning and peer tutoring are commonplace. Myriad objects for concrete learning experiences are arranged on tables. While students work, the teacher moves about the room encouraging, providing feedback, and giving directions. Some students are engaged in small groups; others work independently. Work schedules are arranged to allow students to study different topics at the same time. Rote learning, drills, and passive materials such as worksheets and dittos are shunned.

A common misconception of student-centered classrooms is that they are unstructured. A visitor to a student-centered 4th grade might observe the following scene. Adults and students are scattered throughout the room. In one corner, a parent volunteer is listening to three students take turns reading. Along the perimeter of the room, students in pairs are working at several tables that are labeled "math center," "science center," "art center," and "writing center." In another corner of the room, a student is playing a math game at a computer. Two students are cleaning the gerbil cage. Four students are sitting on pillows and reading library books in the "quiet corner." A student teacher is standing in front of the blackboard reviewing fractions with a group of five students. Finally, the visitor spots the teacher in another corner. Around her is a group of seven students. She is doing a phonics lesson. The room is a beehive of activity. People are talking and walking about. Everybody is busy.

To the untrained eye, the scene may appear disorganized, but there is a complex structure that holds everything together. A student-centered classroom requires a well-thought-out plan for moving students from one center to another; materials and themes at the centers need continual refurbishing; volunteers need direction; student progress must be monitored; and the daily schedule must ensure that all students have a blend of direct and indirect learning experiences. A teacher in a student-directed classroom must be capable of supervising several simultaneous activities. The following models incorporate one or more principles of student-centered learning.

> **SPEEDBUMP—**As you read through these student-centered approaches, make a list of those that resemble teaching methods used by your teachers when you were in elementary or secondary school.

Brain-Compatible Instruction

Educators' efforts to solve the mystery about how students think and learn has in the past been hampered by one critical element: an inability to study the human brain in the process of thinking. With the advent of technologies for direct observation of brain function, the brain slowly is giving up its secrets, and the ramifications for educators is enormous. Consider the following information gleaned from the research on brain function and schooling.

- Students who utilize flash cards for learning will do better if the card is round. A circle is the most recognizable shape. Circular cards allow students to focus better because the round shape is less distracting than squares or rectangles (Barron, 2000).
- Movement is the only experience that unites all brain levels and integrates the right and left hemispheres of young students. Movement increases heart rate and circulation. It provides students with a spatial reference in the classroom, which improves memory. Movement promotes the release of noradrenaline and dopamine. These energizers keep students alert and enhance attention (Barron, 2000; Jensen, 1998).
- Thematic instruction improves learning by helping students to identify patterns and build on prior knowledge. Integrating curriculum areas such as the study of rain forests by combining mathematics, music, biology, and geography into a unit helps students learn more effectively than teaching each of these subjects in isolation (Wagmeister & Shifrin, 2000).
- Abstract ideas are developed by connecting concepts to students' personal experiences. This helps students link new information into preexisting neural patterns. For example, a teacher introduced a lesson on ratios by having students make juice from cans of concentrate (i.e., three cans of water for each can of juice) (Westwater & Wolfe, 2000).
- Analogies, similes, and metaphors enhance learning by linking abstract concepts and visualizations. For example, the terms *million, billion,* and *trillion* have no referent in direct experience. Creating visual analogies makes the numbers comprehensible. For example, a 4-inch stack of tightly bound 1,000 dollar bills would equal a million dollars. A stack that was a city block long would equal $1 billion (Westwater & Wolfe, 2000).
- The brain is not wired for long attention spans. Attention is focused in short bursts. Initially, attention lasts for about 18 seconds. The optimum sustained attention span

is roughly equivalent in minutes to the age of the student. A 1st grader's attention span is 6 minutes, 6th grader's 12 minutes, and high school seniors 17 minutes. Individual lessons should include a variety of components, for example, teacher presentation could be followed by student discussion, seat work, group project, and feedback (Jensen, 1998).

SPEEDBUMP—The previous points are interesting but not everyone agrees with them. What do you think? Do a Web search and see if you can find some interesting new facts about how the human brain learns.

The brain consists of approximately 100 billion neurons. That's a big number that is difficult to grasp. Sylwester explained, "There are about 100,000 hairs on the average human head, so that all of the hair in a population of a million people would be about as many neurons as you have in your brain" (Figgis, 1995). However, individual neurons are not the site of most brain activity. It is the connections that develop between neurons (500 trillion by age 10) that powers human thought. Think of individual computers running software on neurons so small that 70,000 could be contained on the head of a pin (Kotulak, 1996). Now connect all of these computers via the Internet and you have an idea of the exponential brain power produced by neural networks. These neural networks are cultivated by experience. As students mature, patterns develop that link neural networks residing in different locales within the brain. It is this chunking or binding of neurons that we refer to as thought. The cultivating and pruning of these pathways goes throughout life. Sylwester compared the neural landscape to a jungle "where different kinds of neurons and neuronal pathways competed randomly to survive, the way that particular trees or insects do. The message, then, is: for schools to match these messy minds of ours there should be more open-ended work for kids, more conversation, more liveliness—indeed more passion" (Figgis, 1995, 2).

Emotions and Learning

Within the past decade, scientists have learned more about the brain than in the previous 100 years. Gradually, the fields of neuroscience and education are finding common ground. One of the major insights is recent revelations about how emotions affect thought and learning. These findings are particularly relevant to the education of students with mild disabilities because so many of these students have experienced failure in classrooms. Far more neural fibers project from our brain's emotional center up into the logical/rational areas of the brain than the reverse (Sylwester, 2000). A brain that is faced with a perceived threat is likely to "downshift." This is a biological response that focuses the brain on only what is necessary for survival. When students feel threatened by academic material that carries with it a high anxiety quotient, ". . . their brains perseverate, continuously repeating thoughts or unresolved emotional issues" (Caine, 2000, 59). Anyone who can recall his or her mind going "blank" when confronted with a difficult test question has experienced the downshifting that is commonplace among students who are chronic underachievers in school.

Fatigue, frequent illness, distractibility, and defiance are some of the classroom behaviors observed in "downshifted" students. Students who are exposed to a steady regimen of threatening academic work develop "learned helplessness" or habitual avoidance habits. Creating a sense of community and fostering positive relationships in the classroom is one method for countermanding the brain's "downshift" orders. Fostering communal bonds relieves stress and helps students to feel emotionally secure in the classroom. Music, art, drama, and sports help relieve tension and give students opportunities to experience success.

> **SPEEDBUMP—**Read the last paragraph again. Do you agree with this concept of downshifting? Can you think of some ways emotions influence your ability to perform? For example, do you ever experience test anxiety?

One teacher worked as a consultant in alternative high school. Students were placed in this program because of severe behavior problems. Getting these young people to attend to academics and to take responsibility for their behavior was a major chore, yet, while playing basketball during recess, these same recalcitrant youths helped each other, managed frustration, and relished the competition. After each game, there were smiles, sweat, and satisfaction. The physical education teacher observed that "they seem like different kids!" At least for some of the students who attended this alternative school, the basketball court was a welcome stress reliever from the classroom.

Emotions are unconscious responses spurred by chemical reactions to environmental stimuli. *Cortisol*, which is released by the adrenal glands, activates a defensive reaction to stress. A stressful school climate can elevate cortisol and eventually destroy hippocampus neurons that are associated with learning. Activities that put students in positive learning states include class discussions, journal writing, stretching, panel discussions, mind-mapping, reflecting, listening to music, dancing, and games (Jensen, 1998). *Endorphins* are a group of peptides that regulate emotions along the pain-pleasure continuum. They increase euphoria and decrease pain. Exercise, positive social contacts, fun, camaraderie, and a joyful classroom atmosphere activate endorphins and help students tackle difficult academic tasks.

Emotions also play a key role in memory retention. Classroom simulations, presentations, role playing, drama, projects, and group collaborations tie learning to emotional contexts, thus enhancing retention of information (Sylwester, 1994). Unexpressed emotions inhibit learning. Students need opportunities to link their feelings to classroom content. Drama, classroom discussions, singing, writing, music, and drawing help build neural connections and inhibit the release of chemicals that interfere with learning such as cortisol, adrenaline, and vasopressin (Jensen, 1998). Emotions direct attention, and attention leads to better learning (D'Arcangelo, 2000). Students who are emotionally involved will learn better than students who are emotionally uninvolved from the content presented. Even mildly stressful situations (e.g., studying for an impending test) support learning better than a neutral state.

Multiple Intelligence

According to Gardner (1983), there are eight types of intelligence that students acquire as they mature and interact with their environment: linguistic, logical-mathematical, spatial, kinesthetic, musical, interpersonal, intrapersonal, and naturalist. Multiple intelligence theory explains the rich diversity of abilities that individuals demonstrate in society. Gardner's concern related to schooling is that two types of intelligence are emphasized—linguistic and logical-mathematical—at the expense of the six others. Students who demonstrate strengths in linguistic and logical-mathematical intelligence have a distinct advantage over other students, who may be just as intelligent, but are unable to demonstrate their abilities within the traditional curricula. The lack of attention to individual differences between students is demonstrated by one-size-fits-all teaching methods. Gardner said, "What I argue against is the notion that there's only one way to learn how to read, only one way to learn how to compute, only one way to learn about biology. I think that such contentions are nonsense" (cited in Checkley, 1997, 10).

> **SPEEDBUMP**—If President George Bush, the architect of No Child Left Behind, and Howard Gardner sat down for a cup of coffee, do you think they would agree about how to improve schools?

Multiple intelligence emphasizes student movement. Rather than spending prolonged periods of time sitting at desks, students are up and moving around the room. They are engaged in learning stations, group projects, and small-group instruction. Open-ended learning activities that have practical uses such as student-directed newspapers and research activities are highlighted in the multiple intelligence classroom. There are opportunities for socialization as students learn together in pairs or small, cooperative groups. Teachers put a premium on student reflection. Right-and-wrong answers are not as relevant as the thinking processes that lead students to a particular conclusion. Music, art, and dance are prized as an end and a means to help students explore their own unique forms of expression. Above all, the multiple intelligence approach respects the different ways in which students learn. Many educators have embraced the multiple intelligence perspective, yet the theory has its critics as well. The primary criticism is that Gardner's theory is lacking empirical validation and that despite different ways of learning there are some intellectual skills such as critical thinking, information gathering, and presenting one's ideas that all students need to learn.

The following illustration from a high school social studies class illustrates one teacher's approach to incorporating multiple intelligence methods in her lesson (Lambert, 1997, 53). At the end of a unit on early American history, students were allowed to choose presentation formats. The student projects included:

- Writing and performing skits about the Lewis and Clark expedition (verbal, linguistic, and interpersonal intelligence).
- Painting watercolors of birds and other wildlife for a project on John J. Audubon (visual-spatial intelligence).

- Creating a working telegraph (logical-mathematical and bodily-kinesthetic intelligences).
- Developing a board game (visual-spatial intelligence).
- Delivering a eulogy on Davy Crockett (interpersonal intelligence).
- Role playing a historical figure and speaking to the class in character (intrapersonal, verbal-linguistic, and visual-spatial intelligences).

Identifying students' learning style is a good beginning for instruction, but teaching is not a mechanical activity. Teachers cannot fit students to instruction like so many eggs nestled in a carton. To some extent, all students need control over their environment, as well as teacher-directed whole-group instruction and assistance in how to learn.

> **SPEEDBUMP—**Michelangelo said that a block of stone contained the statue. He revealed it by chipping away the unnecessary stone. Can you connect Michelangelo's view to teaching and multiple intelligence?

Rather than emphasizing the "right" way to teach, learning style literature underscores the fact that students are different. Student learning style is a unique blend of individual development and life experience. Teachers who understand learning styles respect the capabilities of their charges. The literature on learning styles provides a sharp contrast to the traditional school norm of student conformity to a single standard of instruction or behavior. As John Holt remarked, "Children are not only extremely good at learning, they are much better at it than we adults are. As a teacher it took me a very long time to find this out" (Holt, 1977, 232). By utilizing an array of instructional models, the teacher builds a bridge between the student and the curriculum. Research on multiple intelligence and learning styles helps us to grasp the complexity of learning and to appreciate the need for teachers to remain flexible when deciding how to teach individual students.

TEACHER-DIRECTED MODELS

Trying to find the best way to teach is a major goal for educators. Educational journals brim with debates about which system of instruction is most effective for teaching reading, math, writing, and appropriate behavior. The search for the best way to teach is tied to many factors. Among these are local leadership, politics, economics, and public support. Education is more like law than like medicine. Absolute cures for educational ills are almost nonexistent. Rather, like law, education must change and adapt to the needs of society; for example, educational policy is shaped at the local level by superintendents, who are hired by school committees. School committees are elected by voters in the community. Consequently, introduction of educational change, along with the necessary budgetary adjustments eventually must have public support.

Each of the following instructional models has been used successfully with students with mild disabilities and nondisabled students. None is foolproof. The selection of a specific instructional model should come after a careful review of educational goals, school-wide resources, and student need.

Direct Instruction

Direct instruction, also referred to as *mastery learning*, refers to a variety of carefully sequenced, teacher-directed methods. The research of Rosenshine and Stevens (1984) indicated that when teachers follow a hierarchy of instructional steps in their lessons, low-achieving students increase achievement in basic skills.

Direct instruction utilizes teacher demonstration, guided practice, and feedback. According to Larivee (1988), direct instruction includes:

1. *Teacher demonstration*—Provide clear, controlled presentations of new material. Model each step of the material to be learned.
2. *Guided practice*—Follow the demonstration, ask questions, and check student understanding of material.
3. *Feedback*—Circulate among students as they work on independent activities related to the new material. Provide corrective feedback on their work. Use frequent cumulative review.

The work of Madeline Hunter and her instructional theory into practice (ITIP) instructional model is an example of a direct instruction program that has been implemented in thousands of schools throughout the country. Hunter stated that teachers were first and foremost decision makers and teaching decisions should be informed by educational research. Hunter's ITIP system divided teaching into practical lists and sublists that teachers follow as they make decisions about how and what to teach. Hunter organized the teaching act into seven components:

1. Knowledge of human growth and development
2. Content
3. Classroom management
4. Materials
5. Planning
6. Human relations
7. Instructional skills

These components identify the kinds of decisions a teacher makes minute-by-minute in the classroom. Hunter encouraged teachers to use data from learning situations to augment teaching decisions and increase student mastery. Hunter summarized her approach in an interview with Mark Goldberg, ". . . all of the 5,000 decisions a teacher makes every day fall neatly into three categories: what you are going to teach, which we call a content category; what the students are going to do to learn it and to let you know that they've learned it, which we call a learning behavior category; and what you as the teacher will do to facilitate and escalate that learning, which is called a teaching behavior category" (Goldberg, 1990, 41).

In their summary of direct instruction for students with mild disabilities, Bickel and Bickel (1986) noted, "Effective teachers take an active role in creating a positive, expectant, and orderly classroom environment in which learning takes place." Teachers' control time management, signal when academic work will begin, maintain a group focus, expect students to be accountable, and provide a variety of instructional tasks. Direct instruction is based on teacher control of instruction and close supervision of student work. It has produced good results in teaching basic skills, and raising standardized test scores. Critics maintain that direct instruction stifles student initiative and doesn't teach higher-level thinking skills. Critics also express concern that direct instruction undercuts motivation by reinforcing student dependence on the teacher (Knapp, Turnbull, & Shields, 1990). The following instructional models are teacher directed, and incorporate one or more principles of direct instruction.

SPEEDBUMP—What teaching goals are best suited for direct instruction and which are best suited for student-centered learning? If you can answer this question, you will be well on your way to a successful teaching career.

Multisensory Instruction

Many students with mild disabilities have severe reading problems. Within the field of learning disabilities, multisensory approaches to teaching reading are well regarded. **Multisensory instruction** is based on the premise that the more senses involved, the more efficient the instruction. There are many specific reading programs that incorporate multisensory approaches. These programs are often referred to as *VAKT instructional methods*. This acronym is formed from the first letter of the words visual, auditory, kinesthetic, and tactile. "To stimulate all of these senses, children hear the teacher say the word, say the word to themselves, hear themselves say the word, feel the muscle movement as they trace the word, feel the tactile surface under their finger tips, see their hands move as they trace the word, and hear themselves say the word as they trace it" (Lerner, 2000, 430).

The Orton–Gillingham method is perhaps the best known VAKT instructional approach. This approach was developed during the 1930s by Samuel Orton. Three colleagues of Orton's, Anna Gillingham, Romalda Spaulding, and Beth Slingerland, worked closely with him to develop a reading instruction program that could help dyslexic students. The focus of the program is to teach sounds and letter names. This phonetic approach is teacher directed and carefully sequenced. Orton's approach was primarily tutorial, Slingerland added a whole-class instruction element for dyslexic students, and Spalding extended the VAKT approach to students without disabilities. Spalding's objective was to prevent reading problems (Farnham-Diggory, 1992). The durability of the VAKT approach to reading is testimony to its usefulness with students with mild disabilities and high-risk learners.

The Wilson Reading Program is closely related to Orton–Gillingham. Students learn encoding and decoding skills through a 12-step, sequenced program. Specifically, the Wilson method focuses on phonological awareness, phonology, and total word structure. The Wilson reading approach is designed for learners after grade 3. A distinctive feature of the Wilson method is a sound tapping system to help students differentiate phonemes.

The linking of decoding skills with multisensory learning activities provides a strong basis for remediation of reading problems. VAKT-type reading programs present a systematic approach to correcting reading difficulties that are neurological-based auditory processing problems that appear as problems related to phonemic awareness, decoding, and encoding.

SPEEDBUMP—Multisensory instruction is deeply ingrained in special education practice. Some techniques go back 50 years or more and are associated with such pioneers in special education as Marianne Frostig, Sam Orton, and Maria Montesorri.

Differentiated Instruction

A teacher differentiates his or her instruction by making adaptations that fit each learner's needs, styles, and abilities. Educators utilizing **differentiated instruction** are acknowledging that students learn at different rates, that they have different learning styles and strengths, and that they differ in their ability to think abstractly or understand complex ideas. Students can explore the same concept or topic; however, each student needs to have the learning experience tailored to increase his or her learning success. This means that in differentiated instruction, teachers make adaptations in one or more of the following ways:

- Content—what you want students to know and be able to do
- Process—how students are going to learn the content
- Product—how students demonstrate what they have learned
- Resources—the media from which students learn (Benjamin, 2003; Instructional Philosophy and Strategies, 2003)

The role of the teacher in a differentiated classroom is that of a planner and facilitator of learning. Teachers give students as much responsibility for their own learning as they are able to manage. Specifically, teachers:

- Assess students' needs and abilities in a variety of ways (e.g., observation, student conference, diagnostic test of a skill).
- Interpret assessment data to determine students' learning needs and styles.
- Design a variety of ways that students can gather information and explore ideas (listening, reading, viewing—resource-based learning).
- Develop a variety of ways that students can express and share their own information and ideas (e.g., orally, in writing, through a visual representation such as a collage or graphic organizer).
- Provide a variety of options for teacher evaluation and student self-assessment.
- Offer students choices as often as possible (1) in their learning arrangement (e.g., working independently or in a group); (2) in the ways that they will learn about the concept and the resources they will use to gather their information and ideas (e.g., print resource—fiction or expository; nonprint—audio, video, human); and (3) in the

ways that they will express, share, or present the ideas and information to others (e.g., oral presentation, visual chart, role play, video production).
■ Keep records to chart students' growth related to the curriculum objectives and concepts being developed. (Instructional Philosophy and Strategies, 2003, 11)

In summary, teachers and students are essentially both learners. Even though teachers may know more about the subject matter than their students, teachers continuously are learning about the diverse ways in which their students learn. Teachers assess students' attainment levels and readiness skills for learning in a variety of ways. Teachers design learning experiences based on their understanding of students' needs and interests. They then present the material in a differentiated manner, and reassess to determine what individual students have learned.

Some new as well as experienced teachers experience difficulty in planning lessons and in adapting their teaching methods in order to allow for differentiation. In addition, many teachers fail to provide a variety of instructional activities for their diverse group of students. Most of these teachers are "teaching to the middle" in their respective classrooms, without addressing the wide range of student abilities at both ends of the continuum—the accelerated learners and the slower learners. The emphasis in these classrooms is in "keeping everyone together" rather than differentiating instruction to meet individual attainment (Holloway, 2000).

Carol Ann Tomlinson (2000) states that educators can recognize differentiated instruction by the following classroom characteristics (p. 2):

■ Teachers begin where the students are.
■ Teachers engage students in instruction through different learning modalities.
■ A student competes more against himself or herself than others.
■ Teachers provide specific ways for each individual to learn.
■ Teachers use classroom time flexibly.

Teachers are diagnosticians, prescribing the best possible instruction for each student.

> **SPEEDBUMP—**Great ideas, but kind of overwhelming, don't you think? Don't worry about it; as a teacher you never stop learning.

Task Analysis

Task analysis is the process of breaking down a learning task into its component parts and teaching each part as a distinct skill. It often is used by sports instructors in teaching such activities as tennis, golf, and skiing. The premise that a hierarchy of subskills underlies mastery of a learning task (e.g., to win a tennis match, to shoot par on a golf course, to ski expert slopes) is the pedagogical foundation of task analysis. By arranging skills in a hierarchy, each skill builds on the next. Task analysis is a sequenced, systematic approach to teaching, which provides opportunities for evaluation of each subskill. When using task analysis, the teacher will need to:

1. write a behavioral statement about the learning task (e.g., to be able to divide three-digit numbers with 90 percent accuracy)
2. design an outline of the learning task broken down into a hierarchy of subskills
3. evaluate the student's abilities in relationship to each of the subskills before instruction
4. select materials and procedures for teaching each subskill
5. provide feedback to students about subskill development
6. evaluate acquisition of each subskill through systematic monitoring

Students generally have some prior knowledge and skills when they begin instruction. Teachers who use task analysis define the task that the student will perform, state the conditions under which the task will occur, and show the criterion measurement required for mastery. Task analysis identifies a sequence of skills needed to perform a task successfully; criterion measurements identify whether the student possesses the necessary skills or knowledge for that task. The level of performance that is acceptable is the criterion level, and it is often specified on the student's IEP.

Through task analysis, the teacher can plan learning activities in the order in which they need to be learned to reach mastery as indicated on the student's IEP. (See Chapter 8 for a description of IEP development.) The criterion set for determining mastery of the behavioral objective can be measured by using criterion-referenced testing, or some other informal, curriculum-based type of assessment.

SPEEDBUMP—Task analysis has been used for years by teachers working with students with moderate to severe disabilities.

Precision Teaching

Ogden Lindsley observed that learning can be enhanced by frequent, self-recorded responses on standardized charts. He encouraged teachers to concentrate on rate of responses instead of percentages of correct responses. Lindsley recommended that teachers teach their students to record their own rate of learning on standardized charts (Lindsley, 1990).

Lindsley designed **precision teaching** around a framework of behavior modification developed by B.F. Skinner. This framework consists of six basic components:

1. By assessing daily performance, teachers can directly measure performance and monitor learning.
2. Calculating rate of response (i.e., the number of correct responses per minute) establishes a consistent measure of behavior.
3. A standard chart format provides a visual display of performance patterns.
4. Definitions of behavior are descriptive and functional.
5. Analysis of instruction is ongoing.
6. The emphasis is on building appropriate and useful behavior, rather than focusing on doing away with undesired or inappropriate behavior.

Jamie is a 5th-grade student at Somewhere Elementary School, U.S.A. Five days a week, Monday through Friday, Jamie reads aloud, answers math problems, and spells words dictated by her teacher. Each of these tasks is timed, and Jamie plots her own scores on separate graphs for reading, math, and spelling. A line is extended from the points where other scores have been plotted (Figure 7.1). This procedure enables her teacher to visually track Jamie's learning rate. Jamie and her classmates are participating in precision teaching. Their teacher is measuring their learning performance daily. By seeing the changes in students' learning each day, Jamie's teacher, and others who utilize precision teaching, can adjust their instructional plans as needed. (White, 1986)

FIGURE 7.1 Precision Learning Chart

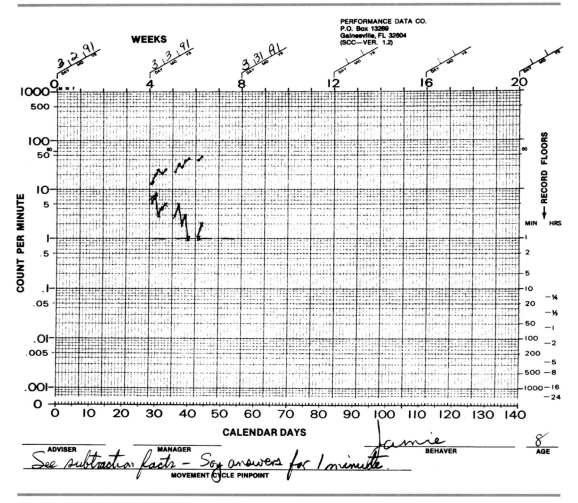

Contributed by Wolking (1991).

When students like Jamie are assessed daily, their changes in performance from one timed assessment to the next guide instruction. The more frequently the timed assessments are made, the more often decisions can be made about the effectiveness of instruction for an individual student. Timings are done each day, thus students have sufficient opportunities to demonstrate skills.

Educators traditionally look for accuracy in student responses. Daily timed assessments provide the data to measure both the accuracy and the rate of learning. Wolking (1991) provided the following description of Jamie:

> At the beginning of this unit of study, Jamie answered 20 subtraction fact problems in a minute. She got 13 correct and made 7 errors. Twelve school days later she answered 47 subtraction facts in a minute. On this timing, she got 45 correct and made 2 errors. The learning line for her correct responses showed that she was improving at a rate of 65% per week. The learning line for her error responses showed she was reducing her errors at a rate of about 70% per week. Overall, Jamie's correct responding has improved by 246% (from 13 to 45 per minute correct), and her error responses have decreased by 250% (from 7 to 2 errors per minute) in just twelve school days.

Precision teaching requires plotting scores on a chart so that changes in student learning can be tracked. This chart is a ratio or logarithmic scale, and referred to as the *standard acceleration chart*. The logarithmic scale displays performance values that are recorded as number of responses per minute. When scores are plotted, an individual's pattern of learning can be seen by drawing a line through the dots. This line of connected points is called a *learning line*. Generally, the steeper the learning line, the faster learning is occurring. Conversely, the more horizontal or flatter the learning line, the slower the rate of learning. The chart is called a *standard* or *acceleration chart* because the same rate of learning is always displayed by the same slope. Lindsley (1990) recommended students self-monitor by plotting their own data on standardized charts. Two innovative self-monitoring approaches are countoons and software spreadsheets.

Countoons.   Daly and Ranalli (2003) use **countoons** to teach self-monitoring skills to students. They contend that young children can learn to count and record their own behaviors, and seem to enjoy doing so. "When you teach children to do the counting and recording themselves in your classroom, you are teaching valuable skills in self-control, as well as freeing up the time devoted to managing the child's behavior for instruction" (p. 30).

Countoons include a simple cartoon representation of a student's appropriate and inappropriate behavior, a reward contingency, and counting frames for recording data. The representations include a picture of the student doing the appropriate behavior and a picture of the student doing the inappropriate behavior (see Figure 7.2). Any behavior that can be described so a student can count it and that can be pictured simply in a cartoon frame can be used for a countoon. A place is provided for students to circle the number of times they demonstrate the behavior. A "consequence frame" pictures the reward.

There are various ways of creating recording devices for these countoons. A teacher can make a sheet of counting frames that can be copied and cut up so new frames can be

FIGURE 7.2   Countoons

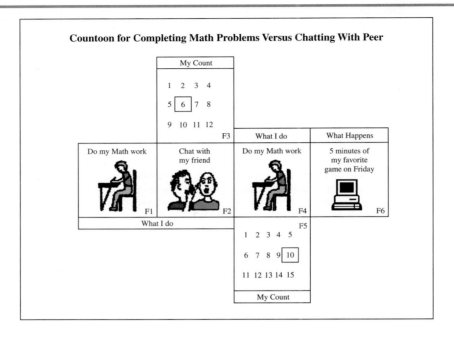

Source: Daly & Ranalli (2003). Reprinted with permission.

added to a countoon for daily data collection. The teacher also can use a file folder and draw the countoon directly onto the inside of the folder. Some teachers use the computer software program Boardmaker (2001) to make countoons. Self-management techniques like countoons appeal to general education teachers who teach in inclusion settings. Both academic and social behaviors can be successfully counted, thus building and reinforcing appropriate behaviors and shaping new ones.

SPEEDBUMP—Getting a student to assess his or her own progress improves the student's accountability—that's a bonus.

Software Charts.   Gunter, Miller, Venn, Thomas, and House (2002) state that "recent simplifications of computer technology software packages have the potential to make it easy for students to record and graph data regarding their academic or social behavior" (p. 30). Gunter and associates used the Microsoft database software Excel and adapted it for self-monitoring by students.

Gunter et al. (2002) outlined the following self-monitoring steps:

1. Identify the academic or social behavior, the data-collection process, and the extent to which the student can contribute to the data-collection process. For gathering data, students can grade their own worksheets and graph the scores. To determine rate such as words read correctly per minute, an audio recording could be made and someone could provide this data to the student for recording and graphing.
2. On the desktop of a classroom computer, a folder can be created for each student. Within each student's folder are files for different academic areas and for social skills. For example, a student can open his folder labeled Manuel Torres's Data and in it find Excel files for subjects like reading, spelling, and math. Each file contains a teacher-generated Excel spreadsheet with an embedded graph for which the student records his or her data.
3. A desired "celebration" line is calculated. The celebration line allows the student to see if the recorded performance meets the criteria necessary to master the objective in the designated amount of time. This visual feedback is important for determining if criteria have been met.

Countoons and software charts promote self-monitoring. The benefits of doing this have been noted over the last 30 years. Moxley (1998) states that self-monitoring by students: (1) provides a clear picture of performance; (2) gives immediate feedback in a clear, visible manner; (3) involves students in selecting behaviors to monitor; (4) enhances communication with parents; and (5) promotes intracomparisons within one's own skills repertoire rather than encouraging intercompetition with peers.

Learning Strategies

A 12-year-old given the task of remembering a list of objects (e.g., milk, bread, soda, candy) might repeat the words several times in order to commit them to memory. **Learning strategies** (also referred to as cognitive strategy, cognitive behavior modification, and meta-cognitive skills) are mental schemes for memorizing, solving problems, planning, or organizing (Pressley & Harris, 1990). Many individuals independently learn these strategies in the normal course of development; others never acquire these strategies on their own. The lack of learning strategy development may be the basis for many of the learning problems encountered by students with mild disabilities.

Alley and Deshler, practitioners in the field of special education, identified learning strategies as "... techniques, principles, or rules that will facilitate the acquisition, manipulation, integration, storage, and retrieval of information across situations and settings" (1979, 13). These authors support the need to teach students how to use learning strategies to improve comprehension and retention of classroom content. Equally important is teaching students how to generalize learning strategies outside of school.

SPEEDBUMP—What are your learning strategies? Can you describe things you do that help improve your own academic progress?

The adage "Give me a fish, and I can eat for a day. Teach me to fish, and I can eat for a lifetime" summarizes the goal of this approach. The intent is to teach students skills that will allow them not only to meet immediate requirements successfully but also to generalize these skills to other situations over time. (Alley & Deshler, 1979, 13)

Learning strategies help students learn to cope with mild disabilities by providing them with a set of directions for improving their ability to learn. Pressley and Harris (1990) present the following guidelines for using learning strategies to improve reading comprehension (p. 13):

1. Summarize the story. Dialogues and classroom discussions enhance memory of plot and characters.
2. Construct an internal visual representation of the story. This procedure can be enhanced through art activities.
3. Relate student experience to a story.
4. Make up questions about the story while reading.

The teaching of learning strategies begins with the teacher modeling the strategy. Students might be assigned an essay, for example, and the teacher would begin by demonstrating how to write an intuitive outline (see Figure 7.3). The purpose of the intuitive outline is to get ideas out before listing them in a sequential outline. An intuitive outline is completed by a student brainstorming by herself. She begins by placing the theme or main idea in an oval, and then writes each idea associated with the main thought on lines that branch out from the center. As a new idea comes to mind, it is added to an existing branch or a new branch is started. Just as a tree branches out spontaneously in different directions, the intuitive outline grows to accommodate the natural progression of ideas. This learning strategy (sometimes called *webbing*) can help solve common problems such as writer's block or test anxiety.

Another example of a learning strategy is *mnemonics*, a system of memory training that helps students remember important concepts by associating ideas to visual stimuli. A student might remember key principles of the U.S. Constitution, for instance, by going for a memory walk down his street and mentally "picking up" due process from the delicatessen, freedom of the press from the newspaper machine, and the right to bear arms from the department store mannequin.

FIGURE 7.3   Intuitive Outline

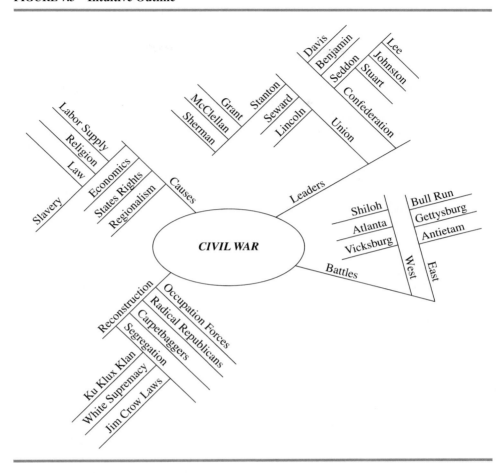

Mann and Sabatino (1985) recommend the following steps for incorporating a learning-strategies approach in the classroom:

1. Describe the strategies needed to solve a classroom problem. (One way to do this is through task analysis; break the solution down into specific steps.)
2. Measure a student's use or nonuse of strategies.
3. Help students implement selected strategies and adjust and revise as needed.
4. Monitor how well the strategy is working.
5. Motivate students to use the strategy.

Selecting the best strategy is a key element in utilizing the learning-strategy approach. Scott (1988) recommends teaching problem-solving skills demonstrated by successful students. She identified concentration, independence, reflection, self-direction, active learning, and persistence as core learning strategies students with mild disabilities could learn to improve their classroom performance. Scott presented a variety of activities to teach each learning strategy to a student. For instance, concentration can be taught by playing chess or other games. Reflection could be taught by having students count to ten before they give an answer.

Story Grammar Marker.   A **story grammar marker** (SGM) is a hands-on manipulative for teaching text structure for oral and written expression. The SGM is designed to be held by the student and teacher while telling, retelling, and writing stories. It is visual, tactile, and kinesthetic, making it a three-dimensional graphic organizer. Use of this tool provides students and teachers with a *common language* that connects language and literacy.

Narrative elements of character, setting, problem, feelings, plans, actions, and consequences are represented by icons along a linear linguistic braid. For example, a star represents the "setting" since sailors at night, when lost, look to the stars to see where they are and what time it is. A heart represents the "feeling" of the character relative to the problem and plan (Figure 7.4).

The teacher can use the SGM with the entire class or a small group to discuss the plot of a story, an episode in a book chapter, a personal experience, or a historical event. When a teacher or student touches an icon, that element of the story is discussed. Connections are made linguistically and visually between the character/setting and the problem (initiating event); the problem, feelings, and plans (critical-thinking triangle); the plans and the actions/attempts; and the attempts and the direct consequence or end of the story.

The visual, tactile, and kinesthetic nature of the manipulative makes it an ideal tool for a variety of learners. The SGM manual contains reproducible maps that serve as graphic organizers modeled after the SGM manipulative. Posters, magnets, an oral/writing activity book, a manual of developmental lessons, a series of card decks, and the ThemeMaker for expository text round out the materials currently available for this link between language and literacy.

Learning strategies teach students how to learn by helping students to organize their thinking and teaching them thinking skills they will use throughout their lives. However, one should be cautious about jumping too quickly on the learning-strategies bandwagon. Much of the seminal work in this area has been conducted under experimental conditions that are unlike classroom conditions. Further research will provide insight into how to teach learning strategies that students can use in different settings; how to integrate learning strategies into the curriculum; and how to design texts to support strategy instruction (Harris & Pressley, 1991).

Instructional Scaffolds

Students come into classrooms at different levels of understanding and skills inherent in academic subjects. Thus, the learning process is a very personal and individual experience for students, as they construct their own meanings and expand their understanding (Instructional Philosophy and Strategies, 2003).

Instructional scaffolding describes a process in which teachers and students work together to design and to provide support as needed. In fact, instructional scaffolds may be

FIGURE 7.4   Story Grammar Marker

Source: The Story Grammar Marker® is a registered trademark of MindWing Concepts, Inc. and may not be reproduced in any form. Copyright © 1994, 2008. The Story Grammar Marker® patent issued. Braidy™ the StoryBraid, U.S. patent pending. MindWing Concepts, Inc. and logo are the registered trademarks. ThemeMaker™, Story Grammar Marker® and Braidy™ the StoryBraid, are U.S. registered trademarks of SGM Productions, Inc. All rights reserved. Reprinted with permission.

designed for individuals (or for groups) to assist them in learning new skills. Teachers learn to anticipate possible difficulties that students might have. As they move about the classroom and work with students on a one-to-one basis, teachers plan which instructional scaffolds might work with individual students on a temporary basis as they learn the new skill. This may include mini-lessons or breaking down the task into subtasks or steps. It also might include the use of prompts or cues for a temporary period of time. Instructional scaffolds can be designed to help students learn how to identify main ideas and supporting details, ask questions, cooperate in groups, predict, infer, summarize, do research, solve problems and so on (Instructional Philosophy and Strategies, 2003). The scaffold support is given temporarily—only as long as needed. Then later, support may be given at another point in the learning process.

TECHNOLOGY

Technology is commonplace in most classrooms. The passage of the Technology-Related Assistance for Individuals with Disabilities Act of 1988, referred to as the Tech Act, is largely responsible for this utilitarian outcome. The Tech Act was designed to enhance the availability and quality of assistive technology (AT) devices and services to all individuals and their families throughout the United States (Behrmann & Jerome, 2003; Blackhurst & Edyburn, 2000).

IDEA uses the same definitions for assistive technology as the Tech Act. IEP teams are required by IDEA to consider whether the child requires AT devices and services. Technology meets another emphasis of IDEA which is access to the general education curriculum for all students with disabilities.

The terminology can be confusing to a teacher who is trying to find the best way to match students with appropriate assistive technology for individual needs. The U.S. Office of Special Education Programs (2002) made the following distinctions for the terms *assistive technology, assistive technology devices, and assistive technology services.* **Assistive technology (AT)** is defined as any tool that helps a student with a disability perform a functional task more easily or more successfully. **Assistive technology devices** are tools that are provided by school districts when assistive technology services are requested in an IEP. It is stated in IDEA, Section 300.5, that the AT devices include

> . . . any item, piece of equipment, or product system, whether acquired commercially off the shelf, modified, or customized, that is used to increase, maintain, or improve the functional capabilities of a child with a disability.

AT services are defined in IDEA as any service that directly assists a child with a disability in the selection, acquisition, or use of an assistive technology device. AT must be considered for all students who have an IEP. The AT services that apply to the classroom teacher, whether a general educator or a special educator, include

> . . . assessment of needs for AT, acquiring AT devices, modification and maintenance of AT devices, coordination of other services related to AT, teaching students and their families to use AT devices, and providing training to professionals who will deliver services to that child to improve functional capabilities. (IDEA, Section 300.5)

AT devices may be categorized as no technology, low technology, or high technology. Any assistive device that is not electronic is called *no technology* or *no tech*. Examples would be teacher-made games and learning tools. Electronic devices that do not have highly sophisticated computer components are referred to as *low technology* or *low tech*. Examples would include electronic audio or voice-recording instruments. *High technology* usually features *high-tech* devices with a computer and software arrayed to perform multiple functions (Behrmann & Jerome, 2003).

Special education literature and professional journals are proliferate with ideas and suggestions about technology available for use with special needs students. The following *high-technology AT devices* were selected from a review of current literature, for possible usage with students in general and special education classes.

WebQuests.   Good teachers use many different strategies to teach students who come to the classroom with differences in readiness, interests, and learning profiles (Albemarle County Public Schools, 2003). When differentiating instruction based on readiness, the learning goals remain constant for all learners; however, learner support, complexity of tasks, and instructional materials are varied according to the individual needs of students. WebQuests are one means of differentiating instruction based on interest. A **WebQuest** is an inquiry-oriented activity. Teachers can show students how to obtain information from resources on the Internet. Within this process, students can learn how to pursue individual interests while working within common content parameters. Last, students' learning profiles are multidimensional and include individual learning preferences. Utilizing multimedia and learning centers in the classroom helps to provide information in multisensory and multiple intelligence formats.

Technology can be employed in the process component of differentiated instruction. The process component is "how students learn the content." The following example is given by Albemarle County Public Schools (2003, 2). Differentiated instruction by process may look like this:

> Some students will be using a traditional print encyclopedia to complete a research task in a classroom, while other students use Internet bookmarks collected by the teacher, and still other students use a multimedia encyclopedia that provides audio support. Each of these learning centers may provide the students with the information necessary to answer the question "What are the three branches of the United States government?" but in very different ways.

SPEEDBUMP—Don't forget how valuable the Web is for lesson plan research.

Widgets.   Miller, Brown, and Robinson (2002) describe how teachers might use what are called "widgets on the Web" as a computerized support tool in the classroom. They state that this type of computerized tool is ". . . easy to use, appeals to students, helps them [the students] learn abstract concepts, and can be found on the Internet" (p. 24). What are widgets? The authors describe them as small computer programs that are created using an authoring software program, and can be stored on CDs or accessed via the Internet.

Widgets are mediation software programs developed to be used by the teacher when interacting with a student in a learning task.

In order to create and develop these widgets, teachers need to consider: (1) what concepts they are teaching; (2) what they need to effectively teach these concepts; and (3) what the student characteristics are that would affect the design. Widgets can be used in an individualized manner or projected onto a screen for group instruction (e.g., an LCD projector). They can be paused during instruction to demonstrate, model, or add further elaboration. The authors state that widgets can be designed to tailor what the students need in contrast to programmed computer software that is controlled and sequenced. This instruction can be developed for a broad range of skills and abilities, thus making it appropriate to use with students who have mild disabilities and need instruction tailored to their unique learning needs.

Get Ready to Read. The National Center for Learning Disabilities (NCLD) has launched a new interactive reading game for preschool children. The program is designed to help preschool children build the literacy skills they need to become successful readers. Gus, the famed rabbit of the PBS Emmy Award–winning show *Between the Lions*, is the lead character.

According to the NCLD (2003), all it takes is Internet access and a click of a mouse to join Gus and his friends in a series of interactive reading games. GetReadytoRead.org is the website for Get Ready to Read!, a national early literacy program developed by the NCLD. The goal of this program is to ensure that all children are equipped with the fundamental skills necessary for learning to read. Families who do not have Internet access can take their children to the public library and access it for free.

Teach How to Learn

Assistive technology (AT) can encourage students in many areas of instruction. In a paper presented at the Annual Council for Exceptional Children Convention in Denver, Colorado, Lahm, and Morissette (1994; cited in Behrmann & Jerome, 2003) outlined six areas: organization, note taking, writing, academic productivity, access to reference and general education materials, and cognitive assistance. In their *ERIC Digest* publication, Behrmann and Jerome (2003) offer some ways in which teachers can incorporate AT into these six areas as they instruct students. The following is a summary of some of their suggestions. (Refer to examples of accommodations, modifications, and strategies in Chapter 8.)

Organization. Both low-tech and high-tech devices can be utilized for teaching students organization of thoughts. Low tech includes manual outlining, color coding, and highlighting. Flow-charting and webbing are also *low-tech* devices. High-tech, graphic, software-based organizers also can be used to accomplish organization of thoughts. Graphic organizers provide students with the means to reconfigure brainstormed ideas and color code and group them in ways that visually represent their thoughts. Color-coded text options and outline capabilities in some word-processing programs are useful to students who have difficulty sorting and sequencing thoughts and ideas (DO-IT, 2002). Another high-tech device is the outline function of word-processing software that allows students to set out major ideas or topics and then add subcategories of information.

Note Taking.   Supplying students with copies of structured outlines in which they can fill in information is one no-tech way of assisting students with note taking. Low- and high-tech methods include videotaping class sessions; sending class notes to students via e-mail; sending Web-cam photography across the Internet in order for students to see and hear what is happening in class; translating print-based notes to voice by using optical character recognition (OCR) software with a voice synthesizer; and using notebook computers, personal digital assistants (PDAs), or portable word-processing keyboards to help students with the mechanics of note taking.

Writing.   Grammar and spell-checkers, dictionaries, and thesaurus programs help with the mechanics of writing. In the writing process, teachers can make suggestions about wording on students' word-processor disks. When computers are networked, students can read each other's work and make recommendations for revisions. Being able to customize their writing with a variety of fonts, graphics, and pictures helps with general motivation to write.

Academic Productivity.   Software- and hardware-based tools can be used to assist with academics. For example, iPods can be separate, multifunction devices or part of a computer's software. Productivity in calculating categorizing, grouping, and predicting events can be enhanced by computer spreadsheets, databases, and graphics software. Productivity in note taking, obtaining assignments, accessing reference material, getting help from experts, and communicating with peers can be assisted via computers, the Internet, and PDAs. Today's students are increasingly sharing documents, using instant messaging, and transferring documents to each other as e-mail attachments.

Access to Reference and General Educational Materials.   Internet communications allow students to engage in interactive learning experiences away from their present learning environment. Students can be taught to access electronic multimedia encyclopedias, library references, and online publications. Information can be made accessible to students through multimedia tools. Multimedia use of text, speech, graphics, pictures, audio, and video in reference-based software is useful in meeting individual learning styles of students (DO-IT, 2002). E-books can motivate students to read. The computer reads each story page aloud, and highlights the words as they are read. Fonts and colors can be changed. Word definitions and pronunciations of syllables can be accessed by additional clicks of the mouse. When a student clicks on a picture, labels appear, with verbal pronunciations of the labels obtained with another click of the mouse. Electronic dictionaries and thesaurus add word definitions. These books are available in multiple languages. This aspect is helpful to students who are acquiring or being exposed to a second language.

Cognitive Assistance.   Many of the assistive technologies just described can be combined with instructional programs to develop and improve cognitive skills. Students can be prompted through PDAs, pagers, and Internet software to remember assignments and important tasks or events. Students can use these to develop to-do lists, and take and retrieve notes.

Both special educators and general education teachers recognize the need to create and tailor instructional materials for students with special needs. Each person with a disability is unique. The challenge is to identify supportive AT that is most beneficial for each learner. Assistive technology is a major avenue for accomplishing this goal (NATRI, 2006).

FUNCTIONAL CURRICULUM

If students with mild disabilities are not anticipating pursuing a postsecondary education, a more practical, applied curriculum may be needed. A **functional curriculum** includes life skills and teaches them both in the classroom and in the community. When using this approach, basic academic skills are reinforced in a practical manner. For example, math could include paying bills, budgeting, and balancing a checkbook. Reading can be related to assembling appliances, cooking, or home repair. Community-based instruction takes students beyond their traditional textbooks and classroom instruction into the community where they learn skills firsthand and have the opportunity to apply those skills in real-life situations. Generally, as students with mild disabilities reach middle and high school years, their needs must be evaluated and their curriculum planned accordingly. Polloway and his colleagues (1989) offer the following suggestions for curriculum planning for students with learning problems:

1. *Adult referenced.* The content should be based on a top-down focus, reflecting curricula alternatives based on successful community adjustment rather than from an elementary-oriented focus upward.
2. *Comprehensive.* Curricula offered to students should include a broad range of topics: generally, a combination of academics, vocational training, social-skills development, and life-skills preparation.
3. *Relevant.* Students at the secondary level need meaningful programs. A student who can relate academic concepts to his or her own experiences is more apt to understand and then apply the concept.
4. *Empirically and socially valid.* Students must acquire skills that are valuable to them personally, appropriate for the communities in which they live, and meaningful to other members of that community.
5. *Flexible.* Curricula must be flexible enough to accommodate a wide variety of diverse student needs as well as the uniqueness of different community settings.
6. *Community based.* Much of the training should occur out of the classroom and in actual community settings to increase the probability that skills will generalize across settings and conditions.

Instead of emphasizing arithmetic problems on worksheets, a functional curriculum teaches budgeting and shopping skills. Although reading often is treated as an isolated subject, a functional curriculum would teach reading throughout the school day by using such everyday materials as newspapers, magazines, and job applications. Apprentice programs, in which high school students spend time in the community working with "mentors" in trades and business, are examples of functional programs that integrate school with on-site job training. Teachers who are successful in implementing functional curricula begin by asking the question, "What do I see this student doing 5 years from now?"

SPEEDBUMP—Because it is based on everyday experience, a functional curriculum works with students who can't make a connection between school work and learning valuable skills.

The Adult Performance Level (APL) curriculum (Figure 7.5) developed at the University of Texas is an example of a functional curriculum. It contains 42 life-skills objectives organized under five major categories: consumer economics, occupational knowledge, health, community resources, and law. The program ranges from elementary to high school and includes reading, writing, speaking, problem solving, interpersonal relationships, and computation skills. Examples of tasks in reading/consumer economics for each level are as follows: elementary—look for ads in the newspaper for toys; junior high school—read an ad for a sale and find the name of the store, location, phone number, and price of the item; and high school—read and compare prices of grocery store ads. The purpose of the curriculum is to develop student competencies necessary for survival in daily life (Patton et al., 1989).

Everyone must ultimately function in a community setting, regardless of the level of schooling pursued or accomplished. This means that life-skills preparation is important for all students at all levels of schooling. Many students figure out skills they need as adults through experience. Students with mild disabilities do not have the ability to problem solve or learn accidentally; therefore, they need to be taught more directly and purposefully (Brolin, 1989; Kokaska & Brolin, 1985; Patton et al., 1989).

COMPREHENSIVE TEACHING

As long as teachers view direct instruction and student-centered learning as philosophical opposites, the debate about which is the best way to teach will continue indefinitely. A 10-minute slide show on the history of U.S. education would resemble a dance with strobe lights. Following every slide of students frozen in their seats listening to the instructor, there would be a slide picturing students spread around the room involved in different activities. Since the early 1900s, the educational pendulum has traced a well-worn track back and forth between direct and student-centered instruction. Teachers who are capable of integrating both approaches into their lessons on a daily basis can attend to the demands of curriculum without forsaking the developmental needs of their young charges.

Glickman (1987) draws a distinction between "effective" schools and "good" schools. Effective schools sponsor teacher-directed learning, narrowing the academic focus. Students are taught in large groups from prescribed instructional objectives. Reviewing, demonstration, checking for student understanding, and frequent tests are standard procedures. Glickman asks the question: Should there be more to school than

FIGURE 7.5   APL Model of Functional Competency: Examples of Tasks (Junior High School)

	Consumer Economics	Occupational Knowledge	Health	Community Resources	Government and Law
Reading	Read an ad for a sale, locating name of store, location, phone number, and price of item	Read a job description	Locate poison control numbers in phone book	Use phone book to locate recreational program in community	Locate and read list of state and U.S. congressmen
Writing	Fill out a magazine order form completely	Practice writing abbreviations for words	Write a menu for a balanced diet	Write letter to TV station about a program they just cancelled	Fill out voter registration form
Speaking, Writing, Viewing	Discuss saving versus spending money	Discuss reasons why people work	Listen to positive and negative feedback on personal appearance	Call library to find out if they have a certain book	Discuss why we need to vote
Problem Solving	Use $10 for the evening, which activity would you choose: movies, bowling, or pizza	Decide on job environment: inside, outside, desk, travel, etc.	Role play appropriate behavior for various places (movies, church, restaurant)	Locate the skating rink on a city map and decide the best way to get there	Decide what items have state and/or local tax
Interpersonal Relations	Ask salesperson for help in purchasing jeans	List questions they would ask in job interview	Discuss honesty, trust, and promise; define each	Call skating rink to inquire about hours	Call to find out what precinct you live in
Computation	Compute the sales tax on a pair of jeans	Compute net income	Calculate and compare the prices of hair washing products	Calculate bus fare to and from the teen center	Calculate the cost of getting a driver's license (fee, gas)

Scholastic Achievement Test (SAT) scores? And, if a school is effective, does that necessarily mean it's a good school? To illustrate his point, Glickman (1987) relates the following story.

> A special education teacher recently told me that she had asked her supervisor for permission to take her students on a five-minute walk to a grocery store to observe transactions at the check-out counter. The supervisor immediately asked, "Which specific objectives will this walk accomplish?" The teacher replied, "I don't know. I simply want my students to see transactions involving real money. Besides, getting out of the classroom for a while would be fun." Responded the supervisor, "I'm sorry. If it's not one of our curriculum objectives, we don't do it!" (p. 623)

Glickman's point is well made. His concern about the overemphasis of one instructional strategy to the exclusion of others is shared by many educators and researchers. Moreover,

Ronald Brandt (1990) observes that teachers have difficulty making changes in their teaching style "like so many compliant windmills on a Kansas prairie." A more comprehensive view of instructional strategies is needed to help teachers integrate seemingly disparate teaching methods.

Harris and Pressley (1991) note that student-centered and teacher-directed strategies are false dichotomies. Students do indeed need opportunities to construct their own knowledge (i.e., student directed), but that does not obviate teacher-directed lessons. As Harris and Pressley (1991) point out, students will direct their own thinking even when exposed to direct instruction.

> . . . children engaged in the rehearsal of mathematics operations may construct new procedural forms, such as arithmetic shortcuts, while practicing. As students develop skill and proficiency, they do not do exactly what they have been taught. This construction of personalized learning has been well recognized among (learning) strategy researchers.

Another element in the discussion of the merits of teaching methods is the uneasy hypothesis that teachers gravitate toward instructional strategies that reflect their personalities. Claudia Cornett (1983) observed that teachers tend to choose instructional strategies based on their personal educational philosophies. The research in this area is thin, but there is ample anecdotal evidence that authoritarian teachers prefer teacher-directed strategies, while student-centered strategies are preferred by teachers who have a developmental view on teaching and learning. More research in this area might produce some uncomfortable insights. While researchers labor to determine the effectiveness of specific strategies and college professors promote strategies based on their utility, it may be that teachers select instructional strategies based on conscious or unconscious personal preferences!

Strong and a small group of colleagues (1990) created a framework to integrate five different instructional strategies: ITIP (Hunter's model of direct instruction), learning strategies, student learning styles, cooperative learning, and reading and writing in content areas. Each member of the group identified a basic operating principle that represented the core premise of an instructional strategy. They called these core principles their "declaration of interdependence." From teacher-directed ITIP, they derived the principle that teachers' decisions should be based on verified educational research. From the learning-strategy approach, they highlighted the need for teachers to incorporate reasoning skills in lesson designs. From the research on student learning style, they emphasized flexibility in using a range of instructional strategies. Cooperative learning underscored the social dimension of learning; that is, the sum total of learning in a small group will surpass the learning each student could accomplish working alone. Finally, from the reading and writing across the curriculum literature, they highlighted the need to appreciate the artfulness of teaching.

In order to make use of Strong's integrative model, teachers need to understand how each system works, have knowledge of the learning characteristics of students, and have administrative support for experimentation. Any time a teacher tries something different in a classroom there is an element of risk. Change is anxiety provoking, and schools are organizations (some would say bureaucracies) that have many built-in mechanisms that resist change. Schedules must be adhered to; school norms must be followed; and principals have most of the power. In a school where teacher-directed learning is the norm, the teacher who attempts to set up student-centered activities is risking failure and ridicule. Without administrative support, teachers must struggle in isolation against the odds. Only in schools where innovation and experimentation are valued will teachers succeed in providing the best of all worlds for their students.

The notion that there is one best way to teach is naïve and limiting. Voluminous research that documents that students have different ways of learning should give any teacher reason to pause before wholeheartedly adopting one method of classroom instruction to the exclusion of others.

SUMMARY

Teachers and students sometimes differ in how they view school. While teachers are concerned with long-range successes, students are more concerned about the here-and-now. As children become adolescents, they often are more concerned about peer acceptance than about adult approval. Too often, we ignore developmental differences between students and adults. Teachers like students to adapt to the often unstated norms of public school life; therefore, students with mild disabilities need to learn the hidden curriculum.

Effective teachers are able to use a variety of instructional approaches. In recent years, teachers have found that students with mild disabilities share many of the same learning problems, and that many of the same instructional models are shared by teachers of students with and without disabilities. Educators are realizing that instructional models like precision teaching, direct instruction, student-centered learning, learning strategies, task analysis, and functional skills hold promise for all students. Rather than matching instructional approaches to types of disabilities, teachers are encouraged to match general curriculum strategies to the characteristics, needs, and learning styles of individual students.

ACTIVITIES

1. Review the advance vignette. Which instructional methods do you think would work best for Jerry and Ann? Discuss the difference between Jerry and Ann. Why was Jerry placed in general education with additional monitoring and Ann was determined eligible for special education?

2. Prepare a short survey that can be used to obtain perceptions about schools and their purposes. Use it to interview classmates, family, neighborhood children, and others. Share the perceptions during class.

3. Divide into small groups. Each group will be assigned a skill to be taught. Outline a task analysis for your particular skill.

4. Divide into five cooperative groups. Ask each group to select a mathematical skill. Select a teaching model from this chapter and design a lesson. Share the lessons with the class.

5. Interview two people who work at various jobs in the community. Ask them about specific tasks and responsibilities that they began acquiring during their school years (e.g., getting to school on time, must be on time to work; being polite and pleasant, customers expect to be treated politely and courteously; and so on). The goal is to help make learning meaningful to future work goals.

6. In small groups, brainstorm the AT devices with which you, as a group, are familiar. Which are more appropriate for the classroom? Talk about how each of these could be used.

7. If your classroom has access to the Internet and a projector, use a search engine to locate 10 terms or names from this chapter. Compare the Web information with the information in this chapter.

CHAPTER EIGHT

INSTRUCTING STUDENTS WITH MILD DISABILITIES

ADVANCE QUESTIONS

Answer the following questions as you read this chapter:

1. How do best instructional practices for students with mild disabilities compare with those used with general classroom students?
2. What is the difference between allocated time, engaged time, and academic learning time?
3. How can teachers help students to improve organizational skills?
4. What are some instructional accommodations that might be utilized in the general education classroom to teach academic subjects like math, reading, and spelling?
5. What are some testing and grading accommodations? Why is cooperative grading productive?
6. What are appropriate guidelines for assigning homework?
7. What is curriculum-based instruction? What are curriculum-based goals and objectives? How are they used effectively?
8. What are some guidelines for writing individual education programs (IEPs)?
9. What is an educator's tool kit? Name items that might be helpful to have when teaching students with special needs. Would these items also be used beneficially with regular classroom students?

VIGNETTE: SHIRLEY ALLEN

It was 3:00 A.M. and Shirley Allen was tossing and turning. Instead of sleeping, she was worrying about the conversation she had with Mr. Kane that afternoon. After 2 years of successful 4th-grade teaching, her principal had asked her to participate in an inclusion program beginning with the new fall term. Shirley considered all the additional responsibilities she would be taking on. Her head buzzed with questions. How could she adapt the curriculum to meet the needs of her special education students? Which best teaching practices could she utilize with both general and special education students in an inclusive classroom? What changes would she make in how she used instructional time? How about grading and homework; should she be consistent with all students or make adjustments for the special needs students?

She was going to be responsible for helping develop individual education programs (IEPs); how was she going to do that? Fortunately she had listened to old professor Moriarty's warning at the end of her undergraduate course in mild disabilities. "Don't sell your text back to the bookstore at the end of the semester," he said. "Someday you are going to need it." Well, the time had come. Shirley got up and rummaged through the cartons she had stashed in the back of her closet. After 15 frantic minutes, she found the text. She breathed a sigh of relief and slowly turned the pages—ah, so many fond memories, the yellow highlighting provided iridescent testimony to her hard-earned A in the course. She found the chapter on instructing students with mild disabilities and began reading. The guidelines for dealing with classroom organization, grading, homework, and IEPs were clear and practical. Half an hour later, she closed the book with a smile. Apprehension was replaced with excitement over the challenge of setting up her inclusion program. "I can do this," she thought as she wearily padded back to bed and dozed off.

Many teachers have tossed and turned at night trying to figure out the solution to difficult educational problems. There is a saying, "you don't have to reinvent the wheel." Whatever problems faced by a teacher, he or she can be sure that others have faced similar challenges—and that others have found solutions. Within the pages of this chapter, there are many useful ideas for adjusting instruction to meet students' individual needs. Although your immediate concern might be remembering this information for a test, don't be shortsighted and discard this information after the course is over. Someday, like Shirley Ann, you will have a class of your own. This book and other resources such as professional organizations, the Internet, and fellow teachers are all there to lend support. So, when you think about the challenges of teaching students with mild disabilities for this course, also keep in mind that you are preparing for your future. Here are some questions to get you started.

1. Do you think Shirley Ann was overreacting to her new challenge?
2. What are some instructional practices that benefit both general education and special education students?
3. Should grading and homework assignments be the same or different for students with and without disabilities?
4. What is a teacher's responsibility in terms of continuing professional development?

5. What is the best source of helpful ideas when trying to figure out educational problems?

BEST TEACHING PRACTICES

There is a common perception that students with mild disabilities require **instructional strategies** that are distinctive from effective general classroom teaching methods. This assumption is based on past practices that characterized the formative years of special education. Just as medicine is geared toward treating diagnosed disorders, past practices in special education were focused on matching an educational treatment to specific types of mild disabilities. There were special instructional approaches to learning disabilities and different approaches for students with mild intellectual disabilities. Students were placed in special education programs based on the assumption that there was something intrinsically wrong with them and that special education instruction would help remediate learning problems symptomatic of specific disabling conditions.

Although some mild disabilities, such as dyslexia, are individually derived, many mild disabilities are the result of a variety of overlapping issues. Poverty, lack of school readiness skills, dysfunctional families, disorganized classrooms, and a mismatch between instruction and learner needs all contribute to a cycle of school failure that can result in a special education placement.

Jenkins, Pious, and Peterson (1988) wanted to determine how students with mild disabilities were different from other students. The researchers analyzed differences between students identified as learning disabled and students identified as underachievers. They compared the instructional levels, learning rates, and learning styles of each group. They found more similarities than differences between the two groups of students. Students with and without disabilities had identical achievement levels. Individual students in each group demonstrated considerable overlap in learning rate and instructional level.

> **SPEEDBUMP—**Do you remember from earlier chapters that identifying mild disabilities is a tricky business. When students are struggling in school it is difficult to be absolutely certain of the cause of the problem.

There are now two discrete sets of instructional methods: one set for use with "special" students and another set for use with "nondisabled" students. As used here, instructional methods refer to basic instructional processes, such as the development of behavioral objectives, curricular-based assessment procedures, task analysis, the arrangement of antecedents and consequences, and open education/discovery learning methods. While some methods need to be tailored to individual characteristics and needs, few, if any, can be clearly dichotomized into those applicable only for special students or only for regular students, (Stainback & Stainback, 1984, 103)

Best teaching practices for general education students are often best teaching practices for students with mild disabilities. The reverse has been found to be true as well. Both classroom and special education teachers have at their disposal instructional strategies to facilitate the learning of students with and without mild disabilities.

When we talk about students with mild disabilities, underachievers, and other hard-to-teach students, qualitative distinctions among groups are difficult to detect. The challenge for educators is to implement instructional strategies that can change school failure to success for all students.

Time Management

Data about **time management** are based primarily on research in general education classrooms. Researchers are interested in discovering how learning is influenced by teachers' use of time. Rich and Ross (1989) found that teachers are allocated approximately 55 percent of the classroom day for instruction, but only half of that time, or 25 percent of the entire day, is utilized by students engaged in learning tasks. The researchers learned that out of an entire school day only one-fourth of the time is spent learning.

SPEEDBUMP—Does the last sentence come as a surprise?

Jacob Kounin's (1977) research on classroom organization in elementary and secondary schools bears testimony to how time is wasted in classrooms. Kounin noted that many teaching behaviors disrupt lessons. He used such terms as *thrusts, dangles, truncations,* and *flip-flops* to describe common time wasters. **Thrusts** refer to intrusions in lessons. Principal announcements over the loudspeaker are an example of *thrusts* that interrupt lessons and make it difficult for teachers to get back on track. One inner-city school teacher was so distracted by PA announcements that his first action of the new school year was to disconnect the speaker from his classroom wall! This minor act of rebellion nearly cost him his job.

Teachers often leave a lesson in midair, for example, when a visitor comes to the classroom door. Students may be left with a perfunctory remark like "I'll be out in the hall for a minute. Turn to page 36 in your workbooks and complete the problems." Kounin called this abrupt change a **dangle**. It is the rare group of students who would not take a teacher's momentary absence as an invitation to relax and catch up on some classroom gossip. The ensuing reprimand upon the teacher's return usually wastes more time and creates an unpleasant mood. After such an incident, teacher and students are hard-pressed to rejoin the lesson with their original enthusiasm.

Teachers **flip-flop** when they reverse direction in a lesson. Flip-flops may be fostered by strategically minded students who would rather hear how Mrs. Jones spent her summer vacation on Cape Cod than hear a lecture on the mollusk family. Teacher anecdotes turn into tangents and digressions, which entertain both teacher and students while instructional time is sliced into smaller pieces. When teachers flip-flop, students with mild disabilities can become confused. This confusion might be misinterpreted as a lack of attention to the lesson. The teacher who begins a lesson on multiplication of fractions and then realizes that some review in fractions is needed, may move back and forth too abruptly for students to keep track of the central ideas. Students with weak listening or attending skills will be unable to follow the teacher's train of thought.

Truncations occur when a teacher abruptly ends a lesson and moves to something else without alerting students to the change. The conclusion of a lesson and transition to the next topic is one of the most critical parts of instructional time. Many behavior problems occur because of disorganized transitions. Dealing with classroom disruptions is a major time waster. By moving smoothly from one lesson to the next, the teacher diminishes management problems and focuses students' attention on the next lesson.

SPEEDBUMP—Write the previous terms in your notebook and observe how many examples you encounter during a week of classes.

Kounin found that teachers who were able to **maintain a group focus** were most successful in using instructional time. These teachers were able to monitor the entire class without being distracted by minor incidents that could cause the entire class to become diverted, like stopping a class discussion because there is a piece of paper on the floor or because someone isn't paying attention. Such teachers demonstrate "with-itness" and "overlapping." They are able to work with an individual student without losing track of the rest of the group. Students describe a teacher who demonstrates "with-itness" as having "eyes in the back of her head."

Academic Learning Time

Berliner (1988) defines **academic learning time** as "time engaged with materials or activities related to the outcome measure being used (e.g., an end-of-unit or achievement test), during which a student experiences a high success rate" (p. 15). When teachers evaluate students specifically on subjects in which students were engaged, academic learning time will improve. If this sounds confusing, let's look at it from a different point of view.

Suppose a 6th-grade teacher allocates 60 minutes a day to whole-language instruction of reading. She has selected this teaching method because she gets higher student involvement. At the end of the year, the school system administers a standardized reading achievement test. There is a vocabulary section in which students are required to give the meaning of solitary words. Also included are timed reading comprehension sections, which include paragraphs of increasing complexity. The test favors students with strong phonetic skills. Her students are going to do poorly on this test because it is measuring a different set of skills than they were taught. If academic learning time is to improve, then curriculum, instruction, learning, and evaluative measures must mesh. The amount of time a student spends demonstrating a specific skill is important to school success. Teachers who are able to monitor student progress through observation, pre- and posttesting, informal testing, and student portfolios are most effective in enhancing academic learning time. This procedure is called **curriculum-based assessment**. (Refer to the section later in this chapter.)

Materials that are too difficult impede academic learning time. This is a particularly nettlesome problem for teachers of students with mild disabilities. What do you give a 15-year-old, street-wise, inner-city youth, who is on a 1st-grade reading level to read? How do you reteach fundamental math concepts to 18-year-olds who need manipulative materials? One solution is high-interest library books (perhaps with brown paper on the covers) for reading and functional activity lessons (measuring, check writing, grocery budgets) for mathematics. Students who have failed with the traditional basal texts are not going to improve through drill and repetition with similar materials.

To improve academic learning time, students require opportunities to practice skills in novel situations. They need to see how skills can be demonstrated and generalized to other settings. It doesn't help to teach students to read if they never pick up a book to read for enjoyment or if they don't know how to read the classified section of the newspaper. Berliner (1988) illustrates the interrelationship between allocated time, engaged time, and academic learning time:

> If 50 minutes of reading instruction per day is allocated to a student who pays attention about one-third of the time (engaged learning) and only one-fourth of the student's reading time is a high level of success, the student will experience only about four minutes of ALT [academic learning time]—engaged reading time at a high success level. Similarly, if 100 minutes per day is allocated [to] reading for a student who pays attention 85 percent of the time and is at a high level of success for almost two-thirds of the time, that student will experience about 52 minutes of ALT. (p. 17)

There are many reasons why students experience lesser amounts of academic learning time. Distractibility, inadequate study skills, emotional problems, disorderly classrooms, and disorganized instruction are samples of the reasons academic learning time is minimal for students (Copple et al., 1992; Kane, 1994; WestEd., 2000). Students with mild disabilities are placed in double jeopardy when they are pulled out of their classroom for special education services. Unless the resource room teacher is duplicating materials and instructional strategies utilized in the general classroom at the time of the student's absence, academic learning time will be lost day after day, week after week, month after month. This is a strong argument for inclusion.

SPEEDBUMP—The authors sincerely hope that by this time they have debunked the myth that the best place for students with mild disabilities to catch up academically is in an alternative special education classroom.

Selecting Instructional Materials

Teachers are faced with difficult decisions about which instructional materials to select for students, especially those with mild disabilities. When given the choice, Ramsey (1988; 1995a) discovered that teachers most often select instructional materials with which they were trained to use and thus are more *familiar* to them. Materials that are more *comfortable* to their teaching style are more readily selected; *availability* also is important in their selection.

Smith (1983) maintains that the most appropriate materials for a teacher to use with students who have learning problems are those that

- have a logical, hierarchical sequence of instructional objectives
- are adaptable to a variety of learning styles (e.g., adventurer, ponderer, drifter)
- cover the same objectives in multiple ways
- pretest to determine where teaching should begin
- have a built-in evaluation mechanism for determining mastery of instructional objectives
- allow students to proceed at their own rate and skip objectives they have already mastered
- have reinforcement activities

To this list, Ramsey (1995a) adds a few additional criteria for the selection of instructional materials. Readers tend to be more interested in reading stories when they see pictures and other illustrations that are representative of themselves, their friends, and their families. *Identification* with one's culture, gender, and age is important. Likewise, content and vocabulary need to be at each *student's reading level*.

Teacher and Student Communication

Effective teaching depends on good communication between teacher and students (Jones & Jones, 1986). The communication process may break down if the message cannot be heard, understood, or is misinterpreted. When any of these happen, communication exchanges are disrupted.

By using effective **communication skills**, a teacher has more assurance that the intended message is getting across to the students. By being a model of a good listener, a teacher can help students learn to listen and respond appropriately to others. Attention is the prerequisite to listening, followed by clarity and the ability to ask probing questions.

> **SPEEDBUMP**—The National Association of College and Employers 2007 survey indicated that good communication skills is the number one attribute employers look for in college graduates. (www.naceweb.org)

Attention.   For some students, special techniques are employed to gain and hold their attention (Morsink, 1984; Jones & Jones, 1981; Ramsey, Dixon, & Smith, 1986; Stephens, 1977). For instance, the teacher might first call the student by name when asking a question to ensure attending by that individual; conversely the teacher can ask the question before calling the name of a student to create greater interest or anticipation from members of the group. Selecting students at random to answer questions helps to keep everybody alert and listening. Enthusiasm and keeping lessons short and interactive assists in maintaining the attention of those students with attending problems. Some students may be better able to focus their attention when environmental distractions are eliminated or at least reduced and nonverbal signals can be used to draw students' attention to the task. Attending skills can be taught through games that encourage active listening. Arranging the classroom so that all students can see the teacher helps direct attention to the appropriate location. Finally, by paying close attention when students speak, teachers become good models for attending skills.

Clarity. Teachers can improve the clarity of their communication in many ways (Gloeckler & Simpson, 1988; Lewis & Doorlag, 1987). One is to give clear, precise directions. Teachers can simplify verbal directions by using shorter sentences, familiar words, and relevant explanations. Asking a student to repeat directions or to demonstrate understanding of them by carrying out the instructions is an effective way of monitoring clarity of expression. In addition, clarification can be achieved by the use of concrete objects and multidimensional teaching aids, and by modeling (i.e., demonstrating) what should be done in a practice situation.

Finally, a teacher can clarify communications by using a variety of vocal inflections. The use of *intonation* (i.e., stresses on certain words or sounds) and *juncture* (i.e., spacing of words) can add clarity to a message. For example, pausing before stating key words or stressing those that convey particular meanings helps students.

In situations involving behavior and feelings, the more immediate the feedback, the more helpful it is. Disturbing situations should be discussed as they occur. For example:

> Buddy's father is a salesman and travels during the week. One Sunday evening, he told Buddy all the things that had bothered him during the weekend. His dad did not feel that Buddy had been glad to see him on Friday evening, and he thought that Buddy spent too much time with his friends instead of with him on Saturday and Sunday. Buddy felt that he was being "dumped on" and that his good traits were overlooked, so he withdrew and pouted. Communication ended and nothing was really resolved between Buddy and his dad during that encounter.

Had Buddy's father talked with him throughout the weekend as things occurred, perhaps his feelings of being left out of his son's life could have been assuaged. Had Buddy known how his father felt earlier, he could have reassured him by doing something special with him.

Johnson (1972) gives several suggestions that teachers can use when providing feedback. First, give a student only the amount of feedback that he or she can understand at that time. Overloading a student with feedback reduces chances that the feedback will be used. Second, describe what happened rather than making judgmental evaluations about the situation. For instance, "You need to be sure to pronounce clearly the words at the end of your sentences," rather than, "You don't make a good public speaker." Last, give objective feedback; avoid moralizing. Do not make personal judgments about statements made by the students or their behavior. Instead, give the students descriptive feedback; for example, "Johnny, the rule says you need your pencil and paper ready to begin work," rather than, "You always forget your notebook!"

Questions. Berliner (1979) noted that the cognitive thinking level of the questions that teachers ask typically is low rather than high. For example, a lower-level question asks for a literal answer, such as "Who was the first astronaut?" A higher-level question requires a student to apply knowledge, analyze and synthesize information, or make evaluations and interpretations. For instance, "Why do astronauts weigh less in space than on Earth?" requires students to apply their knowledge of gravity. Both lower- and higher-level cognitive questions are relevant and are needed in classroom learning; however, teachers may need to focus on asking more higher-level questions.

Asking lower-level questions encourages student participation and builds factual knowledge. From these bases of knowledge, higher-order questions stimulate and facilitate the development of more sophisticated thinking, such as analyzing or evaluating an idea. In the long run, students achieve considerably more when their thinking is heightened and expanded.

Regardless of the level of a question, Belch (1975) suggests strategies for improving teachers' questioning skills.

1. Ask questions that require more than a yes-or-no response.
2. Allow sufficient time for students to deliberate the question.
3. Reword or restate questions when students fail to respond or respond incorrectly.
4. Challenge student responses in a professional way. Avoid giving "put-downs" or other belittling responses.
5. Direct questions to all students and not just to volunteers or the brighter ones.
6. Try to sequence your questions. Encourage students to use logical thinking and build one question on another, or build one question on the answer given to a previous question.

Graphic Organizers

Graphic organizers are specific instructional organization tools that have been used successfully with students in both regular and special education classrooms. These students have learning needs that span across a continuum, yet most are expected to learn the same content as their peers.

Many textbooks and curriculum guides provide reproducible graphic organizers; however, Baxendell (2003) states that often these contain too much information for some learners. He suggests using computer drawing programs or Inspiration 6 (a computer program for creating graphic organizers), in order to design and customize graphic organizers to meet the specific needs of students. To make a main-idea-and-detail chart, Baxendell says to identify the main idea as the central concept and place the details off center. By doing so, the students have a visual reminder of the hierarchical relationship between the concepts. The same approach is used for cause-and-effect diagrams and sequence charts. The use of arrows, lines, and numbers assists students in seeing the flow of ideas. By labeling the relationships and concepts, students can better understand and internalize particular content.

Sequence charts can be used to display the chain of events in various academic areas. Baxendell (2003) states, "We use them in reading to review the key elements in a story, in writing to organize 'how to' paragraphs or short stories, and in social studies to create time lines" (p. 50). Students can be assisted in visualizing steps in math multistep word problems or calculations, as well as procedures in scientific experiments. Baxendell also uses the sequence chart in pre- and post–field-trip activities. Before going on the field trip, the chart helps students to anticipate what they will be doing during the day. After returning from the field trip, students (individually, in small groups, or the class as a whole) can create their own sequence chart of what they did and learned. An essential component in student understanding of the information is to have all flow going in one direction, either from left to right or from top to bottom.

The most common of the compare-and-contrast graphic organizers is the Venn diagram. This diagram offers a visual display of the similarities and differences between two or three main ideas, and can be used across the curriculum in most subject areas. For example, in literature, Venn diagrams can be used to compare characters, stories, genres, problems, and solutions. In science, they can be used to differentiate between animal types or kingdoms, body parts, weather systems, planets, or ecosystems. Social studies, reading, writing, languages, physical education, math—the application to subject matter in all of these areas of the curriculum will be beneficial. Graphic organizers benefit all learners, especially those in inclusive classrooms, because of the wide spectrum of learner skills and needs. Figure 8.1 provides examples of three types of graphic organizers: a KWHL chart, a double cell diagram, and a Venn diagram.

SPEEDBUMP—If you want to see some graphic organizers to download for your student teaching, go to www.eduplace.com/graphicorganizer.

Student Organization

Organization is important for success in the general education classroom, and students with mild disabilities often have organization problems. Particular areas in which organization assistance might be needed include: (1) keeping track of materials and assignments, (2) following directions, (3) completing class assignments, and (4) completing homework assignments.

Keeping Track of Materials and Assignments. *Roberto, a 5th grader, has a problem keeping track of his materials and homework assignments. One day, his English teacher gave him a slip of paper that excused him from that evening's homework in her class. He had earned this waiver by receiving good grades on a specified number of prior homework assignments. When handed this paper, Roberto jammed it into one of his pants pockets. The next day, his teacher asked the students to turn in either their homework assignment or their homework waiver. Roberto suddenly realized that he had neither the excuse nor the homework.*

What can be done in the classroom to help students like Roberto learn responsibility? He could keep all of his schoolwork in a large loose-leaf notebook and not in single folders that can be lost easily. Students with mild disabilities may not have the materials and supplies necessary to begin their class work. This is especially a problem when students move from one classroom to another for different subjects. These students need to be shown how to organize and plan ahead for classroom needs. One way to help students

Double Cell Diagram

K	W	H	L
What do we know?	What do we want to find out?	How can we find out what we want to learn?	What did we learn?

Attributes or characteristics we expect to use:

KWHL Chart

Venn Diagram

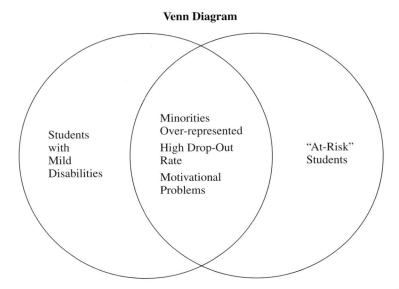

Students
with
Mild
Disabilities

Minorities
Over-represented

High Drop-Out
Rate

Motivational
Problems

"At-Risk"
Students

FIGURE 8.1

develop judgment and planning skills is to teach them strategy games like Monopoly, checkers, or chess. Mnemonic devices and lists help students organize priorities (McCoy & Prehm, 1987).

Following Directions. *Maria has problems following classroom directions. Invariably, Maria answers the wrong set of questions, uses the wrong type of paper, or, in some way, exhibits difficulties following directions.*

Before giving directions to students like Maria, have them clear their desks of distracting objects. A cleared desk helps students to focus attention, as does maintaining eye contact while stating directions. Break directions into parts one, two, and three. Provide visual cues. For example, write key words or steps on the chalkboard or on a large chart. Ask students to restate the directions as they understand them. If directions are written, underline or circle directional words. Gloeckler and Simpson (1988) caution against giving directions to a group several times. Students may "tune out" the initial instructions because they have learned that the directions will be repeated. In addition, the instructions may be reworded the second time, and thus become confusing. Encourage students to ask for clarifications if part of the directions are missed or misunderstood.

Students sometimes experience problems in proper sequencing. To assist with this difficulty, keep the number of directions in a sequence to a minimum. Check to see if the student understands the order in which the directions were given. This can be done by listening to him or her repeat the directions in sequence (Gloeckler & Simpson, 1988).

Completing Class Assignments. *"Class, you have 10 more minutes to finish your assignment," said Mrs. Green. Even that won't help Janice, she thought, as she walked by the girl's desk. Look at her paper—she hasn't even written six math problems on it! I wish I knew what I could do to get her to finish her class assignments!*

Some students, like Janice, have difficulty completing class assignments on time. Before looking for strategies that might be helpful with particular students, teachers might analyze how they are going about assigning work. First, is adequate time being given to finish assigned tasks? Not everyone works at the same pace, and some students require more time than others. Therefore, as in Janice's case, Mrs. Green could assist her in pacing her work. After advising students of exactly how much time is being allowed, Mrs. Green could help Janice set a kitchen timer on her desk that shows her just how much time she has spent on a particular assignment, and how much time is left. Or Janice could be given an assignment sheet with two blank clocks, one for the teacher or student to fill in hands to signify time to begin and one for drawing hands to end that task. With either of these time reminders, a reward system for completed work would help reinforce student efforts.

> **SPEEDBUMP—**Be cautious about using rewards. Used too often, rewards become a distraction for both teachers and students. For an excellent critique on the use of rewards in classrooms, see Alfie Kohn's book, *Punished by Rewards: The Trouble with Gold Stars, Incentive Plans, A's, Praise and Other Bribes* (1999).

Several other strategies help students with mild disabilities complete work. Students need to know exactly when assignments must be turned in. Mini-deadlines set throughout the day periodically alert students to work that is due to be turned in. Scheduling a brief free-time period before work is due allows some catch-up time if needed.

Completing Homework Assignments. *Completing homework assignments is a problem for Doug, a 4th grader. It's not that Doug won't do the work; he does what he can. His problem is that the homework assignments given by his teacher cover new concepts he has yet to master. Why don't his parents help him? Well, his father is a sales representative and travels most week days. His mother works part-time as a nurse at one of the nearby hospitals. The family with whom Doug stays during the evenings while his mom works is so busy with their own activities that no help is possible there.*

The tasks assigned by Doug's teacher are in the category of new tasks, not practice tasks. Because his teacher is overlooking this basic principle, she is placing Doug in a dilemma. Students should be assigned homework that they are capable of completing successfully by themselves with parent monitoring. Tasks that are too difficult instill feelings of frustration and hopelessness in students.

Homework helps in the improvement of students' study skills, attitudes toward school, and an awareness that learning occurs in other places than school. Other non-academic benefits include the fostering of independence and responsibility. Homework involves parents in the school process, makes them more aware of what their child is studying, and signals support of their child's education (Cooper, 1989b).

There can be a negative side to homework. For example, too much work on the same topic leads to boredom. Homework should not deprive a youngster of recreational activities. If parents try to assist their child with homework, their use of different methods from that of the child's teacher can cause confusion. Not understanding what or how to do a homework assignment can result in copying or cheating.

Homework too often accentuates inequities in home environments. For instance, some children do not have quiet, well-lighted places to do their homework; some do not have the necessary materials; and some, like Doug, do not have someone to answer their questions or monitor their homework.

What can be done to reap the benefits of homework, yet make sure individual student abilities and home situations are considered? First, remember that only practice tasks should be given as homework. Second, when deciding on the amount of homework, the objective is for the student to practice things learned at school; thus, too much homework, especially if practiced with errors, can be harmful.

England and Flatley (1985) encourage teachers to talk with their students when homework problems arise. They suggest that teachers ask their students whether they need help or if they are confused about a homework assignment. Legitimate reasons may preclude completing a particular homework assignment. Some homework "do's and don'ts" listed by England and Flatley are given in Figure 8.2.

Coordinate homework with parents. One way to do this is to have students keep a special notebook or folder in which homework assignments are recorded. Such a log would include type of assignment, specific instructions, when it was taken home, and

---

FIGURE 8.2   Do's and Don'ts of Homework

Do try to make homework interesting. For example, practice math by calculating the areas of the living room, bedroom, and kitchen, rather than solving problems on a drill worksheet.

Do explain the specific reason for homework assignments.

Do listen to what students have to say about specific homework assignments.

Do solicit parent feedback about homework. Remember that parents have to enforce homework and may spend time helping with assignments.Don't use homework as punishment.

Don't make up spur-of-the-moment homework assignments.

Don't assume that because there are no questions asked about a homework assignment that students understand it.

Don't expect students (even your best students) always to have their homework assignments completed.

Don't give a homework assignment on a topic unless it has been taught in class.

Source: England & Flatley (1985), pp. 36–37.

when it was completed. Parents might be asked to sign the page on which the day's homework assignments are recorded. Keeping a homework log would ensure that parents know each day what their child is assigned for homework. An alternative is to ask parents to sign the actual homework papers either before they are turned in or after they have been graded and returned to the youngster. Encourage parents to reward successful completion of homework assignments.

> **SPEEDBUMP—**Homework is everyone's bugaboo. Make assignments more manageable for students and parents by using a website such as www.schoolnotes.com.

Student Performance

Self-Esteem.   A person's overall self-appraisal of their self-worth is called **self-esteem**. Teachers may have stereotyped perceptions of students with mild disabilities; likewise, expectations of these students may be less than what is expected of other students (Coleman, 1985; Siperstein & Goding, 1985). Students often pick up on their teachers' perceptions and develop similar negative stereotypes toward classmates with mild disabilities.

Teachers can serve as positive **role models**; that is, model positive behaviors toward students with mild disabilities in order to create an environment of acceptance and support. Teachers do this by conveying that they want to work with the students and by supporting efforts made by the students.

> Sara and Juanita have low self-esteem due to their learning problems. Both girls are in their early teens, come from middle-class backgrounds, and are popular with their peers. Sara experiences difficulty comprehending what she has read. Even though she rereads a passage several times, she still has problems answering questions about the passage she just read. Juanita, on the other hand, has difficulty with written expression. She reads assigned subject content with ease and can tell you what she has read, but cannot write legible responses to short-answer or essay-type questions. Sara has withdrawn and become quiet in class, whereas Juanita acts belligerent and sassy.

Both of these students would benefit from successes in the areas in which they are experiencing difficulties. By following a few practical suggestions, a classroom teacher can help students such as Sara and Juanita.

First, assign tasks in which the students can succeed, and make certain that the assignments are understood so they can be carried out successfully. Point out something favorable about each student's daily work, and praise efforts, even if progress is small. Whenever offering constructive criticism, recognize the effort that was made and explain the desired outcome rather than just calling attention to shortcomings.

Much of a youngster's self-esteem is tied to social acceptance. Students can make contributions to class discussions by explaining a concept or discussing a topic with which they are familiar. Simulations and role-play activities help students to rehearse social responses; cooperative learning provides opportunities to learn with other students. Peer tutoring develops feelings of satisfaction in helping other persons. Grouping students with low self-esteem with classmates who have similar interests enhances social conversation so they can more easily work together on class projects. Providing time for students to share positive accomplishments with classmates and to write daily happenings in a private journal also builds self-confidence.

Encourage students to use computer-based composition so that writing more easily can be edited. Writing on the computer encourages trial, error, and practice. Mark and give credit for students' correct and acceptable work, not just their mistakes and errors (e.g., circle or put checks by correct responses, indicate number correct with a plus symbol).

Study Skills. Knowing how to study is essential to successful performance in school. Students with mild disabilities demonstrate poor study skills (Polloway et al., 1989). Many teachers are either unaware that **study skills** must be taught to these students or do not know how to teach these kinds of skills (Scruggs & Mastropieri, 1986).

> **SPEEDBUMP—**Who hasn't had the experience of spending an hour with a book and on closing it not being able to remember what was read. What do you recall from the last three pages you have read? The more interactive you can make your reading—like writing questions and comments in the margins—the better your recall.

R.J., a 6th grader, exemplifies this problem. During early elementary school years, R.J. had no problem reading assigned stories, doing basic math operations, and spelling weekly spelling words. Therefore, R.J.'s parents were perplexed when he began bringing home low grades in science and social studies. There was no doubt that R.J. was reading the assigned chapters in his science and social studies textbooks but he made failing test scores in these subjects. His parents and teacher discovered that R.J.'s lack of effective study skills left him ill-prepared for tests in these classes.

One way to learn if students need to improve their study skills is to ask them questions about their study habits. Stephens, Blackhurst, and Magliocca (1988) recommend using a checklist for this purpose. See Figure 8.3 for the study habits checklist.

Often, students like R.J. read the pages but don't comprehend what the written passages mean. The SQ3R method of study is effective in helping students to better comprehend what they are reading (Cheek & Cheek, 1983; Mercer & Mercer, 1985). The SQ3R study skill teaches students to:

- *survey or scan* the material: read the title, first paragraph, subheadings, last paragraph
- develop *questions:* change the title and subheadings into questions
- *read* the material: find answers to the questions
- *recite* both the questions and answers
- *review* the material: recite questions and answers daily (Wallace & Kauffman, 1986).

FIGURE 8.3   Study Habits Checklist

_____ Do you have a regular place where you study?
_____ Do you keep a chart that shows the time you spend studying?
_____ Do you have a regular time to study?
_____ Do you keep a homework assignment book?
_____ Do you keep a calendar of tests, reports, and projects?
_____ Do you keep a notebook or folder for each subject?
_____ Do you take class notes?
_____ Do you make notes or highlight material while reading?
_____ Do you review class notes and reading notes regularly?
_____ Do you outline or summarize what you read?
_____ Do you make note of and look up new words?
_____ Do you keep for review all returned papers and tests?
_____ Do you visit and use the library regularly?

Source: Adapted from Stephens, Blackhurst, & Magliocca (1988), pp. 160–161.

The SQ3R method can be modified and used to help students better understand math problems (Georgia Department of Education, 1989). The student procedure is as follows:

- _survey or scan_ the whole problem to determine what needs to be done
- change the math problem into a series of _questions_
- determine the _facts_ that need to be answered
- determine _processes_ needed to answer the facts
- perform _computation_ to solve the problems
- _question_ the answer by checking the computation

Reading comprehension is enhanced when students can relate their personal experiences to what they are reading. Because each reader's background will vary, involve students in firsthand experiences (e.g., field trips) when possible. Another method is to stimulate students' thinking about a topic before oral or silent reading begins (Wilson, 1983). Polloway and colleagues (1989) suggest having the teacher introduce a reading selection by saying, "As you read, think about what you would do if you were caught in a flood like Van is in this story" (p. 229). This helps a student personalize a story.

Active reading is encouraged when a teacher initiates a discussion related to the selection the students are about to read. For example, encourage students to comment on a passage by giving their opinions or by having students read a passage and justify or change their original opinions (Polloway et al., 1989). When students make predictions about the story and generate their own questions, their comprehension is improved.

Students with mild disabilities frequently feel overwhelmed with the amount of material they are expected to learn. The teacher can reduce the amount of written work that is presented or assigned (Carbo, Dunn, & Dunn, 1986; Schulz, Carpenter, & Turnbull, 1991). Students can demonstrate mastery of learning material through projects (Lewis & Doorlag, 1987). For example, students can track the position of planets in relation to the sun by constructing a mobile on which Styrofoam balls representing the planets are scaled in size and distance from a sun. Projects such as these enhance interest in learning.

> **SPEEDBUMP—**Tiny Pluto is no longer a planet. That's probably a good thing because if you tried to do an exact scale of the distance of the Earth from Pluto by reducing the Earth to the size of a pea, Pluto would be a mile and a half away.

INSTRUCTIONAL ACCOMMODATIONS, MODIFICATIONS, AND STRATEGIES

Accommodations, modifications, and strategies are all common terms used in education today. Sometimes these terms have been used interchangeably in the literature to refer to adjustment of the facilities, curriculum, and instruction relating to the education of students with disabilities (Price, Mayfield, McFadden, & Marsh, 2001). Effective teachers need to know what each of these terms means so that the accommodations, modifications, and strategies can be successfully utilized with students in whatever educational setting they are being taught.

Accommodations refer to the actual teaching supports and services that the student may require to demonstrate what has been learned successfully. These include adjustments in the instruction of students, and approaches whereby the learning environment of the students is modified to promote learning. The basic curriculum is not changed. Some examples are additional time for tests, projects, and assignments; oral, open book or take home tests; reports written or given orally; taped stories; paired reading; math charts; use of manipulative objects; preferred seating; study carrel; cooperative groups; peer tutors; use of a scribe; personal note taker; study guides; written notes, outlines and instructions; taped books; audio tape or CD; use of a scribe; calculators; computers; use of a word processor; spelling and grammar assistive devices; specialized computer software; alternative ways of completing assignments; and so on (Department of Student Services, 2007; Special Connections, 2007a).

Modifications refer to changes made to curriculum expectations in order to meet the needs of the student. Generally, modifications are made when the expectations are beyond the student's level of ability. Examples are including a student in the same activity but individualizing the expectations, materials, and/or tasks.

Strategies refer to skills or techniques used to assist in learning. Strategies are individualized to suit the student's learning style and developmental level. Examples include highlighting, rehearsal, color coding, memory joggers, visual cues, number lines, and so on.

If a student has an IEP and is receiving special education, then he or she is receiving accommodations in the general education classroom if they are needed. In addition, students served under Section 504 of Public Law 93-112 are guaranteed the same right to reasonable accommodations. Section 504 is a federal law that provides accommodations for any student with a disability, whether or not he or she is eligible for special education. Accommodations are intended to level the playing field and prevent discrimination. In either case, it was agreed by a multidisciplinary team about which accommodations are reasonable and needed for the student to succeed in the general education classroom (Baumel, 2007; Special Connections, 2007b).

Price and colleagues (2001) state:

> Accommodations may involve the use of modified instructional techniques, more flexible administrative practices, modified academic requirements, or any compensatory activity that emphasizes the use of stronger, more intact capabilities or that provides modified or alternative educational processes and/or goals. (p. 1)

Accommodations are determined on a case-by-case basis. The utilization of accommodations, modifications, and instructional strategies often are looked upon differently by general classroom teachers and special education teachers. For instance, most general education teachers are interested in teaching subject matter content while special educators are concerned with remediating underlying learning deficiencies. Elementary and secondary level teachers have competing influences on them. Regardless, best teaching practices encourage the appropriate use of accommodations, modifications, and strategies so that students reach their potential (Price, et al., 2001).

One type of **math accommodation** that often is needed is a reduced number of problems for seat work. For instance, why require Carlos, who works at a pace much slower than his classmates, to work out 20 long-division problems when he can show he knows how to do the mathematical operations by answering five of these problems correctly? And when Cathy experiences difficulties with division, why not use *error analysis*? That is, pinpoint what she is doing procedurally that is causing the same error to occur in several problems. When error analysis is applied, the student has only one calculation error to correct.

Questioning accommodations are useful as well. For example, the usual way that teachers give spelling tests is by pronouncing words orally and having students write them. Instead, the teacher could give students word choices that are similar and have them underline or circle the correct spelling of words from a multiple-choice format. It also is possible to use the cloze procedure in which the teacher deletes selected letters which must then be filled in by students. Similarly, the teacher can alter the instruction by having students work at learning centers and use picture directions rather than written sentences—or use a buddy system whereby one student reads the instructions, and the other performs the tasks.

Reading accommodations can be made before, during, and after students read (Figure 8.4). One that can be made prior to the actual reading experience is teaching textbook structure (headings, subheadings, different print, introductory and summary paragraphs). Teach students to understand how and for what reasons these items are employed. Preteaching students the vocabulary words in the context in which they will be read is another way of preparing readers before they actually read. Pair question numbers from a study guide with page numbers on which the information can be found. Use advance organizers to help students look for essential ideas as they read. These can later be used for reviewing what was read and for homework activities (CEC Staff, 1997).

FIGURE 8.4   Instructional Accommodations

Textual

- Give students an advance organizer, which also can be used for review or for homework.
- Preteach students vocabulary words in the context in which they will read them.
- Tape record the text. Recorded text segments should be clear and short. You may want to provide an overview of the selection. Also, give the reader page numbers, and summarize important information periodically.
- Teach textbook structure (headings, subheadings, different print, introductory and summary paragraphs).
- Teach active reading. The student reads a paragraph, covers it, and recites the main point and/or important information in his or her own words.
- Highlight important information.
- Give students a partial outline of important information, to be completed while reading.
- Pair question numbers from a study guide with page numbers on which the information can be found.

Sequencing or Assignment Completion

- Break up tasks into workable and obtainable steps and include due dates.
- Provide examples and specific steps to accomplish the task.
- List and/or post requirements necessary to complete each assignment.
- Check assignments frequently.
- Arrange for the student to have a "study buddy" in each subject area.
- Define all requirements of a completed activity (e.g., your math is complete when all five problems are corrected).

Test-Taking Skills

- Allow extra time for testing.
- Teach test-taking skills and strategies.
- Give alternate forms of the test: oral, essay, short answer, multiple choice, fill in the blank.
- Use clear, readable, and uncluttered test forms.
- Provide a scribe.
- Allow students to take tests on computers.
- Give students the opportunity to practice with the accommodations before the test.

Source: CEC Staff, 1997c, p. 15.

Some accommodations can be made to assist readers as they actively read the story or content assigned. One way is to teach active reading. The student reads a paragraph, covers it, and recites the main point and/or important information in his or her own words. Another instructional accommodation is to tape record the text. Recorded text segments should be clear and short. Have an overview of the selection prepared so that the student can review what he or she is going to hear on the tape. Also, while taping, give the reader page numbers and summarize important information periodically.

In order to present content at secondary students' reading and comprehension levels, a teacher might write information presented in textbooks on the blackboard or on an overhead, develop chapter outlines, code paragraphs to chapter questions, and so forth. This is done using magic markers to highlight the main idea, topic, and specific vocabulary words or letters. Another instructional accommodation is to give students a partial outline of important information, and ask them to complete it while they are reading. A review of their responses following the reading exercise is helpful in accomplishing follow-up and provides an after-reading checkup.

Accommodations Using Technology

Audio Text Recordings.   According to Boyle and colleagues (2002), many middle grade and high school students experience difficulty reading and comprehending assigned textbooks because they have poor reading skills and lack effective learning strategies. In addition, assigned textbooks often have readability levels beyond the abilities of students with mild disabilities. Secondary students must read textbooks independently, demonstrate mastery of content information, and apply previously acquired knowledge to new learning situations. Unlike elementary students, secondary students with learning disabilities and other high-incidence cognitive disabilities must "read to learn rather than just learn to read" (p. 50).

> **SPEEDBUMP—**We advance these ideas with trepidation, knowing full well that our readers are no doubt way ahead of your middle-aged authors when it comes to the topic of electronic technology.

Audio texts have become more efficient due to the introduction of DAISY—compatible digital books, like those offered by Recording for the Blind & Dyslexic. A single CD can hold up to 45 hours of recorded material, which is about the size of a standard textbook. The CD can be placed into the playback machine, the desired page number entered, and with a press of a button, the machine quickly advances to the requested page. Moreover, the speed of the reader's voice can be adjusted to be heard more slowly or more rapidly.

E-books and Accommodations.   E-books are electronic texts containing features that can be classified as accommodations (Cavanaugh, 2002). An e-book comprises three different components: an e-book file, software to read the e-book, and a hardware device with which to read it, such as a computer, laptop, or handheld device. E-books can be created from common forms of electronic text with readily available programs. They also are available through online libraries and bookstores.

E-books are available in a variety of formats. Some are specific for certain computer platforms while others are cross-platform. HTML or text-based e-books can be used in standard browsers. With this format, users can adjust text styles, sizes, and colors. They also can search within the e-book, then copy and paste selected text to other programs.

Other formats in which e-books are available include Adobe PDF, Rocket, Palm, MS Reader, Mobi, and eBookMan.

In contrast to school textbooks, which cannot be marked in and are somewhat heavy to transport in book bags, e-books are easier to transport, lightweight, have adjustable text sizes, can be highlighted and bookmarked, can be used with note taking, contain interactive dictionaries, and even read-aloud features. These features allow for many types of special accommodations and adaptations in order to meet the needs of students. The voice output, interactive dictionaries, and note taking are features that provide scaffolding support that many students need.

Speech-Feedback and Word-Prediction Software. Assistive technology, especially in the form of computer software, can be a valuable tool for many students with special needs (Williams, 2002). Furthermore, according to Williams, word processing, speech recognition, and other types of software packages may help students with mild disabilities to participate in classroom writing programs.

One teacher focused on the results obtained with a single subject case study: a student with learning disabilities. Two components were studied: speech feedback and word prediction. The Write:OutLoud program supplied the speech-feedback component. It enabled the computer to "read" selected sections of text to students. In addition, this software highlighted each word as it was being read aloud. This component provided scaffolding support for this particular student who often could not remember what he previously had written. The Co:Writer program has word-prediction capabilities and was used for this reason. After a student typed the first letter or letters in a word, the software predicts the remainder of the word, depending on supplying a word that would be grammatically correct at this point in the sentence. This program originally was developed to limit the amount of keystrokes required for writers with physical disabilities, but offered the spelling assistance needed by this student with learning disabilities.

Test-Taking Skills

Ideas for accommodating test-taking skills include allowing extra time for testing in order for the student to be able to process what is being asked and to formulate an adequate response. Teaching students test-taking skills and strategies helps to avoid test anxiety and to build independent thinking, which allows the student to have clear thoughts about the question. When considering oral testing, essay writing, short-answer responses, multiple-choice selections, and fill-in-the-blanks, consider that students vary in their abilities to do better on different question types. Regardless of whatever type of test is selected, it is essential that clear, readable, and uncluttered test forms be developed or chosen.

If the test requires writing, perhaps a scribe might be useful if the student has difficulty making written responses. In using a scribe, the teacher is able to determine just what the student knows about the question without the response being confounded by writing difficulties. Another alternative to writing difficulties is to allow the student to take the test using a computer software program or word processor if these help to make accommodations for the student's area of disability or weakness. It is important that the student be given opportunities to practice whatever accommodation is deemed necessary in order to best learn what the student knows about the area being tested and to avoid his or her being penalized for a disability.

Testing Accommodations

Methods for testing students with mild disabilities vary in type, structure, and level of response. Students can be asked to respond to tests and quizzes with written answers, verbal responses, or by demonstration. Learner characteristics often dictate the amount that can be tested at one sitting, the time needed for completion, and whether the testing results can best be achieved by giving group or individually administered tests. Responses should be monitored and expanded from simple recognition and recall to higher-level thinking skills, such as inference, analysis, synthesis, evaluation, and appreciation.

Students with mild disabilities may have short attention spans; therefore, schedule intermittent breaks. Read test directions orally and give an example of the expected correct response. Remind students to review their tests, complete any unanswered questions, and to make corrections where needed. For students who have difficulty with traditional tests, alternatives include projects, checklists, discussions, student–teacher interviews, and student-developed portfolios designed to demonstrate student knowledge and understanding of content. Finally, giving brief, frequent tests increases students' opportunities for success. See Figure 8.5.

End-of-year standardized tests often present options for testing accommodations. Some of these include being seated separate from the class; extended time; use of a scribe; the use of a calculator or computer; and so on. If available, these accommodations are written into the directions of the test manual. School personnel can confer with parents about the appropriateness and benefit of an approved accommodation. Parents and older students need to be informed of any restrictions or limitations to the use of test scores if utilizing accommodations.

FIGURE 8.5   Testing Accommodations

Contents of tests should not be altered; accommodations apply to test administration only.

- Segment tests into shorter time periods.
- Space testing over several days.
- Pick the best time of day to administer a test.
- Use enlarged print for visual difficulties.
- Use praise to reinforce perseverance.
- Allow extra time.
- Provide a scribe.
- Allow students to use a computer.
- List multiple choice questions vertically rather than horizontally.
- Use uncluttered test forms.
- Teach test-taking strategies.
- Allow students to practice with accommodations.
- Provide a reader.
- Use alternate test formats, such as oral tests, allowing use of a scribe, or allowing untimed tests.
- Review tests with students to identify test-taking difficulties.
- Provide rubrics for essay tests to give students concrete writing guidelines.

Source: Henley, M. *Creating successful inclusion programs: Guidelines for teachers and administrators.* National Educational Service, 2004. Reprinted with permission.

Rubrics

Jackson and Larkin (2002) explain that the original definition for rubric was "marks in red," but today a rubric refers to "a grading guideline or scoring tool to follow in assessment" (p. 40). Rubrics include predetermined criteria for evaluating student work, and provide specific descriptions of teacher expectations for an assigned task (see Figure 8.6).

The following rubric benefits are stated by Jackson and Larkin (2002, 41):

- Students know before beginning an assignment what the expectations for performance will be. The expectations may be assigned by the teachers or may be determined through class discussions.
- Students monitor their own progress as the assignment progresses.
- Students become aware of the quality of work through judging their own and their peers' assignments against the standards set in the rubric.

Points	1	2	3	4	Total
Title Card or Screen	No title page	Title page is present, but lacks much of the required information	Title page is present but lacks complete information	Title page is present and contains title, author, students' names, and appropriate graphics	
Main Characters	No description of main characters	Incomplete or inadequate description of main characters	Adequate descriptions and character sketches of main characters including a few comparisons among characters	Complete description of main characters including comparisons, contrasts, and complete character sketches	
Setting	No description of setting	Incomplete or inaccurate description of setting	Adequate description of setting including a few visual aids	Complete description of setting. Includes many drawings, maps, and background information	
Brief Summary	Inadequate plot summary	Incomplete plot summary and incomplete or inaccurate story board	Adequate plot summary including some events on a story board	Complete plot summary including story board highlighting major events	
	Grading Scale	**A=40–44 B=35–39**	**C=25–34 D=20–24**	**Total Points:**	

FIGURE 8.6   Book Report Rubric

Source: Adapted from MidLink Magazine (2005).

- Students use the rubric as a final checkpoint before turning in the assignment.
- Students with special needs have the rubric tailored to their learning styles and specific needs.

A number of website resources provide sample rubrics. A tool that can be obtained through the website http://rubistar.4teachers.org is called Rubistar. A tutorial guides teachers and other users through the process of creating rubrics. Rubrics can be customized for oral projects, products, multimedia, science, research and writing, work skills, and math. For the 18 months during which they are saved to the website, the rubrics can be viewed or edited.

Grading

Much debate has centered around grading the performance of students with mild disabilities. Carpenter (1985) suggests using the following questions to guide grading decisions: "On what criteria are grades based? What type of medium should be used? Who should participate in the grading process? How frequently should grades be given?"

Teachers generally include class participation, seat work, tests (e.g., daily, weekly, unit), homework, and special projects in student evaluations. More than one grade could be given to reflect other student attributes, such as effort, attitude, or study skills. Marking correct answers rather than mistakes and giving number grades are other options for grading. Written comments or information can be given or can supplement number and letter grades. Points can be assigned as grades.

> **SPEEDBUMP—**William Farish, a tutor at the University of Cambridge, invented grading in 1792. He got the idea from a factory assembly line where shoe leather was graded by quality.

A major dilemma for teachers is how to grade work that is completed on the student's functioning level in the regular classroom, but not at his or her grade-level placement. It is generally agreed that satisfactorily performed student work should be reinforced if it is at the student's functioning level, even though not his or her grade level. One practice is to link grades to the goals and objectives in a student's IEP (Brantlinger & Guskin, 1988). A criterion-referenced skill list can be used so that specific objectives can be checked as "mastered" or "needs improvement" (Baumel, 2007; Schulz, Carpenter, & Turnbull, 1991).

Another means of assigning grades is to assign the earned grade and check "working below grade level" on the report card. Yet another way is to reward students with the grades earned but coded with actual functioning levels. For example, a 4th-grade student with mild learning disabilities earns an "A" in reading at the 2nd-grade level (the student's actual functioning level in that subject)—thus an "A2" appears on the student's report card as his grade in that subject.

Cograding often occurs when students with disabilities are taught in regular education classrooms. The special educator—whether working in an inclusive, consultative, or resource room setting—may make accommodations and adaptations to daily work, tests, and homework assignments. Vaughn and associates (1997) suggest that grading procedures and guidelines be discussed and agreed upon during the development of the IEP.

They also remind teachers that different grading standards may exist between elementary- and secondary-level classes. For example, whereas at the elementary level, teachers can consider students' ability and progress, at the secondary level, grading often is done on the basis of established academic standards. Charting student progress can help illustrate student gains that might otherwise be overlooked. It may help to involve students in their own grading when possible.

Special educators are encouraged to meet with regular classroom teachers at scheduled times to discuss student progress and achievement. Meetings provide the opportunity to convey to the classroom teacher a clear description of a student's strengths, weaknesses, capabilities, and needs. By doing so, additional data by which to determine grades are provided to the regular classroom teacher. Perhaps most important is the inclusion of the regular classroom teacher in IEP meetings and decisions. Whenever possible, engage in cooperative grading arrangements so that both regular classroom and resource room performances are evaluated. By engaging in cooperative grading arrangements, encouragement and reinforcement for effort and accomplishment is conveyed more effectively.

Curriculum-Based Assessment

Standardized assessment practices often are criticized for their lack of relevance to instruction. Assessment procedures linked to what is taught in school have reemerged as promising alternatives to standardized assessment (Blankenship, 1985; Deno, 1985, 1986, 1989; Tucker, 1985; Wesson, 1991; Ysseldyke & Algozzine, 1982).

Advocates of **curriculum-based assessment** point out the need to target evaluation procedures on content that is taught in the classroom (Algozzine, Ruhl, & Ramsey, 1991). Standardized achievement tests comprise a limited sample of questions that the test-makers believe reflect the classroom's curriculum. Curriculum-based assessment is defined as "the practice of obtaining direct and frequent measures of a student's performance on a series of sequentially arranged objectives derived from the curriculum used in the classroom" (Blankenship, 1985, 234).

SPEEDBUMP—Assessment is misused when it is viewed as an end in itself.

An illustration of curriculum-based assessment follows:

Carol, a kindergarten teacher, decided to teach her students a unit on frogs. Before beginning her lessons she asked her students a series of questions about the amphibians. She tabulated their responses. After the unit, she again quizzed her young charges. She found that they could answer 75% more questions about frogs after the unit than before. By evaluating student progress based on their ability to learn the classroom curriculum, Carol was practicing curriculum-based assessment.

Curriculum-based assessment involves repeated measurement of a student's performance on a sequenced curriculum (Research Brief for Teachers, 1988). Counting and graphing are the best means of tracking student progress. For example, a teacher could ask a student to read a passage from a story that seems to match his present reading level. Each incorrectly read word is marked. A final tally reveals that the student knew two-thirds of the words in the story. This 66 percent figure provides baseline data to measure future progress. Every few days, after instruction, the student's progress in reading again is measured. Graphing the results of each measurement provides a visual means of efficiently marking progress.

Curriculum-based data is collected "prior to instruction, immediately following instruction, and throughout the year to assess long-term retention" (Blankenship, 1985, 238).

Once a lesson has been implemented, teachers *reassess*. There are several reasons for reassessing a student following implementation of instruction. Reassessment occurs so that some determination can be made about the amount of progress a student has made in reaching long-range goals and short-term objectives. Reassessment also occurs so that adjustments can be made in the student's instructional plan, or the teacher's implementation of such, if necessary. Actually, it is important that assessment occur ongoing and accompany daily implementation of instructional programming.

Both the No Child Left Behind Act (2001) and the Reauthorization of IDEA (2004) state that general education teachers need to be able to work with all of the students in their classrooms, including those with special learning needs. It is no longer acceptable for classroom teachers to allege that they cannot teach youngsters with special needs. Knowing effective accommodations for students with special needs assures the general education teacher of a higher success level with all students. (See Table 8.1.)

THE EDUCATOR'S TOOL KIT

Many professionals carry tool kits. Carpenters and repair persons have a collection of tools that enable them to perform carpentry and various types of repair work. Lawyers and

TABLE 8.1   Basic Elements of Effective Teaching

Lesson Introduction	Gain student attention. Review previously learned content and ensure students have the prerequisite knowledge and skills. Provide students a purpose for learning the new content.
Instruction and Modeling	Provide accurate, clear, complete, and concise instruction. Model the less objective. Ask frequent and appropriate questions. Include correct and incorrect examples.
Guided Practice	Provide all students the opportunity to demonstrate lesson objective with assistance. Monitor student performance closely. Apply appropriate error correction procedures when needed.
Independent Practice	Provide all students the opportunity to demonstrate lesson objective independently.
Closure	Review and summarize.

Source: Prater (2003), pp. 58–64.

business people carry their tools of trade in an attaché case. Physicians used to carry a medicine bag when making house calls. We used the tools that mechanics carry in an earlier example when discussing integrative teaching.

Some professors encourage students in methods for learners with mild disabilities courses to construct an educational kit. Many special education teachers go into the regular education classroom to teach students with special learning needs. Others travel from school to school or from room to room in order to teach these students; still others remain in a resource or self-contained classroom of their own. The tools each teacher-in-training makes and places into this kit help that person to be ready with accessible "tools of the trade" to teach students with mild disabilities. The curriculum with which these tools are used includes mathematics, reading, spelling, and social skills. With the tools assembled, teachers are equipped and prepared to provide meaningful learning experiences for each of their students.

Each educational tool kit contains:

Reading
1. A scope-and-sequence or skills hierarchy. (Enables teachers to see where students are functioning on the overall reading skills hierarchy. This is helpful in developing IEPs and in performing other educational planning and programming.)
2. A set of basic sight words (e.g., Dolch word list, survival words). (Useful in building student repertoires in basic word lists. These lists of words contain the words most frequently found in basal readers.)
3. A teacher-made game board. (Provides practice and reinforcement for many reading skills [e.g., long- and short-vowel sounds; initial, medial, and final consonant sounds; consonant blends; word meanings; etc.]).

Mathematics
1. A scope-and-sequence or hierarchy of skills. (Enables teachers to see where students are functioning on the overall math skills hierarchy. The overview is useful when developing IEPs and designing individual plans and programs.)
2. Teacher-made number lines, multiplication table charts (wall or student desk size), and an abacus. (All provide hands-on manipulative materials that help students to learn math in a concrete and meaningful manner. Number lines are useful in acquiring knowledge of math operations [addition, subtraction, multiplication, division], multiplication charts provide visual repetition of math facts that leads to mastery. An abacus is essential when learning borrowing and carrying in subtraction and addition, and regrouping in multiplication and division.)
3. A teacher-made game board. (Provides practice and reinforcement for many math skills [e.g., math facts, math operations, fractions, geometric shapes, decimals, solving word problems, and so on]).

Social Skills
1. A set of classroom rules, few in number and positively directed (wall or student desk size). (Involves students in the development of rules and classroom structure.) The fewer the number, the more likely students will remember and follow them. The positive direction in which they are written enables reinforcement and instills a positive classroom atmosphere.

2. A teacher-made social skills activity. (Encourages role play or simulation opportunities for practicing and reinforcing many social skills.)
3. A teacher-made game board. (Provides practice and reinforcement for many social interaction skills.)

The construction of tools encourages teachers to accommodate students' learning needs. Commercially made materials will not always provide the means for teaching a particular skill to a student; therefore, some teaching aids will need to be tailored and adapted to accommodate special learning or behavioral needs of many students. This activity prepares teachers to have educational tools ready for use with students. It also requires teachers to give thought beforehand about the instruction they will be conducting with their students.

SUMMARY

Effective teachers are able to use a variety of instructional accommodations, modifications, and strategies. In recent years, teachers of inclusive classroom have found that instruction of both general classroom students and special needs students is enhanced when best teaching practices are utilized. Instructional accommodations, modifications, and strategies also enhance learning when appropriately employed. The law requires that special accommodations, when needed, be provided students with IEPs and Section 504 plans. Many of these same accommodations work well with general classroom students.

Numerous studies also have noted the importance of time management, allocated time, engaged time, and academic learning time. Effective teaching also depends on good communication between teacher and students. It is important that: (1) student attention be directed toward the instruction being given, (2) teachers be clear in their instructions and explanations, (3) teacher feedback be appropriate to the purpose, and (4) questioning skills reflect good instructional techniques.

Teachers are effective when they make appropriate accommodations during instruction. Test-taking accommodations more accurately assess what the student has learned. Cooperative grading arrangements offer more encouragement and reinforcement for student progress.

Research has addressed students who have low self-esteem, poor study skills, and weak organizational skills perhaps more than other learning problems. These difficulties can be found on a day-to-day basis within most classrooms with students who have learning disabilities, mild intellectual disabilities, and behavior disorders. These particular problems also are identifiable with low-achieving and at-risk learners, as well as other nondisabled youngsters. Practical strategies for dealing with these difficulties include affirming efforts, enabling successful experiences, and planning interventions that meet individual student needs. Direct teaching of study skills and student organizational skills aid students in maximizing their learning potential. Success in the classroom and social acceptance help students to build self-esteem. The classroom atmosphere has a significant impact on learning. Students tend to accomplish more when they have positive feelings about themselves. Curriculum-based assessment enables both the teacher and student to track academic progress.

ACTIVITIES

1. Reread the vignette about Shirley Allen. Answer the questions that follow the vignette. As an option, answer other questions within the vignette instead.

2. Design a graphic organizer for this chapter. You could do a Venn diagram, double cell diagram, a KWHL chart, or any other visual summary of the chapter that makes sense to you. Compare your organizer with your colleagues'. Discuss the advantages and disadvantages of different types of graphic organizers.

3. Make a list of electronic devices that could be used to enhance classroom instruction. Make a similar list of valuable websites. Share your ideas with your colleagues. Locate the 10 best websites for the beginning teacher.

4. Divide into small groups. Select an area of student performance that could be improved (e.g., self-esteem, study skills, keeping track of materials and assignments, following directions, and completing class and homework assignments). Develop a list of 10 ideas for helping students in each area.

5. Divide into three groups. Assign one academic subject and grade-level math, reading, for each group. Identify a possible instructional need that a student with a mild disability might have (e.g., attention problem). Identify instructional accommodations that would help this student to learn. Be sure to consider accommodations using technology.

6. Divide into three groups. Assign each group one area of the educator's tool kit—reading, math, or social skills. Discuss within your small group how you would use the items in the tool kit to accommodate or modify instruction to meet each student's learning needs. Optional: Construct one or more of the items and demonstrate how you would use it to teach students who needed this accommodation.

CHAPTER NINE

CLASSROOM MANAGEMENT

ADVANCE QUESTIONS

Answer the following questions as you read this chapter:

1. What effects do teacher attitudes have on classroom management?
2. What is proactive discipline?
3. What is positive behavioral support and functional behavioral assessment?
4. What are some commonly used classroom discipline methods?
5. What are some key features of life-space interviews?
6. What are some common behavior modification strategies?
7. What is the difference between verbal and nonverbal classroom interventions?
8. How does classroom organization influence classroom management?
9. What are some advantages and disadvantages of using punishment to control behavior?
10. What discipline procedures are required by federal law (IDEA) for students with mild disabilities?

VIGNETTE: JOE CLARK

Joe Clark was the principal of Eastside High School in Eastside, New Jersey. Each day he patrolled the halls of Eastside with a bullhorn. His motto, "There's only one way—my way," hung on his office door as a stern reminder that Joe Clark was a tough disciplinarian. Before Joe Clark came to Eastside, the school was in chaos. Fights and drug deals were routine in the halls of this inner-city school. Learning was almost nonexistent. Each year, Eastside students tallied pathetically low on standardized tests of achievement.

After his arrival, Clark, a retired U.S. Army sergeant, quickly took charge. In one incident, he suspended 60 students without notifying the school board. He locked school doors—a fire code violation—to bar intruders. As a result of Clark's tough tactics, 1,900 students either dropped out or were expelled from Eastside. To some, including former U.S. Secretary of Education William Bennett, Joe Clark was a hero—an example of a nononsense disciplinarian in action. The remaining students at Eastside walked the school hallways without fear, and their standardized test scores improved. Other educators argued that Joe Clark did not solve problems; he merely transferred them from the halls of his school to the streets of his community. After a deluge of both positive and negative media attention, Joe Clark resigned. He was commended by President Reagan and a movie was made of his exploits as principal of Eastside. Is Joe Clark a pedagogical hero or villain? He got results, but did the end justify his means?

Albert Shanker, past president of the American Federation of Teachers, believed Joe Clark created more problems than he solved. According to Shanker, punishments, suspensions, and expulsions become necessary when schoolwork ceases to be relevant for students. When students are made to sit still and listen quietly for 4 to 6 hours every day, when they are hopelessly behind the rest of the class with no chance to catch up, classroom disruptions are inevitable. Shanker believed many classroom disruptions can be traced to student apathy, student frustration, and lack of student control over daily events. He stated that discipline practices need to be embedded in a classroom management system that empowers students. Students should feel worthwhile and that they have a voice in classroom affairs. He promoted proactive classroom management ideas such as understanding student developmental needs and teaching self-control. The experiences at Eastside typify the debate about how to best manage behavior problems; some like Joe Clark believe that rewards and punishments in order to foster obedience is the best approach. Others like Albert Shanker believe discipline should do more than cultivate compliance; discipline, according to Shanker and other proactive educators, should be a means to help students grow socially and emotionally.

1. What do you believe is the purpose of discipline?
2. Should teachers teach students how to behave responsibly or simply teach them how to read, write, compute, and do other academic content?
3. Are all approaches to classroom management and discipline equally suited for all students?
4. Did you have teachers who resembled Joe Clark? Did you have teachers who practiced Albert Shanker's vision?
5. Do you think that how students feel about their teacher's classroom management practices influences their academic performance?

DISCIPLINE: AN OVERVIEW

Classroom management is an essential teaching skill (see Evertson & Weinstein, 2006, for a comprehensive review of contemporary research, practices, and issues). The most elegant lesson will deteriorate if the teacher is unable to maintain a sense of order and purpose in the classroom. The first signal that a new teacher is experiencing difficulty is usually problems with discipline. Przychodin (1981) notes, "No teacher can teach a class that is out of **control**, and once it is reported that the teacher cannot control the classroom his reputation in the public eye begins to decline." Discipline is consistently among the highest concerns in surveys of public attitudes toward education (cf. Rose & Gallup, 2007).

> **SPEEDBUMP—**During job interviews, prospective first-year teachers often are asked how they would handle discipline problems.

Many special needs programs are populated with youngsters who were referred for discipline problems. Disruptive behavior in the general classroom is a fast track to special education services. Although classroom teachers may have tolerance for weak academic skills, deficiencies in self-control can quickly strain teacher patience. Since 1977, there has been a steady increase in students identified as having some type of behavior or emotional disorder. These students constitute the highest proportion of special needs students in the 12–21 age bracket.

Educators have a penchant for labeling behavior problems, and those labels have a way of intimidating even the most sanguine teacher. Such terms as emotionally disturbed, ADHD, hyperactive, and conduct disordered have a common theme: The youngster needs help with discipline. How is a teacher to manage a classroom with youngsters such as these? The answer actually is quite simple—look behind the label for the child. Labels are deceptive. They obscure the truth by implying that all students with similar labels have similar needs, aspirations, and problems. The teacher who says, "I treat all students the same," and then proceeds to try to get them to conform to the same set of behavioral expectations will be continually frustrated. Like Sisyphus, the mythical king whose eternal punishment was to roll a rock to the top of the hill only to have it roll back down again, the educator who presses for obedience will put much effort into a futile task. Young people are resilient and resourceful. They may bend to a heavy hand, but they will end up resenting any system of discipline that overlooks their culture, their personal needs, or their integrity.

In this chapter, we describe **proactive classroom management** practices. Proactive classroom management is based on the notion that students do their best work in classrooms where they are respected as individuals. When behavior problems do occasionally surface, proactive teachers look for positive solutions that include student input. Punishment as a behavior management technique is eschewed in favor of behavior interventions that teach students to take responsibility for their actions. Many of the behavior strategies described in this chapter have been utilized specifically with youngsters with emotional disturbance. Other strategies were developed within general education. This blend of general and special education management practices will provide a functional guide for managing the behavior of students with mild disabilities.

> **SPEEDBUMP**—Many classroom behaviors problems are avoided when teachers make smooth transitions from one activity to another?

All students, at some time, present **behavioral challenges** to teachers. Incidents can range from a few cases of noncompliance to serious emotional problems. All teachers, whether general or special education, need a diverse array of classroom management skills to facilitate learning (Evertson & Weinstein, 2006). In their survey of teacher burnout, Feiter and Tokar (1982) reported 58 percent of teachers polled said that student misbehavior was the primary cause of their job-related stress (p. 484). The following remarks by Amanda, a graduate student working toward her masters in education, illustrate the psychological impact of discipline problems on a beginning teacher (Leverault, 1990).

> At the breakfast table last week, I was talking incessantly about how well I was doing in my courses at the college and about how all of the information I was getting about teaching was finally coming together. I was sure that I was soon going to be an English teacher extraordinaire, just like Robin Williams' character in the film *Dead Poet's Society*. My husband was staring at me with his cold, calculating eyes and I knew what was coming; we had this conversation before. "What will you do when some kid acts up in your first class?" he asked, a knowing smile on his lips. "Well that's easy," I said, "I will handle it in as mature and responsible a way as you would expect from someone of my obvious mental stature." And I smiled, but my husband did not. "You'll cry," he said, and then he smiled. (p. 1)

Every teacher would like a class full of motivated, well-adjusted young scholars, but as Amanda's breakfast conversation with her husband indicates, the more realistic expectation is that public school teaching requires intestinal fortitude as well as good teaching skills.

Students are impressionable human beings with complex life histories. Some urban schools have metal detectors to screen students for weapons. However, there is no method for screening such **emotional baggage** as hostility or despair. These burdens cannot be checked at the schoolhouse door. Poverty undermines hope. Drug abuse scorches intellectual ability. Dysfunctional families thwart personal development (Menacker, Weldon, & Hurwitz, 1989). Even students who are raised in the best conditions experience emotional ups and downs.

> **SPEEDBUMP**—According to the Children's Defense Fund, every 36 seconds a child is abused or neglected. Every 4 hours, a young person commits suicide.

There is no easy life. All young people must grapple with the distress that accompanies growth. The metaphor "growing pains" refers to more than pinched toes from tight fitting shoes. Personal growth requires persistence, mentoring, and opportunity. It is hard work for both student and teacher. Growth is first an emotional and second an intellectual experience. Before students can learn, they need an emotional base of security, trust, and self-confidence. It is the classroom teacher's responsibility to nurture these feelings in some students and teach them to others.

PROACTIVE DISCIPLINE

Many discussions about school discipline begin with what the teacher should do after a student is disruptive. **Proactive discipline** focuses on teacher actions that will decrease classroom disruptions. *Proactive discipline* is defined as a classroom management system designed to promote student **self-control** by focusing teacher intervention at the cause of discipline problems and by teaching such prosocial skills as cooperation and conflict resolution.

Many proactive teachers use prompts and preinstructional routines to prevent misbehavior. For example, a teacher reminded his students of one of the classroom rules (i.e., keeping hands and feet to self) before transitioning to a new activity. He explained the appropriate behavior for the upcoming task: "OK, now we are going to start something new. You are going to have to move from your seat to the Life Sciences Center. As we are doing this, please remember Rule #3: Keep hands and feet to self. I know we can all do this." Another teacher used a similar preinstructional routine to provide structure and prevent misbehavior. For example, prior to taking her students to the Media Center, she reviewed how she expected them to behave in the hallway and how she expected them to behave in another teacher's room. She asked students for examples of how to behave (and how not to behave) and reminded them of the consequences of inappropriate behavior. Prompts and preinstructional routines are simple ways many teachers reduce the likelihood of misbehavior and prevent discipline problems. Other systematic use of proactive discipline work best when teachers reflect on how their values influence the way they interact with their students.

Teacher Values

Kohn (1991) points out that what a teacher believes about the nature of his or her students can have a profound effect on how classroom management is handled. The teacher who believes students need to be taught obedience will emphasize teacher control of student behavior. The teacher who believes students should learn to work together, to accept individual differences and take responsibility for their behavior will develop routines and procedures that empower students.

Classroom management practices are saturated in **values** (Morse, 1987). Each time a teacher reacts to a classroom disruption, a hidden message is embedded in the teacher's action. Sometimes the message is autocratic, "You need to behave because I say so." With other teachers, the message is humanistic, "I expect you to be responsible for your actions." When teachers act in anger, the hidden message is, "I can't control myself either." This is the most unsettling message of all because students first and foremost need the security of knowing the teacher is in control. When teachers punish students, the embedded message is, "You can't control your behavior, so I must do it for you." **Punishment** accompanied with anger creates stress among students, and increases the likelihood of further discipline problems (Henley, 2005; Kohn, 1991; Kounin, 1977).

> **SPEEDBUMP**—B.F. Skinner, the leading authority on behavior modification, believed that punishment is a weak tool for behavior change because it often produces hostility and resentment.

When adults feel secure, they are more capable of responding to the different developmental needs of youngsters. Conversely, insecure adults may feel threatened by disturbing student behavior that is developmentally normal. Rezmierski (1987) explains:

> . . . adults who are still struggling to develop a sense of power or autonomy are likely to have difficulty dealing with adolescent children for whom this is a natural developmental struggle as well. Such adults may even have difficulty dealing with their two-year-olds who display what some have called the first round of adolescence. . . . (p. 6)

Nichols and Good (2004) maintain that young people get "a bad rap":

> Research evidence shows that a large majority of adults believe the "average" teenager is "wild, rude, and irresponsible." Though some people may embrace a more positive view, more by far view the young suspiciously. Even though adults may fiercely love and support the young people they know, when asked about the "average" youths—those they might run into on the street corner, or see in schools across the country—they are more likely to use words such as "lazy" and "out of control." (p. 42)

Teacher Needs

Discipline practices that take developmental phases of youngsters into account emphasize the needs of the students. Some teachers are predisposed toward authority (i.e., power) practices; others are predisposed toward democratic (i.e., cooperation) practices (Algozzine, Ysseldyke, & Elliott, 1997; Everston & Weinstein, 2006; Lasley, 1989). Before establishing a classroom management system, teachers should understand their own **psychological needs**. This requires **reflection** and honesty. Effective discipline is emotionally disengaged from student behavior. Teachers who respond to individual discipline problems with anger, defensiveness, or hostility create stress among all the students in the classroom. This "ripple effect" will either lead to more discipline problems (Kounin, 1977) or produce a group of obedient but frightened learners.

All teachers have pet peeves. Some dislike tattling; others can't tolerate name calling. Fighting is the worst offense in many teachers' minds. *The key action is not the student transgression, but the teacher reaction* (Long and Morse, 1996). Teachers who know themselves are more effective disciplinarians because they don't take misbehavior personally. Such teachers realize that students need to be taught what is expected of them. Canter (1989) says:

> **SPEEDBUMP**—What are your pet peeves? Make a list of the five student behaviors you would find most annoying as a teacher.

Teachers too often assume that students know how they are expected to behave. Teachers first need to establish specific directions for each activity during the day—lectures, small group work, transitions between activities, and so forth. For each situation, teachers must determine the exact behaviors they expect from them. . . . [Teachers] must teach the students how to follow directions. . . . They must model the behaviors, ask the students to restate the directions, question the students to make sure they understand the directions, and immediately engage the students in the activity to make sure that they understand the directions. (p. 59)

The aim of discipline is to teach students how to behave in a socially responsible manner. Sometimes compliance or noncompliance to classroom routines obscures the real issue. When 10-year-old Jorge consistently argues with his classmates, he is disturbing the classroom, but there is a deeper, more fundamental concern; Jorge lacks the ability to relate with peers. Classroom discipline procedures aimed solely at stopping Jorge from arguing in school miss the point. Jorge needs to learn how to socialize with others both in and out of school. In Chapter 10, strategies that help teachers manage behavior problems while promoting the development of such prosocial skills as maintaining peer relationships are described.

Know Your Students

The Phi Delta Kappa Commission on Discipline (1982) had this to say about proactive discipline:

Educators in well-disciplined schools know that behavior is caused. When misbehavior occurred, the principal and faculty tended to go beyond merely punishing students for the misbehavior. They searched for probable causes and they addressed them. They improved discipline in their schools by taking steps to remove those causes and by establishing activities within their school and community that would result in good behavior. (p. 12)

Discipline is a double-edged sword; it cuts both ways. Students have an obligation to cooperate and allow others to learn. Teachers and administrators have a duty to understand their students and to deal with disruptions in a fair and equitable manner. Teachers who believe students need to learn to be responsible for their own behavior work to help students to develop **inner controls**. These classrooms are characterized by a respect for student differences. Discipline and classroom management are approached as a process rather than an end in itself (Evertson & Weinstein, 2006; Henley, 1987). In this context, students are encouraged to develop social skills that will help them to adapt not only to the classroom, but also to the world at large. Cooperation, decision making, and accountability for behavior are skills emphasized by teachers who believe discipline should be a learning experience.

There is always a reason for misbehavior. Boredom leads to distractibility and inattentiveness. Vandalism is anger erupting in mindless destruction. Impulsivity can signal a learning disability. Teachers who try to understand their students look for the causes of classroom disruptions. They recognize that students are complex human beings with **developmental needs** that can overshadow reading, writing, and calculating. By looking beyond misbehavior and trying to understand why a student is a discipline problem, a teacher can gain insight into the causes of disruptive behavior (Phi Delta Kappa Commission on Discipline, 1982).

Classroom Organization

A well-organized classroom deters discipline problems. Organization includes the total school attitude toward discipline. The principal takes the lead in establishing an atmosphere of trust and respect. Within the classroom, teachers need to manage individual student behavior in group situations. Groups influence individual behavior, and individual behavior shapes group actions. The manner in which a teacher responds to the **group dynamics** of a classroom can contribute to or prevent discipline problems.

Effective classroom management requires attention to teacher behaviors that minimize behavior problems. Jacob Kounin (1977) and other researchers learned that teachers prevent discipline problems through their ability to monitor the entire group without becoming distracted by minor incidents that cause the entire class to become diverted. Such teachers demonstrate "with-itness" and "overlapping."

> **SPEEDBUMP**—Although Kounin's research was done in the mid-1970s, his observations about how teacher miscues contribute to classroom behavior problems are still relevant.

With-itness.   **With-itness** is a keen sense of what is happening throughout the classroom (DeLuke & Knoblock, 1987). Two features of with-itness reduce misbehavior:

1. **Select the right student for a behavior comment.** When a teacher reprimands the wrong student, the rest of the class assumes she does not know what is going on. Kounin found this ripple effect can work to the teacher's disadvantage. Clarity in identifying the correct student and clearly explaining the preferred behavior increases conformity among the rest of the class. Kounin also found that anger, sarcasm, or other roughness in the teacher's reproach upsets younger children. The ripple effect is most pronounced at the beginning of the school year, and it loses its impact as the year goes on.

2. **Attend to the more serious infraction when two problems develop at the same time (Charles, 1989).** Taking steps to stop a misbehavior before it sets off other students is characteristic of with-it teachers. These teachers have the ability to judge the contagibility of student behavior, and they respond accordingly. For example, Eileen is gazing off into space. The with-it teacher takes note of her inattention but does not disrupt the smooth work flow of the rest of the class. Planned ignoring or proximity control work best. However, when a serious disruption occurs, verbal desist is warranted.

Overlapping.   **Overlapping** is aligned closely to with-itness. It refers to the ability to monitor two situations simultaneously. Suppose the teacher is working with a small reading group of seven students, and she lost track of events around the rest of the classroom. This absence of overlapping would almost assuredly result in misbehavior. Students with their hands up would be ignored; students who are done with their work would start looking for something else to do; and a mischievous student would have an opportunity to cause a disturbance. The overlapping teacher keeps the small group on task while at the same time managing the flow of activity throughout the rest of the classroom.

Maintain a Group Focus.   Virtually all of a teacher's day is spent managing students in groups. Kounin (1977) reported that the manner in which teachers conduct their group lessons had a significant impact on discipline problems. Teachers **maintain a group focus** by encouraging cooperation. For example, during a presentation one student demonstrates at the African American board, and students in their seats offer suggestions and comments. Students are encouraged to listen, help others, share ideas, and work toward group goals. Well-managed groups have a high rate of student work involvement. Student boredom and indifference to work assignments is a main cause of discipline problems. Tasks that are repetitious and require minimal thought invite discipline problems. As Morse (1987) observes:

> If school is not inviting, if the tasks are not clear, interesting, and at an appropriate level, how can we expect students to be on task? Adverse student reactions should be expected when classes are dull, teaching is uninspired, and failure is built in. Their oppositional behavior is a sign of personal growth and integrity. (p. 6)

Teachers who find ways to relate learning to student interests and lives outside of school help students to see value in their lessons. When students understand the purpose of tasks, they can make a connection between teacher expectations and their personal needs; this increases group harmony and minimizes classroom disruptions.

POSITIVE BEHAVIOR SUPPORT

Positive behavior support (PBS) is a schoolwide system that defines, teaches, and encourages appropriate behavior in children. In schools that have been successful building PBS systems, the following procedures have been established (cf. Colvin, Kame'enui, & Sugai, 1993; Horner & Sugai, 2000; Horner, Sugai, Todd, & Lewis-Palmer, 2005; Lewis & Sugai, 1999; Sugai & Horner, 1999, 2002; Todd, Horner, Sugai, & Sprague, 1999):

1. Identify a small number of clearly defined behavioral expectations and present them as positive, simple rules. For example:
   - Come to class prepared.
   - Be respectful to yourself and others.
2. Teach social skills using the same instructional formats applied to other curriculum content: Present the social skill, discuss its rationale, describe and rehearse positive examples ("right way"), describe and model negative examples ("wrong way"), and provide opportunities for students to practice the "right way" until they demonstrate fluent performance.
3. Acknowledge appropriate behavior on a regular basis using formal systems (e.g., tickets, rewards) or social events (e.g., Friday Fun Time). When teachers are successful in creating a positive behavior learning environment, their interactions with students are positive four times as often as they are negative.

4. Establish clear procedures for providing information to students when their behavior is unacceptable. Establish limits with logical consequences.

PBS interventions are proactive and designed to teach appropriate alternatives to disruptive behavior (Safran & Oswald, 2003). When universal schoolwide interventions are designed for all students, positive effects also can be achieved for individuals with severe difficulties. PBS can be applied as secondary-level interventions with small groups of students and in specific settings such as hallways, playgrounds, and cafeterias or as tertiary-level interventions with individual students experiencing chronic difficulties. PBS is based on a **problem-solving model** and aims to prevent inappropriate behavior through teaching and reinforcing appropriate behaviors (OSEP Center on Positive Behavioral Interventions and Supports, 2005). PBS is a process that is consistent with the core principles of RTI (see Chapter 5). Similar to RTI, PBS offers a *range of interventions that are systematically applied to students based on their demonstrated level of need*, and addresses the role of the environment as it applies to development and improvement of behavior problems (Sandomierski, Kincaid, & Algozzine, 2007).

Although research offers several guiding principles, individual schools must collaboratively shape PBS to fit their own unique needs. The key factors to be included are using collaborative team problem-solving and research-based interventions, using multiple data sources for planning and evaluating, and using positive strategies to reduce punitive disciplinary practices. To summarize, PBS interventions serve a preventive function by providing antecedent strategies to alter the classroom environment and decrease the likelihood of misbehavior occurring.

Functional Behavioral Assessment

Functional behavioral assessment (FBA) is a key component of PBS. The FBA includes the observations and input of people close to the person exhibiting the problem behavior. This team observes the person's behavior to identify and define the problematic behavior, determine what actions or events precede and follow the behavior, and identify how often the behavior occurs. The FBA serves as an important part of the process in determining appropriate positive behavioral support plans.

IDEA requires that, at a minimum, the FBA be conducted when disciplinary sanctions result in extended periods in which a student is removed from school (i.e., either before or not later than 10 business days after either the first removal beyond 10 cumulative school days in a school year or commencing a removal that constitutes a change in placement). In addition to the IDEA requirements, the FBA gives schools valuable information about the possible causes of problem behavior. Research demonstrates that the process of PBSs and developing behavioral support plans is more effective when the FBA is conducted prior to developing interventions. The FBA is used to (a) define the problem behaviors; (b) describe the settings under which problem behaviors are and are not likely to be observed; (c) identify the function (the why) of the problem behaviors; and (d) collect information from direct observation to support these outcomes.

Many techniques are available to conduct a functional behavioral assessment. All FBA processes include the following key principles:

■ *Collect information* through informal consultation as well as direct observation. Conversations, questionnaires, checklists, and structured interviews with key persons (e.g., teachers, parents, students) who have contact and experiences with the individual student can offer insights into the contexts or conditions under which the behavior occurs. Direct observations also should be made so that observers can watch the behaviors as they are occurring and note the environmental events (environmental factors, antecedent and consequence events) that may initiate or sustain the behaviors. Specific, concrete behaviors are defined after observational assessments have been performed.

■ *Propose testable explanations* of the student's behavior. A *testable explanation* is a hypothesis that may explain the relationship between a problem behavior and environmental factors that seem to be associated with its occurrences. Variables observed may include settings or circumstances that seem either to lead to the problem behavior or reinforce it after the fact. The hypothesis should consider the possible functions of the behavior for the student.

■ *Assess the validity of the hypotheses* to confirm the validity of the testable explanations. In general, additional information is collected about the conditions under which the problem behavior occurs and does not occur. This information should demonstrate that occurrences of the behavior and the presence of these conditions are related and predictable.

The results of the FBA should be used to develop an effective and efficient behavioral intervention/support plan. Although the FBA term was introduced formally in IDEA in 1997, there has been a strong history of using FBA for reducing behavioral problems. It is a critical tool for developing effective behavior intervention and classroom management plans.

Abdul is an inquisitive, resourceful 15-year-old high school student. He has struggled with behavior problems for years. In middle school, when presented with a difficult or complex assignment, he would complain and refuse to work. When reprimanded, Abdul often ran out of the room and, on several occasions, left the school grounds without permission.

Instead of removing Abdul from his neighborhood school, the school personnel conducted an FBA to evaluate the reasons for his problem behavior. The team determined that Abdul acted inappropriately when he was frustrated with the academic demands. Therefore, the school revised his academic program to meet his individual needs. This included an adapted curriculum with individual and small-group tutoring and a revised behavioral support program. The last two years of middle school were a great success for Abdul, his family, and school staff.

MANAGING STUDENT BEHAVIOR

Once there was a school administrator who believed he had hit on the perfect plan for classroom discipline. With the assistance of his daughter who was a graduate student in special education, he embarked on a systematic collection of interventions matched to problem behaviors. His goal was to develop an index card system, compact enough to fit into the top drawer of a teacher's desk. The cards alphabetically listed student discipline problems and briefly explained the correct intervention; for instance, if a student refused to obey, the teacher would flip through the cards, pull out the 3 × 5 labeled "disobedience," and read "student loses free time." His approach was well-meaning, but hopelessly naïve. Student behavior cannot be matched to interventions like a game of dominoes. Every student is different and every situation unique. Therefore, teachers need an array of interventions to meet the changing needs of the classroom.

> **SPEEDBUMP**—Does this story sound far-fetched? It's a true story based on an interview that occurred when one of the authors applied for a job as a special education teacher.

Each of the following strategies is research based (Cooper, Heron, & Heward, 1987; Dreikurs, Grunwald, & Pepper, 1982; Evertson & Weinstein, 2006; Ginott, 1971; Jones, 1987; Redl & Wineman, 1957). Each is useful for eliminating problem behaviors, but none is teacher proof. **Professional judgment** determines the best intervention to use at any given time. Classroom interventions anticipate student disruptions and nullify potential discipline problems. Each category of interventions—behavior modification, nonverbal interventions, and verbal interventions—prevents disruptive behavior while maintaining a sense of mutual respect between teacher and student. None will work all the time. Good classroom management requires the ability to select an appropriate strategy from an array of alternatives. It also means being mindful of the types of problems that require attention or as one principal put it, "Knowing the difference between mountains and molehills." When working with students with behavior disorders, teachers and other professionals often group their problem behaviors into two categories (see Table 9.1): externalizing and internalizing (cf. Walker & Severson, 1999).

TABLE 9.1 Externalizing and Internalizing Behavior Problems

EXTERNALIZING BEHAVIORS

OVERT	COVERT
Fighting	Lying
Disobeying	Cheating
Destroying property	Stealing
Disrupting others	Being truant
Hitting	Being uncooperative
Tantruming	Using drugs and/or alcohol
Bullying	Being passive and noncompliant
Swearing	Being boisterous

INTERNALIZING BEHAVIORS

Acting anxious	Acting timid
Worrying excessively	Acting bashful
Crying easily	Acting shy
Acting tense	Being self-conscious
Acting shy	Acting aloof
Being sad or depressed	Being easily confused
Lacking self-confidence	Being hypersensitive

Behavior Modification

Behavior modification is regularly used to teach prosocial behavior to students with mild disabilities (Ager & Cole, 1991). Behavior modification programs are data based. Target behaviors (i.e., behaviors to be eliminated or shaped) are observed and measured. Prior to initiating a program, the target behavior is described in precise, behaviorally concrete terms. Vague behavior descriptors such as "immature," "aggressive," or "cooperative" are replaced with such target behaviors as "whines," "hits other students," and "shares toys." Baseline data on the frequency of the target behavior are collected for at least a week prior to beginning the program. These data serve as a comparison for determining progress at a later date. Once a target behavior has been selected and counted, the most appropriate consequence is determined (e.g., reinforcement, token economy, extinction, etc.). Next, a schedule to administer consequences is developed (e.g., reinforcement in the form of verbal praise will follow each time a student raises her hand).

The following systems: token economies, contingency contracts, timeout, and cogntive-behavior intervention are well-established in the behavior modification literature and in special education programs.

Token Economies.   A **token** is a general conditioned reinforcer. Tokens are paired with backup reinforcers such as special privileges or toys from a class store. A token is given to a student to reinforce a target behavior. At a later time in the day or week, the student can exchange accumulated tokens for the backup reinforcer. The value of tokens is derived from the student desirability for backup reinforcers. For example, without goods to purchase (backup reinforcers), money (tokens) would be useless. Cooper, Heron, and Heward (1987) provide the following guidelines for implementing a token economy:

1. Select a token that is durable and cheap (e.g., rubber stamp, chips, pennies).
2. Be clear about rules and behavior(s) for earning tokens.
3. Whenever possible, use regularly occurring events or privileges for backup reinforcers.
4. Guard against bootlegging of tokens. Hoarding of tokens is often a signal that students don't understand the token's value.
5. Establish a rate of exchange; begin with a low ratio of token to back up the reinforcer and increase the ratio as the program becomes successful.
6. Decide in advance how to remove the system.

The efficiency and immediacy of token economies make them an attractive motivation tool.

SPEEDBUMP—Did you ever have a teacher who used stamps, play money, points, or a similar token to encourage expected behavior? If so, how well do you think the system worked?

Contingency Contracts. A **contingency contract** is a written agreement between a teacher and student. The contract serves as a positive reinforcer to shape a target behavior. A contingency contract specifies the responsibilities (i.e., the behaviors) of each party and the consequences associated with compliance. Schroeder and Riddle (1991) list five key elements of a contingency contract: detailed privileges and obligations, observable behaviors, sanctions for failure, bonus clauses for consistent compliance, and clear description of methods for administering reinforcers. Contingency contracts are a way of concretely emphasizing student responsibility for behavior. Salend (1987) suggests that responsible behavior can be increased by involving students in making such contractual decisions as determining the target behavior, selecting reinforcers, and evaluating systems.

Timeout. Cooper, Heron, and Heward (1987) describe two types of **timeout**: non-exclusionary and exclusionary. Nonexclusionary timeout consists of planned ignoring, withdrawal of a specific reinforcer, contingent observation, and the timeout ribbon. Planned ignoring is the removal of such social reinforcers as attention, praise, or verbal comments. Withdrawal of a specific reinforcer means that an identified positive stimulus is removed when an undesirable behavior occurs. In one study, researchers turned off classroom music each time students left their seats, thus significantly reducing out-of-seat behavior (Ritschl, Mongrella, & Presbie, 1972).

Contingent observation is the change of seating of a student for a specified period of time following a classroom infraction. During the contingent observation time period, the student is able to observe the activity of the rest of the group, but may not participate. The timeout ribbon is a paired reinforcer. When a youngster wears the ribbon, it is a signal that there are opportunities to receive positive reinforcers. When the ribbon is removed, no reinforcers can be gained.

Exclusionary timeout is the removal of a student to a room outside the classroom for a specified period of time. Release from timeout is contingent on cessation of disturbing behavior. While an effective intervention if used sparingly, exclusionary timeout can be misused and even abused. Procedures for using exclusionary timeout must be spelled out clearly to both students and parents. Exclusionary timeouts are documented with a timeout log. Such data collection protects against abuse and provides information to determine the effectiveness of exclusionary timeout as a means of extinguishing disruptive behavior.

The aim of timeout is to institute a brief, 5–10 minute isolation of a student from classroom activities because of disruptive behavior. Longer periods of timeout are not recommended for several reasons. Instructional time is lost. The student may prefer the timeout, thus it becomes a positive reinforcer. Removing a student from the classroom may be more disturbing than the behavior that prompted the timeout. Finally, timeout can be unnecessarily punitive (Cuenin & Harris, 1986; Council for Children with Behavior Disorders, 1990).

Behavior Modification Pitfalls. The goal of behavior modification is to increase adaptive behavior and to decrease maladaptive behavior. Behavior modification has a certain intuitive appeal. After all, it's common parenting and teaching practice to reward "good" behavior and punish the "bad." Schools are awash in everyday practices that reflect behavior modification. Students who learn their lessons get good grades. Teachers use stickers and progress charts to encourage students to work harder. Detentions, staying after school, and suspensions are everyday procedures for dealing with students who don't abide by school expectations for proper behavior.

When the normal corrective procedures don't seem to work for a student, it's common for a teacher to step up the reward and punishment cycle through the application of a homespun behavior modification program. Some teachers do this without training in specific techniques. Consequently, errors in treatment undercut the effectiveness of the program and add to the unfortunate judgment that it's the student who is at fault. When teachers begin a behavior modification program, they should keep the eight guidelines listed in Figure 9.1 in mind. Some illustrations of behavior modification methods for improving the behavior of students are presented in Table 9.2.

Nonverbal Interventions

An orderly classroom climate is widely acknowledged as a key component of effective instruction. Classroom disruptions are among the greatest obstacles to creating and maintaining a calm and productive classroom environment. A variety of general nonverbal and verbal interventions are available for managing classroom disruptions.

Nonverbal interventions have several advantages over verbal interventions. Silence does not draw attention to the student or inadvertently reinforce the behavior. Classroom activities proceed without interruption when the teacher manages classroom behavior unobtrusively (McDaniel, 1986). Lastly, nonverbal interventions help teachers avoid "power struggles" with students.

Body Carriage.   Frederic Jones (1987) observed teachers in hundreds of secondary and elementary classrooms. He found that teachers conveyed leadership through body language. Posture, eye contact, facial expressions, and gestures conveyed confidence or

FIGURE 9.1   Guidelines for Behavior Modification Programs

1. Identify and describe the disturbing behavior.

2. Count the frequency of the disturbing behavior.

3. Identify the replacement behavior, if possible with student input.

4. Select a reinforcer that is meaningful to the student.

5. Avoid using sugar foods as reinforcers (e.g., cookies, candy, raisins).

6. Don't take away reinforcers for punishment.

7. Do a postfrequency count of the disturbing behavior after a specified period of time to determine the program's effectiveness.

8. If the program isn't working, don't blame the student; change the plan.

TABLE 9.2   Illustrations of Behavior Modification

TACTIC	ILLUSTRATION
Reward students for reducing out-of-seat behavior.	Gather data on the number of times the student is out of his or her seat for 10 class periods. Provide a sticker, star, or other token for each class period that the student is out of seat less than average during the data collection phase. Keep track of improvements and discuss them with the student.
Reward appropriate classroom behavior	Provide your class with an opportunity to earn free time based on their behavior. Start a stopwatch at the beginning of a class period. Each time misbehavior occurs, stop the watch and announce to the class that it will start again when appropriate behavior resumes. At the end of the class period, determine the amount of free time that was earned and allow students to select activities for that time period.
Reward appropriate behavior in other students.	Look for opportunities to reward other students for appropriate behavior. For example, if a student fails to comply with a request you have made, turn to another student, and make a similar request. When the other student complies, provide a reward or special attention for the appropriate behavior.
Ignore inappropriate behavior.	The process of withholding attention or reward from previously rewarded behavior is referred to as *putting the behavior on extinction.* As a general rule, extinction is used for behaviors that are minimally disruptive, attention-seeking types of problems. Often, simply ignoring these behaviors decreases them.
Use contracts to control behavior	Help students set goals for appropriate behavior and then design contracts that detail expectations and rewards for meeting the terms of the agreement.

uncertainty. Students observe teacher body language and make judgments about what they see. Charles (1989) summarizes Jones's findings:

> Good posture and confident carriage suggest strong leadership; a drooping posture and lethargic movements suggest resignation or fearfulness. Effective teachers even when tired or troubled tend to hold themselves erect and move with a measure of vigor. (p. 92)

Teachers who convey authority naturally through body language encounter half the behavior problems of teachers in "loud, unruly" classrooms (Charles, 1989, 90).

Planned Ignoring.   Sometimes disruptive student behaviors are intended to attract the attention of the teacher and other students. When teachers ignore attention-seeking behaviors, the audience is eliminated. Planned ignoring works best for minor classroom disturbances. The teacher who interrupts group lessons or activities with a continual stream of admonitions such as "sit still," or "pick up that piece of paper" disrupts learning while drawing attention to the misbehavior. Paradoxically, this negative attention can reinforce behavior problems.

> **SPEEDBUMP—**A college student once approached a professor and said, "I tried planned ignoring last week in my field site—it didn't work. During recess two students were fighting, I ignored them, and they kept fighting!"

Signal Interference.   Every adult has memories of childhood teachers who could quell minor disturbances with a flick of a light switch or a finger raised to the lips. There are numerous nonverbal signals for quieting a class: eye contact, snapping fingers, a frown, shaking the head, or a quieting gesture with the hand. Visual signals do not disturb students and emphasize the teacher's awareness of all activity in the room.

Proximity Control.   Teachers who stand or sit as if rooted to the front of the room are compelled to issue verbal directions in order to deal with disruptions. Teachers who move around the room merely need to stand near a student or gently place a hand on a student's shoulder to stop a disturbing behavior. Teaching while moving has several advantages; rather than being a separate, remote entity, the teacher becomes physically a part of the group. The teacher is able to monitor students more easily; the teacher projects more of a presence because students can't predict where the teacher will be standing at any given moment; and finally, standing nearby also reassures students that the teacher is in control.

Removal of Seductive Objects.   Manipulation is a strong channel for learning, and in most instances, should be encouraged. However, some students become distracted by objects. Fritz Redl and David Wineman (1951) indicated that the ability to control the impulse to handle, grab, or steal seductive objects was a basic component in the development of self-control. When teachers leave valuables or students leave toys around, youngsters who are prone to "gadgetorial seduction," the objects might disappear. Removing seductive objects decreases the strain on a youngster's burgeoning self-control system.

Verbal Interventions

Because nonverbal interventions are the least intrusive, they are preferred. **Verbal interventions** are useful after it is clear that nonverbal interventions have been unsuccessful in desisting a disruptive behavior.

Humor.   It may sound strange to use humor to calm a disruptive student, but it is a very useful technique. Almost every school has a teacher who is capable of defusing discipline problems with a quip or easy comment. Humor is a basic human need. People watch TV, go to the movies, and pay to watch live performances just to laugh. The teacher who smiles and jokes in the face of adversity sets a strong model for students. A word of caution, however: Avoid sarcasm, cynicism, or teasing. Rather than lightening a moment, sarcasm increases tension and creates resentment. Cynicism and teasing breed resentment.

SPEEDBUMP—On a teacher's first day, his high school class started tossing around a student's bologna sandwich. Recognizing that the class was getting out of control, the teacher confiscated the sandwich, unwrapped it, and ate it. The teacher's unexpected action got a big laugh and for the rest of the period, he had no further control problems. (from "Teacher Man" by Frank McCourt)

Sane Messages. When teachers respond to disruptive behavior with anger, they add to student anxiety, which increases the likelihood of further behavior problems (Kounin, 1977). "I" messages let students know how the teacher feels. Such statements as, "I am frustrated because you keep interrupting this lesson," or "I am disappointed because you didn't maintain control when I left the room," describe the situation rather than attacking a student's character (Charles, 1989, 59). Sane messages are descriptive and model appropriate behavior (Ginott, 1971). Sane messages help students understand how their behavior affects others. They are a direct appeal to change behavior. "Bev, when you talk during silent reading, it disturbs everyone in your group," is an example of a sane message. "Bev, keep quiet," is an example of what Ginott calls an insane message. In the first instance, the reason for a change in behavior is explained to the student. In the second instance, the "insane message," the student feels personally attacked. Such a directive as "keep quiet" or "shut up" may get the intended results, but if the model for expressing needs is abrupt and callous, students will take the same approach in their own conversations.

Restructuring. *Restructuring* means changing a lesson or activity that is floundering without blaming the students. When confronted with student disinterest, the best option may be to move on to another activity. Restructuring is part of the decision-making powers of a teacher. One inner-city 6th-grade teacher gave a spelling test every time the class seemed restless and difficult to manage. "It was amazing," he reported; "one minute they are ready to climb the walls, and the next minute they were quietly and dutifully folding their papers and numbering lines from 1 to 20!"

Hypodermic Affection. Each student from time to time needs a shot of caring. "Hypodermic affection" lets students know that they are valued human beings. Students get frustrated, discouraged, and anxious in school. Students with mild disabilities, in particular, need encouragement to persevere with tasks at which they have failed in the past. Sometimes a smile, a pat on the back, or a kind word can help a student over a psychological hurdle. Showing interest in a student's life outside of school and plainly communicating concern are ways of building trust. A trusting relationship between student and teacher is the key to solving all discipline problems.

Praise. Verbal praise is used frequently to reinforce positive classroom behavior. The aphorism "Catch them being good" describes the most useful approach to praise. For example, some students need attention. Praising their behavior when they are not seeking attention while ignoring disruptive behavior is a useful way to use praise in the classroom. Too much praise can undercut impact; too little praise communicates indifference. Effective praise is directed at student behavior rather than the student personally. "You really are trying hard" encourages student effort. It is a descriptive statement that gives the student guidance in terms of the type of behavior the teacher expects to see.

Ginott (1971) pointed out the "**perils of praise**." Praise directed at a student personally is condescending and manipulative. A statement such as, "You are a good person to have in my class," implies the teacher is making such judgments about all the students. What about the students who don't get the same compliment? Remember there is always a ripple effect in the classroom. Everyone wants to be liked by the teacher. Judgmental praise may make one student feel good, while another may feel rejected. Praise works best when it evaluates behavior instead of the student.

Alerting.   Imagine a group of students during recess playing kickball. They are hot, sweaty, and thoroughly enjoying themselves. All the running around has them excited, and they are eager to continue the game. The teacher looks at her watch and realizes she should have had them back into the classroom 5 minutes ago. What does she do? One approach is to abruptly end the game and rush the entire group back to class. Abrupt changes almost assuredly will result in behavior problems.

In his extensive research on classroom discipline, Kounin (1977) found the manner in which teachers handled transitions to be a key element in effective discipline. Charles (1989) succinctly summarized Kounin's findings: "Teachers' ability to manage smooth transitions and maintain momentum was more important to work involvement and classroom control than any other behavior management technique" (p. 33).

Alerting helps students to make smooth transitions by giving them time to make emotional adjustments to change. This particularly is true for impulsive students or students who are frustrated easily. Alerting takes many forms. One method is to count down the number of minutes before a change will take place. Usually two warnings in 5-minute increments is sufficient. Alerting is useful when moving from a high-student-preference activity (e.g., recess) to a low-student-preference activity (e.g., grammar lesson).

Accepting Student Feelings.   A student walks into class in the morning radiant with the news that the family will be visiting Disneyland. The teacher is pleased to have such a happy youngster in class for the day. It is a pleasure to accept positive feelings and reaffirm their expression. The next day the same youngster walks into class furious. Her dad has been laid off his job, and the trip to Disneyland is canceled. The student is angry and frustrated. She hates her dad; she hates the teacher; and she hates her schoolwork. These feelings are not so easy to accept and reaffirm. Teachers, who have a one-sided view of student feelings, allow for the expression of positive feelings but are reluctant to accept feelings of distress.

Students need to learn how to express such feelings as anger, frustration, and impatience. Students act out these feelings when they lack appropriate verbal skills. The teacher who attempts to put a lid on student behavior that is embedded in anger or frustration is sowing the seeds of further discontent. Distressful feelings cannot be made to disappear. Suppressed feelings will resurface. By providing opportunities for students to express all types of feelings, teachers reaffirm students. Role playing, class discussions, life-space interventions, and journal writing are samples of classroom methods that help students channel difficult feelings into constructive outlets.

MANAGING CONFLICT SITUATIONS

While all students have good and bad days, some students have persistent problems in adapting to school expectations and routines. The intensity and duration of student disruptions will determine the severity of the problem. An emotional disturbance can cause a student to act out feelings of anger, hostility, or isolation. For instance, students who engage in attention-getting behaviors don't know how to relate in socially acceptable ways. Many students who receive special education services for behavior problems are identified as emotionally disturbed.

Most of the causes for emotional problems are outside the classroom teacher's reach. Time is a factor no one can overcome. A student's aggressive behavior may be caused by sexual abuse that happened several years earlier. Childhood difficulties, such as separation of parents or death of a loved one, may be overcome in a positive manner by one student or thrust another student into the depths of depression. What then is a teacher to do when confronted with the awesome obstacles presented by a student's troubled life history?

Although a teacher cannot (and should not) pretend to be a therapist, the teacher can utilize therapeutic strategies that have proved useful with students in conflict. One such strategy is the life-space intervention (Redl, 1971; Wood & Long, 1991).

Life-Space Crisis Intervention

The **life-space crisis intervention** (LSCI) is a technique for turning listening into a plan for student behavior change. If a teacher wants to understand why a student behaves a certain way, the best source of information is the student. The LSCI uses crisis situations to move a youngster toward more constructive behavior. The following five-step procedure summarizes key points of the life-space intervention. For a more thorough analysis, see *Life Space Crisis Intervention* by Long, Wood, and Fecser (2001).

Step 1. Ventilate Feelings. The LSCI is a conversation between student and teacher. Unlike most such conversations, in the first phase the student does most of the talking and the teacher listens. The LSCI is initiated by the teacher after a specific incident. It requires some privacy. A quiet corner of a classroom might work or if the student is out of control, he or she should be removed from the classroom for the interview.

The teacher begins by allowing the student to ventilate feelings. No moral implications are attached to what is said. The teacher is nonjudgmental and supportive of the student's feelings. Such statements as, "I can see you are angry," or "When Alex said that you must have felt hurt," emphasize empathy and communicate that feelings, even negative ones, are important. During Step 1 of the LSCI, the teacher is accepting. This builds trust and helps the teacher to understand the student perspective.

The student may swear, whine, or blame others. It may seem strange not to correct these "inappropriate" comments. Some youngsters lack the verbal skills to express strong feelings in a socially acceptable manner. Strong language is a symptom of frustration. The intention at this stage is to build trust. The subsequent steps aim at behavior change.

Step 2. Clarify the Incident.   Physical signs that the student is beginning to unwind (e.g., relaxed muscle tone; steady, calm breath) will become evident. At this point, the incident that prompted the LSCI is ready to be clarified in two stages.

First, ask the student to explain what happened. The student is likely to place blame on you, other students, other adults, anyone but himself or herself. This is to be expected. The purpose of the LSCI is to help a student learn to accept responsibility for individual behavior. If the student was in the habit of "owning up" to disturbing action, you wouldn't need the life-space intervention.

The student's view is significant data. Action is guided by perception. Attempting to correct the student version would eliminate an important source of information. Right or wrong, distorted or clear, the student perspective is a crucial clue in understanding behavior.

Next, the incident is reviewed again, except this time the teacher assists the student to paint a reality-based picture of the crisis situation. The student is prompted to describe the physical scene and chronological time frame. Comments such as "Where were you standing when Cole threw the eraser?" or "What happened next?" help the student to recall events. You want to find the central issue. A gentle reminder interjected at this point about how the adult saw events unfold can be helpful, but caution is advised because too much "reality rub" will place teacher and student at odds. The student is reflecting, an unaccustomed practice, and he or she will jump at an opportunity to argue over details, and thus derail the LSCI.

Step 3. Look for Patterns.   Once the central issue is identified, use questions such as "Has this happened before?" or gentle reminders such as "Last week it seemed you had the same problem with Sally," to help students gain insight into their own behavior. Many times students with emotional problems will deny their experience. They literally forget past episodes, or they may be unable to learn from experience. The student may be stuck in behavior patterns, continually repeating the mistakes of the past.

Up to this point, the LSCI has focused on affective fallout from the incident. Looking for patterns switches emphasis to the cognitive domain. The student may be well-equipped to deny a history of problems related to the incident. *Projection* (i.e., finding one's own faults in someone else) and *rationalization* (i.e., explaining away behavior) are well-entrenched defenses against change. Initially it is enough at this stage to get agreement that there does seem to be a problem. Future interviews can continue to explore disturbed behavior patterns.

Step 4. Implement a Plan.   The purpose of the life-space intervention is to help a student assume personal responsibility. When a persistent pattern is identified by both the teacher and the student, the next logical step is to consider alternative ways to deal with the problem. Questions such as "What could you have done rather than knock all of your books off the desk?" or "Are there any signals we could arrange for the next time you are feeling frustrated?" move the discussion into the problem-solving stage. Although the teacher provides supportive or clarifying questions, it is up to the student to do the problem solving. The student needs to "own" the behavior and the solution.

Of course, reality rules of the school and common sense also come into play. A student may be overly zealous in terms of self-imposed consequence. Neither punishment nor consequences are part of the solution. The plan is preventive: "Each time I feel frustrated with my work, I'll close my book and count to 10 slowly"; "Every time I lose my temper I'll put a check in my self-monitoring log"; "If I get angry I'll blow off steam by walking around the room."

The intent of the planning stage is to get students thinking and working on their emotional or behavior problems. Student plans are not usually characterized by their elegance. It may be tempting to step in and offer a more reasonable alternative. The student may need to be reminded about such reality concerns as the implausibility of leaving the room when upset. The initial plan might require multiple adjustments, but that is the nature of personal growth. Changing habitual behavior patterns is a difficult endeavor. Whether the mechanics of the plan achieve the objective is secondary; the student is learning to take responsibility for behavior. In the long run, there is no more important goal. The final act of the LSCI is for the teacher and student to write the plan and sign it. The "contract" increases commitment and provides a basis for future life-space interventions (Fagen, 1986).

Step 5. Transition Back to Classroom Activity. A smooth transition back to classroom activities helps the student save face and establishes a routine for further life-space interventions. Wood and Long (1991) suggest preparing the student with the following questions (p. 148):

> "What is your group doing now?"
> "When you left the group they were writing news reports. Do you think they are still at it?"
> "When you go back to your room, what will they be doing?"

Keep in mind that being removed from the classroom during a crisis situation can be embarrassing. Hard-won gains made during the life-space intervention can dissipate if the student or classmates are unable to return to a normal routine. Getting a student returned to work gives the life-space crisis intervention a successful closure. The key points of the LSCI are summarized in Figure 9.2.

SPEEDBUMP—For more information about LSCI and other promising practices for students with emotional problems, go to http://.cecp.air.org.

Long (1990) describes five uses of emotional "first aid": to drain off frustration, to support the management of strong feelings, to maintain communication during stress, to regulate social and behavioral traffic, and to provide umpire service. For example, in a brief episode, Ms. Halpin, a special education teacher, managed all five. She allowed Andy, a 12-year-old upset student, time and space to ventilate his anger. She helped him deal with his anger by her supportive comments. Instead of punishing him for leaving the room, she maintained communication by remaining nonjudgmental and concerned about his feelings. She emphasized social regulations by giving him 5 minutes to return to the classroom, and she emphasized his accountability by handing him the stopwatch. Finally, she recognized that she could not solve Andy's problem for him. Like a good umpire, she remained neutral while requiring Andy to return to the classroom.

FIGURE 9.2   Life-Space Crisis Intervention

PURPOSE: TO DEFUSE CRISIS SITUATION AND SEEK SOLUTIONS

Step. 1. Ventilate Feelings
Teacher behavior: Listens.
Teacher attitude: Accepting, nonjudgmental; allows for ventilation of feelings.
Student behavior: Talks, expresses strong feelings such as anger, hostility, or frustration.

Step 2. Clarify the Incident
Teacher behavior: Asks questions, probes for details of incident.
Teacher attitude: Tries to help student see his or her contribution to the crisis incident.
Student behavior: Attempts to reconstruct a timeline of events that culminated in crisis incident.

Step 3. Look for Patterns
Teacher behavior: Within dialogue helps student to remember similar situations.
Teacher attitude: Problem solving.
Student behavior: Attempts to relate present crisis incident to past problems with adults or peers.

Step 4. Implement a Plan
Teacher behavior: Supports student in searching for alternative ways of handling crisis situations.
Teacher attitude: Helps student take responsibility for actions.
Student behavior: Develops a written contract that describes student solutions.

Step 5. Transition Back to Classroom Activity
Teacher behavior: Discusses what student needs to do in order to rejoin group.
Teacher attitude: Student may need face-saving options or reminder of consequences.
Student behavior: Calmed down and, with support, ready to resume activities.

LSCI is directed at helping students make good choices. The technique takes into account the student's point of view and feelings. LSCI provides support and ultimately points the student in the direction of personal accountability. It also adheres to the principle that behavior management should be nonjudgmental and nonpunitive. It helps students to manage their feelings while working toward solutions to behavior problems.

Discipline and IDEA

The 2004 reauthorization of IDEA created a set of mandates that changed disciplinary procedures for students with special needs. The intent of changes to the law was to modify the perception that a dual system of discipline existed: one for the general education population and another for students with special needs. These changes gave schools more freedom to remove disruptive students whose behavior was not related to their disability. Previously school administrators had to build a case to remove a student to an alternative education setting. The 2004 reauthorization of IDEA allows administrators to remove a student to an alternative placement, and the parents, if they disagree, must appeal the decision. Consider the following scenario.

In 2003, a year before the reauthorization of IDEA, Preston, a 15-year-old middle school student, exhibited both academic and behavioral difficulties. Among other things, Preston had a record of incomplete work, truancy, and arguing with his teachers. Because of his academic problems, Preston's teachers agreed to refer him for a special education evaluation. The evaluation team determined that Preston met the systemwide criteria for a learning disability due to a severe discrepancy between his IQ and academic achievement. (The severe discrepancy formula for determining a learning disability is not recommended in the 2004 reauthorization of IDEA, but this does not change the special education status of students like Preston who were identified with a learning disability prior to the 2004 reauthorization.)

Although special education services appeared to help Preston with his academic difficulties, discipline problems persisted. The principal suspended him for fighting several times during the 2003–2004 year. After one additional episode of disruptive behavior, the principal placed Preston in a temporary alternative program for disruptive students. His parents hired a lawyer who pointed out that because Preston was a student with special needs, his placement could not be changed without a "manifest determination" hearing. This time-consuming investigation was mandated by IDEA to determine if a student's misbehavior was related to his or her disability. If the manifest determination found there was no relationship between his learning disability and his behavior, Preston was subject to the same disciplinary codes as the general education population. However, if it was determined that his behavior was a manifestation of his disability, the school was legally required to follow a series of due process procedures to ensure that Preston's special education services were not interrupted.

When legislators in 2004 were revamping IDEA, it was clear that the complications involved with special education discipline procedures needed to be addressed. Many school administrators complained that mandated legal procedures were too complex. They said that additional hearings, paperwork, IEP revisions, and parental consent had become an overwhelming burden. Delays in fulfilling federal requirements also meant delays in keeping schools safe for all students. While still containing protective due process procedures for students with special needs, the 2004 changes to IDEA were intended to simplify discipline procedures. The following bulleted items include Council for Exceptional Children (2005) highlights of the 2004 IDEA reauthorization in regard to discipline procedures.

- Language has been added giving school personnel authority, on a case-by-case basis, to consider unique circumstances when determining whether to order a change in placement for a child with a disability who violates a code of student conduct.
- The length of time that school personnel may remove a student to an interim alternative setting (without a hearing officer) has been changed from 45 days to 45 school days. In addition, school personnel now may remove a student who "has inflicted serious bodily injury upon another person while at school, on school premises, or at a school function" to such an interim placement without a hearing-officer ruling.
- The provisions related to the criteria for determining whether a behavior was a manifestation of a student's disability has been revised to state: "If the conduct in question

was caused by, or had a direct and substantial relationship to, the child's disability; or if the conduct in question was the direct result of the LEA's failure to implement the IEP. . . ."

■ Timelines have been added for an expedited hearing in matters related to placement during appeals.

■ Under the protections for children who are not yet eligible under IDEA, the provisions related to whether a local education agency (LEA) should have known that a child was a child with a disability have been changed as follows:

Current disciplinary provisions require that a parent must put their concerns in writing to school personnel that their child needs special education services, with an exception for a parent who is illiterate or has a disability impacting on their ability to submit concerns in writing. The new bill eliminates that exception related to the parent's ability to put their concerns in writing.

■ Under the new bill, an LEA shall not be deemed to have knowledge that the child is a child with a disability if the parent of the child has not allowed an evaluation of the child or has refused services, or the child has been evaluated and it was determined that the child was not a child with a disability.

The Council for Exceptional Children told its members to be cautious in interpreting these new requirements until final federal regulations are issued. The special education organization stated (2005):

Examples of specific policy areas that will need to be addressed during the regulatory process include: defining "unique circumstances" as they relate to the authority of school personnel to make a change in placement on a "case by case" basis; clarifying the length of time a student may be removed from school, 45 days vs. 45 school days; providing additional information on the revised criteria for determining whether a behavior was a manifestation of a student's disability; and explaining the significance of deleting the definition of "substantial evidence" from the statute. (p. 21)

SPEEDBUMP—If your brain went into lockdown after reading the legal detail of the previous section, these science answers given by children might help revive you. Q. What does the word "benign" mean? A. Benign is what you will be after you be eight; Q. How can you delay milk turning sour? A. Keep it in the cow; Q. Name the four seasons. A. Salt, pepper, mustard, and vinegar; Q. Name a disease associated with cigarettes. A. Premature death; Q. What is the fibula? A. A small lie. (courtesy of www.adprima.com/humor.htm)

PUNISHMENT

Punishment is one of the most misunderstood reactions to student actions. One of the factors that makes punitive approaches so appealing is that in terms of short-term goals, they appear to work. Such punishments as checks on a blackboard, "timeout," calls to home, or trips to the principal's office may halt disruptions, but too frequently the gains are temporary. Although punishment can temporarily stop misbehavior, it does not change behavior nor does it teach new behaviors (Everston & Weinstein, 2006; Hyman & D'Allesandro, 1984; Kohn, 1991; Morse, 1987). Punishment is most effective when used sparingly and with students who can make a logical connection between offense and consequence.

Sometimes it is difficult to determine where treatment for disruptive behavior ends and abuse begins. This is particularly true when punishment is couched in scientific jargon. For example, the term "negative aversives" is used in special education to label such tactics as blasts of cold water in the face from an atomizer or pinching to thwart disruptive behavior. Whether negative aversives are a euphemism for punishment is a matter of some dispute (Council for Children with Behavior Disorders, 1990). In Rhode Island, parents of children attending a residential program for emotionally disturbed students defended the use of negative aversives. The school served diverse types of behavior disorders from juvenile delinquency to autism. Negative aversives ranged from pinches and hot sauces placed in the mouth to blasts of pressurized air on the side of the face, and, ultimately, restraints. Youngsters were spread-eagled against a wall face first and held fast by strong cloth bands.

SPEEDBUMP—Corporal punishment in schools is banned in every industrialized country with the exception of Australia and 21 states in the United States.

When punishment is used, it should be guided by school policy. Braaten and associates (1988) recommend seven procedural elements to guide the use of punishment in schools (p. 80):

1. Information about the use and abuse of punishment should be provided to teachers.
2. Teachers should be trained in the use of punishment.
3. Punishment procedures should be approved by the school board and be disseminated to teachers, parents, and students.
4. Records of punishment usage should be maintained.
5. Complaint and appeal procedures should be established.
6. Infractions that warrant punishment should be explained to all students and teachers.
7. Procedures for periodic review of punishment procedures should be implemented.

Punishment is commonplace and controversial. Some teachers use it first; others as the last resort. Punishment is effective when used sparingly. Reserve punishment for events or actions that cause physical or psychological harm to students or teacher. Remember, if punishment and its antecedent—threats—are used as a primary discipline tactic, there is nothing left to fall back on when those methods fail to achieve the desired results.

PUTTING THEORY INTO PRACTICE

Rudy is a 6th-grade student. He has been diagnosed as having ADD with hyperactivity. He takes medication for his condition three times a day: before, during, and after school. Rudy also meets with the school adjustment counselor for an hour once a week.

Rudy's school behavior is impulsive. He runs in hallways. He often jumps and hits door frames with his right hand like he's dunking a basketball. He is unable to resist misusing such objects as pens, pencils, and paper clips by taking them apart or using them as "weapons." Rudy also is disorganized and frequently fails to complete assignments.

Transition times are difficult for Rudy, especially unstructured times, such as finishing an assignment and getting ready for lunch. When the class makes the transition from lecture to independent work, it takes Rudy several minutes to settle down and begin the task at hand. Often Rudy will get sidetracked into some other type of activity like cleaning his desk.

Socially Rudy cannot work with other students in such activities as group work or cooperative learning. He tends to be disruptive in his group and prevents the other children from completing assignments. Rudy does not anticipate consequences and seems not to care about the effects of his actions on others.

Rudy's problem is twofold: his behavior is disruptive and his social skills are weak. We further discuss social skills and how to help students learn social skills in the following chapter. For now, concentrate on Rudy's behavior and what to do about his classroom disruptions.

The prevailing expert opinion indicates that Rudy's disorder, ADHD, is neurologically based. This means that Rudy is not intentionally causing behavior problems. His medication may need to be increased, because his teacher does not report any behavior gains despite two dosages each day. On the other hand, Rudy may be one of those youngsters who does not respond to medication and another treatment may be preferred (see information on diet in Chapter 4).

Each time Rudy disrupts the class, the teacher takes him into a corner of the room, which she has set up with a divider to provide some privacy. She has independent work assignments ready for the rest of the class so she and Rudy can have a few private minutes together. She provides *emotional first aid* and highlights the effect of Rudy's behavior using *sane messages*. She encourages Rudy to describe what happened and she *accepts his feelings*. Her goal for these sessions is to maintain communication during stress and to regulate behavior by reminding Rudy in a nonjudgmental fashion that her job is to protect the ongoing classroom programming by using timeout if necessary.

His teacher also understands that Rudy needs a more behavior management plan to help him learn to control his behavior throughout the day. She institutes a *behavior modification program*. She does a *functional assessment* of his most disturbing behavior—running through the halls. After gathering this data, she learns that three out of every four times the class moves from one area of the building to another she has to correct Rudy's behavior. She sets up a *token economy* with Rudy. Each time he walks through the halls in an appropriate manner, she will give him a ticket that he can exchange for a baseball card (baseball is one of his favorite sports) at the end of the day. The use of this *positive reinforcement* is discussed with the class. This alleviates negative student feelings about being left out of the reward system. Additionally, for every 10 baseball cards Rudy earns, the class gets 10 extra minutes of recess. This helps everyone pull for Rudy to succeed. After a month, Rudy's teacher does another behavior frequency count to see if the positive reinforcement program is taking hold.

In order to help prevent Rudy's disruptions, she uses *alerting* to help him get ready for transitions and she uses several nonverbal interventions such as *proximity control*, *signal interference*, and *removal of seductive objects* to provide support without drawing attention to his behavior.

The success of the interventions for Rudy will be based on several factors including administrative and parental support. No guarantees go with this behavior plan for Rudy, but the teacher's knowledge of an array of behavior strategies plus her understanding that all behavior interventions require timely adjustments is movement in the right direction.

SUMMARY

Well-managed classrooms facilitate learning. No one can learn in a class that is constantly disrupted by behavior problems. Discipline problems cause stress in both teachers and students. For the novice teacher, classroom management is a major concern. At one time or another, all students present discipline problems. Although authoritarian discipline tactics hold some appeal, promoting student participation in discipline policies increases their sense of personal responsibility and helps to prevent future behavior problems.

Proactive discipline is based on the premise that many classroom disruptions can be avoided. Teachers who use proactive discipline techniques strive to intervene before a disturbance turns into a full-blown discipline problem. Such teachers are skilled in an array of behavior management tools including behavior modification, nonverbal, and verbal interventions. There are several disadvantages to using punishment as a behavior change method. Included among these is the resentment punishment produces and the fact that modifications of behavior usually are temporary because punishment does not teach new prosocial behaviors. Programming for students with mild disabilities have improved over recent years due to an increased emphasis on positive behavior supports and functional behavior assessment. Before a student can be removed from an educational setting because of a behavior problems related to his or her disability, administrators are required by law to follow specific due process procedures.

ACTIVITIES

1. Arrange to have two classroom teachers speak on how they manage their classrooms. Make note of differences and similarities in their approaches to discipline. Make a checklist of verbal, nonverbal, and behavior modification interventions. See how many of these interventions the classroom teachers utilize.
2. Watch the video *Dangerous Minds*. Find examples of the following interventions: restructuring, planned ignoring, hypodermic affection, humor, accepting feelings, body language, token economy, and punishment. Identify times that a LSCI would have been useful. What do you think about the way Ms. Johnson utilized behavior modification techniques?
3. Watch the video *Lean on Me*, about Joe Clark. Have a class debate. Were his tactics to control student behavior justified? What alternative behavior interventions could Joe Clark have used? Was Joe Clark a hero?

4. Go online and look up two classroom management approaches: the responsive classroom and assertive discipline. Compare and contrast elements of these two approaches. In what ways do these approaches reflect proactive discipline? In what ways do these approaches not reflect proactive discipline?

5. Interview a student who is attending public school. Select students from various levels—primary, elementary, and secondary. Ask the following questions. What does your teacher do when a student misbehaves? Do you think your teacher fairly applies classroom rules with all students? How does your teacher use rewards? Is punishment used to control behavior? Do you think punishment helps teach better behavior? Add any other questions you think should be included. Discuss your findings in class.

6. In small groups of three to four people, generate a list of classroom management approaches used by your teachers. Have each group focus on either elementary, middle, or high school. Compare how teachers at each level deals with behavior problems. Answer the following questions: Can you identify different approaches at the three levels? Do teachers have different expectations for student behavior at each level? How many approaches listed took student developmental differences into account? How many approaches were punishment based? How many approaches used behavior modification? Do nonverbal and verbal alternatives to punishment appear on your lists often? Which of the approaches listed seemed to be the most effective? Which the least effective?

CHAPTER TEN

TEACHING SOCIAL SKILLS

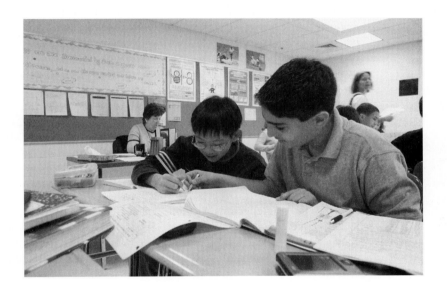

ADVANCE QUESTIONS

Answer the following questions as you read this chapter:

1. What is emotional intelligence?
2. Why is social skill instruction needed in some classrooms?
3. What does "character education" mean?
4. How does values clarification fit into a classroom curriculum?
5. What are some specific social skills that comprise self-control?
6. What problem-solving steps would you follow to develop a social skills program for a specific student?

VIGNETTE: DEBBIE

Debbie is 11 years old, overweight, and in the 5th grade. Her teacher is concerned about Debbie's behavior and her status in the class. She is less mature than the other students and she is impulsive. She is impatient and has difficulty following class rules. She gets out of her seat often and always has an excuse to leave the room. In the hallways, cafeteria, and library, she acts up apparently to get attention from other children. Her teacher believes Debbie needs an evaluation for ADHD and is planning on talking to the principal about it.

Although Debbie likes other students, she spends a great deal of time alone on the playground. Her classmates shy away from her because she tries to relate to them by gossiping, teasing, or doing favors. She enjoys reading and math and her grades would be much better if she could stay focused on her classwork. Her teacher emphasizes rewards and punishment to improve behavior. Unfortunately, due to her lack of social skill development, Debbie is punished more than rewarded. Debbie is a frequent occupant of the classroom timeout area.

1. What social skills does Debbie lack?
2. Do you think Debbie should be removed from her classroom and placed in a self-contained special education class for students with emotional disorders?
3. What could Debbie's classroom teacher do to help Debbie learn the social skills she lacks?

Consider the challenge of classroom management. The typical classroom teacher engages in 1,000 interactions a day (Jackson, 1968), and less than half of these interpersonal exchanges relate to teaching. The majority of time is spent trying to keep the classroom running smoothly. Maintaining a group focus, minimizing disruptions, and encouraging student participation require the organizational skills of Donald Trump and the interpersonal skills of Oprah Winfrey. Each student is a unique human being with likes, dislikes, strengths, and weaknesses. Regardless of the ability or personality of individual students, the classroom teacher is expected to bring each "up to grade level." The public school classroom is one of the best examples of the U.S. democratic tradition. Public education is based on the common school principle that all students should have an equal opportunity to succeed in life—yet all students do not start out equal. The inequity of student life experiences and student social skills imposes a challenge to teachers.

EMOTIONAL INTELLIGENCE

Emotional intelligence refers to an individual's ability to monitor emotions and weigh alternatives before acting. Daniel Goleman (1995) explains the relationship between emotional intelligence and social skills:

> Those who are at the mercy of impulse—who lack self-control—suffer a moral deficiency. The ability to control impulse is the base of will and character. By the same token, the root

of altruism lies in empathy, the ability to read emotions in others; lacking a sense of another's need or despair, there is no caring. And if there are any two moral stances our times call for, they are precisely these, self-restraint and compassion. (p. xii)

Emotional intelligence increases with an individual's ability to consider options before reacting to a stressful situation. Emotionally intelligent individuals control their feelings, rather than letting their feelings control them.

Impulsiveness in childhood is a forerunner of aggression in adolescence and it undercuts social skill development. In the Pittsburg Youth Study (Block, 1995), researchers discovered that impulsivity is nearly three times more powerful an indicator of delinquency than IQ. When child psychologist Walter Mischel tracked the developmental progress of impulsive 4-year-olds into adolescence, he found the teenagers enmeshed in conflict. Impulsive teenagers overreacted. They were easily frustrated, and they provoked fights and arguments with their peers (cited in Goleman, 1995, 80–82). A youngster who is unable to control the impulse to strike out, either in fear or anger, is a walking powder keg. Almost half of the boys identified as bullies in elementary school will have adult felony records by age 24 (Brendtro & Ness, 1996).

Impulsive behavior is a survival mechanism that has been passed down from our ancient forebears. During the Paleolithic era, an impulsive reaction could mean the difference between life and death. Making quick judgments and leaping to action was the best way to eat and avoid being eaten. The biological root of impulsiveness is located in the *amygdala*, a bundle of small almond-shaped glands near the base of the brain. The amygdala acts like a switching device. It instantaneously evaluates input from the senses and either forwards signals to the frontal lobe of the neocortex for further scrutiny or mobilizes the body for immediate response. The structure of this neural alert system is unchanged from the time our ancestors dressed in animal skins and slept in caves. Fate and the speed of cultural change have placed us in a fast-paced, complicated world with the brain of a cave dweller as our guide. Everyday life is filled with challenges to emotional intelligence. Frustrations, misunderstandings, and disappointments test our abilities to stay in control. Thinking before acting or speaking is the crux of emotional intelligence (Goleman, 1995; Jensen, 1998).

Emotional circuits may be configured by nature, but they are cultivated by experience. Practiced consideration helps to strengthen the neural pathways between the amygdala and the frontal lobe. For young people who are raised in households or neighborhoods where abrupt and hostile reactions are common, the neural track between the amygdala and the frontal lobe becomes the path least traveled. The amygdala kick-starts an impulsive youngster into action without regard for the consequences. Daniel Goleman (1995) calls this an "emotional hijacking." An atavistic reaction to a perceived threat elevates, rather than reduces, danger by turning impulse into aggression. An often-cited reason for aggressive behavior is a "knee-jerk" reaction to a perceived slight.

Acting out, aggressive behavior characterizes three-quarters of students placed in special education programs because of a behavior or emotional problem (Report to Congress, 1998). Impulsivity not only characterizes the behavior of many youth with mild disabilities, it also influences how they think about themselves and the world around them. Rather than reflecting on how their impulsive behavior hurts others, aggressive youth rationalize their actions. These rationalizations distort their ability to put their behavior into a proper social perspective. They are unable to see their actions from any other point of view but their own. This "me-centeredness" plays a critical role in their deficient emotional intelligence. Students with behavior disorders in particular utilize self-serving thinking patterns to rationalize their behavior. These "cognitive distortions" serve as a sort of character armor, keeping at bay the slings and arrows of reality (Henley & Long, 1999).

A female jogger was beaten and raped by gang members in Central Park. When interrogated by the police about their motive, the attackers explained that they were "wilding" (i.e., having fun). Several of the guilty youth pointed out that it was the jogger's fault she was attacked, because she should have known better than to be in the park during the evening. Such cognitive distortions twist reality into self-serving observations about victims (Henley & Long, 2003). Thus, a car is stolen because the owner "is too stupid to remove the keys"; a student is beat up during recess because he "dissed" another student; a delivery man is robbed because a youngster wants a new pair of Nikes.

In her article, "Do Conduct Disordered Gang Members Think Differently?," Beverly Lewis (1992) described "errors in criminal thinking." Included among the rationalizations for their actions, aggressive youth blame their victims and cite causes outside their control, such as poverty and insults. Aggressive youth follow their own line of misguided logic, and their egocentric explanations are bereft of social conscience. Such youngsters are delayed in their emotional intelligence. They maximize the fulfillment of immediate physical needs and desires, and they minimize their responsibility for their action.

> **SPEEDBUMP—**Examine a local newspaper for events that appear to be related to a lack of emotional intelligence. Daniel Goleman believes that emotional intelligence is more important for a successful life than IQ. What do you think?

Helping students to develop emotional intelligence is a high priority. Rehabilitation efforts over the past century have produced dismal results. Nearly half of youth who are incarcerated will commit another crime upon release (Brendtro & Ness, 1996). The absence of a comprehensive mental health system in this country, coupled with the staggering number of children (one in six) who grow up in poverty, presents a challenging picture for those who would help at-risk youth develop the social skills they need for success.

TEACHING SOCIAL SKILLS

Teachers want and need harmony in their classrooms. Learning cannot proceed without cooperation, mutual respect, and caring. The "three R's" of the basic school curriculum has been supplemented with a fourth: responsibility. However, teaching personal and social responsibility to a youngster lacking in emotional intelligence is a daunting task. The key is prevention. Early intervention in teaching social skills that form a foundation for emotional intelligence will produce more effective results than trying to remediate patterns of violent and aggressive behavior that have had 15 or more years to develop.

Many general and special educators agree that social skills instruction has a legitimate place in the classroom. Participation in today's changing society requires adaptability and human relations skills. Deficits in social skills have been identified as a source of problems for behavior-disordered, gifted, learning-disabled, and delinquent adolescents (Davis & Rimm, 1985; Hazel, Schumacker, & Sherman, 1982; Marzano et al., 2003). Gresham (1998) defined social skills training as the process of directly teaching students to develop positive relationships with peers and adults.

Through most of the twentieth century, students graduated from high school and found employment in manufacturing. Factory workers needed to follow directions, tend to repetitious work, and accept company rules. The workplace required obedience and conformity. A worker's value was judged on his or her ability to complete an honest day's labor. However, the blue-collar world of work is slowly disappearing from the U.S. scene.

The United States is evolving into a service economy. Many new jobs in the twenty-first century require the ability to handle people instead of machines. Employers want employees who can cooperate with others, solve social problems, and resolve conflicts. Historically, the teaching of these skills was assumed by the family and church, but the changing demographics of society indicates a more central role of schools in teaching social abilities.

London (1987) characterized today's children as potential victims of a "psychosocial epidemic." Consider the following statistics: 715,000 children are born to unwed mothers each year; over a million nonsexual cases of child abuse are reported each year; three million 14- to 17-year-olds may have a drinking problem; half a million children attempt suicide each year, and six thousand die by suicide. Students need help in managing their lives. They need to understand how to make good choices. They need to learn to view problems from the other person's point of view. They need assistance in coping with feelings that drive them to drugs and sex (Garabino, 2000).

Three reasons students have difficulty adjusting to social situations are:

1. The student does not know appropriate behaviors.
2. The student may have knowledge of appropriate behavior but may lack practice.
3. Student emotional reactions to situations may inhibit performance of the desired behavior. (cited in McGinnis & Goldstein, 1984, 4)

Lack of **social competence** is one of the primary reasons that students with mild disabilities have difficulty in general classrooms (Nelson, 1988). More than one special educator has been chagrined at how a student with mild disabilities seemed to "fall apart" when transferred from a special education program to a full-time general classroom placement.

Social skills programs are a **proactive** approach to dealing with behavior problems. Brendtro and Ness (1996) stated that building on strengths, rather than fixing flaws, has been the basis for some of the most significant advances in the treatment of delinquent youth. Jane Addams saw delinquency as a spirit of adventure. Maria Montessori developed inner discipline in slum children. Kurt Hahn nurtured civic spirit through community service. Karl Wilker taught responsibility to youth in Berlin's jails, and then gave them hacksaws to cut off the bars. Janus Korczak developed youth courts with peer governance to teach principles of truth and justice (Brendtro & Ness, 1996, 4).

Some examples of programs that have successfully taught social skills through co-operation include the Capital Offender Program in Texas, which uses psychodrama and role playing to teach empathy to youngsters convicted of rape and murder (Mathews, 1995); Kidsmatter, a national mental health program in Australia; the Youth-Reaching-Youth Project, an acclaimed national substance abuse prevention program based on peer counseling (Dietz, 1992); and the Child Development Project (CDP) in California, which is the first long-term school-based project to teach prosocial skills to children. Instructional methods in the CDP focus on giving students control of their learning. Cooperative learning, peer tutoring, and **bibliotherapy** teach students enrolled in the CDP to help one another while they learn. A report published by the *Journal of the American Medical Association* on the effectiveness of the Second Step social skills program reported decreases in aggressive behavior and increases in prosocial behavior among 750 2nd and 3rd graders in King County, Washington (Grossman et al., 1997). The Second Step Curriculum focused on three areas: empathy training, impulse control, and anger management.

> **SPEEDBUMP—**An alternative approach to teaching social skills are detention "boot camps" for delinquents. These "tough love" programs have been widely criticized for inhumane tactics.

Each of these successful programs respects the resourcefulness of young people and involves them as decision makers in their learning. In his article, "Reframing Gang Violence: A Pro-Youth Strategy," Frederick Mathews wrote: "Recognize that young people learn responsibility by having responsibility. Youth need to have a voice with respect to their schools and education, social services, community programs, and in government policy and planning directed towards them" (1992, 27). A survey of teacher attitudes toward social skills training revealed that 82 percent of teachers agreed that social skills training should be a part of the school curriculum. The majority of these teachers believed that outside of the parents the general education teacher was responsible for social skills instruction (Bain & Farris, 1991).

Selecting a Social Skills Curriculum

In one classroom, social skills means following directions, sitting quietly, and working independently. Such a classroom is organized autocratically—the teacher is in charge, and **compliance** is prized. Students who have difficulty following this regimen will be identified as having social skills problems.

> **SPEEDBUMP—**In your elementary school experience, did you have autocratic teachers?

In another classroom, perhaps right across the hall, the teacher encourages students to be self-directed. There is a buzz of activity in the classroom as students work in cooperative learning groups and move from one learning area to another. This classroom is organized democratically with an expectation that students will take personal responsibility for their behavior. In such a classroom, a student who lacks the ability to work cooperatively is the deviant. Each teacher has different behavior expectations, a different tolerance level for misbehavior, and different methods of handling discipline problems. This lack of consistency undermines school-based efforts to teach social skills.

The expectation that teachers possess the skills and knowledge to teach social skills without the benefit of guidelines or training is an unwarranted assumption, and in some cases, just plain naïve. In order to teach social skills, teachers need a clearly defined curriculum, a method for assessing student abilities, and a model for instruction. Even the most talented teacher would have difficulty teaching science, math, or reading without a curriculum. Curriculums provide goals and objectives, ways of measuring progress, and recommendations for educational activities.

Much time and effort goes into researching school curriculums. The marketing of lesson plans, texts, and tests is a multimillion dollar industry, yet when it comes to classroom discipline practices, for the most part, teachers are on their own. In one way or another, all teachers attempt to teach social skills but there are many different points of view about social skills priorities.

A sound **social skills curriculum** is research based. It is derived from a theory or model of human development. It substitutes adaptive skills for nonconstructive behavior both in and out of school. A social curriculum begins with general goals and then delineates observable student behaviors matched to goal statements. Specific objectives provide a basis for evaluation of student growth and program accountability. See Figure 10.1 for a list of some frequently used social skills programs.

All social curricula emphasize one key point: Scheduling time to teach social skills is a legitimate educational activity. If students are going to change their behavior, they require opportunities to learn new behaviors in an organized and relevant manner. Wood (1986) states, "A (social skills) program must have relevance to the student's world beyond the special classroom, and the skills learned in the program must produce satisfying results in personal, real life situations" (p. 12).

Schumacker and associates (1983) posed five questions to serve as a guide in selecting a social skills curriculum:

1. Does the curriculum promote social competence?
2. Does the curriculum accommodate the learning characteristics of the students for whom it is to be applied?
3. Does the curriculum target the social skills deficits of the students for whom it is to be applied?
4. Does the curriculum provide training in situations as well as skills?
5. Does the curriculum include instructional methodologies found to be effective with the population of students for whom it is to be applied? (cited in Walker & Shea, 1991)

FIGURE 10.1   Social Skills Programs Selected Biography

Campbell, P., & Siperstein, G. N. (1994). *Improving social competence: A resource for elementary school teachers*, Boston: Allyn and Bacon.

Committee for Children (1998). *Second step: A violence prevention curriculum, Grades 1–3*, Seattle, Washington: Author.

Eggert, L. L., Nicholas, L. M., Owen, L. J. & Bendtro, L. (1994). *Reconnecting youth: A peer group approach to building life skills*, Bloomington, IN: National Educational Service.

Gibbs, J. (1995). *Tribes, A new way of learning and being together*, Center Source Publications.

Gibbs, J. C., Potter, G. B., & Goldstein, A. P. (1995). *The equip program: Teaching youth to think and act responsibly through a peer-helping approach*, Champaign, IL: Research Press.

Henley, M. (2003). *Teaching self-control: A curriculum for responsible behavior*, 2nd ed. Bloomington, IN: Solution Tree.

Jackson, N. F., & Jackson, D. A. (1983). *Getting along with others: Teaching social effectiveness to children: Skill lessons and activities*, Champaign, IL: Research Press.

Mannix, D. (1993). *Social skills activities for special children*, **New York:** Prentice-Hall Trade Books.

McGinnis, E. and Goldstein, A. P. (1984). *Skillstreaming the elementary school child: A guide for teaching pro-social Skills*, Champaign, IL: Research Press.

Rockwell, S. (1995). *Back off, cool down, try again: Teaching students how to control aggressive behavior*, Arlington, VA: Council for Exceptional Children.

Taylor, R. (1997). *Curriculum strategies: Social skill interventions for young African-American males*, New York: Praeger Publications.

Walker, H. M., & Holmes, D. (1991). *The Walker social skills curriculum: The ACCESS program: Adolescent curriculum for communication and effective social skills,* Austin, TX: Pro-Ed.

Social skills can be taught directly or indirectly. Direct instruction begins with the identification of a specific skill—for example, making good decisions. For a lesson, a teacher could select a contemporary problem, say, to increase drug awareness. The class is divided into small groups comprised of four students. Each group is given art materials, reference materials, and recent newspaper articles. The students must brainstorm five ways of increasing drug awareness and present their findings to the entire class.

Advocates of direct teaching of social skills develop curricula for both general and special education. Such books as *Skill-streaming the Elementary School Child* (McGinnis & Goldstein, 1984), *The Responsive Classroom* (Northeast Foundation for Children, 2002), and *Teaching Self-Control: A Curriculum for Responsible Behavior* (Henley, 2003) provide goals, instructional objectives, learning activities, and consulting guidelines. The aim of each program is to teach social skills that can be generalized beyond the secure confines of special education programs.

Each of these books is based on the premise that social skills training of students with special needs requires cooperation between general and special educators. Students cannot be "fixed" in self-contained special education programs and then shipped as finished products into general classrooms. (See Chapter 6 for guidelines about inclusion.) In order to develop appropriate social skills, students with mild disabilities need time to learn with and from nondisabled students. Social skills training requires agreement by general and special educators on specific areas of competence to be developed.

Developmental skills, those that cut across many settings, are preferred to context specific skills. Youngsters must be able to cope with social demands in many different environments. Training a youngster with low-frustration tolerance finish math worksheets is a school-context skill. Teaching the same youngster to verbalize rather than act out feelings of frustration is a developmental skill that is useful in many settings (Fagen & Hill, 1987). Although following directions, completing assignments, taking notes and other "school survival skills" are important, unless these skills are embedded in a more comprehensive framework, students will leave school without the tools to manage the broader social demands of work, family, and the community (Figure 10.2).

A SAMPLE SOCIAL SKILLS CURRICULUM

Fagen and Long (1975) defined self-control as the ability to direct and regulate personal behavior flexibly and realistically in a given situation. The work of Redl and Wineman

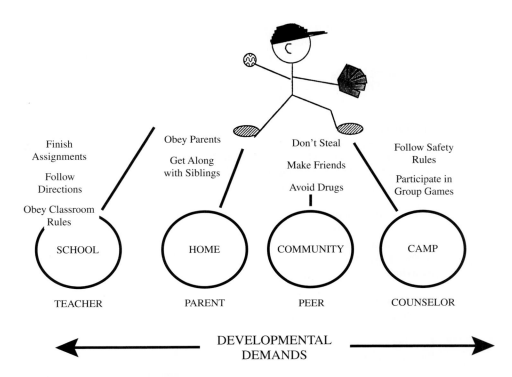

FIGURE 10.2   Development Demands

(1951) presented a structural model for describing a self-control curriculum. In their quest to unveil the "anatomy of self-control," Redl and Wineman detailed a list of specific **self-control skills** that children normally develop as they learn to restrain their impulses and relate to the world at large. Redl and Wineman's detailed descriptions provide the classroom teacher with a paradigm of self-control (1951). As children mature, they must learn to control their impulses, assess social reality, manage group pressure, deal with stress, and solve social problems (Henley, 2003).

What follows is a brief description of the social skills entailed in each of these areas (see Figure 10.3). The items describe self-control developmental milestones. The descriptions can help the classroom teacher in the following ways:

FIGURE 10.3   Self-Control Skills

Impulse Control
Resisting Temptation
Using Materials Properly
Spontaneously Establishing Self-Control
Tolerating Frustration

Assessment of Social Reality
Anticipating Consequences
Evaluating the Effect of Behavior on Others
Appreciating Feelings
Accepting Praise and Affection
Taking Care of Personal Possessions

Manage Group Pressure
Resisting Group Contagion
Maintaining Control Under Impact of Peer Pressure
Adapting to Competitive Challenge
Participating in Group Activities

Stress Management
Coping with Anxiety
Controlling the Floodgates of the Past
Adapting to New Situations
Relaxing

Solve Social Problems
Recalling Disruptive Actions
Learning from Experience
Drawing Inferences from Others' Experiences
Resolving Conflicts

Sources: Adapted from Redl & Wineman, 1951; Fagen, Long, & Stevens, 1975; Henley, 2003.

1. To identify individual student self-control strengths and weaknesses
2. To anticipate situations when a student might lose control
3. To establish goals and objectives for a social skills program

Impulse Control

Impulses are powerful psychological motivators. A student may have an impulse to hit another student or an impulse to throw a textbook in frustration. Impulses are derived from an infant's need for immediate gratification. As children grow and mature, they learn to delay gratification. A student with self-control is capable of restraining impulses. Situations or conditions can strain the impulse control abilities of students and cause classroom disruptions. The following self-control skills are a subset of impulse control:

1. *Resisting Temptation.* As they grow and mature socially, students learn to control the impulses brought on by tempting situations or objects. A student who sees an examination lying on the teacher's desk and resists the urge to pick it up to survey the questions is practicing self-control. Schools are filled with alluring objects. Equipment, toys, and learning materials can present strong temptations to students who lack temptation resistance. Students with emotional problems sometimes steal with no idea about what to do with the object once it is in their possession. One youngster in a program for students with emotional problems was literally seduced by gadgets of any sort. He was so predictable that the teaching staff always knew to go to Peter's "treasure hole" under the schoolyard fence to check for missing items.

Space has its own attraction. Open spaces invite running. Enclosed spaces invite yelling. Field trips, in particular, offer myriad possibilities for disruptive behavior for a youngster who has difficulty curbing impulses.

2. *Using Materials Properly.* Most students understand the purpose of classroom materials. Books are for reading. Erasers are for cleaning chalkboards. Clay is for modeling. Chisels are for scraping wood. Other students use classroom materials as props to act out feelings. An impulsive toss of an eraser across the room at an offensive peer or jabbing an adjacent student with a pencil illustrates how students misuse materials. These students are unable to restrain the impulse to "send a message" with the closest object available. Care should be taken to keep a close watch on materials that could be used to injure another student in a sudden outburst of anger or frustration.

3. *Spontaneously Establishing Self-Control.* Many a substitute teacher has been greeted by a spontaneous, "Oh boy, a sub"; or in other words, "Let the fun and games commence." The substitute teacher scenario is an example of how in certain situations even well-mannered students can fail to spontaneously establish self-control. Controlling one's own behavior when there is no authority figure around to monitor is a sign of maturity and emotional development. Conversely, the absence of spontaneous self-control skills indicates that a youngster is motivated by impulses rather than a sense of social responsibility. Organized classroom activities and routines support the student in maintaining self-control. When schedules indicate a change in routine, particularly from structured to open-ended activities, the impulsive youngster does not have the inner resources to substitute internal for external controls. Transition times, in particular, challenge the impulse control system of the students.

4. *Tolerating Frustration.* Frustration can be overwhelming for a youngster who lacks impulse control. Such a mundane obligation as waiting for help with a classroom assignment can culminate in a display of anger. When a 4-year-old child cries because she loses in a game, that is acceptable. When an unhappy 9-year-old throws a board game aside, sending everyone's pieces flying because someone else bought Boardwalk, there is a problem. It is quite remarkable to behold how children learn to accept minor frustrations and persevere as they mature. Learning to swim, ride a bike, and play a musical instrument are all building blocks toward perseverance, an essential quality for success in life.

For many children, frustration-tolerance happens naturally and gracefully. Others need to be taught how to handle frustration. Usually low self-esteem exemplified by an "I can't do it" attitude is characteristic of students with low frustration tolerance.

SPEEDBUMP—Can you think of any other impulse control skills?

Assessment of Social Reality

All students learn to take measure of **social reality**. For instance, behavior that is accepted by one teacher may be forbidden by another. Developing children are remarkably adaptable, and their insight into behaviors that are acceptable and unacceptable is a determinant of how they are accepted by others. Well-adjusted children are capable of maintaining relationships. They interpret social cues and make adjustments in their behavior based on what a situation demands. Deficiencies in their assessment of social reality will result in persistent conflicts with peers or adults.

1. *Anticipating Consequences.* In the classroom, as elsewhere, rules and routines organize activity and keep harmony. Students may not like rules, but they understand why rules are necessary. They know there are consequences for breaking rules. In society, norms substitute for rules, and laws are legislated codes of behavior. Social consequences follow violation of norms, and legal action is the consequence for breaking the law. Students who have an unrealistic notion of rules, norms, and laws interpret them as personal affronts to their integrity or well-being. They resent consequences. Such students, when confronted with consequences for their behavior, may become hostile.

2. *Evaluating the Effect of Behavior on Others.* Youngsters learn that their actions stir up corresponding reactions in others. Without this insight, a student will fail to recognize how personal behavior shapes the way that others act. A youngster who is "mean" to another may show remorse or at least understand why a friend has decided to leave. Some students with behavioral or emotional difficulties are unable to untrack their self-centered thinking. To such a student, interpersonal problems are always the fault of others.

3. *Appreciating Feelings.* Students with emotional problems have difficulty accepting the feelings of others. This is not surprising because their own feelings are such a mystery to them. Their ability to identify and describe feelings in themselves and others is deficient. Low self-esteem coupled with a naïve grasp of the significance of feelings leaves a student with emotional disturbance at a loss to contemplate his or her own life experience.

4. *Accepting Praise and Affection.* Trust is a basic requirement for social exchange between teacher and student. A student who has difficulty trusting adults will have difficulty forming attachments to others. Expression of care and interest may be reciprocated by hostility or resentment. Many students with emotional problems have well-entrenched defenses against what they consider a hostile world. Such youngsters need to learn to accept and give affection.

5. *Taking Care of Personal Possessions.* A bike that is left unlocked may get stolen. Carelessness in keeping track of assignments can mean coming to school unprepared. Personal responsibility in managing day-to-day activities is important for school success. Students who can manage their daily lives do well in school. Other students need to learn how to organize themselves. They are undermined by their own unintentional carelessness.

Manage Group Influence

Virtually everything in a classroom happens in a **group situation**. Group dynamics have a powerful impact on young people both in and out of school. The need to belong and the need to socialize with like-minded people are strong forces that can impel a youngster to make good or bad choices. Why does one youngster join Boy Scouts while another joins a gang? Why does one youngster look for mystical experience with drugs and another choose religion? In many cases, the answer is the power of peer pressure to shape young people's choices. The ability to handle group pressure is a hallmark of self-control. Students who are overly influenced by peer groups give up control of their lives. These students need to learn how to manage group pressure.

1. *Resisting Group Contagion.* Excitability is contagious. When a class is out of control, one or more students set off others with their disruptive behavior. Overstimulated students become leaders in pandemonium, and the teacher is hard-pressed to restore order. Some students have the internal strength to maintain internal control while others around them are out of control. Meanwhile, other students are swept away by the excitement. Such students need to learn how to appraise situations reasonably and to strengthen their sense of themselves as agents of their own control.

2. *Maintaining Control Under Impact of Peer Pressure.* For young people, particularly adolescents, peer pressure is a powerful shaper of attitude and behavior. When confronted with peer pressure, students may be hard-pressed to make the types of decisions that adults would advocate. Self-control within groups means being able to steer an individual course of action, even though it may be the opposite of group expectations. By helping students learn to make pro-social decisions despite group pressure, teachers not only enhance classroom management but also provide students with the tools to deal with myriad group pressures outside of school.

3. *Adapting to Competitive Challenge.* Competition is a basic fact of life in U.S. society. Keeping a balanced perspective about winning and losing is necessary to productivity both in and out of school. Winning and losing gracefully require self-control and positive self-regard. Competition in school, both obvious (e.g., tests) and unobtrusive (e.g., art displays), are factors that all students must learn to accept. Resilience, perseverance, and task commitment are basic to success. Students who avoid competition or think of themselves as "losers" need help in learning how to handle competitive challenge.

4. *Participating in Group Activities.* Cooperative group work is prevalent in all levels of society. Learning to help others, resolve conflicts, and share resources are signs of personal growth. Each of these skills requires the ability to "decenter"; that is, to consider the other person's perspective. Although these skills develop naturally in some students, others become fixated on their own point of view. This impedes their ability to cooperate and maintain group harmony. Such students need opportunities to learn to set aside their own personal agendas and focus on the concerns of the group.

Stress Management

Stress is the electricity of life. Through a combination of perception and biochemical reactions, stress energizes us to action. Schultz and Heuchen (1983) succinctly state, "All life events carry the potential for introducing stress into a person's life" (cited in Knoblock, 1987, 216). Hans Seyle (1975) defined stress as the nonspecific response of the body to any demand, pleasant or unpleasant. For a student, a pleasant prospect, such as anticipating a field trip to the zoo, causes stress just as surely as the unpleasant prospect of going to school without assigned homework.

Learning to **manage stress** is an important adaptive and survival skill. Perception plays a key role in inducing a stress reaction of fight or flight. Students with emotional disabilities often misinterpret social cues. Overreaction to mild stressors is commonplace with these students. An ordinary task, such as reading aloud in class, can bring on a temper tantrum (i.e., fight) or refusal to perform (i.e., flight). Learning to adapt to stressful classroom situations can help prepare students for life outside of school. Essentially, there are four characteristic stressful conditions that challenge the self-control abilities of students.

1. *Coping with Anxiety.* Some students are so ridden with *anxiety* (painful apprehension or sense of foreboding) that they are unable to decipher reality-based threats from normal expressions of feeling. Their reaction may be to strike out or verbally assault the perceived protagonist. Many teachers have difficulty understanding that overreaction to routine situations, brought on by a student's inability to cope with anxiety, is a symptom of his or her disability. In the section on the life-space interview, the value of gathering information on how a youngster perceives events in the classroom was emphasized. Through the use of LSCI and other active listening techniques, it is possible to identify specific stressors that set a youngster off into a fight-or-flight reaction.

2. *Controlling the Floodgates of the Past.* Fortunately, most students have the capacity to separate present events from past unpleasant situations. For example, a student will attempt to persevere in a mathematics assignment despite past difficulties with arithmetic. Given this situation, even a well-adjusted youngster will need support and will at times get frustrated. Students with behavioral disorders have life histories replete with failure or trauma. A minor dose of recall is all that is needed to set off a severe stress reaction.

3. *Adapting to New Situations.* Learning to adjust to unfamiliar situations or people is an essential adaptive skill. Adaptive responses to stress caused by new situations include questions, verbalization of apprehensions, and caution. When students have not learned these adaptive skills, their reactions can be disturbing. Pretenses of familiarity, avoidant behaviors, and unwarranted hostility are samples of how students overreact to new situations or people.

4. *Relaxing.* After a hard day at school, a youngster might look forward to going home and playing with friends. On a rainy day, such a child might pick up a favorite book or get back to completing a model. Relaxation reduces stress. Relaxation is an emotional and biochemical state. Numerous body signs indicate an individual is relaxed: The pulse rate goes down, skin temperature is warm to the touch, breathing is paced and easy. Chronic stress disables the immune system; chronic stress can cause disease. Students with emotional difficulties are rarely able to achieve a prolonged state of relaxation. Even games dissolve into a series of petty disputes. Alone, they have difficulty sustaining solitary activity. Television, alcohol, and drugs are pastimes of youth that are nonadaptive attempts to relax.

Solve Social Problems

Interpersonal problems are difficult to solve. The negotiating of relationships requires the ability to reflect on one's own behavior. One must be able to apply the lessons of the past to present situations. Once a problem is identified, it is necessary to consider various options and eventually choose a course of action. Ultimately, **social problem solving** requires evaluation of goals and the means to achieve those goals. A student must be able to apply these skills in both individual and group situations. The final achievement is measured by a student's ability to develop and maintain relationships. When a student lacks these skills, interpersonal conflicts are frequent, and a student becomes isolated by his or her own futile social gestures.

1. *Recalling Disruptive Actions.* Every teacher and parent is familiar with the refrain, "It wasn't my fault." Denial of personal culpability is normal in young children. As students develop better insight into their own behavior, they begin to accept responsibility for their actions. Students with emotional problems sometimes literally "forget" their own behavior. Redl and Wineman (1951) called this forgetfulness "evaporation of self-contributed links to the causal chain." The youngster is unable to perceive how his or her actions culminated in a classroom disturbance. This lack of recall should not be confused with lying to avoid punishment. Rather the deficiency rests in the inability to perceive personal feelings or behavior clear enough to review a series of events.

2. *Learning from Experience.* Students should be able to apply past experiences to present situations. Learning from past mistakes is a basic strategy for solving social problems. Natural consequences play a significant role in social maturity and development. Children learn to modify their behavior based on reactions from peers: Teasing is returned in kind; selfishness keeps others away. Students with behavior or emotional problems may persist in the same social errors regardless of the consequences. Even positive social experiences provide few clues for future behaviors. These students seem unable to learn from their experiences in order to piece together the behavioral steps needed to work out social problems to their advantage.

3. *Drawing Inference from the Experiences of Others.* Some students learn and profit from other students' mistakes or successes. This modeling is a basic style of learning for young people. Adults count on the fact that one youngster may be an example to others. This is the premise behind severe punishment (e.g., expulsions), and it is a premise behind awards and honors. Many youngsters do in fact learn from others and use the experience so gained to guide future actions. A student who cannot learn from the mistakes and successes of others is handicapped by shortsightedness. Adults cringe when they hear a youngster say, "It can't happen to me." The ever-increasing numbers of pregnant teenagers and drug-dependent youngsters are stern reminders that a key social problem-solving skill is drawing inference from what happens to others.

4. *Resolving Conflicts.* You don't change a lightbulb with a hammer, and you don't solve social problems with aggressive behavior. Many youngsters need to learn conflict resolution, negotiation, and cooperation as social tools. The need for students to be able to appraise social situations and develop peaceful strategies for solving problems has never been greater. Racism and teen violence are commonplace in today's society. Every classroom discipline system should help provide students with the human relations tools needed for functioning as a productive member of a democratic society.

CHARACTER EDUCATION

Schools are the only places where children are ensured constant adult supervision. If today's youngster is to successfully navigate the moral storms that await outside school, they will need adult help. According to advocates, **character education** can provide students with a moral compass. *Character education* (Kohn, 1991; Lickona, 1988; London, 1987) is a term that best seems to suit the evolving notion that many students need a booster shot of civility and ethics. Proponents of character education stress the teaching of cooperation and mutual respect. Moral development, with its attendant emphasis on caring for others, is emphasized in character education, as is reflection and commitment to moral principles. London lists two primary components of character education: (1) education in civic virtue and in the qualities that teach children the forms and rules of citizenship in a just society, and (2) education in personal adjustment, chiefly in the qualities that enable children to become productive and dependable citizens (London, 1987). Figure 10.4 lists 11 principles of character education.

Schools that emphasize character education follow different paths in their quest to develop characteristics that exemplify good citizenship. The following examples are winners of the 2000 National Schools of Character awards presented by the Character Sample Education Partnerships, a Washington, D.C.–based national, nonprofit coalition that provides advocacy and leadership for character education.

- Coswold Elementary School, Charlotte, North Carolina—With the motto "Hope means having faith in yourself" as a guide, the school system established a program to recognize character traits among students. School morale went up, and suspensions declined by 40 percent in 2 years.

FIGURE 10.4   Eleven Principles of Character Education

Core ethical values, such as caring, honesty, fairness, responsibility, and respect for self and others, form the basis of good character and should be the focus of character education.

"Character" must be comprehensively defined to include thinking, feeling, and behavior. Knowing the good, loving the good, and doing the good are the ultimate goals of character education.

Character education should be woven into the fabric of school life in a planned, proactive way, and it must be seen as central to the school's mission and purpose.

The school must be a caring community. The daily life of classrooms and all other parts of the school (corridors, cafeteria, playground, school bus) must be imbued with the core values.

To develop character, students need opportunities for moral action. Through repeated moral experiences, students can develop and practice the moral skills and behavioral habits of good character.

Character development and learning should be viewed as inseparable. Effective character education includes a meaningful and challenging academic curriculum that respects all learners and helps them to succeed.

Character education should strive to develop students' intrinsic motivation and commitment to do what is right.

All school staff—teachers, administrators, counselors, coaches, secretaries, cafeteria workers, playground aides, and bus drivers—must be involved in learning about, discussing, and sharing responsibility for character education.

Character education requires moral leadership from both staff and students. A character education committee is often helpful in the initial stages.

Parents and community members should be full partners in the character-building effort.

Effective character education must include an effort to assess progress.

Source: Character Education Partnership, 1997.

- Columbine Elementary School, Woodland Park, Colorado—Beginning with a project to study the culture of Nepal, students' increased understanding of empathy led to support of inclusion programs for students with special needs. The school adopted standards for personal and social responsibility. A 1999 survey indicated gains in students' attitudes toward school and each other.
- Morgan Road Elementary School, Liverpool, New York—Morgan Road used its motto "To grow academically and to become the best people we can be" as inspiration for its Character and Enrichment Committee team to teach character through language arts and literature. Success for increased achievement in math and science was credited to enhanced classroom climate, which increased focused instructional time.
- South Carroll High School, Sykesville, Maryland—Both adults and students are encouraged to be role models for good character. South Carroll established a student leadership program and student SAT scores have risen steadily over the past 5 years.

Character education can be included in any lesson. Lickona describes how a 2nd-grade teacher merged character education with a science lesson. For a science project, the class was incubating 20 chicken eggs. The teacher suggested that the students might want to open one egg to observe embryonic development. Later that day, Nathaniel, 7 years old, expressed reservations, "Mrs. Williams, I've been thinking about this for a long time. It's just too *cruel* to open an egg and kill the chick inside!" Mrs. Williams listened and decided to bring the topic up for a class discussion. Some students agreed with Nathaniel; others wondered how you could kill a chick if it hadn't been born yet. Mrs. Williams gave her students the night to think it over. The next day, the majority decided not to open the egg (Lickona, 1988, 422).

Several variations on these themes appear in other character education models. Edwards (1991) emphasized a modified version of the 1921 Dalton Plan, in which students determine their own schedules from subject lab alternatives. The purpose of the Dalton Plan is to teach students to assume responsibility for their own learning in a noncompetitive atmosphere. Kohn (1991) stresses a caring curriculum. He encourages teachers to develop empathetic relationships with their students; to promote cooperation over competition; and to allow students to participate in the governing of the classroom. Each of these conditions, Kohn maintains, increases academic skills by investing students in their day-to-day learning.

SPEEDBUMP—Do you see similarities between character education and social skills curricula? Do you see differences between the two approaches?

MORAL DEVELOPMENT

The notion of **moral development** in the classroom is not a novel idea. Moral development is a cornerstone of Western philosophy. The eighteenth-century philosopher, Immanuel Kant, believed that moral behavior was directed by reason. He provided the following "categorical imperative" to guide reason and actions: "Act only on that maxim through which you can at the same time will that it should become a universal law" (Seldes, 1985, 223). According to the categorical imperative, the rightness of behavior depended on the reasoning behind the act, not the consequences (Benniga, 1988). This focus on the internalization of judgment is what sets advocates of character education apart from teachers who believe students are best trained through external manipulation such as rewards and punishment.

No educator in the twentieth century was a more ardent advocate of character education than John Dewey. In 1909, Dewey published *Moral Principles in Education* in which he advocated the teaching of initiative, courage, judgment, and persistence. He maintained that external control of students instills dependence on the judgment of authority figures. Dewey believed that the purpose of education was to help students develop social consciousness. According to Dewey, concern for the social good required nurturing. Students needed opportunities to help their classmates, participate in classroom decisions, and discuss moral questions.

Classrooms don't have to be inclined toward character education to teach values. All classrooms are saturated in values. Either covertly or overtly, U.S. students for generations have been instilled with values educators believed crucial to success. Consider the following excerpt from the 1920 *McGuffey's Fourth Eclectic Reader:*

LAZY NED

" 'Tis royal fun," cried lazy Ned,
"To coast upon my fine, new sled,
And beat the other boys;
But then, I cannot bear to climb
The tiresome hill, for every time
It more and more annoys."
So while his schoolmates glided by,
And gladly tugged uphill, to try
Another merry race;
Too indolent to share their plays,
Ned was compelled to stand and gaze,
While shivering in his place.
Thus, he would never take the pains
To seek the prize that labor gains,
Until the time had passed;
For, all his life, he dreaded still
The silly bugbear of uphill,
And died a dunce at last.
(cited in Benniga, 416)

Unobtrusive artifacts of values permeate life in classrooms. For example, tests promote competition, while stringent behavior codes demand conformity. Benniga provides insight on the pervasiveness of covert moral education. "Whether or not they offer specific programs, schools provide moral education. In many schools and districts the curriculum in morality is informal and unwritten. It pervades the school and classroom rules (Benniga, 1988). As an illustration, consider the recent change in how scholars depict Christopher Columbus. For years, Columbus was portrayed in U.S. textbooks as a prototype of U.S. values. Against all odds, the story goes, he altered our conception of the world and discovered America. He brought Christianity to the native "Indians" and opened the gates to a "new world." So esteemed was Columbus that the Knights of Columbus promoted him for sainthood.

Now compare this traditional tale of Columbus with the view held by some Native Americans. According to Russell Means of the American Indian Movement, Columbus practiced genocide with the fervor of a despot. Under Columbus's administration, Indians living in what is now the Dominican Republic were shipped to Europe as slaves; thousands of others were raped, tortured, and murdered. Recent disclosures of Columbus's misadventures prompted the United Nations to cancel a celebration of his quincentenary. The

National Council of Churches stated that the 500th anniversary of Columbus's discovery should be a time of penitence instead of jubilation. Cultural values are shaped by textbook writers and teachers. In the case of Columbus, the atrocities committed against Native Americans were paved over by historians eager to promote Columbus as an icon of U.S. values.

SPEEDBUMP—Can you think of any other prominent historical figures whose contributions have been questioned on moral grounds?

Moral education is as basic to schools as mathematics and reading. What type of moral education do we want to pass on to our students? Advocates of character education believe school should emphasize ethical behavior and civility. These educators prefer co-operation to competition, altruism to individualism, and empathy to egocentrism.

The teaching of character education and social skills especially is relevant for students with mild disabilities. Students with mild mental retardation are characterized by deficits in adaptive behavior; students with learning disabilities have difficulty deciphering social cues; and students with emotional or behavioral disorders act out their emotions in disruptive ways. Teaching students with mild disabilities how to regulate their behavior in socially acceptable ways is a worthwhile goal for educators and parents.

SOCIOMETRICS

Sociometrics is the study of how groups and individuals interact and form patterns of relationships. For example, *cliques* are small social groups embedded in larger groups. Cliques are common in classrooms. From a sociometric point of view, cliques are neither good nor bad, but a natural event in group dynamics. However, cliques can have a powerful influence on student behavior. A teacher can identify cliques by using sociometric techniques to examine student affiliations and the effect of those affiliations on the class as a whole. The most common method is called a **sociogram**. A sociogram is a visual representation of classroom relationships. There are three kinds of sociograms: graphically plotted patterns, visual displays, and statistical analysis.

There are two steps to plotting a sociogram. The first step is to gather information about student affiliation patterns. This is accomplished by asking students about classmate preferences. Students answer such questions as who would you like to sit next to on the way to a field trip, or who do you like to play with during recess? Usually a student is asked to identify three preferences. The second step is displaying the data in a format that provides a succinct summary of the data. Figure 10.5 is an example of a visual sociogram. Sociograms can be used to identify specific roles such as popular or neglected children. Because sociograms outline preferences (i.e., the arrow in Figure 10.5), they are useful for spotting cliques. Sociometric findings can be used to arrange seating in a class, organizing cooperative groups, and to identify students in need of social skill instruction. In Figure

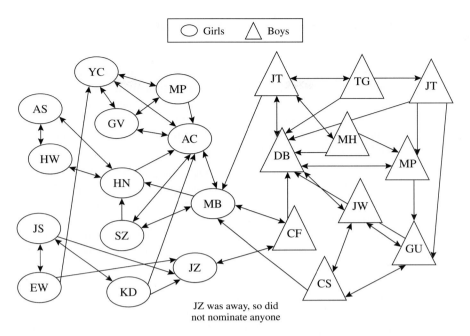

FIGURE 10.5   Sociometric results for Class A, displayed as a sociogram

Source: Copyright © Smith, D. (2004). *Practical strategies that work using sociograms as a behavior management tool.*

10.5, initials represent individual students. The arrows denote their choices. A one-way arrows mean a student selected another student. Reciprocal arrows mean two students chose each other. JZ was absent and did not nominate anyone. Note that among the boys JW, CS, and GU form a closed unit. This indicates a clique.

> **SPEEDBUMP—**What other patterns can you see in the sociogram? Can you spot a neglected student? Are there gender differences in affiliations? Who are the most popular children?

In addition to analyzing individual relationships with groups, sociograms can be used to evaluate behavior interventions, detect changes in group dynamics, and determine effectiveness of social skill instruction. Using sociograms as a tool to trace personal affiliations teachers can investigate such questions as are students accepting classmates who are culturally different; are students with special needs included in unsupervised activities like recess; and how are newcomers to the class treated (Smith, 2004)?

A FUNCTIONAL MODEL FOR PROBLEM BEHAVIOR

Teachers in general and special education classrooms are confronted with a variety of behavior problems. Some students, often those with more intense emotional or behavioral problems, require an organized **intervention plan**. Dealing with chronic disruptive behaviors requires a systematic problem-solving method based on a functional assessment and proactive interventions. The following procedure is a model for responding to persistent classroom disturbances, and it incorporates elements from this chapter and the preceding classroom management chapter.

1. *Describe Student Behavior.* Disturbing behavior should be described, not evaluated. Avoid clinical-sounding terms that interpret behavior. Rather than saying that a student is "distractible," describe his behavior; for example, "Steven typically sits still for about 5 minutes, then he starts sliding books around on his desk, dropping pencils, and talking to other students." Common evaluative comments to be avoided are: hyperactive, immature, aggressive, noncompliant, attention-seeker, and withdrawn. Evaluative terms are too abstract to clearly communicate a problem. A behavior that is "aggressive" to one teacher may be "assertive" to another teacher and "immature" to a third teacher. Description enhances communication among teacher, parents, and student. It ensures that everybody is talking about the same behavior, and it prevents the misunderstandings that arise when behavior is labeled. Moreover, descriptions of behavior can be counted. Interpretations cannot. You cannot observe "hyperactivity," but you can see and count how many times a youngster gets up from his desk.

2. *Count Behavior.* Educators use a tool called a **behavior frequency chart** to count behavior (Figure 10.6). This sort of chart is another type of functional assessment described in Chapter 9. Disturbing behaviors are listed next to a series of boxes for each day of the week. Each time a student demonstrates a disturbing behavior, the time is written in the appropriate box. This checklist can be located on the teacher's desk or some other convenient spot in the classroom.

The purpose of the behavior frequency chart is to provide a database for determining the severity of a classroom problem. The more frequent the disturbing behavior, the more likely it is a disturbance in the classroom. The chart gives the teacher an objective way of calculating the frequency of the behavior. The data can provide other important information. Perhaps many of the disruptions occur during a specific time of the day; this could provide some insight into its cause. Knowing when a disturbing behavior occurs helps the teacher determine antecedents. For example, the student might be most disturbing after transitions from preferred to nonpreferred activities. Finally, no program can be properly evaluated without initial baseline data. In a few months, do another count to determine whether the intervention program is working.

3. *Empathize with the Student.* All behavior occurs for a reason. Put yourself in the student's shoes. What does he or she feel? A life-space intervention (Chapter 9) would be helpful at this juncture to elicit the student's perspective.

Consider physiological causes first. Is the student getting enough sleep? How about diet? The average American teenager eats 120 pounds of refined sugar a year. What is your

Student: __Sylvia__   Week: __September 7–14__

Describe Behaviors	Mon.	Tue.	Wed.	Thu.	Fri.
Verbal taunts directed at teacher	10:00 10:07 10:08 11:15 1:05	9:45 12:57 2:10 2:19	10:12 10:13 10:23 2:19	11:45 11:47 2:29	10:28 10:51 11:12 11:13 11:17
Verbal taunts directed at other students	9:13 12:19 12:20	None	None	11:46 11:51 11:58	None
Moving around the room without permission	10:01 10:08 11:17	2:11 2:21	None	11:45 11:47	10:27 10:53

Comments:

FIGURE 10.6   Behavior Frequency Chart

student eating? Is lead poisoning a possibility? When was the last time the student's vision and hearing were checked? Some attention problems are traced to hearing impairments.

What about the student's family? Are there problems at home? Does the student have a home? For that matter, does the student have a family? Don't forget drug and alcohol abuse. Does the student come to school with frequent bruises? Emotional neglect is more difficult to determine than physical abuse, but no less important. Talking to students provides useful information about his or her family and life after school.

Empathizing means trying to understand the problem from the student's point of view. Disturbing behavior in class, if it's serious enough to require a specific plan, will show up outside of school too. Enlist the aid of family members. Empathy alone will not solve the problem, but it will change your perspective. Judgments of the student change from a classroom nuisance to a real person with a complicated life. Empathizing helps the teacher to depersonalize the classroom disruptions. Approaching the issue with professional detachment ensures that an intervention plan is professionally prepared without anger or resentment.

4. *A Proactive Plan: Behavior Interventions and Teaching Social Skills.* After describing, charting, and counting the disturbing behavior, the next step is to determine the best intervention to curb the disturbing behavior, and to identify a social skill to replace the disturbing behavior.

Teresa, a 6th-grade teacher, has completed a behavior frequency chart on a female student, Sylvia (see Figure 10.6). Sylvia is 12 years old. She is verbal, bright, and impulsive. Sylvia's quick tongue is matched by her fast mood changes. Teresa has counted Sylvia's verbal taunts and sarcastic remarks. They usually are directed at Teresa; and when Sylvia launches these verbal missiles, everything in the classroom stops. Watching Teresa and Sylvia match wits has become a great source of entertainment for the rest of the class.

Through her charting, Teresa sees that Sylvia starts her day out well, then, around 10:00 A.M., she warms to her task of harassing the teacher. By lunchtime, Sylvia has made on average five unprovoked and disturbing remarks aimed at Teresa and other students. Sylvia also moves about the room without permission. Empathizing with Sylvia, Teresa considered the possibility that Sylvia might resent her—but why? A conversation in the teacher's lounge with some of the faculty reveals that Sylvia formed a close attachment to Ms. Collins, her 5th-grade teacher. Sylvia asked Ms. Collins to fail her so she could spend another year with her.

Teresa decided to adopt a couple of interventions. First, she would restructure Sylvia's morning. Teresa worked out an arrangement for Sylvia to do peer tutoring each morning in a 3rd-grade classroom from 9:45 to 10:15. Sylvia had no problem with academics, and she had a sensitive side that Teresa hoped could be capitalized on to nurture younger children. Second, Teresa determined to bolster her relationship with Sylvia through hypodermic affection and sane messages. She wanted Sylvia to learn that she was a valued classroom member, but at the same time, Teresa knew it was important for Sylvia to understand the effect of her taunts.

Teresa decided to direct her social skills activities toward helping Sylvia assess social reality. Sylvia needed help specifically in evaluating the effect of her behavior on others. The more she thought about it, the more Teresa realized that the other students could learn about how their behavior affects people. Teresa determined to develop a unit for the entire class. She would do values clarification, role playing, cooperative learning activities, and additional peer tutoring.

5. *Evaluate the Plan.* How many times do teachers settle on a system for changing student behavior without ever evaluating the plan? In most experiences, this happens far too often. W.H. Auden had this to say about changing human behavior

> *We would rather be ruined than changed*
> *We would rather live in our dread*
> *Than climb the cross of the moment,*
> *And let our illusions die.*
> *(Seldes, 1985, 23)*

Changing behavior is a difficult enterprise. A behavior change plan that is elegant on paper can mislead a teacher into overlooking periodic evaluations. Every behavior intervention plan should be evaluated on a regular basis. Three months is a reasonable amount of time to look for some change. Another evaluation requires another behavior frequency count. If there is no decrease in disturbing behaviors, a new plan may be needed. Go back and review the steps outlined in this chapter. Did you miss anything in terms of empathizing with the student? Did you, for instance, fail to talk with family members? Perhaps you need to try some different interventions. If the problem is more serious, you might consider life-space interventions.

If you are seeing a change in behavior, you hit the mark on your first try. That is a good start. Success in working with a youngster to learn socially adept skills is well worth the effort. Twenty years from now, your students may have forgotten how to multiply mixed numbers; but if they can listen to another person's point of view, you will have left them a valuable legacy.

SUMMARY

Students with behavior problems are limited by their lack of emotional intelligence and lack of social competence. Often these youngsters have been identified by the school system as having a mild disability, and sometimes the student is viewed simply as a chronic discipline problem. Regardless of the label, disruptive classroom behavior has a profound negative effect on teacher and students. Social skills instruction and character education is an educational strategy for helping students with persistent behavior problems learn more appropriate ways of interacting with others. Character education, which overlaps with social skills development, helps students cultivate pro-social values.

Character education and values clarification are two approaches that have been utilized in classrooms for many years in the attempt to shape student attitudes and behavior. When applied to students with behavior problems, social skills instruction often is combined with behavior interventions. The application of a problem-solving approach in order to select specific social skills and behavior interventions helps teachers respond to persistent classroom disturbances in a systematic fashion.

ACTIVITIES

1. Recall your favorite class in elementary or high school. What social skills did your teacher expect you to demonstrate? Did you meet those expectations? What social skills did you develop outside the classroom?
2. In a cooperative learning group, brainstorm 10 social skills you think students should learn. Give a rationale for each. Present the results to the class. Discuss similarities and differences in perspective.
3. The following is known as the Heinz Dilemma, a classic problem in ethics.

    A woman was near death from a special kind of cancer. There was one drug that the doctors thought might save her. It was a form of radium that a druggist in the same town had recently discovered. The drug was expensive to make, but the druggist was charging 10 times what the drug cost him to produce. He paid $200 for the radium and charged $2,000 for a small dose of the drug. The sick woman's husband, Heinz, went to everyone he knew to borrow the money, but he could only get together about $1,000, which is half of what it cost. He told the druggist that his wife was dying and asked him to sell it cheaper or let him pay later. But the druggist said, "No, I discovered the drug and I'm going to make money from it." So Heinz got desperate and broke into the man's store to steal the drug for his wife.

Should Heinz have broken into the laboratory to steal the drug for his wife? Why or why not?

4. Research old public school textbooks—history, reading, and health would be good choices. Look for values that were highlighted in these texts (e.g., typical American family had mother taking care of children and father working, while Spot romped around).

5. Keep a diary for a week. Record events where your emotional intelligence was tested.

CHAPTER ELEVEN

BUILDING FAMILY PARTNERSHIPS

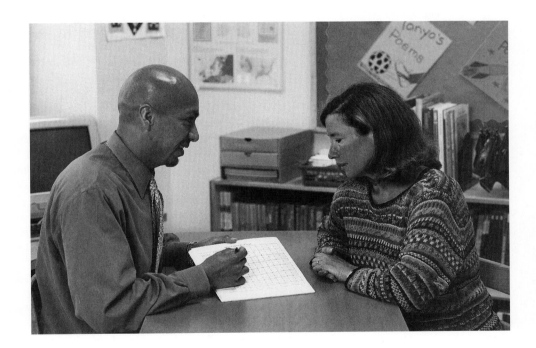

ADVANCE QUESTIONS

Answer the following questions as you read this chapter:

1. How do social and economic conditions affect the quality of life of children in the United States?
2. What are some barriers to family-school communication?
3. What are some ways that schools have overcome communication barriers that impede family member participation in their students' schooling?

4. What is the emotional impact on family members of having a youngster with a mild disability?

5. What are some ways that family members can gain additional information about their role in their students' schooling?

6. How do government-funded programs enhance opportunities for youth?

7. What are some due process rights of family members when a student is placed in a special education program?

VIGNETTE: EILEEN

Eileen slowly climbed the steps of the rundown, two-family house. She felt apprehensive in this poor neighborhood where every house seemed to need a new coat of paint. As she reached for the doorbell, Eileen reviewed why she was here.

Her student, Alexis, a pretty 12-year-old, seemed to be compensating for her weak academic skills by playing the role of class clown. Every time Eileen gave an assignment, Alexis had a comment. "You never showed us how to do this," or "This is stupid; why do we have to do it?" were typical of the disturbing remarks Alexis directed at Eileen on a regular basis.

Perhaps this home visit would help. After a moment's hesitation, Eileen knocked on the front door. Within a few seconds, the door swung open. Alexis stood in the doorway. "Hi, Ms. Morrison; my mother is in the living room." Alexis led Eileen into a sunny room with blue muslin curtains. Standing with teapot in hand was Alexis's mother. "I'm Mrs. Taylor; I'm pleased you could visit us. Alexis tells me so many wonderful things about you." Eileen glanced at Alexis whose face had suddenly turned three shades brighter. "Please sit down and have some tea," invited Mrs. Taylor. She turned to Alexis, and said, "Go into the kitchen and get some oatmeal cookies for your teacher." "Yes, momma," was the quick reply, and Alexis breezed into the other room. Eileen watched in astonishment. "Is this the same child who has been carrying out a single-handed verbal assault on me in class?" she wondered.

Mrs. Taylor smiled, "It's been difficult for Alexis ever since her daddy died, but she tries hard and she's a good girl."

"I'm sorry, Mrs. Taylor. I didn't realize your husband had passed away," responded Eileen.

Mrs. Taylor's smile slowly melted away. "Alexis needs help with her schoolwork, I know, but trying to raise her and her younger brother and sister on my waitress salary has been difficult for all of us," said Mrs. Taylor. "Tell me, what can I do at home to help Alexis with her reading? I didn't get past 8th grade, and I want Alexis to earn her high school diploma," continued Mrs. Taylor. Eileen sat down and the two women spent the next hour discussing how together they could help Alexis improve her schoolwork.

As Eileen drove home, she reviewed her home visit. After school, Alexis makes dinner for her 7-year-old brother and 9-year-old sister. Her mother is trying to raise three children on a waitress's salary. They can't afford health insurance. Perhaps most surprising of all, Alexis is not the disruptive child at home that she appears to be in the classroom. Eileen smiled to herself. She knew that her classroom strategy for handling Alexis would change. The insights she gained from this visit would help her to better manage Alexis's attention-seeking behavior in school. As she drove toward her condominium in the sub-urbs, Eileen vowed to make more home visits. An hour in a student's home, she realized, could eliminate countless hours of misunderstanding in school.

1. Do you think Eileen's apprehension about visiting homes in a low-income neighborhood is shared by other teachers?
2. Why don't more teachers visit with their students' families?
3. Do you think school systems should require home visits?
4. What are some reasons for making home visits? What are some reasons for not making home visits?

Eileen's home visit highlights a little-appreciated fact; students' lives do not begin and end at the schoolhouse door. Student experiences outside school have a profound influence on student behavior in the classroom. If a student is having difficulty in school, a home visit can provide a teacher with useful insights into how to handle the problem. In today's public schools, there are many communication gaps between students and teachers. Language, cultural, and ethnic differences lead to misunderstandings. Communication is a vital link to bridge this gap. Families are the best source of information about a student's likes and dislikes, emotional peaks and valleys, motivation, and activities outside of school.

AMERICA'S CHILDREN

Children, James Coleman (1990) noted, require "**social capital**" in order to grow, learn, and prosper. *Social capital* refers to the social networks and adult relationships that nurture children during their development. Coleman found, for instance, a lower dropout rate among students in Catholic schools (3.4 percent) than among students in public schools (14.3 percent). He explained the discrepancy in terms of social capital in the Catholic schools. The community of school and church helped families keep students in school. Because of the additional adult support outside the family, the students attending Catholic schools had a strong incentive to stay in school. Coleman highlighted the bonding together of adults through shared goals and beliefs as a primary source of social capital.

Social capital has steadily eroded since the turn of the century. In early-twentieth-century agricultural society, children were mentored by extended families, neighbors, and community members. Informal relationships between adults outside the family were commonplace. Home visits, teacher–family member meetings, and school socials were once frequent aspects of life in the United States. James Comer's (1986) memories of his neighborhood recall a time when the authority of family members was transferred to teachers through proximity.

When I went into the grocery store with my mother and father in the 1940s, it was a rare day that we did not encounter someone from my elementary school—the custodian, the principal, the secretary, or a teacher. There would always be an exchange of pleasantries and sometimes an exchange about my school behavior or achievement. The knowledge that my family members knew and appeared to like and respect the people at my school had a profound impact on my behavior. (p. 442)

During the era of the neighborhood school, indirect involvement of family members in school activity was underscored at each chance meeting of teachers and family members at the grocery store, bus stop, park, or library. Trust and mutual respect between school and home was a by-product of close-knit communities. The transformation to an industrial society disconnected children from the lives of adults. Fathers returned home from factories tired from hours of mind-numbing toil on assembly lines. Soon mothers followed fathers into the workplace. The family unit as a source of social capital began to unravel as the pressure to maintain a decent standard of living increased each year. With more time spent in work, adults had less time to spend in community activities such as family member–teacher organizations (PTOs) and Scouting (Coleman, 1987). The overall effect has been an alienation of children from basic nurturing elements in society that were common throughout history.

> **SPEEDBUMP**—Thinking back to your childhood, what elements of social capital can you remember?

The Children's Defense Fund (2007) reported that every 36 seconds, a child is born into poverty. African American children have the highest poverty rate, followed by Hispanic children, white children, and Asian/Pacific Islander children. Infant mortality for children born into poverty is 50 percent higher than for children above the poverty guidelines listed by the U.S. Department of Health and Human Services (i.e., $20,650 for a family of four living in the contiguous 48 states (*Federal Register*, 2007). African American children have almost twice the mortality rate of white children: 16.5 deaths compared with 6.5 deaths per live births. Poverty and transiency are the two most critical factors influencing the well-being of children in the United States.

Up to 40 million Americans move each year. **Mobility** is a significant factor in classroom composition. Hodgkinson (2001) reported, "Many teachers have 22 students in the fall and 22 in the following spring, but 20 out of the 22 are different students. Hospitals in these regions spend most of their time taking case histories from strangers. Each Sunday, ministers preach to a congregation, a third of whose members are new" (p. 8). California, Texas, and Florida are the main havens for a million immigrants a year. Sharon Dreyfus, a 2nd-grade teacher in Gaithersburg, Maryland, saw a new face in her classroom every few weeks. Typically the youngster spoke little English and came from a family of recent immigrants. "The biggest challenge is to keep constantly changing the program around to meet the needs of the kids," said Dreyfus. "Not only are they learning a new language, but learning about life in the United States" (Armas, 2001, A5). Other significant demographic data about children include the following:

> **SPEEDBUMP**—The problem of transient children in urban schools is so serious that a superintendent jokingly commented that the number one thing on his wish list was a transmitter planted under the skin of kids so he could keep track of them.

- An estimated 3 million children were reported as suspected victims of child abuse and neglect and referred for investigation or assessment in 2003; approximately 900,000 children were confirmed as victims of child abuse and neglect. In other words, a child is abused or neglected every 35 seconds.
- Fewer than 6 out of 10 (57.1%) of these children who were abused or neglected receive any post-investigation services. Several reasons are given for why only some children and families receive post-investigation services, including unavailability of services and long waiting lists.
- Neglect is the most common form of child maltreatment. Three times as many children are victims of neglect (63.2 percent) as are victims of physical abuse (18.9 percent). Another 9.9 percent are recorded as victims of sexual abuse; 4.9 percent emotional and psychological maltreatment; and 16.9 percent other.
- Research indicates that children who live in families with annual incomes less than $15,000 are 22 times more likely to be abused or neglected than children living in families with annual incomes of $30,000 or more. This higher rate can be attributed to the stress that poverty places on parents and to the increased likelihood that child abuse and neglect will be detected, reported, and substantiated in low-income homes that are more closely supervised by social services and law enforcement agencies. (www.childrendefensefund.org, 2007)

The teenage birth rate has also declined in the 15-year to 17-year-age bracket from 38.7 live births per 1,000 females in 1991 to 32.1 live births per 1,000 females in 1997. Children born to teenage mothers are at risk of developing intellectual disabilities. Tragically, government assistance for poor children in the United States falls far behind that provided by other countries. See Table 11.1 for a comparison of the United States and other countries' poverty rate before and after government assistance (U.S. Bureau of the Census, 1995).

SPEEDBUMP—These statistics can be overwhelming. What you should understand is that millions of U.S. children have much bigger problems to deal with on a daily basis than such things as grades and test scores.

Most family members care deeply about their children. A few family members are indifferent and, unfortunately, a small minority of family members harm their children. Neglect and abuse are a sad reality in some homes. Early medical and educational intervention for youth should be a national priority. As a society, the United States is at risk of squandering its most precious national resource: its children. Without a major shift in U.S. national priorities, many youngsters will mature without hope for success in life.

FAMILY MEMBERS AND TEACHERS: VALUABLE PARTNERS

The erosion of school-neighborhood linkages began in the 1960s with the advent of racial integration through busing. This process of detachment continued in the 1970s with the

TABLE 11.1   Child Poverty in 17 Developed Countries Before and After Government Assistance

COUNTRY	YEAR	BEFORE ASSISTANCE (%)	AFTER ASSISTANCE (%)	PERCENT OF CHILDREN LIFTED OUT OF POVERTY BY GOVERNMENT ASSISTANCE
United States	1991	26	22	17
Australia	1989	20	14	29
Canada	1991	23	14	40
Ireland	1987	30	12	60
Israel	1986	24	11	54
United Kingdom	1991	30	10	67
Italy	1991	12	10	17
Germany	1989	9	7	24
France	1984	25	7	74
Netherlands	1991	14	6	55
Norway	1991	13	5	64
Luxembourg	1985	12	4	77
Belgium	1992	16	4	77
Denmark	1992	16	4	77
Switzerland	1982	5	3	35
Sweden	1992	19	3	86
Finland	1991	12	3	78

Source: Rainwater & Smeeding (1995).

middle-class exodus to the suburbs and subsequent regionalization of small-town schools. Today, separation of school and family is a pervasive condition. Sometimes, the only time a family member has direct contact with the school is when there is a problem. Although such measures as school open houses provide some assurance that teachers and family members get an opportunity for personal meetings, these usually large-group activities preclude personal conversation between family members and teachers.

SPEEDBUMP—Throughout this chapter, terminology has changed from parents to family members. Many schoolchildren are raised by their parents, but many others are raised by aunts, uncles, and grandparents. Still others are raised in foster homes.

A common teacher complaint when family members are missing conferences or open houses is that family members "don't care." There are many explanations for family members not attending school functions. Their own education may have left them with negative feelings about school. Perhaps the family member is illiterate or a school dropout. Family members may not have a phone or transportation. There may be a language barrier or a communication problem (the message doesn't reach the family member). A family member might miss a meeting or school function due to an inability to obtain child care. When schools provide child care, family member attendance increases. Family members may be working when meetings are held. Many IEP meetings, for example, are held during the day, which can conflict with family work schedules.

The isolation of school and family continues at the same time that schools and teachers are being asked to take on responsibilities that used to be the sole domain of the family. Social skill curriculums, character education, and school safety have found a larger role in school curricula. Sex and drug education have become major concerns in schools. In many urban and suburban school districts, "Johnny" can't read because he's too "high" to care. When schools find ways to work with family members on problems of youth, the results are impressive.

BENEFITS OF FAMILY-TEACHER COOPERATION

The National Committee for Citizens in Education (NCCE) learned that when teachers maintain frequent contact with family members, students profit. Family member–teacher partnerships produce measurable gains in student achievement. "Some of the major benefits of family member involvement include higher grades and test scores, better long-term academic achievement, positive attitudes and behavior, more successful programs, and more effective schools" (Henderson, 1987, 149). The greater the degree of familial involvement, the greater the likelihood that students will succeed in school. In a review of 53 studies that measured the impact of family member–teacher partnerships, the NCCE did not find a single negative report. The evidence also indicated that students who were at risk for educational failure gained the most from family member–teacher collaboration (Mapp, 1997).

At-risk students include the disadvantaged, the students with mild disabilities, and underachievers. These students frequently are absent from school. Some are behavior problems. Almost all lack the motivation to persevere. By age 16, the at-risk student is a prime dropout candidate. Research on at-risk students indicated that "by the time students are in the third grade we can fairly reliably predict which students will drop out and which will complete their schooling" (Slavin, 1989, 5). The early onset of school failure underscores the need for close school-family partnerships at the beginning of formal schooling. Successful preschool programs, such as Head Start, place a premium on family member involvement.

SPEEDBUMP—Have you heard of the marshmallow test? Walter Mischel developed an experiment with preschoolers to determine the long-range effects of impulsivity. The researcher put a marshmallow in front of the child and said, "If you don't eat this and wait until I get back I'll give you a second marshmallow." Some sang to themselves, played with toys, stared at the marshmallow, and tried to occupy the time successfully. Others ate the marshmallow. Mischel followed the development of these children for many years. Which group do you think fared better? See www.columbia.edu/cu/psychology/indiv_pages/mischel.html.

Disadvantaged students who participate in preschool programs with strong family member involvement components outperform their peers through high school. Despite the documented benefits of family member participation in preschools, the carryover of family member participation in education is uneven. Some educators believe the best place for family members is at a bake sale or car wash. Williams (1988) reported that principals and teachers preferred that family member involvement be limited to extracurricular activities. The educators in Williams's study did not view family member involvement in educational decisions as either useful or appropriate.

Leitch and Tangri (1988) investigated barriers to school-family partnerships in two poor, inner-city, Washington, D.C., junior high schools. Twenty-nine teachers and 60 families participated in the study. The researchers found that a family member from a single-family household was less likely to be involved than one from a two-family member household. The larger the family (six members or more), the more likely the involvement. Extended families, both single- and two-family member, were the most involved. Members of foster families were highly involved. Employment made it difficult for almost half the family members to get to school functions. Among the unemployed, poor health was the most frequent reason for lack of participation. Education did not seem to be a factor; family members who finished and those who did not finish high school were involved on an equal basis.

From the teachers' perspective, their own family responsibilities were factors that impeded setting aside time for family members. Teachers who enjoyed their work tended to value family member involvement more than teachers who were unhappy or disgruntled. Some familial attributes listed by discontented teachers were: unrealistic expectations about the school's role; familial jealousy of teacher's upward mobility; poor family member attitudes about school; large families (although the data showed large families participated more frequently); and lack of familial skills to help with schoolwork. Other teachers listed the following school barriers to family member involvement: absence of school activities, teachers' suspicions of family members, and teacher apathy. All the teachers recognized that changes in society had diminished the familial role. They felt that the schools needed to change to meet the changing social fabric of families and the community.

SPEEDBUMP—Were your family members closely involved with your schooling? Ask them if they felt accepted and valued by your teachers and school administrators.

Family members believed teachers looked down on them. "One family member said that teachers have the attitude, 'I got mine, and you got yours to get' " (p. 74). Family members characterized school attempts to get them involved as meager. Family member–teacher organization meetings were the most commonly reported school invitation, although many family members said they never received such notices. The same small group of family members seemed to control most activities. Despite the negative attitudes attributed to both teachers and family members, Leitch and Tangri summarized their report by stating that a lack of specific planning about how to organize and utilize family member resources was the major barrier to school-home collaboration.

When administrators and teachers make a commitment to family member involvement, results have followed. In many schools, family members volunteer in classrooms. They sponsor orientation programs, conduct alcohol education classes, welcome new families, arrange for guest speakers, provide library assistance, and much more. The principal is the catalyst in these ventures. The principal allocates resources, persists in family member recruiting efforts, and establishes a schoolwide norm that family members are welcome. In order for family member–school partnerships to flourish, family members need to make decisions about school policies. Treating family members as teacher aides and doling out menial tasks works against collaboration. It's not how much time family members spend in school that counts, it's the responsibilities they assume (Sandford, 1987). A well-planned and comprehensive family member–school partnership can have a positive impact on both individual students and the school (Henderson, 1987).

James Comer built school–family member partnerships in approximately 100 urban schools throughout the country. His goal was to create school management teams comprising of family members, teachers, and mental health professionals. These schools enhance teachers' knowledge of their students, draw family members into the educational process, especially governance and management, and combine school and community services (Reed & Sauter, 1990). In 1991, the School Development Program formed **CoZi**, a family support model that enhances families' efforts to participate in their children's schooling (Comer, Zigler, & Stern, 1997). Other such programs throughout the country bear witness to the ability of teachers and family members to work together to improve schools.

In San Francisco and Redwood City, California, Henry Levine's accelerated schools model established specific achievement goals for all elementary school children. Including family members as educational decision makers is a key component in this program. Joyce Epstein developed other family member involvement models that emphasize reciprocal relationships—the family members within the school and the school within the community. Family member involvement projects share the following values: No child is labeled a potential failure because of social or economic factors; social and physical development of children is as important as academic and cognitive gains; and children's development is a shared obligation of school, family, and community. These principles are exemplified in the work of the League of Schools Reaching Out, a confederation of 41 urban schools that span 13 states and Puerto Rico (Davies, 1991).

The league takes an enlarged view on the meaning of family member involvement. The term "family member" is broadened to "family," which may include grandfamily members, uncles, aunts, and other significant adults in a youngster's life. The league advocates coordinating with social agencies that provide assistance and support to families—for example, agencies that administer housing, mental health, and public health services. Hard-to-reach families are targeted. Included in this group are the non-English speakers, the unemployed, and the indigent. League members recognize that the families that are least responsive are precisely the ones that most need to get involved with educational affairs. The League of Schools Reaching Out is attempting to revitalize Coleman's concept of social capital by abandoning the deficiency view of urban life and identifying strengths in families. Cultural diversity is prized and families are encouraged to establish their own priorities for school-community partnerships.

Just as the opening vignette described, Eileen's home visit deepened her insight into Alexis and her school behavior, educators throughout the country are learning that families are a teacher's best source of information about students. Families can provide information on developmental, social, and academic problems. Student attitudes toward school are shaped in the home. When families value the educational process, students succeed. If teacher and family are at odds, students are left without direction. However, when teachers and families cooperate, they are able to help a student focus on productive goals. Each year, teachers begin anew the hope of helping their students grow and learn. Building family member partnerships has proved to be one of the most effective means of turning this hope into reality.

UNDERSTANDING FAMILIES

Cooperation begins with understanding. How does it feel to have a child identified as disabled? What is the impact of a child with special needs on the family? What type of support is available to family members of students with mild disabilities? Family membering is complex and difficult. Family members of children with disabilities must deal with all the tensions and pressures familiar to other families, plus the extra stress of raising a child with special needs.

Family Member Feelings

Few children with mild disabilities are identified as requiring special services until they enter school and begin to encounter academic or discipline problems. Suddenly, family members are faced with an array of demands as they attempt to cope with the burden imposed by their child's inability to fit into the normal routine of school life. Excerpts from a family's journal help to convey the feelings experienced by family members whose child became a school "problem."

September. David began school today. The house seemed so quiet when the three left. David was so happy when he got home. Bubbling away about how much fun it is to ride the bus and have "lots of kids to play with."

October 1. David's teacher told us that David has no self-control. He has been having a lot of trouble getting along with the kids in his class. We spoke to him, but he says it is all the other kids' fault.

May 4. The complaints about David in school never stop. His teacher says she doesn't know what to do with him. Maybe adjustment to school was just difficult. Maybe 1st grade will be better.

January 1. The school called work today and left a message with the switchboard that they need to set up a conference about David's problem behavior. This is just great. Now people at work also know that something is wrong.

November 1. We just came from talking with the [school] psychologist. He thinks David would be better off if we let him enter a special class. David seems smarter than that, but something has to change. He will be starting in the next few weeks, if some [school] committee says that's what should be done.

December 1. The meeting of the Committee on Special Education was like the Inquisition. We got there and had to face seven school people. It seemed like they wanted to know everything. The meeting better be confidential and we hope we don't have to go through that again. David is going to the special class in a couple of days. We hope this is the answer, but what does emotionally disturbed mean? What did we do wrong? How can we tell the family about this?

Guilt, denial, anger, and despair frequently are mentioned in professional literature as family member reactions to a child with a disability. The extent to which a family member will experience these feelings is contingent on many factors, including finances, the severity of the disability, the age of the child, availability of child care, and support from family and professionals.

SPEEDBUMP—Has it occurred to you that family members could be intimidated by teachers?

Family members need to be treated as individuals. Each family member has a unique view of his or her child's disability. In order to work effectively, educators need to understand the family member's perspective. This is difficult to do if the family member is pitied or patronized. Trust and respect are essential for communication between family member and teacher. Federal law has made family members key decision makers in determining the type of educational services that will best suit their youngster.

The Family Unit

The universal role of the family is to nurture the young child. Within the family milieu, the child learns the social and intellectual competencies needed to succeed in society. When a family has a child with a special need, all family members are affected. Mother, father, and siblings must learn to cope with the unique stress of living with the child. A child with a disability imposes demands that strain the family's ability to function. Families must cope with several critical periods in the life of a child with a disability (Gloecker & Simpson, 1988):

1. Birth, when family members, usually of children with moderate to severe disabilities, first realize their child is disabled.
2. When the disability is first diagnosed and treatment begins. For family members of children with mild disabilities, this is usually the beginning school years.
3. When the child is placed in a special education program. Placement in segregated special class, pull-out program, or mainstreamed regular classroom can influence family memberal perceptions about the severity of their child's disability.
4. When the child reaches adolescence, peer acceptance or rejection becomes a central concern.

5. As the child nears the end of the public school years, family members must make transitional plans for their child's future.
6. If by adulthood the son or daughter has not been able to live independently, family members begin worrying about what will happen when their child outlives them.

The family's ability to manage these stress points depends on the severity of the disability, their emotional resources, and the type of support the family receives.

Sometimes the stress can be too much. For example, studies have found that family members of children with intellectual disabilities have higher suicide and divorce rates than families without disabled children. It also appears that children with disabilities are at greater risk of child abuse. In some instances, child abuse or neglect is the cause of the disability. Other problems encountered by families include increased financial burdens, isolation, chronic fatigue, and emotional problems (Gallagher, Beckman, & Cross, 1983).

Coping with the demands of raising a child with a mild disability begins with the husband-wife relationship. Friedrich (1979) found that marital satisfaction is the single best predictor of a family's ability to rear a child with a disability. When husband and wife share the nurturance and physical care of a son or daughter, their marriage can become stronger.

Rick Bennion's (1983) comments about his child with a disability highlights the need for fathers and mothers to support each other during difficult times.

> Finding out you have a retarded child is somewhat analogous to walking through a mine field. You remain in constant shock and fear as you grope along an uncharted course. The next step is always tenuous, and the lack of a clear-cut path adds to an incessant mental fatigue. For us the initial reactions were, I suppose, rather the norm: Why us? How about a second diagnosis? Is there a miracle cure lurking on the horizon? In the midst of continuous anguish, much solace can be derived from a few words of compassion from friends, loved ones, and particularly each other. No matter how trying, an ongoing dialogue between husband and wife is a must to breach the abyss of despair that envelops your being. (p. 39)

Gallagher, Cross, and Schartman (1981) studied families who made a successful adjustment to having a child with a disability. Their data suggested that the quality of the husband-wife relationship was an instrumental factor in helping the family cope with stress. Two personal characteristics that the researchers found associated with adjustment were the mother's self-confidence and a "set of supporting values" (e.g., strong religious beliefs).

Working Family Members.   The majority of U.S. women are now part of the workforce. This shift in family dynamics presents problems to husbands and wives in their roles as family members. Among some of the problems facing working family members are day care, after-school care, and job responsibilities. Employer sensitivity to the needs of family members is a key factor in how involved they will become in school activities, conferences, or family member organizations. Keep in mind that some family members work evenings and others may work two jobs. Employers who provide employees with flexible short-term leave help promote school–family member relationships. Without an employeeleave arrangement, a family member has to choose between attending a teacher conference and losing a day's pay!

Child care is a pressing problem. Particularly difficult is obtaining child care for older youngsters. Espinoza (1988) reported that in a sample of 79 children ages 8 to 13 years, 42 percent were latchkey children (left to care for themselves after school). Family members were anxious about their children returning from school to a home with no adult supervision. An additional 20 percent of the youngsters were supervised by an older sibling, many of whom were just a year or so older. Schools can support working family members by providing after-school child care, arranging evening IEP conferences, and providing an evening telephone service for family member questions regarding homework and other school issues.

Single Family Members.   Kathleen McCoy, author of *Solo Parenting: Your Essential Guide* (1987), called single family parenting the toughest job in the world. The demographics on single family members indicate that it may be not only the toughest job, but the lowest paying as well. According to the census bureau, two-thirds of female-headed families with children under 18 received some sort of welfare benefits (Zinmeister, 1990). Some researchers and policy makers have dubbed this phenomenon "the feminization of poverty" (Pearce, 1978).

Mothers who care for their children alone struggle to make ends meet. Shelter, food, clothing, medical care, and child care are top priorities. Most single mothers work. Two-thirds of single mothers with school-aged children and one-half of single mothers of preschool-aged children are employed. The U.S. Department of Agriculture found that almost 10 percent of the average single mother's income goes for child care (Vadasy, 1986). Although day care is a necessity for all working mothers, mothers of children with a disability have the combined problem of finding a safe place for their child while they work, and locating someone to provide respite care. The more severe a child's disability, the greater the need for respite. Vadasy (1986) noted that 73 percent of single mothers with children who have special needs received some type of social welfare support, but respite care was not included.

Single family members of either sex experience more stress than married couples (Beckman, 1983). Daily chores such as shopping and doing laundry are compounded by non-stop family member duties. Social isolation, particularly when a child with special needs is involved, increases the loneliness of a single family member. The most obvious impact of single family membering is financial hardship. Family members who must work full time have less time to spend with their children. These families are buffeted by the constant strain of struggling to make ends meet. Older children get recruited as surrogate caregivers as mothers try to balance impossible schedules. **Latchkey children** are common in single family member families. Without a partner to provide emotional support, the family member may be less capable of providing nurturance to a difficult-to-care-for child. This means that normal developmental milestones, such as "the terrible twos" and adolescent rebelliousness, can become the source of severe stress in the single family member family.

Single family members may cope with their loneliness by relating to their child as an adult friend. Single family members are more likely than married couples to treat their children as confidants. Strong emotional bonds can develop between family member and child when that child becomes decision maker, friend, and helper. Children in single family member families grow up faster than children in two family member families.

There are negative consequences from relating to a child as an adult friend. The child may be unable to cope with the responsibility of providing emotional support. The family member may become possessive of the child and restrict opportunities for independence. Outside support from friends and other family members can lessen a family member's dependence on his or her child to fulfill the need for companionship.

Many separated or divorced couples continue to share family membering responsibilities. Splitting child-raising schedules is a common practice that ensures that a child will continue to get family membering from both father and mother. The manner in which each family member is able to make the transition from married to separate life while continuing the respective family membering role is a key variable in the emotional development of a child.

SUPPORT FOR FAMILIES

Help for families who have a child with a disability can be broadly divided into three categories: emotional support, information, and federal government programs. Emotional support for family members of children with mild disabilities begins with the immediate family, branches out to grandfamily members and other relatives, and continues with friends and neighbors. Professional support agencies complement "grassroot" networks by providing information and services that train families to help themselves. The stronger their support system, the more capable the family will be in coping with the daily stresses of raising a child with a disability.

Federal programs are primarily targeted at low-income families. Poverty continues to play a significant role in the development of mild disabilities, particularly mild mental retardation and behavior disorders. Children without adequate nutrition and health care are at-risk populations. Environmental threats to normal development include heavy-metal poisoning, child abuse, child neglect, community violence, lack of proper educational experiences at home, and drug abuse. Government programs, when funded properly, can prevent and/or remediate medical and environmental conditions that contribute to mild disabilities.

Emotional Support

Support groups help family members cope with isolation. When family members have an opportunity to discuss their problems with other family members of children with disabilities, they learn they are not alone. Over the years, many self-help, support groups for family members have sprung up in local communities. Sometimes leadership for these groups comes from local professionals; more often family members themselves are the organizers.

Support groups provide family members with an emotional lifeline as they discover that others share their experiences. When family members talk to family members, a sense of comradeship supplants feelings of loneliness and isolation. The Federation of Families for Children's Mental Health, for example, has assisted many family-run organizations in getting started (Bullock & Gable, 1997). Support groups also help family members learn how to use their influence to get the best educational services for their children. Many school systems have family member advisory councils. These advocacy groups are comprised of family members with disabled children and representatives from the local educational agency. They meet on a regular basis to discuss issues pertaining to delivery of special education services in their community. How much influence a family member advisory council has is largely determined by the political activism of member family members. Some typical activities of a family member advisory council include regular review of special education policy in their school system, dissemination of information to family members of special needs children, and the writing of grants to improve educational services for children with disabilities.

Information

Recent federal legislation has enabled family member–organized groups to develop a national networking system. A federal grant program to support organized family member efforts to provide information and training is the Federation for Children with Special Needs (www.fcsn.org). The purpose of the federation is to disseminate information regarding special needs to family members and families.

The National Information Center for Children and Youth with Disabilities (NICHCY, www.nichcy.org) provides educational information and technical assistance to family members, advocates, and professionals. NICHCY maintains a collection of resource publications and fact sheets that help family members locate assistance in their local communities. Since 1922, the Council for Exceptional Children (CEC, www.cec.sped.org) has provided both family members and professionals with support services, including national and regional conferences, journals, and political activism on behalf of children with disabilities. While CEC provides support activities for all types of disabling conditions, other national organizations provide support services for families of children with specific disabilities. Chapters of the Learning Disabilities Association (www.ldanatl.org) and Association for Retarded Citizens exist throughout the country (www.thearc.org). These organizations provide family members with information on recent developments in research and teaching children with specific impairments. Family members or educators who wish to contact any of these organizations can get the necessary information from websites and state department of education offices.

Many organizations and agencies are eager to help support families (see Table 11.2 for a list of Internet addresses), yet each year countless family members struggle alone, unaware of the support network that is available to help them. By providing family members with names of local and regional support agencies, teachers can help ensure that their classroom efforts are complemented by help outside of school. Mild disabilities are more than just a school problem; learning disabilities, mild emotional disorders are family problems. When families are supported at home, children with special needs have a better opportunity to overcome their intellectual disability in school and in the community.

TABLE 11.2   Agencies and Organizations that Support Families

American Association of Mental Retardation www.aamr.org	Internet Resource for Special Children www.irsc.org
American Council of the Blind www.acb.org	Learning Disabilities Associations www.Ldonline.org
American Speech and Hearing Association www.asha.org	Education Development Center www.edc.org
Autism National Committee www.autcom.org	National Educational Service (at-risk and behavior disorders) www.nes.org
Children and Adults with Attention Deficit Disorder (CHADD) www.chadd.org	National Information Center for Children and Youth with Disabilities (NICHCY) www.nichcy.org
Children's Defense Fund–Family Member Resource Network www.childrensdefense.org	National Deaf Education Network www.clerccenter.gallaudet.org
Council for Exceptional Children www.cec.sped.org	Office of Special Education and Rehabilitation Services www.ed.gov/offices/OSERS
Federation for Children with Special Needs www.fcsn.org	U.S. Department of Education www.ed.gov

Compiled by Linda Nober, Education Department, Westfield State College.

Government Programs

Because federal grant funding is cyclical and subject to legislative approval, changes in funding priorities and appropriations are frequent. Updated information regarding federal assistance to enhance families involvement in schooling can be obtained through the U.S. Department of Education website at www.ed.gov. The following is a brief list of important federal assistance programs.

WIC (www.fns.usda.gov).   The Special Food Supplemental Program for Women, Infants, and Children (WIC) is a federal grant program for which Congress authorizes a specific amount of funds each year. A family of four that earns $31,593.00 or less annually meets WIC assistance guidelines. The WIC target population is low-income, nutritionally at-risk women and children. Specifically included are:

- Pregnant women (through pregnancy and up to 6 weeks after birth or after pregnancy ends); one in four new mothers participates in WIC
- Breast-feeding women (up to infant's 1st birthday)
- Non–breast-feeding postpartum women (up to 6 months after the birth of an infant or after pregnancy ends)
- Infants (up to 1st birthday); WIC serves 45 percent of all infants born in the United States
- Children up to their 5th birthday

WIC operates through 2,000 local agencies in 10,000 clinic sites and in 50 state health departments. WIC provides nutritional assistance to pregnant women and children through supplemental nutritious foods purchased at retailers with vouchers, nutrition education and counseling in WIC clinics, and screening and referrals to other health, welfare, and social services.

CHIP (www.cms.nhs.gov/home/schip.asp). In 1997, Congress enacted the Children's Health Insurance Program (CHIP). Eligible working families are those whose income is too high to qualify for Medicaid, but too low to afford private coverage. More than 90 percent of eligible children live in working families. In most states, children age 18 and younger in a working family of four earning up to $34,100 annually would qualify. The Children's Defense Fund estimated that in 1999, 10.8 million children under 18 lacked health insurance. Of the uninsured, 4.4 million were white, 3.4 million Hispanic, and 2.1 million were African American. Compared with the insured, children without health insurance are four times more likely to have an unmet medical problem, three times as likely to have an unmet dental need, and almost twice as likely to have an unmet vision problem. Lack of health insurance is a leading contributor to mild mental retardation and behavior disorders.

EPSDT (www.hrsa.gov/epsdt/default.htm). Medicaid and Early Periodic Screening, Diagnosis and Treatment (EPSDT) provide health services to families who are unable to afford health insurance. Prenatal care, increased birth weight, decreased neonatal deaths, and fewer abnormalities are some of the benefits of EPSDT for poor children. Screening for lead poisoning is a required component of EPSDT treatment for all Medicaid-eligible children from 24 to 72 months. Childhood immunization programs, which prevent measles, rubella, mumps, polio, diphtheria, tetanus, and pertussis, are funded. As a result of EPSDT, in 1997, an estimated 37,177,000 recipients including low-income persons over 65, disabled, low-income children, and pregnant women received medical assistance (Federal Domestic Assistance Catalog, 1997).

Head Start (www.nhsa.org). Head Start is a federally funded program that provides preschoolers with a range of crucial services. The Head Start educational programs help youngsters learn school readiness skills, thus increasing their chances for academic success when they enter public school. Nutrition and medical screening, including EPSDT and dental checkups, are components of Head Start. Family member involvement is built into every Head Start program. Family members are encouraged to attend family membering workshops on such topics as nutrition and developmental play at home. Some Head Start programs are home based. Head Start teachers visit youngsters' homes and demonstrate early childhood activities for family members.

The most notable accomplishment of a Head Start preschool was attributed to the Perry Preschool Program in Ypsilanti, Michigan. By age 19, students who had attended the Perry program "were more likely to have finished high school, were dramatically less likely to have committed a crime, were less likely to be on welfare, and were earning more money" when compared to peers who had not attended the Perry program (Stein, Leinhardt, & Bickel, 1989, 149). Head Start children have demonstrated better school readiness skills, higher verbal achievement, and enhanced social competence when compared to other low-income children (www.nhsa.org).

Federal programs make significant contributions to strengthening the ability of family members to improve the health and education of their children. Only the federal government has the financial and political leadership required to make children a national priority. In order to provide for the needs of youth, a new vision of community is needed. A community is a network of people working together toward common goals. This new vision would promote community organizations as extended families. Services such as youth clubs, athletic organizations, schools, mental health clinics, and family member resource centers can help family members and children. All of these ventures are woefully underfunded.

SPEEDBUMP—Tip: Keep an active list of these resources. Many family members are unaware of available support.

Although the country can't turn back the clock to the neighborhood school memories of James Comer, there are many paths to the goal of providing for the nation's children. WIC, CHIP, and EPSDT are based on the premise that children need to be healthy to learn. Head Start integrates health services, family member involvement, and education to help at-risk children succeed in school. Innovative programs and family member involvement provide a decision-making role for family members in schools, establish support for family members to assist children to learn at home, and enhance family member–teacher communication.

TEACHER–FAMILY MEMBER COMMUNICATION

Good communication with family members serves three useful purposes. First, it provides teachers with information about their students and family member expectations for school. Second, family members get reliable and up-to-date information to help them make decisions about their child's special education. Finally, when family members and teachers communicate and work together, they develop trust and a sense of shared commitment. Trust helps the school and family support each other and share expectations for student achievement. This is the type of social capital that can make a significant difference in a youngster's life (Bryk & Schneider, 2002).

Communication means more than simply relaying information. The medium of exchange tells family members how the school system feels about them. Schools and teachers who seek minimum family member involvement do the least to attract a family member's attention to important issues. For instance, one school system was obligated by state special education regulations to form a special needs family member advisory board. Instead of sending letters of invitation to family members describing the need for family member participation, the superintendent and special education director squeezed the message on the back of the weekly school lunch menu. As expected, there was minimal family member response. Did this mean that the family members in this school system were apathetic? Of course not, but judgments about family member behavior sometimes are based on such transactions.

Understanding family members of children with mild disabilities requires treating each family member as an individual. Teachers communicate their respect through words and actions. One strategy is to make telephone calls to family members notifying them of their child's positive classroom contributions. This offsets the family member expectation that the only time they will hear from school is when there is a problem.

The following description of an exceptional teacher by a family member highlights the anxiety and hope that family members harbor when they first meet their child's teacher.

> I just met a talented and gifted teacher, and I'm still tingling with joy. He invited the family members to a meeting, before the beginning of school, to introduce himself and to discuss the year. I wouldn't have missed it for the world, but I went with fear. What if I didn't like the man? Within half an hour, however, I felt the tension drain from my body to be replaced with excitement. Before me was a talented and gifted teacher. I knew other exceptional teachers before, and this time I could identify the qualities they had in common. (Williams, 1988, 61)

Linda Williams described a teacher who loves to learn, is not afraid to take risks, believes teaching is helping children to learn, conveys the message that family members are important, and respects children. Family members need to know what kind of person is teaching their child.

Conferences

When family members and professionals meet to discuss a child, family members need to feel that they are valued participants. Teachers who treat family members with respect create the best climate for a cooperative partnership. It wasn't long ago that professionals placed the majority of the blame for a child's learning problem on inferior parenting skills. Professionals viewed family members as part of the problem rather than part of the solution. A one-sided view that says 'it's all the family members fault' bred a condescending attitude toward family members of children with disabilities. In order to avoid barriers to effective communication, teachers should keep in mind the following pointers outlined by Gloeckler and Simpson (1988):

1. *Family members of exceptional children are more like family members of nondisabled children than they are different.* There are no generalizations about families of children with mild disabilities. Each situation is unique. The majority of special needs children come from families in which other children do not have learning problems.
2. *Family members of children with mild disabilities, in general, are not the cause of their children's disabilities.* Mild disabilities have been traced to many sources, including poor instruction, faulty assessment practices, neurological impairments, and poverty. To view family members as the single contributor to a child's disability is misleading and unfair. Teachers may encounter some family members who are inadequate. These individuals need support and help, rather than condemnation.

3. *Family members are interested in their child's welfare and will react positively to those they believe are genuinely interested in their children.* Family members need someone to listen more than someone to tell them what to do. Listening indicates concern and interest in each individual situation. Listening helps professionals to problem-solve with family members. When family members feel their point of view is respected, they are more likely to be open and honest in their conversations.

4. *The family is a social unit.* When a child is identified as having a learning disability, mild intellectual disability, or emotional disturbance, each member of the family—mother, father, siblings, and relatives—will have individual reactions. The interrelationship among family members will have an impact on how a student behaves in school.

5. *Family members have the greatest impact on their own children.* No matter how many professionals are involved with a youngster, the specialist is still the family member. Family members need accurate and full knowledge of their child's status in school. Explanations of classroom actions, test results, and professional judgments should be honest and direct. Describing student actions in descriptive, nontechnical language helps the family member to understand discrepancies between home and school behavior.

An initial family member–teacher conference sets the tone for all future contacts. In order to prepare for a conference, imagine how the family member feels driving or walking to the conference. What will be on his or her mind? Think about feelings that precede a visit to a doctor, dentist, lawyer, or professor. A common concern is that something is wrong. Some family members, particularly those of children with mild disabilities, approach a conference with apprehension. They might be concerned that they appear to be "bad" family members, or they hope the teacher has some magic up his or her sleeve that is going to turn things around for their child. Their schooling may have been a negative experience, so the simple task of walking into a classroom and sitting down with a teacher can be anxiety provoking.

The first step to a productive family member–teacher conference is preparation. The following are some practical suggestions for family member–teacher meetings.

1. *Physical preparation.* Physical preparation means attending to the accoutrements of the conference. Don't sit behind a desk. If you are an early childhood teacher, provide adult-sized chairs. Have concrete samples of student work available to highlight topics you want to cover. Sit at a table that is wide enough to display student work. Be organized.

2. *Mental preparation.* Have a mental or written checklist of specific items you want to review. Avoid using materials, such as test profiles, that require educational jargon to explain. Talk in plain language. If the family member is a non-English speaker, make an attempt to communicate in a way that will help set the person at ease. A smile and cheery "Buenas tardes," for example, can go a long way toward helping a Spanish-speaking family member to relax.

3. *Establish a mood.* Begin a conference with good news. This will set a positive tone and help smooth the waters for any trouble spots that need to be reviewed. Be can-

did and direct with family members. Honesty helps establish trust. Don't dominate the conference. At least 50 percent of the talk should come from family members. Remember that the purpose of the conference is for both of you to learn about each other. Use active listening skills. Encourage family members to give examples of their concerns by talking about what happens at home. Remember that you might be the only adult outside the family that a family member can confide in about his or her child. This is an opportunity for family members, but they need your nonjudgmental support in order to express their concerns. Finally, don't be defensive. If a family member makes what appears to be a negative remark about your teaching or the curriculum, listen to what they have to say. Listening demonstrates respect.

4. *Carryover.* Teachers can use a family member conference to assist family members with their children at home. Many family members would like to do more but they need guidance. Table 11.3 offers ideas for family members to improve their children's school performance. Give a family member a reading list of children's books, or refer a family member to another resource such as the WIC program or Head Start. A teacher's credibility rides on follow-up. After the conference is over, make a careful written record of the conversation. Include suggestions and questions that were discussed, and the type of follow-up you agreed on.

Written Communication

Newsletters, family member handbooks, and bulletins provide families with information regarding their rights and obligations under IDEA. Teachers and administrators usually assume that family members understand this information. Given the importance of family member involvement in special education decisions, it is clearly in the school's best interests to disseminate readable information to family members.

In order to fulfill their obligations, family members need a working knowledge of special education law and regulations. They should understand notification, evaluation, and placement procedures. Family members also must be aware of due process procedures established to protect their rights. Family members should know how to utilize family member advocates. Finally, family members need to understand their role in developing and implementing an IEP.

Roit and Pfohl (1984) assessed the readability of written information disseminated to family members regarding their involvement in special education meetings. The researchers hypothesized that family members did not clearly understand information presented in school information materials. Their supposition had particular significance for family members of students with mild intellectual disabilities and behavior disorders because a disproportionate percentage of these children come from either non-English–speaking or culturally different families. Additionally, Educational Testing Service data on adult literacy indicated that between 18 and 23 million adults cannot read a daily newspaper.

The results of the readability study indicated that large pages filled with small print made reading overwhelming and unappealing. The use of examples, samples, charts, and pictures enhanced the readability of printed materials. The researchers found that bold headings and outlines did not communicate information as effectively as paragraphs that related

TABLE 11.3   Helping Family Members Help Their Children

1. You Can Help Your Child Mentally by
_ praising your child for work well done and for good effort.
_ eliminating comparisons of your child to another child.
_ showing confidence in your child's abilities.
_ being realistic in your expectations of your child.

2. You Can Help Your Child Physically by
_ seeing that your child gets adequate sleep.
_ providing a schedule or fixed routine for your child to follow during school days.
_ seeing that your child has an appropriate diet with limitations on the amount of junk food consumed.
_ encouraging your child to exercise regularly.
_ seeing that your child visits his or her dentist and doctor on a regular basis.
_ showing your child a great deal of love.

3. You Can Help Your Child Academically by
_ talking with your child. Have your child talk about the day's activities or future plans for the weekend or any other subject of interest.
_ listening to your child. Responding to questions encourages curiosity and motivation in a child.
_ reading to your child and having your child read to you.
_ seeing that your child does assigned homework.
_ establishing a regular time and place for your child to study.
_ providing materials to use while studying (e.g., pencils, paper, dictionary, etc.).
_ allowing your child to do his or her own work, but being available to provide assistance if needed.
_ taking your child to the library often.
_ playing vocabulary games with your child, such as naming common objects around the house and their uses; going to the grocery store and naming fruits and vegetables.

_ playing question games with your child. Ask your child questions that begin "What if" or "How will."
_ having your child memorize some vital pieces of information, such as a family telephone number, home address, your place of employment, the police emergency number, and other information needed for your child's safety and well-being.
_ serving as a positive role model for your child by reading, using appropriate speech, writing notes or letters, watching educational television programs.

4. You Can Help Your Child in Test Taking by
_ ensuring your child gets a good night of sleep so as to be alert the next day.
_ seeing that your child eats breakfast.
_ seeing that your child dresses appropriately for outside weather conditions.
_ getting your child to school on time (so there will be no last-minute problems).
_ encouraging your child to do his or her best on the test, but not placing undue pressure on your child.
_ demonstrating verbally and nonverbally that you have confidence in your child's abilities to perform well on the test.

5. You Can Help Your Child in Other Ways by
_ seeing that your child turns in assigned homework.
_ keeping up-to-date on your child's progress in school.
_ getting to know your child's teacher(s).
_ volunteering to work in a school classroom or making materials for use in the classroom.
_ participating in school-sponsored activities.
_ reviewing your child's work folder as it is sent home from school.
_ supporting the family member–teacher organization of the school that your child attends.

Source: Whiting & Aultman (1990).

concepts to specific situations. Finally, Roit and Pfohl recommended organizing the content of printed material into five broad categories: (a) disabling conditions (e.g., what is a learning disability and how does it affect a youngster developmentally, socially, and academically); (b) normal child development; (c) legal issues and trends in litigation; (d) assessment and placement procedures; and (e) the role of family members in the educational process.

Although family member conferences, the telephone, and newsletters represent the traditional approach to school-family communication, educators realize that the electronic media has tremendous potential for interconnecting families and teachers.

THE INDIVIDUAL EDUCATION PLAN MEETING

One of the remarkable aspects of IDEA that family members are required to collaborate with educators to determine the appropriateness of their student's IEP. The law requires family memberal involvement in deciding the:

1. Type of special services required (e.g., speech therapy, counseling)
2. Educational placement (e.g., full-time regular class with support, resource room, special class)
3. Makeup of the individual education program (e.g., annual goals)

Students with mild disabilities cannot be evaluated or placed in a special education program without family member's consent. If family members do not agree with educational decisions about their child, they have the due process right to mediation and appeal. Figure 11.1 lists family member's due process rights. The fact that several family member–school disagreements about special education services have reached the Supreme Court highlights the importance of family member–school cooperation.

The IEP begins with the initial referral and concludes with the family members

FIGURE 11.1   Family Members' Due Process Rights

1. The right to examine school records.
2. The right to request a special education evaluation.
3. The right to refuse the school permission to do a special education evaluation.
4. The right of child to remain in a general education until family members agree to special education services.
5. The right to request an independent educational evaluation.
6. The right to bring an advocate to all meetings.
7. The right to participate in the development of an IEP.
8. The right to disagree with the IEP.
9. The right to appeal decisions made by the school system regarding special education services.
10. The right to review and amend the IEP.
11. The right to have a child educated in the least restrictive environment.

agreeing to special education services outlined in the program. The IEP is a management tool designed to ensure that special education services match a student's individual needs and that special education services are monitored. It contains annual goals, a statement about a student's educational strengths and weaknesses, and a description of special education and related services. Figure 11.2 lists the basic components of the IEP. The individual education program must be approved by family members before a student can be placed in a special education program. (See a sample IEP in Appendix D.)

In theory, the IEP meeting provides for maximum family member input into a child's special education program. Unfortunately, the reality often is different. Sometimes, family members are not viewed by educators as colleagues at the meeting. A survey of several hundred families (Lynch & Stein, 1987) reported that 50 percent of family members did not feel they were active participants and only 34 percent of family members made suggestions during the meeting. Sometimes, because of time conflicts, transportation problems, child care needs, or work commitments, family members are unable to attend the meeting. When family members are absent, the IEP usually is mailed to them for their signature.

When family members attend the IEP meeting, a variety of factors impede participation. Consider the following scene. A group of professionals are sitting around a table facing the family members. Each professional takes a turn reporting on the educational failure of their child. The family members are deluged with educational jargon like "subaverage IQ," "deficient adaptive behavior skills," "dyslexic," and "behavior disordered." Education jargon places the family members at a serious disadvantage as they attempt to follow what is being said. Without an advocate to help the family members sort out what is happening, the family members are in jeopardy of consenting to an IEP that is unclear.

All IEP meetings are not as muddled for family members as the one just described. When educators are sensitive to family members' feelings and take the time to explain what they are talking about, family members have an opportunity to be involved. Educators need to remember that it takes a good deal of resolve for a family member to participate in a meeting that is intended to analyze what is wrong with his or her child. One family member expressed her feelings this way (Roberts, 1986):

FIGURE 11.2 Components of an Individual Education Program

An IEP is a written plan provision of special education services for a student who is disabled.

Each IEP must contain:

1. A statement of the child's present level of educational performance.
2. A statement of annual goals.
3. A statement of the specific special educational and related services to be provided the child, and the extent to which the child will be able to participate in regular educational programs.
4. The projected dates for initiation of services and the anticipated duration of the services.
5. Appropriate criteria and evaluation procedures.

The IEP process was something that was really hard for me to accept and get into, because I'm not by nature an assertive person. In a group I don't speak up that much, but as a family member in an IEP conference, I have to. I have to be totally prepared. I may have a lot of confidence in the staff that's working with him; they're all great people. But I have to know what each is doing with Geoff and where they're headed with him. I need to review my concerns when I go to the conference, to speak up, and really be his advocate. I have to do that. I think the family member is the one who has the best whole concept of the child, with regard to where he's been and where he's going. And the family member has a lot to offer the staff members—knowledge and understanding of the child. (p. 206)

The IEP planning meeting is an important event in a family member's life. By following a few basic guidelines, educators can ensure that the meeting enhances rather than diminishes family member–teacher communication.

1. Before the meeting, tell family members how the meeting will be conducted, who will be attending, and what they can do to be effective participants.
2. Arrange seating so family members are not sitting on one side of a table, "squared off" against the professionals.
3. Avoid general negative statements like "Carlos is 8 but has a mental age of 5." There is enough valid criticism of educational assessment procedures to warrant tempering of professional enthusiasm for the accuracy of test results.
4. Encourage family member questions after each professional makes a contribution.
5. Be conscious of the group dynamics. Is one person dominating? Are there hidden agendas? Are the professionals communicating their views in plain language? Are family members giving off distress signals with body language? Most important, are family members being given ample opportunity to verbally participate?
6. When the meeting is over, summarize the group's conclusions and indicate one professional that the family members can contact to answer questions that may occur to them on the way home.

In order to ensure an appropriate education for students with disabilities, Congress mandated family member participation in IEP meetings. By encouraging active family memberal participation, educators not only fulfill their legal responsibilities, they also provide students with their best opportunity for success.

> **SPEEDBUMP—**You finished the book, congratulations! The authors sincerely hope it has met your needs. We would like to hear from you. Contact us at mhenley21@comcast.net.

SUMMARY

Teachers and families share a common vision. Both want children to develop the social and intellectual skills needed to function as contributing citizens. Homes, schools, and communities are besieged by the ravages of poverty, drugs, and alcohol. Schools and families need each other. When educators reach out to families and seek their involvement, schools improve, students achieve, and communities grow closer together.

Family members of children with mild disabilities need support and understanding as they deal with the daily stresses of modern life. When a child is evaluated by the school as having a mild disability, it affects all members of the family. This ripple effect in turn influences the family's ability to cope with the demands of family membering and education. There are many organizations that support families, yet many families struggle on in isolation, unaware of the network of help that is available to them. Family members need opportunities to communicate with others who share their problems. Family members need information about their rights and responsibilities as codeterminers of their child's appropriate education. Successful experiences with the schools are needed in order for family members to believe in their ability to promote their child's education. Most of all, family members need teachers who respect them and value their role in shaping the education of their children.

ACTIVITIES

1. Do a community survey of organizations in your community that provide support services to families. Visit a local Head Start program and inquire about the wraparound services offered by Head Start.

2. Ask the following to visit your class and participate in a panel discussion about school-family partnerships: school administrator (e.g., superintendent or principal), PTO parent, elementary teacher, middle or high school teacher, special education teacher, and a family member with a child in special education program.

3. Go to the Center for School Family and Community Partnerships website: www.csos.jhu.edu. Follow the TIPS link. Make a list of ideas for getting families more involved in their child's education. Use a search engine for other useful links and do a class presentation on fostering positive school-family partnerships.

4. Contact a local agency that provides support for family members who have children in special education. If you are unfamiliar with local agencies, go to www.ldamerica.org and type in your state in the search engine; this will provide a name of a contact person. Another good site is the Federation of Families for Children's Mental Health: www.ffcmh.org. Go to the "who we are" link which will take you to the local chapter link. From there, locate an individual who will be happy to visit your class.

5. Go to your college or university library. Review several issues of *Exceptional Parent*. Select an article that you think is relevant to your studies. Make a report to the class about your findings.

Appendix A: A Chronology

Appendix B: Commonly Used Psychoactive Medications

Appendix C: Tests

Appendix D: Sample Individualized Education Plan (IEP)

Appendix A   A Chronology

Date	Intellectual Disabilities	Emotional Disturbance	Learning Disabilities	Generic to General and Special Education
1799		Jean Itard's attempts to train Victor, the Wild Boy of Aveyron (France). Treatment centered around sensory stimulation exercises coupled with systematic teaching procedures.		
1792		Philippe Pinel appointed head of Bicêtre Hospital of mentally ill in Paris, France. Pinel influenced humane treatment.		
1802			Franz Joseph Gall speculated that specific regions of the brain control certain mental activities.	
1817				Thomas Gallaudet became principal of the first residential school for the deaf and mute persons in Hartford, CT.
1820s	Almshouses erected in America for the destitute, originally designed to provide humane and moral care for the poor; became catchalls for the retarded, insane, ill, and other afflicted.			
1828		Horace Mann influenced authorization of funds for state hospitals for the insane in Massachusetts.		
1831				Samuel Howe became director of the Perkins School, formerly called the New England Asylum for the Blind.
1834				Louis Braille publishes the first Braille code.
1830s & 1840s		Conditions in state hospitals were little better than almshouses. Other forms of treatment included public		Horace Mann set economic and legal foundations of American public education, while Secretary of Massachusetts Board of Education (1837–1848), he wrote bills which became national standard

(continued)

APPENDIX A   Continued

Date	Intellectual Disabilities	Emotional Disturbance	Learning Disabilities	Generic to General and Special Education
1830s & 1840s (*continued*)		auctions, selling of chattel slaves, and abandonment.		(e.g., lengths of school year, tax base for financial support of schools, standardized teacher training, standardized school curriculum, political selection of school superintendent, and so on). Established first state normal (teacher training) school (1839).
1837	Samuel Howe began a class for training retarded children at Perkins Institute in Boston, Massachusetts.			
1839				The first state normal school opens in Massachusetts. Elementary level teachers receive 11 weeks to one year of preparation.
1842	Edward Sequin was instrumental in founding the first school for care and education of mentally retarded (MR) students in Paris, France.			
1843		Dorothea Dix reported cruel and inhumane treatment to the Massachusetts Legislature (e.g., chains, locks, cages, bloodletting practices). Influenced construction of special asylums some improvement over prisons and poorhouses. Nonexistent rehabilitation and education programs.		
1846		First educational facility (Westborough, Massachusetts) for socially maladjusted youth. Established with reformatory and educational goals in mind; thus called a "reform school."		

Date			
1848	Massachusetts was the first to support state schools for the mentally retarded in the United States.		Depression brought financial strains. Dorothea Dix reveals shocking conditions in asylums.
1850s	Overcrowding doubled clientele of reform school. Custodial rather than instructional services rendered.		
1851	Harvey Willus was the first state-supported school for MR in New York (transferred from Albany to Syracuse in 1855). Other such schools followed in the northeastern and New England states: Ohio (1857); Connecticut (1858); Pennsylvania (1859); Kentucky (1860); Illinois (1865).		
1850s	Edward Sequin believed retardation to be treatable and curable. Environmental factors (e.g., health, diet) considered important.	Paul Broca demonstrated that speech disorders were the result of damage to the frontal convolutions of the brain. He proposed that the functions of the brain's left and right hemispheres were different.	
1860s	Prevailing belief that social deviance was inevitable product of immigrant population, largely poor and uneducated.		
Mid-1860s	Rise of Darwinist thought. Environmental view gave way to emphasis on innate deficiencies. Mood of pessimism became dominant. State institutions became more custodial. Samuel Howe was discouraged with the		National Deaf-Mute College opened, later renamed Gallaudet College.

(continued)

APPENDIX A   Continued

Date	Intellectual Disabilities	Emotional Disturbance	Learning Disabilities	Generic to General and Special Education
Mid-1860s (*continued*)	results of the Perkins Institute.			
1866		Samuel Howe became discouraged by increased size and bureaucratization of mental hospitals and reform schools.		
1870s		Establishment of "ungraded schools" for mischievous and disruptive children in New Haven, Connecticut (1871); New York City (1874); Cleveland, Ohio (1875).		
1870–1890	Herbert Spencer (Britain) developed a "philosophy of natural selection" (weaker members of society pose threat to future of mankind, thus only the most fit of human species be allowed to survive).			
1875–1900		Classes for socially maladjusted children grew rapidly.		
1887				Anne Sullivan begins work with Helen Keller.
1890s	Increased advocacy efforts for special classes or schools for recalcitrant or mentally deficient children.			More stringent administration of compulsory attendance laws. Educational Commission of the City of Chicago (Hapur Report) urged the establishment of ungraded classes for unmanageable children.
Late 1800s	First public school programs for the MR in Providence, Rhode Island (1896); Springfield, Massachusetts (1897); Chicago, Illinois (1898);			

Year		
1896	Boston, Massachusetts (1899); New York City (1900). Called classes for "backward" children.	First U.S. psychological clinic for children opened at the U. of PA by Lightner Witmer.
1897		National Education Association (NEA) approves the Department of Special Education.
1898		Alexander Graham Bell states that children with handicaps have a right to education in the public schools.
Turn of Century	Establishment of special classes to cope with children who presented problems for regular classrooms.	Anti-immigrant attitude perpetuated Social Darwinism.
1900		Special class programs for gifted begun in NYC and Worcester, Mass.
		Day classes are provided children with blindness in Chicago.
		The first electrical amplifying device is developed for persons with hearing impairments.
		Term "special education" used by Alexander Graham Bell at the NEA convention.
Early 1900s	MR children frequently assigned to foreign-speaking "steamer" classes; many normal foreign children placed in classes for the mentally deficient.	
1902	Ungraded classes in New Haven, Connecticut, reported to serve three distinct types of children grouped together: incorrigible boys, mentally defective children, and non-English-speaking youth.	
1904	Alfred Binet creates the first paper intelligence test.	Preparatory schools opened for gifted students in Worcester, Mass. New Jersey's Vineland Training School held summer classes for teachers of students with M.R. Public Law 58–171, promoted circulation of reading materials for persons with blindness.
	G. Stanley Hall, founder of the American Psychological Association and originator of child-study movement, published *Adolescence*, a two-volume study of youth development and adaptation to the environment.	

(continued)

APPENDIX A Continued

Date	Intellectual Disabilities	Emotional Disturbance	Learning Disabilities	Generic to General and Special Education
1905				Maximillian P.E. Groszman became the founder and director of the National Association for the Study and Education of Exceptional Children; was first to use term "exceptional." E. L. Thorndike planned a scale to measure educational achievement.
1907	Indiana passed first sterilization law for mental defectives.			
1908	Henry G. Goddard, while Director of Research at the Training School in Vineland, New Jersey, translated the Binet intelligence scales into English and made adaptations for their use in the United States.	Clifford Beers published personal experiences in mental institutions for a depressive mental disorder. Exposed inhumane and inadequate treatment.		
1909		Elizabeth Farrell helped establish the first special education class in New York City.		
1911	Goddard published own version of the Binet–Simon Test. New Jersey was the first state to pass legislation concerning the education of MR children in the public schools. Defined MR as "three or more years retarded in mental development."			
1911	New Jersey mandated special classes when number of students with MR in district totaled 10 or more.			

1912	Devereau School Founded in Philadelphia for treating youth with mental retardation and emotional disturbance.
1912	Publication of "The Kallikak Family," which gave fuel to the prevailing eugenics theory. Portrayed the "feebleminded" as a menace to society and to the future of the human race. Proposed that social undesirables (e.g., criminals, paupers, drunkards) arose from the genetic stock of the mentally deficient.
1914	Charles Scott Berry set up the first teacher-training program in special education at a residential school for MR in Michigan. St. Louis, Missouri, public school system adopted eligibility standards for special schools for the severely MR and ungraded classes for borderline and backward students.
1915	Connecticut Board of Education hired Arnold Gesell as first official school psychologist to examine slow-learning children and to devise better methods for their school instruction.
1915	*Laggards in Our Schools* by Leonard P. Ayres, used as one of first special education texts.
1916	Lewis Terman produced the Stanford–Binet Scale of Intelligence.
1917	James Hinshelwood, a French physician, defined "word blindness" as a condition in which an individual with normal vision is unable to interpret written or

(continued)

APPENDIX A Continued

Date	Intellectual Disabilities	Emotional Disturbance	Learning Disabilities	Generic to General and Special Education
1917 (continued)			printed language. Hinshelwood theorized that this difficulty is caused by a defect in the left hemisphere of the brain, the portion that stores memories of words and letters.	
Between 1852 and 1918				Compulsory school attendance required in all states of the Union, beginning with Massachusetts (1852) and ending with Mississippi (1918).
1918	Wyoming appointed State Director of Special Education responsible for MR, crippled, and speech-defective children.			
1919	St. Louis eligibility standards of 1914 were adopted statewide and subsequently adopted by other states.			
Years prior to 1920	Relatively small number of teachers trained to work with mentally or socially handicapped. Most facilities were residential with staff members trained on the premises. Technology was not yet developed for assessing individual differences, and special education was not included in curricula at teacher colleges.			
1920s		August Aichhorn, student of Sigmund Freud, developed residential facility for aggressive, delinquent boys.		Columbia University Teachers College prepared teachers of the gifted.
1922	W.E. Fernald persuaded Mass. to set up statewide system of mental clinics for diagnosing children with MR.			The International Council for the Education of Exceptional Children (CEC) founded with NYC. Original purposes for establishing the CEC organization included:

1924	Estimated 43,000 persons with MR reside in institutions; 40 state institutions nationwide in existence.	American Orthopsychiatric Association founded. Concerned with early prevention and correction of children's behavior disorders.	1) To emphasize the education of the special child rather than his identification or classification; 2) To establish professional standards for teachers in the field of special education; 3) To unite those interested in the problem of the special child.
			Classification of exceptionalities published by John Lewis Horn in the *Education of Exceptional Children*.
1925		Samuel Orton coined the word "strephosymbolia" (twisted symbols).	
1926		Sir Henry Head theorized that disorders in language could not be dichotomized as sensory or motor.	Hollingsworth implemented enrichment programs for the gifted in New York public schools.
1922–1932	MR enrollment in separate facilities within public school systems more than tripled.	Growth of separate facilities within public school systems for deviant children.	
1928			Seeing-eye dogs for the blind are introduced in the U.S.
			Courses in special education offered at 43 teacher training institutions.
1929		Special classes for socially maladjusted frequently called "disciplinary classes." Employed strong arm rather than education or rehabilitation approach.	Samuel T. Orton speculated that one side of the brain dominated the language processes; therefore, he concluded that disabled children who had no demonstrable brain injury had failed to establish hemispheric dominance.
By 1930	Sixteen states passed legislation regarding education of the mentally handicapped.		U.S. Office of Education established a section of Exceptional Children and Youth administered by Elise Martens.

(continued)

APPENDIX A Continued

Date	Intellectual Disabilities	Emotional Disturbance	Learning Disabilities	Generic to General and Special Education
Early 1930s			Kurt Goldstein observed meticulosity, perseveration, figure-ground configuration, forced responses to stimuli, and catastrophic reaction in adult, brain-injured patients.	
The 1930s	Decrease in special programs for MR and socially deviant youth due to: 1) Less money for special programs; and 2) Dissatisfaction with the quality of education in special classes.			
	Public schools more likely to provide separate facilities for MR children than for any other exceptionality group, especially the northeast and north central states.	Establishment of disciplinary classes for truant and incorrigible youth in the schools.		
	Building principals often experienced difficulty in distinguishing between pupils who were "fit subjects" for disciplinary classes and those who were mentally retarded.			
1932				Thirteen states established a state director in charge of administrative special education services.
1933				The first teaching certificates for special education are issued (Mental Retardation, Deaf, Speech Defective, Partially Sighted, Blind, and Crippled).
				The International Council for the Education of Exceptional Children was shortened to the International Council for the Exceptional Children (ICEC).
1934				*The Board of Education of Cleveland Heights v. State ex rel. Goldman* ruled that the exclusion of a child with low mental functioning, on the basis of tests prescribed by the State Department of Education, was unauthorized.

Year			
1935	Edgar Arnold Doll publishes the Vineland Social Maturity Scale. New York was the first state to certify school psychologists. Roles consisted largely of evaluating and making recommendations for placement in special services of children viewed as "backward" or MR.		Certification guidelines are established by the American Association of Instructors of the Blind. Talking books on phonograph records are produced.
Late 1930s and Early 1940s		Alfred A. Strauss and Heinz Werner investigated brain-injured, mentally retarded children. Findings led to the identification of the exogenous subgroup of retarded children (externally brain-injured).	
1943		Grace Fernald used the VAKT (visual-auditory-kinesthetic-tactile) approach in the development of remedial reading programs.	
1944		The Sonja Shankman Orthogenic School opened in Chicago under Bruno Bettelheim for children with emotional disturbance.	
The 1940s-W.W.II years	Use of handicapped (including MR) in many jobs due to able-bodied men being away at war.	Laura Lehtinen collaborated with Strauss to develop teaching procedures. Strauss and Lehtinen coauthored *Psychopathology and Education of the Brain-Injured*	World War II years necessitated man power.

(continued)

APPENDIX A   Continued

Date	Intellectual Disabilities	Emotional Disturbance	Learning Disabilities	Generic to General and Special Education
The 1940s-W.W.II years (*continued*)			*Child* (1947) in which two interventions were suggested: 1) Manipulation and controlling the environment, and 2) Teaching the child voluntary control.	
1946		Division of Child Welfare in NYC organized "600 schools" for children viewed as emotionally disturbed or socially maladjusted. Despite therapeutic intent, these schools were operated as warehouses for uncontrollable boys and were custodial in nature. Fritz Redl and David Wineman opened Pioneer House, a residential treatment center for severely aggressive adolescents. Developed the Life Space Interview intervention.		
Until Early 1950s	Nearly all schools had policies that excluded children with I.Q.s below the mild range. Parents of these children were expected to educate them at home or place them in state or private residential facilities.	Pearl Berkowitz and Esther Rothman extended psychotherapy into the classroom at Bellevue Hospital in N.Y.		
Early 1950s	Federal funding for teacher preparation in MR enacted.	William Morse designed mental-health milieu in camp setting.		
1948 to 1952 to 1958	Number of children enrolled in special public school programs increased from			

Year			
1950	87,000 to 113,000 to over 213,000.		
	National Association for Retarded Citizens (NARC) first organized in Minneapolis, Minnesota. This organization was considered the primary source of help to families with retarded children, as well as a major information disseminating and legislative lobbying force.		
The 1950s			William M. Cruikshank facilitated the transfer of brain-injured research from exogenous retarded children to children with normal intelligence.
			Cruikshank conducted the Montgomery County Project in Maryland.
1951		Fritz Redl and David Wineman publish *Children Who Hate*.	
1953	P.L. 83–531 Cooperative Research Act. Funds earmarked for research with students with MR.	B.F. Skinner published *Science and Human Behavior*. Proposed operant conditioning as treatment model for B.D.	
1954			Cooperative Research Act of 1954 (P.L. 85–531) authorized support for cooperative research in education; funding was granted for this in 1957.
1955			Helmer R. Myklebust defined language as symbolic behavior (i.e., using words as symbols for expressing ideas and feelings and labeling objects). Strauss and Newell C. Kephart coauthored Vol. II of

(continued)

APPENDIX A   Continued

Date	Intellectual Disabilities	Emotional Disturbance	Learning Disabilities	Generic to General and Special Education
1955 (*continued*)			*Psychopathology* . . . in which comparisons were made of research on brain-injured children of normal intelligence with research on mentally retarded brain-injured children.	All 48 states had established legal provisions for some sort of state assistance, advisory and/or financial, to local special education programs. The degree of involvement and support varied from state to state, and the growth of special education services has not been at the same rate for all types of exceptional programs.
1956			Spaulding presented an approach to written language disability called Unified Phonics Methods. Words are pronounced and component sounds are written in accordance with the rules of English spelling. Jerome Bruner coauthored *A Study of Thinking* (Bruner, Goodnow, & Austin), which stressed the importance of studying covert cognitive processes.	
1957				Public attitude toward education for all children was spurred by general concern of the populace for American education after the Russian launching of Sputnik.
1958 & 1959	P.L. 85–926 and P.L. 86–158 authorized fellowship awards for graduate students intent on careers as teacher-trainers or administrators of the mentally retarded.		Noam Chomsky gave support to "inner thinking processes."	
1950s & 1960s	Improved education and training of MR occurred under the Kennedy administration.			

1960		CEC publishes first set of professional standards for special education. U.S. Office of Education funds grant for CEC to operate the ERIC Clearinghouse on Exceptional Children. Federal Bureau of Education for the Handicapped (BEH) formed. Encouraged training, research, demonstration, etc.
	Richard Whelan used token reinforcement methods at the Children's Rehabilitation Unit. Association for the Advancement of Behavior Therapy founded.	
1960s	Edward L. Thorndike, called the "father of reinforcement theory," believed the connection between stimulus and response represented all learning.	J. M. Wepman postulated that the language "transmission" process is divided into receptive and expressive modes. "Integration" provides for the decoding and encoding of previously learned patterns to give meaning to the stimulus. Emphasized role of recall, transmission (receptive and expressive modes), and integration (the decoding and encoding of previously learned language patterns).
		Beginnings of educational focus on children with learning difficulties. Ogden R. Lindsley developed a comprehensive set of measuring procedures, called "precision teaching," which includes pinpointing behavior, counting and charting performance, and making instructional decisions based on performance data.
Early to Mid-1960s	Norris Haring and E. Lakin Phillips combined Cruickshank's structured-environment classroom and B.F. Skinner's operant conditioning to develop educational programs for emotionally disturbed children.	

(continued)

381

APPENDIX A Continued

Date	Intellectual Disabilities	Emotional Disturbance	Learning Disabilities	Generic to General and Special Education
Early to Mid-1960s *(continued)*		The Council for Children with Behavioral Disorders (CCBD) was founded as a division of CEC.		
1962		Nicholas Long became Director of Hillcrest Children's Center, Washington, D.C. (residential school for B.D.). Long trained teachers in psycho-educational principles. Norris Haring and E. Lakin Phillips applied behaviorism in their Arlington Project for educating students with behavior disorders.	Term "learning disabilities" was introduced by Samuel Kirk at a national conference of parent organizations and subsequently adopted. Association for Children with Learning Disabilities (ACLD) was formed as a parent, teacher, professional interest group.	
1963	Passage of P.L. 88–164 increased support for training of personnel and extended support for professional training to severe areas of childhood exceptionality, including mental retardation and emotional disturbance; authorized use of funds for research and demonstration projects in field of handicapped education.		Department of Health, Education, and Welfare sponsored several task forces to study brain-injured children with learning problems. Term "minimal brain dysfunction" (MBD) was introduced.	
Mid-1960s				Host of domestic legislation was enacted at the federal level, aimed at launching "War on Poverty" and achieving the "Great Society."

1964	Council for Children with Behavior Disorders established as a division under CEC.
1965	P.L. 89–313 encouraged programs to educate children with disabilities residing in institutions and other state-supported residential facilities. P.L. 89–105, added to P.L. 88–164, permitted the construction and operation of research facilities and related programs, including the training of special personnel. National Society for Autistic Children (NSAC) was founded. Was one of the first major parent-interest groups devoted to concerns of the emotionally disturbed child. Organization has sought public school involvement for autistic children and has opposed their placement in private or residential facilities.	P.L. 89–10, Elementary and Secondary Education Act, Title VI (ESEA) provided assistance to children in "disadvantaged" areas (including handicapped children). Act was part of the "Great Society's" legislative package and was considered a significant effort to alleviate poverty through schooling. Eleven colleges and universities received funding by the U.S. Office of Education to help support training of personnel in this field. Office of Economic Opportunity (OEO) established to aid the culturally disadvantaged or deprived child. Head Start, an OEO-funded project, along with remedial reading, counseling, and tutorial services was begun. Student Council for Exceptional Children (SCEC) is organized.
1965	Burton Blatt publishes exposé on institutions "Christmas in Purgatory."	A separate Bureau for the Education of the Handicapped (BEH) was created within the U.S. Office of Education. Special Education was included in the top policy-making levels for the first time.
1967	Hobson v. Hanson litigation resulted in finding the "tracking" system in Washington, D.C., to be unconstitutional. Based on standardized test results, children were placed in honors, general, or special programs. Relying on Brown v. Board of Education, the court held that assessment measures were culturally biased and sustained an	

(continued)

APPENDIX A Continued

Date	Intellectual Disabilities	Emotional Disturbance	Learning Disabilities	Generic to General and Special Education
1967 (*continued*)	unjustifiable racial separation of students. A disproportionate number of African American children were enrolled in special classes.			P.L. 90–538 authorized the negotiation of grants and contracts with both private and public agencies to establish experimental preschool and early education programs for special needs students.
1968	Lloyd Dunn questioned the wisdom of special self-contained class placement for students with MR.	Joint Commission on Mental Health of children estimated at least 100,000 children were in residential treatment institutions for B.D., and 1.5 million children and youth were in need of psychiatric services. Frank M. Hewett designed the "engineered" classroom using developmental sequence of educational goals known as the Santa Monica Project.	The Division for Children with Learning Disabilities (DCLD) (now Council for Learning Disabilities) was organized as a professional division within the CEC. The National Advisory Committee of Handicapped Children (NACHC) was formed to develop a definition for learning disabilities. *Journal of Learning Disabilities* was published.	P.L. 90–583 (Handicapped Children's Early Education Assistance Act), established experimental demonstration centers for the education of preschool children with disabilities.
1969			P.L. 91–230, the Specific Learning Disabilities Act of 1969, was passed along with all of the categories of programs and services for educating children with special needs who receive federal assistance. The definition developed by the NACHC under Kirk's leadership was used in this act.	P.L. 91–61 provided the authority to the Secretary of health, education, and welfare to contract a university to develop, construct, and operate a national center of educational media and materials for persons with disabilities.
Late 1960s & 1970s	Skinner defined two types of learned behavior: respondent (involuntary) and operant (voluntary). Transferred work with animals in the laboratory (1950s) to observable, measurable events in the educational arena (1960s and 1970s).			"Right to fair classification" cases filed as class action suits. Parents and other interested parties argued that the labeling and placement procedure by which children are processed into special education is culturally discriminatory and a violation of the 14th

	Amendment's Constitutional guarantee for due process and equal protection under the law.
	Jean Piaget's developmental theory suggested that instruction should recognize maturational growth and not require students to perform skills for which they are not ready.
Early 1970s	The optacon, an optical scan of a printed page, generates a tactile impression of letters for persons with blindness.
The 1970s	Juvenile justice system dealt with 900,000 youth ages 10 to 17, which was 3 percent of this age group.
	NARC organized effective lobbying forces and succeeded in bringing about massive increases in school services for children previously thought to be "unteachable."
1971	Pennsylvania Association for Retarded Children alleged violations of due process and equal protection under the 14th Amendment of the U.S. Constitution regarding barring of low I.Q children from public schools in that state. Similar "right-to-education" suits initiated in other states.
1971	*Larry P. v. Riles* was filed as a class action suit in California on behalf of several African American children who had been placed and retained in EMR classes. Plaintiffs alleged use of racially and culturally biased testing procedures, which violated the Civil Rights Act of 1871 and the right to equal protection under the California Constitution and the 14th Amendment of the U.S. Constitution.

(continued)

Date	Intellectual Disabilities	Emotional Disturbance	Learning Disabilities	Generic to General and Special Education
1972	A preliminary injunction was issued by the court halting the use of I.Q. tests in the state of California for placing African American children in classes for the EMR.			P.L. 92–424, mandated a minimum of 10 percent of the enrollment slots in Head Start programs be made available to students with disabilities. *Mills v. the Board of Education* mandated the District of Columbia serve all students with disabilities.
1973		Peter Knoblock promotes open education for disturbed children.		P.L. 93–112, Section 504, specified that no individual with a disability should be excluded from the participation in, be denied benefits of, or subjected to discrimination under any program or activity receiving federal financial assistance.
1974	Carl Fenichel developed the League School in Brooklyn (first day school for psychotic children). Enlisted parents as partners.			P.L. 93–380, Title VI, extended the Education of Handicapped Act. Required states to locate and serve all children with handicaps. Assured an education with one's peers, if possible, and mandated nondiscriminatory evaluation materials. Included in law was Family Educational Rights and Privacy Act of 1974, referred to as Buckley Act. This Act protects the confidentiality of school records and provides procedures to challenge questionable information in student records.
1975		U.S. Senate report (subcommittee to Investigate Juvenile Delinquency, 1975) documented growth of violence and crime in schools.		Public Law 94–142, Education for All Handicapped Children Act (EHA), provided for a free, appropriate public education for all handicapped children, and defined special education and related services. Mandated that an individualized education plan (IEP) or an individualized family services plan (IFSP) be developed for every child found eligible for special education or early intervention.

1975	P.L. 94–142, The Education for Handicapped Childrens Act, is enacted into Federal Law
1976	CEC revised Professional Standards and Guidelines in Special Education.
	The Kurzweil Reader, a prototype translator of printed text into speech for readers with blindness, is invented.
	Gifted and Talented Children's Act (Title IX-A), provides funds to state and local education agencies and public and private agencies to meet the needs of gifted and talented students.
1978	Formation of the National Joint Commission for Learning Disabilities (NJCLD).
Late 1970s	The Reagan Administration attempted to deregulate and decentralize all phases of public education; however, most categorical services and mandates regulating special education survived this initiative.
	Department of Education established by Congress.
	A separate U.S. Department of Education established, removing responsibilities from the Department of Health, Education, and Welfare.
1980	U.S. Dept. of Health and Human Services reported 15,000 children ages 14 and under admitted to inpatient facilities and over a quarter million seen in outpatient psychiatric clinics.
1981	S-1 v. Turlington rules that complete cessation of services for students with disabilities is not allowed; expulsion is allowable under some circumstances.
1982	The DCLD membership voted to withdraw from CEC and form an independent organization, the Council for Learning Disabilities (CLD). A cadre of former DCLD members began a new CEC division called the Division for Learning Disabilities (DLD).
1983	Office of Special Education and Rehabilitative Services (OSERS) created under the newly established Department of Education.

(continued)

APPENDIX A   Continued

Date	Intellectual Disabilities	Emotional Disturbance	Learning Disabilities	Generic to General and Special Education
1983 *(continued)*				Public Law 98–199 (EHA Amendments) passed. Reaffirmed the federal role in special education by expanding P.L. 94–142 with supported preschool, secondary, and post secondary programs for the handicapped, and support for special education teacher preparation, early childhood education, parent training, and information dissemination.
1985				Children "at risk"—poor, nonwhite, disabled, and female become the focus of education reform.
1986				Public Law 99–457 (EHA Amendments) reauthorized existing EHA, amended PL 94–142 to include financial incentives for states to educate children ages 3 to 5 by the 1990–91 school year, and established incentive grants to promote programs serving handicapped infants (birth to age 2).
1988				The Gifted and Talented Students Education Act of 1988 authorized funding of a National Research Center and demonstration programs to build the nation-wide capability to meet the needs of gifted and talented students, especially those from traditionally underserved populations.
1989				Academic standards take the spotlight. The National Council of Teachers of Mathematics is the first to state its curriculum standards.
1990				P.L. 101–336, Americans with Disabilities Act (ADA), gives civil rights protection to individuals with disabilities in private sector employment, all public services, public accommodations, transportation, and telecommunications. Patterned after (and extends) to Section 504 of the Rehabilitation Act of 1973. Prohibits discrimination on the basis of disability and requires agencies to provide "reasonable accommodations."

Year	
	P.L. 101–392 (Carl D. Perkins Vocational and Technology Education Act) provides resources to improve educational programs needed in order to work in a technologically advanced society. Guarantees full vocational, educational opportunities for all special needs populations.
1990 to 1991	The U.S. House of Representatives opened for citizen comment the issue of a separate exceptionality category for students with attention deficit disorders. The issue died without legislative action.
	Public Law 101–476, Individuals with Disabilities Education Act (IDEA), reauthorized and renamed existing EHA. This amendment to EHA changed the term "handicap" to "disability," expanded related services, and required individual education programs (IEPs) to contain transitional goals and objectives for adolescents (ages 16 and above, special situations age 14). The exceptionality categories of autism and traumatic brain injury were added.
1991	National Education Goals 2000 are adopted. Encourages involvement of reform-minded communities, national examinations, and parental choices including private schools.
1992	Rehabilitation Act amendments establish the presumption that anyone can be employed and increase the focus on vocational rehabilitation services for minorities.
1994	P.L. 103–239 (School to Work Opportunities Act) promotes collaboration and problem solving by the Department of Education and Labor. Encourages partnership models between school-based and employment-based sites at the local level. Promotes interagency agreements, technical assistance, and services to employers, educators, case managers, and others.
1995	CEC published its third set of standards for the preparation and certification of special education teachers.

(continued)

APPENDIX A Continued

Date	Intellectual Disabilities	Emotional Disturbance	Learning Disabilities	Generic to General and Special Education
1997				P.L. 105–17 (Amendment to and reauthorization of IDEA) adds general education curriculum to student's IEP, modifies alternative placement options pending discipline determinations, and modifies transition requirements.
2002				No Child Left Behind Act (NCLB). Reauthorization of the Elementary and Secondary Education Act. Mandates standardized testing of students with disabilities. Sets specific goals for progress in reading, math, and science.
2004				P.L. 108–446 reauthorization of IDEA. Establishes new criteria for identifying learning disabilities and disciplining students with special needs. Reduces paperwork and streamlines due process procedures. Addresses standards for qualified special education teachers.
2007	American Association of Individuals with Developmental Disabilities changed terminology from "mental retardation" to "intellectual disability."			

Bibliography

Cullinan, D., Epstein, M.H., & Lloyd, J.W. (1983). *Behavior disorders of children and adolescents.* Englewood Cliffs, NJ: Prentice-Hall, Inc.

Gearheart, B.R. (1974). *Organization and administration of educational programs for exceptional children.* Springfield, IL: Charles C Thomas, Publisher.

Rhodes, W.C., & Tracy, M.L. (1966). *A study of child variance: Conceptual models* (Vols. 1 & 2). Ann Arbor, MI: University of Michigan.

The Council for Exceptional Children. (1997, May & June), *Teaching Exceptional Children,* 29(5), 5–49.

Appendix B: Commonly Used Psychoactive Medications*

Stimulants

Expected Classroom Effects

Stimulants are the most widely used drugs in the treatment of students with mild disabilities. Their intended effects are to make the students more ready to learn rather than to make the students learn. They have their so-called "paradoxical effect" of decreasing symptoms by increasing behaviors that inhibit hyperactivity, distractibility, and inattention, which often interfere with a readiness to learn.

Stimulants Commonly Used with Students with Mild Disabilities

Dextroamphetamine sulfate.   (Dexedrine) is usually administered in 5 milligram dosages (daily at 8 A.M. and 12 noon). Less classroom restlessness, increased attention span, and improvements in social and emotional behavior patterns are the expected effects. Most common side effects are loss of appetite and loss of sleep; less common are headaches with blurred vision, apathy, stupor, tiredness, dry mouth, and drug tolerance over long periods of use.

Methylphenidate hydrochloride.   (Ritalin) is usually administered in a single 20 milligram dose in the morning or in two 10 milligram doses in the morning and afternoon; it is generally taken before a meal. Less classroom restlessness, increased attention span, and improvements in social and emotional behavior patterns are the expected effects. Most common side effects are loss of sleep; less common are headaches with blurred vision, apathy, stupor, tiredness, dry mouth, and drug tolerance over long periods of use. Ritalin does not suppress appetite as much as Dexedrine.

Magnesium pemoline.   (Cylert) is usually administered once a day in a 37.5 milligram dosage and is considered slower acting than other stimulants. Less classroom restlessness, increased attention span, and improvements in social and emotional behavior patterns are the expected effects. Most common side effects are loss of appetite and loss of sleep; less common are headaches with blurred vision, apathy, stupor, tiredness, dry mouth, and drug tolerance over long periods of use. Cylert is preferred over Dexedrine because it does not suppress most children's appetites as much.

---

* *Source:* B. Algozzine, *Behavior Problem Management: Educator's Resource Service.* Rockville, MD: Aspen Publishers, 1997.

Minor Tranquilizers

Expected Classroom Effects

Minor tranquilizers are the second most commonly used drugs in the treatment of students with mild disabilities. Their intended effects are to reduce anxiety and agitation associated with some emotional and learning problems. The goal again is to help students become more receptive to instruction.

Minor Tranquilizers Commonly Used with Students with Mild Disabilities

Amitriptyline hydrochloride.   (Elavil) is usually administered in varying dosages according to level of problems, but is not recommended for students under 12. Expected effects include antidepressant and sedative action. Most common side effects are sleepiness, dry mouth, blurred vision, nightmares, dizziness when first standing up, and weight gain.

Maprotilene hydrochloride.   (Ludiomil) is usually administered in initial dosage of 75 milligrams daily that can be divided; dosages of as low as 25 milligrams are recommended for some. It is indicated for treatment of depressive illness and relief of anxiety associated with depression. Expected effects include antidepressant and sedative action. Most common side effects are sleepiness, dry mouth, blurred vision, nightmares, dizziness when first standing up, and weight gain.

Imapramine hydrochloride.   (Tofranil) is usually administered in one 10–25 milligram dose an hour before bed to control enuresis or 75 milligrams once a day for more serious problem behaviors. It is the most widely recognized and recommended antidepressant for children under 12 years of age; there can be as much as a three-week lag before effects are noticed. Controlled bed-wetting and improved emotional and social patterns result in children who are depressed or overly anxious. Most common side effects are dry mouth, urinary retention, blurred vision, tremors, drowsiness, sweating, and some postural rigidity.

Chlordiazepoxide hydrochloride.   (Librium) is usually administered in divided doses up to 30 milligrams a day; it is not recommended for children under six. Expected effects include reduction in anxiety, general relaxation, sense of well-being, and general drowsiness. Most common side effects are confusion, skin eruptions, edema, gastrointestinal symptoms, unwanted drowsiness, jaundice, and some changes in electroencephalogram patterns.

Hydroxine hydrochloride.   (Atarax) is usually administered in varying doses according to the level of the individual's problems. Expected effects include reduction in anxiety, aggressiveness, and hyperactivity. Most common side effects are tolerance, dependence, and dry mouth.

Meprobamate.   (Equanil) is usually administered 2 or 3 times a day in 100–200 milligram dosages. Expected effects include reduction in anxiety; it is used for its sedative effects. Most common side effects are unwanted drowsiness, dependency, and hematologic disorders.

Deanol acetamid obenzoate. (Deaner) is usually administered in one 100 milligram dose in the morning. Improved emotional and social patterns result in children who are immature or anxious. Most common side effects are headaches, constipation, insomnia, and skin rashes.

Major Tranquilizers

Expected Classroom Effects

Major tranquilizers are less commonly used than stimulants and minor tranquilizers in the treatment of students with mild disabilities. Their intended effects are to reduce symptoms associated with more severe disabilities, including depression, psychotic behavior, and delusions associated with clinical forms of emotional disturbance. The reduction in symptoms is associated with a more favorable clinical receptiveness for behavioral intervention.

Major Tranquilizers Commonly Used with Students with Mild Disabilities

Haloperidol. (Haldol) is usually administered in 1 milligram dosages several times a day; it is not recommended for children. Haldol is used to treat mania, paranoia, social withdrawal, and aggressive problems associated with schizophrenia. Most common side effects are skin reactions, jaundice, and impaired vision.

Chlorpromazine hydrochloride. (Thorazine) is usually administered in 10–24 milligram dosages two or three times a day; it can be increased to 50 milligrams for adolescents. Expected effects include reduction in activity and general reduction in aggressive, negative symptoms commonly seen in seriously disturbed individuals. Most common side effects are skin reactions, impaired vision, and weight gain.

Thioridiazine hydrochloride. (Mellaril) is usually administered in 10 milligram dosages three or four times a day for preschoolers and in 25 milligram dosages three or four times a day for older children. Expected effects include antidepressive symptoms, reduced anxiety, aggression reduction, and less overall activity. Most common side effects are sexual dysfunction in males, disturbed color vision, and weight gain.

Anticonvulsants

Expected Classroom Effects

Anticonvulsants are commonly used in the treatment of students with sudden, brief, localized seizures or widespread convulsive seizures associated with epilepsy and some types of mild disabilities. Therapeutic effects do not cure convulsive disorders, but do not control seizures without altering other functions of the Central Nervous System.

Anticonvulsants Commonly Used with Students with Mild Disabilities

Phenobarbital.   (Luminal) is usually administered in 100 milligram dosages and may require as long as 15 minutes to take effect. Expected effects include control of grand mal seizures. Most common side effects are sedation, rashes, slurred speech.

Diphenylhydantoin.   (Dilantin) is usually administered in varying milligram dosages dependent on age of individual, ranging from 50 milligrams for 1–2 year olds to 300–400 milligrams for adolescents. Expected effects include control of grand mal seizures; generally considered drug of choice for most forms of epilepsy (except petit mal seizures). Most common side effects are ataxia, nystagmus, vertigo, blurred vision, confusion, hallucinations, nausea, and urinary incontinence.

Ethosuximide.   (Zarontin) is usually administered in 0.5–1.0 milligram dosages two or three times a day. Expected effects include control of petit mal seizures; generally considered drug of choice for this form of seizures. Most common side effects are gastric distress, nausea, vomiting, anorexia, headaches, fatigue, dizziness, and blood disorders.

Carbamazepine.   (Tegretol) is usually administered in varying dosages relative to diagnosis and age. Expected effects include reduction of psychomotor and grand mal seizures. Most common side effects are drowsiness, double vision, uncoordination, rapid eye movement, nausea, and skin rashes.

Ethosuximide.   (Zarontin) is usually administered in 0.5–1.0 milligram dosages two or three times a day. Expected effects include contol of petit mal seizures; generally considered drug of choice for this form of seizures. Most common side effects are gastric distress, nausea, vomiting, anorexia, headaches, fatigue, dizziness, and blood disorders.

Appendix C: Tests

Frequently Used Achievement Tests

Test	Major Areas	Type of Test		Standardization		Administration	
Name	Tested	Formal	Informal	Norm-Referenced	Criterion-Referenced	Individual	Group
Brigance-R Diagnostic Inventories	reading, writing, spelling, mathematics, language, motor skills		X		X	X	
Diagnostic Achievement Battery (DAB)	listening, speaking, reading, writing, mathematics	X		X		X	
Kaufman Test of Educational Achievement (KTEA)	reading, spelling, mathematics	X		X		X	
Peabody Individual Achievement Test-Revised (PIAT-R)	mathematics, reading, spelling, general information	X		X		X	
Wide Range Achievement Test-Revised (WRAT-R)	reading, spelling, arithmetic	X		X		X	
Gilmore Oral Reading Test (GORT)	oral reading	X		X		X	
Durrell Analysis of Reading Difficulty	oral and silent reading, listening, comprehension, word analysis, spelling, handwriting	X		X		X	
Gates-Mac-Ginitie Reading Tests	silent reading, vocabulary, and comprehension	X		X			X

(continued)

Frequently Used Achievement Tests *(continued)*

Test	Major Areas	Type of Test		Standardization		Administration	
Name	*Tested*	*Formal*	*Informal*	*Norm-Referenced*	*Criterion-Referenced*	*Individual*	*Group*
Gray Oral Reading Tests-Revised (GORT-R)	oral reading	X		X		X	
Slosson Oral Reading Test	word reading	X		X		X	
Test of Reading Comprehension (TORC)	reading comprehension	X		X		X	
Woodcock Reading Mastery Tests-Revised (WRMT-R)	reading	X		X		X	
The Boder Test of Reading-Spelling Patterns	reading, spelling		X			X	
Test of Written Language (TOWL)	written language	X		X		X	X
Larsen-Hammill Test of Written Spelling (TWS-2)	written spelling	X		X		X	X
Enright R Diagnostic Inventory of Basic Arithmetic Skills	math computation	X			X	X	X
Key Math-Revised	mathematics	X			X	X	

Frequently Used Intelligence Tests

Test	Major Areas	Type of Test		Standardization		Administration	
Name	*Tested*	*Formal*	*Informal*	*Norm-Referenced*	*Criterion-Referenced*	*Individual*	*Group*
Coloured Progressive Matrices (CPM)	visual perception and analogous reasoning	X		X		X	
Denver Developmental Screening Test-Revised (DDST)	social, fine motor, gross motor, and language skills	X				X	
Detroit Tests of Learning Aptitude-Revised (DTLA-2)	vocabulary sequencing, detail recognition, and memory	X		X		X	
Detroit Tests of Learning Aptitude-Primary (DTLA-P)	verbal and nonverbal aptitudes, structural and conceptual aptitudes, memory and motor skills	X		X		X	
Goodenough-Harris Drawing Test	conceptual and intellectual maturity and personality characteristics	X				X	X
Kaufman Assessment Battery for Children (K-ABC)	cognitive ability and achievement	X		X		X	
McCarthy Scales of Children's Abilities (MSCA)	general intellectual ability	X		X		X	

(continued)

Frequently Used Intelligence Tests *(continued)*

Test	Major Areas	Type of Test		Standardization		Administration	
Name	*Tested*	*Formal*	*Informal*	*Norm-Referenced*	*Criterion-Referenced*	*Individual*	*Group*
Slosson Intelligence Test for Children and Adults (SIT)	mental ability	X		X		X	
Stanford-Binet Intelligence Scale (4th ed.) (SB)	verbal reasoning, quantitative reasoning, abstract/ reasoning, short-term memory	X		X		X	
System of Multicultural Pluristic Assessment (SOMPA)	cognitive abilities, sensory-motor skills, and adaptive behavior	X		X		X	
Wechsler Intelligence Scale for Children-Revised (WISC-R)	general intelligence	X		X		X	
Woodcock-Johnson Psycho-Educational Battery-Revised (WJ-R)	cognitive ability and academic skills in reading, writing, mathematics, and general knowledge	X		X		X	

Frequently Used Language Tests

Test	Major Areas	Type of Test		Standardization		Administration	
Name	*Tested*	*Formal*	*Informal*	*Norm-Referenced*	*Criterion-Referenced*	*Individual*	*Group*
The Goldman-Fristoe Test of Articulation (GIFTA)	articulation	X			X	X	
Auditory-Visual Single Word Picture Vocabulary Test-Adolescent (VSWPVT-A)	receptive picture vocabulary		X			X	X
Boehm Test of Basic Concepts-Revised (BTBC-R)	basic relational and space, quantity, and time concepts	X				X	X
Clinical Evaluation of Language Fundamentals Revised (CELF-R)	word meaning; word & sentence structure; recall and retrieval	X		X		X	
Expressive One-Word Picture Vocabulary Test (EOW-PVT)	expressive vocabulary	X		X		X	
Expressive One-Word Picture Vocabulary Test-Upper Extension (EOW-PVT-UE)	expressive vocabulary	X		X		X	
Peabody Picture Vocabulary Test-Revised (PPVT-R)	receptive single-word vocabulary	X		X		X	

(continued)

Frequently Used Language Tests *(continued)*

Name	Tested	Formal	Informal	Norm-Referenced	Criterion-Referenced	Individual	Group
Preschool Language Scale (PLS)	receptive and expressive language; articulation	X		X	X	X	
Test of Adolescent Language (TOAL-2)	receptive and expressive language, spoken and written	X		X		X	X
Test of Language Development-2-Primary (TOLD-2-P)	receptive and expressive language	X		X		X	
Test of Language Development-2 Intermediate (TOLD-2-I)	receptive and expressive language	X		X		X	
Test of Word Finding (TWF)	accuracy and speed of naming	X		X		X	
The Word Test	expressive language	X		X		X	

The header spans: **Type of Test** (Formal, Informal), **Standardization** (Norm-Referenced, Criterion-Referenced), **Administration** (Individual, Group).

Frequently Used Perceptual/Perceptual-Motor Tests

| Test | Major Areas | Type of Test | | Standardization | | Administration | |
Name	Tested	Formal	Informal	Norm-Referenced	Criterion-Referenced	Individual	Group
Test of Visual Motor Skills (TVMS)	visual perception and eye-motor coordination	X		X		X	X
Test of Visual-Perceptual Skills (Non-Motor)	visual perception (all types)	X				X	
Bruininks-Oseretsky Test of Motor Proficiency	motor proficiency, gross and fine motor skills	X				X	
Miller Assessment for Preschoolers (MAP)	sensory and motor abilities; verbal and non-verbal cognitive abilities	X		X		X	
Peabody Developmental Motor Scales (PDMS)	gross and fine motor skills	X				X	X
Marianne Frostig Developmental Test of Visual Perception (DTVP)	visual perception	X				X	X
Purdue Perceptual-Motor Survey	laterality, directionality, perceptual-motor skills	X			X	X	
Wepman Auditory Discrimination Test	auditory discrimination	X				X	

Appendix D: Sample Individualized Education Plan (IEP)

Special Education Department   Type of Staffing

Individualized Education Program (IEP)   Initial____

Review_____

Student: <u>Jerry Smith</u>   B'date <u>5/15/00</u>   School/Grade <u>Lake Park/3</u>   Date <u>2/23/08</u>

Student Attendance #_____   Parent/Guardian <u>Janet Smith</u>   Work Phone <u>324-1168</u>

Date of Original Program Entry <u>2/23/05</u>   Address <u>1421 McGill Street</u>   Home Phone <u>322-7722</u>

I. Present Level of Performance

Test results indicate average intelligence. Academic performance in reading vocabulary and comprehension below second grade expectancy levels. Parents describe Jerry as well-meaning, but overactive and immature.

II. Prioritized Annual Goals (see attached page(s) for short-term objectives)

1. Jerry will increase his reading comprehension to 2nd grade level, as measured by the Woodcock Reading Mastery Tests–Revised.
2. Jerry will increase his word recognition skills from 2nd to 3rd grade level, as measured by the Woodcock Reading Mastery Tests–Revised.

III. Recommended Special Education and/or Related Services

Service/Program	Implementation Date (Projected)	Hours/Week	Anticipated Duration	Review Date
Resource Room	2/30/08	5 hrs	One school year	2/23/09

Regular Class Placement: <u>25 </u>Hours/Week   Transportation: ___Yes <u>x </u>No   Documentation of Attempts to

Adaptive Physical Education ___Yes <u>x </u>No   Involve Parent/Guardian

Committee Members Present:
_____Chairperson
_____
_____
_____
_____

This is to certify that I was invited to participate in the writing of this IEP & that I understand its contents. Due process rights & procedures have been explained & I have been provided a copy of these rights. I understand that a copy of this IEP will be given to me upon my request.

Date	Comment
1/10/08	note sent home
1/30/08	phone call

_____   Date <u>2/23/08</u>
Parent/Guardian Signature

Page 2 of 2   Individualized Education Program (IEP)

Short-Term Objectives

(Complete at least one objective for each goal)

Student: <u>Jerry Smith</u>   B'date <u>5/15/00</u>   Program: <u>LD Resource</u>   Date <u>2/23/08</u>

Person to Provide Service <u>Nora Clark</u>

Annual Goal: <u>Jerry will increase his reading comprehension to 2nd grade level, as measured by the</u> <u>Woodcock Reading Mastery Tests-Revised</u>.

Short-Term Instructional Objectives	Criteria for Mastery	Date Reviewed	Method of Evaluation	Mastery Yes No
1. Given a selected 2nd grade reading passage, Jerry will verbally answer literal and inferential comprehension questions about the content.	80% accuracy	3/15/08	Teacher prepared list of literal and inferential comprehension questions drawn from a reading passage	Yes
2. Given a selected story from a 2nd grade reading book, Jerry will write correct answers to 8 of the 10 questions.	80% accuracy			

Annual Goal: <u>Jerry will increase his word recognition skills from 2nd to 3rd grade level, as measured by the Wood-cock Reading Mastery Tests-Revised</u>.

3. Jerry will use the context of sentences from a 2nd grade reading passage to identify unknown words.	85% accuracy	4/15/08	Teacher observation	Yes
4. Given a list of 20 vocabulary words from a selected 3rd grade reading story, Jerry will read 18 correctly.	90% accuracy			

REFERENCES

AAMR Ad Hoc Committee on Terminology and Classification. (2002). *Mental retardation: Definition, classification, and systems of support* (10th ed.). Washington, DC: American Association on Mental Retardation.

Achenbach, T. M., & Edelbrook, C. S. (1981). Behavioral problems and competencies reported by parents of normal and disturbed children aged 4 through 16. *Monographs of the Society for Research in Child Development, 46* (Serial No. 188).

Ager, C. L., & Cole, C. L. (1991). A review of cognitive-behavioral interventions for children and adolescents with behavioral disorders. *Behavioral Disorders, 16*(4), 260–275.

Ainsworth, M. (1989). Attachments beyond infancy. *American Psychologist, 44*(4), 709–716.

Albemarle County Public Schools. (2003). *Technology and differentiated instruction web resources.* Available at www.lakelandschools.org/EDTECH/Differentiation/home.htm.

Algozzine, B., & Korinek, L. (1985). Where is special education for students with high prevalence handicaps going? *Exceptional Children, 51,* 388–394.

Algozzine, B., & Maheady, L. (1986). When all else fails, teach. *Exceptional Children, 52*(6), 287–300.

Algozzine, B., Ruhl, K., & Ramsey, R. (1991). *Behaviorally disordered? Assessment for identification and instruction.* Reston, VA: The Council for Exceptional Children.

Algozzine, B., Serna, L., & Patton, J. (2001). *Childhood behavior disorders: Applied research and practice.* Austin, TX: Pro-Ed.

Algozzine, B., Ysseldyke, J., & Elliot, J. (1997). *Strategies and tactics for effective instruction* (2nd ed.). Longmont, CO: Sopris West.

Alley, G., & Deshler, D. (1979). *Teaching learning disabled adolescent: Strategies and methods.* Denver, CO: Love Publishing.

American Association on Intellectual Disabilities (2007). Frequently asked questions on intellectual disability and the AAID definition. Available at www.aidd.org/policies/faq_intellectual_disability.html.

American Psychiatric Association. (1994). *Diagnostic and statistical manual of mental disorders* (4th ed.). Washington, DC: Author.

Apter, S. J. (1982). *Troubled children, troubled systems.* New York: Pergamon.

Armas, G. C. (2001). Schools look for help as Hispanics flood in. *Springfield* [MA] *Sunday Republican*, Oct. 20, A5.

Armor, D. J. (2003). Environmental effects on IQ: From the family or from the schools? *Education Week 23*(12), 32–33.

Armor, D., Conry-Oseguera, P., Cox, M., King, N., McDonnell, L., Pascal, A., Pualy, E., & Zellman, G. (1976). *Analysis of the school preferred reading program in selected Los Angeles minority schools.* (Report No. R–2007–LAUSFD). Santa Monica, CA: The Rand Corporation. (ERIC Document Reproduction No. ED 130–243).

Armstrong, T. (1998). To empower, not control! A holistic approach to AD/HD. *Reaching Today's Youth: The Community Circle of Caring Journal 2*(2), 3–5.

Augard, T. (Ed.). (1991). The Oxford Dictionary of Modern Quotations. Oxford, England: Oxford University Press.

Baca, L., & Harris, K. D. (1988). Teaching migrant exceptional students. *Teaching Exceptional Children, 24*(4), 32–35.

Bailey, D. B., Skinner, D., Rodriguez, P., Gut, D., & Correa, V. (1999). Awareness, use, and satisfaction with services for Latino parents of young children with disabilities. *Exceptional Children, 65,* 367–381.

Bain, A., & Farris, H. (1991). Teacher attitudes toward social skill training. *Teacher Education and Special Education 14*(1), 49–56.

Baker, E. T., Wang, M. C., & Walberg, J. J. (1994). The effects of inclusion on learning. *Educational Leadership 52*(4), 33–35.

Baker, K. (1985). Research evidence of a school discipline problem. *Phi Delta Kappan 66*(7), 482–488.

Banks, J. (1993). Multicultural education: Development, dimensions, and challenges. *Phi Delta Kappan 75*(1), 22–28.

Barkley, R. A. (1977). A review of stimulant drug research with hyperactive children. *Journal of Child Psychology and Psychiatry 18,* 137–165.

Barresi, J. (1984). Interstate migrant council. National policy workshop on special education needs of migrant handicapped students. *Proceedings Report.* Denver, CO: Education Commission of the States.

Barron, M. A. (2000). Surprising truths: The implications of brain research. Available at http://nauticom.net/www/cokids/brain.html.

Barsch, R. H. (1968). *Perspectives on learning disabilities: The vectors of a new convergence.*

Bartoli, J. S. (1989). An ecological response to Cole's interactivity alternative. *Journal of Learning Disabilities 22*(5), 292–297.

Baumel, J. (2007, September). General education accommodations. A parent's guide to helping kids with learning difficulties. Schwab Learning.org. Available at www.schwablearning.org/articles.aspx?r=77.

Baxendell, B. W. (2003). Consistent, coherent, creative: The 3 C's of graphic organizers. *Teaching Exceptional Children 35*(3), 46–53.

Beckman, P. J. (1983). Influence of selected child characteristics on stress in the family of handicapped infants. *American Journal of Medical Deficiency 88*, 150–156.

Behrmann, M., & Jerome, M. K. (2003). Assistive technology for students with mild disabilities: Arlington, VA: ERIC Clearinghouse on disabilities and gifted education. ERIC Identifier: ED463595. Available at www.ericdigests.org/2003-1/assistive.htm.

Belch, P. (1975). The question of teachers' questions. *Teaching Exceptional Children 1*, 46–47.

Benjamin, A. (2003). *Differentiated instruction: A guide for middle and high school teachers.* Available atwww.eyeoneducation.com/Merchant2/merchant.mv?Screen=PROD&Store_Code=st. Accessed September 16, 2003.

Bennett, T., DeLuca, D. A., & Allen, R. W. (1996). Families of children with disabilities: Positive adaptation across the lifecycle. *Social Work in Education 18*, 31–44.

Benniga, J. S. (1988). An emerging synthesis in moral education. *Phi Delta Kappan 69*(6), 415–418.

Benson, D., Edwards, L., Rosell, J., & White, M. (1986). Inclusion of socially maladjusted children and youth in the legal definition of the behaviorally disordered population: A debate. *Behavioral Disorders 11*(3), 213–222.

Bereiter, C., & Englemann, S. (1966). *Teaching disadvantaged children in the preschool.* Upper Saddle River, NJ: Prentice Hall.

Berliner, D. C. (1979). Tempus educare. In P. L. Peterson & H. J. Walberg (Eds.), *Research on Teaching: Concepts Findings and Implications.* Berkeley, CA: McCutchan Publishing.

Berliner, D. C. (1988). The half-full glass: A review of research on teaching. In E. L. Meyen, G. A. Vergason, & R. J. Whelan (Eds.), *Effective Instructional Strategies for Exceptional Children.* Denver, CO: Love Publishing.

Berman, P., McLaughlin, M., Bass, G., Pauly, E., & Zelman, G. (1977). Federal programs supporting educational change. Vol. 7: Factors affecting the implementation and continuation. Santa Monica, CA: The Rand Corporation. (ERIC Document Reproduction Service No. ED 140 432).

Bernstein, B. (1961). Social class and linguistic development: A theory of social learning. In A. H. Halsey, J. Flored, & C. A. Anderson (Eds.), *Education, Economy and Society.* New York: Free Press.

Bickel, W. E., & Bickel, D. P. (1986). Effective schools, classrooms, and instruction: Implications for special education. *Exceptional Children 52*(6), 489–499.

Blacher, J., Lopez, S., Shapiro, J., & Fusco, J. (1997). Contributions to depression in Latino mothers with and without children with retardation: Implications for caregiving. *Family Relations 46*, 325–334.

Blackhurst, A. E., & Edyburn, D. L. (2000). A brief history of special education technology. *Special Education Technology Practice 2*(1), 21–36. Available at www.setp.net/pdf/SEThistory.pdf.

Blackman, H. P. (1989). Special education placement: Is it what you know or where you live? *Exceptional Children 55*, 459–462.

Blankenship, C. (1985). Using curriculum based assessment data to make instructional decisions. *Exceptional Children 52*(3), 233–238.

Block, J. (1995). On the relationship between IQ, impulsivity, and delinquency. *Journal of Abnormal Psychology 104*(3), 45–48.

Bly, R. (1990). *Iron John: A book about men.* Reading, MA: Addison-Wesley Publishing.

Boardmaker. (2001). *Picture Communication Symbols.* [Computer Software]. Solana Beach, CA: Mayer-Johnson, Inc.

Boder, E., & Jarrico, S. (1982). *The Boder test of reading-spelling patterns.* New York: Grune & Stratton.

Boyle, E. A., Washburn, S. G., Rosenberg, M. S., Connelly, V. J., Brinckerhoff, L. C., & Banerjee, M. (2002). Reading's SLiCK with new audio texts and strategies. *Teaching Exceptional Children 35*(2), 50–55.

Braaten, S., Simpson, R., Rosell, J., & Reilly, T. (1988). Using punishment with exceptional children. *Teaching Exceptional Children 20*(2), 79–81.

Brandt, R. (1990). Overview: Making connections. *Exceptional Leadership 47*(5), 3.

Brantlinger, E. A., & Guskin, S. L. (1988). Implications of social and cultural differences for special education. In E. L. Meyen, G. A. Vergason, & R. J. Whelan (Eds.). *Effective Instructional Strategies for Exceptional Children.* Denver, CO: Love Publishing.

Brendtro, L. K., & Ness, A. E. (1996). Fixing flaws or building strengths? *Journal of Emotional and Behavioral Problems 4*(2), 2–7.

Brolin, D. E. (Ed.) (1989). *Life centered career education: A competency based approach.* Reston, VA: The Council for Exceptional Children.

Brooks, D. (2007). The waning of I.Q. *The New York Times,* September 14, p. C5.

Brown v. Topeka, Kansas, Board of Education (1954). 347 U.S. 483, 745. Ct. 98 L. Ed.

Bruininks, V. L. (1978). Actual and perceived peer status of disabled students in mainstream programs. *The Journal of Emotional Special Education 12,* 51–58.

Bruner, J., Cole, M., & Lloyd, B. (1978). *The developing child series.* In S. Farnham-Diggory. *Learning Disabilities: A Psychological Perspective.* Cambridge, MA: Harvard University Press.

Bryan, T. H. (1974). Peer popularity of learning disabled children. *Journal of Learning Disabilities 7,* 621–625.

Bryan, T., Donohue, M., & Pearl, R. (1981). Studies of learning disabled children's pragmatic competence. *Topics in Learning and Learning Disabilities 1,* 29–39.

Bryan, T., Werner, M., & Pearl, R. (1982). Learning disabled students conformity responses to prosocial and antisocial situations. *Learning Disability Quarterly 5,* 344–352.

Bryen, D. N. (1982). *Injuries into child language.* Boston: Allyn and Bacon.

Bryk, A. S., & Schneider, B. L. (2002). *Trust in schools: A core resource for improvement.* New York: Russell Sage Foundation.

Bullock, L. M., & Gable, R. A. (Eds.). (1997). *Making collaboration work for children, youth, families, schools, and communities.* Reston, VA: The Council for Exceptional Children.

Burrello, L. C., Burrello, J. M., & Friend, M. (1996). *The power of 2: Making a difference through co-teaching.* (Videotape). Elephant Rock Productions, Inc., and Indiana University Educational Series.

Buscaglia, L. (1975). *The disabled and their parents: A counseling challenge.* Thorofare, NJ: Leo F. Buscaglia.

Bush, W. I., & Waugh, K. W. (1982). *Diagnosing learning problems* (3rd ed.). Columbus, OH: Charles E. Merrill.

Caine, R. N. (2000). Building the bridge from research to classroom. *Educational Leadership 58*(3), 59–61.

Canter, L. (1989). Assertive discipline: More than names

on the board and marbles in a jar. *Phi Delta Kappan 71*(1), 57–60.

Carbo, M. (1987). Reading styles research: What works isn't always phonics. *Phi Delta Kappan 68*(6), 431–435.

Carbo, M., Dunn, R., & Dunn, K. (1986). *Teaching students to read through their individual learning styles.* Upper Saddle River, NJ: Prentice Hall.

Carlson, C. I. (1987). Social interaction goals and strategies of children with learning disabil-ities. *Journal of Learning Disabilities 20*(5), 306–311.

Carpenter, D. (1985). Grading handicapped pupils: Review and position statement. *Remedial and Special Education 6*(4), 54–59.

Cavanaugh, T. (2002). E-books and accommodations: Is this the future of print accommodation? *Teaching Exceptional Children 35*(2), 56–61.

CEC Staff. (1997a). CEC testifies before Congress, calls for quick IDEA reauthorization. *CEC Today 3*(8) 1, 7, 9.

CEC Staff. (1997b). IDEA sails through Congress. *CEC Today 3*(10), 1, 9, 15.

CEC Staff. (1997c) Instructional accommodations. *CEC Today 4*(3), 15.

CEC Staff. (2003). CEC issues, IDEA recommendations. *CEC Today,* April/May, 1.

Cegelka, P., Lewis, R., & Rodriguez, A. (1987). Status of educational services to handicapped students with limited English proficiency: Report of a statewide study in California. *Exceptional Children 54*(3), 220–227.

Center for the Improvement of Early Reading Achievement. (2003). *Put reading first: The research building blocks for teaching children to read.* Washington, DC: Partnership for Reading.

Center on Budget & Policy Priorities. (2000). *Poverty rate hits all time lowest level since 1979 as unemployment reaches 30-year low.* Available at www.cbpp.org/9-26-00pov.htm.

Centers for Disease Control. (2008). *Lead poisoning prevention programs.* Available at www.cdc.gov/nceh.lead/

Chalfant, J. C., & Scheffelin, M. A. (1969). *Central processing dysfunction in children: A review of the research.* National Institute of Neurological Diseases and Stroke, Monograph #9. Bethesda, MD: U.S. Department of Health, Education, and Welfare.

Character Education Partnership. (1997). Available at www.character.org/site/

Charles, C. M. (1989). *Building classroom discipline: From models to practice* (3rd ed.). New York: Longman.

Checkley, K. (1997). The first seven . . . and the eighth

conversation with Howard Gardner. *Educational Leadership 55*(1), 8–13.

Cheek, E. H., & Cheek, M. C. (1983). *Reading instruction through content teaching.* Columbus, OH: Merrill Publishing.

Children's Defense Fund. (1971). *The way we go to school: The exclusion in Boston.* Boston: Beacon Press.

Children's Defense Fund (2007). Child welfare and mental health research. Available at www .childrensdefense.org/site/pageserver?pagename =research_CWMH.

Chmelynski, C. (1990). All-black, all-male classes. *The Educator 12*(10), 16–18.

Chrispeels, J. H. (1991). District leadership in parent involvement—Policies and actions in San Diego. *Phi Delta Kappan 72*, 367–371.

Cicci, R. (1983). Disorders of written language. In H. R. Myklebust (Ed.), *Progress in Learning Disabilities.* New York: Grune & Stratton.

Cincinnati [Ohio] Public Schools Department of Student Services. (2007). *ABCs of adaptations and accommodations.* Available at www.cps-k12.org/programs/speced/ABCs.html.

Coleman, J. (1987, August/September). Families and schools. *Educational Researchers*, 31–38.

Coleman, J. M. (1985). Achievement level, social class, and the self-concepts of mildly handicapped children. *Journal of Learning Disabilities 18*(1), 26–30.

Coles, G. S. (1989). The learning mystique: A critical look at "learning disabilities." *Journal of Learning Disabilities 22*(5), 267–273, 277–278.

Colvin, G., Kame'enui, E. J., and Sugai, G. (1993). School-wide and classroom management: Re-conceptualizing the integration and management of students with behavior problems in general education. *Education and Treatment of Children 16*, 361–381.

Comer, J. P. (1986). Parent participation in the schools. *Phi Delta Kappan 67*(6), 442–446.

Comer, J. P., Zigler, E. F., and Stern, B. M. (1997). Supporting today's families in the elementary school. *Reaching Today's Youth. The Community Circle of Caring Journal 1*(3), 37–43.

Conner, M. G. (2003, September 7). Understanding and dealing with pervasive developmental disorders. Available at www.CrisisCounseling.org.

Connors, J. L., & Donnellan, A. M. (1998). Walk in beauty: Western perspectives on disability and Navajo family/cultural resilience. In H. I. McCubbin, E. A. Thompson, A. I. Thompson, & J. E. Fromer (Eds.), *Resiliency in Native American and Immigrant Families* (pp. 159–182). Thousand Oaks, CA: Sage.

Cooper, H. M. (1989a). Synthesis of research on homework. *Educational Leadership 47*(3), 85–91.

Cooper, J. O., Heron, T. E., & Heward, W. L. (1987). *Applied behavior analysis.* Columbus, OH: Merrill Publishing.

Copple, C., Yante, M., Levin, D., & Cohen, S. (1992). *Briefing paper.* Washington, DC: Pelavin Associates, Inc.

Cornett, C. E. (1983). *What you should know about teaching and learning styles.* Bloomington, IN: Phi Delta Kappan. (Phi Delta Kappa Fastback Series #191.)

Council for Children with Behavior Disorders (1990). Position paper on use of behavior education strategies with children with behavioral disorders. *Behavioral Disorders 15*(4), 243–260.

Council for Exceptional Children. (2003a). Advocacy in action: House Bill on IDEA contains CEC recommendations, but CEC remains cautious. *Today 9*(7), 4–5, 14.

Council for Exceptional Children. (2003b). CEC says all students must be included in assessments. *Today 9*(7), 1, 5, 14–15.

Council for Exceptional Children. (2004). Changing the way we identify learning disabilities. *CEC Today* Jan–Feb, March p. 14.

Council for Exceptional Children (2005). *CEC provides comments on IDEA proposed regulations.* Available at www.sped.org.

Cremin, L., (1961). *The transformation of the school.* New York: Vintage Books.

Crook, W. G. (1980). Can what a child eats make him dull, stupid, or hyperactive? *Journal of Learning Disabilities 13*, 53–58.

Croser, M., & Seiter, M. (Eds.). (2003). *Pollution, toxic chemicals, and mental retardation: Framing a national blueprint for health promotion and disability prevention:* Proceedings of a national Wingspanel summit, July 22–24. Available at www. aamr.org/ToxinsandMentalRetardation/pdf.

Cruickshank, W. M. (1967). *The brain injured child in home, school, and community.* Syracuse, NY: Syracuse University Press.

Cruickshank, W. M. (1986). The learning disabled hyperactive child. *Perceptions 1*, 7–9.

Cuenin, L. H., & Harris, K. R. (1986). Planning, implementing, and evaluating time out interventions with exceptional students. *Teaching Exceptional Children 18*(4), 272–276.

D'Arcangelo, M. (2000). The scientist in the crib: A conversation with Andrew Metzloff. *Educational Leadership 58*(2), 8–13.

Daly, P. M., & Ranalli, P. (2003). Using countoons to

teach self-monitoring skills. *Teaching Exceptional Children 35*(5), 30–35.

Daniel R. R. v. State Board of Education. (1989). 874 F.2d 1036 (5th Cir.).

Davies, R. (1991). Schools reaching out. *Phi Delta Kappan 72*(5), 376–382.

Davis, G. A., & Rimm, S. B. (1985). *Education of the gifted and talented.* Upper Saddle River, NJ: Prentice Hall.

DeLuke, S. V., & Knoblock, P. (1987). Teacher behavior as preventive discipline. *Teaching Exceptional Children 19*, 18–24.

Dennison, G. (1969). *The lives of children: The Story of the first street school.* New York: Random House.

Deno, S. (1989). Curriculum-based measurement and special education services: A fundamental and direct relationship. In M. Shinn (Ed.), *Curriculum-Based Measurement: Assessing Special Children.* New York: Guilford Press.

Deno, S. L. (1985). Curriculum-based measurement: The emerging alternative. *Exceptional Children 52*(3), 219–232.

Deno, S. L. (1986). Formative evaluation of individual student programs: A new role for school psychologists. *School Psychology Review 15*(3), 358–374.

Derr, A. M. (1986). How learning disabled adolescent boys make moral judgments. *Journal of Learning Disabilities 19*(3), 160–164.

Deshler, D. D. (1978). Psychoeducational aspects of learning disabled adolescents. In L. Mann, L. Goodman, & J. L. Wiederholt (Eds.), *Teaching the Learning Disabled Adolescent.* Boston: Houghton Mifflin.

Deshler, D. D., & Schumaker, J. B. (1983). Social skills of learning disabled adolescents: Characteristics and intervention. *Topics in Learning Disabilities 3*, 15–23.

Deshler, D. D., Schumaker, J. B., & Lenz, B. K. (1984). Academic and cognitive interventions for LD adolescents: Part 1. *Journal of Learning Disabilities 17*(2), 108–117.

Deshler, D. D., Warner, M. M., Schumaker, J. B., & Alley, G. R. (1983). Learning strategies intervention model: Key components and current status. In J. D. McKinney & L. Feagans (Eds.), *Current Topics in Learning Disabilities.* Norwood, NJ: Ablex.

Diana v. State Board of Education. No. C-70-37 Rfp (n.d. Calif. 1970).

Dietz, M. P. (1992). Youth-reaching-youth project. *Journal of Emotional and Behavioral Problems 1*(3), 28–29.

DiGangi, S. A., Perryman, P., & Rutherford, R. B., Jr. (1990). Juvenile offenders in the 90's: A descriptive analysis. *Perceptions, 25*(4), 5–8.

Digest for Education Statistics. (2007). Available at http://nces.ed.gov/pubsearch/.

Dobbins, D. A., & Rarick, G. L. (1977). The performance of intellectually normal and educable mentally retarded boys on throwing accuracy. *Journal of Motor Behavior 9*, 23–28.

DO-IT Staff. (2002). *Working together: Computers and people with learning disabilities.* Available at www.washington.edu/doit/Brochures/Technology/atpwld.html.

Dover, W. (1994). *The inclusion facilitator.* Manhattan, KS: The MASTER Teacher, Inc.

Dreikurs, R., Grunwald, B., & Pepper, F. (1982). *Maintaining sanity in the classroom.* New York: Harper & Row.

Dupont, H. (1978). *Counseling and human development.* Denver, CO: Love Publishing.

Dykens, E., & Kasari, C. (1997). Maladaptive behavior in children with Prader-Willi syndrome, Down syndrome, and nonspecific mental retardation. *American Journal on Mental Retardation 102*(3), 228–237.

Dykens, E., & Rosner, B. A. (1999). Refining behavioral phenotypes: Personality-motivation in Williams and Prader-Willi syndromes. *American Journal on Mental Retardation 104*(2), 158–169.

Eden, A. (2003, July). *National Center for Learning Disabilities launches new interactive game for learning disabilities.* Press release. Available at www.ncld.org.

Edge, D., & Burton, G. (1986). Helping learning disabled middle school students learn about money. *Journal of Learning Disabilities 19*(1), 46–51.

Edgerton, R. B. (1979). *Mental retardation.* Cambridge, MA: Harvard University Press.

Edwards, J. (1991). To teach responsibility, bring back the Dalton Plan. *Phi Delta Kappan 72*(5), 398–401.

Elkind, D. (1986). Formal education and early childhood education: An essential difference. *Phi Delta Kappan 67*(9), 631–637.

Ellis, N. R. (1963). The stimulus trace and behavioral inadequacy. In N. Ellis (Ed.), *Handbook of Mental Deficiency.* New York: McGraw-Hill.

England, D. A., & Flatley, J. K. (1985). *Homework—Any why.* Bloomington, IN: Phi Delta Kappa Educational Foundation (Monograph, Fastback 218).

Epstein, M. H., Cullinan, D., & Polloway, E. A. (1986). Patterns of maladjustment among mentally retarded children and youth. *American Journal of Mental Deficiency 2*(2), 127–134.

Erickson, M. T. (1998). *Behavior disorders of children and adolescents* (3rd ed.). Upper Saddle River, NJ: Prentice Hall.

Espinoza, R. (1988). Working parents, employees, and schools. *Educational Horizons.* Winter, 62–65.

Evertson, C. M., & Weinstein, C. S. (Eds.) (2006). *Handbook of classroom management: Research, practice, and contemporary issues.* Mahwah, NJ: Lawrence Erlbaum Associates, Publishers.

Executive Committee of the Council for Children with Behavioral Disorders. (1987). Position paper on definition and identification of students with behavioral disorders. *Behavioral Disorders 13*(1), 9–18.

Fagen, S. (1986). Conducting an LSI: A process model. *Perceptions* 4–5.

Fagen, S. A., & Hill, J. M. (1987). Teaching acceptance of frustration. *Teaching Exceptional Children 19*(4), 49–51.

Fagen, S. A., & Long, N. J. (1975). Teaching children self-control: A new responsibility for teachers. *Focus on Exceptional Children 7*(8), 1–10.

Farley, J. W. (1986). An analysis of written dialogue of educable mentally retarded writers. *Education and Training of the Mentally Retarded 21*(3), 181–191.

Farnham-Diggory, S. (1978). *Learning disabilities: A psychological perspective.* Cambridge, MA: Harvard University Press.

Farnham-Diggory, S. (1992). *The learning-disabled child.* Cambridge, MA: Harvard University Press.

Farrell, E. E. (1908–1909). Special classes in the New York city schools. *Journal of Psycho-Asthenics 13*(1–4), 91–96.

Featherstone, H. (1980). *A difference in the family.* New York: Basic Books.

Federal Domestic Assistance Catalog. (1997). Available at www.gsa.gov/fdac/query fdac.htm.

Federal Register. (2007). V72, #15, Jan. 24, pp. 3147–3148.

Fein, E. B. (1995, January 6). An educational oasis on Rikers Island. *The New York Times,* B1.

Feingold, B. (1975). *Why your child is hyperactive.* New York: Random House.

Feiter, F., & Tokar, E. (1982). Getting a handle on teacher stress. *Educational Leadership 39*(6), 456–457.

Feurenstein, R. (1980). *Instrumental enrichment: An intervention program for cognitive modifiability.* Baltimore, MD: University Park Press.

Figgis, J. (1995). *A new book about how our brains function.* (Interview with Robert Sylwester), ABC Radio National, Education Report Transcript, November 15. Available at www.abc.net.au/rn/talks/8:30/edurpt/estories/er151102.htm.

Fine, E. (1987). Are we preparing adolescents with learning disabilities to cope with social issues? *Journal of Learning Disabilities 20*(10), 633–635.

Fishbaugh, M. S. E. (1997). *Models of collaboration.* Boston: Allyn and Bacon.

Fiske, E. B. (1988, February 12). Standardized test scores: Voodoo statistics? *The New York Times,* B1.

Flick, G. F. (1998). 24 ways to manage AD/HD in the classroom without medication. *Reaching Today's Youth: The Community Circle of Caring Journal 2*(2), 37–40.

Ford, B. A. (1992). *Multicultural education training for special educators working with African-American youth. Exceptional Children 59*(2), 107–114.

Forness, S. R. (2001). *Schools and the identification of mental health needs.* Report of the Surgeon General's Conference on Children's Mental Health: A National Action Agenda. Available at www.surgeongeneral.gov/topics/cmh/childrenreport.htm. Accessed December 19, 2003.

Fowler, M. (2002). *Attention deficit/hyperactivity disorder. NICHY briefing paper.* Washington, DC: National Information Center for Children and Youth with Disabilities.

Frankenberger, W. (1998). Wonder drug or quick fix? *Reaching Today's Youth: The Community Circle of Caring Journal 2*(2), 11–15.

Freisleben-Cook, L. (2003a, September). A more down-to-earth description. In *What Is Asperger Syndrome?* Asperger Syndrome Information and Support (O.A.S.I.S.). Available at www.udel.edu/bkirby/asperger/aswhatisit.html.

Freisleben-Cook, L. (2003b). A more down-to-earth description. In V. Gonzalez, R. Brusca-Vega, & T. Yawkey. (1997). *Assessment and instruction of culturally and linguistically diverse students with or at-risk of learning problems.* Boston: Allyn and Bacon.

Friedrich, W. N. (1979). Predictors of the coping behavior of the mothers of handicapped children. *Journal of Consulting and Clinical Psychology 47,* 1140–1141.

Friend, M., & Bursuck, W. D. (1999). *Including students with special needs: A practical guide for classroom teachers* (2nd ed.). Boston: Allyn and Bacon.

Friend, M., & Cook, L. (2000). *Interactions: Collaboration skills for school professionals* (3rd ed.). New York: Addison Wesley/Longman, Inc.

Fuchs, L., & Fuchs, D. (1986). Effects of systematic formative evaluation: A Meta-analysis. *Exceptional Children 53*(3), 199–208.

Fujiura, G. T., & Yamaki, K. (2000). Trends in demography of childhood poverty and disability. *Exceptional Children 66,* 187–199.

Fujiura, G. T., Yamaki, K., & Czechowicz, S. (1998). Disability among ethnic and racial minorities in the United States: A summary of economic status and family structure. *Journal of Disability Policy Studies 9*(2), 111–130.

Gallagher, J. J., Cross, A., & Schartman, W. (1981). Parental adaptation to a young handicapped child: The father's role. *Journal to the Division for Early Childhood 3,* 3–14.

Garabino, J. (2000). *Lost boys: Why our sons turn violent and how we can save them.* New York: Anchor Books.

Gardner, H. (1993). *Multiple intelligences: The theory into practice.* New York: Basic Books.

Gazaway, R. (1969). *The longest mile.* Garden City, NY: Doubleday.

Gelb, S. (1997). The problem of typological thinking in mental retardation. *Mental Retardation 35*(6), 448–457.

Gelzheiser, L., & Meyers, J. (1990). Special and remedial education in the classroom: Theme and variations. *Journal of Reading, Writing, and Learning Disabilities 6*, 419–436.

Georgia Department of Education. (1989). Revised flow chart. Personal correspondence with Dr. Joan Jordan, State Director of Special Education.

Gilbert, S. (2000, June 20). Gains in diagnosing hyperactivity. *New York Times*, D8.

Ginott, H. (1971). *Teacher and child.* New York: Macmillan.

Ginsburg, H. (1972). *The myth of the deprived child: Poor children's intellect and education.* Upper Saddle River, NJ: Prentice Hall.

Glasser, W. (1985). *Control theory in the classroom.* New York: Perennial Library.

Glickman, C. D. (1987). Good and/or effective schools: What do we want? *Phi Delta Kappan 68*(8), 622–624.

Glidewell, J., & Swallow, C. (1968). *The prevalence of maladjustment in elementary schools.* Chicago: University of Chicago Press.

Gloeckler, T., & Simpson, C. (1988). *Exceptional students in regular classrooms: Challenges, services, and methods.* Mountain View, CA: Mayfield Publishing.

Goddard, H. H. (1912). How shall we educate mental defectives? *Training School Bulletin 9*, 43.

Goldberg, M. F. (1990). Portrait of Madeline Hunter. *Educational Leadership 47*(5), 41–43.

Goldstein, H. (1974). *Social learning curriculum.* Columbus, OH: Charles E. Merrill.

Goldstein, K. (1942). *After effects of brain injuries in war.* New York: Grune & Stratton.

Goleman, D. (1995). *Emotional intelligence: Why it can matter more than I.Q.* New York: Bantam Books.

Goodlad, J. I. (1984). *A place called school.* New York: McGraw-Hill.

Gough, P. B. (1987). The key to improving schools: An interview with William Glasser. *Phi Delta Kappan 68*(9), 656–662.

Gould, S. J. (1981). *The mismeasure of man.* New York: W. W. Norton.

Greenbaum, P. E., Dedrick, R. M., Freidman, K. K.,

Brown, E. L., Lardieri, S. P., & Pugh, A. M. (1998). National adolescent and child treatment study (NACTS): Outcomes for children with serious emotional and behavioral disturbance. In M. H. Epstein, K. Kutash, & A. Duchnowdki, (Eds.), *Outcomes for Children and Youth with Behavioral and Emotional Disorders.* Austin, TX: Pro-Ed.

Greenberg, G. S. (1998). Answers to six of them most frequently asked questions about ADHD. *Reaching Today's Youth: The Community Circle of Caring Journal 2*(2), 16–18.

Gresham, F. M. (1989). Utility of cognitive-behavioral procedures for social skills training with children: A critical review. *Journal of Abnormal Child Psychology 13*, 411–423.

Gresham, F., MacMillan, D., & Bocian, K. (1996). Behavioral earthquakes—Low frequency salient behavioral events that differentiate students at-risk of behavioral disorders. *Behavioral Disorders 21*(4), 277–292.

Gresham, F. M., VanDerHeyden, A., & Witt, J. C. (2005). Response to intervention in the identification of learning disabilities: Empirical support and future challenges. Available at www.joewitt.org.

Grosenick, J. K., & Huntze, S. L. (1979). *National needs analysis in behavior disorders.* Columbia, MO: University of Missouri, Department of Special Education.

Grossman, C., Neckerman, H., Koepsell, T., Liu, P., Asher, K., Beland, K., Frey, K., & Rivara, P. (1997). Effectiveness of a violence prevention curriculum among children in elementary school. A randomized controlled trial. *Journal of the American Medical Association 277*(20), 1605–1611.

Grunwald, P. (1990). The new generation of information systems. *Phi Delta Kappan 72*(2), 113–114.

Guetzloe, E. (1988). Suicide and depression: Special education's responsibility. *Teaching Exceptional Children 20*(4), 25–28.

Gunter, P. L., Miller, K. A., Venn, M. L., Thomas, K., & House, S. (2002). Self-graphing to success: Computerized data management. *Teaching Exceptional Children 35*(2), 30–34.

Gus and Inky's underwater adventure. (2003). Available at www.getreadytoread.org.2003.

Hallahan, D., & Cruickshank, W. (1973). *Psychoeducational foundations of learning disabilities.* Upper Saddle River, NJ: Prentice Hall.

Hallahan, D. P., & Kauffman, J. M. (1977). Categories, labels, behavioral characteristics: ED, LD, and ENR reconsidered. *Journal of Special Education 11*, 139–149.

Hallahan, D. P., & Kauffman, J. M. (1982). *Exceptional*

children: Introduction to special education (3rd ed.). Upper Saddle River, NJ: Prentice Hall.

Hallahan, D. P., & Kauffman, J. M. (1994). *Exceptional children: Introduction to special education* (6th ed.). Boston: Allyn and Bacon.

Hallahan, D. P., Keller, C. E., Martinez, E. A., Byrd, E. S., Gelman, J. A., & Fan, X. (2007). How variable are interstate prevalence rates of learning disabilities and other special education categories? A longitudinal comparison. *Exceptional Children 73*(2), 136–146.

Haring, N. G., & Phillips, E. L. (1962). *Educating emotionally disturbed children.* New York: McGraw-Hill.

Harris, I. B. (1996). Children in jeopardy: Can we break the cycle of poverty. *The Yale Child Study Center Monograph Series on Child Psychology. Child Development and Social Policy,* Vol. 1. New Haven, CT: Yale University Press.

Harris, K. R., & Pressley, M. (1991). The nature of cognitive strategy instruction: Interactive strategy instruction. *Exceptional Children 57,* 392–401.

Hazel, J. S., Schumacker, J. B., & Sherman, J. S. (1982). Application of a group training program in social skills and problem solving to learning disabled and non-learning disabled youth. *Learning Disabled Quarterly 5,* 398–414.

Healthy Children's Project. (2005). Available at www.healthychildrensproject.org/exposures/index.html.

Hebb, D. O. (1966). *A textbook on psychology* (2nd ed.). Philadelphia: W. B. Saunders.

Heller, K., & Monahan, J. (1977). *Psychology and community change.* Homewood, IL: Dorsey Press.

Henderson, A. (1987). *The evidence continues to grow: Parent involvement improves student achievement.* Columbia, MD: National Committee for Citizens in Education.

Hendrick, I. G., & MacMillan, D. L. (1987). Coping with diversity in city school systems: The role of mental testing in shaping special classes for MR children in Los Angeles, 1900–1930. *Education and Training in Mental Retardation 22,* 10–17.

Henley, M. (1985). *Teaching mildly retarded children in the regular classroom.* (Phi Delta Kappan Fastback series #220). Bloomington, IN: Phi Delta Kappan.

Henley, M. (1986). Training teachers to manage the feelings and behavior of emotionally disturbed students. Paper presented at the National Adolescent Conference, Minneapolis, MN., November 17–21.

Henley, M. (1987). Ego function and dysfunction: A guide to understanding discipline problems. *The Pointer 31*(4), 24–30.

Henley, M. (2003). *Teaching self-control: A curriculum for responsible behavior.* (2d ed.). Bloomington, IN: Solution Tree.

Henley, M. (2004). *Creating successful inclusion programs: A guide for teachers and administrators.* Bloomington, IN: National Educational Service.

Henley, M. (2005). *Classroom management: A proactive approach.* Columbus, OH: Merrill/Prentice Hall.

Henley, M., & Long, N. (1999). Teaching emotional intelligence to impulsive-aggressive youth. *Reclaiming Children and Youth: Journal of Emotional and Behavioral Problems 7*(4), 224–229.

Henley, M., & Long, N. (2003).

Hersch, P. (1998). *A tribe apart: A journey into the heart of American adolescence.* New York: The Ballantine Publishing Group.

Hewett, F. M., & Taylor, F. D. (1980). *The emotionally disturbed child in the classroom: The orchestration of success.* Boston: Allyn and Bacon.

Hobbs, N. (1966). Helping disturbed children: Ecological psychological strategies. *American Psychologist 21,* 1105–1115.

Hobbs, N. (1982). Help's on the way for the learning disabled. *Salt Lake [UT] Tribune,* 102.

Hodgkinson, H. (2001). Educational demographics: What teachers should know. *Educational Leadership 58*(4), 6–11.

Holland, B. V. (1987). Fundamental motor skill performance of non-handicapped and educable mentally impaired students. *Education and Training in Mental Retardation 22*(3), 197–203.

Holloway, J. H. (2000, September). Research link—Preparing teachers for differentiated instruction. *Educational Leadership 58*(1), 1–3.

Holt, J. (1977). *How children fail.* New York: Dell.

Hops, H. (1983). Children's social competence and skill: Research practices and future direction. *Behavior Therapy 14,* 3–18.

Horn, J. L. (1924). *The education of exceptional children: A consideration of public school problems and policies in the field of differentiated education.* New York: Century.

Horn, J. L., O'Donnell, J. P., & Leicht, D. J. (1988). Phonetically inaccurate spelling among learning-disabled, head-injured, and nondisabled young adults. *Brain and Language 33*(1), 55–64.

Horner, R. H. (2000). Positive behavior supports. *Focus on Autism and Other Developmental Disabilities, 15*(2), 97–105.

Horner, R. H., & Sugai, G. (2000). School-wide behavior support: An emerging initiative (special issue). *Journal of Positive Behavioral Interventions 2,* 231–233.

Horner, R. H., Sugai, G., Todd, A. W., & Lewis-Palmer, T. (2005). School-wide positive behavior support. In L. Bambara & L. Kern (Eds.), *Individualized Supports for Students with Problem Behaviors: Designing Positive Behavior Plans* (pp. 359–390). New York: Guilford Press.

Houts, P. L. (1977). *The myth of measurability.* New York: Hart Publishing.

Hu-DeHart, E. (1993). The history, development, and future of ethnic studies. *Phi Delta Kappan 75*(1), 50–54.

Huefner, D. S. (2000). *Getting comfortable with special education.* Norwood, MA: Christopher-Gordon Publishers.

Hughes, C., Copeland, S. R., Wehmeyer, M. L., Agran, M., Cai, X., & Hwang, B. (2002). Increasing social interaction between general education high school students and their peers with mental retardation. *Journal of Developmental and Physical Disabilities 14*, 387–402.

Hyman, I., & D'Alessandro, J. (1984). Good old fashioned discipline: The politics of punitiveness. *Phi Delta Kappan 66*(1), 39–45.

Hynd, G. W., & Hynd, C. R. (1984). Dyslexia: Neuroanatomical/neurolinguistic perspectives. *Reading Research Quarterly 19*(4), 482–498.

Jackson, P. W. (1968). *Life in the classrooms.* New York: Holt, Rinehart, & Winston.

Jackson, W. J., & Larkin, M. J. (2002). Rubric: Teaching students to use grading rubrics. *Teaching Exceptional Children 35*(1), 40–45.

Jacobs, L. (1984). Cognition and learning disabilities. *Teaching Exceptional Children 16*(3), 213–216.

Jenkins, J. R., & Jenkins, L. M. (1981). *Cross age and peer tutoring: Help for children with learning problems.* Reston, VA: The Council for Exceptional Children.

Jenkins, J. R., Pious, C. G., & Peterson, D. L. (1988). Categorical programs for remedial and handicapped students: Issues of validity. *Exceptional Children 55*(2), 147–158.

Jensen, E. (1998). How Julie's brain learns. In *The Best of Educational Leadership: 1998–1999.* Alexandria, VA: Association of Supervision and Curriculum Development.

Johnson, D. W. (1972). *Reaching out: Interpersonal effectiveness and self-actualization.* Upper Saddle River, NJ: Prentice Hall.

Johnson, D. W., & Johnson, R. T. (1986). Mainstreaming and cooperative learning strategies. *Exceptional Children 52*(6), 553–561.

Johnson, D. W., & Johnson, R. T. (1990). Social skills for successful group work. *Educational Leadership 47*(4), 29–33.

Johnstone, E. R. (1908). The functions of the special class. *National Education Association Journal of Proceedings and Address of the 46th Annual Meeting, 114–118.*

Jones, F. (1987). *Positive classroom discipline.* New York: McGraw-Hill.

Jones, V. F., & Jones, L. S. (1981). *Responsible classroom discipline: Creating positive learning environments and solving problems.* Boston: Allyn and Bacon.

Jones, V. F., & Jones, L. S. (1986). *Comprehensive classroom management: Creating positive learning environments* (2nd ed.). Boston: Allyn and Bacon.

Kane, C. (1994). *Prisoners of time research: What we know and what we need to know.* Washington, DC: National Education Commission on Time and Learning.

Kauffman, J. M. (1997). *Characteristics of emotional and behavioral disorders of children and youth* (6th ed.). Columbus, OH: Merrill.

Kauffman, J. M. (1999). Comments on social development research in EBD. *Journal of Emotional and Behavioral Disorders 7*, 189–191.

Kelly, T., Bullock, L., & Dykes, M. K. (1974). *Teacher perceptions of behavioral disorders in children.* Gainesville, FL: Florida Educational Research and Development Council.

Kephart, N. C. (1971). Foreword. In T. S. Ball (Ed.), *Itard, Sequin, and Kephart: Sensory Education, A Learning Interpretation.* Columbus, OH: Charles E. Merrill.

Kilborn, P. T. (2000, July 27). Illiteracy pulls Appalachia back, and efforts to overcome it grow. *The New York Times,* A1, A14.

Kirby, B. L. (2003, September). *What is Asperger's syndrome?* In Asperger Syndrome Information and Support (O.A.S.I.S.). Available at www.udel.edu/bkirby/asperger/aswhatisit.html.

Kirk, S. A. (1976). In J. K. Kauffman & D. P. Hallahan, *Teaching Children with Learning Disabilities: Personal Perspectives.* Columbus, OH: Charles E. Merrill.

Knapp, M. S., Turnbull, B. J., & Shields, P. M. (1990). New directions for educating the children of poverty. *Educational Leadership 48*(1), 4–8.

Knitzer, J., Steinberg, Z., & Fleisch, B. (1990). *At the schoolhouse door: An examination of programs and policies for children with behavioral and emotional problems.* New York: Bank Street College of Education.

Knoblock, P. (1983). Teaching emotionally disturbed children. Dallas, TX: Houghton Mifflin.

Knoblock, P. (1987). *Understanding exceptional children and youth.* Boston: Little, Brown.

Kohl, H. (1967). *36 children.* New York: New American Express.

Kohn, A. (1988, November). Suffer the restless children. *The Atlantic Monthly,* 90–100.

Kohn, A. (1991). Caring kids: The role of schools. *Phi Delta Kappan 72*(7), 496–506

Kohn, A. (1999). *Punished by rewards: The trouble with gold stars, incentive plans, A's, praise, and other bribes.* Boston: Houghton Mifflin.

Kokaska, C. J., & Brolin, D. E. (1985). *Career education for handicapped individuals* (2nd ed.). Columbus, OH: Charles E. Merrill.

Koppitz, E. M. (1972–1973). Special class pupils with learning disabilities: A five year follow-up study. *Academic Therapy 8,* 133–138.

Kotulak, R. (1996, June 13.). *Learning how to use the brain.* Paper presented at the Brain Development in Young Children: New Frontiers for Research, Policy, and Practice Conference, Chicago, IL. Available at www.newhorizons.org/otc_21chusebrain.html.

Kounin, J. (1977). *Discipline and group management in classrooms.* New York: Holt, Rinehart and Winston.

Kozol, J. (1991). *Savage inequalities: Children in America's schools.* New York: Crown Publishers.

Kozol, J. (1995). *Amazing grace: Lives of children and the conscience of a nation.* New York: Crown Publishers.

Kuveke, S. (1983). School behaviors of educable mentally retarded children. *Education and Training of the Mentally Retarded 14*(2), 134–137.

Lahm, E., & Morrissette, S. (1994, April). *Zap 'em with assistive technology.* Paper presented at the annual meeting of the Council for Exceptional Children, Denver, CO.

Lambert, W. E. (1997). From Crockett to Tubman: Investigating historical perspectives. *Educational Leadership 55*(1), 51–54.

Langdon, H. (1983). Assessment and intervention strategies for the bilingual language-disordered student. *Exceptional Children 50*(1), 37–46.

Larivee, B. (1988). Effective strategies for academically handicapped students in the regular classroom. In R. E. Slavin, N. L. Karweit, & N. E. Madden (Eds.), *Effective Programs for Students at Risk.* Boston: Allyn and Bacon.

Larry P. v. Riles, Civil Action No. C-70-37 (n.d. Calif. 1971).

Larson, K. A., Gerber, M. M. (1987). Effects of social metacognitive training for enhancing overt behavior in learning disabled and low achieving delinquents. *Exceptional Children 54*(3), 201–211.

Lasley, T. J. (1989). A teacher development model for classroom management. *Phi Delta Kappan 7*(1), 36–38.

Leitch, L. M., & Tangri, S. S. (1988). Barriers to home-school collaboration. *Educational Horizons,* Winter, 70–74.

Lemeshow, S. (1982). *Handbook of clinical types in mental retardation.* Boston: Allyn and Bacon.

Lerner, J. (1997). *Learning disabilities: Theories, diagnosis, and teaching strategies.* (7th ed). Boston Houghton Mifflin Publishing.

Lerner, J. (2000). *Learning disabilities: Theories, diagnosis, and teaching strategies.* (8th ed.) Boston: Houghton Mifflin Publishing.

Lerner, J. (2003). *Learning disabilities: Theories, diagnosis and teaching strategies.* (9th ed.). Boston: Houghton Mifflin.

Lerner, J. W., Lowenthal, B., & Lerner, S. R. (1995). *Attention deficit disorder: Assessment and teaching.* Pacific Grove, CA: Brooks/Cole Publishing.

Leverault, A. H. (1990). Preventive discipline in the secondary school. Unpublished research paper.

Levine, M. (1990). *Learning disorders and the flow of expectations.* Their World. National Center for Learning Disabilities. Available at www.ldonline.org/ld/ld_indepth/general_info/gen-1.html.

Lewis, A. C. (1990). Tracking the national goals. *Phi Delta Kappan 72*(7), 496–506.

Lewis, B. L. (1992). Do conduct disordered gang members think differently? *Journal of Emotional and Behavioral Problems 1*(1), 17–20.

Lewis, R. B., & Doorlag, D. H. (1987). *Teaching special students in the mainstream* (2nd ed.). Columbus, OH: Merrill Publishing.

Lewis, T. J., and Sugai, G. (1999). Effective behavior support: A systems approach to proactive school-wide management. *Focus on Exceptional Children 31*(6), 1–24.

Lickona, T. (1988). Four strategies for fostering character development in children. *Phi Delta Kappan 69*(6), 419–423.

Lindsley, O. R. (1964). Direct measurement and prothesis of retarded behavior. *Journal of Education 147,* 62–81.

Lindsley, O. R. (1990). Precision teaching: By teachers for children. *Teaching Exceptional Children 22*(3), 10–15.

Lloyd, J. (1980). Academic instruction and cognitive behavior modification: The need for attack strategy training. *Exceptional Education Quarterly 1*(1), 53–63.

Lobav, W., Cohen, C., & Lewis, J. (1968). *A study of the non-standard English of Negro and Puerto Rican speakers in New York City.* New York: Columbia University (Research Project No. 3288).

Lokerson, J. (1996). *Learning disabilities.* Council for Exceptional Children, ERIC Clearinghouse on

Handicapped and Gifted Children, Reston, VA. (ERIC Digest #E516). Available at www.ldonline .org/ld_indepth/general_info/eric_ldgen.html.

London, P. (1987). Character education and clinical intervention: A paradigm shift for U.S. schools. *Phi Delta Kappan 68*(9), 667–673.

Long, N. (1990). Life space interviewing. *Beyond 2*(1), 10–15.

Long, N. J., Wood, M. M., & Fecser, F. A. (2001). *Life space crisis intervention: Talking with students in conflict* (2nd ed.). Austin, TX: Pro-Ed.

Long, N. L. (1986). The nine psychoeducational stages of helping emotionally disturbed students through the reeducation process. *The Pointer 30*(3), 5–20.

Lovitt, T. C. (1989). *Introduction to learning disabilities.* Boston: Allyn and Bacon.

Lund, N. J., & Duchan, J. F. (1988). *Assessing children's language in naturalistic contexts.* Upper Saddle River, NJ: Prentice Hall.

Lynch, E. W., & Stein, R. C. (1987). Parent participation by ethnicity: A comparison of Hispanic, black, and Anglo families. *Exceptional Children 54*(2), 105–111.

Lyon, G. R. (1996). Special education for students with disabilities: The future of children. *Learning Disabilities 6* (1), 1–20. Available at www.ldonline.org/ ld_indepth/general_info/future_children.html.

Maheady, L., Sacca, K. M., & Harper, G. F. (1988). Classwide peer tutoring with mildly handicapped high school students. *Exceptional Children 55*(1), 52–59.

Mandelbaum, L. H. (1989). Reading. In G. A. Robinson, J. R. Patton, E. A. Polloway, & L. R. Sargent (Eds.), *Best Practices in Mild Mental Retardation.* Reston, VA: The Division of Mental Retardation Council for Exceptional Children.

Mangrum, C. T., & Strichart, S. S. (1984). *College and the learning disabled student.* London: Grune & Stratton.

Mann, L., & Sabatino, D. (1985). *Foundations of cognitive process in remedial and special education.* Rockville, MD: Aspen Systems.

Mapp, K. (1997). Mating the connection between families and schools. *The Harvard Education Letter 8*(5), Cambridge, MA: Harvard Graduate School of Education.

Margolis, R. J. (1988). *Out of harm's way: The emancipation of juvenile justice.* New York: Edna McConnel Clark Foundation.

Marston, D. (1988). The effectiveness of special education: A time series analysis of reading performance in regular and special education settings. *Journal of Education 21*, 13–26.

Marzano, R. J., Marzano, J. S., & Pickering, D. J. (2003). *Classroom management that works: Research-based strategies for every teacher.* Alexandria, VA: Association for Supervision and Curriculum Development.

Massachusetts Department of Education (1991). Tracking: It's bad practice to identify ability groups, educators told. *Massachusetts Education Today 6*(5), 1, 7.

Mastropieri, M. A., & Scruggs, T. E. (2000). *The inclusive classroom: Strategies for effective instruction.* Upper Saddle River, NJ: Merrill/Prentice Hall.

Mathews, F. (1992). Reframing gang violence: A pro-youth strategy. *Journal of Emotional and Behavioral Problems 1*(3), 24–28.

Mathews, S. (1995). Juvenile capital offenders on empathy. *Journal of Emotional and Behavioral Problems 4*(2), 10–12.

Mayron, L. (1979). *Correlates of success in transition of mentally retarded to regular class* (vols. I and II). Los Angeles, CA: New Psychiatric Institute, Pacific State Hospital.

McConaughy, S. H. (1986). Social competence and behavioral problems of learning disabled adolescents. *Journal of Learning Disabilities 19*(2), 101–106.

McCourt, F. (2005). *Teacher man: A memoir.* New York: Scribner.

McCoy, K. (1987). *Solo parenting: Your essential guide.* New York: Signet.

McCoy, K. M., & Prehm, H. J. (1987). *Teaching mainstreamed students: Methods and techniques.* Denver, CO: Love Publishing.

McCubbin, H. I., McCubbin, M. A., Thompson, A. I., & Thompson, E. A. (1998). Resiliency in ethnic families: A conceptual model for predicting family adjustment and adaptation. In H. I. McCubbin, E. A. McCubbin, A. J. Thompson, & J. E. Fromer (Eds.), *Resiliency in Native American and Immigrant Families* (pp. 3–48). Thousand Oaks, CA: Sage.

McDaniel, E. A., & Diella-McCarthy (1989). Enhancing teacher efficacy in special education. *Teaching Exceptional Children 21*(4), 34–38.

McDaniel, T. R. (1986). A primer on classroom discipline: Principles old and new. *Phi Delta Kappan 68*(1), 63–67.

McFall, R. M. (1982). A review and reformulation of the concept of social skills. *Behavioral Assessment 4*, 1–33.

McGinnis, E., & Goldstein, P. (1984). *Skillstreaming the elementary school child: A guide for teaching prosocial skills.* Champaign, IL: Research Press.

McGuffey's Fourth Eclectic Reader (1920). New York: H. H. Vail, 38–39.

McKinney, J. D., McClure, S., & Feagans, L. (1982). Classroom behavior of learning disabled children. *Learning Quarterly 5*(1), 45–52.

McWhirter, J. J., McWhirter, R. J., & McWhirter, M. C. (1985). The learning disabled child: A retrospective review. *Journal of Learning Disabilities 18*(6), 315–318.

Meese, R. L. (1994). *Teaching learners with mild disabilities.* Pacific Grove, CA: Wadsworth.

Meichenbaum, D. (1977). *Cognitive behavior modification: An integrative approach.* New York: Plenum.

Meichenbaum, D., & Goodman, J. (1971). Training impulsive children to talk to themselves: A means of developing self-control. *Journal of Abnormal Psychology 77*, 115–126.

Menacker, J., Weldon, W., & Hurwitz, E. (1989). School order and safety as community issues. *Phi Delta Kappan 71*(1), 39–40, 55–56.

Mercer, C. D., & Mercer, A. R. (1985). *Teaching children with learning problems* (2nd ed.). Columbus, OH: Charles E. Merrill.

Mercer, J. (1973). The pluralistic assessment project. *School Psychology Digest 2*, 10–18.

Miller, D., Brown, A., & Robinson, L. (2002). Widgets on the web: Using computer based learning tools. *Teaching Exceptional Children 35*(2), 24–28.

Miller, E. (1996). Changing the way we think about kids with disabilities: A conversation with Tom Hehir. *Harvard Education Letter 10*(4), 5–7.

Mills v. the Board of Education of the District of Columbia, 348F. Supp. 866 (D.C. 1972).

Moores, D. F. (1982). *Educating the deaf: Psychology, principles, and practices* (2nd ed.). Boston: Houghton Mifflin.

Morrison, J. (1995). *DSM-IV made easy: The clinician's guide to diagnosis.* New York: Guilford Press.

Morse, W. (1987). Introduction. *Teaching Exceptional Children 19*(4), 4–6.

Morse, W. C. (1985). *Pursuit of excellence for educating the behavior disordered.* Paper presented at the Midwest Symposium for Leadership in Behavioral Disorders. Kansas City, MO.

Morsink, C. V. (1984). *Teaching special needs students in regular classrooms.* Boston: Little, Brown.

Mostert, M. P. (1998). *Interprofessional collaboration in schools.* Boston: Allyn and Bacon.

Moxley, R. A. (1998). Treatment-only designs and student self-recording as strategies for public school teachers. *Education and Treatment of Children 21*, 37–61.

Myers, P. I., & Hammill, D. D. (1982). *Learning disabilities: Basic concepts, assessment practices, and instructional strategies.* Austin, TX: Pro-Ed.

Myklebust, H. R. (1964). Learning disorders: Psychoneurological disturbances in childhood. *Rehabilitation Literature 25*, 354–359.

National Assistive Technology Research Institute. (2006). *A functional approach to the delivery of assistive technology services.* Available at http://natri.uky.edu/resources/reports/function.html.

National Association of Colleges and Employers. (2007). *Job survey.* Available at www.naceweb.org.

National Center for Learning Disabilities. (2007). *IDEA 2004 Parent Guide.* Available at www.ncld.org/content/view/924/456087/.

National Center for Learning Disabilities. (2006). *A parent's guide to response-to-intervention.* Parent Advocacy Brief. Available at www.LD.org.

National Education Association (2001). Where the stakes are high for students. In L. Washburn-Moses (2003, March/April). What every special educator should know about high-stakes testing. *Teaching Exceptional Children 35*(4), 12–15.

National Head Start Programs. (2008). Benefits of Head Start (HS) and early Head Start (HS) programs. Available at www.nhsa.org.download/research/REDFactSheets/.pdf.

National Information Center for Children and Youth with Disabilities. (2000). *Learning strategies for students with learning disabilities.* Washington, DC: NICHCY. Available at www.ldonline.org/ld_indepth/teaching_techniques/nichcy_interventions_bib.html.

National Institute of Child Health and Development. (2007). *Learning disabilities.* Available at www.education.com/reference/article/RefDisabilities 2/.

National Institute of Mental Health. (1996). *Learning disabilities: Decade of the brain* (NIH). Available at www.ldonline.org/ld_indepth/general_info/gennimh-booklet.html.

National Research Council, Committee on Educational Interventions for Children with Autism, Division of Behavioral and Social Sciences and Education. (2001). *Educating children with autism.* Washington, DC: National Academy Press.

National Research Council, Committee on Minority Representation in Special Education. (2002). M. Suzanne Donovan & Christopher T. Cross (Eds.), *Minority Students in Special and Gifted Education.* Washington, DC: National Academy Press.

Neill, M. D., & Medina, N. J. (1989). Standardized testing: Harmful to educational health. *Phi Delta Kappan 70*(9), 668–697.

Neisworth, J. T., & Greer, J. G. (1975). Functional similarities of learning disability and mild retardation. *Exceptional Children 42*, 17–21.

Nelson, C. M. (1988). Social skills training for handicapped students. *Teaching Exceptional Children 20*(4), 19–22.

Nelson, M. C., Rutherford, R. B., Jr., & Wolford, B. I. (Eds.). (1987). *Special education in the criminal justice system.* Columbus, OH: Charles E. Merrill.

New York Times. (1999, September 7). *Scientists find the first gene for dyslexia. New York Times*, D1.

Nichols, S. L., & Good, T. L. (2004). Why today's young children are viewed so negatively. *Education Week 23*(31), 42.

NLDline News. (2003, September). *NLD letter and information packet.* Available at www.nldline.com/welcome.htm.

Nonverbal Learning Disorders Association. (2003, September). *What is NLD?* Available at www.nlda/whatis.html.

Noyes, K. G., & McAndrew, G. L. (1971). Is this what schools are for? In M. L. Silberman (Ed.), *The Experience of Schooling.* New York: Holt, Rinehart, & Winston.

O'Brien, G. V. (1999). Protecting the social body: Use of the organism in fighting the menace of the feeble-minded. *Mental Retardation 37*(3), 188–200.

Obiakor, F. E. (1994). *The eight step multicultural approach: Learning and teaching with a smile.* Dubuque, IA: Kendall/Hunt.

Obiakor, F. E. (1999). Teacher expectations of minority exceptional learners: Impact on "accuracy" of self-concepts. *Exceptional Children 66*, 39–53.

Obiakor, F. E. (2001). *It even happens in "good" schools: Responding to cultural diversity in today's classrooms.* Thousand Oaks, CA: Corwin Press.

Ornstein, R. (1978, May). The split and the whole brain. *Human Nature*, 76–83.

OSEP Center on Positive Behavioral Interventions and Supports. (2005). *School-wide positive behavior support: Implementers' blueprint and self assessment.* Eugene, OR: Author.

Osman, B. B. (1979). *Learning disabilities: A family affair.* New York: Warner.

Palinesar, A. S. (1982). *Improving the reading comprehension of junior high students through reciprocal teaching of comprehension-monitoring strategies.* Unpublished doctoral dissertation, University of Illinois, Urbana-Champaign.

Pallas, A. M., Natriello, G., & McDill, E. L. (1989, June/July). *The changing nature of disadvantaged population: Current dimensions and future trends. Educational Leadership*, 16–22.

Pasamanick, B., & Knoblock, H. (1973). The epidemiology of reproductive casualty. In S. Sapir & A. Nitzburg (Eds.), *Children with Learning Problems.* New York: Brunner/Mazel.

Patton, J. R., Cronin, M. E., Polloway, E. A., Hutchison, D., & Robinson, G. A. (1989). Curricular considerations: A life skills orientation. In G. A. Robinson, J. R. Patton, E. A. Polloway, & L. R. Sargent (Eds.), *Best Practices in Mental Disabilities.* Des Moines: Iowa Department of Education, Bureau of Special Education.

Patton, J. R., Kauffman, J. M., Blackbourn, J. M., & Brown, B. G. (1991). *Exceptional children in focus* (5th ed.). New York: Macmillan.

Paul, J. L., & Epanchin, B. C. (1991). *Educating emotionally disturbed children and youth: Theories and practices for teachers* (2nd ed.). New York: Merrill Publishing.

Pennsylvania Association for Retarded Children (PARC) v. Commonwealth of Pennsylvania, 334 F. Supp. 1257 (E.D. PA 1971).

Pervasive Developmental Disorder. (2003, September). *An AskERIC InfoGuide.* Available at www.askeric.org/Old_Askeric/InfoGuides/alpha_list/ppd12_96.html.

Peterson, N. L. (1987). *Early intervention for handicapped and at-risk children.* Denver, CO: Love Publishing.

Phi Delta Kappa Commission on Discipline. (1982). *Handbook for developing schools with good discipline.* Bloomington, IN: Phi Delta Kappa.

Phillips, V., & McCullough, L. (1990). Consultation based programming: Instituting the collaborative work ethic. *Exceptional Children 56*(4), 291–304.

Piaget, J. (1950). *The psychology of intelligence.* New York: International Universities Press.

Plessy v. Ferguson, 163 U.S. 537 (1896).

Polloway, E. A., Patton, J. R., Payne, J. S., & Payne, R. A. (1989). *Strategies for teaching learners with special needs* (4th ed.). Columbus, OH: Charles E. Merrill.

Poplin, M. S. (1989). The reductionistic fallacy in learning disabilities: Replicating the past by reducing the present. *Journal of Learning Disabilities 21*(7), 389–400.

Prater, M. A. (2003). She will succeed! Strategies for success in inclusive classrooms. *Teaching Exceptional Children 35*(5), 58–64.

Pressley, M., & Harris, K. R. (1990). What we really know about strategy instruction. *Educational Leadership 48*(1), 31–33.

Price, Mayfield, McFadden, & Marsh. (2001). *Accommodation strategies.* Available at www.parrotpublishing.com/Inclusion_Chapter_6.htm.

Pruchno, R., Patrick, J. H., & Burant, C. J. (1997). African American and white mothers of adults with chronic disabilities: Caregiving burden and satisfaction. *Family Relations 46*, 335–346.

Przychodin, J. (1981). Improving classroom discipline. *Clearing House 55*(1), 16.

Pugach, M. C., & Johnson, L. J. (1989a). The challenge of implementing collaboration between general and special education. *Exceptional Children 56*(3), 232–235.

Pugach, M. C., & Johnson, L. J. (1989b). Prereferral interventions: Progress, problems, and challenges. *Exceptional Children 56*(3), 217–226.

Putnam, J. W., Rynders, J. E., Johnson, R. T., & Johnson, D. W. (1989). Collaborative skill instruction for promoting positive interactions between mentally handicapped and nonhandicapped children. *Exceptional Children 55*(6), 550–558.

Ramsey, R. S. (1981). *Perceptions of disturbed and disturbing behavioral characteristics by school personnel.* Unpublished doctoral dissertation, University of Florida, Gainesville.

Ramsey, R. S. (1995a). Preparatory guide for special education teacher competency tests-revised. Boston: Allyn and Bacon.

Ramsey, R. S. (1995b). *Students with learning disabilities in college.* Presentation to Andrew College Faculty, Cuthbert, Georgia, April 12 and September 6, 1995.

Ramsey, R. S. (1996). Working with college students with learning disabilities. Session Presenter at the Georgia Council for Exceptional Children State Conference, Columbus, Georgia, November 8, 1996.

Ramsey, R. S. (1997). *Learning disabilities and young adults in college.* Unpublished manuscript.

Ramsey, R. S. (1998). *Co-teaching/collaboration.* A session for the Block Academy, Muscogee County School District, Columbus, Georgia, June 11, 1998.

Ramsey, R. S., Dixon, M. J., & Smith, G. G. B. (1986). *Eyes on the special education: Professional knowledge teacher competency test.* Albany, GA: Southwest Georgia Learning Resources System Center.

Ratekin, N. (1979). Reading achievement of disabled learners. *Exceptional Children 45*(16), 454–458.

Redl, F. (1971). The concept of the life space interview. In N. Long, W. Morse, & R. Newman (Eds.), *Conflict in the Classroom.* Belmont, CA: Wadsworth Publishing.

Redl, F., & Wineman, D. (1951). *Children who hate.* Glencoe, IL: The Free Press.

Redl, F., & Wineman, D. (1957). *The aggressive child.* Glencoe, IL: The Free Press.

Reed, S., & Sauter, C. R. (1990). Children of poverty, the status of 12 million young children. *Phi Delta Kappan*, K1–K12.

Reid, D. (1978). *Toward the application of development epistemology to the education of exceptional children.* Proceedings of the Eighth Annual Conference on Piagetian Theory and the Helping Professions. Los Angeles, California.

Reid, D. K., & Hresko, W. P. (1981a). Thinking about it in that way: Test data and instruction. *Exceptional Education Quarterly 1*(3), 47–57.

Reid, D. K., & Hresko, W. P. (1981b). *A cognitive approach to learning disabilities.* New York: McGraw-Hill.

Reif, S. (1998). Redefining "structure" for students with AD/HD. Reclaiming today's youth. *Journal of Emotional and Behavioral Problems 2*(2), 24–28.

Reinert, H. (1976). *Children in conflict.* St. Louis, MO: C. V. Mosby.

Renzulli, J. S., Reis, S. M., & Smith, L. H. (1981). *The revolving door identification model.* Mansfield Center, CT Creative Learning.

Report of the National Reading Panel. (1999). *Teaching children to read: An evidence-based assessment of the scientific research literature on reading and its implications for reading instruction.* Washington, DC: Author.

Reschly, D. J. (1989). Incorporating adaptive behavior deficits into instructional programs. In G. A. Robinson, J. R. Patton, E. A. Polloway, & L. R. Sargent (Eds.), *Best Practices in Mild Mental Retardation.* Reston, VA: The Division of Mental Retardation Council for Exceptional Children.

Research Brief for Teachers. (1988). *Curriculum based assessment.* (ERIC/OSEP Special Project). Reston, VA: The Council for Exceptional Children.

Restak, R. M. (1984). *The brain.* New York: Bantam Books.

Reynolds, W. M., & Miller, K. L. (1985). Depression and learned helplessness in mentally retarded and nonmentally retarded adolescents: An initial investigation. *Applied Research in Mental Retardation 6*(3), 295–306.

Rezmierski, V. E. (1987). Discipline: Neither the steel nor the velvet, but the maturity inside the glove, that makes the difference. *The Pointer 31*(4), 5–13.

Rhodes, W. C. (1967). The disturbing child: A problem of ecological management. *Exceptional Children 33*, 449–455.

Rhodes, W. C., & Tracy, M. L. (1972a). *A study of child variance: Conceptual models* (vol. 1). Ann Arbor: University of Michigan.

Rhodes, W. C., & Tracy, M. L. (1972b). *A study of child variance: Interventions* (vol. 2). Ann Arbor: University of Michigan.

Rich, H. L., & Ross, S. M. (1989). Students' time on learning tasks in special education. *Exceptional Children 55*(6), 508–515.

Ritschl, C., Mongrella, A. J., & Presbie, R. L. (1972).

Group time out from rock and roll music and out of seat behavior of handicapped children while riding a school bus. *Psychological Reports 31*, 967–873.

Roberts, M. (1986). Three mothers: Life span experiences. In R. Fewell & P. Vadasy (Eds.), *Families of Handicapped Children: Needs and Supports Across the Life Span* (pp. 193–218). Austin, TX: Pro-Ed.

Roberts, S. (1983). A focus on learning disabilities at the college level. *Times-Argus*, Montpelier, VT, 89, 90.

Robinson, S. M. (1989). Oral language: Developing pragmatic skills and communicational competence. In G. A. Robinson, J. R. Patton, E. A. Polloway, & L. R. Sargent (Eds.), *Best Practices in Mild Mental Retardation*. Reston, VA: The Division of Mental Retardation Council for Exceptional Children.

Robinson, W. A. (1965). The elaborated code in working class language. *Language and Speech 8*, 243–252.

Rogers-Dulan, J., & Blacher, J. (1995). African American families, religion, and disability: A conceptual framework. *Mental Retardation 33*, 226–238.

Roit, M. L., & Pfohl, W. (1984). The readability of P.L. 94–142. Parent materials: Are parents truly informed? *Exceptional Children 50*(6), 496–504.

Rose, L. C., & Gallup, A. M. (2006). The 38th annual Phi Delta Kappa/Gallup Poll of the public's attitudes toward the public schools. *Phi Delta Kappan 88*, 41–53.

Rosenshine, B., & Stevens, R. (1984). *Classroom instruction in a reading research*. New York: Longman.

Rothstein, L. F. (1995). *Special education law* (2nd ed.). New York: Longman Publishers.

Rubin, R., & Balow, B. (1971). Learning and behavior disorders: A longitudinal study. *Exceptional Children 38*, 293–299.

Rutter, M., Giller, H., & Hagell, A. (1998). *Antisocial behavior by young people*. New York: Cambridge University Press.

Ryan, E. B., Short, E. J., & Weed, K. A. (1986). The role of cognitive strategy training in improving the academic performance of learning disabled children. *Journal of Learning Possibilities 18*, 521–529.

Safran, S. P., & Oswald, K. (2003). Positive behavior supports: Can schools reshape disciplinary practices? *Exceptional Children 69*, 361–373.

Salend, S. J. (1987). Contingency management systems. *Academic Therapy 22*(3), 245–253.

Salend, S. J. (2001). *Creating inclusive classrooms: Effective and reflective practices* (4th ed.). Upper Saddle River, NJ: Merrill/Prentice Hall.

Salend, S. J., & Lutz, J. G. (1984). Mainstreaming or mainlining: A competency based approach to mainstreaming. *Journal of Learning Disabilities 17*, 27–29.

Sandford, J. A. (1987). Putting parents in their place in public schools. *NASSP Bulletin*, 47.99–103.

Sandomierski, T., Kincaid, D., & Algozzine, B. (2007). Response to intervention and positive behavior support: Brothers from different mothers or sisters with different misters? *Positive Behavior Interventions and Supports Newsletter 4*(2).

Sarason, S. B., & Doris, J. (1979). *Educational handicap, public policy, and social history*. New York: Free Press.

Satcher, D. (2000). Keynote address. Conference of children's mental health. Available at www.surgeongeneral.gov/library/speeches/ChildMentalHealth.htm.

Scanlon, D. M., Vellutino, F. R., Small, S. G., & Fanuele, D. P., & Sweeney, J. (2003). *The short and long term effects of different types of early literacy intervention on reading comprehension*. Paper presented at the annual conference of the Society for the Scientific Study of Reading. June 2003, Boulder, CO.

Schloss, P. J., & Smith, M. A. (1998). *Applied behavior analysis in the classroom* (2nd ed.). Boston: Allyn and Bacon.

Schroeder, C. S., & Riddle, D. B. (1991). Behavior theory and practice. In J. L. Paul & B. C. Epanchin (Eds.), *Educating Emotionally Disturbed Children and Youth: Theories and Practices for Teachers* (2nd ed.). New York: Merrill Publishing.

Schultz, E. W., & Heuchen, C. M. (1983). *Child stress and the school experience*. New York: Human Sciences Press.

Schulz, J. B., Carpenter, C. D., & Turnbull, A. P. (1991). *Mainstreaming exceptional students: A guide for classroom teachers*. Boston: Allyn and Bacon.

Schumaker, J. B., & Hazel, J. S. (1984). Social skills assessment and training for the learning disabled: What's on second? Part I. *Journal of Learning Disabilities 17*(7), 422–431.

Schumaker, J. B., Pederson, C. J., Hazel, J. S., & Meyen, E. L. (1983). Social skills curricula for mildly handicapped adolescents: A review. *Focus on Exceptional Children 16*(4), 1–16.

Schwartz, L. W. (1979). *Psychopathology of childhood*. New York: Holt, Rinehart & Winston.

Scott, M. E. (1988). Learning strategies can help. *Teaching Exceptional Children 20*(3), 30–34.

Scruggs, T. E., & Mastropieri, M. A. (1986). Improving the test-taking skills of behaviorally disordered and learning disabled children. *Exceptional Children 53*(1), 63–68.

Section 504 of the Rehabilitation Act of 1973, as amended, 29 U.S.C. 793(a), 794 (1973).

Seldes, C. (1985). *The great thoughts.* New York: Ballantine.

Seligman, M. (1999). Childhood disability and the family. In V. L. Schwean & D. H. Saklofske (Eds.), *Handbook of Psychosocial Characteristics of Exceptional Children* (pp. 111–131). New York: Plenum.

Selman, R. L. (1980). *The growth of interpersonal understanding: Developmental and clinical analysis.* New York: Academic Press.

Seyle, H. (1975). *Stress without distress.* New York: Signet.

Shaw, P., Eckstrand, W., Sharp, J. Bluementhal, J. P., Lerch, D., Greenstein, L., Clasen, A., Evans, A., Giedd, J., & Rapoport, J. L. (2007). *Attention-deficit/hyperactivity disorder is characterized by a delay in cortical maturation.* Proceedings of the National Academy of Sciences of the United States of America. Available at www.pnas.org/cgi/content.

Sherry, L. (1982). Non-task oriented behaviors of educable mentally retarded, emotionally handicapped, and learning disabled students. *Educational Research Quarterly 4,* 19–29.

Sigmon, S. B. (1989). Reaction to excerpts from *The Learning Mystique:* A rational appeal for change. *Journal of Learning Disabilities 22*(5), 298–300, 327.

Silver, H., Strong, R., & Perini, M. (1997). Integrating learning styles and multiple intelligences. *Educational Leadership 55*(1), 22–27.

Silver, L. B. (1975). Acceptable and controversial approaches to treating the child with learning disabilities. *Pediatrics 55*(3), 406–415.

Silver, L. B. (1989). Frequency of adoption of children and adolescents with learning disabilities. *Journal of Learning Disabilities 22*(5), 325–327.

Siperstein, G. N., & Goding, M. J. (1985). Teachers' behavior toward LD and non-LD children: A strategy for change. *Journal of Learning Disabilities 18*(3), 139–144.

Skiba, R. J., Michael, R. S., Nardo, A. C, & Peterson, R. L. (2002). The color of discipline: Sources of racial and gender disproportionality in school punishment. *Urban Review 34.* 317–342.

Skiba, R. J., Poloni-Staudinger, L., Gallini, S., Simmons, A. B., & Feggins-Azziz, L. R. (2005). Disparate access: The disproportionality of African American students with disabilities across educational environments. *Exceptional Children 72,* 411–424.

Skiba, R. J., Poloni-Staudinger, L., Simmons, A. B., Feggins-Azziz, L. R., & Chung, C. G. (2005). Unproven links: Can poverty explain ethnic disproportionality in special education? *Journal of Special Education 39,* 130–144.

Skiba, R. J., Wu, T. C., Kohler, K., Chung, C. G., & Simmons, A. B. (2001). *Disproportionality and discipline among Indiana's students with disabilities.* Bloomington, IN: Indiana Education Policy Center.

Skiba, R., Simmons, A., Ritter, S., Kohler, K., Henderson, M., & Wu, T. (2006). The context of minority disproportionality: Practitioner perspectives on special education referral. *Teachers College Record 108,* 1424–1459.

Skinner, D., Bailey, D. B., Correa, V., & Rodriguez, P. (1999). Narrating self and disability: Latino mothers construction of identities vis-à-vis their child with special needs. *Exceptional Children 65,* 481–495.

Slavin, R. E., Madden, N. A., & Leavey, M. (1984). Effects of cooperative learning and individualized instruction on mainstreamed students. *Exceptional Children 50*(5), 434–443.

Smith, C. R. (1983). *Learning disabilities: The interaction of learner, task, and setting.* Boston: Little, Brown.

Smith, C. R. (1991). *Learning disabilities: The interaction of learner, task, and setting.* Boston: Allyn and Bacon.

Smith, D. (2004). *Practical strategies that work: Using sociograms as a behaviour management tool.* Available at www.aase.edu.au/2004_Conf_papers/.

Smith, J. E., & Patton, J. M. (1989). *A resource module on adverse causes of mild mental retardation.* Prepared for the President's Committee on Mental Retardation. Available at www.archives.gov/federal-register /codification/exe.

Smith, R. A. (1987). A teacher's views on cooperative learning. *Phi Delta Kappan 68*(9), 663–666.

Smith, S. (1980). *No easy answers: The learning disabled child at school and home.* New York: Bantam Books.

Smith, S. (2005). *The lab school of Washington.* Available at www.labschool.org.

Smith, S. L. (1979). *No easy answers.* Cambridge, MA: Winthrop.

Smith, T. E. C., Finn, D. M., & Dowdy, C. A. (1993). *Teaching students with mild disabilities.* Fort Worth: TX: Harcourt Brace Jovanovich.

Smith, T. E. C., Price, B. J., & Marsh, G. E., II. (1986). *Mildly handicapped children and adults.* St. Paul, MN: West Publishing.

Smith-Davis, J. (1989a, April). *A national perspective on special education.* Keynote presentation at the GLRS/College/University Forum, Macon, GA.

Smith-Davis, J. (1989b). Exceptional children in tomorrow's schools. In E. L. Meyen (Ed.), *Exceptional Children in Today's Schools.* Denver, CO: Love Publishing.

Special Connections. (2007a). *Accommodations: Considerations for assessment and instruction.* Available at www.specialconnections.ku.edu/cgi-bin/cgiwrap/specconn/main.php?cat=instruction.

Special Connections. (2007b). Accommodations: Keys to accessing the general education curriculum for inclusion students. Available at www.specialconnections.ku.edu.

Speece, S. L., McKinney, J. D., & Appelbaum, M. I. (1986). Longitudinal development of conservation skills in learning disabled children. *Journal of Learning Disabilities 19*(5), 302–307.

Sperry, R. W. (1968). Hemisphere deconnection and unity in conscious awareness. *American Psychologist 23*, 723–733.

Stafford, P., & Klein, N. (1977). Application of Piaget's theory to the study of thinking of the mentally retarded: A review of the research. *Journal of Special Education 11*(2), 201–216.

Stainback, D., Stainback, W., & Forest, M. (1989). *Educating all students in the mainstream of regular education.* Baltimore, MD: Brookes.

Stainback, W., & Stainback, S. (1984). A rationale for the merger of special and regular education. *Exceptional Children 51*(2), 102–111.

Staub, D., & Peck, C. A. (1994). What are the outcomes for nondisabled students? *Educational Leadership 52*(4), 36–40.

Stein, K. S., Leinhardt, B., & Bickel, W. (1989). Instructional issues for teaching students at risk. In R. E. Slavin, N. L. Karweit, & N. A. Madden (Eds.), *Effective Programs for Students at Risk.* Boston: Allyn and Bacon.

Stephens, R. J., & Slavin, R. E. (1991). When cooperative learning improves the achievement of students with mild disabilities: A response to Tateyama-Sniezek. *Exceptional Children 57*(1), 9–23.

Stephens, T. (1977). *Teaching skills to children with learning and behavior disorders.* Columbus, OH: Charles E. Merrill.

Stephens, T. M., Blackhurst, A. E., & Magliocca, L. A. (1988). *Teaching mainstreamed students* (2nd ed.). New York: Pergamon Press.

Sternberg, R. J. (1990). Thinking styles: Key to understanding performance. *Phi Delta Kappan 71*(5), 366–371.

Still, G. (1902). Goulstonian lectures. March 4, 6, 11. Available at www.georgestillforam.co.uk/

Strauss, A., & Lehtinen, L. S. (1947). Psychopathology and education of the brain injured child. New York: Grune & Stratton.

Strong, R. W., Silver, H. F., Hanson, J. R., Marzano, R. J., Wolfe, P., Dewing, T., & Brock, W. (1990). Thoughtful education: Staff development for the 1990s. *Educational Leadership 47*(5), 25–29.

Sugai, G., & Horner, R. H. (1999). Discipline and behavioral support: Practices, pitfalls, promises. *Effective School Practices 17*(4), 10–22.

Sugai, G., & Horner, R. H. (2002). The evolution of discipline practices: School-wide positive behavior supports. *Child and Family Behavior Therapy 24*, 23–50.

Sylwester, R. (1994). How emotions affect learning. *Educational Leadership 52*(2), 60–65.

Sylwester, R. (2000). Unconscious emotions, conscious feelings. *Educational Leadership 58*(3), 20–24.

Tarver, S. G. (1986). Cognitive behavior modification, direct instruction and holistic approaches to the education of students with learning disabilities. *Journal of Learning Disabilities 19*(6), 368–375.

Task Force of Children Out of School. (1970). *The way we go to school: The exclusion of children in Boston.* Boston: Beacon Press.

Tateyama-Sniezek, K. M. (1990). Cooperative learning: Does it improve the academic achievement of students with handicaps? *Exceptional Children 57*(2), 426–427.

Taylor, S. (2007). Mental retardation is no more; New name is intellectual and developmental disabilities. Available at www.aamr.org/Abour AIDD/MR name change.htm.

Taylor, S. J., & Searle, S. J. (1987). The disabled in America: History, policy and trends. In P. Knoblock (Ed.), *Understanding Exceptional Children and Youth.* Boston: Little, Brown.

The Condition of Education. (2007). Available at http://nces.ed.gov/programs/coe/.

Thomas, A., & Chess, S. (1977). Temperament and development. New York: Bruner/Mazel.

Thomas, C. C., Correa, V. I., & Morsink, C. V. (2001). *Interactive teaming: Enhancing programs for students with special needs* (3rd ed.). Upper Saddle River, NJ: Merrill/Prentice Hall.

Todd, A. W., Horner, R. H., Sugai, G., and Sprague, J. R. (1999). Effective behavior support: Strengthening school-wide systems through a team-based approach. *Effective School Practices 17*(4), 23–27.

Tomlinson, C. (2000). Reconcilable differences? Standards-based teaching and differentiation. *Educational Leadership 58*(1), 6–11.

Torgesen, J. K. (1977). Memorization processes in reading disabled children. *Journal of Educational Psychology 69*, 571–578.

Treible, C. (1996, February). Unpublished interview with Director of Learning Disability Support Services, Andrew College, Cuthbert, Georgia.

Tucker, J. (1985). Curriculum-based assessment: An introduction. *Exceptional Children 52*, 199–204.

U.S. Bureau of the Census. (1995). Health insurance coverage: 1994. *Current Population Reports*, Series P60–P190. Washington, DC: U.S. Government Printing Office.

U.S. Department of Education. (1996). *Eighteenth annual report on the implementation of the Individuals with Disabilities Education Act.* Washington, DC: Author.

U.S. Department of Education. (1997). *Nineteenth annual report to Congress on the implementation of the Individuals with Disabilities Education Act.* Washington, DC: Author.

U.S. Department of Education. (1998). *Twentieth annual report to Congress on the implementation of the Individuals with Disabilities Education Act.* Washington, DC: Author.

U.S. Department of Education. (2000). *Twenty-first annual report to Congress on the implementation of the Individuals with Disabilities Education Act.* Washington, DC: Author.

U.S. Department of Education. (2001). *Twenty-second annual report to Congress on the Implementation of the Individuals with Disabilities Education Act.* Washington, DC: Author

U.S. Department of Education. (2002). *Twenty-third annual report to Congress on the Implementation of the Individuals with Disabilities Education Act.* Washington, DC: Author.

U.S. Department of Education. (2003). *Twenty-fourth annual report to Congress on the implementation of the Individuals with Disabilities Education Act.* Washington, DC: Author.

U.S. Department of Education. (2004). *Twenty-fifth annual report to Congress on the implementation of the individuals with disabilities education act*, vol 1. Washington, DC: Author.

U.S. Department of Education. (2006). Assistance to states for the education of children with disabilities and preschool grants for children with disabilities; final rule. *Federal Register* part II 34 CFR Parts 300 and 301. Washington, DC: Author.

U.S. Department of Education. (2007a). *Alignment of IDEA and NCLB.* Washington, DC: Author, Office of Special Education Programs.

U.S. Department of Education. (2007b). *Twenty-seventh annual report to Congress on the implementation of the Individuals with Disabilities Education Act* (vol. 1). Washington, DC: Author.

U.S. Department of Education, National Center of Education Statistics. (2007). The condition of education 2007 (NCES 2007–064). Washington, DC: U.S. Government Printing Office.

U.S. Department of Education. (2008). Reauthorization of No Child Left Behind. Available at www.ed.gov/nclb/anding.jhtml.

U.S. Office of Special Education Programs. (2002, Nov./Dec.). *A new resource to help IEP teams.* Available at www.nea.org/special/ed/resources.

Uecker, A., & Nadel, L. (1998). Spatial but not object memory impairments in children with fetal alcohol syndrome. *American Journal on Mental Retardation 103*(1), 12–18.

Umbreit, J., & Ostrow, L. S. (1980). The fetal alcohol syndrome. *Mental Retardation 18*(3), 109–111.

Utley, C. A., & Obiakor, F. E. (2001). *Special education, multicultural education, and school reform: Components of quality for learners with mild disabilities.* Springfield, IL: Charles C. Thomas.

Vadasy, P. F. (1986). Single mothers: A social phenomenon and population in need. In R. Fewell & P. Vadasy (Eds.), *Families of Handicapped Children: Needs and Supports Across the Life Span* (pp. 221–249). Austin, TX: Pro-Ed.

Van Sickle, J. H. (1908–1909). Provision for exceptional children in the public schools. *Psychological Clinic 2*, 102–111.

Vaughn, S., Bos, C. S., & Lund, K. A. (1986). But they can do it in my room: Strategies for promoting generalization. *Teaching Exceptional Children 18*(3), 176–180.

Vaughn, S., Bos, C. S., & Schumm, J. S. (1997). *Teaching mainstreamed, diverse, and at-risk students in the general education classroom.* Boston: Allyn and Bacon.

Vaughn, S., Schumm, J. S., & Arguelles, M. E. (1997). The ABCDEs of co-teaching. *Teaching Exceptional Children 30*(2), 4–10.

Villa, R., Thousand, J., Stainback, W., & Stainback, W. (1999). Restructuring for caring and effective educators, (2nd ed.). Baltimore, MD: Brooks Publishing.

Wagmeister, J., & Shifrin, B. (2000). Thinking differently, learning differently. *Educational Leadership 58*(3), 45–48.

Wagner, M., Carneto, R., & Guzman, A. (2003). Who are secondary students in special education today? *Reports from the National Longitudinal Transition Study 2*(1). Available at www.ncset.org/publications/viewdesc.asp?id=1008.

Walker, H., Ramsey, E., & Gresham, F. (2004). *Antisocial behavior in school: Evidence based practices.* (2nd ed.). Belmont, CA: Thomson Wadsworth.

Walker, H. M., & Severson, H. H. (1999). *Systematic screening for behavior disorders (SSBD): User's guide and administration manual* (2nd ed.). Longmont, CO: Sopris West.

Walker, J. E., & Shea, T. M. (1991). *Behavior management: A practical approach for educators.* New York: MacMillan.

Wallace, G., & Kauffman, J. M. (1986). *Teaching students with learning and behavior problems* (3rd ed.). Columbus, OH: Charles E. Merrill.

Wallace, H. (1972, October). The epidemiology of development disabilities. Paper delivered to the Annual Meeting of United Cerebral Palsy, Louisville, Kentucky.

Wang, M. C., & Baker, E. T. (1986). Mainstreaming programs: Design features and effects. *Journal of Special Education 19*(4), 503–520.

Warner, I. (1991). Parents in touch—District leadership for parent involvement. *Phi Delta Kappan 72*(5), 372–375.

Washburn-Moses, L. (2003). What every special educator should know about high-stakes testing. *Teaching Exceptional Children 35*(4), 12–15.

Watson, S. (2003, May). *Special education terminology.* Available at www.specialed.about.com/cs/teacher-strategies/a/terminology.htm.

Wehmeyer, M., & Schwartz, M. (1997). Self-determination and positive adult outcomes: A follow-up study of youth with mental retardation or learning disabilities. *Exceptional Children, 63*, 245–255.

Wehmeyer, M. L., Kelchner, K., & Richards, S. (1996). Essential characteristics of self determined behavior of individuals with mental retardation. *American Journal on Mental Retardation 100*, 632–642.

Weller, C., Strawser, S., & Buchanan, M. (1985). Adaptive behavior: Designator of a continuum of severity of learning disabled individuals. *Journal of Learning Disabilities 18*(4), 200–203.

Werner, H. (1944). Development of visuo-motor performance on the marble board test in mentally retarded children. *Journal of Genetic Psychology 64*, 269–279.

Wesson, C. L. (1991). Curriculum-based measurement and two models of follow-up consultation. *Exceptional Children 57*(3), 246–256.

WestEd. (2000). *Improving student achievement by extending school: Is it just a matter of time.* Available at http://web.wested.org/online_pubs/timeandlearning/TAL_PV.html.

Westwater, A., & Wolfe, P. (2000). The brain-compatible curriculum. *Educational Leadership 58*(3), 49–52.

White, M. A. (1971). The view from the pupil's desk. In M. L. Silberman (Ed.), *The Experience of Schooling.* New York: Holt, Rinehart, and Winston.

White, O. R. (1986). Precision teaching—precision learning. *Exceptional Children 52*, 522–534.

Whiting, J., & Aultman, L. (1990). *Workshop for parents* (Workshop materials). Albany, GA: Southwest Georgia Learning Resources System Center.

Wickman, E. K. (1929). *Children's behavior and teachers' attitudes.* New York: The Commonwealth Fund.

Will, M. (1986). *Educating students with learning problems: A shared responsibility.* Washington, DC: U.S. Department of Education.

Williams, L. D. (1988). A parent's opinion: Exceptional teachers. *Teaching K–8, 9–10*, 88.

Williams, S. (2002). How speech feedback and word prediction software can help students write. *Teaching Exceptional Children 34*(3), 72–78.

Wilson, C. R. (1983). Teaching reading comprehension by connecting the known to the new. *Reading Teacher 36*, 382–390.

Winick, M. (1976). *Malnutrition and brain development.* New York: Oxford Press.

Winzer, M. A., & Mazurek, K. (1998). *Special education in multicultural contexts.* Columbus, OH: Merrill.

Wojnilower, D. A., & Gross, A. M. (1988). Knowledge, perception, and performance of assertive behavior in children with learning disabilities. *Journal of Learning Disabilities 21*(2), 109–117.

Wolking, B. (1991). Personal correspondence.

Wong, B. Y. L. (1979). Increasing retention of main ideas through questioning strategies. *Learning Disability Quarterly 2*, 42–47.

Wong, B. Y. L. (1985). Potential means of enhancing content skills acquisition in learning disabled adolescents. *Focus on Exceptional Children 17*(5), 1–8.

Wood, M. (1986). *Developmental therapy* (2nd ed.). Austin, TX: Pro-Ed.

Wood, M. M., & Long, N. J. (1991). *Life space intervention: Talking with children and youth in crisis.* Austin, TX: Pro-Ed.

Wrightslaw. (2007), *What you need to know about IDEA 2004 response to intervention (RTI): New ways to identify specific learning disabilities.* Available at www.wrightslaw.com/Info/rti.Index.htm.

Wyne, M. D., & O'Connor, P. D. (1979). *Exceptional children: A developmental view.* Lexington, MA: D. C. Heath.

Ysseldyke, J. E., & Algozzine, B. (1982). *Critical issues in special and remedial education.* Boston: Houghton Mifflin.

Ysseldyke, J. E., & Algozzine, B. (1984). *Introduction to special education.* Boston: Houghton Mifflin.

Ysseldyke, J. E., & Algozzine, B. (1990). *Introduction to special education* (2nd ed.). Boston: Houghton Mifflin.

Ysseldyke, J. E., & Algozzine, B. (1995). *Special education: A practical approach for teachers.* Boston: Houghton Mifflin.

Ysseldyke, J., Algozzine, B., & Thurlow, M. (1983). On interpreting institute research: A response to McKinney. *Exceptional Education Quarterly 4*(1), 145–147.

Ysseldyke, J. E., Algozzine, B., & Thurlow, M. L. (2000). *Critical issues in special education* (3rd ed.). Boston: Houghton Mifflin.

Ysseldyke, J. E., Algozzine, B., Shinn, M. R., & McGue, M. (1982). Similarities and differences between low achievers and students classified learning disabled. *Journal of Special Education 16*(1), 73–85.

Zigmond, N., Levin, E., & Laurie, T. (1985). Managing the mainstream: An analysis of teacher attitudes and student performance in mainstream high school programs. *Journal of Learning Disabilities 18*, 505–568.

Zinmeister, K. (1990). Growing up scared. *The Atlantic 265*(6), 49–66.

Zucker, S. H., & Polloway, E. A. (1987). Issues in identification and assessment in mental retardation. *Education and Training in Mental Retardation 22*(2), 69–76.

INDEX

PHOTO CREDITS